LONDON COUNTY COUNCIL.

RECORD OF SERVICE

in the Great War 1914-18 by Members of the Council's Staff.

PUBLISHED BY THE LONDON COUNTY COUNCIL,
and may be purchased, either directly or through any Bookseller, from
P. S. KING AND SON, LIMITED,
2 AND 4, GREAT SMITH STREET, VICTORIA STREET,
WESTMINSTER, S.W.1,
Agents for the sale of the Publications of the London County Council.
1922.

No. 2113. Price 5s. [21955.]

PREFACE.

The Council on 9th November, 1920, decided, as a mark of its appreciation, to present to each member of the staff who served in the Great War, or to the next-of-kin of those who died on service, a short history of the war so far as the staff were concerned, with brief particulars of their service. Accordingly the *Record of Service* which gives effect to this decision has been prepared under my supervision by Mr. V. A. Weeks, B.A. (late Lieut., R. West Kent Rgt.), of my department. The sketch plans, which show practically every place mentioned in the battle areas, have been drawn by Capt. A. G. Harding, O.B.E. (late R.A.O.C.), also of my department.

Authorities for the statements made have not, as a rule, been given. To do this adequately would have required an elaborate series of footnotes, and these in a simple summary of the facts did not seem to be called for. The narrative and the comments thereon are based for the most part on the despatches of the various commanders-in-chief, the works referred to in the text, and H. C. O'Neill's *History of the Var,* Sir Henry Newbolt's *Naval History of the War,* H. W. Nevinson's *Dardanelles Campaign,* E. Dane's *British Campaigns in the Near East,* and Brig.-Gen. J. H. V. Crowe's *General Smuts' Campaign in East Africa.* The chapter on the Royal Air Force is based on an official *Short History of the R.A.F.* [F.S. 136], kindly supplied by the Air Ministry.

As far as practicable the recommendations of the Battles Nomenclature Committee [Cmd. 1138] have been adopted.

The *Record* deals only with the Council's staff, but it is not fitting that it should be issued without mention of the two members of the Council who lost their lives on active service, Captain R. M. Sebag-Montefiore, of the Royal East Kent (The Duke of Connaught's Own) (Mounted Rifles), who died at Alexandria on 19th November, 1915, from wounds received in Gallipoli, and Lieut.-Col. Lord Alexander Boteville Thynne, D.S.O., M.P., who was killed in France on 15th September, 1918, whilst commanding a battalion of the Duke of Edinburgh's (Wiltshire Regiment).

JAMES BIRD,
Clerk of the Council.

COUNTY HALL, S.W.
January, 1922.

CONTENTS

CHAP.		PAGE
I.	INTRODUCTION	1
II.	WESTERN FRONT, 1914.—Mons and the Retreat, the Marne and the Aisne, Antwerp, La Bassée and Armentières, Ypres	5
III.	WESTERN FRONT, 1915.—Neuve Chapelle, Hill 60, Ypres, Aubers Ridge, Festubert, Loos and Hulluch	19
IV.	WESTERN FRONT, 1916.—The Bluff and St. Eloi, Vimy Ridge, the Somme, and the Ancre	32
V.	WESTERN FRONT, 1917.—The Ancre and the German retreat, Arras and Vimy Ridge, Messines, Lombartzyde, Ypres, Lens, Cambrai	53
VI.	WESTERN FRONT, 1918.—The Somme (German offensive), the Lys, the Aisne, the Marne, Amiens, the Somme (Allied offensive), Arras, Havrincourt and Epéhy, Cambrai and the Hindenburg line, Flanders, Le Cateau, the Selle and the Sambre, Armistice	90
VII.	THE ROYAL NAVY	130
VIII.	THE ROYAL AIR FORCE	140
IX.	GALLIPOLI	148
X.	EGYPT AND PALESTINE	158
XI.	MESOPOTAMIA	167
XII.	SALONICA	174
XIII.	BRITISH TROOPS IN ITALY	180
XIV.	BRITISH TROOPS IN RUSSIA	185
XV.	BRITISH TROOPS IN AFRICA	187
XVI.	DEATHS FROM DISEASE	192
XVII.	SUMMARY	197
	Index of names of the Council's staff mentioned in the text	202
APPENDIX giving brief details of the war service of the Council's staff:		
	Clerk of the Council	1
	Comptroller of the Council	3
	Chief Engineer	10
	Architect	15
	Solicitor	25
	London Fire Brigade	26
	Public Health	34
	Estates and Valuation	37
	Public Control	38
	Parks	40

APPENDIX giving brief details of the war service of the Council's staff (*continued*):

	PAGE
Tramways	49
Housing	114
Education Officer:	
Central Administrative Staff	116
Industrial and Special Schools	124
Secondary Schools and Training Colleges	125
Technical Institutes and Schools of Art	126
School Attendance Officers	126
Botany Scheme	129
Stocktakers, etc.	129
Schoolkeepers	129
Teaching Staff	134
Stores	181
Parliamentary	184
Asylums and Mental Deficiency	184
Asylums Engineer	203

NOTE.-

The Divisions in the British Army on active service during the Great War were as follows:

Regular. Guards, 1st to the 8th, 27th, 28th, 29th, 1st, 2nd and 3rd Cavalry Divisions.

Service. 9th (Scottish), 10th (Irish), 11th (Northern), 12th (Eastern), 13th (Western), 14th (Light), 15th (Scottish), 16th (Irish), 17th (Northern), 18th (Eastern), 19th (Western), 20th (Light), 21st, 22nd (Western), 23rd (Northern), 24th (Eastern), 25th, 26th (Scottish), 30th, 31st, 32nd, 33rd, 34th, 35th, 36th (Ulster), 37th, 38th (Welsh), 39th, 40th, 41st (Eastern), 63rd (R. Naval).

Territorial. 42nd (E. Lancs), 43rd (Wessex), 46th (N. Midland), 47th (London), 48th (S. Midland), 49th (W. Riding), 50th (Northumbrian), 51st (Highland), 52nd (Lowland), 53rd (Welsh), 54th (E. Anglian), 55th (W. Lancs), 56th (London), 57th (W. Lancs), 58th (London), 59th (N. Midland), 60th (London), 61st (S. Midland), 62nd (W. Riding), 66th (E. Lancs.), 74th (Yeomanry dismounted), 75th.

In accordance with official practice the Battalions of the London Regiment are referred to throughout by numbers only. Their names were as follows:

1st, 2nd, 3rd and 4th (Royal Fusiliers), 5th (London Rifle Brigade), 6th (Rifles), 8th (Post Office Rifles), 9th (Queen Victoria's Rifles), 10th (Hackney), 11th (Finsbury Rifles), 12th (The Rangers), 13th (Princess Louise's Kensington Battalion), 14th (London Scottish), 15th (Prince of Wales's Own, Civil Service Rifles), 16th (Queen's Westminster Rifles), 17th (Poplar and Stepney Rifles), 18th (London Irish Rifles), 19th (St. Pancras), 20th (Blackheath and Woolwich), 21st (First Surrey Rifles), 22nd and 24th (The Queen's), 25th (Cyclist) and 28th (Artists' Rifles).

RECORD OF WAR SERVICE

CHAPTER I.

EVENTS LEADING UP TO THE GREAT WAR

IT would be a long task to refer even in outline to all the causes, direct and indirect, of the Great War and the attempt to do so would raise many controversial questions. Here it must suffice to state that the Franco-German War of 1870 had been succeeded by a period of international jealousy and suspicion, and that, so far from abating, these feelings of unrest had spread during the early part of the twentieth century widely throughout Europe. A serious crisis in 1905, leading up to the Algeciras conference, had been followed by another in 1908 when Austria, in defiance of the Treaty of Berlin, annexed Bosnia and Herzegovina, and by a third in 1911 arising out of the Agadir incident. Each had threatened to lead to war and, although war had been averted, it began to be clear that efforts to maintain peace could not continue to be successful. In most of the chief states there was no inconsiderable number of people who desired war, some in order to unite to their own country people of kindred race or language, others for the sake of territorial or political gain, others in mere self-defence before those plotting against their country became invincible. So deep were the feelings of distrust that any incident might result in a crisis for which no peaceful solution could be found. Such an incident was forthcoming on 28th June, 1914, when the Archduke Francis Ferdinand, heir to the Austrian Empire, was assassinated with his wife while on a visit to Sarajevo, the capital of

Bosnia. The effects of the outrage were not at once apparent, for no public action was taken by Austria until 23rd July. Then, however, it presented to Serbia a peremptory note and demanded a reply by the evening of the 25th. On this note Sir Edward Grey, the Foreign Secretary, remarked in a despatch to the British Ambassador at Vienna that he "had never before seen one State address to another independent State a document of so formidable a character" and that one of the demands "would be hardly consistent with the maintenance of Serbia's independent sovereignty." [1] Serbia's reply, delivered within the stipulated time, accepted in principle, though with reservations, most of the Austrian demands. This, however, was not considered satisfactory, diplomatic relations were broken off, orders were given for the mobilisation of the army, and on the 28th war was declared against Serbia. Germany supported Austria, while Serbia was supported by Russia, thus bringing in France, the latter's ally. Diplomatic negotiations to avert war or to localise its effects having proved fruitless, Germany on 1st August declared war on Russia and France, and on the 6th Austria declared war on Russia.

Great Britain of course had no direct interest in the quarrel between Austria and Serbia, or even in that between Austria and Russia, but, when other issues were raised and Germany and France were involved, it became vitally affected. The two main questions were the maintenance of the integrity of France and of the neutrality of Belgium. Great Britain was under no treaty obligation to France, but it had been agreed in November, 1912,[2] that, if either Government had grave reason to expect an unprovoked attack, or something threatened the general peace, it would immediately discuss whether

[1] Correspondence respecting the European Crisis, 1914 [Cd. 7467], p. 9.
[2] *Ibid.*, p. 57.

both Governments should act together to prevent aggression and to preserve peace. The German Chancellor's suggestion on 29th July that Great Britain should remain neutral on condition that Germany took no territory from France except in her colonies was indignantly rejected, and on 2nd August France was informed that, if the German fleet came into the English Channel or the North Sea to attack the French coasts or shipping, the British fleet would give all the protection in its power. The second question, Belgian neutrality and the respect of that neutrality by all belligerents, was even more important. By the Treaty of London, 1839, Great Britain, Austria, Prussia, France and Russia had agreed that Belgium should form an independent and perpetually neutral state, and that it should be bound to observe such neutrality towards all other states. This treaty had been strictly adhered to during the Franco-German War, and accordingly on 31st July, 1914, when hostilities between France and Germany became imminent, the two countries were asked whether, so long as no other power violated it, they would respect the neutrality of Belgium. France gave the necessary undertaking, but no reply was received from Germany. In fact on 2nd August the latter presented an ultimatum to Belgium demanding facilities for military operations, and on the 4th German troops actually invaded Belgian territory. On this date Germany was again asked to give the assurance already given by France and was informed that, unless a satisfactory reply was received, Great Britain would take all steps in its power to uphold the neutrality of Belgium. Germany made no reply and accordingly from 11 o'clock on the night of 4th/5th August, 1914, Great Britain was at war with Germany.

Approximate limits of German advance 1914.

Approximate front line, winter of 1914-15.

10 5 0 10 20 30 40 50 Miles

MONS, THE MARNE AND THE AISNE, 1914.

CHAPTER II.

THE WESTERN FRONT, 1914.

FROM 18th to 20th July, as part of a test mobilisation, a great naval display had been given at Spithead by the British Fleet at which some 200 vessels, manned by 70,000 officers and men, were present. After the manœuvres it was thought advisable, as affairs in Europe appeared so threatening, that the vessels should not disperse. Consequently at the outbreak of war the fleet was fully mobilised, ready at once for active service. The army was not mobilised until 3rd August, when it became clear that Germany was about to invade Belgium.

War between Great Britain and Germany having been declared, an Expeditionary Force, consisting at first of only four divisions, with some cavalry and a few aeroplanes, was sent to the assistance of the French. The troops embarked chiefly at Southampton, the bulk of them crossing to Boulogne or Havre on the nights of 12th and 13th August. They concentrated at Amiens and between 17th and 20th August were assembled under the command of Sir John French to the south of Maubeuge.

Mons and the Retreat.

By the morning of Sunday, the 23rd, they were in position at Mons with a front of about twenty miles on the extreme left of the Allies, the 1st Corps, commanded by Sir Douglas Haig, being to the east of the town, the 2nd Corps, under Sir Horace Smith-Dorrien, holding the town itself and the line to the west, and the cavalry, under Sir Edmund Allenby, being mostly in reserve.

During the morning the Germans attacked with five corps and three cavalry divisions, thus outnumbering our men by more than two to one. Although the enemy suffered heavy losses the attack achieved only a moderate success, the British 2nd Corps, which was chiefly involved, retiring, late in the day, to prepared positions in rear. Towards evening, however, Sir John French learned that Namur, thirty-five miles to the east, had fallen on the 22nd, that, in consequence, the French on his right had retired and that his left was being outflanked. In addition therefore to being outnumbered in front he was in grave danger of being surrounded on both flanks, so that immediate retreat was essential. This began the next day, the direction taken being roughly south-west. The 1st Corps retired to the east of Bavai and thence through Landrecies, Venerolles, La Fère, and Villers-Cotterets, while the route of the 2nd Corps lay to the west of Bavai, and through Le Quesnoy, Le Cateau, St. Quentin, Ham, Noyon and Compiègne. At Betz on 1st September, the two corps were re-united and crossing the Marne next day fell back towards the Seine.

Apart from an attack at Landrecies on the night of 25th/26th August, when the Guards drove off with heavy losses a force which advanced through the Forêt de Mormal, the 1st Corps was not seriously molested, but the 2nd Corps was much harassed. As his men were too weary to continue their march, Sir Horace felt it necessary, in order to gain time, to disregard the orders he had received not to fight, and on the 26th near Le Cateau turned and faced the enemy. Accordingly a line was formed to the south of the Cambrai—Le Cateau road with the 5th Division on the right, immediately west of the latter town, the 3rd in the centre and the 4th on the left, the whole front measuring some nine or ten miles. The fighting lasted from dawn until well into the afternoon when the 5th Division, having lost many of its guns, was forced back and the two other divisions had to conform. The retirement in some disorder gave rise at the time to disconcerting rumours in England but these, as usual, greatly exaggerated the facts, and, although there was much confusion, the retreat never degenerated into a rout.

The mobilisation of H.M. Forces led to the calling up from the Council's staff of 436 naval reservists, 870 army reservists and 590 members of the Territorial force. During August and September eighteen of the staff joined the Navy and 1664 the Army, so that, after two months of war, the staff on service numbered 3578. There were casualties amongst these from the first, for on 23rd August George Baker (4th R. Fus., Asylums) and Lance-Corp. E. W. Stretton (2nd R. Ir. Rgt., Tram.) were reported as missing, on the 24th John Yates (1st R. Scots Fus., Tram.) died of wounds, and on the 26th J. A. Goodwin (R.F.A., Tram.) was killed at Le Cateau, while before the end of the month A. G. Mitchell (1st Lincs, Ch. Engr.) died of wounds and W. J. Thynne (1st E. Surr., Tram.) was missing. P. S. T. Marshall (1st Lincs, Tram.) died on 11th September of wounds received near Mons, Corp. Frederick Lait (R.G.A., Educ.) on the same date of wounds received towards the end of the retreat, and S. C. Good (4th Dragoon Gds., Tram.) on 2nd October of wounds received on 3rd September near Lagny. Randall Kirk (Coldstr. Gds., Asylums), wounded and taken prisoner near Mons, died at Laon on 14th September.

The first member of the Council's staff to win a decoration was Sergt. A. J. Tilney (4th Drag. Gds., Clerk) to whom was awarded the Croix de Guerre. During the retreat towards the end of August he was accidentally left behind by his regiment. While making his way back he rescued a wounded comrade, taking him on his horse, and later picked up a straggler. Eventually he fell in with some French troops with whom he remained some days before he was able to rejoin his regiment.

Battle of the Marne, 1914.

The German forces advancing from Mons to the Marne were commanded by Von Kluck, who appeared to think that our troops had been so roughly handled that for the time being they might be ignored. Accordingly in the early days of September, instead of continuing his advance to the south and south-west, he turned to the south-east from the neighbourhood of Amiens, and crossed the Marne between Meaux and Château-Thierry seemingly with the intention of attacking the left of what he considered to be the main body of the Allies. He thus exposed his right flank, guarded only by comparatively small detachments, to the full assaults of the British and of a French army, commanded by General Maunoury, on their left. These assaults proved successful and, in the face of vigorous opposition, the British by 7th September had advanced to Coulommiers on the Grand Morin, and by the 8th to the Petit Morin, both these streams being tributaries of the Marne which was crossed on the 9th to the west of Château-Thierry. Von Kluck was now in considerable danger and a general retreat of the Germans to the Aisne was ordered. This retreat was followed up by the British through Oulchy and Fère-en-Tardenois, and on the 12th they were again in touch with the main German forces.

The operations from 6th September onwards, which formed a part of important engagements by several French armies, culminating in General Foch's successful attack at St. Gond, 40 miles to the east, are usually known as the first Battle of the Marne. By it the German advance was definitely checked and, indeed, pushed back for thirty miles and the threat on Paris was removed, so that it is rightly regarded as one of the decisive battles of the war.

9

Battle of the Aisne, 1914.

The passage of the Aisne, on a front of fifteen miles between Bourg on the east and Soissons on the west, was forced on 13th September. This was a difficult task, for the river is both broad and deep and, as many of the bridges had been blown up, some troops had to cross on rafts or pontoons, others on the girders of the broken bridges, and all this under continuous fire. Facing the British and three or four miles to the north of the river was a line of chalk hills on the summit of which was the Chemin-des-Dames.[1] As the scene of prolonged fighting throughout the war, this was destined to become one of the most famous positions on the whole front. The 1st Corps on the right advanced nearly to the top of the ridge, the 2nd Corps in the centre near Vailly was not so successful, while the 3rd Corps (which had been formed under Sir William Pulteney towards the end of the retreat from Mons) could do little more than hold its ground immediately across the river. Here both sides dug themselves in and, in spite of attacks and counter-attacks, the line remained unaltered for many months. After 18th September, although local encounters were frequent, the general fighting died down and early in October the British were relieved by the French and moved northwards to the flank of the Allied advance.

The casualties amongst the Council's staff were Alfred Luker (Northld. Fus., Asylums) killed on 9th September at the Marne, while those killed or missing at the Aisne were: 13th September, E. S. Harrison (1st R.W. Kent, Tram.); 14th September, C. A. Dickens (4th R. Fus., Asylums), Lance-Corp. S. Andrews (R.W. Surr., Parks), F. A. G. Daysh (1st Coldstr. Gds., Housing), Lance-Corp. James Walker (2nd R. Suss., Asylums); 15th September, H. G. Davis

[1] Constructed for the journeys of the daughters of Louis XV. between the royal châteaus at Compiègne and Bouconville.

(2nd W. Riding, Educ.); 16th September, John Ryan (1st Irish Gds., Tram.), C. J. Morley (4th Worcesters, Asylums); 20th September, W. A. Farley (1st S. Lancs., Clerk); 21st September, F. W. Adams (3rd Worcesters, L.F.B.); 22nd September, H. H. Chitty (2nd R. Fus., Parks); 4th October, W. J. Plater (1st Coldstr. Gds., Tram.), I. W. Bradford (1st Coldstr. Gds., Housing) died as a prisoner of war on 21st October of wounds received on 14th September.

Antwerp.

In the latter part of August the main Belgian army had withdrawn northwards to the neighbourhood of Antwerp but, using this as a base, it continued by frequent sallies to harass the enemy. The Germans were thus compelled to retain in the district troops which could have been more usefully employed elsewhere, and accordingly, at the end of September, after several weeks of desultory warfare, the reduction of the Belgian position was seriously undertaken. The defence fared badly against heavy artillery of the kind which had been so successful at Liège and Namur, and the Allies were appealed to for assistance. The only troops immediately available were a brigade of Royal Marines and two brigades of the R.N.V.R., which were despatched to Antwerp in the early part of October. A breach had already been made in the outer defences of the town and, as the Germans were greatly superior in numbers, no striking success was probable. The British forces, however, did good service by aiding the Belgians in holding up the attack for several days, and also by covering the Belgian withdrawal from the town. In this fighting Sergt. T. York (Educ.) was killed on the 6th, Percy Haggis (Arch.) on the 7th, and W. F. Forse (Tram.) on 9th October. The 7th Division and some cavalry landing at Zeebrugge covered the retreat along the coast.

La Bassée and Armentières.

Early in October, when a dead-lock had been reached on the Aisne, Sir John French suggested that, if his forces were transferred to the left of the Allied line, his lines of communication would be much shortened and he might be in a position to outflank the Germans. General Joffre consented and, as already mentioned, the British were relieved by the French and moved northward. Stated thus the problem which confronted the British commander appears simple enough to need no comment, but it must be remembered that his forces numbered about 100,000 men with horses, guns and baggage. One division alone, containing at full strength about 19,000 men with some 5,600 horses, 75 guns and 650 wagons, occupies in column of route about ten miles of road and takes three hours to pass a given point, while to transport it by rail about 90 trains are needed. It was therefore a formidable task, requiring much skill and organisation on the part of a staff unpractised in the handling of large bodies of men, to disengage so large a force from a vigilant and energetic enemy, and to convey it across the lines of communication of other troops. This intricate movement was, however, accomplished without mishap and by the 11th of the month the 2nd Corps was operating near La Bassée with the 3rd Corps on its left to the east of St. Omer. With much hard fighting and in spite of a strong resistance the line slowly advanced eastward until, towards the end of the month, the two corps were held up to the east of Béthune, Laventie and Armentières in positions which were maintained with little or no alteration almost to the end of the war.

In this fighting B. A. Edlin (2nd Bedfords, Asylums) was killed on 13th October, J. P. Knights (1st Notts. and Derby, Asylums) on the 20th, A. G. Martin (Wilts., Tram.) on the 24th, E. W. Moore (4th R. Fus., Tram.) and Joseph Knowles (2nd Border,

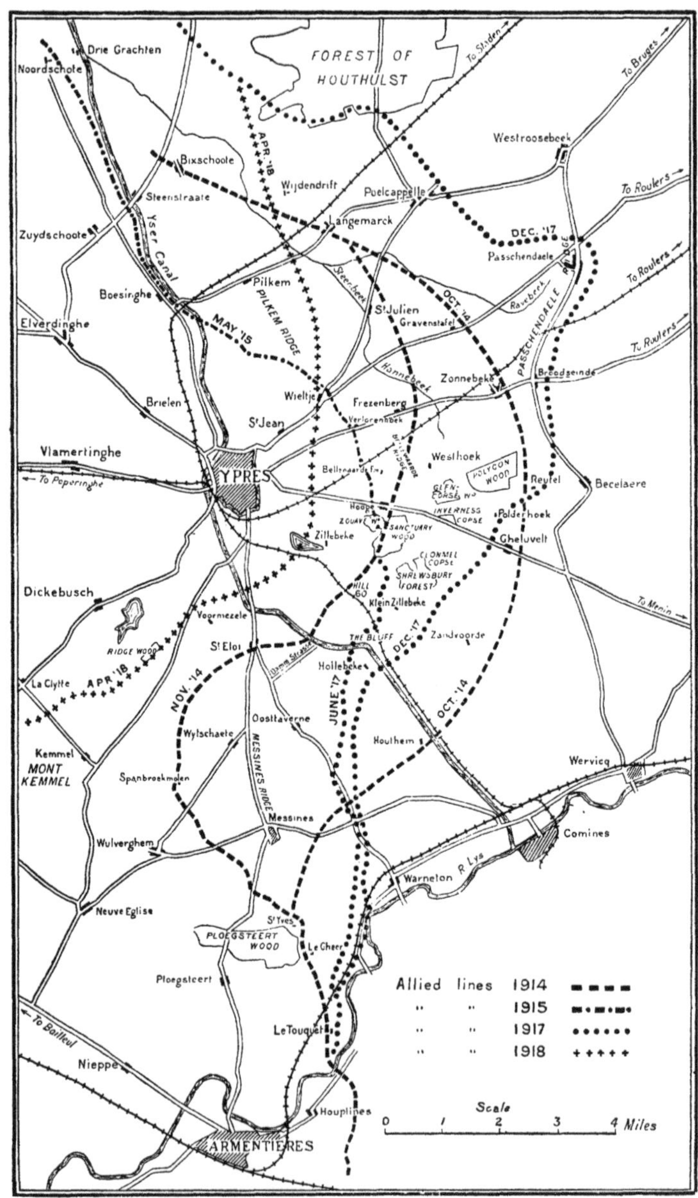

YPRES, 1914–18.

L.F.B.) on the 26th, and F. C. Hyde (1st Wilts, Tram.) on the 31st. J. W. Otton (4th Middx., Tram.) was awarded the D.C.M. for an attempt near Neuve Chapelle on 5th November in which he lost his life, to rescue a wounded non-commissioned officer. Corporal O. J. T. Smith (Yorks. L.I., L.F.B.) died on 7th January, 1915, of wounds received near La Bassée on 22nd October.

Battles of Ypres, 1914.

The 1st Corps which also detrained at St. Omer, but later than the 3rd Corps, pressed on to the east of Ypres, where it took up a position on the left (*i.e.*, to the north) of the 4th Corps. The latter had been despatched from England to aid the Belgians but, arriving too late to alter the course of events at Antwerp, had, after the fall of the city, retired in a south-westerly direction along the coast. An advance was made to the line Zandvoorde—Gheluvelt—Zonnebeke—Langemarck (see map opposite) with the intention of striking to the south-east at Menin, an important point in the German communications, and to the north-east through Poelcappelle and Passchendaele in the direction of Bruges. The Germans, however, had collected great numbers of troops in this district, partly in order to make a diversion and so relieve the pressure on their line further south, but chiefly with the object of breaking through and of capturing Calais and the adjacent coast-line and so hampering the British bases of supply. The British were outnumbered in the proportion of three or four to one and, instead of advancing, found themselves hard put to it to hold their ground.

Ypres, which in this way came to be the scene for four years of such desperate fighting and obstinate bravery, both in attack and defence, as can scarcely have been surpassed in all history, was before the war an ancient and beautiful but decayed city of 17,000 inhabitants. Situated in an extensive and fertile plain it had become a centre for agriculture instead of for weaving, its former industry, and it was also a rail and road centre of importance. Its historical monuments included the famous Cloth Hall and Belfry, dating from the 13th century, the finest Gothic public building in the country, the 13th-century Church of St. Martin (formerly the Cathedral), the 14th-century Town Hall and numerous quaint and picturesque houses of the Renaissance. All were destroyed, and the town during its four years partial siege was so completely wrecked that when the enemy was at length driven off not a house, scarcely even a room, was habitable. In its defence 300,000 British and Dominion troops died and a million were wounded.[1]

To the north, east and south the ground rises, but it is only on the south, near Messines and Wytschaete, that any really considerable hills exist. There the highest parts, 260 feet high, are nearly 200 feet above the level of the plain, while to the east the average rise is only about 80 or 100 feet, and to the north it is even less. In modern warfare in so flat a country the possession of the higher ground confers great advantages upon the side which hold it. First and foremost they have very much better opportunities for observing the movements of their opponents and the effect of their own shell-fire. Secondly they can secretly mass troops on the reverse side of the slopes, and so launch surprise attacks without warning to their opponents. Finally, and this is not the least important benefit in a marshy area, they can drain their trenches more or less effectively, and thus prevent them from becoming so many muddy pools or water-courses. It was for possession of these ridges, therefore, that the fiercest fighting took place, and a brief outline of the opening phases of this struggle will now be attempted.

As already stated, the British had advanced to

[1] Findlay Muirhead, *Belgium and the Western Front*, p. 38.

the line Zandvoorde—Gheluvelt—Zonnebeke—Langemarck which was reached about 20th October, although isolated advances were made even later at different parts. After much fighting, which daily increased in severity, the main German assault opened on 29th October. In face of the overwhelming attacks on that and the next day Gheluvelt, Reutel and Zonnebeke were lost and the line was withdrawn on the average about one mile to Messines, Hollebeke and Klein Zillebeke. On the 31st the famous counter-attack by the 2nd Worcesters at a very critical time recovered much of the ground up to Gheluvelt, but further south Messines fell and Wytschaete was threatened. On 1st November the Germans developed their success and captured the whole of the Messines-Wytschaete ridge, the British retiring to Wulverghem. After this the fighting on the British front slackened for some days, the brunt of the attacks being borne by the French and Belgians to the north. On 11th November, however, their sector was once more ablaze for, after a terrific bombardment lasting several hours, the attack culminated in an assault by the Prussian Guard, aided by troops of the line, along the Ypres-Menin road. This was almost successful, for the line was pierced in several places, but the advance was stemmed by the 2nd Oxford and Bucks L.I., the 1st Northamptons, the Connaught Rangers and others, and a new line formed some distance to the rear.[1] Wytschaete, which had changed hands several times since the beginning of the month, now finally passed into the possession of the Germans. This day's attack proved to be the final attempt by the enemy to break through, and the British were therefore able to consolidate their position on the line of St. Eloi—Hooge—Frezenberg—Langemarck.

As the result of three weeks' desperate fighting,

[1] The enemy's losses were enormous, those of the Prussian Guard alone in killed, wounded and missing amounting to nearly 7,000.

the Germans, with the loss of 150,000 men, had succeeded in advancing at the most a distance of four miles on a front of about fifteen. It is true that, especially from the east round to the south, they had secured positions which enabled them to overlook and even to enfilade the British lines, both to the south and south-east of Ypres and to the north-east of Armentières, but they had definitely failed in their attempt to break through to the Channel coast or even in their subsidiary effort to capture Ypres.

On 21st October Sergt. A. J. Toole (2nd Drag. Gds., Educ.) was killed near Zonnebeke, and Charles Walker (R.F.A., Tram.) at some place unknown; on 23rd October, Francis Greygoose (2nd K.R.R., Tram.) near Pilkem; E. S. Moth (3rd Rif. Bde., Asylums) died of wounds on the 25th; on 30th October, W. R. Henderson (1st Dragoons, Asylums) and T. H. Broom (1st Life Gds., L.F.B.) were missing, and Walter Bell and Lance-Corp. M. M. Humphreys, both of 1st S. Wales Bord. and Asylums, were killed near Gheluvelt; on 31st October, Lance-Corp. Daniel Reilly (1st R. W. Surr., Tram.) was killed, W. Curtis (1st R. W. Surr., Parks), W. J. Basterfield (1st R. W. Surr., Educ.) and A. G. Perryman (2nd K.R.R., Tram.) were missing near Gheluvelt, and H. J. F. White (2nd Life Gds., Tram.) was missing near Messines. It was on this last date that the 14th Londons won their laurels near Messines, the first occasion when a Territorial battalion had fought as a complete unit by the side of the Regular Army. The killed or missing included R. T. M. Wyllie and M. S. Bryce (Arch.) and A. B. C. Sarll (Educ.), while Lance-Corp. James Carey (Arch.) died a few days later as a prisoner of war of wounds received on that date.

The casualties in November were: 1st November, A. R. Shearing (Highd. L.I., L.F.B.) killed; 7th, Thomas Foss (2nd R. Innisk. Fus., Tram.) killed; 8th, Corp. H. H. Jeffries (1st Northld. Fus., Parks), and

C. D. Cater (1st Northld. Fus., Educ.) missing; 9th, John Rafter (Irish Gds., Asylums) killed; 10th, C. R. Kenchatt (W. Riding, Parks) killed; 11th, Sergt. Hubert McShane (1st Scots Gds., Parks) missing, and William Simmonds (4th R. Fus., Clerk) killed; 13th, Lance-Corp. Ernest Andrews (3rd Worcest., Educ.) killed; 15th, E. T. Benson (R.F.A., Stores) wounded near Dickebusch subsequently died of his wounds; 19th, Charles Clarke (1st Northld. Fus., Parks) killed. Lance-Corp. C. E. J. Martin (R. W. Surr., Tram.) wounded and taken prisoner on 31st October died at Wervick on 4th December, and J. G. Hicks (2nd Drag. Gds., Asylums) wounded and taken prisoner near Messines died at Ghent on 9th December.

Fighting in Winter of 1914-15.

After the Battles of Ypres the fighting died down for some months into ordinary trench warfare with its unremitting watch and guard even in the quietest sectors, with its mud and slime and vermin, with its patrols in No Man's Land, with its nightly ration parties, working parties and burying parties, with its continual casualties from shell, bomb, mine and sniper, with its sudden bombardments and raids and minor attacks, with its hours of cold and wet, boredom and discomfort, punctuated by minutes of deadly peril. The casualties included W. H. Ayton (R. W. Surr., Tram.) killed on 17th December in a British attack at Le Touquet to the north of Armentières, Corp. W. H. Cowan (Scots Gds., Educ.) on the 18th in a raid near Rouges Bancs to the east of Laventie, C.Q.M.S. G. Malcolm (1st Gren. Gds., Educ.) on the 20th in the neighbourhood of Armentières or Sailly-sur-la-Lys, W. S. Liddle (14th Lond., Parks) on the 24th and A. J. Webb (3rd Gren. Gds., Asylums) on the 29th near La Bassée.

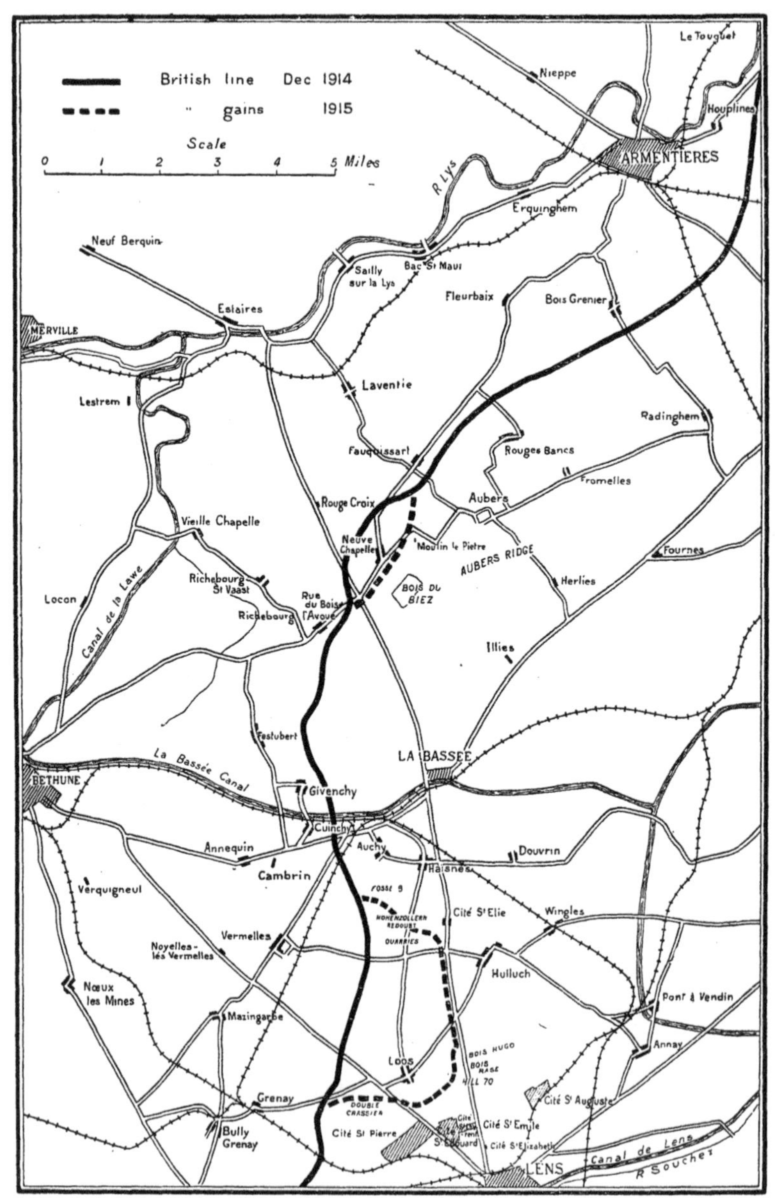

NEUVE CHAPELLE AND LOOS, 1915.

CHAPTER III.

Western Front, 1915.

Although the opening months of 1915 were not marked by any important fighting minor engagements were frequent and casualties heavy. The latter included O. S. Dawson (1st Cameronians, Asylums) killed near Bois Grenier on 6th January and A. E. Wilton and F. W. Clarke, both of the 1st Coldstream Gds. and the Stores Department, killed in a German attack at Cuinchy on the 25th, while on the same date William Maxim (R.F.A., Estates and Valn.) died of syncope at Zevecote. On 4th February Sergt. H. W. E. Jarratt (2nd Coldstr. Gds., Educ.) was killed near Givenchy, on the 8th Joseph Huggins (3rd R. Fus., Tram.) near Ypres, and E. H. Palmer (2nd Essex, Tram.) at Le Gheer in Ploegsteert Wood, on the 11th Corporal H. T. Cordery (1st Life Gds., Asylums) probably near La Bassée and on the 22nd Lieut. H. F. Heatly, B.Sc. (Yorks., attached 2nd E. Lancs, Educ.). Lance-Corp. W. J. Mott (1st R. W. Surr., Tram.) was killed on 9th March and on the 10th T. G. Pitt (1st Life Gds., Tram.) died at Boulogne of wounds received near La Bassée on 16th February. Capt. J. H. Stokes (R. W. Kents, attached R. Berks, Educ.), one of the first to be awarded the newly instituted decoration of the M.C., died at Boulogne on 22nd March of wounds received on 13th February. G. E. Romer (2nd E. Surr., Tram.) was killed at Ypres on 25th March, and A. E. Mears (R.F.A., Comp.) died at St. Omer on the 28th of meningitis. Corp. E. S. Carpenter (6th Lond., Educ.) was killed on 21st April near Cuinchy, and D. Angus (2nd Warw., Tram.) was missing a few days later. A. Seal (2nd Scots Gds , Asylums) died on 15th May of illness.

Neuve Chapelle.

During the fighting of October, 1914, by the 3rd Corps (see p. 11) the village of Neuve Chapelle, guarding the Aubers ridge, had changed hands several times but remained finally in the possession of the Germans. In March, 1915, in order to test the spirit of our troops after the losses of the preceding six months and so that all ranks and all arms might obtain experience of the offensive in trench warfare, it was decided to attack the place. Accordingly at 8 o'clock in the morning of 10th March, after a heavy bombardment by 300 guns, British and Indian troops attacked on a front of about 2,000 yards; at the same time demonstrations on each flank kept the enemy occupied. On the right of the main attack the advance was at once successful, but on the left it was held up for a time by broad belts of uncut wire. However, by noon the village had been seized and during the afternoon our troops debouched to the east, where they were held up at the Bois du Biez and the Moulin du Piètre. Heavy mists on the 11th and 12th, while preventing a further advance, enabled the Germans to bring up reinforcements for several counter-attacks, but these were all beaten off. (See map on p. 18).

For conspicuous gallantry and devotion to duty, especially on the 11th, Staff Sergt. W. C. Minchin (4th Seaf. Highdrs., Arch.) was awarded the D.C.M., the official notice stating that "he was always to the fore when volunteers were required for arduous and dangerous work, leaving cover on more than one occasion voluntarily to take the place of wounded stretcher-bearers."

Our gains were the village and 3,000 yards of the enemy's position to a depth of 1,000 yards. The casualties were nearly 13,000 and included Sergt. H. J. Stevens (2nd Durham L.I., Educ.) killed on the 10th in some subsidiary fighting at Houplines near

Armentières, C. E. Russell (1st Grenadier Gds., Educ.) on the 10th or 11th, Sergt. A. E. Coster (Border, Tram.), A. F. Samuels (2nd Yorks., Tram.) and J. D. Hale (2nd Yorks, Housing) on the 12th, and H. Gostling (2nd Midd., Tram.) on the 14th. L. Foy (13th Lond., Tram.) died at Boulogne on 5th April of wounds received on 12th March.

Hill 60.

The fighting at Hill 60, which lasted for a fortnight or more from 17th April, may be taken as an example of the attacks made by each side with varying success upon points up and down the line which were, or were held to be, of importance. This modest feature is a spoil-heap, rather more than 2½ miles to the south-east of Ypres, by the side of the Ypres-Comines railway. At the most only fifty feet high, it was useful as an observation post, and so, at dusk on the evening of 17th April, after the explosion of several mines, it was rushed by the 1st R. W. Kents and the 2nd Scottish Borderers. By the next morning the Germans had recovered part of the crest from which, however, during the night of the 18th/19th they were again driven by the 2nd W. Ridings and the 2nd Yorks L.I. For some time, in spite of heavy bombardments and numerous counter-attacks, the hill, defended by the 1st E. Surreys, the 1st Bedfords and the 9th Londons, remained with the British. In the early part of May the Germans renewed their attacks, this time with poison gas, against which our men were not then protected. One such attack on the 1st failed, but a second on the 5th was more successful, and the main part of the hill had to be given up.

Battles of Ypres, 1915.

In the first Battles of Ypres the Germans concentrated on the line to the east and south-east of the city, but in the second they attacked chiefly the sector to the north-east. The assault opened on 22nd April,

1915, with a discharge of poison gas against the trenches at, and to the north-west of, Langemarck held by French Colonial troops. This was the first occasion on which such gas had been used, at all events on a considerable scale, the troops were quite unprepared, and those that survived fled in terror. A gap, several miles wide, was made in the line and, if the enemy had properly exploited the success purchased by ignoring the conventions of civilised warfare, the position of the Allies would have been most serious. The Germans, however, paused to consolidate their gains, and the Canadians, who formed the left of the British line next to the French, had time to defend their flank and even to make a counter-attack. Isolated detachments were hurried up as reinforcements, and by the morning of the 23rd the gap to the left of the Canadians had been somehow bridged by a line in rear of the original position. Part of the area abandoned was regained by counter-attacks, but eventually the loss of St. Julien, Pilkem Ridge, Langemarck and Bixschoote had to be accepted, and a new line was formed just to the east of Wieltje and Boesinghe. At the same time the dangerous projection which was thus formed to the north-east was given up. The latter movement was completed by 4th May, and on the 8th a fierce attack broke out on the sector to the south of Wieltje. The line was pierced at Wieltje and near Frezenberg, but the former was recaptured and at the latter a new line was formed to the west. A German attack on the 24th near Bellewaarde and another at the end of the month near Hooge were equally fruitless.

The fighting died down with the Allies holding the line St. Eloi—Hooge—Wieltje—Boesinghe (see p. 21). On the north and north-east the Germans had advanced, at the most, two miles nearer Ypres and had secured positions overlooking the town, but their efforts to capture it had failed and were now finally abandoned. The casualties included F. H. Stanton (12th Lond.,

Arch.) on the 24th, and George Hood (2nd D. of Cornwall's L.I., Tram.) on 28th April, both killed near St. Julien, while on the 29th Lance-Corp. J. T. Pascoe (1st Somerset L.I., Tram.) died near Vlamertinghe and M. H. Woodhead (Middlx., Ch. Engr.) at Boulogne of wounds which they had received probably in this district. On 3rd May John Kirkwood (Educ.) and E. W. Baldwin (Pub. Cont.), both of the 5th Londons, were killed to the south of St. Julien and A. A. Ridlington (2nd Buffs, Tram.) was killed probably to the north-east of that village. On the 4th Lance-Corp. C. W. H. Juniper (2nd Essex, Tram.) was killed near St. Jean and on the 8th C. L. Rizzi (12th Lond., Arch.) probably near Frezenberg. W. F. West (5th Lond., Educ.) died on 12th May of wounds received near St. Julien on 25th April. On 13th May John Pearce (1st Rif. Bde., Comp.) and W. C. R. Boughton (5th Lond., Educ.) were killed near Wieltje and Corporal G. Guyver (Tram.) and H. L. J. Christiansen (Parks), both of the 10th R. Hussars, and Lance-Corp. Benjamin Hambly (2nd Life Gds., Asylums) near the Ypres-Roulers road. G. A. Jenkins (12th Lancers, Asylums) was wounded on the 14th probably at the same place and died at Hazebrouck on the 17th. Sergt. A. J. Shepherd (4th R. Fus., Tram.) was killed near St. Eloi on the 20th, and on the 24th Lieut. Thomas Roberts (Cheshires, Educ.), Walter Everitt (4th Drag. Gds., Tram.), Lance-Corp. F. G. Griffin (3rd R. Fus., Tram.) and W. T. Ellner (3rd R. Fus., Tram.), all in front of Ypres. George Moore (2nd E. Surr., Tram.) was killed on the 28th and on the same date Lance-Corp. Sidney Clark (3rd R. Fus., Tram.) died of wounds received at Ypres on the 8th. Edward Moore (4th Huss., Tram.) died at Dublin on 10th January, 1916, from the effects of a wound received in this sector on 24th May, 1915.

Aubers Ridge and Festubert.

Early in May the French took the offensive between Loos and the Vimy Ridge to the north of

Arras and, in order to engage the enemy's attention, the British on 9th May opened an attack on a front of about ten miles between Laventie and Richebourg l'Avoué. In the north near Rouges Bancs the 13th Londons seized a mine crater and several lines of trenches beyond, and in the south the 2nd R. Munster Fus. captured some trenches near the Rue du Bois. The rest of the attack failed and these two battalions, being unsupported on their flanks, had to withdraw. Further attacks on the night of 15th/16th May at Richebourg l'Avoué and Festubert were less unsuccessful but, though the operation continued for several days, the total gains were negligible for, apart from the casualties inflicted on the enemy, an advance of a few hundred yards in so flat a country was of no advantage.

The Germans seem to have had warning of the attack and to have been fully prepared for it, and, owing to the demands for guns and ammunition at Ypres, our artillery preparation was far from being effective. It is therefore not surprising that the casualties in this, the first engagement in which Territorial and New Army units were employed on a considerable scale, were very heavy. On the first day alone they exceeded 12,000, most of the battalions engaged losing over half their effectives. This at the time seemed a very heavy proportion, but later such losses became so frequent as scarcely to arouse comment. The undermentioned members of the Council's staff were killed on 9th May: V. J. Macartney (Comp.), H. C. C. Whitwell (Solr.) and F. M. Macrae (Educ.) all of the 13th Londons near Rouges Bancs, W. H. Ferry (1st Northamptons, Tram.), John Whittam (Solr.) and Sergt. William Keys (Educ.) both of the 4th Seaforth Highrs. near Rouges Bancs, James Bailey (2nd R. Suss., Educ.) at Richebourg l'Avoué, W. G. Dickens (24th Lond., Tram.) near the Rue du Bois, Sergt. H. J. Lock (2nd Middx., Tram.), and John Tott

(2nd Cameronians, Tram.). Albert Forse (24th Lond., Tram.) died on the 10th of wounds received on the 9th. Joseph Gray (1st Lond., Tram.) was killed on the 10th and Lance-Corp. A. E. Keeling, B.Sc. (7th Lond., Educ.) on the 16th near Festubert. On the same day and probably at the same place Lance-Corp. George Cox (2nd R. W. Surr., Tram.) and Corporal Herbert Parker (8th Lond., Educ.) were also killed, and on the 17th J. E. Petherick (13th Lond., Comptr.) died of wounds received near Rouges Bancs on the 9th. On the 18th W. A. V. Luckhurst (7th Lond., Tram.), H. F. Buckby (4th Cam. Highrs., Educ.) and Lance-Corp. Edward Carey (1st Irish Gds., Housing) were killed near Festubert. C. E. Pearson (15th Lond., Solr.) died on the 23rd of wounds received on the 20th. Lieut. H. E. Handley (Educ.) was killed on the 24th and Lance-Corp. G. T. Boxall (Educ.), Lance-Corp. H. S. Burton (Educ.), Lance-Corp. Frederick Rushton (Tram.), Lance-Corp. T. S. Waterhouse (Tram.), J. C. Terrett (Educ.), T. H. Dibble (Educ.), A. J. Hammond (Educ.), R. J. H. Maley (Educ.), V. K. Mallpress (Educ.) and H. C. Turner (Estates and Valn.) on the 25th, all these falling at Givenchy with the 23rd Londons. On the same day and at the same place were killed W. S. Curtis (Educ.) of the 15th and R. C. Beale (Stores), Archibald Herriott (Tram.), Corporal George Klein (Tram.), of the 24th Londons. Those in the 23rd Londons killed on the 26th included Douglas Waterland (Educ.), J. L. Aubury (Tram.), Arthur Bickmore (Tram.), F. M. Carson (Educ.), and H. G. Pugh (Educ.). Corp. A. E. W. Chappell (24th Lond., Arch.) was killed on the 26th and W. Allan (1st R. W. Surr., Tram.) died on the 27th of wounds received the day before.

Summer of 1915.

The summer of 1915 was taken up with various local encounters which led to no more definite result than the occasional gain or loss of a trench. Thus on

15th June about eight battalions attacked opposite Givenchy; some failed to reach their objective and the others suffered such heavy casualties that they were unable to maintain themselves in the captured trenches. Trenches captured at Hooge on 16th June were retaken by the Germans with the aid of liquid fire on 30th July, and again captured by us on 9th August.

On a date in July Staff-Sergt. N. Mapham (R.A.V.C., Educ.), in charge of some N.C.O.'s and men, was ordered to entrain at Béthune a large number of sick and wounded horses. There was a two hours' wait for the train and during all this time the station was heavily shelled. In these trying circumstances and in spite of many casualties he successfully carried out this difficult operation, and for his gallantry was awarded the D.C.M.

In the general warfare during the middle of 1915 J. J. Shrimpton (H.M.S. *Vernon*, Tram.) was killed on 23rd May near Dunkirk while employed in connection with some naval guns which were in use on shore. On 8th June J. H. Rowe (16th Lond., Tram.) died at Vlamertinghe of wounds received the previous day in front of Ypres, on the 15th H. E. Bailey (5th Seaforth Highrs., Arch.) was shot at Givenchy while aiding a wounded comrade, on the 16th Harry Jackson (1st R. Scots Fus., Tram.) and W. G. Squires (R.F.A., Asylums) were killed at Hooge and on the 20th William Allison (1st Middx., Tram.) died of wounds received probably near Armentières. On 6th July Corporal J. E. Butler (1st Rif. Bde., Tram.) was killed near Boesinghe, on the 19th J. E. Matthews (4th Middx., Tram.) at Hooge and on the 30th S. W. Jones (24th Lond., Tram.) died of wounds received on the 26th and Harry Fuller (1st N. Staffs, Tram.) of wounds received near Ypres on the 27th. R. Payne (E. Surr., Parks) was reported as missing about this time. Walter Pearson (H.A.C., Educ.) was killed at

Hooge on 25th August, J. R. Marshall (2nd Worcs., Tram.) in front of Béthune on the 26th and Corporal W. W. Davis (R.E., Tram.) at Grenay on the 30th.

During September Lieut. F. W. Quilter (6th Lond., Comp.) was killed on the 1st near Vermelles, Lance-Corp. Albert Jackson (2nd Yorks. L.I., Asylums) on the 4th, Lieut. S. B. Walsh, M.D., D.P.H. (R.A.M.C., Pub. Health) died at Calais on the 8th owing to an accident on 28th August when his horse, frightened by a shell, threw him, Sergt. F. C. Dixon (12th Rif. Bde., Parks) at Boulogne on the 9th of wounds received near Laventie on the 5th, Charles White (2nd Drag. Gds., Stores) in a railway accident on the 18th, and G. A. E. Searle (4th Oxf. and Bucks L.I., Educ.) near Hébuterne,[1] south of Arras, on the 24th.

Loos and Hulluch.

In September, the French decided, in conjunction with a great attack in Champagne, to renew their offensive against the Vimy Ridge, and the British were asked to co-operate by attacking between Lens and the La Bassée Canal (see plan p. 18). The preliminary bombardment occupied four days and, immediately before the advance, large quantities of asphyxiating gas were released, this being the first time that gas was used by us. The main attack was launched at 6.30 a.m. on the 25th, and in some parts suffered much from coming upon large belts of uncut wire and drifting clouds of our own gas. On the extreme right the 47th Division (with the 18th Londons dribbling a football across No Man's Land), captured the Double Crassier [2] and part of Loos. On their left the 15th Division captured the remainder of Loos, pressed on a mile or so farther to Hill 70 and even attempted an attack beyond (*i.e.*, to the east of) the

[1] During the first half of 1915 the portion of line held by the British in France was gradually extended southwards as far as Lens. About July, 1915, they also took over a sector to the south of Arras extending to the north of Albert.

[2] This was a pit bank or slag-heap.

hill. In the centre the 1st Division got as far as Hulluch and the 7th up to Cité [1] St. Elie but the latter had to withdraw to the Quarries. Further north the 9th Division, although held up by the Hohenzollern Redoubt and Fosse 8,[2] reached the outskirts of Haisnes. They were much impeded, however, by the failure of the 2nd Division on the extreme left to deal with the very strong works at Auchy which were thus able to enfilade sections of the advance.

During the following night the Quarries were lost, and on the 26th the 15th Division was forced to give up most of Hill 70. The reserves in this latter part consisted of the 21st and 24th Divisions. These, being newly arrived from England, had never been under fire; they were wearied with a series of night marches along roads crammed with traffic; they were short of food and water and drenched with rain; it has been stated [3] that the officers had no precise orders or detailed information.[4] In this state these two divisions on the 26th were thrown into the conflict between Hulluch and the Bois Hugo. Both succeeded in advancing, but suffered so terribly that they were unable to maintain their gains and had to fall back. The 8th Buffs for instance, and the 8th R. West Kents each lost nearly 600 officers and men, and the brigade, the 72nd, of which they formed part, lost 2,000 men out of 3,600. On the 27th Fosse 8 was lost and the Hohenzollern Redoubt which it commanded was threatened. As a set-off to this reverse the newly-formed Guards Division retook Hill 70. Desultory

[1] Cité usually means a city or a division thereof, but in the Lens neighbourhood it denotes a group of miners' cottages.

[2] A fosse is a coal-pit, but it was the accompanying slag-heap with its commanding sites for observation and fire which made such positions formidable.

[3] Sir A. Conan Doyle, *British Campaign in France*, 1915, p. 197.

[4] Concerning these operations it has been remarked, without excess of emphasis, that " the problem of bringing up reserves in time through the confusion of a modern battle had not yet been solved."—*British Campaigns in the West* (p. xliv.) by Maj.-Gen. Sir F. Maurice in Findlay Muirhead's *Belgium and the Western Front.*

fighting proceeded for several days, a strong German counter-attack on 8th October being beaten off and renewed efforts by the British on the 13th to clear the redoubt and to take Fosse 8 being unsuccessful.

After this the fighting died down into ordinary trench warfare with the British holding a line (see plan on p. 18) running almost due eastward from Grenay as far as the Lens-Hulluch road, then northward along this road and finally turning westward through the Hohenzollern Redoubt to the original front line. The area captured, although less than that gained in the first assault, represented an advance of about two miles on a front of about four, and the advance formed a permanent threat to the German occupation of Lens in the south and La Bassée in the north. Some 3,000 prisoners with 26 field guns were taken.

Major (afterwards Lt.-Col.) Ernest Eton (R.F.A., Educ.) was awarded the D.S.O. for excellent service throughout the summer when, although constantly shelled out of observation stations, he always managed to command his guns with success. He also did good work at Loos at the end of September. In the latter fighting the D.C.M. was gained by Sergt. A. A. W. Gray (M.G.C., Tram.) on the 25th when "he carried his machine-gun forward . . . when only two men of the gun team were left, and selected the gun position in the most able way. His coolness and gallantry . . . afforded a fine example to all ranks." Co. Sergt.-Maj. (afterwards Captain) P. E. Fairley (18th Lond., Educ.) was awarded the same decoration for conspicuous bravery and devotion to duty under heavy shell fire during the repair of trenches that had been blown in. For excellent work on night patrols, both at Festubert and Loos, Rgt. Sergt.-Maj. J. W. Fisher (22nd Lond., L.F.B.) was awarded the D.C.M. Sergt. A. E. Kitchen (R.A.M.C., Educ.), Sergt. J. V. Jeanes (Gren. Gds., Asylums), and F. J. Bulcraig (23rd Lond., Stores) were awarded the M.M.

On 25th September W. A. G. Davey (18th Lond., Stores), S. J. Farley (20th Lond., L.F.B.) and Harold Marsh (6th Lond., Tram.) were killed with the 47th Division, Sergt. H. B. Richardson (12th Highd. L.I., Educ.) with the 15th Division somewhere near Hill 70, Claude Challice (8th Devons, Educ.) near Hulluch, Capt. L. G. Coward (Comp.) and H. E. Cannard (Tram.) near Auchy with the 1st Middlesex and S. H. Townsend (R.F.A., Tram.). On the same day G. James (1st R.W. Surr., Tram.) was killed in a subsidiary attack near Givenchy and Henri Willem Dussauze (French Army, Educ). was killed at Aubérive-sur-Suippes during the French assault in Champagne. For his gallantry on this occasion he was awarded the Croix de Guerre (highest class). J. S. Walker (1st R. Welch Fus., Tram.) died on the 26th of wounds received the previous day. On the same day Sergt. P. J. Gould and Albert Ingram, both of the 9th E. Surreys and Asylums, were killed to the south of Hulluch, Lieut. Edgar Faulks (R.A.M.C., Asylums) near Loos, B. G. Turner (1st Colds. Gds., L.F.B.) near the Bois Hugo and E. T. Havell (10th R. Suss., Educ.) near Fosse 8. On the 27th E. C. Barklamb (2nd E. Surr., Housing) was killed in the Hohenzollern Redoubt, and on the 30th Frank Ashby (R.A.M.C., Tram.) died at Nœux-les-Mines of wounds received on the 26th. On 13th October Sergt. Henry Eason (14th Lond., Educ.) was killed while reconnoitring, and Sergt. A. T. O'Meara and Sergt. E. Hart, both 7th Norfolks and Education, and Lance-Corp. A. J. King (5th R. Berks., Tram.) near the Quarries. On the 14th B. L. Bilcliffe (15th Lond., Educ.) was killed near Loos.

Autumn of 1915.

During the autumn of 1915 there were no serious engagements, but casualties on the long front now held by the British were numerous. They included Lance-Corp. H. J. Simons (8th E. Surr., Tram.) killed at Fricourt to the east of Albert on 15th October, Sergt. James

Shrewsbury (12th K.R.R., Educ.) at Laventie on the 16th, William Fox (1st Buffs, Parks) on the 17th, Crowther Morton (15th Lond., Educ.) on the 24th near Loos, S. J. Baker (23rd Lond., Tram.) on the 28th of wounds received on the 25th, A. S. Plumb (8th Rif. Bde., Tram.) on the 30th of wounds received near Ypres on the 13th, and Sergt. J. G. Jones (21st Lond., Tram.) near Hulluch on the 31st. During November E. S. Meredith (15th Lond., Estates and Valn.) was killed near Loos on the 1st, L. H. T. Williams (15th Lond., Solr.) near Loos on the 2nd, and A. E. Coventry (6th R. Berks, Tram.) near Albert on the 27th. P. H. Rivers (R.E., Tram.) died on 4th December of wounds received on 20th November, Arthur Cooper (11th Essex, Tram.) probably near Hulluch on 19th December, and C. R. S. Aplin (22nd Lond., Tram.) on the 30th.

Edward Gimble (1st Middx., Tram.) was awarded the Albert Medal, second class, for his gallantry on 26th October, when he assisted Lieut.-Com. Warden in quenching a fire which had broken out on the s.s. *Maine*. The vessel, loaded with high explosives, was lying at the time in the Bassin Loubet, Boulogne, and a serious, possibly disastrous, explosion was averted by their action.

Sergt. A. J. Tilney (4th Drag. Gds., Clerk) received the D.C.M. for repeated acts of gallantry, particularly on a night in January, 1916, when he accompanied an officer and two men in an attempt upon a mine crater in the Hohenzollern Redoubt. The officer was killed and one of the men wounded, but Sergt. Tilney seized and held the position. Corp. S. C. P. Drury (R.E., Educ.) was awarded the D.C.M. for consistent gallantry and good work about this time when in charge of sap and wire entanglement work. During an engagement in the Ypres salient he also displayed great courage and coolness.

CHAPTER IV.

Western Front, 1916.

In December, 1915, Sir John French returned to England, and on the 19th of the month Sir Douglas Haig was appointed commander-in-chief of the British forces. During the winter the British took over from the French the sector from Lens to Arras, so that in the early part of 1916 the line held by them started north of Ypres, passed near Armentières, Béthune, Lens and Arras and reached practically to the river Somme. The length was about 90 miles, out of a total length from the North Sea to Switzerland of about 350 miles, and for its defence in July 660,000 infantry and cavalry were available. In addition there were great numbers of artillery as well as of units, near the front and at the various bases, dealing with health services, supply, transport, etc.

The first serious operation in 1916 in the British sector was the capture by the Germans on 14th February, after a heavy bombardment and the explosion of several mines, of the Bluff, a low bank on the Comines canal nearly three miles S.S.E. from Ypres. Like Hill 60, about one mile to the north, it conferred upon the side holding it facilities for observation and so was the scene of fierce fighting. In fact one trench changed hands so frequently that it gained the name of " International Trench." A British counter-attack in a rain-storm on the night of the 15th/16th failed, but in another attack just before dawn on 2nd March not only the lost ground but an additional area was captured.

At St. Eloi, a mile or more to the west, the positions were reversed. On 27th March six mines were exploded under the German trenches, portions of which were seized. The consolidation of the new position proved difficult and, after numerous bombardments and counter-attacks during the next four weeks, our men withdrew on 27th April to the line held before the operations began.

Of the remaining operations the most notable were the fighting, chiefly by the 12th Division, in the Loos salient in April and May, a German attack at the Vimy Ridge near Souchez in the middle of May, and a German attack near Hooge and Zouave and Sanctuary Woods early in June. The last two were undertaken in the hope that troops and munitions would be diverted to the threatened points, and that the preparations, then well advanced, for the Battle of the Somme would be impeded. To prevent this no effort was made to recover the ground lost near Souchez, and at Hooge only the area essential for the safety of the line was attacked and captured.

In these [1] or in similar engagements the casualties mentioned below occurred during the first half of 1916. On 6th January H. E. L. White (9th Rif. Bde., Tram.) was killed near Ypres, on the 11th J. G. J. Waite (7th K.R.R., Tram.) probably in the same neighbourhood, and S. A. Parkington (15th R. Welch Fus., Tram.) near Richebourg, and on the 21st Sergt. E. W. Lord (8th Glouc., Educ.). On 27th January Corporal James Skeggs (9th R. Fus., Tram.) died at Netley Hospital of wounds received on 4th November, 1915. Lieut. E. T. Morgan (15th R. Welch Fus., Educ.) died at Merville on 7th February of wounds received near Richebourg two days before, Lance-Corp. A. G. Rose (15th Lond., Educ.) on the 12th, and J. A. Braybrooke (18th Middx., Tram.) near Cambrin on the 29th. G. E. Rolfe (11th Middx., Tram.) died at Abbeville on 16th March of wounds received on the 5th, G. H. Downie (5th Drag. Gds., Asylums) on the 16th, Lance-Corp. George Wright (1st Middx., Tram.) near Cambrin on the 18th, Cecil Hodgkinson (R.E.,

[1] The casualties in the fighting at Vimy Ridge are dealt with later in a separate paragraph.

Tram.) at Aveluy near Albert on the 25th, and H. G. Ashdown (4th R. Fus., Parks) on the 27th. P. T. Ketcher (20th Lond., Educ.) died at Camiers near Boulogne on the 29th of wounds received on the 20th.

In April H. M. F. Quick (9th R. Fus., Tram.) was killed near Loos on the 5th, A. W. Roberts (5th Wilts, Tram.) on the 8th, W. A. Butlin (6th R. Berks, Tram.) near Albert on the 19th, Lance-Corp. James Smythe (R.W. Surr., Tram.) near Vermelles on the 20th, and Sergt. Frank Sturtridge (6th Lond., Educ.) near Vimy on the 30th. Capt. P. E. Fairley, D.C.M. (18th Lond., Educ.) wounded on 6th April lingered on until 4th February, 1919, when he died in hospital in Co. Armagh. Lieut. B. R. Baker (17th R. Fus., Educ.) was killed near Bully Grenay on 3rd May, Sergt. Mark Cutler (2nd Gren. Gds., Tram.) probably near St. Jean on the 6th, William Swainsbury (R.F.A., Parks) near Arras on the 7th and A. F. Canivet, B-ès-L., B-ès-Sc., (French Army, Educ.) on the 31st. Sergt. E. C. Laver (R.F.A., Tram.), wounded near Arras on 11th March, died in England on 19th June. Michael Doolin (2nd R. Munster Fus., Tram.) was killed on 25th June in a raid on the enemy's trenches south of Hulluch, Sergt. E. J. Perry (7th Middx., Educ.) near Hébuterne on the 26th, and Lieut. P. F. Gethin (8th Devons, Educ.) near Mametz on the 28th. Lieut. L. H. Kenny (8th Suff., Educ.) was missing after a trench raid on the night of 26th/27th June. Sergt. V. M. Elliott (2/4th Oxf. and Bucks L.I., Educ.) died at Merville on 1st July of wounds received in a raid on the enemy's trenches near Laventie.

Sergt. R. W. Braham (R.F.A., Educ.) was awarded the M.M. for gallantry during April at Vimy Ridge and Co. Sergt.-Maj. C. W. Froome (16th Lond., Educ.) the D.C.M. on 2nd June, the details not being known. Sergt. A. Prentice and Corporals A. E. Brereton and W. H. Nash, all of the Oxf. and Bucks L.I. and Education, received the M.M., the first named for rescuing a wounded comrade, and the others for various acts of gallantry during a trench raid in front of Laventie on 29th June.

Vimy Ridge.

The fighting on Vimy Ridge to the south of Souchez in May, 1916, when many of the Council's staff were killed, was briefly as follows. At evening on 15th May the British exploded several mines in No Man's Land and the craters were occupied by troops from the 25th Division. On the 21st the Germans heavily bombarded the position, and during the night of the 21st/22nd, while the 47th Division was relieving the 25th, they captured the craters and even parts of our trench system in rear. As already stated, it was not thought worth while to drive them out. The casualties included Sergt. Arthur Favell (21st Lond., Educ.) killed on the 18th, Sergt. T. P. Chick (15th Lond., Comp.), H. W. Babington (15th Lond., Educ.), A. H. Russell (15th Lond., Arch.) and J. A. Wynne (15th Lond., Educ.) on the 22nd, Sergt. L. S. Duck (21st Lond., Solr.), Lance-Corp. Albert Burgess (21st Lond., Pub. Cont.) and Sergt. S. E. Hill, B.Sc., (20th Lond., Educ.) on the 23rd, and Corp. Ebenezer Kirby (R.F.A., Tram.) on the 24th. Lance-Corp. L. J. Mayer (20th Lond., Pub. Cont.) died at Abbeville on the 31st of wounds received on the 21st, and on 3rd June Lieut. L. T. Taylor (8th Loyal N. Lancs., Educ.) died at Aubigny of wounds received on 21st May.

Battle of the Somme, 1916.

Since February, Verdun, an important point in the French line of defence, had been furiously assaulted but, although the defence severely taxed the French resources, the Germans, even at the cost of more than 300,000 casualties, achieved no definite result. To relieve the pressure and also to prevent the transfer of German troops to the Italian or Russian fronts an offensive by the French and British was planned at

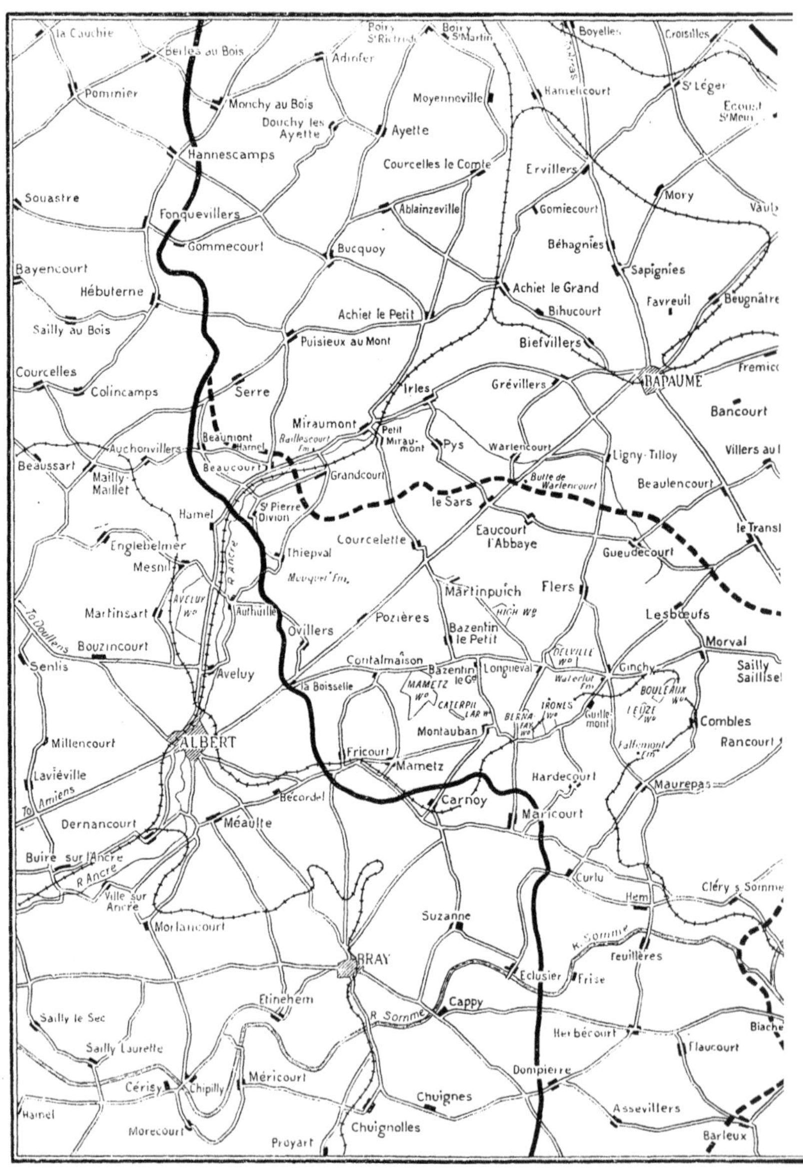

THE SOMME, 1916, AND

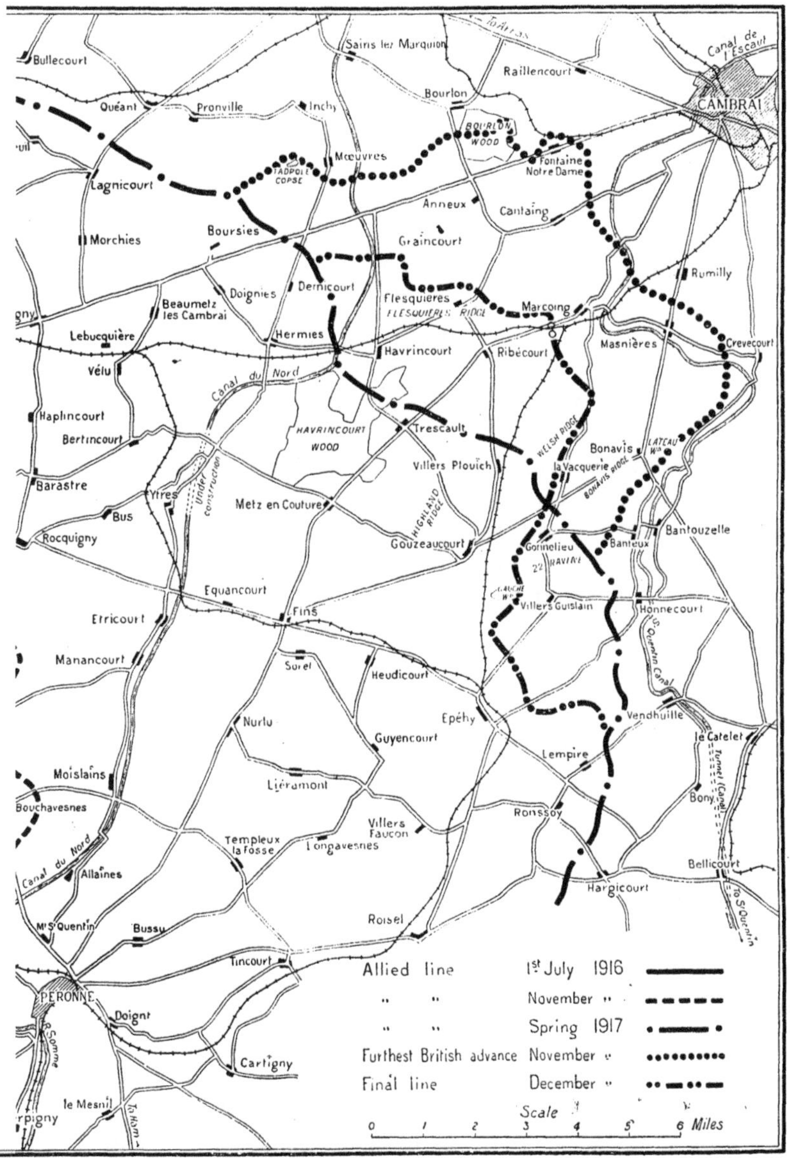

CAMBRAI, 1917

the junction of the two armies in the valley of the Somme.

Modern armies consume such great quantities of supplies that even in stationary warfare very careful arrangements have to be made to maintain them; during an offensive their needs are increased out of all proportion. For the Battle of the Somme vast stocks of ammunition and stores had to be accumulated, and on the British front alone many miles of new railways were constructed, more than 120 miles of water mains were laid, new roads and bridges were built and old ones were improved. In addition many miles of communication trenches, assembly trenches, assault trenches and trenches for telephone wires had to be dug.

The country from Ypres to Loos, formerly part of the province of Flanders, which witnessed the British conflicts at the end of 1914 and throughout 1915 is not unlike certain portions of the eastern districts of England. It is flat or gently undulating, and divided into fields by ditches, small streams and high hedges, with many farms dotted about. The country to the south, the scene of new and greater conflicts, is a rolling, chalk country, for the most part waterless, which rises steadily to heights of 500 feet or more. It is quite open, except for woods on many of the hill-crests, and the farms are grouped into small compact villages situated every mile or so at road junctions. In such country the defenders have good observation and good fields of fire, while the attackers, even if they find it difficult or impossible to obtain cover, are able, in ordinary weather and under ordinary conditions, to move their infantry freely in any direction.

The position to be attacked by the British was the high land running north-westward from the Somme to St. Pierre Divion, where it was cut by the valley of the Ancre, and then northward to Gommecourt. The German first system of trenches was on the forward, that is the southern and western, slopes, their second on the hill-crests 3,000 to 5,000 yards in rear, and still farther back there were the elements of a third line. The first two lines were exceptionally strong. The chalk soil enabled dug-outs to be prepared at a depth which made them practically safe from bombardment, the villages and woods had been turned into fortresses, the trenches were protected by belts, forty feet wide or more, of barbed wire often as thick as a man's finger.

The battle is usually regarded in three phases, the first from 1st to 17th July when a footing was gained on the hill-crest between Delville Wood and Bazentin-le-Petit (see plan on p. 36), the second from 17th July to the first week of September when violent counter-attacks were beaten off and our position on the whole of the high land was made good, and the third from September to November when an advance was made down the further, that is the eastern and northern, slopes, and our gains were extended on both flanks.

First Phase, 1st/17th July.

From 24th June the enemy's line from Maricourt to Gommecourt, a distance of twenty miles, was bombarded almost continuously, and gas was discharged at frequent intervals. At 7.30 a.m. on 1st July, a calm summer day, after a short final bombardment of exceptional violence accompanied by the discharge of smoke and the explosion of many mines, the attack was launched. Counting from the right, the 30th, 18th and 7th Divisions were successful at Montauban and Mametz, a distance of about five miles, and the 21st, 34th and 8th were partially successful at Fricourt, La Boisselle and Ovillers. On the left, in spite of initial successes, the 32nd and 36th failed near Thiepval, the 29th and the 4th near Beaumont Hamel, the 31st at Serre and the 56th and 46th near Gommecourt. One cause of the failure was that the Germans expected that the main attack would be in this sector and consequently they had greatly strengthened their defences and had brought up large numbers of guns. Even as it was, our men at Thiepval, Serre, Gommecourt, and elsewhere reached points to which British troops did not penetrate again until after several months of weary fighting. These scattered groups, cut off from their supports and supplies by a heavy barrage, were attacked in rear by parties of the enemy who, by withdrawing to positions of safety, had escaped our bombardments. It is not surprising that, outnumbered and short of ammunition and bombs, they had to withdraw, and that few of them regained their own lines in safety.

In spite of heavy counter-attacks the success on the right was exploited and during the next few days Fricourt, Bernafay and Caterpillar Woods and La Boisselle fell. About the 5th the weather broke and to the horrors of the battle were added the misery and discomfort of heavy rain. Contalmaison and Mametz Wood were captured on 10th July and, as some progress had been made at Trônes Wood on the right and Ovillers on the left, a general attack on the enemy's second line was possible.

Accordingly on the night of 13th/14th July our troops advanced nearly a mile and in the darkness took up position unobserved just below the crest. At 3.25 on the morning of the 14th, when there was only sufficient light to distinguish friend from foe, the attack opened. Trônes Wood was captured by the 18th Division, Longueval by the 9th, the Bazentins by the 3rd and 7th, and ground to the west of Bazentin-le-Petit by the 21st, 1st and 34th, while some troops even reached High Wood but were ordered to retire. On the 15th Delville Wood [1] and Waterlot Farm to the south were captured, and on the 16th Ovillers, after a heroic resistance for more than two weeks, surrendered.

Capt. (afterwards Major) A. C. Hancock (R.A.M.C.,

[1] Often known as Devil's Wood.

Asylums) received the M.C. for devotion to duty at Montauban when he led a rescue party in the open under heavy fire and rescued twenty-eight wounded men. Lieut. John Lever (13th R. Fus., Educ.) won the M.C. for conspicuous bravery at Mametz Wood. Major C. C. B. Morris (R.A.S.C., L.F.B.) also won the MC.. about this time but details are lacking. The M.M. was awarded to Corp. A. S. Devis (12th M.G.C., Tram.) for rescuing a wounded man, and to Sergt. J. E. Bailey (1st R. Welch Fus., Asylums) for his gallantry at the capture of Bazentin-le-Petit.

The fighting up to 17th July resulted in the capture of seven miles of the enemy's front system and three of his second, numerous strongly-fortified villages and woods, 54 guns, 82 machine-guns and trench mortars, and over 10,000 prisoners.

These varying successes and failures were of course accompanied by long lists of casualties, and on 1st July alone twenty-three of the Council's staff were killed, namely Sergt. J. E. Simons (8th E. Surr., Tram.) near Montauban, M. W. Bevan (1st Dorsets, L.F.B.) near Albert, Capt. John Foley (25th Northld. Fus., Educ.) near La Boisselle, Lieut. R. M. Stainton (10th York and Lancs, Educ.) near Ovillers, Capt. F. S. Blake (2nd S. Wales Borderers, Comp.), and Sergt. Douglas Kirkcaldy (1st Borders, Asylums) near Beaumont Hamel, Lieut. F. W. Wareham, Lieut. F. B. Freeman and Corporal T. G. Jeynes, all of them 8th R. Warwicks and Education, between Beaumont Hamel and Serre, Lieut. Thomas Moody, B.Sc. (4th Lond., Educ.), Corporal S. A. Ebbetts (5th Lond., Educ.), Alfred Cook (5th Lond., Educ.), V. J. Terrell (5th Lond., Educ.), James Leverington (9th Lond., Tram.), Lance-Corp. E. W. Hatcher (9th Lond., Educ.), W. G. Rowland (9th Lond., Compt.), Reginald Shears, A.R.I.B.A. (9th Lond., Arch.), Lance-Corp. H. Williams (14th Lond., Educ.), G. A. C. Moxley (14th Lond., Educ.), Arthur Alderton (14th Lond., Asylums),

F. M. Sampford (16th Lond., Tram.), Co. Sergt.-Maj. C. W. Froome, D.C.M. (16th Lond., Educ.) and Sec. Corp. C. W. Shipton (R.E., Ch. Engr.) at or near Gommecourt.

Capt. H. C. Harris (6th R. W. Kents, Educ.) was killed on the 3rd at Ovillers and S. G. Barnes (9th Lond., Educ.) died on the 4th of wounds received at Bayencourt to the west of Hébuterne on the 2nd. On the 7th Lieut. E. L. J. Stockdale, B.Sc. (10th Lanc. Fus., Pub. Health) was killed near Contalmaison, and Lieut. A. D. G. Procter (8th R. Fus., Educ.), Samuel Lower (8th R. Fus., Tram.), Lance-Corp. Richard Elliott (9th R. Fus., Tram.) and C. H. Edwards (9th R. Fus., Tram.) near Ovillers. Capt. E. A. Haselden (11th W. Yorks, Educ.) died on the 9th of wounds received near Contalmaison on the 4th. On the 10th E. J. Davies (15th R. Welch Fus., Tram.) and Frank Pearce (14th R. Welch Fus., Tram.) were killed, both at Mametz Wood, W. C. Rice (13th Rif. Bde., Tram.) on the 11th near La Boisselle, and on the 12th Lance-Corp. H. A. Cole (6th Dorsets, Tram.) died of wounds received two days before at Mametz Wood. Mark Humphrey (R.F.A., Tram.) died on the 15th of wounds received on the 14th, probably in this sector. Acting-Quartermaster C. A. W. Walpole (R.F.A., Tram.) was killed on the 15th, and Alfred Ridgewell (1st Middx., Asylums) on the same date near Bazentin-le-Petit. Ernest Davis (10th R Fus., Educ.) died on the 23rd of wounds received near Pozières on the 15th.

Second Phase, 17th July to 9th September.

By this time the enemy had brought up strong reserves and, as our line formed a pronounced salient, it was almost a question, not whether the position could be improved, but whether even it could be maintained. Longueval and Delville Wood, at the apex of the salient, were under fire from three sides, and during a violent attack on the 18th the Germans captured part of the village and of the wood. As a set off against this we gained a footing in High Wood on the 20th, and advanced on the 23rd along much of the front between Guillemont and Pozières. On the 25th the last named place fell, and between the 27th and the 29th Delville Wood and Longueval were cleared. Our attacks on Falfemont Farm and Guillemont on 30th July and 8th and 16th August with the object of straightening out the salient all failed, but on the 18th Guillemont station and part of the village were captured, and on 3rd September the whole passed into our hands.

In the meantime our men had fought their way almost step by step towards Mouquet Farm near Thiepval and to the high ground which enabled them to overlook Martinpuich and Courcelette. Following upon a general attack on 3rd September along the line as far north as the Ancre, Falfemont Farm and Leuze Wood were captured on the 5th, and another general attack on the 9th gave us possession of Bouleaux Wood and Ginchy. The two months' fighting from 17th July yielded little more than the two weeks before that date, but the enemy's resistance was now broken and henceforward the advance was comparatively rapid.

Lieut. (afterwards Lt.-Col.) W. Parkes (S. Wales Bord., Educ.) won the M.C. for conspicuous gallantry in action. "He rallied troops which had lost their officers . . . and displayed great coolness and courage. He continued to do fine work till he was severely wounded." Capt. (afterwards Lt.-Col.) C. F. Healey (8th R. Dub. Fus., Educ.) was awarded the M.C. for conspicuous bravery at Ginchy on 9th September. On the same date Sergt. W. Brawn (Lond., Educ.) won the D.C.M. when at Leuze Wood he assumed command of three companies, re-organised them and superintended the consolidation of the captured position under very heavy fire for thirty hours. J. H. Counter (1st Devons, Ch. Engr.) won the M.M. for digging out, under heavy shell fire, several of his comrades who had been buried in a dug-out by the explosion of a shell. Lieut. T. E. Cresswell (R.N. Div., Arch.) was awarded the M.C. for conspicuous gallantry in action at Beaucourt on 13th September when, although severely wounded, he continued to lead his men with great courage and determination.

In this fighting the undermentioned members of the staff were killed: Sergt. Percy Walton (R.F.A., Asylums) on the 18th to the west of Fricourt, Lieut. C. J. Fox (1st R.W. Kents, Educ.) and S. V. Scutt (1st R.W. Kents, Tram.), on the 22nd at Longueval, Lieut. W. F. B. Willis (1st D.C.L.I., Educ.) and Sergt. F. C. Lambert (1st D.C.L.I., Asylums) near Delville Wood, and Charles Archer (2nd R. Suss., Educ.) on the 23rd, Corporal George Bull (1st E. Surr., Tram.) on the 26th, D. A. Cole (24th R. Fus., Educ.) on the 27th, Lance-Corp. J. H. Taylor, A.R.I.B.A. (R.A.M.C., Arch.) on the 28th, and Lieut. H. L. Petrie (2nd K.O.S.B., Educ.) on the 30th, all near Longueval, and H. J. Ash (24th R. Fus., Educ.) on the 31st near Delville Wood. Bombr. Tom Rose (R.F.A., Educ.) died at Rouen on 2nd August of wounds received near Mametz Wood on 19th July.

Capt. O. H. Peters, M.B., B.S., D.P.H. (R.A.M.C., Pub. Health) died at Corbie-sur-Somme on 4th August of wounds received in this sector a few days before, and J. B. Owens (9th R. Fus., Tram.) at Boulogne on the 11th of wounds received near Pozières on the 5th. Sergt. A. E. Bristowe (13th Rif. Bde., Educ.) was killed on the 7th near Mametz Wood and Sergt. J. H. B. Cope (17th Middx., Educ.) on the 8th, Albert Martin (9th E. Surr., Tram.) on the 12th, Lance-Corp. Sidney Priest (8th Buffs, Tram.) on the 13th and Sergt. F. J. Whiteley (7th Rif. Bde., Educ.) on the 18th, all near Delville Wood, Herbert Miller (13th Middx., Tram.) on the 18th near Guillemont, Lieut. W. H. Bissley (8th R. Berks., Educ.) on the 19th near High Wood, A. B. Cope (R.F.A., Comp.) on the 20th at Montauban, C. J. Denly (R.F.A., Educ.) on the 23rd near Mametz Wood, Sergt. W. A. Lowes (R.F.A., Asylums) on the 25th at Bazentin-le-Petit, Sergt. F. C. Pocock (3rd Worc., Tram.) also on the 25th, Henry Crane (9th Rif. Bde., Parks) on the 29th near Delville Wood, David Haslum (R.F.A., Tram.) on the 31st near Longueval.

On 3rd September Sergt. E. A. Head (Parks), Corporal H. W. Veaser (Parks) and Corporal G. W. J. Holt (Ch. Engr.), all of the 17th K.R.R., were killed near Beaumont Hamel, Sergt. G. E. Corkett and P. H. Edwards, both of the 16th Rif. Bde. and Tramways, near Hamel, and Lieut. P. A. Bick (2nd R. Irish Rgt., Arch.) and Sergt. Jacob Robinson (9th E. Surr., Parks) near Ginchy. On the 4th Capt. H. S. Cameron, B.Sc. (Educ.) and Sergt. A. W. Sterry (Tram.), both of the 1st Norfolks, were killed near Falfemont Farm, and Lieut. P. S. Worner (9th Devons, Educ.) near Ginchy, on the 7th Sergt. R. H. Newbold (2nd Lond., Educ.) near Guillemont and E. P. Finnessy (R.F.A., Tram.) near Montauban and on the 9th Robert Jessop (5th Lond., Educ.) near Guillemont. On this same day Corporal T. B. Butler (M.G.C., Asylums) died at Rouen of wounds received on 18th August near Martinpuich.

Third Phase, September to November.

In another general attack on 15th September Flers was captured by the 41st Division and New Zealand troops assisted by several tanks,[1] Martinpuich by the 15th and Courcelette by the Canadians. High Wood, reached by cavalry during the fighting on 14th July, had been attacked by the 33rd and 51st Divisions later in the month and by the 1st on 3rd September, but each time without permanent success. Outflanked by the fall of Flers, it was at length captured on the 15th by the 47th Division after sharp fighting. On the 18th an advance was made towards Morval.

[1] This was the first occasion on which these new engines of war were used.

These were the best results which, since the beginning of the battle, had been obtained in any one operation. A further advance on the 25th resulted in the capture of Morval by the 5th Division, and Les Bœufs by the 6th and the Guards, while next day Gueudecourt fell to the 21st Division and Combles to the 56th.

The enemy was thus cleared from much of the high land which he had held for the previous two years and instead of overlooking our trenches was now overlooked by them. Thiepval, on the left of the advance, where the attack had failed on 1st July, still continued to offer a resolute and obstinate resistance. However on the 26th, in conjunction with the operations on the right at Gueudecourt and Combles, Mouquet Farm was captured by the Canadians and the 11th Division, and by the morning of the next day the whole of Thiepval had been seized by the 18th Division.

Lieut. A. C. Dancer (5th Dorsets, Educ.) for conspicuous gallantry in the fighting at Thiepval and Mouquet Farm was awarded the M.C. "He established and maintained communications throughout the operations with great courage and skill. On one occasion he himself killed several enemy snipers." About this time also Sergt. J. H. Taylor (R.W. Surr., Parks) was awarded the D.C.M. "for conspicuous gallantry in action. He commanded his men with great courage and initiative, holding a front line position until relieved." Sergt. T. F. Watkins (R.F.A., L.F.B.) was awarded the M.M.

Between 1st and 3rd October the enemy's fourth system of defences was breached by the 47th Division, at and near Eaucourt l'Abbaye, and on the 7th the 23rd captured Le Sars and the 20th advanced to the east of Gueudecourt.

At this point when great results were in prospect, even the cutting off or enforced withdrawal of the enemy as far as Arras and the river Scarpe, the weather, which for some time had been unfavourable, completely broke up. A month's incessant rain made the roads, already much damaged by the traffic and shell-fire, almost impassable either for troops or supplies, and in the mists aeroplane reconnaissance was impracticable. The enemy thus had time in which to re-organise his troops and to construct new defences. Except therefore for the operations in the valley of the Ancre (see p. 50) the battle, after more than three months' continuous fighting, died down with our line on the forward slope of the ridge running through Les Bœufs, Gueudecourt and Le Sars.

Sergt. L. Willey (1st E. Surr., Housing) was awarded the M.M. for bravery shown at Combles on 25th September when, after all the officers of his company had become casualties, he re-organised half the company, consolidated the new position and held it until relieved on the night of the 26th. Sergt. F. Hills (Lond., Educ.) gained the M.M. at Eaucourt l'Abbaye on 8th October when he carried out a most successful reconnaissance under heavy fire, and about this time Sergt. S. Simpson (Lond., Educ.) also received the same decoration. Captain A. B. Raffle (R.A.M.C., Pub. Health) was awarded the M.C. for general distinguished service.

The casualty lists were very heavy, the deaths among the Council's staff being as follows: On 10th September W. H. Hird (5th Lond., Educ.) was killed near Guillemont, B. E. Clarke (7th Middx., Educ.) on the 11th and J. G. Armes (3rd Lond., Tram.) on the 12th, both near Leuze Wood, while H. O. Wood (1st Middx., Stores) and Sergt. T. W. Peel (8th Middx., Asylums) died on the latter date of wounds received on the 10th and 11th respectively. On the 15th Sergt. H. G. Maidment (2nd Lond., Educ.) was killed near Combles, James Gleadall, Sergt. C. J. Cotter, and A. F. Warren, all 7th Middx. and Educ., at Leuze Wood, A. E. Hentsch (10th R.W. Surr., Parks) and Corporal G. W. Stannard (2nd Gren. Gds., Educ.) at Flers, and at High Wood Corporal B. A. Geis (7th

Lond., Estates and Valn.), Lieut. W. A. Burrows (8th Lond., Educ.), A. T. Harling (Arch.), H. A. W. Knight (Educ.) and Lancelot Palmer (Educ.), all of the 15th Londons, Sergt. G. O. Patterson (17th Lond., Parks), Lieut. T. H. Rowson (19th Lond., Educ.), Lieut. C. H. H. Roberts, M.C. (21st Lond., Educ.), Sergt. J. C. Mills (23rd Lond., Tram.), and H. O. Beardmore (25th Lond., Parliamentary). On the same date Harry Ashley (R.F.A., Tram.) was killed near Mametz, and J. A. Clarke (5th Rif. Bde., Pub. Health) and Walter Cappleman (10th Rif. Bde., Tram.) probably near Gueudecourt. W. A. Head (23rd Lond., Educ.), Sergt. G. T. Springbett (11th R.W. Kents, Educ.) and Lance-Corp. H. A. Overton (15th Lond., Stores), wounded on this date, died on the 16th, the 17th and the 18th respectively.

Frank Russell (Educ.), Norman Lynes (Educ.), W. W. Beverley (Tram.) and Lance-Corp. Fred Wholey (Educ.), all of the 7th Middx., and G. F. Pearson, B.Sc. (5th Lond., Educ.) were killed on the 16th at Leuze Wood, and Alfred Page (15th Lond., Solr.), H. G. Rees (15th Lond., Educ.) and Alfred Reeve (23rd Lond., Tram.) at High Wood. Lieut. W. G. Beaumont-Edmonds (22nd Lond., Clerk) was killed on the 17th at High Wood and Lance-Corp. A. V. Weston (13th E. Surr., Tram.) near Flers. P. St. C. Selman (17th Lond., Pub. Health) wounded at High Wood about this date died at Rouen on the 18th and on the latter date Capt. T. S. Rushworth, A.R.I.B.A. (7th Lond., Housing) was killed at High Wood. W. G. N. Hannaford (R. Engrs., Arch.) died at Rouen on the 23rd of wounds received in the Somme area on the 18th, and J. W. W. Powlesland, M.M. (4th Grenadier Gds., Tram.) at Gueudecourt on the 25th. The losses at Thiepval included Lance-Corp. J. Woodcock (12th Middx., Stores) on the 26th, and John Thompson, M.M., and C. J. Jeffery, both of the 7th Buffs and Tramways, on the 30th.

S. J. Best (20th Lond., Ch. Engr.) was killed at Flers on 1st October, C.Q.M.S. Fred Woodhouse (6th R. Berks., Educ.) near Thiepval on the 2nd, E. A. Trew (18th K.R.R., Educ.) at Eaucourt l'Abbaye on the 3rd and G. H. Gordon (R.F.A., Educ.) died at Rouen on the 4th of wounds received near Combles a week before, and Co. Sergt.-Maj. J. P. Edwards (26th R. Fus., Arch.) in England on the 7th October of wounds received near Flers on 15th September.

Another day on which the staff suffered heavily was 7th October. Lieut. J. H. Allender (1st Lond., Comp.), Lieut. L. C. Haycraft (Educ.), and Co. Sergt.-Maj. T. C. Pope (Educ.) of the 4th Londons, Lance-Corp. J. F. Ore and Lance-Corp. A. J. Ames (7th Midx., Educ.), and probably D. Daly (7th Lond., Educ.), and E. J. Titcomb (7th Lond., Tram.) were killed near Les Bœufs, Lance-Corp. R. W. Daly (6th R.W. Kents, Parks), C. M. Coleman (9th R. Fus., Tram.) and Corp. C. J. Mitchell (9th R. Fus., Asylums) near Gueudecourt, F. W. Trotman, B.Sc. (Comp.), Corp. R. A. McMillan (Pub. Health) and H. W. Lawrance (Arch.) of the 15th Londons, and F. W. Peterson and S. H. Potter, both of the 11th R.W. Kents and Tramways, at Eaucourt l'Abbaye.

On the 8th Lance-Corp. C. A. Raymond (11th R.W. Surr., Educ.) was killed, probably near Eaucourt l'Abbaye, E. R. Porter (5th Lond., Clerk) and A. E. Haward (5th Lond., Educ.) near Le Transloy, and G. A. Gaywood (M.G.C., Tram.) probably near Gueudecourt. On the 10th Lieut. R. E. Brewer (R.F.A., Educ.) was killed near Carnoy, and Nelson Laurence (1st Lond., Asylums) in the area of the Somme, and on the same date Battery Q.M.S. Harry Kelcey (R.F.A., L.F.B.) died at Rouen of wounds received at High Wood at the beginning of the month, and Lance-Corp. Arthur Clark (16th Lond., Stores) of wounds received on the 9th. Lieut. Charles Sizeland (7th Norfolks, Educ.) was killed near Le Transloy on the 12th, Lieut.

S. S. Boden (M.G.C., Educ.) near Le Sars and Corporal L. M. Marks (11th Essex, Tram.) near Gueudecourt on the 15th, Lieut. William Davis (9th Middx., Educ.) near Gueudecourt on the 18th, Lance-Corp. W. E. Stower (16th Middx., Asylums) near Flers on the 20th, Lieut. T. E. Parry (2nd Lanc. Fus., Educ.) near Gueudecourt, and E. J. P. Longley (2nd Rif. Bde., Est. and Valn.) near Les Bœufs on the 23rd, and Lieut. Archibald Steven (8th Glouc., Educ.) near Thiepval on the 25th.

Bombardier F. J. Archer (R.F.A., Tram.), wounded on 2nd November near Sailly, died the same day and W. T. Chesterman (1st R.W. Surr., Tram.) was killed on the 3rd between Les Bœufs and Combles.

Battle of the Ancre.

The failure at Thiepval and Beaumont Hamel on 1st July and the partial success at the former on 26th September have already been referred to (see pp. 39 and 46). Our advance over the high land east of Thiepval to the line Les Bœufs—Gueudecourt—Le Sars threatened to cut off the Germans in the valley of the Ancre round about Hamel and Beaucourt, but the continual rain put an end to that advance. It was therefore decided to deal with the enemy positions on the Ancre by direct assault.[1] Early in November the weather improved, with frost in place of rain. On 13th November, after a bombardment lasting 48 hours, the attack was launched in a mist and at almost every point was completely successful. On this or succeeding days the 19th and 39th Divisions captured St. Pierre Divion and land to the east, the 63rd was successful at Beaucourt, the 51st at Beaumont Hamel and the 2nd to the north thereof. The number of prisoners taken was 7,200.

In the fighting near Beaumont Hamel Lieut. (afterwards Captain) F. G. Bull (23rd R. Fus., Clerk) gained the M.C., and in the same neighbourhood Sergt. T. J.

[1] For plan, see p. 36.

Sevier (R.A.M.C., Educ.) gained the M.M. on 16th November for rescuing wounded under heavy shell fire.

On 13th November H. F. Bentley (R.N.V.R., Tram.) was killed near Beaucourt and S. H. Boot (5th Seaforth Highdrs., Arch.) near Beaumont Hamel, on the 14th H. J. Dunford (Hon. Artillery Co., Educ.) near Beaucourt and on the same date C. J. L. Jewell (R.G.A., Tram.) died near Albert of wounds received the day before, probably in this sector.

Summary.

The net immediate result of the Battle of the Somme was the piercing of the enemy's lines on a front of some seven miles and to an average depth of three or four miles, and the capture of 38,000 prisoners, 29 heavy guns, 96 field guns, 136 trench mortars and 514 machine guns. The enemy's withdrawal in the spring of 1917 (see p. 56) south of the Scarpe and in the valley of the Somme was a further direct result. Of much more importance, however, than the gain of ground or the capture of prisoners, was the moral effect of the fact that our men had driven the Germans out of strongly fortified positions and had held the positions so won against frequent counter-attacks. Casualties of course had been heavy but the enemy's losses both in men and material were not much less than ours.[1] In the second place the pressure on Verdun was relieved so effectually that in the latter part of the year the French were able to win back much of the ground lost in the earlier part and to capture many prisoners and guns. Finally the enemy was prevented from moving troops to the Italian or Russian fronts

[1] The losses admitted by the Germans were 444,933 which, in view of their methods, might have to be increased by 50 per cent. (*Times Literary Supplement*, 20th January, 1921, p. 34). The British losses in July, 1916, were 196,081 (Capt. P. E. Wright, *At the Supreme War Council*, p. 121), but this rate was far from being maintained. Our total losses were 499,476 (*ibid.*, p. 33). The French losses were less than the British. It must be remembered, however, that the British casualty lists included the names of those who received very light wounds; usually such light cases were not included in the lists of the other belligerents.

for, at the end of the year, his strength in France was greater than in July.

Although only British operations are dealt with in this sketch it should be stated that throughout the battle the French played a most prominent part. The Germans were not expecting an attack from them so that their advance on our right was most successful, particularly at first, and carried them almost as far as Péronne. Then the German resistance stiffened, but all through the operations the French continued to assist the right of our advance and to push the enemy back on both sides of the Somme. Their total advance was from four to six miles on a front of about fourteen miles.

General Fighting during the latter half of 1916.

Sergt. F. King (R.F.A., L.F.B.) was awarded the D.C.M. for gallantry and devotion to duty in action at Laventie on 23rd August, 1916, and Sergt. E. M. Cronyn (R. Fus., Asylums) the same decoration for bravery at some place unknown. Sergt. J. V. Jeanes, M.M. (Gren. Gds., Asylums) for bravery at Ypres was awarded a bar to his M.M.

The list of those killed in France during the latter half of 1916, apart from those who lost their lives in the Battles of the Somme and the Ancre, includes Corporal A. E. Stevens (2/15th Lond., Educ.) killed at Neuville St. Vaast on 3rd August, Lance-Corp. George Dormon (2nd Hamps., Tram.) in a gas attack near Ypres on the 9th, Sergt. F. G. Golding (6th Lond., Arch.) on the 21st of wounds received the day before, C. H. Barnes (9th R.W. Surr., Tram.) on the night of the 21st/22nd, Louis Green (R.E., Educ.) on the 24th, Alfred Warren (17th K.R.R., Asylums) on the 25th of wounds received on 21st June, and F. J. B. Saunders (2/15th Lond., Educ.) on the 31st near Arras.

W. J. Fell (10th R. Fus., Educ.) was killed on 8th September, Lance-Corp. H. R. Horwood (23rd Lond., Tram.) died at Havre on the 15th of tetanus, and

Lieut. J. C. Chalmers, M.M., (20th Northd. Fus., Educ.) was killed, probably near Armentières, on 16th October.

Chas. E. Palmer (4th R. Fus., Tram.) died of wounds on 6th November, Lieut. F. W. Lambe (4th R. Berks., Educ.) died at Rouen on the 10th of wounds received the day before, Lieut. W. L. Elliott (9th Rif. Bde., Educ.) was killed near Arras on the 21st, and Capt. G. N. Higginson (16th R. Fus., Educ.) on the 23rd near Beaumont Hamel. A. P. Phenix (12th K.R.R., Tram.) died of exhaustion when leaving the line at Les Bœufs on 15th December, and J. A. Walker, B.Sc. (R.A.M.C., Educ.) and C. W. King (M.G.C., Educ.) were both killed to the south-east of Ypres on 24th December.

CHAPTER V.

Western Front, 1917.

During the winter of 1916–17 the British took over a further section of the line, principally that which had fallen to the French at the Battle of the Somme. With the completion of this operation the British sector extended from the north of Ypres to the Amiens-Roye road, a distance of about 115 miles. The undermentioned deaths among the staff on service occurred about this time. H. W. Cooper (13th Lond., Tram.) died on 6th January of wounds received the day before, and F. W. Groombridge (Army Cyclists Corps, Tram.) was killed near Bullecourt on the 26th, Walter Peters (R.A.M.C., Asylums) died of bronchitis at Etaples on the 11th, and Lieut. J. A. Monkhouse (R.A.M.C., Educ.) on the 23rd, of heart trouble following trench fever. During February Frank Bailey (16th Middx., Tram.) was killed near Combles on the 4th, Corporal C. G. Adams (2/5th Lond., Pub. Health) died on the 6th of wounds received near Arras on the 2nd, Sergt. S. R. Bence, M.M. (3rd Lond., Educ.), on the 17th, probably near Neuve Chapelle, C. T. Harris (3rd Cold. Gds., Parks) on the 22nd near Combles, Lance-Corp. A. R. Hart (7th Middx., Educ.) on the 23rd near Neuve Chapelle, and F. H. H. Taylor (7th Buffs, Educ.) on the 27th. Lieut. J. V. Amos (R.F.A., Parks) died at Béthune on the 13th of illness, and W. J. Power (9th R. Fus., Educ.) on the 17th of appendicitis. Bombr. J. A. George (R.G.A., Asylums), wounded near Arras on 14th February, died in England on 25th January, 1918.

G. W. Sapsworth (17th Lond., Educ.) died at Poperinghe on 1st March of wounds received the day before near Ypres, C. W. Bishop (2nd R. Berks, Tram.) on the 4th near Péronne, Capt. D. F. Goodwin (R.F.A., Arch.) near Rozières, and H. G. Brice (6th Lond., Tram.) near Arras on the 7th, E. W. Vince (20th Lond., Parks) near Dickebusch and C. R. Darkens (13th E. Surr., Tram.) in the area of the Somme on the 14th, and Ernest Lewis (23rd Lond., Educ.) near Zillebeke on the 15th.

Capt. A. C. Hancock, M.C., (R.A.M.C., Asylums) was awarded a bar to his M.C. for conspicuous good work in advanced dressing stations, near the Butte de Warlencourt early in 1917, "notably when he successfully conducted evacuation of wounded under heavy shell fire and adverse circumstances. . . . By his initiative, personal courage and devotion to duty he was responsible for the able carrying out of wounded through a barrage of shell fire for six days. He was then severely gassed, but persisted in attempting duty until physically incapable."

Fighting in the Valley of the Ancre.

The fighting at the end of 1916 closed with the capture of Beaumont Hamel and Beaucourt in the valley of the Ancre. This advance, if continued, would enable the enemy's strong positions at Serre and Gommecourt, which had repulsed all assaults in 1916, to be attacked in flank or in rear, and it was natural that, in the spring of 1917, the fighting should commence at the same point.[1] During January our position at Beaumont Hamel was extended and consolidated, and on 6th February, Grandcourt, and on the 7th Baillescourt Farm were occupied. A further advance on the 17th up to Petit Miraumont led to the evacuation by the enemy of the defences of Pys, Miraumont and Serre, and on the 25th these places with Warlencourt to the east were occupied. On the 27th Gommecourt fell, followed by Puisieux-au-Mont on the 28th. After a week's delay to enable artillery to be brought up and communications to be put in order, Irles was attacked and captured at dawn on 10th March.

In an attempted advance in February up the valley of the Ancre towards Pys, Capt. J. W. Woods (2nd Yorks L.I., Educ.) "accompanied by six men . . . pushed forward in front of his company, thereby effecting the capture of 60 prisoners. Later, he took charge of the right-half battalion and consolidated his position under the most difficult conditions." For this gallantry he was awarded the M.C. For his gallant conduct and devotion to duty on 17th February during operations near Miraumont, Sergt. Thomas Eaves (8th Suff., Tram.) was awarded the M.M.

In this fighting Lieut. L. T. Despicht, M.C. (4th Beds, Educ.) was killed on 11th February, Capt. Leon Simons, M.C., B.Sc. (22nd R. Fus., Educ.), Sergt. Frank Trevett, M.M. (1st K.R.R., Tram.), Sergt. E. G. Stanbrough (22nd R. Fus., Arch.) and A. E. Lassetter (11th R. Fus., Educ.) on the 17th in the advance on Miraumont, and Sergt. Frederick Prior (23rd R. Fus., Tram.) on the 18th. Lieut. S. D. Lang, B.A. (2/5th Yorks L.I., Educ.), wounded in this neighbourhood on the 20th, died on the 23rd.

German Retreat.

For some time it had been suspected that the German withdrawal in the valley of the Ancre would

[1] For plan, see p. 36.

be extended to other parts of their front. A constant watch was maintained, and on 14th March portions of the enemy's lines to the south of Sailly-Saillisel were found to be empty. A general advance between Roye and Arras was ordered for the 17th when Chaulnes and Bapaume were entered; next day Nesle and Péronne fell. The advance continued on succeeding days, but great care had to be exercised so that progress was slow.

It was known that the enemy was falling back upon fortified positions, carefully selected, and possessing ample communications for the movement of troops and supplies. Our men, on the other hand, had to abandon their defences, and to move forward more or less in the open; their communications lay across a desolate region which for four months recently had been the scene of most destructive fighting. Sudden counter-attacks were to be expected at almost any time or any place, and such attacks, if successful, would have far-reaching results. To add to the difficulties, roads and railways had been mined, bridges blown up and stores and farm stocks removed. Shelter of any kind was hard to find, for all buildings, both public and private, including several of great historical or archæological interest, had been pillaged and destroyed or at least rendered uninhabitable. In some of them mines with delayed action had been left, which exploded after the arrival of our men and caused many casualties. All this of course was legitimate warfare. Less legitimate, and, indeed, completely opposed to civilised practice, were the poisoning and pollution of wells, which occurred in so many places that the work must have been done under orders. The destruction of the numerous orchards was of no military advantage, but was rather a proof of a petty and spiteful disposition in those who planned the work.

In face of growing resistance the pursuit gradually slackened, and about 8th April our troops were definitely held up on a line (see pp. 92 and 37) which, starting from opposite St. Quentin on our right, passed to the east of Epéhy, near Havrincourt Wood and Croisilles, to the eastern suburbs of Arras where it joined the original line. The withdrawal extended much farther than this, in fact from Soissons in the south to Arras in the north, a distance of 70 miles, or, allowing for the curves in the line, a battle front of 120 miles. Two-thirds of this was opposite the British, the remainder being opposite the French. The greatest distance through which the line was withdrawn was about 20 miles, this being near Roye; elsewhere, except of course at the extremities, the withdrawal averaged about 15 miles.

Lieut. S. J. F. Philpott, (R.G.A., Educ.) gained the M.C. on 6th April, when a magazine containing cartridges and fuses was set on fire, and the enemy proceeded to shell the spot. With two others he rushed into the blazing mass and extricated boxes of fuses from the fuse store.

Although there was no prolonged resistance during the retreat, there was sharp fighting at various points and Sergt. W. A. Williams (12th Middlx., Stores) was killed on 17th March near Bapaume, H. E. Lawrance (2nd H.A.C., Arch.) near Ecoust St. Mein on the 31st, C. A. Sanderson (R. Inn. Fus., Educ.) on 1st April, George Saunders (8th R. Fus., Tram.) near Arras on the 4th, Corporal W. J. Burford (4th Oxf. and Bucks L.I., Educ.) near Ronssoy on the 5th, and Sergt. Bertie Elliott (2/4th Oxf. and Bucks L.I., Educ.) near St. Quentin on the 7th.

Battles of Arras, 1917.

For the spring of 1917 the French, now under General Nivelle in succession to General Joffre, had planned in the Champagne area north-west of Rheims an ambitious scheme of attack from which great results were expected. To ensure concerted action the British army was to some extent placed under the orders of

British line 8th April 1917
" " end of April 1917
" " December 1917
Scale
0 1 2 3 Miles
Loos
Grenay
Bully Grenay
To Bethune
Aix-Noulette
Liévin
LENS
Cité St Auguste
Cité St Pierre
Cité St Emile
Cité St Elizabeth
Cité du Bois de Liévin
R Souchez
Canal de Lens
Avion
Givenchy
Ablain St Nazaire
Souchez
Givenchy en Gohelle
Carency
Vimy
Mericourt
Drocourt
Arleux en Gohelle
Fresnoy
Quiéry la Motte
Farbus
Neuville St Vaast
Mont St Eloy
Thélus
Oppy
Bailleul
To Douai
Gavrelle
Vitry en Artois
Roclincourt
Marœuil
Anzin St Aubin
Point du Jour
To St Pol
Fampoux
ARRAS
Blangy
Feuchy
Rœux
R Scarpe
Dainville
Infantry Hill
Tilloy lez Mofflaines
Monchy le Preux
Orange Hill
To Doullens
Achicourt
Telegraph Hill
Agny
Beaurains
Guémappe
Wailly
Wancourt
R Cojeul
Neuville Vitasse
To Cambrai
Héninel
Ficheux
Mercatel
St Martin sur Cojeul
Chérisy
Henin sur Cojeul
Blairville
Fontaine lez Croisilles
Boisleux au Mont
Boisleux St Marc
Hendecourt
Boyelles
Boiry St Martin
Boiry St Rictude
Croisilles
Adinfer
Bullecourt
To Bapaume
St Léger
Moyenneville
Ecous St Mein
Quéant
Ayette

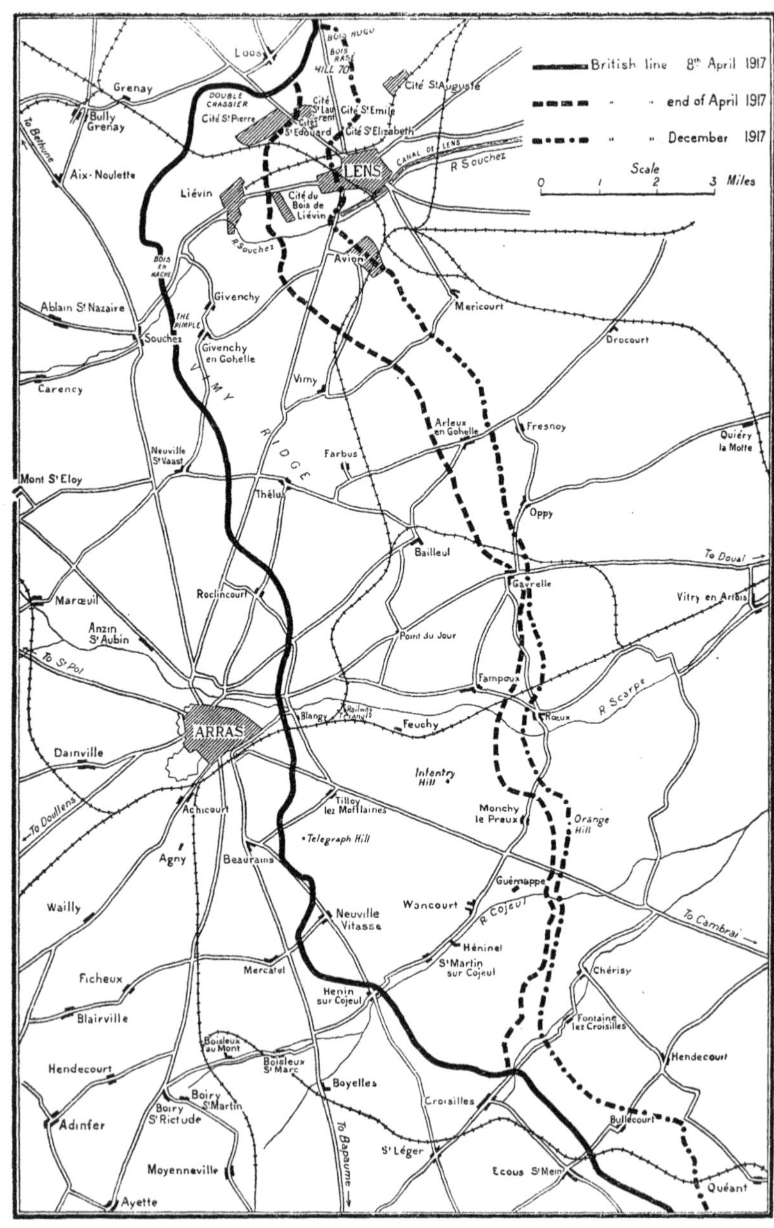

ARRAS, 1917.

General Nivelle, and it was arranged that it should attract the enemy's reserves by opening an offensive to the east of Arras. The enemy had obtained an inkling of what was proposed and the retreat, just referred to, between Soissons and Arras was carried out partly with the intention of dislocating the Allies' plans. Fortunately the withdrawal near Arras was slight and the British plans were hardly interfered with.

Arras, as the principal city in the British sector of the front and also as the French city which, after Rheims, sustained most damage from the war, merits a brief description. It is situated on the river Scarpe, a canalised stream flowing through a marshy valley and from this point eastwards navigable for barges. The surrounding country is much like the Somme country—bare sloping uplands, the chief points in which are Vimy Ridge on the north with a height of 475 feet and Monchy-le-Preux to the south-east with a height of 350 feet. Arras had been an important place for over 2,000 years for, in the time of Julius Cæsar, it was the capital of the Atrebates from whom, like the surrounding province of Artois, it derived its name, and in the 6th century it became the seat of a bishopric. After various vicissitudes in the Hundred Years' War between England and France, it passed into the power of the Spaniards but was taken from them by the French in 1640.[1] In the Middle Ages it gave its name of "arras" to the special kind of tapestry for the manufacture of which it was noted.

Overlooked by the enemy from the high ground to the north-east and south-east, and closely hemmed in on three sides by trenches dug through several of the suburbs, it suffered terribly from the war. The early 16th-century *Hôtel de Ville*, regarded as one of the most beautiful buildings in northern France, was completely destroyed. The *Grande-Place* and the

[1] Some of the architecture has been said to show Spanish influence, but this seems to be incorrect. (*Notes and Queries*, 7th Jan., 1922.)

Petite-Place, surrounded by gabled houses dating from the 17th century or earlier, with charming arcades, were wrecked. The cathedral became a roofless ruin, piled with débris to a height of ten or twenty feet. Extensive areas near the station and in the middle of the city were so damaged as to be uninhabitable.

As at the Somme our preparations included the construction of many miles of ordinary and narrow gauge railways, the formation of new roads, the provision of accommodation and water for tens of thousands of troops, and the accumulation of immense quantities of guns, ammunition and supplies. In the chalk under the city were immense catacombs dating from very early times. These were linked up into one system, lit by electricity, and connected with the trenches. A few days before the attack large bodies of troops, brought up to the city under cover of darkness, were concealed in these catacombs with the result that at the opening of the assault the British were in much greater strength than the Germans expected.

The front attacked extended for fifteen miles, from Croisilles in the south to the northern end of the Vimy Ridge. For most of this distance the enemy's defences consisted of three separate trench systems forming a highly organised belt, and to deal with these a heavy bombardment was necessary. This commenced three weeks before the date fixed for the assault and gradually increased in intensity, while from time to time extensive discharges of gas were made. The assault was launched in a storm of sleet and wind at 5.30 on the morning of Easter Monday, 9th April, and, differing from the opening of the Battle of the Somme nine months earlier, was everywhere successful. By 7.20 the first objective had been captured and by noon most of the second, while before the end of the day wide gaps had been forced in the enemy's third system. Counting from the south, that is from the right of the advance, the troops responsible for these excellent results were the 30th Division at St. Martin-sur-Cojeul, the 56th at Neuville Vitasse, the 14th at Telegraph Hill, the 3rd and the 12th along the Arras-Cambrai road followed by the 37th towards Orange Hill, the 15th at Railway Triangle and Feuchy, the 9th at Blangy followed by the 4th at Fampoux, the 34th at Point du Jour and the 51st further north. Tanks co-operated in the capture of Tilloy and Railway Triangle. The attack on Vimy Ridge was brilliantly carried out by the Canadian Corps of four Canadian divisions.

In spite of heavy falls of snow and rain the success was extended on the 10th by the capture of Orange Hill and the summit of Vimy Ridge, on the 11th by the capture of Monchy and by an attempt on Bullecourt and on the 12th by the capture of Héninel and Wancourt in the south, and two hills known as the Pimple and the Bois-en-Hache in the valley of the Souchez south-west of Lens. During the next few days the enemy vacated many of his trenches to the south, west and north of Lens, and these were promptly occupied.

Altogether the fighting between 9th and 16th April yielded the most important results achieved by us up to that time. The front was advanced an average of four miles on a length of fifteen. The gains included about 8,500 yards, near the Scarpe, of the Hindenburg line, a system of trenches which had been very strongly constructed in positions specially suitable for defence. Moreover the British position was much improved by the seizure of high ground by which it had previously been dominated. The prisoners numbered 13,000 and over 200 guns were captured.

In the fighting near Gavrelle on the 24th, Corporal A. C. Batchelor (10th R. Fus., Comp.), before communication by signal could be established and when nearly all the officers had become casualties, maintained touch between battalion headquarters and the front line, and in doing so he thrice made his way through very heavy fire and returned with valuable information. For this gallantry he was awarded the M.M.

Those who lost their lives in the first eight days of the battle included Herbert Stagnell (13th K.R.R., Stores) killed near Feuchy, G. E. Downham (1st Rif. Bde., Pub. Cont.) north of Fampoux, Sergt. W. E. Newton (R.G.A., Parks) near Arras, and Lance-Corp. Benjamin Rotenberg (Wilts Yeo., Educ.) on Vimy Ridge, all on 9th April. On the 10th Lance-Corp. A. G. Greenwood (8th Middx., Educ.) was killed to the east of Neuville Vitasse and C. H. Plummer (10th R. Fus., Tram.) near Monchy, and on the 11th Capt. B. T. Bryant (5th Linc., Educ.). B. A. Savage (11th Middx., Parks.) wounded on the 9th, and A. E. Newton (3rd Lond., Educ.) on the 12th, died on the 12th and 13th respectively. On the 14th Sergt. A. G. Chick (Educ.) and Corporal C. J. Brunning (Tram.) of the 9th Londons, and James Scowcroft (Educ.) and Lance-Corp. Arthur Bradbury (Solr.) of the 16th Londons, were killed between Héninel and Chérisy.

Continuation of the Battle.

In the ordinary way the battle would now have been broken off and the bulk of our men transferred to the neighbourhood of Ypres in preparation for the fighting which will be described later. The French offensive, however, near Rheims had been held up by the bad weather and it was therefore desirable to continue to engage the enemy at Arras. Accordingly on 23rd April a fresh assault was opened between Croisilles and Gavrelle and also near Lens. The 30th and 50th Divisions advanced near Chérisy, the 15th took, but lost, Guémappe, the 29th advanced to the east of Monchy, the 51st was heavily engaged at Rœux, the 63rd captured Gavrelle, and the 5th was successful in a minor operation south-west of Lens. Guémappe was retaken by us next day

On the 28th the attack was renewed on a front of eight miles north of Monchy, when the 12th Division was successful between Monchy and the Scarpe, the 2nd near Oppy and the Canadians at Arleux. On 3rd May in an attack extending from Bullecourt to Fresnoy ground was gained at each of these places, at the former by the Australians and at the latter by the Canadians. The Australians, being open to attack on three sides, were hard pressed, but in spite of many counter-attacks held their ground for two weeks until the advance of troops on each flank relieved the pressure.

On 5th May the French captured the Chemin-des-Dames, to the east of Soissons, and, General Pétain having now succeeded General Nivelle, it was agreed that the main effort of the British should be shifted from Arras northward to the neighbourhood of Ypres. The attention of the enemy continued to be engaged, but now various feints were employed for the purpose. One of the most amusing consisted of a heavy bombardment of the German lines followed by the appearance in No Man's Land of numerous troops and tanks. These were all dummies manipulated by ropes but they effectually deceived the enemy, for in a subsequent *communiqué* he claimed that the attack had been annihilated. There was still serious fighting, however, and on the 8th our men gained a footing in Bullecourt, but did not capture the whole until ten days later. On the 8th Fresnoy was lost but Rœux and the adjoining chemical works, which had been continually changing hands for over a month, were, between the 12th and the 14th, finally captured and held. Between 20th May and 16th June possession was gradually obtained of a sector of the enemy's line from Bullecourt to the west of Fontaine-lez-Croisilles. On 14th June the crest of Orange Hill to the east of Monchy was captured by a surprise attack. Many fierce counter-attacks followed but, although advanced posts changed hands frequently, the main line, which gave important facilities for observation, remained permanently in our possession.

In the second phase of the battle the line was advanced only about a mile, but 8,000 prisoners were captured, with 57 guns, bringing the total gains up to 21,000 prisoners and 257 guns, in addition to many machine-guns and trench mortars and immense quantities of war material. About twelve miles of the Hindenburg line or of systems allied to it were captured. Our total casualties amounted to 196,110.[1]

Captain A. C. Hancock, M.C. and bar (R.A.M.C., Asylums) received a second bar to his M.C. when " he established his advanced dressing station in a village, although it was under very heavy shell fire. He attended and evacuated a very large number of wounded, working all night, finally going out himself along the front to see if there were any left." In the fighting at Oppy Lieut. (afterwards Captain) F. G. Bull (23rd R. Fus., Clerk) was awarded a bar to his M.C., " for his conspicuous gallantry . . . as battalion signalling officer when, in spite of continuous heavy shelling and constant moves over difficult ground, he maintained communications." Capt. A. A. Riley (7th Middx., Comp.) received the M.C. for his conspicuous gallantry near Monchy on 3rd May when " an assault having failed, and most of his officers being casualties, he collected and re-organised all the men he could find and formed a strong front against counter-attacks by occupying and linking up a line of shell-holes. After his battalion was relieved he remained behind to guide the stretcher-bearers to the wounded, thereby saving many lives." On the same date near the river Cojeul Co. Sergt-Maj. E. J. P. Dainty (2nd Lond., Educ.) won the D.C.M., " for conspicuous gallantry and devotion to duty in consolidating and defending a position which had become almost

[1] Capt. P. E. Wright, *At the Supreme War Council*, p. 33.

untenable through flanking and frontal fire. His total indifference to danger restored the situation at a very critical moment when no officers were on the spot."

The M.M. was awarded to R. Bristow (R.A.M.C., Educ.), for attending to wounded men during a four days' continuous attack by the British, to J. Etherington (6th R. W. Kents, Asylums) when "in charge of a bombing section . . . with the help of his comrades he put enemy's machine gun out of action and held the trench until reinforcements arrived," and to Lance-Corp. W. W. Cracknell (1st Bord., Comp.) who, on 19th/20th May at Monchy "carried messages . . . all night through the heaviest barrages. At one time, when things were critical, he carried a message through a terrific machine-gun fire and, . . . though wounded, carried on and delivered the message. . . . When his officer was knocked out he acted as N.C.O., and by his great courage, coolness and tireless energy was invaluable to his company commander." Staff-Sergt. D. Keenan (R.A.M.C., Asylums) and Bombr. W. T. Mills (R.F.A., L.F.B.) won the M.M. for gallantry in action.

In the later fighting Corporal H. J. Hollins (9th E. Surr., Tram.) was killed near Lens on 17th April, and William Johnston (R.G.A., Educ.) near Arras on the 19th, W. G. Udall (R.E., Educ.) wounded in this sector on the 20th, died on the 22nd. On the 23rd Lieut. R. D. Wills, M.M. (5th Bord., Arch.), was killed near Wancourt, G. E. F. Gray (19th Manch., Parks) near Monchy, and C. T. Barker (R.N. Div., Parks) near Gavrelle, and on the 24th Victor Williams (2nd R. Fus., Asylums) near Monchy, while on the 28th P. J. Martin (7th R. Fus., Parks) died of wounds received two days before in the Gavrelle sector. On the 29th Lieut. M. E. Wardley (22nd R. Fus., Educ.) and H. F. Ponton, A.R.I.B.A. (17th R. Fus., Arch.) were killed near Oppy or Gavrelle and on the 30th A. H. Brownsword (R.G.A., Estates and Val.) died of wounds received at Vimy Ridge on the 21st.

On 1st May T. W. Burton (7th E. Surr., Tram.) was killed near Monchy, on the 2nd Percy Chorley (R.E., Educ.) near Guémappe, on the 3rd Corporal R. R. Summers, B.A. (2nd H.A.C., Educ.) near Bullecourt, Sergt. George Harland (5th Lond., Educ.), Sergt. W. G. White (12th Middx., Trams.) and L. H. Pert (8th Rif. Bde., Educ.), all near Chérisy, T. V. Thorpe (6th Buffs, Educ.) near Monchy, Lieut. G. W. Coombes (1st R. Lanc., Comp.) and A. S. T. Wright (2nd Essex, Tram.) near Rœux, and Sergt. J. R. Pardew (8th R. Fus., Tram.), J. G. Keyworth (8th E. Surr., Tram.), S. T. Wakeford (9th Lond., Educ.), and H. C. J. Clifton (R.G.A., Pub. Cont.), all in the Arras sector. Corporal A. C. Batchelor, M.M. (10th R. Fus., Comp.) wounded near Gavrelle on 24th April died on 4th May, and C. W. Almeroth (1st R. Berks., Tram.) wounded at Oppy on 29th April died a prisoner of war on 5th May.

E. A. Wright (1st Lond., Tram.), Lance.-Corp. H. F. C. Jones (2/5th Lond., Educ.) and A. J. Bain (Stores) and Sergt. S. J. Wale (Educ.) both of the 2/6th Londons, were killed near Bullecourt on 13th, 16th and 21st May respectively, and on the 18th Lieut. S. C. Tremeer (7th Beds, Educ.) died of wounds received near Chérisy on the 3rd. On the 20th F. N. Brooker (6th Buffs, Parks) died of wounds received near Arras, Lance-Corp. W. H. Hamer (2nd R. Fus., Educ.) was killed on the 21st at Monchy, Bomdr. A. C. Colborne (R.F.A., Tram.) on the 24th near Arras, L. J. Friday (R.A.M.C., Asylums) on the 25th, and on the 27th P. T. Williams (12th Lond., Tram.) died of wounds received the day before. Sergt. T. W. Bedwell (16th Middx., Tram.) was killed on the 31st.

On 15th June Lieut. S. M. Williams (2/4th Lond., Educ.) was missing, probably near Bullecourt, on the 16th Frederick Spencley (Ch. Engr.) and Corporal J. L. Hancock (Educ.), both of the 2/2nd Londons, were killed between Croisilles and Ecoust St. Mein, and S. L. Fasham (2/4th Lond., Tram.) at Bullecourt, and on the 17th Lance-Corp. Fred Holloway (2/5th Lond., Educ.) was killed near Bullecourt. Lieut. G. D. Turk (1st Essex, Comp.) died a prisoner of war on the 23rd of wounds received near Monchy on 14th April.

Battle of Messines, 1917.

It has been explained (see p. 15) how during the first Battles of Ypres the Germans pressed the British back from the Messines-Wytschaete ridge, the highest ground near the city, and how they were thus able to overlook and, in places, to enfilade the British lines to the south and south-east of Ypres and to the north-east of Armentières.

The enemy's position here, already of great natural strength, had been so well fortified that it might have been regarded as impregnable. One system of trenches skirted the western foot of the ridge, a second, to the west of Messines and Wytschaete, defended the crest, and a third, to the east of Oost-taverne, protected the eastern part of the ridge. In addition, numerous woods, hamlets and farmhouses had been converted with great skill and industry into strong points which would form centres for rallying or defence.[1]

The usual preparations for bringing forward troops, guns, ammunition and stores were of course much impeded by the fact that the enemy had direct observation over our movements. These labours had also to be supplemented by the construction of a series of mines. In all twenty-four were formed, nineteen of which were used for the assault. The enemy, aware of his danger, tried to avert it by means of counter-mines, and at Hill 60 and the Bluff in particular underground fighting continued for months. In spite of this and of difficulties from springs and streams which

[1] For plan, see p. 12.

were liable to flood the work, over 8,000 yards of gallery were driven and one million pounds of explosive were stored therein.

At 3.10 a.m. on 7th June the nineteen mines were exploded, one at Spanbroekmolen forming a crater 140 yards across and another, near Hill 60, taking up with it a whole company of Wurtembergers. Simultaneously the final bombardment opened and the attack was launched on a front of ten miles from the north of Ploegsteert Wood to a point just north of Hill 60. The front system offered practically no resistance and by noon the Anzac Corps on the right had captured Messines, the 36th and 16th Divisions had captured Wytschaete, the 41st had reached a formidable position in a sunken road known as the Dammstrasse, and the 47th had fought its way from the Bluff along the Ypres-Comines canal. The infantry made such rapid progress that, over the broken ground, the artillery and tanks could hardly keep pace with them, and when, early in the afternoon, the Oosttaverne line was reached they halted there to enable a new assault to be organised. This was as successful as the former, and by the evening the whole line was in our hands. A violent counter-attack on the 8th was repulsed at all points. The progress on the right caused the Germans to the north of the river Lys to vacate their trenches which were promptly occupied. Also on the 14th we made a slight advance along most of the line reached on the 7th, but thereafter no further efforts were made to exploit the success.

By this victory a standing menace to two sections of our line was removed, the enemy was deprived of a commanding position on the defence of which he had lavished much skill and labour, his lines were pierced to a depth in some parts of three miles, and in addition to many killed and wounded he lost 7,200 prisoners. Much material and stores, including 67 guns, were captured. Our total casualties were about 16,000.

The effect of the initial success was not marred, as at the Somme, at Arras, and later in the year at Passchendaele, by long and costly attempts to carry on the action without effective artillery preparation and ample supplies of all kinds. Mr. John Buchan in his *History* (vol. xx. p. 71) says of this brilliant engagement that it will rank "with Nivelle's two victories at Verdun, in the winter of 1916, as a perfect instance of the success of the limited objective."

Lieut. W. J. Field (1st R. Fus., Educ.) in the attack on the 7th opposite the Dammstrasse ". . . showed great promptness and good leadership in capturing two machine-guns. . . . He also captured many prisoners and by his determination and resource many casualties were avoided." He was awarded the M.C. G. F. Bell (14th Northld. Fus., Asylums) received the M.M. for bravery under heavy fire when, though wounded, he brought in a wounded officer and kept up constant communications for three days and two nights.

On the 7th, the opening day of the battle, the Council lost only two of its staff, Harry Amos (Tramways) and H. S. Zoller (Education), both of the 21st Londons, who were killed in the advance along the Ypres-Comines canal. Lieut. E. N. Makeham (13th Middx., Clerk) who was wounded and missing on the 10th, died a prisoner of war on an unknown date. Sergt. J. E. Hughes (12th R. Fus., Pub. H.) was killed, probably in this part, on the 16th, as his division, the 24th, was in reserve behind St. Eloi on the 9th.

Lombartzyde.

The following incident is worthy of mention. Towards the end of June, in preparation for the third Battle of Ypres, the British took over from the French a short sector of the front extending from the Belgian coast to the south of Nieuport. The part near the coast was defended by breastworks in the sand dunes, and, being intersected by several canals and approached from the rear only by floating bridges, did not form a satisfactory position. The enemy, realising this and suspecting an attack along the coast, took the initiative, and on 10th July opened an intense bombardment which flattened out the breastworks and destroyed all the bridges. It is said that as many as 182 batteries were available for this, while only 13 were ready for the defence.[1] An attack in great strength then followed which so completely overwhelmed the 1st Northamptons and the 2nd K.R.R., which were holding the line, that out of the two battalions, numbering perhaps from 1,200 to 1,500 men, only 74 escaped by swimming the Yser in rear.

H. H. Chaplin (K.R.R., Asylums) was awarded the M.M. for bravery shown in this engagement.

Battles of Ypres, 1917.

It will be remembered that in the first Battle of Ypres the enemy captured ground to the south of the city, and, in the second ground to the north and east which completely commanded the defences. The enemy was superior in numbers and in gun-power and, as it was not possible to regain the lost positions, it was suggested more than once that the place should be abandoned, and that a new line which could be defended more easily and with fewer losses should be taken up on higher ground to the west. This was not agreed to and so, for well over two years, our men continued, at the price of heavy casualties, to hold on to their inferior positions. Early in 1917 it was decided to commence operations in the summer for freeing the salient and for dealing with the submarine peril by capturing the Passchendaele ridge from which long range guns could fire upon the enemy's submarine bases at Bruges, Zeebrugge and Ostend. This plan had to be subordinated to the French offensive, and to meet their wishes the fighting at Arras was prolonged into the early part of the summer. As it

[1] Sir A. Conan Doyle, *British Campaign in France*, 1917, p. 130.

was not possible for our forces to conduct at the same time two offensives on a large scale, this led to the work at Ypres being postponed. However, in June, the fighting at Arras died down and by the capture of the Messines ridge the way was, to some extent, cleared for the proposed attack further north. The preparations for this were more than usually difficult, for, as the commander-in-chief wrote in his despatch, " on no previous occasion . . . had the whole of the ground from which we had to attack been so completely exposed to the enemy's observation."

All preliminaries having been at length completed, the opening of the attack was fixed for 25th July, but a few days before that date the Germans withdrew many of their batteries to safer positions. The attack was therefore postponed while these new positions were being identified by the airmen and dealt with by the artillery, and a succession of cloudy days led to a further postponement until the 31st. On the 27th the enemy's trenches near the Yser canal were found to be empty, so that this formidable obstacle was at once crossed and the position occupied by the French to the north of Boesinghe and by the Guards Division to the east.

The main battle may be conveniently divided into five phases corresponding with our chief attacks as follows: (1) 31st July to 15th August, (2) 16th August to 19th September, (3) 20th September to 3rd October, (4) 4th to 25th October, and (5) 26th October to the early part of November.[1]

First Phase, 31st July to 15th August.

The battle opened on 31st July with an attack on a front of fifteen miles between the river Lys to the south and Steenstraat on the north, the main attack being directed upon the sector, seven and a half miles wide, from the Zillebeke-Zandvoorde road to Boesinghe. On the right, where the attack was not pressed, only the

[1] For plan, see p. 12.

enemy's front line was captured, but on the northern half of the advance both his first and second systems were taken. In detail, the 24th Division captured part of Shrewsbury Forest, the 30th Sanctuary Wood, the 8th Hooge and Bellewaarde ridge, the 15th Frezenberg, the 55th and 39th St. Julien, the 51st land to the north-west of that village, and the 38th Pilckem. Two French divisions on our left were equally successful, advancing to the Steenbeek and capturing Bixschoote, and all these gains were held against numerous counter-attacks. Our men took over 6,000 prisoners and 25 guns.

During the afternoon rain began to fall and continued with hardly a break for four days. This put an end to all reconnaissance by aeroplane, and it also turned the low-lying shell-torn area over which we had just advanced into a morass. Movement through this was possible only along well-defined tracks which soon became marks for the enemy artillery. On the enemy's side the ground was as yet comparatively undamaged, and he was therefore able with comparative freedom to re-organise his defences, and to bring up reinforcements and supplies.

During the preliminary operations Corp. A. G. Buck (R.F.A., Ch. Engr.) won the M.M., for conspicuous gallantry near Armentières on 28th/29th July, when at great personal risk, and although suffering from the effects of gas, he remained at work repairing telephone lines which were repeatedly cut by shell fire. Sergt. J. Orrin (R.E., Housing) gained the M.M. on 30th/31st July, when an emplacement for firing projectors for oil bombs was heavily shelled. Although the officer in charge was killed, Sergt. Orrin carried on with his work, and by his bravery and example encouraged all other ranks who were engaged with him. On many previous occasions he had performed excellent service under adverse conditions.

On 31st July A. I. Brown (18th K.R.R., Tram.)

was killed near Hollebeke, Lieut. W. J. Field, M.C. (1st R. Fus., Educ.) near Clonmel Copse to the north of Shrewsbury Forest, Co. Sergt.-Maj. H. P. McAlister (2nd Rif. Bde., Educ.) near Verlorenhoek, and Lance-Corp. J. I. Cohen (2nd Wilts., Educ.) and W. B. Lewis (12th R. Fus., Tram.) at places unknown. M. W. Churchill (12th R. Fus., Tram.) was killed between 31st July and 3rd August, George Penfold (R.G.A., Asylums) was killed near Zillebeke on 4th August, Lance-Corp. A. E. Bennett (12th E. Surr., Asylums) on the 5th, John White (R. Ir. Rif., Ch. Engr.) near Frezenberg on the 6th, Victor Bown (R.F.A., Asylums) on the 10th, and Corporal J. F. Patterson (M.G.C., Tram.) near Zillebeke on the 14th. W. J. Colverd (R.F.A., Tram.) died on the 16th of wounds received the day before. W. E. Goddard (R.F.A., Tram.) died on the 29th of wounds received on the 5th.

Second Phase, 16th August to 19th September.

On 16th August the attack was resumed on a line forming roughly a quadrant of a circle from the Menin road round through St. Julien to the French north-west of Langemarck. The enemy in the southern part of this sector had adopted a new method of defence, and, instead of manning a series of trenches, he divided his troops among numerous "pill-boxes" very strongly built of reinforced concrete. These were distributed in depth and, being stoutly defended with machine-guns, formed a serious obstacle. From the Menin road through Frezenberg to St. Julien little progress was made by the 8th and 56th Divisions, but to the north-west of the latter village we were more successful, the 11th and 48th Divisions getting a footing in the third trench system, and the 20th and 29th Divisions capturing Wijdendrift and Langemarck. On our left the French were also successful as far north as Drie Grachten. Thirty guns were taken and over 2,100 prisoners. The weather again broke up and, as no big attack was practicable in so water-logged a country, the rest of the month was devoted to local operations against various strong points.

Lieut. H. W. Fisher (R.F.A., Educ.) won the M.C. near Polygon Wood on 17th August when "he was in charge of an observation party attached to an assaulting battalion. He followed the infantry closely in the attack, and twice went to the most forward position under heavy fire and brought back information of the utmost value." Co. Sergt.-Maj. J. C. Cairns (Oxf. and Bucks L.I., Educ.) was awarded the D.C.M. on 22nd August and Co. Sergt.-Maj. W. A. Humphreys (R.E., Educ.) the M.M. about this time, but no details are available. In the fighting at Westhoek the latter gained a bar to his M.M.

The 16th of August was a day of heavy casualties among the staff. W. J. Relf (1st R. Dub. Fus., Tram.) F. C. Brook (8th R. Dub. Fus., Asylums) Sergt. E. C. Brown (R.H.A., Parks) and Corp. G. A. J. Clarkson (7th Yorks L.I., Tram.) were killed in the salient at various places unknown, Sergt. Ernest Swanson (5th Lond., Educ.) at Glencorse Wood, C. P. Norby (13th R. Irish Rif., Tram.), G. K. Lenney (13th R. Irish Rif., Parks) and Lance-Corp. H. W. Baker (12th R. Irish Rif., Parks) at the Frezenberg ridge, Alfred Chaney (2nd R. Dub. Fus., Parks) at the Hannebeek and A. J. Madden (8th Northd. Fus., Tram.) and W. J. Skipp (8th Northd. Fus., Tram.) between St. Julien and Poelcappelle.

H. T. J. Kenyon (R.A.M.C., Educ.) was killed on the 17th, F. T. Townsend (2nd Middx., Asylums) wounded that day near the Hannebeek, died on the 18th, Corp. George Brooker (20th Lond., Educ.) on the night of 20th/21st, Lieut. William Hornsby (6th Somers. L.I., Educ.) at Glencorse Wood on the 21st, Patrick Fitzgerald (7th Worc., Asylums) on the 26th. W. J. Potter (18th K.R.R., Educ.) was killed on 19th September near Shrewsbury Forest.

Third Phase, 20th September to 3rd October.

Early in September the weather improved and enabled the artillery and other preparations for another attack to proceed. This was launched, after a night of rain, in a mist on the morning of 20th September on a front of eight miles between the Comines canal on the south and the Ypres-Staden railway on the north. Few points which can be identified on a sketch map were included in the objectives, so here it must suffice to say that at all parts the advance to an average depth of 1,000 yards was successful, the victorious divisions, counting from the south, being the 19th, 39th, 4th and 23rd between the canal and the Menin road, the Australian Corps between the Menin road and the Ypres-Roulers railway (in which sector they captured Inverness Copse and Glencorse Wood and gained a footing in Polygon Wood) and the 9th, 55th, 58th, 51st, and 20th between the Ypres-Roulers and Ypres-Staden railways. The high ground, crossed by the Menin road, which had so long formed the object of very fierce fighting now passed into our possession. In addition, over 3,000 prisoners and a number of guns were taken. Numerous counter-attacks followed which, though gaining local successes, were eventually beaten off.

On the 26th the advance was resumed on a front of six miles from the Menin road northwards to the north-east of St. Julien. The Australians captured Polygon Wood, the 3rd Division Zonnebeke and the 59th and 58th Divisions a series of positions to the east and north-east of St. Julien. The prisoners numbered 1,600.

Lieut. (afterwards Capt.) R. A. Nicholl (R.E., Educ.) was awarded the M.C. about this time for his gallantry in laying " a pipe-line forward under incessant shell fire. It was due to his energy and encouragement that the line was completed in time for operations." Q.M. and Hon. Lt. F. Poole (R.A.M.C., Asylums) won the M.C. "He remained at the advanced collecting station for several days organising the rationing of the wounded, and daily visited the relay posts and regimental aid posts. . . . During heavy shelling he helped to withdraw the wounded, and lives were saved by his action and example." Sergt. E. A. Rose (R.E., Educ.) was awarded the D.C.M. for exceptional gallantry and devotion to duty between March and September. "On September 18th and 19th he worked day and night under incessant fire to put through a buried cable route to the front line."

On 20th September Lieut. H. P. Oates (5th King's Liverpool, Educ.) and T. H. Tigg (R.A.M.C., Tram.) were killed near the Menin road, Co. Sergt-Maj. W. H. Carr (2/6th Lond., Educ.) near St. Julien and F. W. A. Smith (12th R. Suss., Educ.) at some place unknown, Co. Sgt.-Maj. L. Dimond (2/5th Lond., Educ.), wounded near St. Julien, and Lieut. S. P. Siebert (16th Rif. Bde., Educ.), wounded near the Menin road, died on the 21st, and on the same day were killed Charles Miller (12th E. Surr., Tram.), Lance-Corp. L. H. Hymans (13th Lond., Educ.) and Sergt. T. W. Turner (R.F.A., Tram.). Lieut. E. T. Winbush, B.Sc. (R.F.A., Educ.), was killed on the 24th east of Zillebeke, H. G. Joyce (1st R.W. Surr., Asylums), on the 25th near the Menin road. On the 26th Lieut. H. C. Hattam, F.R.H.S. (4th Suff., Educ). was killed near Inverness Copse, and Harry Birch (14th Hamp., Asylums) near the Menin road, Lance-Corp. S. E. Helyar (2/6th S. Staffs, Educ.) on the 27th near Polygon Wood and Lieut. James Wrigley (R.G.A., Educ.) on the 29th. F. W. Keeler (13th K.R.R., Tram.) was killed on 1st October near the Menin road, and on the 2nd, Corp. E. R. Jolly (4th E. Surr., Educ.) near Polygon Wood and Lieut. D. J. Williams (M.G.C., Educ.) near Polderhoek.

Fourth Phase, 4th to 25th October.

The weather had now cleared again and it was decided to make a further advance between the Menin road and the Ypres-Staden railway. Before the advance began, however, the weather broke once more, and on the night of the 3rd/4th the troops assembled for the assault in a storm of wind and rain. Notwithstanding these conditions the attack next morning was successful, the 5th Division capturing Polderhoek, the 21st Reutel, the Australians Broodseinde, the New Zealanders Gravenstafel, and the 11th and 4th parts of Poelcappelle. The prisoners amounted to more than 5,000 and, as the enemy was preparing an attack and had moved up large forces into the battle area, great numbers of his troops came under our fire and suffered heavy casualties; in fact, Ludendorff speaks of the German losses as "enormous." [1]

Rain continued to fall for several days, but on the 9th the assault was resumed, the right flank of the advance being at Zonnebeke. The Australians and some English troops made progress towards Passchendaele, the 11th Division at Poelcappelle and the 4th and 29th along the Ypres-Staden railway, while the Guards reached the southern outskirts of Houthulst Forest. Persistent rain put an end to further operations except for slight advances on very limited frontages. On 22nd October the 18th and 34th Divisions gained important posts east of Poelcappelle and the 35th with the French secured a footing in Houthulst Forest.

During this fighting the M.M. was won by H. Johnston (Beds, Asylums) at Hooge, and by Sergt. J. A. Lingwood (H.A.C., L.F.B.) but no details are available.

On 4th October, Co. Sergt.-Maj. H. C. Robson (3/4th R.W. Surr., Educ.) was killed near Broodseinde and Capt. A. C. Dancer, M.C. (5th Dorset, Educ.) near Poelcappelle, on the 5th Co. Sergt.-Maj.

[1] *My War Memories*, 1914–18, vol. ii. p. 490.

H. S. Hodges (3/10th Middx., Educ.) near Poelcappelle, on the 7th Lieut. C. J. Chamberlain (1st Rif. Bde., Educ.) near Poelcappelle, on the 9th J. G. Davis (2nd Irish Gds., Educ.) and Lieut. Cecil Prophet (2/5th E. Lancs, Compr.), on the 10th Lance-Corp. George Ayles (M.G.C., Educ.) and Arthur Vale (R.F.A., Tram.), on the 12th Sergt. Thomas Eaves, M.M., (8th Suff., Tram.) north of Poelcappelle, on the 14th Sergt. James Wynn (R.F.A., Tram.) and Bombr. G. W. Key (R.F.A., Asylums), on the 15th Co. Q.M.S. E. R. Johnson (7th K.R.R., Asylums) and Harry Parks (2nd Gren. Gds., Tram.) near Houthulst Forest. C. J. Lee (8th Manch., Asylums), wounded on the 10th, and J. J. Gilroy (R.A.M.C., Tram.), wounded on the 14th, both died on the 19th. Edward Cox (R.F.A., Parks) was killed on the 21st, George Gaunt (R.E., Asylums) near Zillebeke on the 23rd, and William Clark (R.F.A., Ch. Engr.) on the 24th.

Fifth Phase, 26th October to early November.

Words are hardly adequate to describe the state of the battlefield at this time. The continual shell fire and the almost continual rain had reduced the country for several miles on our side of the line to one immense swamp. Only the lips of the craters divided one shell hole from another, and all were filled with mud. In many places, where peaceful agriculture had flourished for centuries, there remained not one sign of the useful activities of mankind; not a vestige could be seen of crops or of orchards or of pasture lands; houses and villages had been entirely blotted out; roads could be traced only by the stumps of trees which once had formed pleasant avenues along their sides; the woods had been levelled and the fragments of their trees used for gun-pits or to form tracks across the waste. Away from the roads and the duck-board tracks movement was hardly possible. At each step men sank to the knee or the thigh, not a few stumbled into the shell holes and, encumbered with their rifle, ammunition and equipment, were drowned. Scores of tanks were engulfed in the mud.

In such conditions it is not surprising that the word Passchendaele came to be used by many, and these were not all civilians, as a symbol of waste and useless suffering. But in battles and campaigns, as in all other human affairs, it is not always the immediate object which must be regarded, and in the Passchendaele operations other considerations, several of which could not then be made public, had to be taken into account.[1] In the main these centred in the fact that it was essential for the Allies to maintain the initiative and at all costs to prevent the enemy from moving troops to other fronts. The other Allies were faced with important crises, and could not give much assistance. The failure of the French offensive in Champagne (see p. 62) was succeeded in May and June by serious mutinies in their army. This, in the opinion of Gen. Gouraud, was the most critical period of the war.[2] The Russian revolution in March was followed by the rapid decay of discipline, so that by July the Russian armies had ceased to be a fighting force. In the latter part of October the Italians were defeated at Caporetto with the loss of 200,000 prisoners and 2,000 guns. The Americans who had entered the war in April, 1917, were still training the troops who were to fight for them. Of all the Allies, therefore, only the British were capable at the time of engaging the enemy's attention, and it was specially necessary for them to do this because plans were afoot for the surprise attack at Cambrai (see p. 82) from which great results were expected.

The battle therefore had to proceed, and on 26th October, in a downpour of rain which lasted all day, the Canadians advanced along the Ravebeek towards Passchendaele. On their left the R. Naval and the

[1] "Passchendaele, 1917," by Maj.-Gen. Sir J. Davidson, M.P., in *Nineteenth Century and After*, for February, 1921.

[2] Mrs. Humphry Ward, *Fields of Victory*, p. 104.

58th Divisions were successful to the east and north of Poelcappelle. The 5th and 7th Divisions captured Gheluvelt which had been lost three years before, but their rifles, choked with mud during the advance, were useless and they had to withdraw. On the 30th the attack was continued, when the Canadians reached the outskirts of Passchendaele and the R. Naval and 58th Divisions made what little progress was possible across the swamps on the lower ground to the north-west. On 6th November the Canadians rushed the village and high ground to the north and north-west, and on the 10th, having consolidated their gains, made a further advance to the north.

The capture of this high ground marks the close of the battle which, except for the short intervals enforced by the weather or by the need of preparing for the separate phases of the attack, had been carried on continuously for more than three months. In this gigantic conflict some 45 British divisions "by the exercise," in the words of the commander-in-chief, "of courage, determination and endurance to a degree which has never been surpassed in war," defeated 78 German divisions with the loss of 24,065 prisoners, 74 guns and over 1,000 machine-guns, etc. On a front of ten miles and in face of every kind of difficulty they advanced to a depth varying from one to nearly six miles, and by wresting from the enemy practically all the high land near the city freed our communications through Ypres from the dangers which had so long threatened them. But these gains were made at a terrible cost, for our casualties, including the comparatively slight losses at Cambrai (see p. 82), are said to have been 454,463.[1]

Capt. P. F. Watts (4th Beds, Educ.) was awarded the M.C. for conspicuous gallantry in the advance on Passchendaele on 30th October when he re-organised and consolidated a line of posts after all other officers

[1] Capt. P. E. Wright, *At the Supreme War Council*, pp. 33-4.

in his sector had become casualties. Petty Offr. W. Jarman (R. Nav. Div., Ch. Engr.) was awarded the M.M. for his gallantry in the same neighbourhood, when during a heavy counter-attack he defended with a machine-gun a trench which had been abandoned by other troops. Lance-Corp. T. J. Gunter (R.E., Oxf. and Bucks L.I., Educ.) won the M.M. for his gallantry in action at Houthulst Forest during the early part of November, and Sergt. H. E. Hayward (R.F.A., Asylums) for bravery in action in front of Ypres.

Lieut. W. J. Reed (8th Devons, Educ.), wounded near Gheluvelt on 26th October, died two days later as a prisoner of war, W. D. Shea (2/28th Lond., Educ.) and H. N. Field (4th Beds, Arch.) were killed on the 30th near Passchendaele, and Provost-Sergt. W. J. Laird in the same neighbourhood on 4th November, J. H. Counter, M.M. (1st Devons, Ch. Engr.), near Polderhoek on the 6th, and Bombr. Henry Lilburn (R.F.A., Tram.) near Passchendaele on the 8th.

Lens.

In the Battle of Arras and in the fighting which followed it much ground was gained near Lens. Towards the middle of August, in order to prevent the enemy from concentrating all his attention on resisting our advance from Ypres, the assault was renewed to the north-west of the town. On the 15th the Canadians, attacking on a front of about 2½ miles, captured Hill 70, which had been won but lost again in the Battle of Loos, the mining suburbs of Cité Ste. Elizabeth, Cité St. Emile and Cité St. Laurent, the whole of Bois Rasé and the western half of Bois Hugo which had also figured in the earlier battle. Six days later they closed in upon the town from the west and south-west.[1]

[1] For plan, see p. 58.

Battle of Cambrai.

It was well known that, in order to withstand the advance at Ypres, the enemy had withdrawn troops from other portions of the front, and a surprise attack was therefore planned on a part of the defences thus weakened. The sector near Cambrai, where several important roads and railways converged, was selected for the attempt. In order to increase the surprise, it was decided not to prelude the attack by a long bombardment, but to rely upon tanks for smashing the enemy's wire and for dealing with his strong posts and machine-guns. Our line here, opposite the Hindenburg line, ran, roughly, south-east and north-west. Facing it across a slight dip was the Flesquières ridge defended by the Hindenburg support line, and behind that again was another dip, the high ground on the further side of which was crowned by Bourlon Wood.[1]

Some 400 tanks were assembled with great secrecy just behind the line between Gonnelieu and Hermies, chiefly in Havrincourt Wood, and at 6.20 on the morning of 20th November the attack was opened. Although there was no rain the sky was cloudy, and the enemy's chances of observation were diminished by the smoke barrage which preceded the tanks. At the same time, to add to his confusion and to prevent him from moving reinforcements to the part actually threatened, subsidiary attacks were launched east of Epéhy (see plan on p. 37) and between Bullecourt and Fontaine-lez-Croisilles (see plan on p. 58) and demonstrations were made with smoke, gas and artillery on most of the British front south of the Scarpe. Of these subsidiary attacks it will be sufficient to say that at Bullecourt the 3rd and 16th Divisions captured and held a very strong sector of trenches, and took 700 prisoners.

The main attack on a front of six miles was brilliantly

[1] For plan, see p. 37.

successful. The 12th Division, on the right, moving along the Bonavis ridge, captured Lateau Wood, the 20th La Vacquerie and Welsh Ridge, the 6th Ribécourt, the 51st pushed forward as far as Flesquières, the 62nd captured Havrincourt, Graincourt and Anneux and the 36th trenches to the west of the Canal du Nord. The 51st Division was held up at Flesquières, where a number of tanks were knocked out, as mentioned by the commander-in-chief, " by a German artillery officer who, remaining alone at his battery, served a field-gun single-handed until killed at his gun." The 29th Division passing between the 20th and 6th Divisions, seized Masnières and Marcoing, thus securing bridgeheads over the Canal de l'Escaut (Scheldt Canal), which in this part formed the chief defence of Cambrai. At Masnières the bridge had been damaged and unfortunately it broke down under the weight of the first tank which attempted to cross it. This left only one bridge for the advancing troops and the accident, with the check at Flesquières, went far towards limiting the success of the day's fighting. Early on the 21st Flesquières fell, the 51st Division pressing forward reached the southern outskirts of Bourlon Wood and, with the help of other troops, captured Cantaing and Fontaine-notre-Dame. The latter was lost next day, but as some set-off the 56th Division stormed a strong point known as Tadpole Copse, on the left of our advance.

Owing to the comparatively few troops available it was originally proposed not to continue the advance after forty-eight hours, but when that period had elapsed the enemy was still holding Fontaine and Bourlon Wood. As these completely commanded our position north of Flesquières it was essential either that they should be stormed or that, giving up some of our gains, we should retire to the Flesquières ridge. The capture of Bourlon Wood would seriously threaten the enemy's line to the north if, indeed, it did not make it quite untenable, and with so great a prize within reach it was decided to press on. On the 23rd therefore the 51st Division made another attempt, which eventually failed, on Fontaine, while the 40th captured Bourlon Wood and part of the village beyond. During the next few days these two villages changed hands several times, but by about the 30th the enemy appeared to have a firm hold of the villages while we had an equally firm hold of the wood.

By that date the ten days' fighting had yielded 10,500 prisoners, half of whom were taken on the first day, 142 guns and over 400 machine-guns, etc., with great quantities of ammunition, stores and material. The enemy's elaborate trenches were penetrated to a depth of 4½ miles, as great a distance as was gained in more than three months' fighting on the Somme or at Ypres.

Towards the end of November it was clear that the enemy intended to counter-attack on an ambitious scale. This opened on the 30th, the main attack being from the north between Bourlon Wood and Tadpole Copse, but it was preceded by a subsidiary attack westwards upon our line to the south of Masnières. The hollows and folds usual in chalk country enabled the enemy, assisted by a ground mist, to assemble, without attracting notice, large bodies of infantry. After a short bombardment, numbers of low-flying aeroplanes rained machine-gun fire upon our trenches, and immediately afterwards the attack was launched. The left of the 55th Division was driven in and the enemy, making great progress up 22 Ravine and across the northern end of Bonavis Ridge, was able to take the 12th and 20th Divisions in flank and rear. Villers Guislain, Gonnelieu and Bonavis soon fell, and the enemy even reached Gouzeaucourt, but was gallantly driven out by the Guards Division which, on its way to rest billets after heavy fighting at Fontaine and Bourlon, was hurried into the conflict.

In the main assault further north the 29th Division at Masnières, the 47th at Fontaine, the 2nd at Bourlon, and the 56th at Mœuvres and Tadpole Copse beat off numerous attacks with very heavy losses. Here and there posts were overwhelmed or driven back by superior numbers, but any important points were regained by counter-attacks and the line was everywhere maintained.

On 1st December the Guards retook Gonnelieu and Gauche Wood and even reached Villers Guislain, but next day our troops were forced out of Gonnelieu. During these two days many attacks in this sector and in the Bourlon sector were driven off, but on the 3rd the Germans succeeded in capturing La Vacquerie.

Owing to the Germans' success at Villers Guislain our position at Masnières and Bourlon now formed a dangerous salient. Troops were not available for another offensive on a large scale, and it was therefore decided to contract the line by withdrawing to the northern slopes of the Flesquières ridge and to make the necessary adjustments further south. The withdrawal was commenced on the night of 4th/5th December and was completed by the 7th without molestation. The net result of the fighting since 20th November was an advance of about 2½ miles and the capture in addition to the prisoners, guns, material, etc., already mentioned, of 12,000 yards of the enemy's front line, a rather shorter length of the Hindenburg and Hindenburg support lines and the villages of Ribécourt, Flesquières and Havrincourt. On the other hand we lost an unimportant section of line near Gonnelieu with 6,000 prisoners and 100 guns.

On 30th November J. C. Buckley (R.A.M.C., Educ.) won the M.M. for attending single-handed to the wounded under heavy shell fire, although he himself was at the time severely wounded. At Tadpole Copse on 2nd December Corporal (afterwards Sergt.) C. A. Dearing, B.Sc. (5th Lond., Educ.) earned the M.M.

" Under intense bombardment, he worked in the open repairing lines and keeping communication between the front line and battalion H.Q. Regardless of danger he carried out this work throughout the day, and after the battalion was relieved he remained behind for several hours, again repairing the lines in order to hand over communications to the relieving battalion."

In later fighting at this part Lieut. F. N. Stone (21st Lond., Educ.) won the M.C. on 9th December when the enemy attacked an adjoining battalion and he " led a counter attack to relieve the pressure. Though he was met by a superior force of the enemy, he drove them back with great courage and skill and held on to the ground gained until the line was re-established." On the same date at Graincourt Lieut. A. D. Barnes (23rd Lond., Educ.) won the M.C. " for conspicuous gallantry and devotion to duty in an advanced post which was repeatedly attacked by the enemy. Time after time they obtained a footing in it only to be driven out. He went about calmly encouraging the men and organising counter-attacks, and was fighting continuously for six hours."

These striking results were obtained at a low cost in casualties, and on 20th November, the opening day of the attack, only two of the Council's staff were killed, namely, Lance-Corp. S. F. Howard (11th Rif. Bde., Stores) to the southward of Masnières and R. H. Barker (R.W. Surr., Tram.). Sergt. R. A. Wood (16th Lond., Educ.) at Tadpole Copse, and Arthur Ireland (15th R. Irish Rif., Parks) possibly near Bullecourt, were killed on the 22nd, I. C. Rixon (R.F.A., Tram.) on the 23rd, Lieut. F. G. Wheatcroft (13th E. Surr., Educ.) on the 25th near Bourlon. On 30th Nov. or 1st Dec. Sergt. Charles Brown, M.M. (4th Gren. Gds., Parks) was killed at Gonnelieu, William Griffiths (16th R. Fus., Trams.) near Masnières, Lance-Corp. W. A. Legg (15th Lond., Educ.) near Bourlon, and Lieut J. W. Johnson, B.Sc. (Educ.) and Lance-Corp. W. P.

Brill (Asylums), both of the 8th Middlesex, near Tadpole Copse. Thomas Thomas (15th Lond., Est. and Valn.) died on 2nd December of wounds received near Fontaine on 29th November, and Lance-Corp. S. F. Long (23rd Lond., Tram.) on the 9th of wounds received some days before.

General Fighting.

About this time Major F. W. Jackson (R.A.S.C., Educ.) was awarded the D.S.O. for the general excellence of his work, and Major V. L. Connolly (R.A.M.C., Asylums) the M.C. for gallantry in action.

Apart from the decorations awarded in the course of the set engagements at Arras, Ypres and Cambrai, E. Campion (R.A.M.C., Educ.) earned the M.M. for courageous conduct during an enemy air raid at Bandaghem, and Sub-Lieut. F. C. Stacey (R. Nav. Div., Pub. Health) the M.C. for gallantry in action at Welsh Ridge, near Cambrai, on 30th December.

The general casualties during the spring and the latter half of the year included Sergt. S. M. C. Bonfield (R.E., Educ.) killed by a gas explosion on 6th April, Capt. J. W. Woods, M.C. (2nd Yorks. L.I., Educ.) in an attack upon Fayet near St. Quentin on the 14th, C. W. Law (R.G.A., Parks) south of Vermelles on the 25th, and Capt. J. L. Warry, A.R.I.B.A. (2/8th Notts and Derby, Arch.) on the 27th.

Arthur Crawley (R.E., Educ.) was killed on 4th May near Neuve Chapelle, W. H. Smith (R.F.A., Trams.) on the 9th, probably to the north of Lens, H. T. Page (H.A.C., Educ.) on the 11th, W. M. Timpson (R.A.M.C., Educ.) near Ypres on the 12th, A. C. Steadman (2/3rd Lond., Tram.) on the 13th, and Frank Diamond (Norfolks, Asylums) on the 19th. On the 23rd Lieut. R. W. W. Vaughan, M.B., B.S. (R.A.M.C., Asylums) was killed at some place unknown.

T. E. Dyer (12th K.R.R., Tram.) was killed on 1st June, Corp. F. Barnes (R.F.A., Educ.) on the 4th, and on the same day G. W. Parker (R.G.A., Trams.) near Ypres. On the 17th Corp. H. H. Haynes (L.N. Lancs, Educ.) died of wounds received the day before near Ypres. On the 23rd E. V. Ament (1st Rif. Bde., Trams.) was killed, and on the 25th H. E. Woolley (R.F.A., Trams.) died of wounds received on 31st May near Messines. On the 27th Lieut. Arthur Richards (1st Mon., Solr.) died of wounds received the same day near Liévin, Sergt. Herbert Thorn, D.C.M. (17th R. Fus., Educ.) also died on this day of wounds received in April, possibly near Arras. James Pearson (R.F.A., Trams.) was killed on the 30th near Ypres.

On 1st July Lieut. W. H. Davis (2nd Notts and Derby, Educ.) was killed near Lens, Sgt. C. H. Pardoe (15th Lond., Tram.) on the 3rd/4th near Ypres, Lieut. Wilfred Bishop (11th Bord., Educ.) on the 5th near the coast, Sgt. A. J. Bright (20th Lond., Educ.) on the 6th near Messines, and on the same day Corp. W. J. May (R.E., Educ.) died of wounds received on the 3rd near Ypres. On the 7th Corp. H. D. Turner (R.F.A., Asylums) was killed near the Menin road, Ypres, and Lieut. Harry Warren (15th Hamps., Educ.) near Hill 60, W. G. Daniel (1st E. Surr., Asylums) on the 18th, John Kelly (15th Lond., Educ.) on the 19th to the south-east of Ypres, William Clifford (R.G.A., Asylums) and Harry Tysoe (R.E., Tram.) on the 20th, H. C. Guy (Gren. Gds., Educ.) on the 23rd near Ypres, and L. A. Davis (12th R. Suss., Educ.) and Leonard Groves (15th Lond., Educ.) on the 24th also near Ypres. Lieut. J. R. Carne (12th R. Suss., Educ.) wounded that day died on the 25th, A. W. Scarf (2nd H.A.C., Comp.) on the 26th near Bullecourt, Lance-Corp. Cornelius Duggan (14th Rif. Bde., Tram.) on the 28th, and H. C. Kelsey (R.F.A., Tram.) on the 29th near Ypres.

Sergt. W. Channel (M.G.C., Asylums) died on 6th August of wounds received near Armentières, Batt.-Sergt.-Maj. J. G. Thomas (R.G.A., Educ.) on the

11th near Béthune, and Lance-Corp. F. S. Sçott (12th K.R.R., Tram.) on the 18th, Henry Webb (18th K.R.R., Tram.) was killed, probably on 19th September, Capt. H. H. E. Ferguson (14th Highd. L.I., Educ.), wounded to the south-west of Cambrai on the night of the 22nd/23rd, died on the 23rd. Harry Ediker (2/6th Notts and Derby, Educ.) was killed on the 26th, probably near Arras.

E. G. Thomas (R.F.A., Tram.) was killed on 2nd October, and R. E. Kemp (7th Beds, Arch.) on the 30th at places unknown, and on the 28th W. P. Whitfield (2/5th R. Lancaster, Educ.) died near Poperinghe, of wounds received near Ypres on the 26th. F. W. Hutson (R.F.A., Educ.) died on 3rd November as the result of an accident in the Ypres salient, Co. Sergt.-Maj. E. J. P. Dainty, D.C.M. (2nd Lond., Educ.) was killed on 8th November in an accident near Lebucquière to the east of Bapaume, Herbert Page (R.F.A., Ch. Engr.) on the 12th near the Menin road, and on the 21st George Young (11th Rif. Bde., Stores) died of wounds received on the 8th near Gouzeaucourt. W. J. Smithers (2nd Middx., Asylums) was killed on the 28th at some place unknown, and on the same date C. W. Tagg (Labour Corps, Parks) died at Boulogne of pneumonia.

F. J. Keane (2nd Rif. Bde., Clerk) was killed on 2nd December near Passchendaele, Lieut. W. A. Wilkinson, B.Sc. (R.F.A., Educ.) on the same date at some place unknown, Lieut. R. E. Simmons (R.G.A., Educ.) on the 5th north of Ypres, George Pavitt (R.F.A., Tram.) on the 13th near Cambrai, H. C. Brazil (8th K.R.R., Tram.) on the 26th near Passchendaele, and H. E. Leighton (7th K.R.R., Tram.) on the same date and probably at the same place, and Corporal C. V. Golle (28th Lond., Ch. Engr.) on the 27th near Cambrai.

CHAPTER VI.

WESTERN FRONT, 1918.

IN the prolonged fighting which lasted for about six months of the year 1917, the losses among the British and Dominion troops were very heavy, and as an army had to be maintained for home defence, these could not be made good. Early in 1918, in order to meet this shortage, the number of battalions in a division was reduced from 13 to 10, and the troops surplus to this establishment were used to make up the deficiencies in the remaining battalions. The Germans had suffered as much, or perhaps more, but Russia had now disappeared as a belligerent, and copious reinforcements could be brought from the eastern to the western front. The difficulties of the situation were much increased because troops had been sent to aid the Italians after their serious defeat at Caporetto in 1917 (see p. 181), and because the British Government decided to relieve the French of the defence of a further sector of the front. This decision was carried out during the winter of 1917–18 when the front from St. Quentin southwards to Barisis on the Oise was taken over. The sector measured 28 miles, bringing the total length held by the British up to 125 miles. The French troops thus relieved were formed into a reserve available for the support of either army.

Early in 1918 it was obvious that the enemy would soon be superior in numbers, and probably in munitions. The United States had declared war on Germany on 5th April, 1917, and it was decided, pending the arrival of their troops to redress the balance, to act on the defensive. Casualties became less numerous, and in January only two of the Council's staff were killed, Corporal A. A. Withey (2nd K.R.R., Tram.) on the 16th and S. G. Blay (7th Buffs, Tram.) on the 19th, in February none, and in March, before the opening of the German offensive, only three, namely, John Lamont (14th Lond., Asylums) on the 12th north of Arras, and Lance-Corp. P. W. T. Holmes (R.A.M.C., Educ.) and Lance-Corp. T. E. Fox (1st Cameronians, Tram.) who both died on the 13th of wounds received the day before near Arras and Ypres respectively.

Captain G. Clark (General List, Educ.) was awarded the M.C. for great zeal and efficiency about this time in a forward area subject to shell-fire.

First Battles of the Somme, 1918.

In February it became clear that the enemy proposed to take the offensive. It was known that many divisions transferred from Russia and Italy were receiving special training, and aerial reconnaissances showed that communications were being improved, and ammunition and supply dumps increased. To meet this attack existing defences had to be strengthened and new ones to be prepared, and communications, especially in the Somme area, had to be improved. These works entailed much extra labour, and, as a greater length of line was being held with fewer troops than heretofore, the opportunities for training such new drafts as were being received were very limited.

The enemy's preparations covered most of our front and, as all this could not be defended in equal strength, it was necessary to decide at what points ground could be yielded with least harm. In the north the battle lines were only fifteen miles from Dunkirk, and forty from Calais, and the possession of these and the other Channel ports was essential to our safety. The middle sector defended the few remaining collieries in northern France still held by the Allies, and also important railway points such as Béthune and Arras. In either of these sectors any extensive withdrawal would clearly be most dangerous. The southern sector in front of Cambrai and St. Quentin had in its rear the area devastated during the

Somme fighting in 1916 and the German retreat in 1917, and here retreat was possible without greatly improving the enemy's position or seriously harming

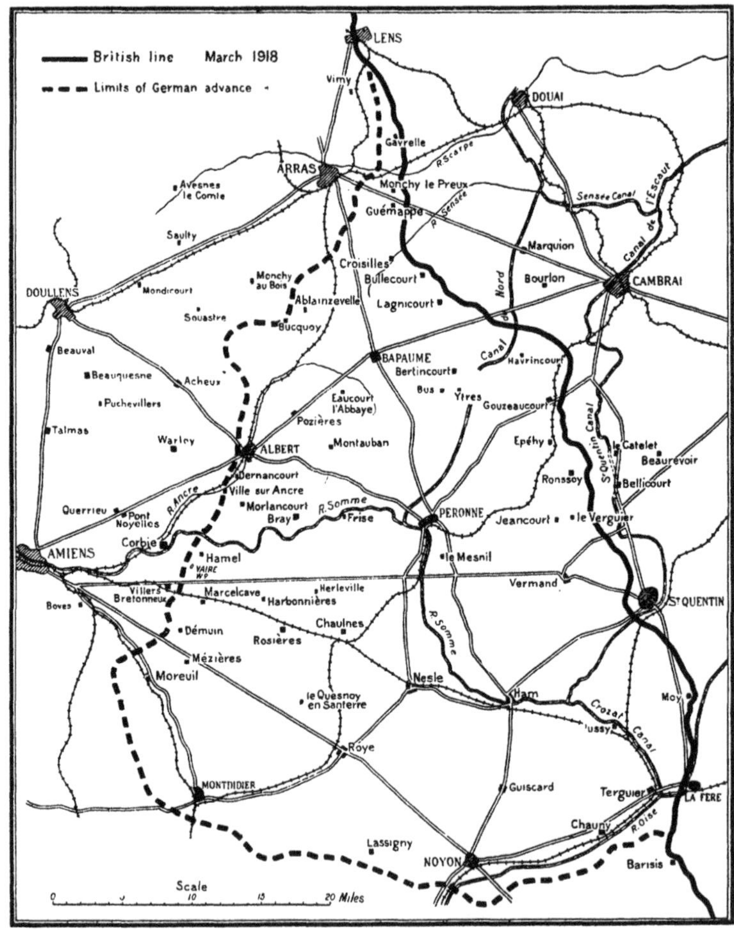

FIRST BATTLES OF THE SOMME, 1918.

our own. This sector was therefore held most lightly.

On the morning of 21st March, after a violent bombardment lasting some hours, the long expected assault opened on a front of about fifty miles from the Oise nearly to the Scarpe. Until midday the battlefield was obscured by a thick mist which greatly favoured the assailants by completely covering them from the view of our artillery and machine-guns. The enemy outnumbered our men in the proportion of five or more to one and, in face of such numbers, the outpost line was soon surrounded, although the posts themselves held out with the utmost gallantry for many hours. In the words of the commander-in-chief: "The prolonged defence of these different localities, under conditions which left little hope of any relief, deserves to rank among the most heroic actions in the history of the British Army."

Several weeks of fine weather had made the marshes between St. Quentin and La Fère easily passable by infantry, so that the enemy in this part was able to effect some sort of a surprise and to make good progress. This led to a withdrawal (58th and 18th Divs.) being ordered to the Crozat Canal connecting the Oise at La Fère with the Somme to the east of Ham. The enemy was also successful at Ronssoy (16th Div.) to the south of Cambrai, and at Lagnicourt and Bullecourt to the west (6th and 59th Divs.), and orders were given for part of the salient thus formed opposite Cambrai to be vacated. Elsewhere the attack was held up by our battle positions, the 24th Division at Le Verguier, the 21st at Epéhy, and the 17th on the Canal du Nord showing particular gallantry.

On the 22nd the attack was renewed all along the line in a dense mist, which as before greatly aided the advance. The passage of the Crozat Canal was forced at several points, but for the time the enemy was prevented by a vigorous defence (58th Div.) from developing his advantage. Further north, that is to the west and north-west of St. Quentin, he was more successful, advancing four or five miles and causing us to vacate Epéhy. He also made a substantial advance to the west of Fontaine-lez-Croisilles.

On the 23rd the troops south of Ham were ordered to withdraw across the Somme, but it was hoped to hold, north of that town, the position which had been specially laid out for the defence of the Péronne bridge-head. Later the Fifth Army decided to abandon these lines. This decision had far-reaching results and it was criticised by the commander-in-chief on the ground that, taken somewhat hurriedly, it greatly interfered with the withdrawal of troops and stores, with the destruction of the various bridges, and generally with putting the river line into an adequate state of defence. Other misfortunes followed during the day, for our men were driven away from the Crozat Canal and the enemy crossed the Somme near Ham forcing a passage from the north. Further north some confusion arose at the junction of the Third and Fifth Armies, and near Ytres a gap was left through which the enemy pressed. On the extreme right of the enemy's advance Monchy and Guémappe were evacuated by our troops.

On the 24th the enemy continued to develop the success which he had gained at the junction of the two armies, with the result that the part of the Fifth Army to the north of the Somme was driven back and, in the effort to keep in touch with it, the right of the Third Army had to retire across the battle fields of 1916. Higher up, that is to the south-east, the river, owing to the dry weather, was not a very formidable obstacle, and it was crossed at many points to the north-west of Ham. On the right of our line we were driven out of Chauny in a fog.

On the 25th strong attacks on the line to the north of Bapaume were driven off but, although the left of the Fifth Army was transferred to the Third Army who were entrusted with the command of all troops north of the Somme, the enemy continued to force his way through the gap formed on the 23rd. In spite of all efforts this was so far from being closed that reinforcements, moved up on the 25th from the Ancre to Pozières, found themselves unsupported on both flanks and had to fall back upon the river. To the south of the Somme where the French had now taken over the defence, including the control of what British troops still survived, the enemy captured Noyon and Nesle and pushed us back from the part of the line situated to the east and south of Frise.

On the 26th the defence to the north of Albert became stabilised roughly on the line held before the Battle of the Somme in 1916 except near Arras, where some of the gains made to the south-east of the city in April, 1917, were maintained. Further south the situation was less satisfactory. The troops there were so reduced in numbers and so exhausted by the continual marching and fighting that they were ordered to withdraw to the line Le Quesnoy—Rosières—Bray, but, owing to a misunderstanding, Bray was vacated and the retreat on the north side of the Somme was continued westward. Another gap was formed, this time near Roye between us and the French, and it was only with very great difficulty that the enemy was prevented from thrusting at once towards the important railway junction of Montdidier. It was on this day that General Foch was placed in supreme control of the Allied troops in France and Belgium.

During the night of the 26th/27th Albert which, although it was for two years immediately behind the front line, had been free from the enemy since September, 1914, again fell into his hands. Our retreat from Bray enabled troops on the 27th to be passed across to the south side of the Somme in rear of the Rosières—Bray line. Rosières stood fast, but the line to the north as far as the river was withdrawn to Hamel and to the south to Montdidier, which was taken by the enemy from the French.

The next day, the 28th, was marked by a signal success. With the object of capturing Arras, retaking the Vimy ridge, and so of relieving Lens, the enemy shifted his main assault from the Somme to the Scarpe, and early in the morning launched an attack with great forces on both sides of the river.[1] The methods which had obtained such great results further south were again adopted, but this time, unaided by fog or mist, failed completely. The 4th and 56th Divisions to the north of the river held their main positions against five German divisions, and to the south the 3rd and 15th Divisions were equally successful against four German divisions. The attack was continued southwards at various points but everywhere failed, with enormous losses to the enemy.

To return to the southern area, a force, organised under the orders of the Fifth Army Commander, out of details, stragglers, army troops, etc., and placed under the command of General Carey, had been stationed on the 26th on the line Mezières—Marcelcave—Hamel and, as practically the only reserves available in this part, came into action on the 28th. The enemy continued to press back the French on our right and this advance, combined with the advance along the Somme, made the salient with Harbonnières and Rosières at its apex so dangerous that it had to be vacated, and our troops were withdrawn to a line running roughly due south from Hamel.

By this time the enemy's attack had lost much of its weight and on the 29th Carey's Force, assisted by cavalry, took over the defence south of the Somme and so enabled some of the much harassed divisions to re-organise. On the 30th Démuin was lost and on the 31st Moreuil. For some days after this the line was comparatively quiet, but on 4th April in the course of an attack between the Somme and our right at

[1] The enemy troops were evidently prepared for an advance on an ambitious scale, for one prisoner was found to be carrying six days' rations, two blankets and a pair of new boots.

Hangard and upon the French south of that point we lost Hamel. Strong attacks next day at Hangard and between Dernancourt, to the south of Albert, and Bucquoy, to the north, were completely repulsed at practically all points. When the fighting at length died down we were holding south of the Somme a line which passed to the west of Hamel and east of Villers Bretonneux and Hangard.

Frequent local attacks ensued on different sectors, and finally the Germans on 24th April attempted to advance upon the whole of our front south of the Somme. After a conflict between tanks, the first of which there is record, and fierce fighting along the whole front, the enemy broke through at Villers Bretonneux and gained positions commanding Amiens. This threat on so important a point was not to be tolerated and a brilliant counter-attack, undertaken at short notice on the following night (the 24th/25th) by the Australians aided by the 18th Division, drove the enemy back to the east of the village almost to the line from which he had set out in the morning.

Thus ended the second Battle of the Somme, the most serious defeat sustained by us during the war. In about ten days of actual fighting the enemy advanced on a front of forty miles to a depth of twenty to forty miles, regained large areas which had been won by the Allies only after months of desperate fighting in 1916 and 1917, and captured and held such places as Albert, Bray, Rosières and Montdidier which had not been in his possession since the opening of the war and then only temporarily. He claimed to have taken, chiefly from us, 70,000 prisoners and 1,100 guns. Immense quantities of stores and material, which in so hurried a retreat were not destroyed, fell into his hands. Our casualties in this battle, and immediately afterwards at the Lys (see p. 102) amounted to 400,000,[1] most of them in the Somme area.

[1] *British Campaigns in the West*, by Sir F. Maurice (p. liii), in Findlay Muirhead's *Belgium and Western Front*.

The German casualties were about the same, for they have admitted[1] the loss of 300,000 wounded and, as the proportion of wounded to killed throughout the war was usually three to one, these figures imply a loss in killed of about 100,000. It is clear that the legend, at one time current, that the defence collapsed is a legend and nothing more. Only the most resolute defence could have inflicted such enormous casualties and have foiled the plan, supported by a great superiority in numbers and munitions, of capturing Amiens and of separating the British and French armies.

To meet these losses troops and munitions were hurried out from England, troops were recalled to France from Italy, Salonica, Palestine and elsewhere, and President Wilson gave orders that the partially trained American troops in France should be temporarily incorporated with English or French brigades.

In the operations described above the M.C. was won by four of the Council's staff:

(i) Lieut. H. T. Maddocks (M.G.C., Comp.) on 21st March during a withdrawal at Le Mesnil, near Péronne, " held on unsupported by infantry, until almost surrounded, when he withdrew in good order doing great execution as he retired. He was the last to cross a bridge before its destruction."

(ii) Capt L. K. Spencer (Lond., Educ.) on 28th March " handled his company in a difficult counter-attack with great ability, and later, when it was necessary to clear up the situation, he personally reconnoitred in the face of machine-gun fire and sniping, sending back invaluable information as to the enemy's position. He was wounded while doing this, but insisted on carrying on until the advance and consolidation had been effected."

[1] *General Staff and Its Problems,* by Gen. Ludendorff, translated by F. A. Holt (vol. i. p. 139).

(iii) Lieut. A. P. Comyns (10th R. Welch Fus., Clerk) at Hamel on 30th March, "when a considerable length of trench on both sides had been evacuated, held the trench with a Lewis gun and three men, keeping up a steady fire and inflicting many casualties until reinforcements arrived."

(iv) Lieut. D. J. Davies (R. Welch Fus., Educ.). "By his personal example, and by the excellent fire control which he maintained, he kept his front intact against repeated enemy attacks. At night he went out on patrol on three occasions, capturing a prisoner and killing a machine-gun crew and bringing in the gun."

Co. Sergt.-Maj. J. C. Cairns, D.C.M. (Oxf. and Bucks L.I., Educ.) received a bar to his D.C.M., but details are lacking. Co. Sergt.-Maj. S. C. P. Drury, D.C.M. (R.E., Educ.) received a bar to his D.C.M. for his gallantry at Highland Ridge. "When his company were advancing in the open and were met by very heavy machine-gun fire, he walked up and down in front of the line encouraging the men and ensuring that the line was maintained in good order. Later, under heavy fire, he withdrew the company in good order, and assisted a pioneer battalion to fight a rear-guard action." Sergt. (afterwards Regt. Sergt.-Maj.) J. Wild (R.E., Asylums) won the D.C.M. near Albert, but no details are available.

Corp. (afterwards Sergt.) F. Hills, M.M. (Lond., Educ.) received a bar to his M.M. Towards the end of March, between Bus and Bertincourt, he "carried out patrol work under exceptionally trying conditions and extreme closeness of contact with the enemy, securing valuable information which enabled the battalion to get clear when practically surrounded. Throughout the whole of the withdrawal of March and April he had charge of a platoon, and, by his own coolness and courage, kept up the *moral* of his men at all times."

The M.M. was won by the undermentioned members of the Council's staff:

(i) Sergt. E. Strugnell (15th Lond., Solr.) for bravery in action near Cambrai on 21st March.

(ii) Sergt. (afterwards Co. Q.M.S.) P. J. W. Pollard (Beds, Educ.) near Jussy on 22nd March, " volunteered to take field kitchens and supplies to troops in the line, under enemy observation and shell fire."

(iii) Sergt. J. R. Austin (R.G.A., Parks) for bravery at Bois Hullot, on 22nd March.

(iv) Sergt. P. H. Spowage (R. Fus., Educ.) on 23rd March, for the successful manner in which he assumed command at Eaucourt l'Abbaye after all his officers had become casualties.

(v) F. H. W. Briggs (R.A.M.C., Asylums) on 24th March, near Guiscard " where, after he had been on duty continuously for 36 hours, he voluntarily searched for some French wounded who had been left behind, and brought them to safety."

(vi) Sec.-Corp. E. H. Knowles (R.E., Housing) near Ytres, for rescuing a wounded man under heavy machine-gun fire and, the nearest dressing stations having been evacuated, carrying him a long distance to a train.

(vii) R. A. P. Willmer (7th Manch., Educ.) for obtaining at Ablainzeville, under heavy fire, useful information concerning the enemy's movements.

Capt. S. A. French (7th R.W. Kent, Clerk) was killed at Moy during the preliminary bombardment on 20th March and Capt. H. T. Rapson (7th R.W. Kent, Educ.) wounded next day died on the 23rd. The long list of those missing on the 21st or succeeding days, the actual date of death being often unknown, included Lance-Corp. P. Ford (1st R. Dub. Fus., Tram.), Sergt. L. N. Wright (11th Leic., Asylums), O. J. Pikett (16th Rif. Bde., Tram.) W. J. Peake (23rd Northd. Fus., Tram.), Paul Sherard

(R.E., Educ.), A. J. Troke (12th K.R.R., Parks), Alfred Huddart (2/5th Notts and Derby, Educ.), W. E. Carritt (2nd Rif. Bde., Parks), S. A. Lewis (R.F.A., Tram.), A. E. Miller (1st Lond., Educ.), K. L. Baxter (2nd Suffolk, Comp.), Jesse Gebbett (19th Northd. Fus., Tram.), Lieut. S. J. Jennings, B.Sc., (E. Surr. and R.E., Educ.), W. J. Brinklow (9th Rif. Bde., Parks), Edward Quinlan (18th Lond., Ch. Engr.), Edward Hems (24th Lond., Tram.), Ernest Whybrow (8th Rif. Bde., Tram.), Frank Richardson (21st Lond., Arch.), Sergt. W. Kennedy (8th R.W. Kent, Asylums).

Definite particulars are known of the undermentioned: Bomdr. W. J. Plumridge (R.H.A., Asylums) killed on 21st March near Jeancourt, Sec.-Corp. R. A. Howes (R.E., Ch. Engr.) died of wounds received the same day at Lagnicourt; on the 23rd J. R. Baker (23rd Lond., Educ.) was killed, probably near Gouzeaucourt, F. F. Drewett (2/5th R.W. Surr., Tram.) south of St. Quentin, Lieut. W. T. S. Hard (3rd Lond., Educ.) at Tergnier and W. F. Jewers (11th K.R.R., Comp.) near Nesle; on the 24th H. J. Sanders (28th Lond., Pub. H.) at Ytres and H. W. Burwood (R.A.M.C., Educ.) north of Arras; on the 25th Richard Jones (1st R. Drag., Tram.) near the Oise, H. F. Coombes (2nd Drag. Gds., Asylums) probably at Montauban; on the 27th A. G. Barber (R.E., Tram.) at Harbonnières, and T. H. Taylor (E. Yorks, Tram.); on the 28th Corporal Jack Hill (16th Lond., Educ.) and J. F. B. Barrett (5th Lond., Comp.) and R. V. Butcher (5th Lond., Arch.) at Gavrelle and F. B. Rammage R.F.A., Arch.) and Frank Dolan (R.E., Ch. Engr.) south of Arras; on the 29th Thomas Parsons (R.H.A., Tram.) died in hospital of wounds and Corporal H. V. Lane (28th Lond., Educ.) died as a prisoner of war of wounds received at Ytres on the 23rd. On 3rd April John Toby (5th Oxf. and Bucks, Tram.) died as a prisoner of war of wounds received on 25th

March, and on the 4th Corporal F. J. Hatton (R.F.A., Educ.) was killed near Corbie; Sergt. C. A. Dearing M.M., B.Sc. (5th Lond., Educ.) died on 16th April of wounds received at Gavrelle on 28th March and Corporal W. E. Martin (2nd R. Scots, Educ.) wounded on the 12th died on 20th April, H. W. K. Mason (7th R.W. Kent, Educ.) was killed at Villers Bretonneux on the 24th, and Sergt. W. E. Long (3rd Lond., Educ.) wounded this day, probably at the same place, died on the 25th. P. F. Archer (R.H.A., Tram.), wounded near St. Quentin on 28th March, died in England on 1st September.

Battle of the Lys.

Although an attack north of La Bassée was not unexpected, the crisis on the Somme made it necessary to weaken the defence in this sector. Many divisions were sent to the south, and others which needed a respite from the desperate fighting there were made up to strength with drafts fresh from England and put into the line in their place. The attack opened on 9th April on a front of some 12 or 15 miles between the La Bassée Canal and Armentières which had been the scene of so much fighting in 1915. Again aided by a thick mist the enemy over-ran Portuguese divisions which were being relieved and, pressing rapidly forward, reached the river Lys at and near Sailly. The withdrawal of the Portuguese opened up the British divisions on each side of them to attack in flank and

BATTLE OF THE LYS, 1918.

rear. The 55th, north of the La Bassée Canal, stood fast, but the 40th to the south of Armentières were compelled to give ground. Towards evening the Germans near Estaires and Bac St. Maur forced passages over the river, the former being driven back by the 51st and 50th Divisions who were in reserve behind the Portuguese.

Next day the enemy captured Estaires and, although driven out, succeeded later in regaining the town. On this day the battle spread northwards to the neighbourhood of Hill 60. Aided once more by mist the Germans pushed back the 25th Division north of Armentières and the 19th on the east side of the Messines ridge, but the situation at the latter point was somewhat restored in a counter-attack by the 9th Division. Armentières, thus threatened from the north and from the south, was vacated during the evening by the 34th Division.

On the 11th Messines, Neuf Berquin and Merville were captured, and with the object of reducing the length of line held to the north our troops, under orders, vacated the Messines ridge and withdrew to the line Wulverghem—Neuve Eglise. On the 12th the Germans attacked in great strength to the north-west of the salient they had formed and seized Merris, but were checked by the 29th Division. Renewing the attack next day they pushed back the 29th and 31st Divisions which had already suffered heavy losses, and, in an effort to reach the important railway junction at Hazebrouck, got as far as the eastern edge of Nieppe Forest. Here they were finally held by Australian troops brought up from the Somme. Neuve Eglise, after changing hands several times, finally passed to the enemy on the 14th, and on the 15th the enemy developed his success by capturing Bailleul. During these latter days a previously arranged plan for the evacuation of the Passchendaele salient was carried out, the operation being completed by the night of the

15th/16th, when our line, starting from the west and south of Langemarck, passed through St. Julien and to the east of Frezenberg.

On the 16th Wytschaete was lost, but the 9th Division held on to the outskirts of the village, and an attack next day on the commanding feature known as Kemmel Hill was repulsed by the 34th, 49th and 19th Divisions. On the 18th a renewal of the attack at Givenchy and Festubert was successfully met by the 1st Division, while to the west the 4th and 61st Divisions defeated other attacks with heavy losses.

Some days of comparative quiet now intervened during which French reinforcements took over the Kemmel sector. On the 25th the battle was renewed between the Comines Canal and the north of Bailleul, with the result that the 21st and 9th Divisions were forced back along the Canal and at Wytschaete, and the French lost Kemmel village and hill. Next day French and British troops recaptured Kemmel village, but being unsupported on the flanks had to withdraw. The loss of Kemmel Hill seriously threatened our positions in the Ypres salient where the communications and defences were under direct observation, and as a precaution, on the night of the 26th/27th, our troops were withdrawn to a point south of La Clytte, the line passing thence to the west of Zillebeke and through Wieltje and Pilckem. Thus on the east round to the south and south-west the enemy approached Ypres nearer than at any time since the fighting line became stabilised in the autumn of 1914. On the 29th very fierce attacks delivered between Locre and Voormezeele by almost overwhelming numbers of troops were completely defeated by the 21st, 49th and 25th Divisions.

The casualties on both sides have already been dealt with under the Battles of the Somme, 1918 (see p. 97). In this, our second serious defeat on the western front, the Germans advanced a maximum of ten miles on a front of twenty. By the capture of Kemmel and the recapture of the Messines ridge they caused us to vacate most of the ground won in more than three months' bitter fighting during the summer and autumn of 1917. Their advance brought them close to Béthune, Hazebrouck and Poperinghe, and enabled them to harass with gun-fire at moderate range those important points in our communications by road and rail.

The fate of Merville, Merris, Bailleul and many other little towns and villages was a pathetic feature of the fighting. As the line in this part had hardly varied, their only association with the war had been to provide peaceful quarters for advanced depots, hospitals, rest billets and the like. The inhabitants might therefore hope that such good fortune would continue to the end, and that their homes, although sometimes threatened, would escape destruction. Such hopes were rudely shattered for, after a respite of nearly four years, these places suddenly found themselves in the thick of the struggle, and in a few days were as utterly wrecked as though they had been for years in the forward battle area.

Capt. (afterwards Lt.-Col.) W. Parkes, M.C. (8th Glouc., Educ.) in fighting near Messines gained a bar to the M.C. "When the enemy penetrated the line . . . he led forward the battalion and such other details as he was able to rally and restored the situation. His initiative and coolness saved a general withdrawal."

Lieut. F. Morgan (R.G.A., Educ.) for gallantry at Kemmel and Mont Noir was awarded the M.C. "As senior subaltern of his battery he did splendid work on many occasions and commanded the battery very efficiently for some time." Capt. R. E. Licence (2nd Durh. L.I., Educ.), as adjutant of his battalion, rendered most valuable assistance throughout the operations, and received the Croix de Guerre. S. Seaman (R.F.A., Asylums) was awarded the M.M. for his gallantry at Kemmel Hill on 25th April.

In this fighting Thos. C. Truman (R.G.A., Educ.) was killed on 10th April, Lieut. and Quart.-Mast. A. H. Jibb (R.A.M.C., Asylums) on the 12th, A. H. Hampton (R.A.M.C., Asylums) on the 13th probably in this sector, A. W. May (8th R.W. Surr., Tram.) on the same day, Lance-Corp. A. J. Thomas (R.E., Tram.) near Meteren on the 14th, and Lieut. Robert Findon (R.E., Estates and Val.) near Béthune on the 18th. Charles Herd (R.F.A., Tram.), wounded near Armentières earlier in the month, died on the 19th, and on the same date Lieut. E. W. Standerwick (2nd Essex, Stores) was killed near Béthune. Sergt. Jack Heritage, M.M. (R.G.A., Tram.) was killed on the 21st. Lieut. R. T. Wood (M.G.C., Comp.) was killed near Wytschaete, Bomdr. Victor Zoller (R.G.A., Educ.) near Kemmel, Sergt. T. Bailey (12th Glos., Asylums) near Merville and Lieut. C. S. Day (R.F.A., Educ.) east of Béthune, all on the 25th, Lieut. C. W. Clark (13th Rif. Bde., Educ.), and A. E. Broad (4th R. Fus., Parks) on the 26th, and H. G. Lewin (15th Dur. L.I., Educ.) near Wytschaete on the 27th. G. H. Jones (R.F.A., Tram.), wounded and taken prisoner at Kemmel Hill, died on an unknown date some months later.

Battle of the Aisne, 1918.

An attack was quite possible on practically any part of the British front, and this prevented troops from being completely withdrawn from the fighting area. On the French front, however, there were thought to be several quiet sectors and to one of these, to the north-west of Rheims, were transferred a few divisions with the hope that they would have a period of comparative rest in which, after their heavy losses on the Somme and the Lys, to refit and to re-organise. This hope was not realised for on 27th May, after only a few weeks, the Germans opened an attack on a front of some forty miles between Rheims and the north-west of Soissons.[1] The 21st Division near Loivre, the

[1] For plan, see p. 108.

8th at Berry-au-Bac on the Aisne, and the 50th near Ville-aux-Bois, the 25th being in general reserve, were driven back across the Aisne, the Vesle and the Ardre with enormous losses, the 8th for instance losing 7,000 infantry out of 9,000. At the same time the French on our left were driven from the Chemin des Dames where the British had been held up in September, 1914 (see p. 9), but which had been captured by the French in the spring of 1917. After a week's fighting the Germans had taken 45,000 prisoners and 400 guns and had advanced some thirty miles to Villers-Cotterets and to Château-Thierry on the Marne. There the defence by the French and the Americans, aided by the 19th Division, prevented any further success.

During the fighting on the 27th Lieut. R. T. Boyes (R. Suss., Educ.) "re-organised men of his company and stragglers, dug a line, and held off enemy attacks throughout the night and again in the morning. He himself brought down with rifle fire a low-flying enemy aeroplane. . . . " He was awarded the M.C.

Those killed included Mark Farrow (2nd Devons, Asylums) near Berry-au-Bac on 26th May and Sergt. R. W. Stevens (2nd Northants, Tram.) at Berry-au-Bac, William Pollock (4th S. Staffs, Educ.) and Bernard Sibbitt (R.A.M.C., Comp.) all on the 27th. Walter Butler (8th Border, Educ.) who was taken prisoner on the latter date died in Germany on 8th September.

General Casualties.

J. R. McBean (R.E., Clerk) died on 22nd April as the result of an accident on the railway at Audruicq, Frank Wiscombe (2nd Wilts, Asylums) was missing on 8th May, Sergt. G. O. King (R.G.A., Educ.) died at Rouen on the 11th of heart failure, Lieut. L. F. Brown, B.A. (M.G.C., Educ.) died on the 14th of wounds received on the 10th, S. E. Martin (Gren. Gds., Tram.) on the 27th of wounds received near

Arras, and Lieut. A. L. Tongue (R.F.A., Educ.) was killed on the 28th in the same neighbourhood.

On 2nd June, Lieut. Benjamin Downes (2nd Lond., Educ.) was killed, on the 6th Lieut. G. H. Spicer (17th R. Fus., Tram.) was killed at Monchy-au-Bois,

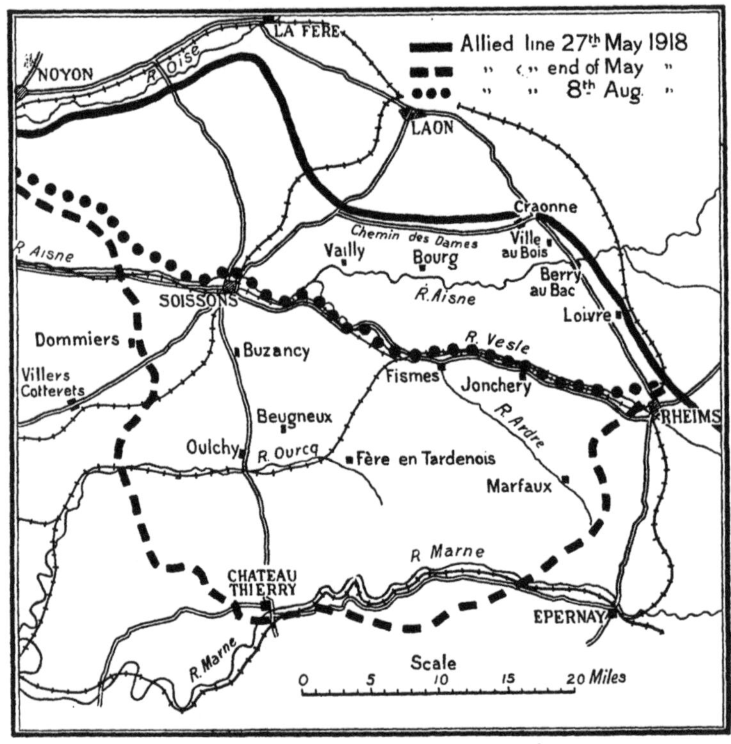

THE AISNE AND THE MARNE, 1918.

to the south of Arras, on the 9th Bombdr. F. H. Voak (R.F.A., Tram.) was killed near Verdun, on the 13th Samuel Goss (R.F.A., Stores) died of wounds received sometime before, on the 15th S. V. Duncton (4th R. Fus., Tram.) died of wounds received near Béthune, on the 17th Co. Sergt.-Maj. F. A. Kingham (15th Lond., P. Cont.) was killed near Albert, and on the 18th Capt. D. T. O'Flynn (R.A.M.C., Asylums) died of appendicitis. H. E. Bishop (Rif. Bde., Tram.) taken prisoner on 21st March died of pneumonia on 29th June near Péronne.

On 15th July John Reynolds (R.E., Asylums) was killed as the result of an accident at Etaples, on the 20th W. H. Green (R. Ir. Rif., Parks) was killed to the south or south-west of Ypres, and on the 25th Co. Sergt.-Maj. J. G. S. Adam (8th Lond., Educ.) was killed in a trench raid south of Albert. Sergt. E. Hook (9th R. Innisk. Fus., Educ.) was killed on 4th August near Poperinghe, A. J. Suckling (6th Lond., Tram.) died on the 10th of wounds probably received near Arras, A. E. Richards (51st M.G.C., Comp.) on the 28th of wounds received on the 25th, and F. S. N. Lediard (13th R. Fus., Asylums) also on the 28th near Beaumetz. On the 14th Sergt. A. C. Wilby (8th Buffs, Tram.) who had been wounded and taken prisoner at the Battle of Loos in September, 1915, died of pneumonia near The Hague whither he had been transferred from Germany.

G. E. Wybrow (R.A.M.C., Arch.) was killed on 5th September to the south-west of Ypres, H. H. Dean (M.G.C., Tram.) on the 10th of gas poisoning, Bombr. R. Butland (R.G.A., Asylums) on the 25th near Arras, and T. T. Jackaman (2nd Devons, Parks) on the 27th probably in front of Vimy Ridge. Lance-Corp. R. A. Hale (1st R. Berks, Educ.) was killed near Noyelles on 3rd October, and R. C. Tovey (R.F.A., Educ.) on the 12th. F. W. Earl (R.G.A., Parks) died on the 20th of gas poisoning.

Battle of the Marne, 1918.

To make clear what follows it will be well at this point to survey the general position and to glance at events on the French front. In two months the enemy had made three great and successful attacks; one, chiefly against the British in the valley of the Somme, had brought him nearly to Amiens, a second, also against the British in the valley of the Lys, had brought him nearly to Hazebrouck, and a third, chiefly against the French in the valleys of the Aisne and the Marne, had brought him to within forty miles of Paris. Although each assault, successful at first, had been foiled, he continued his efforts to make that breach in the Allied lines which would lead to complete victory. Early in June the French, attacked between Montdidier and Noyon, were pressed back, but only for a few miles, and finally on 15th July the last great assault by the enemy was opened. Rheims, which being at the apex of a sharp salient could be attacked on two sides, was the main objective, but the whole offensive covered a front of more than fifty miles. To the west and south-west of the city there were some slight gains, but to the east the assault, owing to the skilful tactics of General Gouraud, was completely shattered.

On 18th July General Foch, judging that the Germans had now committed the bulk of their remaining reserves to this last attack, launched his counter-offensive, directing it at first against the western half of the great salient formed in the German line by their success in the recent Battle of the Aisne. French and American troops, secretly assembled in the woods near Villers-Cotterets, were successful between Château-Thierry and Soissons.[1] The British 15th Division, having relieved the Americans near Dommiers to the south-west of Soissons, captured Buzancy after a fluctuating struggle, and on their right the 34th Division took Beugneux. Meanwhile on the east side of the salient the 51st and 62nd Divisions advanced along the valley of the Ardre. In about ten days of this fighting the Germans were driven back to the Aisne with the loss of 20,000 prisoners and 400 guns. Once again the Marne proved to be the point at which an advance seriously threatening Paris had been arrested and thrown back, but

[1] For plan see p. 108.

whereas in 1914 the French, who on both occasions bore the brunt of the attack, were aided only by a few British divisions, in 1918 they were aided also by Americans and Italians.

In the fighting on the east of the salient Sergt. P. Clark (R.A.S.C., Tram.) was awarded the Croix de Guerre. He " organised . . . a service of cars between loading posts and aid posts, going and coming continuously by bombarded roads, establishing control posts and regulating the circulation of cars." W. T. F. Stiff (62nd M.G.C., P. Health) won the M.M. " Despite almost insuperable difficulties, he maintained communication between brigade, battalions and his own company. He repeatedly repaired wires under heavy shell fire."

Only two of the Council's staff lost their lives during these operations, H. W. Drewett (2/4th Hamps., Tram.) who was killed on 20th July near Jonchery to the west of Rheims, and Lieut. C. F. Wilson (2/4th Hamps., Educ.) who was wounded on the 23rd near Marfaux and died on the 27th at Epernay.

Minor Operations on British Front.

Advantage was taken of the lull in the fighting on the main British front to re-organise the defences, and, as a preliminary, eight divisions, the 14th, 16th, 31st, 34th, 39th, 40th, 59th, and 66th, which, having suffered the most, had been reduced to cadres were temporarily written off as fighting units. To relieve the situation at Amiens, Béthune, Hazebrouck and even at St. Pol, twenty miles to the west of Arras, where much-used railway junctions were under shell fire, three routes for north and south traffic were provided, this making it necessary to lay some 500 miles of broad gauge track. New lines of defence in rear consisting of about 5000 miles of trench had also to be constructed by the weary troops.

As, however, the numbers of our men increased and their confidence and training improved, various minor operations were undertaken. These included the capture of Ville-sur-Ancre on 19th May, and an advance near Morlancourt, to the south of Albert, on 10th June, both by the Australians. An advance

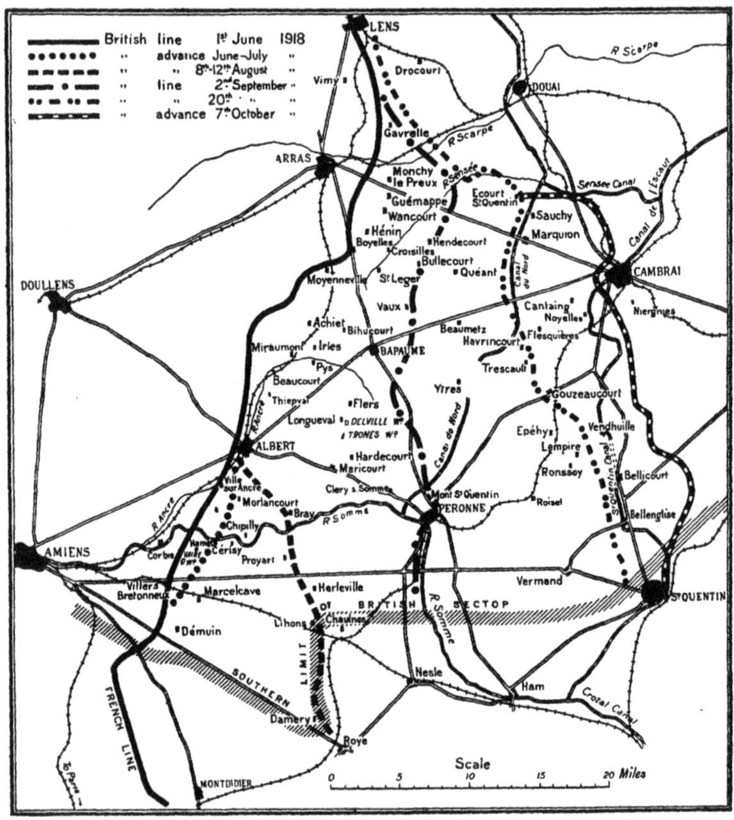

FIRST PART OF BRITISH ADVANCE, 1918.

by the French near Locre Hospice on 20th May was followed early in July by the capture of the Hospice, and on the 14th of the month by the final capture of Ridge Wood in the same neighbourhood by the 6th Division. On 3rd June the Australians and the 29th Division captured Mont de Merris, west of Merris village. On 28th June the 5th and 31st Divisions made a successful surprise attack to the east of the Forest of Nieppe, capturing the enemy's defences on a front of 6,000 yards and taking 450 prisoners. The plateau of Villers-Bretonneux was cleared by the Australians, and Hamel and Vaire Wood were recaptured with 1,500 prisoners on 4th July. A week later some slight advances were made near Merris, on the 19th the 9th Division recaptured Meteren, and on the night of the 28th/29th Merris was recaptured by the Australians.

The Battle of Amiens.

The failure of the enemy's attack on Rheims on 15th July and the success, three days later, of the counter-offensive at the Marne and the Aisne transferred the initiative to the Allies. In order to maintain this advantage it was arranged that the French, American and British armies should undertake separate local offensives, the task assigned to the British being an advance to the east and south-east of Amiens so as to free the railway communications through the city from enemy pressure. It was desirable that the attack should be a surprise, and elaborate precautions were therefore taken to lead the enemy to suppose that any effort contemplated would be at the other, that is the northern, end of our line. With this object, headquarters and casualty clearing stations were built in conspicuous positions in Flanders, and training and general activity behind that part of the line were simulated. Meanwhile preparations were made rapidly and secretly for the advance at Amiens, and on 8th August the attack opened at dawn in a thick mist. The Canadians were on the right immediately north of the Amiens—Roye road, the Australians in the centre at Villers-Bretonneux and to the south of the Somme, and the 58th, 18th and 12th Divisions on the left to the north of the river. Within a very short time these troops, aided by 400 tanks, had pushed forward two miles to the line Démuin—Marcelcave—Cérisy, where the Cavalry Corps joined in the advance. By nightfall the infantry were six or seven miles from their starting point, the only check being at Chipilly which was not stormed until the next day, 13,000 prisoners had been captured with nearly 400 guns and stores of ammunition, etc.[1]

On the 9th the enemy's resistance stiffened, but this was overcome and by the 12th, when the battle was broken off, we had reached the line Damery—Lihons—Proyart—Bray. This represented an advance of some twelve miles with the capture of a total of 22,000 prisoners and over 400 guns. The Amiens—Paris railway was freed from enemy fire and, by seizing Montdidier and by bringing Chaulnes under shell-fire, the Allies greatly hampered the enemy's arrangements for the movement of troops and munitions.

In the fighting on 8th August Sergt. E. C. Dare (Lond., Educ.) won the D.C.M. for capturing, with the help of about thirty men, mostly stragglers from different regiments, a German strong point with twenty machine-guns and nearly 300 prisoners, and Corp. R. B. Williams (Lond., Educ.) won the M.M. for his bravery near Chipilly. Batty. Q.M.S. E. W. Martin (R.F.A., Educ.) also won the M.M. about this time.

Lieut. P. C. Cleall B.A. (10th Essex, Educ.), wounded and taken prisoner on the 8th, died of his wounds on 26th August.

Second Battles of the Somme, 1918.

The attack was now shifted northwards to the line between Albert and Arras where the ground was suitable for tanks and where an advance to the south-

[1] General Ludendorff described 8th August as "the black day of the German Army in the history of this war." To it he attributed the defection of Bulgaria and the general discouragement of Germany's allies and on 14th August he advised his government to seek for avenues of peace. (*My War Memories*, 1914-18, vol. ii. p. 679).

east, in conjunction with the recent success at Villers-Bretonneux, might produce far-reaching results. As a preliminary, on 21st August the line from Beaucourt and Miraumont, in the valley of the Ancre, northwards to Moyenneville, was successfully attacked by the 21st, 42nd, New Zealand, 37th, 2nd and Guards Divisions. The 5th, 63rd and 3rd Divisions, passing through them, continued the advance, and by the end of the day the Arras railway had been reached, and in some places crossed, between Miraumont and Achiet. As the result of an attack, early next morning, by the Australians and the 32nd, 47th, 12th, 18th and 38th Divisions with a few tanks on the sector between the Somme and the Ancre, Albert was captured by the 18th Division, and our front was advanced to the east of the Bray—Albert road. The fighting on these two days yielded 4,400 prisoners and a few guns.

The way was thus cleared for a general attack between Chaulnes and Arras, which opened on 23rd August on a front of 33 miles. The divisions in action on the 21st and 22nd continued their advance in a general easterly direction, while on the left the attack was taken up by the 56th and 52nd Divisions. The assault was everywhere successful, particularly to the east and north-east of Achiet, and the enemy began to show signs of confusion. Soon after midnight on the 23rd/24th the advance was resumed, the Australians capturing Bray, the 12th and 18th Divisions positions to the north, the 38th Thiepval which held out for three months during the Somme fighting in 1916, the 42nd Miraumont and Pys, the 5th Irles, the Guards St. Leger, the 56th positions near Croisilles and the 52nd Hénin. These successes were followed up, and on the 27th the 18th Division captured Trônes Wood, on the 28th the 12th and 58th Divisions captured Hardecourt, and the 38th and 17th advanced near Delville Wood towards Flers. On the 29th Bapaume fell to the New Zealanders, and the 56th and 57th Divisions reached Bullecourt and Hendecourt. The enemy's resistance was now increasing, but, notwithstanding this, the Australians, in the night of 30th/31st August, stormed Mont St. Quentin to the north-west of Péronne, beat off numerous counter-attacks and on 1st September occupied the town.

After this achievement the advance halted for a time. Sir Douglas Haig summarised the operations in the following words: "Twenty-three British divisions . . . had driven 35 German divisions from one side of the old Somme battlefield to the other. . . . They had inflicted upon the enemy the heaviest losses in killed and wounded, and had taken . . . over 34,000 prisoners and 270 guns." Part of the retirement was to some extent voluntary, but the victories of 8th and 21st August had disorganised the enemy's defences and greatly accelerated his retreat.

The M.C. was gained by five of the Council's staff as follows:

(i) Lieut. A. H. Collins (32nd M.G.C., Educ.) at Herleville, south of the Somme, on the 23rd "went forward with the first wave, selecting positions for his guns. . . . As a result of his forward observation under heavy fire, he was able to place his guns so that effective neutralising fire was brought to bear on the enemy."

(ii) Lieut. C. L. Henstridge (4th Lond., Educ.) on the 23rd at Boyelles, almost due south of Arras, "seeing that the leading company was held up, pushed his platoon round the enemy's flank and enfiladed part of the trench."

(iii) Capt. A. W. K. Burnett (R.F.A., Educ.). Near Bihucourt on the 25th, while his "battery was firing a barrage, the enemy commenced a heavy bombardment. He sent all spare men away to cover and remained moving about the battery encouraging the men."

(iv) Lieut. E. C. Yalden (7th Middx., Educ.) at Bullecourt "during heavy fighting which lasted several days, displayed marked powers of leadership. . . . When his company was almost surrounded, he held on to his position with great resolution, repelling several attacks."

(v) Capt. G. Ames (R.H.A., Educ.) in connection with operations, details of which are not known, leading to the fall of Bapaume.

Co. Sergt.-Maj. T. Archdeacon (7th Lond., Educ.) won the D.C.M. on the 26th when, near Maricourt to the east of Albert, "with an officer and eighteen men, he secured a commanding position about 1,000 yards in front of the main line. The party was subjected to heavy enfilade machine-gun fire, the officer and twelve men becoming casualties. He immediately took command . . . and beat off an enemy counter-attack. He subsequently held on for eight hours."

The M.M. was won by C. W. Shrimpton (R.F.A., Estates and Valn.) at Morlancourt, near the Somme, for his gallantry in taking up ammunition under heavy fire, and by G. J. Willcocks (R.A.M.C., Educ.) for his devotion to duty near Clery-sur-Somme on 1st September.

The casualties included Sergt. A. G. Beavis (Yorks L.I., Tram.) killed on 19th August near Herleville, A. V. Veasey (R.G.A., Tram.) near Albert on the 21st, Lieut. J. C. Stevenson (6th R.W. Surr., Educ.) near Morlancourt, and Lieut. P. T. Sutton, B.A., B.Sc. (R.G.A., Educ.) to the south of that place, both on the 24th, W. H. D. Cole (1st Norf., Tram.) near Achiet on the 25th, Lieut. S. N. Brown (8th R. Berks, Educ.) at Longueval on the 27th, and Capt. E. C. Duprès (9th R. Fus., Educ.) near Hardecourt and Co. Sergt.-Maj. F. G. Weston (16th Lond., Educ.) near Hendecourt, both on the 28th. Bombdr. G. A. Percival (R.F.A., Tram.) was killed near Clery-sur-Somme and L. A. Reardon, B.Sc. (15th Lond., Educ.)

near Péronne, both on 1st September, and Corp. E. W. C. Hayes (20th Lond., Tram.) near the latter place on the 2nd.

Second Battles of Arras, 1918.

The enemy's position in front of Arras had now been turned into a salient, and an attack against it was opened on 26th August. The Canadians, who had been brought up from near Chaulnes, stormed Wancourt, Guémappe and Monchy-le-Preux, and the 51st Division was equally successful, recapturing most of the area, on the north of the Scarpe, lost during the German advance five months earlier. By the end of the month our troops were in touch with the southern part of the elaborate system of trenches known as the Quéant—Drocourt Switch, between the Hindenburg Line at Quéant, to the south-east of Arras, and Drocourt, to the south-east of Lens. On 2nd September the 52nd and 57th Divisions and the Canadians with tanks, cavalry and motor machine-guns broke through this sector, and the 4th and 63rd Divisions following up exploited the victory. Altogether in about eight days ten British divisions defeated thirteen German divisions and captured some 16,000 prisoners and 200 guns.

Battles of Havrincourt and Epéhy.

As a result of his defeats at Amiens, Bapaume and the Scarpe the enemy now found himself so dangerously situated that an immediate retirement became necessary. The first withdrawal, on the night of 2nd/3rd September, was to a line from Péronne along the Canal du Nord to Ytres and thence northwards to the river Sensée, but within a few days the retreat had been continued to the line Vermand—Epéhy—Havrincourt—Ecourt St. Quentin. Much of this defensive position consisted of the Hindenburg Line to which the enemy had retired in the spring of 1917 (see p. 56) and portions of which had been captured in the Battles of Arras and Cambrai (see pp. 61 and 85).

The neighbourhood of Epéhy and Havrincourt had been strongly fortified as a sort of outpost line, and this had to be dealt with before the main position could be attacked. The assault upon the sector at Havrincourt opened on 12th September, when the 37th Division, with the New Zealanders on its right, stormed Trescault, and the 62nd,[1] with the 2nd on its left, stormed Havrincourt. The Epéhy sector was attacked on the 18th when, to render the defence more difficult, the assault extended over a front of twenty-seven miles from near St. Quentin to Gouzeaucourt. The Australians and 74th Division were successful on the right, the 18th at Ronssoy and Lempire, the 12th, after a temporary check, at Epéhy, and the 58th to the north of that village. In these two battles fifteen British divisions defeated twenty German divisions, capturing nearly 12,000 prisoners and 100 guns.

In the attack on Gouzeaucourt on the 18th Lieut. John Evans (R. Welch Fus., Educ.) reached his objective with twenty men but, as the troops on each side failed to get up into line, he was cut off from his supports. During the night he collected some fifty men, beat off six counter-attacks and captured a machine gun. His force held out until, after thirty hours' fighting, their ammunition was exhausted, when the enemy rushed the position, killing or capturing all the survivors. Lieut. Evans was amongst those taken prisoner, but he died of his wounds on the 22nd. For his gallantry he was awarded the M.C.

Battles of Cambrai and the Hindenburg Line.

It had now been decided that, as part of a general scheme for dislocating the enemy's communications by rail, the British should attack on the St. Quentin—Cambrai front in the general direction of Maubeuge, an important point in those communications. The

[1] Curiously enough the same division captured the same position ten months earlier at the Battle of Cambrai (see p. 83).

main position guarding this point was the Hindenburg Line, known to the Germans as the Siegfried Line, with subsidiary systems such as the Brunnhilde, Wotan, Hunding, etc., Lines, named after various individuals in German mythology. The whole was a powerful series of field works, dug in 1916–18 by the forced labour of civilians and prisoners of war, with many concrete shelters and emplacements, and protected by broad belts of wire. It extended from the Chemin des Dames, past La Fère, St. Quentin and Cambrai to near Arras with a depth varying from 7,000 to 10,000 yards. Included in the defences were parts of the Canal du Nord and the Canal de l'Escaut. The former connects the Somme at Péronne with the Sensée midway between Cambrai and Douai, and the latter connects the Somme near St. Quentin with the Escaut (or Scheldt) to the north of Valenciennes.[1] When bridges had been destroyed, the long stretches of water were a formidable obstacle to all arms, but especially to tanks, and the difficulties of crossing were greatly increased by the fact that considerable lengths were in cuttings as much as sixty feet deep, the steep sides of which, faced with brick or masonry, gave little or no foothold.

The less difficult sector, about thirteen miles long, containing part of the Canal du Nord, was dealt with first, the battle opening on 27th September. The 5th, 42nd, 3rd and 62nd Divisions on the right were already across the canal, and their advance on a front between Gouzeaucourt and Flesquières was comparatively easy. To the north of Flesquières the 2nd Division, the Guards, the 52nd, 63rd and 57th Divisions and the Canadians had to force passages on a narrow front and, having done so, most of them, instead of continuing on their original line, had to debouch to the south-east or north-east in order to gain room.

The part of this canal immediately to the north of St. Quentin is also known as the St. Quentin Canal.

The enemy's defence being thus thrown into confusion, the 11th and 56th Divisions crossed near Marquion and Sauchy without great difficulty. In spite of strong resistance the troops throughout the sector pressed on all that day and the next, the average gain being rather less than five miles in depth.

On the 29th the attack was transferred to the sector north of St. Quentin which contained part of the Canal de L'Escaut. This was the scene of one of the most striking exploits of the whole war, described by the commander-in-chief in the following words: "Equipped with life-belts, and carrying mats and rafts, the 46th Division stormed the western arm of the canal at Bellenglise and to the north of it, some crossing the canal on footbridges which the enemy was given no time to destroy, others dropping down the sheer sides of the canal wall, and, having swum or waded to the far side, climbing up the farther wall to the German trench lines. . . . So gallantly, rapidly and well was the attack executed . . . that this one division took on this day over 4,000 prisoners and 70 guns." On this and subsequent days the attack was also successful at other points, namely the 6th and 1st Divisions to the north of St. Quentin, the Americans and Australians at Bellicourt and the 18th and 12th Divisions at Vendhuille.

In these two battles thirty-one British and two American divisions defeated thirty-nine German divisions and captured 36,000 prisoners and 380 guns. Of more importance than the material gains was the loss of *moral* among the enemy troops and civilian population owing to the fact that the last and strongest of his prepared positions had been shattered and that the threat to his communications was now instant and direct.

For gallantry shown when, as just narrated, the 46th Division stormed the enemy's lines at Bellenglise, Capt. W. L. Bass (4th Leic., Educ.) was awarded the

SKETCH MAP OF BRITISH ADVANCE, 1918.

M.C. Sergt. H. Tester (R.F.A., Parks) received the M.M. for exceptional bravery in action at different times during September.

During preliminary fighting to the north of St. Quentin H. P. Obendorf (K.R.R., Educ.) was awarded the M.M. for conspicuous bravery in action on 20th September, and on the 26th Sergt. W. T. G. Jacobs (Lab. Corps, P. Cont.) won the M.S.M. when, although the immediate vicinity of the ammunition dump at which he was working was subjected to heavy bursts of shell fire, he encouraged his men to continue their work of unloading ammunition from a train and reloading into lorries, a very urgent task.

The only serious casualties amongst the Council's staff in these battles were Thomas Bayliss (1st Gren. Gds., Housing) killed near Flesquières on 27th September, Sergt. A. S. Devis, M.M. (Tank Corps, Tram.) on the 29th, H. J. Batchelor (6th York and Lanc., Educ.) to the north-west of Cambrai and Lieut. A. Tinniswood (R.E., Arch.) near Cantaing on 1st October, and H. O. Tichener (R.F.A., Asylums) near Cambrai on the 3rd. G. A. Bull (R.F.A., Tram.), wounded near Cambrai on 3rd October, died in England on 15th November.

Fighting in Flanders.

The effect of this succession of victories was felt further north. During August the enemy gradually vacated the Lys salient (see map on p. 102), and on the 19th we occupied Merville, and on the 30th Bailleul. Later the movement became more hurried, and, although the 36th and 29th Divisions were stoutly opposed near Neuve Eglise, by 6th September Kemmel Hill had been recaptured and we were back on the line Givenchy—Neuve Chapelle—Ploegsteert.

On 28th September, in an attack by British, French and Belgian troops under the general command of H.M. the King of the Belgians, the 14th, 35th, 29th and 9th Divisions, aided by the 41st and 36th Divisions, were completely successful to the south of the Ypres—Zonnebeke road, sweeping the enemy back in one day far beyond the limits of the fighting in 1917. At the same time the 31st, 30th and 34th Divisions captured Wytschaete and reached the outskirts of Messines. In all 5,000 prisoners and 100 guns were taken. Next day the advance was continued, and on 2nd October the enemy fell back along the front between Lens and Armentières. The restoration of roads across the shell-torn salient at Ypres occupied a fortnight, and on 14th October the advance was resumed. The 30th, 34th, 41st and 35th Divisions reached the high ground overlooking Wervicq and Menin, and the 36th, 29th and 9th Divisions on their left were equally successful. Ostend fell on the 17th to the Belgians, who during the next few days drove the Germans from the rest of the coast as far as the Dutch frontier. On the 17th the 8th Division entered Douai, and on the 18th the 57th and 59th Divisions entered Lille, the 40th Roubaix, and the 31st Tourcoing.

Lieut. T. J. Malone (1st R. Innisk. Fus., Educ.) earned the M.C. at Dadizeele on 1st and 2nd October, by his conspicuous gallantry and coolness under fire and by his devotion to duty under most trying conditions. Lieut. A. A. Angel (36th M.G.C., Educ.) won the same decoration at the same time and place. "He was attached to the infantry with four guns and when the enemy put down a heavy barrage . . . he had one put out of action and the team of another disorganised. . . . Paying no attention to the bombardment he set matters right."

W. E. Price (1st Rif. Bde., Tram.) was killed on 20th August near Merville, Corp. J. S. Hall (2/17th Lond., Tram.) on 28th September near Wytschaete Ridge, Lance-Corp. E. H. Heard, B.A. (12th E. Surr., Educ.) near Gheluwe on 2nd October, Corp. J. Heskett (2nd R. Fus., Comp.) near Courtrai and Sergt. H. H. Perry, B.A. (2/23rd Lond., Educ.) near Wervicq on the 14th, and Corp. H. C. Johnson (4th N. Lancs, Comp.) near Tournai on the 22nd.

Battles of Le Cateau, the Selle and the Sambre.

In the south the enemy had now been driven out of the last of his elaborate defences so that the remainder of the fighting was in open country and progress became more rapid. On 8th October the attack was resumed on the St. Quentin—Cambrai line, the successful divisions reckoning from the right being the 66th, 25th, 38th, New Zealand, 3rd, 2nd and 63rd. Next day the 57th Division and the Canadians occupied Cambrai, and our troops almost reached Le Cateau. In this fighting twenty-two British and two American divisions routed twenty-four German divisions and captured 12,000 prisoners and 250 guns.

The next task was the forcing of the line of the river Selle. This, after hard fighting, was accomplished to the east of Le Cateau on 19th October by the 46th, 1st, 6th, Americans, 50th and 66th Divisions, and to the north of the town on the 20th by the 38th, 17th, 5th, 42nd, 62nd, Guards, 19th and 4th Divisions. Further extensive fighting ensued on the 23rd and succeeding days, and by the end of the month our troops had reached the Forêt de Mormal and were in the western outskirts of Valenciennes. In this battle twenty-four British and two American divisions defeated thirty-one German divisions and captured 20,000 prisoners and 475 guns.

As a preliminary to the Battle of the Sambre the 61st, 49th and 9th Divisions successfully attacked on 1st November to the south of Valenciennes, the town itself falling to the Canadians. The main assault opened on the 4th when the 1st, 46th and 32nd Divisions crossed the Sambre, the 25th, 50th, 18th, 38th, 17th and 37th penetrated the Forêt de Mormal, the New Zealanders took Le Quesnoy, scaling the ramparts in mediæval fashion by means of ladders, and the 62nd, Guards, 24th, 19th, 11th and 56th were successful to the north of the town. The average advance on this and the next day was about seven miles, and 19,000 prisoners and 450 guns were taken.

The enemy's resistance was now broken and he began to fall back in disorder, closely pursued by our men and harried by aeroplanes with bombs and machine-gun fire. Bavai was occupied on the 7th, Avesnes, the German advanced G.H.Q., on the 8th, and Tournai and the fortress of Maubeuge on the 9th. In the early morning of the 11th the Canadians captured Mons so that for the British the fighting on the western front began and ended at the same spot.

Lt.-Col. W. Parkes, M.C. and bar (8th Glouc., Educ.) was awarded the D.S.O. for gallantry and good leadership. " His battalion was twice ordered to carry out an attack [near Haussy] on the 20th and 23rd October respectively. He personally led the leading platoons across the Selle River under machine-gun and rifle fire. Throughout he showed great courage and ability to command."

The M.C. was won by the undermentioned:

(i) Lieut. T. A. Edwards (R.N. Div., Educ.) at Niergnies, south-east of Cambrai, on 8th October.

(ii) Lieut. H. R. Oswald (13th Welch, Educ.). " He was indefatigable on the night of 19th/20th October in carrying out reconnaissances across the river Selle in face of the enemy. . . . During the attack he rushed an enemy machine-gun."

(iii) Capt. W. J. Campion (Beds, Educ.) north of Le Cateau on 23rd October when " by his cool courage and fearless leadership he held his company together under a very heavy fire. Later . . . he broke down the enemy resistance and successfully led the line . . . to the final objective, capturing eighty prisoners."

(iv) Lieut. E. T. G. Hancock (R.G.A., Educ.) for conspicuous gallantry early in November between Lille and Tournai.

Corp. E. E. Huntley (Gren. Gds., Pub. H.) was awarded the M.M. for bravery in action near Maubeuge.

Lieut. F. Nevey, M.A. (9th W. Rid., Educ.) and J. F. Auker (9th W. Rid., Tram.) were killed in front of Le Cateau on 12th October, B. W. Muscutt (4th York and Lanc., Tram.) south-west of Valenciennes on the 13th, Sergt. S. J. Boucher (1st Dev., Educ.) near Le Cateau on the 20th, Corp. H. V. Harvey, M.M. (R.F.A., Tram.) and E. C. Yeldham (5th W. Yorks, Tram.) near Valenciennes on 1st November, Capt. E. L. Blunt (R.G.A., Educ.) east of Le Cateau, and Lieut. A. J. Gaskell (Norf. Yeo., Educ.) in Belgium on the 2nd, F. E. Elliott (1st Midx., Tram.) near Valenciennes on the 6th, and F. Watkins (20th Huss., Asylums) near Avesnes on the 7th. Lance-Corp. E. C. Pike (10th R. Warw., Tram.), wounded on the 7th near Mons, died on the 9th.[1]

The Armistice.

After the Battle of Amiens in August, General Ludendorff urged the necessity for an immediate peace. The German Government accordingly decided that, following their army's next victory, negotiations for peace would be opened, but such a victory was not forthcoming. Bulgaria surrendered at the end of September, and on 4th October the German Chancellor, Prince Max of Baden, appealed to President Wilson for an armistice. While notes and replies were passing between them Turkey collapsed, and on the 20th Germany accepted the terms upon which the President was willing to submit the correspondence to the Allies. On 4th November Austria surrendered, on the 5th the President notified Germany that the Allies were willing

[1] Throughout the war the British fighting on the western front was mainly in the ancient provinces of Flanders, Artois and Picardy. Chaucer, five hundred years ago, in the Prologue to the *Canterbury Tales*, wrote:

> " With him ther was his sone, a yong Squyer
> * * * * *
> And he had been somtyme in chivachye
> In Flaundres, in Artoys, and Picardye."

to make peace, and on the 7th the German delegates, travelling by direction of Marshal Foch along the Fourmies—La Capelle—Guise road (see map on p. 122), reached the French lines. They were accommodated for the night near Compiègne, and next morning presented themselves at Marshal Foch's headquarters in a train near Réthondes four miles east of the town, General Weygand, his Chief of Staff, Sir Rosslyn Wemyss, the First Sea Lord, and Vice-Admiral Sims of the American Navy being also present.

Mr. Buchan [1] has given a vivid account of the interview. "The French Marshal asked, 'Qu'est-ce que vous désirez, Messieurs?' and they replied that they had come to receive the Allied proposals for an armistice. To this Foch answered that the Allies were not seeking any armistice, but were content to finish the war in the field. The Germans looked nonplussed, and stammered something about the urgent need for the cessation of hostilities. 'Ah,' said Foch, 'I understand—you have come to *beg for an armistice*.' They admitted the correction, and explicitly begged for an armistice." They were then presented with the Allied terms which had to be accepted within seventy-two hours.

The chief terms were (i) all occupied territories to be evacuated and all deported inhabitants to be repatriated at once; (ii) 2,500 heavy and 2,500 field guns, 25,000 machine guns and 17,000 aeroplanes to be surrendered; (iii) all German territory on the left bank of the Rhine and all territory on the right bank within a radius of 30 kilometres (about 19 miles) from the three bridge-heads at Cologne, Coblenz and Mainz to be evacuated; (iv) 5,000 locomotives, 150,000 wagons and 5,000 motor lorries to be surrendered; (v) all submarines and the bulk of the surface fleet to be surrendered; (vi) all Allied prisoners to be repatriated; (vii) the treaties of Brest-Litovsk with

[1] *Nelson's History of the War*, vol. xxiv., p. 78.

Russia and Bukharest with Roumania to be renounced and (viii) Allied merchant shipping to be restored.

A courier with the text was despatched to the German headquarters, which he reached only after much difficulty and delay. The terms were accepted and were signed at 5 o'clock on the morning of Monday, 11th November, by the German delegates, by Marshal Foch and by Sir Rosslyn Wemyss, and at the eleventh hour of the eleventh day of the eleventh month of the year 1918 the Great War, which had lasted for four years and ninety-nine days, came to an end.

After a few days' delay in which to rest the troops and to bring up supplies, the advance was resumed on 17th November, the frontier was crossed on 1st December and on 6th December our troops entered Cologne. To the Belgians on our left was entrusted the defence of the district to the north of Düsseldorf, to the Americans on our right the bridge-head at Coblenz, and to the French on their right the bridge-head at Mainz.

General Casualties.

Lance-Corp. J. F. Winter, M.A. (R.E., Educ.) was killed on 28th October near the Aisne where apparently his unit was serving with the French. The deaths from influenza (see also p. 196) and kindred diseases were: H. J. A. Vellensworth (R.E., Comp.) on 1st Nov., Lance-Corp. A. Clark (1st Gren. Gds , Asylums) on the 2nd, G. T. White (R.A.S.C., Tram.) at Rouen and H. C. Gatehouse (R.A.M.C., Educ.) at Havre on the 6th, G. F. Potter (7th Shrop. L.I., Clerk) at Rouen on the 15th, P. Martin (13th R. Fus., Tram.) on the 20th, Corp. H. J. Poate (R.A.S.C., Parks) at Dieppe, M. B. Hutchins (8th R.W. Kent, Parks) at Cambrai, and Corp. J. Rosen (R.E., Educ.) at Tourcoing, all on the 25th, H. J. Salmon (42nd M.G.C., Stores) on the 27th, E. C. Moore (R.A.F., Asylums) near Boulogne on the 27th, R. C. Moss (R.A.S.C., Tram.) on 2nd December, H. A. Carter (R.A.S.C., Tram.) at Boulogne on the 3rd,

W. E. King (R.A.S.C., Tram.) at Mons on the 11th, and D. Parry M.S.M. (R.A.F., Arch.) at Paris on the 25th.

Alfred Wright (Educ.), perhaps of the 23rd Londons, died in France during December, but neither the place nor the cause nor the exact date of his death is known.

CHAPTER VII.

Royal Navy.

The fate of the countries engaged in the Great War was determined on the western front, and the fighting there has merited the most attention, but in no other conflict was it so true that, in the words of the Articles of War: " It is upon the Navy that, under the good Providence of God, the wealth, prosperity, and peace of these islands and of the Empire do mainly depend." Without the Navy's powerful aid our country, if not conquered by invasion, would almost certainly have been starved into surrender, nor could our armies in France, and still less those farther away, have been supplied with reinforcements and munitions. Its position at the opening of the war has already been referred to (see p. 5). Although its influence was felt in all our operations, it will be convenient to give here a separate summary of its great work.

Early in 1914 a test mobilisation of the Home Fleets had been ordered for 16th July. In the ordinary way the ships would have dispersed on the 27th, but on the 26th, three days after Austria's ultimatum to Serbia, the dispersal was countermanded. On the 29th the British First Fleet sailed for Scapa Flow in the Orkneys, and on 1st August our full naval forces were mobilised. Action followed close upon the declaration of war, for on the 5th the *Königin Luise,* while laying mines some distance off the East Coast, was chased and sunk by H.M.S. *Amphion.* A few hours later the latter struck one of the mines and went down with most of her crew and some prisoners from the *Luise*. On the 6th H.M.S. *Birmingham* rammed and sank two enemy submarines.

A brief account may here be given of the Navy's duties during the war. These were summarised by Mr. Balfour, as First Lord of the Admiralty, in July, 1915, as follows:—

(i) To drive the enemy's commerce off the sea. This was accomplished by stationing strong forces in Scapa Flow and the English Channel, so as to cut off all egress from the North Sea. The area thus enclosed was then systematically patrolled by light craft, Harwich and Dover being two of the chief bases.

(ii) To protect British commerce. To do this it was necessary to have control in all parts of the world. The Atlantic was the main avenue of supply, but routes had also to be considered to and from Australia, New Zealand, India and China. Also a northern patrol was necessary to insure the passage from Denmark, Norway, Sweden and north Russia. Mine-sweepers and trawlers had to be provided to deal with the mines laid by the enemy in the main traffic routes. Finally, when the unrestricted submarine campaign against trading vessels was undertaken, anti-submarine patrols and escorts both for ships-of-war and the mercantile marine had to be organised.

(iii) To render the enemy's fleet impotent and (iv) to prevent the landing of enemy troops. These were brought about by the forces and patrols referred to under (i) and (ii) at Scapa, in the English Channel and elsewhere. Later the battle-cruiser and other squadrons were stationed in the Firth of Forth.

(v) To enable our troops to be transported across the sea. This entailed the escort of several millions of troops between the British Isles, France, India, Australia, New Zealand, East, West and South Africa, Gallipoli, Egypt, Palestine, Salonica and latterly America and Russia.

(vi) To secure supplies for troops in all theatres of war.

(vii) In fitting circumstances to assist military operations such as those at Gallipoli and at different times on the Belgian coast.

In the space available it is not possible to do more than to give a list of the chief actions in which the Navy was engaged.[1]

On 28th August a sweep by destroyers and light cruisers, aided later by battle cruisers, into the Heligoland Bight was organised. After some confused fighting V187, an enemy destroyer, and the light cruisers *Köln*, *Mainz* and *Ariadne* were sunk with the loss of over 1,000 men. Four enemy raiders were sunk, the *Kaiser Wilhelm der Grosse* by H.M.S. *Highflyer* on 26th August at Rio de Oro on the west coast of Africa, the *Cap Trafalgar* by H.M.S. *Carmania* on 14th September off Trinidada Island, Brazil, the *Emden* by H.M.S. *Sydney* on 9th November at the Cocos or Keeling Islands, in the Indian Ocean, and the *Königsberg* on 11th July, 1915, by monitors in the River Rufiji, East Africa, where she had been shut up by H.M.S. *Chatham* six months before. H.M.S. *Audacious* struck a mine on 27th October and sank, and on 1st January, 1915, the *Formidable* was torpedoed off Start Point, Devon. Several destroyers and monitors aided the Allied left at Lombartzyde on the Belgian coast during the first Battle of Ypres in October. On 3rd November, Yarmouth, and on 14th December, Scarborough, Whitby and the Hartlepools, were bombarded, while on 24th January, 1915, another attempted raid was driven off with the loss of the *Blücher* and severe damage to the *Seydlitz*.

During September, 1915, the *Royal Edward* carrying reinforcements to Gallipoli was torpedoed with the loss of 1,000 out of 1,600 officers and men. In October

[1] The actions in which members of the Council's staff lost their lives are dealt with separately at the end of the chapter.

the transports *Ramazan* and *Marquette* were sunk in the Ægean, on the 28th H.M.S. *Argyll* ran aground on the Scotch coast, and on 30th December the *Persia* was torpedoed in the Mediterranean. The German battleship *Pommern* was torpedoed in the Baltic on 2nd July.

On 25th April, 1916, Lowestoft and Yarmouth were again bombarded, in June H.M.S. *Hampshire*, carrying Lord Kitchener and his staff to Russia, struck a mine off the Orkneys and sank with the loss of nearly all on board, and during the latter part of the year several vessels of no great importance were damaged or destroyed on each side.

On 31st January, 1917, the Germans proclaimed unrestricted action by their U-boats. This danger was met by developing the destroyer patrols and patrols by armed trawlers, smacks, drifters, fast motor boats, etc., by the use of strongly-armed vessels disguised as tramps, by the arming of merchantmen, by the use of depth charges which were constructed so as to explode at any depth desired, and by the use of seaplanes and airships to detect submarines even when submerged. Commanders of merchant vessels were instructed as to routes to be taken or avoided. The vessels were grouped into convoys and many of them were dazzle-painted so as to deceive the enemy as to their type and construction, and even as to their course and speed. Many ships after being sunk were raised by the salvage service; during the last three years of the war over a million and a half tons were so raised, the value of the ships and contents being about £50,000,000.

The opening of 1918 was marked on 14th January by the third bombardment of Yarmouth. Ostend and Zeebrugge were of great assistance to the Germans as submarine bases, and one object of the Passchendaele fighting was to bring them under gunfire (see p. 70). On 23rd April, 1918, gallant efforts were made to seal the entrances to the harbours. At Zeebrugge, the *Vindictive*, under cover of a smoke screen, and accompanied by a flotilla of destroyers, monitors and motor launches, was driven on to the mole to serve as a landing-stage for a storming party. The latter, having landed, silenced a number of batteries, destroyed hangars and store-sheds and sank a destroyer. The submarine C3 was run into the piles of the railway and, by its explosion, caused very great damage. Three block ships were sunk in the channel leading to the Bruges canal. The crews of the submarine and block ships, after accomplishing their tasks, were taken off their vessels in motor boats. The attack at Ostend on the same night was not so successful, as the wind, changing suddenly, dispersed the smoke screen, and the block ships were blown up in the wrong place. In a second attempt on 9th May, the *Vindictive* was successfully blown up and sunk across the channel.

As 1918 advanced the U-boats, partly owing to the reduction in numbers caused by losses and damage at sea, and partly owing to the success of our defensive measures, became much less effective. In October, 1918, when it was clear that the Germans had lost the war, their War Cabinet undertook that the principles of cruiser warfare should be observed and that the lives of non-combatants would be assured. At the end of the month their fleet, ordered out to sea in the hope that some desperate stroke might retrieve the situation, mutinied and it was realised that an offensive was impossible.

In accordance with the terms of the Armistice fourteen battleships, seven cruisers and fifty destroyers surrendered on 21st November to the British Navy and were taken as prizes to the Firth of Forth. Submarines to the number of 150 were also surrendered and taken into Harwich.

Casualties amongst the Council's staff.

The actions in which members of the Council's staff perished were as follows:

H.M.S. Aboukir, Cressy and Hogue.

On 22nd September, 1914, H.M.S. *Aboukir, Cressy,* and *Hogue,* armoured cruisers of 12,000 tons displacement, were torpedoed and sunk in the North Sea to the south of the Dogger Bank with a loss of 60 officers and over 1,300 men. The sinking of the *Aboukir* was an ordinary hazard of patrolling duty, but the *Hogue* and the *Cressy* were sunk because they proceeded to the assistance of their consort, and remained, with engines stopped, endeavouring to save life, thus presenting an easy and certain target to further submarine attacks. All the men behaved extraordinarily well, obeying orders even when in the water swimming for their lives, and many acts of great self-sacrifice and gallantry were witnessed.

Fifteen employees of the Council lost their lives in the sinking of these ships. They were Henry Arnold, J. E. Rawlings, A. S. Keeler, R. G. Grist, C. H. Boys, Walter Challis and A. A. Gaiger (Tramways), E. V. White, F. J. Owen, Westly Livingstone (L.F.B.), G. D. Davis and F. C. Chapman (Education), R. W. Medhurst (Ch. Engr.), William Lawrence (Asylums) and J. W. Curry (Pub. Cont.).

H.M.S. Hawke.

On 15th October, 1914, H.M.S. *Hawke* was torpedoed and sunk in the northern waters of the North Sea. The *Hawke* was a cruiser with a displacement of 7,350 tons, and carried a crew of about 500, of whom only 4 officers and 69 men were saved. At about 11 a.m. the *Hawke* sighted a collier flying the Norwegian flag, and changed her course slightly in order to investigate the character of the vessel. The cruiser was moving through the water at a moderate speed when an explosion occurred and part of the ship's side was torn away. One boat only was got away and her crew pulled about endeavouring to save those in the water. Many men clambered on to life-saving rafts, but the cold was extreme and numbers of them fell from the rafts into the water. Three officers and forty-nine men were saved in this boat and were picked up ultimately by a trawler. One officer and twenty men were also picked up later from a raft.

Six employees of the Council were among those who were lost, namely G. A. B. Allum and T. W. Jackson (Ch. Engr.), F. T. Hemming and C. W. Waite (L.F.B.), P. W. Hepworth (Asylums) and A. W. Woods (Tram.).

Battles of Coronel and the Falkland Isles.

Towards the evening of 1st November, 1914, H.M.S. *Good Hope*, an armoured cruiser of 14,100 tons and flagship of Admiral Sir C. Cradock, accompanied by H.M.S. *Monmouth*, an armoured cruiser of 9,800 tons, H.M.S. *Glasgow*, a light cruiser of 4,800 tons, and H.M.S. *Otranto*, an auxiliary cruiser, came up off Coronel on the coast of Chile with the squadron of Admiral von Spee, consisting of the armoured cruisers *Scharnhorst* and *Gneisenau* of 11,400 tons, and the light cruisers *Dresden*, *Nürnberg* and *Leipzig*, 3,540, 3,350 and 3,200 tons respectively. The enemy declined action until sunset, when the light gave them an important advantage. During the action, which began about 7 p.m. and lasted for an hour, darkness and the head sea made firing difficult. At an early stage both the *Good Hope* and *Monmouth* caught fire, but fought on until, at 7.50 p.m., a great explosion took place on the *Good Hope*, flames shooting 200 feet into the air, and the ship foundered with the loss of all on board. The *Monmouth*, accompanied by the *Glasgow*, hauled off at dark, but was unable to steam away. She was then attacked by the enemy and sank, all on board perishing. The *Glasgow* and *Otranto* escaped. The result of this action is attributed to the superior weight of metal possessed by the enemy and to the advantages of position. The British ships fought with gallantry, but the odds were too great. F. H. Field and W. J. Brooker (Tram.), and J. E. Blake (Parks) lost their lives on the *Good Hope*.

After the battle the *Glasgow* and the *Otranto* fell in with H.M.S. *Canopus*, of 12,950 tons, which also belonged to Cradock's squadron but had been left behind for repairs, and the three vessels made for the South Atlantic. Meanwhile a squadron, consisting of the battle cruisers H.M.S. *Invincible* and *Inflexible*, each of 17,250 tons, and the three armoured cruisers H.M.S. *Carnarvon* of 10,850 tons, and *Kent* and *Cornwall*, each of 9,800 tons, was dispatched from England under Rear-Admiral Sir F. D. Sturdee, and arrived on 7th December at the Falkland Isles off the extreme south-eastern coast of S. America. Next day, just as the combined squadrons had finished coaling, von Spee arrived expecting to find only the remnants of Cradock's force. When he realised his error he attempted to escape, but was compelled by the superior speed of the British ships to give battle. His vessels were overpowered; the *Scharnhorst* and *Gneisenau* were sunk by the battle cruisers, the *Nürnberg* by the *Kent* and the *Leipzig* by the *Glasgow* and *Cornwall*. About 200 of the crews were rescued, the rest with von Spee himself going down with their ships. The *Dresden* escaped for the time being, but on 14th March, 1915, was sunk by the *Kent* and the *Glasgow* off the island of Juan Fernandez.

Battle of Jutland.

The facts relating to the Battle of Jutland have been the subject of so much controversy that it must suffice to say here merely that on 31st May, 1916, the British Battle-cruiser Fleet, under the command of Vice-Admiral Sir David Beatty, was cruising to the west of the Jutland peninsula when the Battle-cruiser Fleet of Vice-Admiral Hipper was sighted. A fierce battle commenced, and had lasted for nearly an hour when the main body of the German High Sea Fleet appeared and took part in the conflict. From the first sighting of the enemy two hours elapsed before the main British fleet could appear on the scene of action, and during the latter part of this time Sir David Beatty's force was engaged against overwhelming odds. Though it successfully held the German fleet and inflicted very heavy damage on the enemy, it necessarily sustained great losses in the unequal conflict. All the might of the German fleet was concentrated in turn against the leading ships of the British line. H.M.S. *Queen Mary* in particular received the full force of the enemy's fire, and after a stubborn fight the vessel was destroyed as the result of an explosion. Very few of the crew were saved and amongst those missing were George Doling (L.F.B.) who was serving as a gunner and E. W. Whitlock (Tram.) who was serving with the R.M.L.I. H.M.S. *Tipperary* formed a unit of the fourth torpedo flotilla attached to the main Battle Fleet. On the night (31st May/1st June, 1916) following the battle the Fourth, Eleventh and Twelfth Flotillas delivered a series of attacks on the enemy, causing him severe losses. In the course of these attacks H.M.S. *Tipperary* was sunk. Only 20 men were saved, and among others Leading Stoker E. W. Ponting (L.F.B.) lost his life.

The Germans claimed the battle as a victory, but the grounds on which this claim was based are not obvious. It is difficult to estimate their losses, but they seem to have equalled ours.[1] Their fleet did not continue the contest, but in the darkness of the early morning of 1st June returned to port. Our blockade was maintained, and never again did they venture to dispute our naval supremacy.

General Casualties.

I. J. Miller (R.N., L.F.B.) was on H.M.S. *Viknor* when she was lost in January, 1915, and F. A. Halliday

[1] H. C. O'Neill, *History of the British Navy during the War*, pp. 257–8.

(Educ.) and W. S. Entwistle (L.F.B.) were on H.M.S. *Clan McNaughton*, an armed merchant cruiser employed on patrol duty, when she disappeared, having probably foundered in heavy weather during February. James Waddingham (R.M.L.I., L.F.B.) was killed by a gunshot on 29th February, 1916, when H.M.S. *Alcantara* was sunk by the *Greif*, a German raider, and Alfred Bolt (Tram.) serving on Torpedo-boat No. 11 as a gunner lost his life on 7th March, 1916, when, having struck a mine off the East Coast, his vessel sank with most of her crew.

H.M.S. *Foyle* struck a mine in the English Channel on 15th March, 1917, and sank with the loss of 29 men, one of whom was Arthur Roake, D.S.M. (R.F.R., L.F.B.). Henry Carpenter (R.F.R., L.F.B.) lost his life on 30th June, 1917, when H.M.S. *Cheerful*, while employed on escort duty, struck a mine and foundered in the North Sea. H.M.S. *Ettrick*, engaged in convoying transports, was torpedoed and sank on 7th July, 1917, off Beachy Head, those killed including James New (R.F.R., Tram.). C. J. C. Bastian (R.N., Educ.) was killed on 9th July, 1917, when H.M.S. *Vanguard* blew up in harbour as the result of an internal explosion. A. C. Jones (R.N.R., L.F.B.) was drowned on 30th July, 1917, when the s.s. *Besswood* on which he was serving as a gunner sank in the Irish Sea after a collision. H.M.S. *Wolverine* sank on 12th December, 1917, as a result of a collision, and John Richards (R.N., Tram.) was among the very few who lost their lives.

J. W. Helps (Educ.) lost his life in the very gallant action on 20th January, 1918, when H.M.S. *Raglan*, a monitor of 4,500 tons, on which he was serving, aided by a smaller vessel of the same type, engaged the *Goeben* (22,640 tons) and the *Breslau* (4,480 tons) off the Dardanelles. The British vessels, hopelessly outgunned, were both sunk, but the *Breslau*, retreating after the engagement, struck a mine and sank, and the *Goeben* also struck a mine and to avoid destruction had to be beached in the Narrows. C. L. Pain (Tram.) was serving on H.M.S. *Eleanor* when on 12th February, 1918, while carrying a cargo of 2,000 mines, she blew up with the loss of all hands. W. F. Harden (Educ.) lost his life on 16th September, 1918, when an explosion occurred on board H.M.S. *Glatton* which, having caught fire, had to be destroyed in Dover Harbour so as to prevent damage to the shipping and the town.

Decorations.

Lieut. A. G. Dodman (R.N.R., Ch. Engr.) received the D.S.C. for the gallantry with which, while on patrol duty in the east Mediterranean on 6th December, 1916, he went to the defence of the s.s. *Camberwell*, his skilful action probably leading to the destruction of the submarine making the attack. The facts relating to other naval decorations gained by members of the Council's staff are described under the various fronts.

CHAPTER VIII.

Royal Air Force.

Like the Royal Navy the Royal Air Force served on all fronts, but, in view of its extraordinary development during the war, its achievements can best be dealt with as a whole.

Balloons, manned by detachments from the Royal Engineers, were used in the British Army in 1879, and rendered good service in the Bechuanaland Expedition in 1884 and during the South African War, 1899–1902. The first British dirigible, the *Nulli Secundus*, was commenced in 1902 but did not make its first flight until 1907. Experiments with army aeroplanes began in 1911 or perhaps a little earlier. The Navy's experiments with dirigibles and aeroplanes date from 1908 and 1911 respectively.[1] About

[1] It is interesting to compare these dates with the dates of the inventions. The balloon was invented by the Montgolfier brothers, the first man to make an ascent being Jean de Rozier in 1783, the

this time only two small airships and fewer than twelve efficient aeroplanes were available for all purposes, but the new service rapidly developed, and on 13th May, 1912, the Royal Flying Corps, with naval and military wings, and a central flying school, reserve and factory, was established. In 1913 the dirigibles were transferred to the Navy, and in June, 1914, the naval wing became an independent force under the name of the Royal Naval Air Service.

At the outbreak of war practically all the available machines of the R.F.C., forming rather more than three squadrons, crossed to France on 13th August, 1914, under the late Sir David Henderson, the majority landing near Amiens. On the 16th they moved to Maubeuge, and on the 19th made their first reconnaissances. Their value was soon proved for at Mons they were the first to give warning of the French defeat on the British right and of the German attempt to outflank the British left (see p. 6). They also reported Von Kluck's swerve to the south-east from Amiens (see p. 8) and the enemy's entrenchments on the Aisne (see p. 9).

When the opposing armies settled down into trench warfare, reconnaissance, although still most important, became a matter of routine and new features were developed. One of these was the regular photographing of the enemy's lines; by comparing later with earlier photographs the position and nature of his works and the progress made could be recorded. Another task was watching for the gun-flashes which revealed the position of enemy batteries. The fire of our guns was then brought to bear upon these points, corrections to the officers controlling the fire being

first successful dirigible was flown at Paris in 1852, the Wright brothers made their first aeroplane flight in America on 17th December, 1903, and in Europe, at Le Mans, some 100 miles south-west of Paris, in August, 1908. On 30th September, 1908, Henri Farman made the first cross-country flight from Châlons to Rheims and on 25th July, 1909, Bleriot crossed the English Channel from Calais to Dover.

signalled at first by coloured lights, later by lamps flashing the Morse code, and finally by wireless telegraphy. There had been fights in the air even during the retreat from Mons, but these isolated combats soon developed into systematic attempts to prevent the enemy's machines from reaching our lines. Generally speaking, in the early fights, for fear of shooting away the propeller, only rifles or machine-guns firing to the side could be used. About the end of 1915 a German aeroplane was captured on which the action of the machine-gun trigger was synchronised with the engine, so that bullets could be fired, without damage to the blades, between the moving arms of the propeller. This device was copied and fitted to most of our machines, greatly improving their capacity for the offensive. Small bombs for attacking ground targets were also used as early as the retreat but they were very primitive in construction and limited in action. Their size and efficiency, as well as the distance which they could be carried, were rapidly increased, so that from Neuve Chapelle in 1915 all important battles were preceded by aerial bombardments of railway and road centres, dumps, batteries, troop trains, etc. Night flying was introduced early in 1916.

These developments, spread over 1915 and the early part of 1916, culminated in the preparations for the Battle of the Somme. In this battle also one most useful service was performed by the Corps for the first time. An army's communications are always difficult to maintain, and, during a big battle, the difficulties are increased a hundredfold. The heavy fire cuts all telephone wires, the continual explosions raise clouds of smoke and dust through which no signals can be seen, runners with messages cannot pass to and fro through the artillery barrage. Attacking troops soon get out of touch with the higher commanders, sometimes they are fired upon by their own artillery, at others they are overwhelmed by counter-attacks of which their artillery cannot be warned. The aeroplane contact patrols altered all this. The assault troops, by lighting flares in the bottom of the captured trenches, signalled their position to aeroplanes overhead, and a code of signals was devised covering the most urgent of their needs. The higher command were thus kept informed of the phases of the battle and could do what was best to help the advance.

Apart from what was done at Kut (see p. 170) aeroplanes were rarely used for conveying stores; this work was not undertaken until the end of the war and then only upon a small scale. Propaganda literature was often dropped, and from the Battle of Messines, 1917, onwards, enemy troops, whether in trenches, in camps or on the march, were frequently engaged by low-flying planes. One purpose to which aeroplanes were put is of special interest. Our agents were taken behind the enemy's lines, dropped by parachute, and not infrequently supplied with carrier pigeons by the same means. There were rumours that occasionally agents were even picked up after they had completed their task and brought back.

In the latter part of the war much of the work of artillery observation and of watching enemy movements in forward areas was done by observers from captive balloons. The most successful type was the stream-line shape,[1] designed by Capt. Caquot, a French officer, in which stability was secured by an air-inflated tail with three air-inflated fins of equal size set at angles of 120 deg. In France these balloons were stationed at frequent intervals along the front, three miles or so in rear of the line, eight or ten being usually in sight at once; they were used on other fronts as well. The occupants ran special risks, for the balloons were tempting targets for the enemy's artillery and aeroplanes, some were struck by lightning and others broke loose in high winds. At sea an adapted

[1] Known to the troops as "sausages."

type was used for convoy escort work. They were towed by one of the convoy to which they could telephone information concerning enemy submarines. They were also used to support, at a height of some 10,000 feet, the aprons of steel cables with which London was surrounded as a protection against aeroplane attacks.

The R.N.A.S. was used chiefly for long distance bombing raids, for maintaining coastal patrols by airships and aeroplanes against submarines, for scouting at sea, and for the defence of London and the coast against attacks by air. A list of the raids would fill several pages, so it must suffice to mention here by way of illustration in 1914 alone the attacks on 22nd September on Zeppelin sheds at Düsseldorf and Cologne, and on 21st November on the Zeppelin base at Friedrichschafen on Lake Constance, the combined attack by sea and land on Cuxhaven on Christmas Day and the incessant attacks upon submarine, etc., bases at Ostend, Zeebrugge and Bruges. On 7th June 1915, Flight Sub.-Lieut. R. A. Warneford at Ghent earned the distinction of being the first airman to destroy a Zeppelin in the air, a feat for which he was awarded the V.C. An officer of the R.N.A.S. was also the first airman to sink a submarine at sea, this happening on 26th August, 1915.

Both the R.F.C. and the R.N.A.S. served in all the main theatres of war, and in each had to encounter new dangers and difficulties. In hot countries, such as Mesopotamia and the tropics for instance, the machines were liable to be clogged with sand, and water in the radiators boiled so easily that flying was usually possible only in the early morning. The intense heat also caused wood-work to warp, and machines of a special pattern in which metal was used instead of wood had to be designed. In Northern Russia, on the other hand, the water in the radiators was liable to freeze and difficult problems connected with lubrication and ignition arose. At sea, and in Egypt and tropical Africa, there was always the risk that the airman might be compelled by engine or other trouble to alight upon the sea or in the desert or jungle far from human aid. This danger was partly guarded against by carrying on the planes pigeons which could be released with messages for help.

The division of the air force into two independent parts engendered a healthy spirit of emulation but it also had grave drawbacks. It is obvious that there would be much overlapping, little or no standardisation of equipment, and such keen competition for limited supplies as to prevent either from obtaining all that was desired. To meet these difficulties the Joint War Air Committee was set up in February, 1916, to co-ordinate questions of supplies and design, and three months later an advisory Air Board was formed. The Board's functions gradually expanded, in 1917 supplies were pooled, and at the end of the year Parliament authorised the amalgamation of the two services. The Royal Air Force as thus constituted came into being on 1st April, 1918.

The R.A.F. continued to develop the work of its predecessors but no details call for special notice except perhaps the part played by the Force in the final defeat of the Turks in Palestine (see p. 165). The neighbourhood of the enemy's aerodromes was patrolled so effectively that none of their machines would venture out. After the main battle on 19th September, 1918, our aeroplanes patrolled the only road leading to the crossings of the Jordan and, by systematic bombing and machine-gun fire, reduced the defeated troops into a mere rabble which on the arrival of the cavalry and infantry surrendered without attempting to resist. Similar but less complete results followed the defeats of the Bulgarians at Lake Doiran in September, 1918 (see p. 179), and the Austrians at Vittorio Veneto in October, 1918 (see p. 184). The Germans in their final retreat on the western front were protected by rain and ground mists from a like fate.

In June, 1918, the Independent Air Force, succeeding long-distance bombing units of the R.N.A.S., was formed for a definite purpose—the bombing of German munition works. Much good work had already been done, for during the previous eight months, which included the severe winter of 1917–18, 142 raids, of which 57 were in Germany, had been made. The work of the I.A.F. can best be summarised by stating that in five months 550 tons of bombs were dropped, 160 by day and 390 by night, and that of this amount 220 tons were dropped on aerodromes. Special attention was devoted to railways and to blast furnaces, the reason for this being that the Germans were very short of rolling stock, and serious damage would therefore lead to important results. A section was formed for bombing Berlin. The necessary machines, each with four engines of 375 horse power, were not received until the end of October, and, although all ranks worked day and night to equip them for their task, they were not ready until the Armistice was about to be signed.

A few figures will help to illustrate the surprising growth of the R.A.F. and its equipment. At the beginning of the war the R.F.C. and the R.N.A.S. comprised only a few hundred officers and men; at the Armistice there were in the R.A.F. some 28,000 officers and 264,000 other ranks, making a total of nearly 300,000. In 1914 only 40 pupils could be dealt with at a time; in 1918 30,000 cadets were under instruction at once. In 1914 the R.F.C. had four squadrons [1] up to strength and the R.N.A.S. rather fewer. In 1916 the R.F.C. had 21 squadrons in France, eight in the Middle East and a number at home. By March, 1918, these numbers had risen to 76 and 14 respectively, with 22 for home defence and special training. In November, 1918, the

[1] The R.A.F. was organised as follows: six machines to a flight, three flights to a squadron, three or four squadrons to a wing, two or more wings to a brigade.

number of squadrons was over 200, with another 200 for cadet training. The number of machines had increased from less than 100 to about 22,000. The machines had also improved. In 1914 the best machine had a speed of 73 miles an hour and a climbing capacity of 3,000 feet in nine minutes; by 1917 speed had been doubled and climbing capacity trebled. In place of a single engine of 70 horse power, the most powerful machines were fitted with two engines of 275 horse power each and even four engines of 375 horse power each. The potential output of complete machines rose from 50 to 3,500 a month and of engines from 14 to 3,000 a month. The weight of the heaviest aerial bomb, which in 1914 was about 14 lbs., increased in 1915 to 100 lbs., in 1916 to 336 lbs., and in 1918 to 1,600 lbs., or three-quarters of a ton. The seven airships of 1914 had increased by 1918 to 103, including five rigids.

H. G. Hughes (R.N.A.S., Tram.) was killed on 26th April, 1915, in a flying accident at Southampton Water, Lieut. F. E. Hollingsworth (R.F.C., Stores) on night patrol in France on 15th September, 1916, Lieut. A. I. McKimmie (R.F.C., Educ.) on 23rd May, 1917, in a flying accident near Poperinghe, Lieut. E. Churcher (R.F.C., Educ.) on 14th July, 1917, in the same way at the same place, Lieut. J. W. Todd (R.F.C., Tram.) on 28th September, 1917, in a flying accident in Norfolk, Lieut H. V. Thornton (R.A.F., Educ.) on 10th May, 1918, while flying over the Austrian lines in Italy, Lieut. S. W. James (R.A.F., Educ.) on 9th June, 1918, in a flying accident near Taranto in Italy, Lieut. C. V. Todman (R.A.F., Educ.) on 3rd August, 1918, in a fight against three German aeroplanes, and Capt. F. Jefcoate, M.B.E. (R.A.F., Educ.) on 14th February, 1919, in a flying accident in Palestine.

CHAPTER IX.

GALLIPOLI.

BRITISH influence with Turkey, at one time considerable, had, during the last thirty years or so, been much weakened. One cause of this was the occupation of Egypt and Cyprus, another was the resentment aroused by the spirited condemnations in England of Turkish misrule, a third was the support given by Great Britain after the first Balkan war in 1912-13 to the successful claims of Bulgaria and Greece to Turkish territory, a fourth was the growing understanding between Great Britain and Russia, the hereditary enemy of Turkey. While British influence waned, that of Germany increased. German capital was forthcoming both for public and private purposes, Germany aided the negotiations for the construction of the Bagdad railway, a German general with a German staff was appointed to re-organise the army.

When the Great War broke out Great Britain was seen to side with Russia, and the Turks were further annoyed and alarmed by the fact that two battleships, built for them and intended to strengthen their very weak navy, were detained in England. At the same time the German war vessels *Goeben* and *Breslau*, eluding the Allied fleet in the Mediterranean, escaped to Constantinople, and, when their dismantlement was demanded, were sold or given to Turkey. After three months' hesitation, Turkey on 31st October, asserting that her fleet had been fired upon by Russians, declared war.

The Allies soon dealt with the new combatant, and decided to do this by means of a naval attack on Constantinople. They realised that the fall of the city would check Turkish activities in the Caucasus, Mesopotamia and Egypt, would ensure the passage of munitions to, and of food from, Russia, and also would lead to the neutrality, if not the assistance, of Bulgaria, the safety of Serbia and the co-operation of Greece.

The approach to Constantinople from the Mediterranean lies through the Dardanelles, the strait, from one to six miles wide, which separates the peninsula of Gallipoli [1] from Asia Minor. To make clear what follows it will be convenient to introduce here a brief description of the district. The length of Gallipoli (see plan on p. 150) is a little over fifty miles, and its breadth varies from about three miles at Bulair in the north-east to twenty-four east of Suvla and about seven in the south-west; south of Suvla and west of Maidos the width for a short distance drops to less than five miles. It is a rolling, waterless country, very beautiful in the spring when the hills are covered with flowers, but, as these fade under the summer sun, it takes on a tawny, dusty hue. There is little cultivation, the southern half being covered chiefly with heather and scrub. Most of the coast line consists of steep cliffs, a hundred feet high or more, pierced here and there by gullies which open out into narrow strips of beach two or three hundred yards wide. The chief hills are Sari Bair, nearly a thousand feet high, to the south of Suvla and commanding Suvla Bay and Anzac Cove, and Achi Baba, six hundred feet high, which commands the beaches near Cape Helles at the southern end of the peninsula. Some of the latter, if not all, can also be fired upon from the mainland of Asia Minor.

As a preliminary to the attack upon Constantinople

[1] The peninsula was known to the Greeks in ancient times as the Thracian Chersonesus (literally "land island," which is equivalent to peninsula) and the strait as the Hellespont. It was across the Narrows that, according to the legend, Leander swam to visit Hero and that Xerxes in B.C. 480 built the bridge of boats over which he led his army to invade Greece. On the mainland of Asia Minor, three or four miles from the south-western end of the Hellespont, were "reedy Simois" and the "plains of windy Troy" of which Homer, the first pagan poet whose works have come down to us, sang in the *Iliad*.

Suvla Pt.
SUVLA BAY
SCIMITAR HILL
10th AUG.
SARI BAIR RIDGE
To Gallipoli and Bulaïr
Ocean Beach
26th Apr.
Boghali
Anzac Cove ('Z' Beach)
Brighton Beach
Ravine
Gaba Tepe
KHELIA BAY
Maïdos
ÆGEAN SEA
THE NARROWS
Kalid Bahr
Chanak
Krithia
ACHI BABA
'Y' Beach
Ravine
7th July
Ravine
27th Apr.
26th Apr.
DARDANELLES
'X' Beach
Tekke Burnu
'S' Beach
MORTO BAY
'W' Beach (Lancashire Landing)
C. Helles
'V' Beach
Sedd el Bahr
Kum Kale
Allied lines.
★ The line before Krithia was advanced nearly to the final position (as shown) early in May.
Scale of Miles.
0 1 2 3 4 5 6 7
BULGARIA
TURKEY IN EUROPE
Constantinople
SEA OF MARMORA
SAMOTHRACE
Gallipoli
Bulair
IMBROS
Chanak
LEMNOS
Mudros
TURKEY IN ASIA (ASIA MINOR)
MITYLENE
0 10 20 30 40 50 Miles

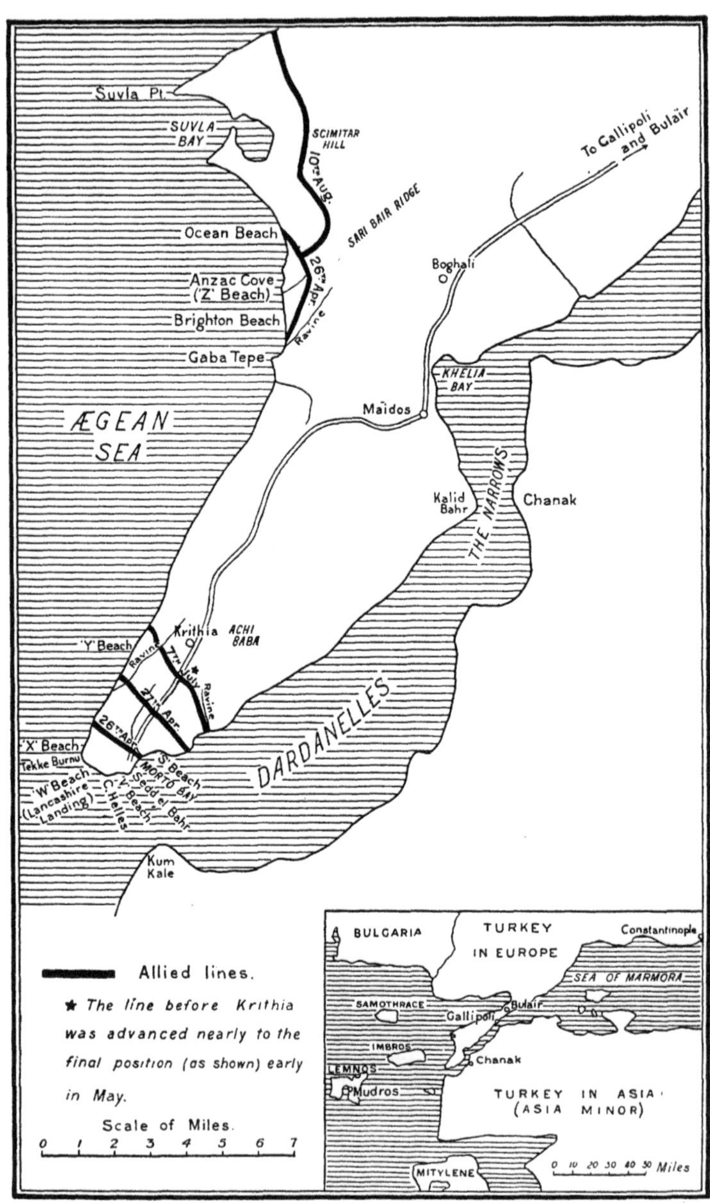

GALLIPOLI.

forts guarding the entrance to the Dardanelles were bombarded from the Ægean on 3rd November, 1914, but it was not until 19th February, 1915, after what appeared to be much vacillation in the higher conduct of the enterprise, that the reduction of the defences was seriously undertaken by the British and French navies, acting alone. When the weather permitted during the next four weeks the bombardment was renewed, and several of the forts were at least silenced, if not destroyed. An attempt, however, on 18th March to force the Narrows failed with the loss of several ships, and it was then determined that the next assault should be in conjunction with troops on land.

The nearest place at which troops or stores could be collected was Egypt, 700 miles away. To facilitate the work an advanced base was formed at Mudros, in the island of Lemnos, but even this was fifty miles from Gallipoli, and only the simplest equipment could be provided there. As the peninsula was for the most part barren and waterless it was necessary, in addition to arranging for the transport of the attacking troops with their guns and ammunition, to make complete arrangements for supplying them with all the food and water they required, and for providing food and water for the transport animals and shelter and medical stores for the sick. These preparations occupied four weeks, although some of the delay would not have been necessary if, owing to faulty organisation, men had not been conveyed separately from their ammunition, guns from the gun-carriages, and wagons from their horses. As it was, many of the transports, when they arrived at Mudros, had to be taken back to Egypt, where their contents were re-arranged. The Turks, warned by the naval bombardments and by the traffic at sea, to expect an attack, had every opportunity to complete their preparations. Troops and guns were hurried into the peninsula, stores and ammunition were collected, trenches were dug on commanding sites, and the few and narrow approaches, including even the shallow parts of the sea, were obstructed with strong wire entanglements.

The landing, under Sir Ian Hamilton as commander-in-chief, was attempted at dawn on Sunday, 25th April, at five points around the southern end of the peninsula and at one to the north of Gaba Tepe on the western coast. The assault on the former was entrusted to the 29th Division, composed of units of the Regular Army, and to the newly formed R. Naval Division, and that on the latter to troops from Australia and New Zealand. Each landing, so far as possible, was to be protected by the guns of the ships. The French effected a diversion by landing at Kum Kale in Asia Minor opposite Helles. Having done this they withdrew some days later and took over the right of the British line at Helles. Reckoning from the east, the positions assailed on the peninsula were S beach, or De Tott's Battery, V Beach near Sedd-el-Bahr, W Beach (or " Lancashire Landing," from the heroism displayed by the 1st Lancashire Fus.) between Capes Helles and Tekke, X Beach to the north of Cape Tekke, Y Beach three miles further north, and Z Beach, afterwards known as Anzac,[1] ten miles north of Y Beach.

At V Beach three companies of the 1st R. Dublin Fus., and a party from the Anson Battalion, R.N.D., while being landed from boats were shot down. The collier *River Clyde* was run aground, and the troops on board endeavoured to reach the shore across a bridge of boats. In doing this and in maintaining the bridge, three companies of the 1st R. Munster Fus. and two of the 2nd Hants were almost destroyed, only a remnant finding, under a low sand-bank, protection from the terrible rifle and machine-gun fire which

[1] The word was coined from the initial letters of the title " Australian and New Zealand Army Corps."

swept the beach. The remainder of these three battalions stayed on board under continual fire until nightfall, when they managed to land. Having joined the survivors on shore they attacked the village and old fort of Sedd-el-Bahr, but in the darkness and unknown country the attack miscarried, and the force was almost overwhelmed by a counter-attack. Early on the morning of the 26th the attempt was renewed, and, aided by the guns from the fleet, was successful.

At W Beach the 1st Lancashire Fus., supported by the 4th Worcesters and the 1st Essex, and at X Beach the 2nd R. Fusiliers, with a working-party from the Anson Battalion, R.N.D., and assisted by the 1st R. Inniskilling Fus., were even more successful, and the landings were secured on the first day with casualties which, though heavy, were not so heavy as at V Beach. The attacks at S and Y Beaches were planned chiefly with the object of diverting the enemy's reserves and of thus protecting the main attack at V, W and X Beaches. That at S Beach by the 2nd S. Wales Borderers succeeded, and the ground won was permanently held, but at Y Beach the 1st K.O. Scottish Borderers and the Plymouth Battalion, R.N.D., having accomplished their purpose, were withdrawn on the 26th. At Anzac the troops forced a landing, pressed on up steep gullies, beat off numerous counter-attacks, and by the evening of the 26th had made good their advance on a front of over two miles to a depth in parts of nearly one mile. Units of the R.N.D., supported by the Navy, made a feint attack upon the enemy's lines at Bulair at the neck of the peninsula, but no landing was seriously attempted.

When the positions gained on the various beaches had been consolidated and while stores and ammunition were being landed our men had some sort of a respite. This was badly needed, for many, exhausted by lack of food, water and sleep, by the toil of digging for most of the day under a hot sun and of carrying heavy loads most of the night, and by the strain of frequent counter-attacks, were nearing the limits of their endurance. About this time some Indian troops and units from the 42nd Division arrived as reinforcements. During May the line was slowly advanced from Helles towards Krithia, a village on the slopes of Achi Baba, the chief assaults being on 6th–8th May and on 4th and 28th June. Counter-attacks were frequent and in particular one on the night of 19th/20th May at Anzac, where the lines had been stationary since the landing, was so violent and the Turkish losses so heavy that they were granted an armistice in which to bury their dead. Two British submarines, E11 and E14, gallantly penetrating the minefields in the straits torpedoed several Turkish transports carrying reinforcements. By the end of the month, that is, in six weeks from the first landing, the casualties among the British and Anzacs amounted to nearly 40,000, a number which exceeded the total battle casualties in the whole of the South African War.

The next two months were marked by frequent attacks and counter-attacks, leading to no definite result, and it became clear that, although our forces had been strengthened by the arrival of the 13th and 52nd Divisions, the Turkish line could not be carried by direct assault. A plan was therefore formed to land a force at Suvla Bay three miles to the north of Anzac, and then to advance from Anzac upon the Sari Bair ridge. It was hoped in this way to cut the enemy's communications and to turn his position. Accordingly on 6th August the enemy's attention was engaged near Helles by an attack (which happened just to forestall an attack which he was planning) and during the night following a landing was effected at Suvla by part of the 10th and by the 11th Divisions. The 53rd and 54th Divisions landed later. The opposition was comparatively slight, and, if prompt action had been taken, a great success might have been achieved. The delay in pressing our advantage was due partly to the exhaustion of the soldiers who, notwithstanding elaborate precautions, suffered terribly from lack of water, but still more to inertia and confusion in the local higher command upon which Sir Ian Hamilton commented somewhat severely in his despatch. The 6th E. Yorks who had occupied Scimitar Hill with hardly any fighting were, in error, withdrawn in order to attack elsewhere. The Turks were able to bring up reinforcements and the advance which might with so little loss of life have led to great results was checked. Meanwhile the advance from Anzac by British, Dominion and Indian troops, although impeded by the partial failure at Suvla, proceeded slowly up almost precipitous heights covered with scrub, and early in the morning of 8th August a ridge near Chunuk Bair was seized which commanded a view across the peninsula to the Narrows. The 6th S. Lancs from the 13th Division and some Gurkhas, however, who so gallantly captured it came under the fire of their own guns, troops which should have supported them lost their way, and under heavy counter-attacks the ridge had to be abandoned. Although the attack thus failed, the area held at Anzac was enlarged from less than one mile to about eight.

The troops having been reinforced by a dismounted Yeomanry division from Egypt, a further attempt to advance from Suvla Bay was made on 21st August. After severe fighting which continued during the night, positions were gained on Scimitar Hill. It was decided that these would be untenable by day and our men were withdrawn.

After the failure at Suvla the fighting died down into the routine of trench warfare. Early in October two of the English and one of the French divisions were sent to Salonica (see p. 176) and towards the middle of the month Sir Ian Hamilton was ordered to advise upon the evacuation of the peninsula. A few days later he was recalled to England and Sir Charles Monro was appointed in his place. This officer reported strongly in favour of evacuation and his opinion was confirmed by Lord Kitchener who, towards the middle of November, inspected portions of the lines at Helles, Anzac and Suvla.

A striking incident showed the risk of remaining during the winter. On 27th November a sudden gale from the south-west destroyed several piers and landing stages and did much damage among the smaller transports. At the same time a deluge of rain converted the trenches into torrents in which friend and foe, stores and mules, were swept away. This was followed by a blizzard, lasting for nearly two days and nights, and this again by a heavy frost. The troops suffered terribly from the unusual cold, many died, and about 10,000 sick had to be removed.

The evacuation was begun at Anzac and Suvla and was completed there on the night of 19th/20th December, just in time to avoid a storm which arose a few hours later. More than 83,000 men were embarked (with the accidental loss of only two men), with 5,000 horses and mules, 2,000 wagons and 200 guns. At Helles our men were even more fortunate, for a south-westerly gale was beginning to blow as the last of them left the shore. There the evacuation was completed in the early morning of 9th January, 1916, and included 35,000 men, 4,000 animals and 110 guns.

The assault upon the peninsula, urged with such gallantry for so many months and in face of so many difficulties, thus ended in failure. This was not due to any lack of bravery, daring, skill or endurance on the part of the rank and file, but rather to the inability of the superior commands to meet the demands of so great an enterprise and to the fact that, in spite of repeated requests, adequate reinforcements were not forthcoming. In the House of Commons on 20th March, 1917, Mr. Asquith, commenting upon the report of the Dardanelles Commission, claimed that the expedition had saved the position of Russia in the Caucasus, had delayed for months the defection of Bulgaria, had kept immobilised at least 300,000 Turks, and had contributed to the favourable development of events in Egypt, Mesopotamia and Persia.

Arthur Roake (R.N.R., L.F.B.) was awarded the D.S.M. for his gallantry on 25th April, 1915, when, being one of a small party which had been landed to reconnoitre, he carried a wounded officer under heavy fire back to the boats, and the next day acted as a guide to a second party. Sergt. W. F. Bird (1st Co. of Lond. Yeo., Educ.) was awarded the D.C.M. for conspicuous gallantry, on 21st August, 1915, at Suvla, when, as medical orderly, he remained under fire attending the wounded, and displayed great bravery and devotion to duty. E. Griffiths (R.F.R., L.F.B.) won the D.S.M.

The casualties were: killed 28,200, wounded 78,095, missing 11,254, making a total of 117,549; there were also nearly 100,000 sick, chiefly cases of dysentery, malaria, and, towards the end of the occupation, frost-bite. The deaths among the Council's staff were: 25th April, J. G. Everett (H.M.S. *Euryalus*, Tram.) killed at W Beach; 28th, F. A. Dolan (R.E., Ch. Engr.); 29th, G. H. Morgan (R. Naval Div., Tram.); 6th May, C. E. Hutchings (R. Naval Div., L.F.B.) of wounds received on the 3rd, and William West (R. Naval Div., Asylums); 25th, Sergt. F. Blanchard (R. Naval Div., Educ.); 4th June, William Perriman (H.M.S. *Bacchante*, Ch. Engr.) of wounds received on 25th April at the landing at Anzac; 21st, James Childs (Hamps, Asylums); 28th, Albert Cox (Essex, Tram.); 6th August, Captain Francis Falcon (4th Worcesters, Ch. Engr.) and Samuel Russell (2nd Hamps., Tram.), both at Helles, and Sergt. E. D. Long (Wilts, Tram.) near Anzac; 7th, Capt. C. S. Blake (S. Lancs, attd. 6th Lancs Fus.) near Helles; 8th,

William Tuffey (7th Glouc., Stores) near Chunuk Bair; 13th, Lance-Corp. S. H. Butler (W. Riding, Asylums) of wounds received near Suvla on the 10th; 14th, Arthur Olney (R.A.S.C., Tram.) on H.M.S. *Royal Edward* when she was torpedoed; 15th, Lieut. H. J. Hoare, B.Sc. (Econ.), LL.B. (10th Lond., Clerk) and Sergt. A. T. F. Beaumont (10th Lond., Tram.) both near Suvla; 21st, E. S. Miller (City of London Yeo., Educ.), near Suvla; 27th September, William Wilson (2nd Scottish Horse, Tram.); 4th November, W. J. Filbee (R. Fus., Tram.), near Suvla; 11th, Capt. A. M. Philips (Yorks L.I., attached 9th W. Yorks., Arch.), near Suvla; 27th, Edwin Barnard (R.E., Arch.), near Suvla. Frank Murrell (H.M.S. *Glory*, L.F.B.) on 15th August, D. G. King (Essex, Asylums) on 22nd November and H. J. R. Marson (Essex, Tram.) on 24th November, died of dysentery. T. H. Baker (R.F.A., Asylums) died on 6th December of tuberculosis.

CHAPTER X.

Egypt and Palestine.

At the outbreak of war with Turkey it was estimated that about 140,000 troops were concentrated at Damascus, and it was anticipated that a part of these would be used for an attempt upon the Suez Canal. It was true that to reach the canal the enemy would have to cross the Sinai Peninsula, a waterless desert 120 miles wide, and that failure would be disastrous. On the other hand the enterprise, if successful, would sever a vital link in the British communications with India and the East, and such a possibility, however remote, had to be guarded against.

At the end of January, 1915, a Turkish column reached El Arish, passed through Wadi-el-Arish,[1] and on 3rd February endeavoured to cross the Canal

[1] A wadi is a rocky watercourse, dry except in the rainy season.

south of Ismalia. Our troops, fully warned, easily repulsed the attack, killed large numbers of the enemy and took 600 prisoners.

The British now pushed forward a railway from Kantara, and early in 1916 Qatia was reached. In April the Turks tried to interfere with the work but were driven off. In July an expedition of 18,000 men, hugging the coast, made some progress, but, bombarded

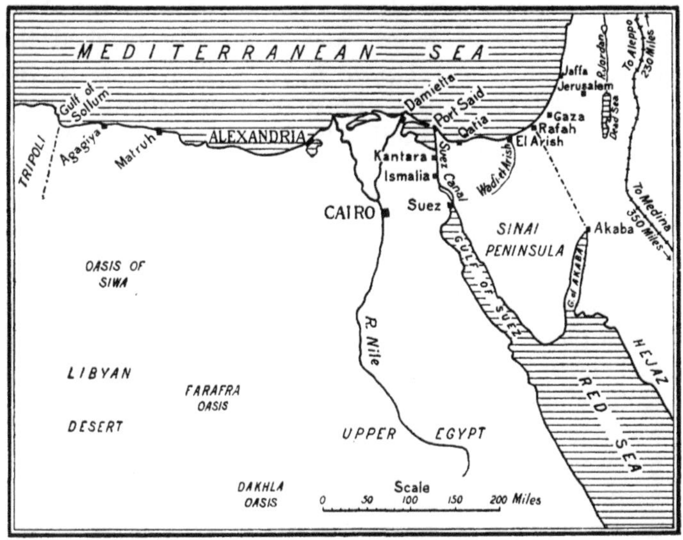

EGYPT, 1915-17.

from British monitors at sea, and harried by mounted troops on its left and rear, it was completely defeated on 4th/5th August with the loss of half its number in casualties and prisoners.

The Senussi of Sollum.

Trouble also arose with the Senussi on the western frontier. These were Arabs, nominally subject to the Turks, and, as they acknowledge in a loose way the religious authority of the Sultan, they were easily aroused against the Infidel. Early in December, 1915, a composite force, which included the 2/7th and 2/8th

Middlesex, occupied Matruh midway between the Nile and the western frontier and defeated the enemy several times in the neighbourhood. A defeat in February, 1916, at Agagiya, sixty miles to the west, drove them back to Sollum where they were dispersed, with the loss of all their equipment, by armoured cars. Some of the fugitives fled 500 miles to the south-east along the oases which form a rough natural boundary between the desert plateau to the west of the Nile, and the Libyan Desert, and eventually reached the Dakhla oasis, near Upper Egypt. They were driven out in October, 1916, and a remnant which reached the Siwa oasis, 150 miles from Sollum, was defeated in February, 1917.

Palestine.

As a preliminary to the invasion of Palestine the Turks in January, 1917, were driven out of El Arish and Rafah and the Qatia railway was continued to the latter place. Anticipating an attack they strongly fortified Gaza, Beersheba and the district between the Wadi Ghuzze and the Wadi es Sheria. In March our assault was launched. A few cavalry entered Gaza on the 26th but were cut off and, although the 53rd and part of the 54th Divisions surrounded the town, they were withdrawn a day or so later. On 17th April the attack was renewed, the 53rd Division attacking along the coast with the 52nd and 54th on their right. The assault seems to have been even less successful than the earlier attempt and, after two days' hard fighting, our men were withdrawn.

It was probably in this fighting that Co.-Sergt.-Maj. (afterwards Lieut.) W. A. Trumble (7th Essex, Arch.) was awarded the D.C.M. for his " marked ability and courage in handling his section in two engagements."

R. H. Lunn (Essex, Educ.) was killed near Gaza on 26th March, and M. T. Lucas (2/10th Middx., Educ.) near the same place on 19th April. Lieut. H. J. Payne, (4th Suss., Comp.) and F. A. Toseland (Highd. L.I.,

Asylums) on their way to Egypt were drowned on 4th May, 1917, when the transport *Transylvania* was torpedoed in the Mediterranean.

Capture of Gaza and Beersheba.

The Turks took the opportunity to strengthen their defences which were held by ten divisions. General Sir Edmund Allenby, now in command, determined to assault a point to the west of Beersheba where the country was so rugged that the enemy considered elaborate fortifications to be unnecessary. The preparations, which included the construction of many miles of roads and branch railways, the laying of rabbit wire on long stretches of sand so as to provide passable tracks for traffic, and the formation of depots for stores and munitions, occupied three months.

By October all was ready and on the 27th Gaza was heavily bombarded from the land and the sea, while a sortie from the town was beaten off. The enemy's attention being thus concentrated upon the right of his line, the 60th and 74th Divisions advanced by a night march, and at dawn on the 31st attacked the sector west of Beersheba. By the early afternoon the defences had been breached, and later in the day the town, with 2,000 prisoners, was seized by Australian Horse which had made a wide detour to the east. On 1st November Tuweil-abu-Jerwal, a commanding height north of the town, was occupied by the 53rd Division, and the Tel-Kuweilfe pass, still further to the north, was blocked. Turning west the 10th and 60th Divisions on the 6th captured a sector of the defences towards Gaza, and the 60th at Sheria also cut the railway leading to Jerusalem. The Turks had been held in Gaza by the 52nd Division, which advanced before dawn on the 2nd, but the situation was now desperate and they retreated in disorder along the coast. The town was occupied on the 7th. Thus in one week Gaza and Beersheba were captured, and the enemy was driven out of the whole of the very formidable positions between those two towns. Some 9,000 prisoners and 80 guns were captured.

Corp. G. Kirkby (1st Co. of Lond. Yeo., Educ.) was awarded the D.C.M. for gallantry and devotion to duty at Gaza. " He rendered splendid service during

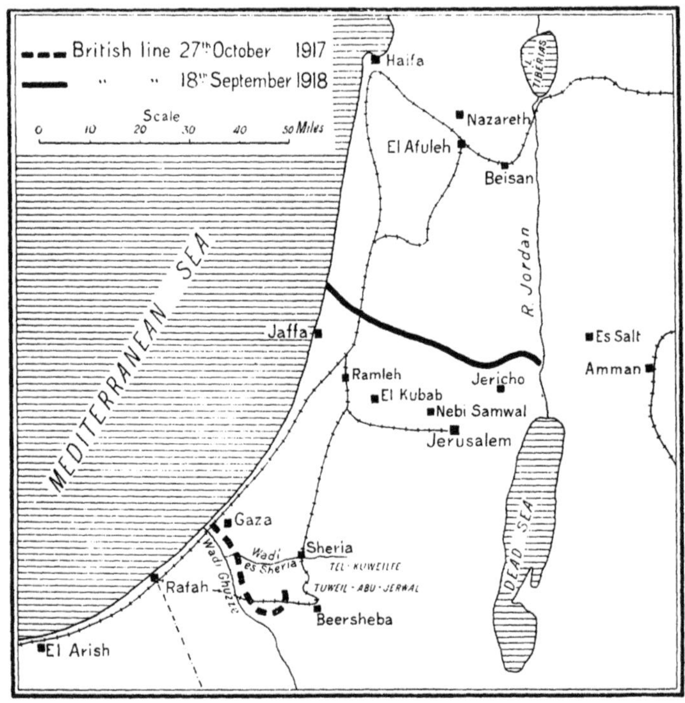

PALESTINE.

two actions, and on many other occasions, under the most difficult conditions."

C. J. Hitchcock (M.G.C , Educ.) died of wounds on 28th October near Beersheba, John McGrath (2/15th Lond., Estates and Valn.) was killed near the same place on the 31st, W. J. Howes (10th Lond., Tram.) near Gaza on 2nd November, Lieut. F J. Miles (R.F.A., Educ.) near Sheria on the 6th, and Bomdr. W. C. Hygate (R.F.A., Tram.) near Sheria on the 7th. P. C.

Bernard, wounded on 4th November, died in hospital on 5th March, 1918.

Fall of Jerusalem and Jericho.

The Turks next attempted to make a stand at El Kubab on high ground guarding Jerusalem and the railway thereto, but were driven out by the 52nd Division. Ramleh was seized on the 15th and Jaffa on the 16th, the latter forming a useful base for supplies by sea. The enemy were now hemmed in on the high ground to the east and south-east of Jerusalem. Avoiding any frontal attack on this main position, General Allenby on the 20th seized the Nebi Samwal ridge north of Jerusalem by means of the 75th Division. On 8th December the 53rd Division advanced from the south and east and the 60th and 74th from the west, east and north. Next day the city surrendered and on the 11th it was entered by our victorious troops.

Fresh enemy troops advancing towards the city were driven off on 27th December by yeomanry and the 10th Division and, following up this success, our troops next day pushed the enemy back some miles. Several weeks of rain caused hostilities to be suspended and time was thus given for putting roads and railways into repair. Towards the end of February, 1918, fighting commenced again, and the 60th Division with Anzac horse fought their way towards Jericho which was entered on the 21st.

C. E. West (2/14th Lond., Educ.), wounded on 8th December in the advance upon Jerusalem, died on 28th March, W. J. Templeman (R.F.A., Tram.) died at Cairo on 7th December of malaria or enteric, Lieut. A. E. Pragnell (2/21st Lond., Educ.) was drowned on the 30th when the transport *Aragon* was torpedoed in the eastern Mediterranean, A. H. B. Barnard (2/15th Lond., Educ.) was killed on 20th February, 1918, to the north of Jerusalem, C. J. F. Dockett (2/15th Lond., Comp.) died of wounds on the 21st, and F. B. Neate (2/24th Lond., Parks) was killed on 9th March.

Raids across the Jordan.

Early in the war many Arab tribes in Hejaz, to the east of the Red Sea, threw off the Turkish suzerainty, which for long they had barely acknowledged, and a force under Feisal, son of the King of Hejaz, in addition to protecting the right flank of Allenby's advance, also attacked various posts between the Red Sea and the Dead Sea and harried the Turkish lines of communication along the railway from Damascus to Mecca.[1] To assist these columns the 60th Division and Anzacs on 21st March, 1918, forced the passage of the Jordan and pushed on to Es Salt which was occupied on the 25th. Attempts during the next few days to reach the railway in strength failed, but small raiding parties cut it in several places and on 2nd April the troops were withdrawn. On the 30th the attack was renewed when mounted troops again occupied Es Salt and the 60th Division assaulted positions to the south-west. A Turkish counter-attack upon the left flank of the expedition was successful and forced our men to retire with the loss of nine guns. As a set-off nearly one thousand Turks were captured.

Capt. F. V. Harris (10th Lond., Solr.) won the M.C. on 26th March but no details are available. Co.-Sergt.-Maj. B. C. Hales (2/23rd Lond., Educ.) was awarded the D.C.M. for his gallantry during the first raid. "He took command of his company, when all the officers had been wounded. Under intense rifle and machine-gun fire he moved fearlessly about, encouraging and organising his much depleted company. Afterwards, he was placed in command of the left of the battalion line, when his courage and resource under heavy fire materially assisted in beating off two strong counter-attacks."

Co.-Sergt.-Maj. S. T. Watson (2/23rd Lond., Educ.)

[1] The fighting in the Hejaz cannot be gone into in detail, but the British gave some assistance, and for continuous and consistent good service whilst commanding an armoured car from April, 1917, onwards Lieut. E. H. Wade (M.G.C., Tram.) was awarded the M.C.

was killed near Es Salt on 28th March, Sergt. A. A. Clements (R.A.V.C., Educ.) near Jericho on 2nd April, and Corp. A. Symons (2/20th Lond., Educ.), Lance-Corp. H. Osborn (2/16th Lond., Educ.) and J. W. H. Woodward (2/20th Lond., Comp.) on the 30th.

Battle of Megiddo.

The success of the German offensives in France from March onwards led to the recall of the 52nd and 74th and the bulk of the 60th Divisions, their place being taken by Indian troops, chiefly from Mesopotamia. Large Turkish forces were detached for service in Persia and elsewhere, so that for once the Allies had the advantage in numbers. As soon as his new troops were properly incorporated in the army General Allenby decided to seize the opportunity for overwhelming the enemy in this part. Accordingly on 18th September the 10th and 53rd Divisions made a feint on the right of our line to the north of Jerusalem, and next day the main attack was launched against the enemy's positions on the coastal plain north of Jaffa. This was completely successful; two important lines of defence were overrun, and on the 20th three cavalry divisions, pushing forward through the gap thus formed and wheeling eastward, cut the enemy's lines of retreat at El Afuleh and Beisan and seized the crossings over the Jordan. Liman von Sanders, the German commander-in-chief, narrowly escaped capture at Nazareth, his headquarters. Under attacks by the 10th and 53rd, aided by several Indian divisions, from the south and west the enemy now turned and fled, and, as the main outlets were already held by our troops, escape was possible only for small scattered bodies using the rough and narrow hill tracks. The disorganisation was completed by the airmen who dispersed the fugitives with bombs and machine-gun fire. Such of the enemy as escaped were relentlessly pursued, and Damascus surrendered on 1st October and Beirut on the 7th. In less than three weeks from the opening of the attack 75,000 prisoners (including 3,000 Germans and Austrians) and 300 guns were captured; out of three Turkish armies only some 17,000 escaped death or capture.

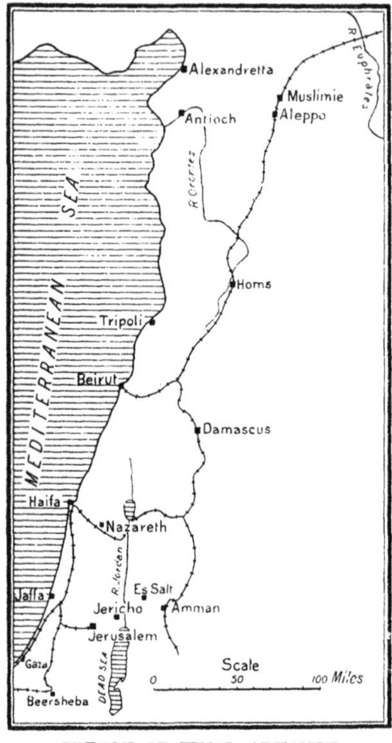

SKETCH OF FINAL ADVANCE.

The advance still continued and, as the enemy offered little resistance, progress was rapid. Tripoli surrendered on 13th October and Homs on the 16th, while on the 26th Aleppo and Muslimie, the latter an important railway centre, were captured after a brisk skirmish with enemy rearguards. General Townshend, who had been taken prisoner at Kut (see p. 170), was now released with the request that he would arrange an immediate armistice. This was signed on the 30th when the Turks agreed to open the Dardanelles and Bosphorus, to surrender all prisoners, to demobilise their army and to transfer to the Allies the control of all railways.

During this fighting no members of the Council's staff were killed, but Lieut. W. A. Trumble, D.C.M. (6th Essex, Arch.) died in Egypt on 9th October, and W. Jackson (2/22nd Lond., Educ.) near Jerusalem of malaria on the 13th, and Corp. E. M. Stiller (R.F.A., Tram.) died in hospital at Alexandria of pneumonia on 14th December.

CHAPTER XI.

Mesopotamia.

When war broke out with Turkey the occupation of Basra was urged as a means of diverting Turkish troops from the threatened attack on the Suez Canal and Egypt, and of protecting the Anglo-Persian oil line, an important source of supply for the British Navy. Accordingly a mixed British and Indian Force, which was despatched to Mesopotamia with this object, defeated the Turks at Sahil, and on 22nd November, 1914, entered Basra. On 9th December the garrison of Qurna, 40 miles higher up, surrendered with nine guns.

Much of Mesopotamia is waste sandy loam, subject to sand storms during the hot weather and turning into an adhesive mud during the wet season. As there are few roads or even tracks, the rivers are the chief means of communication, but they have swift currents, are liable to floods and are encumbered with numerous shallows. Few troops were available for further operations, and the difficulties of transporting them and their supplies were very great.

Some months elapsed before reinforcements arrived, and the Turks, encouraged by the delay, took the initiative, but were driven back at Shaiba on 14th April, 1915. During May Gen. Townshend, having collected or improvised some sort of water transport, advanced with one division up the Tigris and, taking the garrison of Amara more or less by surprise, occupied the town on the 29th. At the same time the advance was consolidated by troops under General Gorringe which cleared the enemy from the district between Ahwaz and Amara and in July advanced up the Euphrates and took Nasiriya.

The water transport, barely sufficient for the original expedition, had now to serve twice the number of men, and the problem of supplying the troops with food and ammunition and of dealing with the sick and wounded became very serious. Nevertheless General Townshend was ordered to advance. On 29th September he defeated the enemy at Kut, captured the town with 1,700 prisoners and much war material, and followed

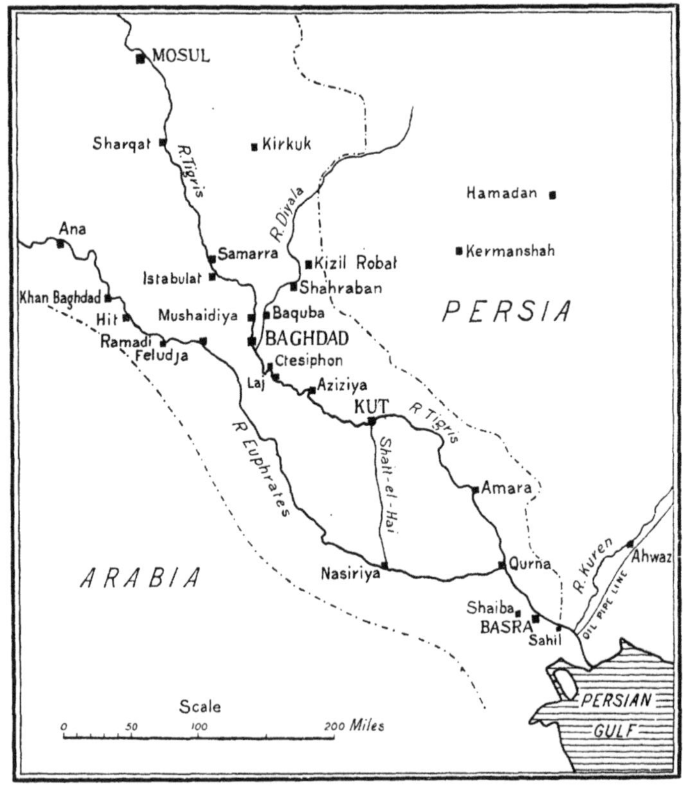

LOWER MESOPOTAMIA.

up the victory by sending his cavalry in pursuit to Aziziya, 50 miles farther up the river.

It was generally considered that to continue the advance, without substantial reinforcements and greatly improved transport, would be unwise, even disastrous, and early in October the Government of India ordered a halt. Why this order was afterwards waived is not clear. The British Government seem to have represented that, prospects in Gallipoli being uncertain, a striking success in the East was desirable, and the military authorities may have been too sanguine. Whatever the reason, a few reinforcements were sent but no transport, and in November, when the Turks had organised their defences, the advance was renewed. On the 21st our men drove the enemy out of Laj, pushed on nine miles, and on the 22nd attacked the main position at Ctesiphon, only sixteen miles from Baghdad. Two lines of trenches were captured, but enemy reinforcements compelled the British to retire to the first line. They were now outnumbered by about two to one, and on the night of the 25th/26th a retreat was ordered. On 3rd December, after a series of rear-guard actions, Kut was reached in safety.

The town lies on a strip of land, one mile broad and two deep, with the Tigris on three sides of it (see plan on p. 170). Across the neck of this strip entrenchments were dug, and buildings on the farther, that is the south side of the river,[1] were also fortified. On the 9th the Turks commenced the assault and drove in the southern outpost. Four attacks on 10th December were beaten back and, after a period of comparative rest, a fifth on the 24th, supported by heavy reinforcements, met with a like fate. Meanwhile the enemy, in order to hold up any relieving expedition, erected strong fortifications below the town, chiefly at Es Sinn on the south bank and at Hanna and Sanna-i-Yat on the north bank where there were extensive marshes.

The winter rains now set in, turning much of the country into a morass, but early in January, 1916, a relieving column under General Aylmer, although hampered by lack of transport, reached Hanna, twenty miles away, where it was checked and had to

[1] The general direction of the Tigris is from north-west to south-east, but at Kut it flows almost due east.

retire. A second attempt on the night of the 9th/10th March, this time on the south side of the river towards the Dujaila Redoubt, miscarried in the darkness, and, after severe fighting, the troops were withdrawn. At the third attempt the 13th Division, under Gen. Maude, captured five lines of trenches at Hanna on 5th April, and on the 9th, after the advance had been held up by floods, breached the Sanna-i-Yat defences.

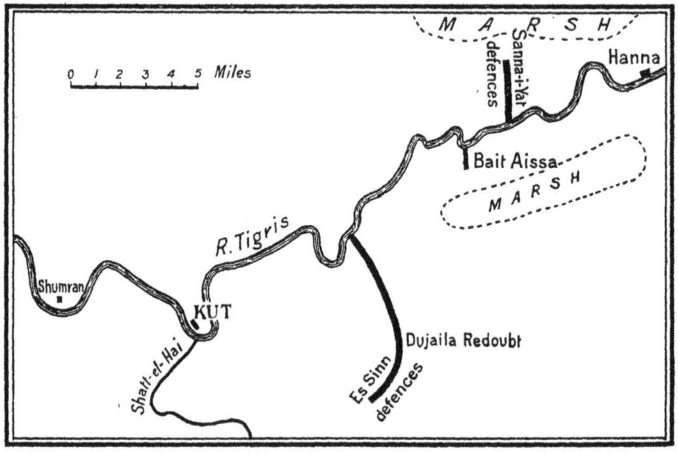

KUT.

South of the river our troops reached Bait Aissa, but neither body could get any farther.

Although rations had been reduced to a half and then to a fourth, and supplies had been dropped from æroplanes, all food in Kut, including the battery bullocks and mules, had now been consumed, and on 29th April, arms and ammunition having been destroyed, the town, after a siege of five months, surrendered.

Corp. H. J. Belben (4th Hants, Educ.), serving with one of the relieving columns, died of disease at Amara on 19th January, 1916.

The British spent the summer and autumn of 1916 on the defensive, but the time was fully occupied by Sir Stanley Maude, now commander-in-chief, in organising transport, in accumulating stores, in training the reinforcements which were being freely sent, and generally in preparing for an advance. The Turks also laboured incessantly, constructing on the south side of the river at Kut, one within the other, four elaborate trench systems, the outermost of which extended for about thirty miles. The British attack opened on 13th December with a bombardment of the Sanna-i-Yat defences. This was only a feint, for the main body, crossing the desert, advanced towards Kut along both banks of the Shatt-el-Hai which connects the Tigris with the Euphrates. The ruse succeeded and the defending troops were taken by surprise. Heavy rains now fell for several weeks, but the troops pressed on and by 19th January, 1917, after much desperate fighting, had cleared the enemy from the four trench systems east of the Hai and had reached the Tigris. This success was followed on 3rd February by the storming of the defences which covered the junction of the Tigris and the Hai, and by the 15th the enemy had been cleared from the elaborate defences west of the Hai. On the 16th the attack at Sanna-i-Yat was resumed with success and, while the enemy's attention was engaged there, the Tigris was crossed on the 23rd at Shumran to the west of Kut. Next day the British broke through at Sanna-i-Yat and the Turks everywhere retreated in disorder, the retreat being hastened by our cavalry and by gunboats on the river.

Aziziya was reached on the 27th and, after a brief halt while the lines of communication were being organised, the troops went forward again, occupying Ctesiphon on 6th March without resistance. The Diyala was crossed on the night of the 8th/9th, and on the 11th our troops entered Baghdad.

At each stage of the advance many prisoners were taken and at Baghdad, the terminus of the railway from Constantinople, much war material, including railway and hospital equipment, arms and munitions, was seized.

Major G. R. Treadwell (6th E. Lancs, Educ.) was killed on 5th February, 1917, and Lance-Corp. A. E. Morris (8th R. Welch Fus., Educ.) and Arthur Walker (8th R. Welch Fus., Tram.) on the 15th, all to the west of Kut.

Operations in Upper Mesopotamia.

The capture of Baghdad was immediately consolidated by stationing strong outposts up the Tigris,

MESOPOTAMIA AND PERSIA.

Diyala and Euphrates. Mushaidiya,[1] situated on the first, was seized on 16th March after a sharp encounter with the enemy; Baquba, on the second, on the 18th; and Feludja, on the third, on the 19th. On the 23rd a force from Baquba occupied Shahraban, twenty miles to the north-east, and, after several conflicts with the Turks who were being driven out of Persia by the Russians, established touch with the latter at Kizil Robat, on 2nd April. On the 21st the enemy were defeated at Istabulat in front of Samarra, an important position on the Tigris and the railway, and two days

[1] See plan on p. 168.

later that place was seized as well as more war material. The first attack, on 11th July, upon Ramadi, thirty miles up the Euphrates from Feludja, was a failure, but a second attempt succeeded on 29th September, when 3,500 prisoners and the bulk of the enemy's remaining stores in this part were captured.

In the midst of these striking successes Sir Stanley Maude, to whom so much of their credit was due, died of cholera at Baghdad on 18th November, 1917 General Sir W. R. Marshall, his second-in-command, was entrusted with the conduct of affairs and during 1918 Hit and Khan Baghdad on the Euphrates were captured in March with 4,000 prisoners, and the enemy was routed and pursued to a point beyond Ana This put an end to any risk of an attack down the Euphrates. At the end of April the Turks were defeated at Kirkuk, north of the Diyala, with further heavy losses. The offensive up the Tigris was resumed in October, and on the 27th the enemy were attacked by our infantry at Sharqat, while cavalry and armoured cars blocked the lines of retreat. On the 30th the whole force to the number of about 7,000 with all stores, etc., surrendered. Mosul, 550 miles from Basra, and 200 from Baghdad, was occupied a few days later. The terms of the armistice with Turkey have already been given (see p. 166).

Capt. J. T. Snelgar (5th Wilts, Educ.) was awarded the M.B.E. for general good work as adjutant and for staff work in connection with the capture and occupation of Kirkuk.

Sergt. A. Peters (7th Glouc., Tram.) died of typhus on 10th July, G. F. Jago (R.A.S.C., Educ.) of typhoid on 30th November, and B. A. M. Dunning (R.E., Tram.) of dysentery on 6th December.

Persia and Caucasia.

After hostilities between Germany and Russia had definitely ceased towards the end of 1917, it was feared that the enemy might penetrate through the southern parts of Asiatic Russia, and so threaten our positions in Mesopotamia and to the north-west of India. A military mission, despatched from India in the early part of 1918, therefore occupied Meshed and established posts on the railway at Krasnovodsk, Askhabad and Merv. These four places are all to the east of the Caspian Sea.[1]

For the same reasons it was necessary to strengthen our positions up, and to the north-east of, the Diyala. Hamadan, in north-west Persia, and Rasht were occupied, the occupation of the latter involving us in conflict with the native tribes. Access was secured to Enzali, a port on the Caspian near Rasht, and a small expedition was sent in August to help in the defence of Baku, the important centre for oil on the west coast of the Caspian. The local levies proved to be quite unreliable, so that the brunt of the fighting fell upon our troops, and in September they were withdrawn to Enzali. The expedition, however, had the result of inducing the ex-Russian fleet on the Caspian to side with the Allies, and so checked German or Turkish hopes of an advance to the east.

After the armistice with Turkey a British force was stationed between the Caspian and the Black Sea in order to keep open the Batum—Tiflis—Baku railway, and to maintain communications across the Caspian with the British force, mentioned above, at, and near, Krasnovodsk.

Lieut. H. A. King (Camel Corps, Educ.) died in east Persia on 4th November, 1918, of enteric.

CHAPTER XII.

Salonica.

Before describing the British share in the Allied expedition to Salonica it should be mentioned that the

[1] For plan see p. 172.

Austrians followed up their declaration of war on Serbia by bombarding Belgrade, the capital, and on 13th August crossed the Danube at Shabatz, 40 miles to the west. Within a few days they were driven out, and a more threatening attack in November and December, which reached Valjevo, 30 miles to the south of the Danube, and led to the fall of Belgrade on 2nd December, was also completely repulsed.

After the first Balkan war, waged by the Bulgarians with the help of Serbians and Greeks against the Turks in 1913, the Bulgarians fell out with their allies, and, in the war which followed, lost most of their gains. It was feared that they might take advantage of the general European war to avenge themselves upon the Serbians, and the latter were urged to secure their neutrality or even alliance, by conceding the territory in dispute. Naturally the Serbians were unwilling to do this, and Germany and Austria by counter proposals, including a substantial loan, obtained the promise of assistance from the Bulgarians. During September, 1915, when the crops had been harvested, their army was mobilised, ostensibly to maintain an armed neutrality. Early in October an Austro-German expedition under Von Mackensen invaded Serbia from the north and the Bulgarians, at length throwing aside all pretence, attacked the Serbians from the east. The Serbian army, already reduced by a year's fighting to about 100,000, was thus set upon by forces four or five times as numerous, and, in spite of an heroic resistance, was rapidly driven back. By the end of November, having lost practically all its guns, ammunition and stores, it had ceased to exist as an organised unit.

The Greeks were parties to a treaty which required them to assist the Serbians but, under the guidance of King Constantine, whose wife was a sister of the Kaiser, had no great scruples in ignoring their responsibilities. France and Great Britain, however, were ready to assist, and Salonica, a Greek port of some 140,000 inhabitants, was offered and accepted as a base. A French force, which included the British 10th Division from Gallipoli, was landed in October, 1915, and endeavoured to join hands with the retreating Serbians by advancing up the valley of the Vardar along the railway from Salonica to Uskub and Nish. After severe fighting by the French, an attempt to

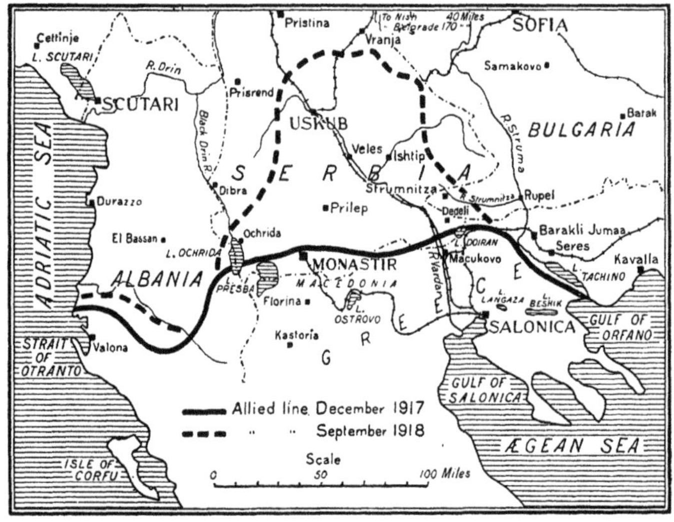

SALONICA.

reach Veles failed and the force returned, through dreadful hardships, to Salonica. The British, who were stationed between Lake Doiran and Dedeli to the north-west to cover the retreat, were heavily attacked early in December during a fog and somewhat roughly handled. They were able, however, to complete their task, and to retire into Greek territory. The Bulgarians did not cross the frontier and the Allies, being unmolested, spent the winter of 1915/16 in constructing very strong defensive works from Lakes Beshik and Langaza to the Vardar.

There was much else to be done. " When you step

out of Salonica you step into a virtual desert, roadless, treeless, uncultivated, populated only by scattered villages . . . inhabited by a low-grade peasantry."[1] Only two roads, both quite inadequate for heavy traffic, and three lines of single railway led from the town towards the enemy. "Winter, right up to the beginning of April, is a season of snow, rain, and, above all, mud. Tracks dissolve into quagmires, main roads break up into holes and ridges, impassable for motor traffic." Roads and bridges were therefore made, wells sunk, supplies stored, hospitals and buildings of all sorts erected, and to enable it to cope with the extra traffic the harbour was deepened and improved. Although the Allies had been officially invited to Salonica, an influential party among the Greeks opposed their work in every way. Worse followed, for on 26th May, 1916, Rupel, commanding the valley of the Struma, was seized by the Bulgarians, the Greeks apparently conniving. In reply the French commander-in-chief placed Salonica under martial law, and on 30th August the town definitely sided with the Allies.

A strangely composite force, comprising French, British, Russians, Italians, Serbians, Portuguese, contingents from French and British colonies and Greek volunteers, was gradually collected. To the British 10th Division were added the 22nd, 26th, 27th, 28th and 60th Divisions, but of these the 10th left in 1916 and the 60th in 1917 for Palestine. After a quiet winter and spring the line was slowly advanced during the summer of 1916, with the British in general in the sector between the Struma and the Vardar, but the Bulgarians captured Kavalla on our right and were successful at Lake Ostrovo on our left. The British made captures to the west of Lake Doiran on the night of 17th/18th August, and on 11th September successfully attacked the Macukovo salient on the left bank of the Vardar, and crossed the Struma at and

[1] G. W. Price, *The Story of the Salonica Army*, p. 2.

near Orliak. These affairs were a prelude to an advance on the left by the French, who stormed Florina on 18th September and Monastir on 19th November. On 30th September and succeeding days British troops captured Zir, and other positions towards Seres, and on 31st October captured Barakli Jumaa.

The campaign of 1917 was marked by a determined British attack on the enemy's position in front of the Petit Couronné to the west of Lake Doiran. Front line trenches were captured in a night attack on 24th/25th April, but most of them were commanded by the enemy's reserve trenches and had to be evacuated, and an attack on the night of 8th/9th May had a similar result. The total British casualties were about 10,000. During the summer, in order to escape the malaria and other diseases which infested the low-lying ground, both sides retired to the hills which line the valley of the Struma, forward positions being held only by outposts.

Lieut. T. W. Greenstreet (R. Irish Fus., Educ.) was awarded the M.C. for his gallantry, on the night of 20th/21st April, to the east of Lake Doiran. While he was guiding an attacking party over difficult country an alarm was given and, the party being much broken up, he was left alone near the enemy's position. "He then, single-handed, kept the enemy at bay, and it was due to his great gallantry that very severe casualties to the retiring party were prevented. Having exhausted his ammunition, he clubbed a rifle and continued to fight until, wounded and overcome, he was captured."

Co.-Sergt.-Maj. A. E. Dawes (2/20th Lond., Educ.) received the D.C.M. for his gallantry during a raid on 23rd April, when, "although wounded, he organised a bombing party, and succeeded in knocking a machine-gun out. Afterwards, though wounded three times, he carried out his duties with the utmost coolness and gallantry."

Lance-Corp. W. G. Gosford (R.A.S.C., Educ.) died of malaria on 3rd September, 1916. Lieut. H. F. Bartram (7th Wilts, Comp.) was killed during the attack on 24th April, 1917, and Lieut. W. I. Partridge (10th Devons, Comp.) and Daniel Conley (2/20th Lond., Ch. Engr.) on the 25th. Lance-Corp. J. D. Allen (2/16th Lond., Educ.) died on 10th May of wounds received two days earlier. W. F. Fish (R.A.M.C., Asylums) who was gassed in March, died on 24th May of paraplegia, E. H. Doherty (Durh. L.I., Tram.) died of malaria on 25th August and Staff-Sergt.-Farrier G. M. Dobson (R.A.S.C., Ch. Engr.) of the same disease on 16th October.

The front was quiet during the spring and summer of 1918, but on 15th September the French and Serbians broke through on a front of seven miles, and rapidly extending their success, within a few days advanced some twenty miles. The British and Greeks prevented the transfer of reinforcements by attacking near Lake Doiran, and on the 27th captured Strumnitza. Prilep fell to the French and Serbians on the 23rd, Ishtip on the 25th, and Uskub on the 29th. The Bulgarians, with their communications cut, were thus threatened with annihilation and applied for an armistice. This was signed at Salonica, Bulgaria evacuating Greece and Serbia, demobilising her army, surrendering all arms and munitions, making over to the Allies all means of transport and receiving Allied garrisons into various parts of her territory. Even after the surrender of Bulgaria a few German and Austrian troops attempted to oppose the Allies, but this resistance was brushed aside, and the Serbians entered Nish on 12th October, and Belgrade on 1st November. In four weeks from the opening of the offensive 90,000 prisoners and 2,000 guns were captured.[1]

[1] General Ludendorff seems to have regarded this defeat as more disastrous for the cause of Germany and her allies than any of the others experienced about this time (*My War Memories*, 1914–18, vol. ii. p. 715).

Lieut. W. R. Reeve (E. Surr., Educ.) received the M.C. for his gallantry on the night of 26th/27th September during two successful patrols when the company under his command had to locate and occupy a strong enemy position. Capt. and Qr.-Master E. A. Beattie (R.A.M.C., Educ.) received the M.B.E. in recognition of his gallantry in saving a man's life at Kavalla on 17th December, 1918.

Co.-Sergt. Maj. F. Challen (9th Bord., Educ.) was awarded the D.C.M. "He took charge of officers' parties, and it was mainly due to his courage, energy and determination that long lengths of wire entanglements were erected in a very short space of time."

Richard Lloyd (R.A.S.C., Stores) died of nephritis on 16th January, 1918, Corp. C. J. Bateman (R.A.M.C., Asylums) of hæmorrhage on 16th March, Percy Berridge (R.F.A., Stores) of pneumonia on 14th April, Lance-Corp. D. C. Belcher (R.A.M.C., Pub. H.) of dysentery on 5th July, Lance-Corp. T. S. Tonkin, B.Sc. (R.A.M.C., Solr.), of malaria on 17th October, E. Chauvin (R.G.A., Educ.) of malaria and pneumonia on 17th November, S. Swindells (R.N.A.S., Tram.) on the 18th of pneumonia, T. H. G. Willcock (R.A.M.C., Parks) on the 28th of pneumonia on his way home, and A. D. Cripps (R.G.A., Pub. H.) on 17th December, also of pneumonia. In January, 1919, Lance-Corp. G. G. Smith (R.A.M.C., Educ.) died on the 9th and Staff-Sergt. W. Dobson (R.A.O.C., Parks) on the 16th, both of pneumonia.

CHAPTER XIII.

British Troops in Italy.

Italy had two main reasons for declaring war upon Austria. First, she was alarmed by the latter's designs upon Serbia and the east coast of the Adriatic; the success of these would naturally gravely impair Italian influence in the Mediterranean. Secondly, she was anxious to recover Italian lands, held by the Austrians, such as the Trentino in South Tirol, and Trieste and Istria north-east of the Adriatic. In the spring of 1915, Austria made certain vague offers which were regarded as quite insufficient, and on 23rd May, 1915, after further indecisive parleyings, Italy declared war.

The Trentino projects into Italy in a great salient, so that the danger of the Austrians secretly collecting troops for a sudden attack had to be guarded against. Fortunately the frontier around this salient and to the east lies along the crests of the Alps, which are crossed by only a few passes. The Italians were satisfied with containing, by frequent local attacks, a number of the enemy in this part, while they made their chief attacks through open country on the east towards the Isonzo. During 1915 no fewer than five great assaults were launched in this direction. In June, 1916, an Austrian counter-offensive from the Trentino, which at first seemed very threatening, was driven back, and in August the attacks upon the Isonzo were resumed, with the result that Gorizia was taken, and the line carried forward across the Carso plateau south of the town. A further advance there and across the Bainsizza plateau north of the town in May, 1917, was checked by the Austrians, but the attack, in which a few British heavy batteries assisted, was resumed later with some success.

Towards the end of October, 1917, the Austrians, aided by Germans, attacked the Italian 2nd Army near Caporetto to the north of Gorizia. The defence, war-weary and much discouraged by troubles amongst the civil population, offered little resistance,[1] and on the 26th, in order to ensure the safety of the rest of the line, a general retreat was ordered. This continued until 12th November when the river Piave

[1] There were some brilliant exceptions. At least one group of Alpini near Gorizia were reported by airmen to be still holding out as late as 4th November, although they were then 100 miles or more behind the line.

was reached. The Italians lost 200,000 men and 2,000 guns, and their gains in the Trentino and near the Isonzo, as well as a district, at least 100 miles deep and of the same breadth, out of their own territory. In their extremity they turned to the Allies for assistance, and five British divisions, the 5th, 7th, 23rd, 41st and 48th, under Sir Henry Plumer,[1] in addition to French divisions under French generals were sent. The line of the Piave was fiercely attacked during

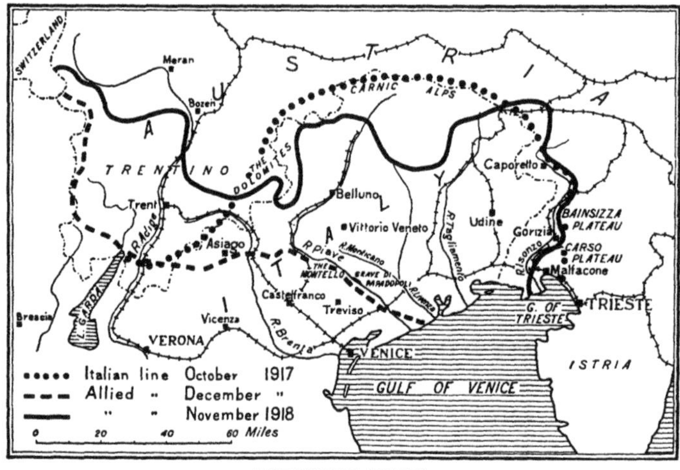

NORTHERN ITALY.

November but remained firm, and the enemy, content with their gains, at length broke off the engagement. About this time General Diaz succeeded General Cadorna as Italian commander-in-chief.

The spring of 1918 was quiet, but on 15th June the Austrians resumed the offensive with an attack upon the British 23rd and 48th Divisions on the Asiago plateau, immediately west of the river Brenta. The attack did not succeed, for the positions lost by us were promptly regained by counter-attacks. Attacks

[1] In March, 1918, he was recalled to resume command in Flanders and was succeeded by the Earl of Cavan; somewhat later the 5th and 41st Divisions returned to France.

upon the Italian lines along the Piave were at first more promising, for crossings were forced at several points. Reinforcements, however, were brought up, and these, aided by a sudden rise of the river which seriously hampered the Austrian lines of transport, retook the lost positions.

During the autumn, signs of a loss of *moral* among the Austrians began to be noted, and General Diaz, although his forces were fewer in number, decided to attempt a break through. He first ordered an attack up the valley of the Brenta and, when the enemy's reserves were thoroughly engaged in that sector, directed a general attack to the east. As part of this the Earl of Cavan, now commanding the 10th Italian Army which included the 7th and 23rd British Divisions, was ordered to cross the Piave. The river, on the front of attack, was over a mile wide, but it was broken up by numerous islands, the chief of which, the Grave di Papadopoli, was three miles long by one broad.

On the night of 23rd/24th October, the 2nd H.A.C. and the 1st R. Welch Fus., crossing in small boats, surprised the garrison and captured part of the island; next night the conquest was completed by the 7th and an Italian division. On the 27th, the 7th and 23rd Divisions, under cover of a heavy bombardment, attacked the enemy on the farther bank of the river. Bridges to connect our lines with Papadopoli had been constructed, but, beyond the island, the troops had to use fords. These were often five feet deep, and, as the river was in flood and the currents strong, many men were swept away and drowned. After a stout resistance, the passage was forced, the bridges were carried forward across the river, and the advance was continued. On the British left the 8th Italian Army was held up, and, for a time, that flank was in some danger. However, the river, still higher up, was crossed by other Italian troops, and eventually the district between us and them was cleared, and on the 28th the 8th Italian Army was able to complete its crossing. On the 29th it reached Vittorio, a very important point in the Austrian lines of communication, while the 10th Army reached the Monticano. A great wedge had thus been driven into the Austrian front, completely dividing the troops in the plains from those in the hill country to the north. The retreat rapidly degenerated into a rout, the enemy abandoning all stores, and surrendering in great numbers, often by whole units at a time. By 4th November Cavan had crossed the Tagliamento, the 6th Army, which included the British 48th Division, was on the outskirts of Trent, and Trieste had been occupied from the sea.

The Austrians had now lost at least 300,000 prisoners and 5,000 guns,[1] most of the nations which formed their straggling empire were in a state of revolution, and further resistance was hopeless. Under an armistice, concluded on 4th November, they demobilised their army, surrendered half their artillery, the bulk of their navy, and all prisoners of war, and, leaving in position all military and railway equipment, evacuated all invaded territory, as well as strips of what, till then, had formed part of their own country.

Sergt. G. Burnett (H.A.C., Educ.) was awarded the M.M. for bravery in action at Papadopoli, and Sergt. A. P. Paveley (R.F.A., Asylums) for bravery in action at Cesuna.

During 1917 Harry Carben (R.A.M.C., Tram.) died at Taranto of dysentery on 20th July, and during 1918 Charles Gristwood (R.F.A., Tram.) died of rupture on 24th January, Capt. R. P. Buxton (4th Oxf. and Bucks L.I., Educ.) was killed in action on the Asiago plateau on 15th June, and V. E. T. Salmon (2nd H.A.C., Educ.) died on 3rd November of influenza.

[1] The British 7th and 23rd Divisions alone captured 28,000 prisoners and 219 guns, and the 48th Division at least 20,000 prisoners and 500 guns.

CHAPTER XIV

British Troops in Russia.

During the war Murmansk in North Russia was greatly developed, with the help of the Allies, as a port for supplying the Russians with munitions, and, at the same time, it was connected with Petrograd by a railway some 600 miles long. In order to prevent the Germans from establishing submarine bases there and at Archangel, Allied detachments were landed in August, 1918. That at Murmansk, assisted by local levies, defeated White Finn and German detachments in several engagements, and drove them from North Karelia. The force at Archangel was also successful and advanced 200 miles up the Dwina and about 100 miles up the Vologda railway. On 18th October, our advanced troops on the Dwina were driven back, but other attacks then and early in December were beaten off with heavy loss to the enemy. In April, 1919, the Bolsheviks initiated further attacks near Archangel, and our force at Murmansk which had been unmolested for several months was also attacked. Neither attempt succeeded, but in July, some of the local levies having mutinied, the situation became so threatening that

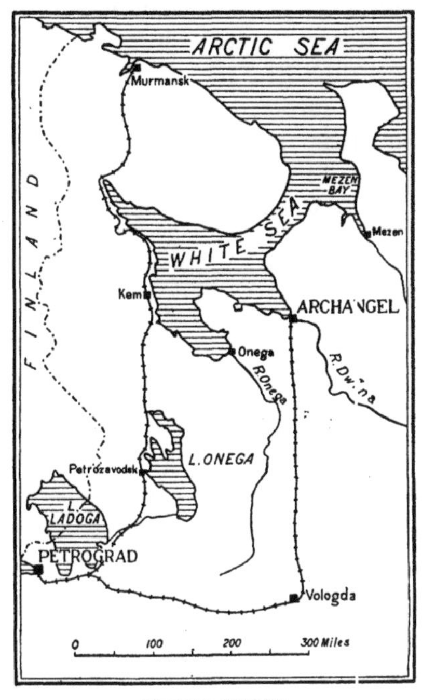

NORTH RUSSIA.

Sir Henry (afterwards Lord) Rawlinson was sent out with reinforcements. By their help the objects of the expedition were finally achieved and, as the Allied Council was opposed to further operations, Archangel was voluntarily evacuated at the end of September and Murmansk early in October.

Major A. G. Church (R.G.A., Educ.), M.C., was awarded the D.S.O. and the order of St. Vladimir (with crossed swords and bow) "for conspicuous gallantry and zeal during the operations from . . . June 8th to July 26th, 1919. When the Russian infantry were driven back . . . he pushed his guns up to the front line and restored the situation by his accurate shooting. . . . On June 22nd under heavy shelling he kept his guns in action, silencing the enemy and causing them to move their guns."

Siberia.

Serving with the Russian army was a Czecho-Slovak Corps composed for the most part of troops who had deserted to the Russians. After peace was signed between Russia and Germany this corps determined to continue fighting for the Allies. Accordingly they proposed to make their way across Siberia to Vladivostok so that they might take ship thence for Europe. Several thousand reached that port by May, 1918, but the middle and rear of the force were drawn into conflict with local Bolsheviks along the trans-Siberian railway. By the end of October they were much exhausted, but the enemy attacks then slackened and they were able to withdraw. Their withdrawal along the railway was aided and covered by a labour battalion of the Middlesex Regiment under Lt.-Col. John Ward, M.P.

CHAPTER XV.

BRITISH TROOPS IN AFRICA.

German East Africa.

GERMAN EAST AFRICA, immediately to the south of the Equator, has a coast line of about 450 miles to the Indian Ocean, extends inland for some 700 miles in the north and 400 miles in the south, and in area is about six times the size of England and Wales, with a population estimated at 8,000,000. The chief ports are Tanga (pop. 6,000) in the north and Dar-es-Salaam (pop. 24,000) in the centre, these being the termini of railways running north-westward to the Kilimanjaro district and westwards to Kigoma, which adjoins Ujiji, on Lake Tanganyika. Tabora (pop. 37,000), 250 miles east of Tanganyika, is the chief town in the interior. A belt, twenty or thirty miles wide, along the coast is flat and low-lying, but the interior gradually rises to a series of barren plateaux at a height of 4,000 or 5,000 feet. There are no roads, but only unmetalled tracks through the bush, dusty in the dry, and almost impassable in the wet seasons. Under the conditions of active service, malaria and dysentery are frequent, and the prevalence of the tsetse fly throughout much of the country makes horses or oxen almost useless for transport.

The enemy's force originally consisted of about 5,000 native troops and police, with a reserve of 3,000, all officered by Germans and under the command of General Von Lettow-Vorbeck. There were also some 1,500 European settlers. By energetic recruiting the total strength was eventually raised during the war to over 30,000 with 2,300 Europeans, the arms and ammunition for these increased numbers being chiefly supplied by the *Königsberg* (see p. 132) and other vessels which ran the weak blockade. Precise details as to our troops are lacking; they seem to have been fewer than the enemy at first, but at the height of the campaign were more numerous and better equipped. They were, however, a heterogeneous assortment, consisting of British and South African troops and settlers,

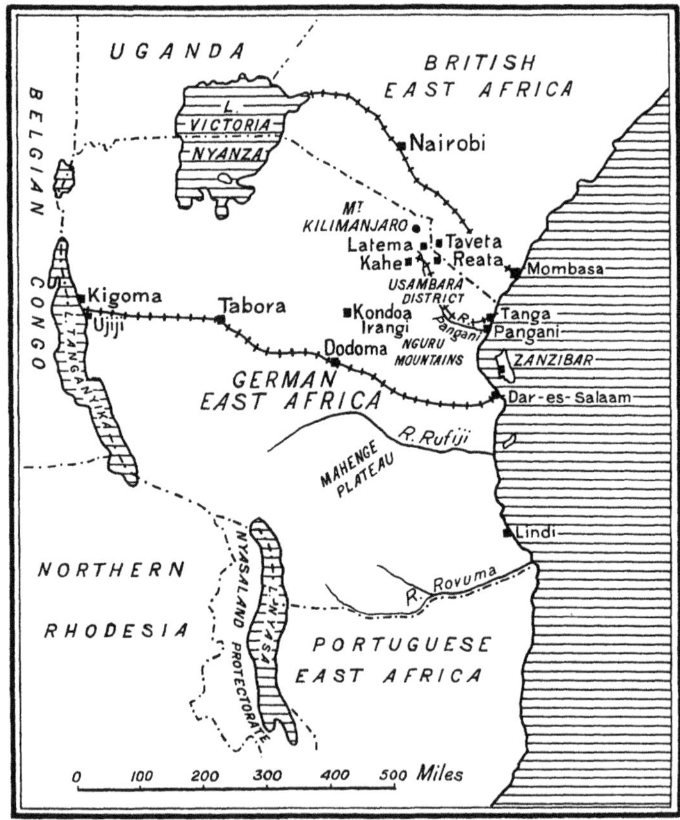

GERMAN EAST AFRICA.

native troops from many different parts of India and native troops from East Africa, Uganda, the Gold Coast, Nigeria and even the West Indies. The languages spoken included English, Dutch, Hindustani, Swahili and several West Coast and East Coast dialects. Some had uniforms almost the same as those worn by the enemy, and, to enable them to be recognised, they were provided with the familiar blue and white bands worn by the Metropolitan Police or with red armlets bearing the letters G.R.

At the outbreak of war the Germans, being the stronger, took the initiative, seized Taveta in British East Africa and, until the end of 1915, frequently raided the railway connecting Mombasa, the principal port of the colony, with Nairobi, the capital. An enemy attack on Mombasa early in October, 1914, was repulsed, and our attempts on Tanga early in November failed with nearly 1,000 casualties. The whole of the campaigning season of 1915 was taken up with raids and counter raids across the various frontiers.

After several changes, Lt.-Gen. J. C. Smuts from South Africa, succeeding Sir Horace Smith-Dorrien who, owing to ill-health, had resigned on his way out from England, was appointed commander in February, 1916, and started a vigorous offensive. In March the German position at Taveta was outflanked and seized, the Latema—Reata ridge was forced and Kahe was captured. Kondoa Irangi was seized by General Van Deventer on 19th April. While a large body of the enemy was engaged in checking our further progress to the south of the latter place, Smuts turned south-east from Kahe, cleared the Usambara district and occupied Tanga and Pangani. Belgian and British troops by July drove the enemy from the district between Lakes Victoria and Tanganyika, and at the same time Van Deventer reached the central railway at Dodoma. The Germans, who had retreated to a strong position in the Nguru Mountains, were out-flanked and driven south in August, on 3rd September Dar-es-Salaam fell and by the end of the month the coast as far south as the Portuguese frontier had been occupied. During the autumn the Germans under General Wahle were driven out of Tabora and nearly surrounded, but, with the loss of more than half their numbers, managed to break through and join the main body on the Mahenge plateau.

Our losses from sickness were very heavy. In one week in September there were 9,000 in hospital, of whom 4,000 were whites, and between October and December from 12,000 to 15,000 patients, mostly malaria cases, were evacuated from the hospitals along the central railway alone. The wastage among animals for two months from the middle of September was, horses 10,000, mules 10,000, oxen 11,000, donkeys 2,500.

In January, 1917, when Lettow-Vorbeck had been hemmed in in the south-eastern part of the colony, Smuts was recalled to take part in the Imperial Conference, and about this time all white infantry and mounted troops were withdrawn. He was succeeded by General Hoskins who, in May, was succeeded by General Van Deventer. At the end of the latter month a sortie to the north-west was met and driven back by the Belgians who, during the summer, continued their advance and in October drove a German force from Mahenge. Van Deventer, working from Lindi on the coast, defeated the Germans in several engagements in November, captured some 5,000 prisoners, and forced Lettow-Vorbeck with the remnants of his troops across the Rovuma into Portuguese territory. In 1918 the British, with assistance from the Portuguese, carried out active operations in Portuguese territory against the Germans, who sometimes made daring raids but more often fled further and further afield. One detachment under General Wahle returned northward into German East Africa and was captured. The main body eventually got into Northern Rhodesia and was there at the conclusion of hostilities when, in accordance with the Armistice, Lettow-Vorbeck was ordered by his Government to surrender.

G. A. Hogg (R.N., Tram.), gunlayer on board H.M.S. *Severn*, received the D.S.M. for his devotion to duty during the destruction of the *Königsberg* in July, 1915. A. W. Henderson (R.N., L.F.B.) was killed by an explosion on H.M.S. *Mersey* which was taking part in the attack.

Cameroon.

Cameroon was a German colony on the west coast of Africa just to the north of the equator. It has a coast

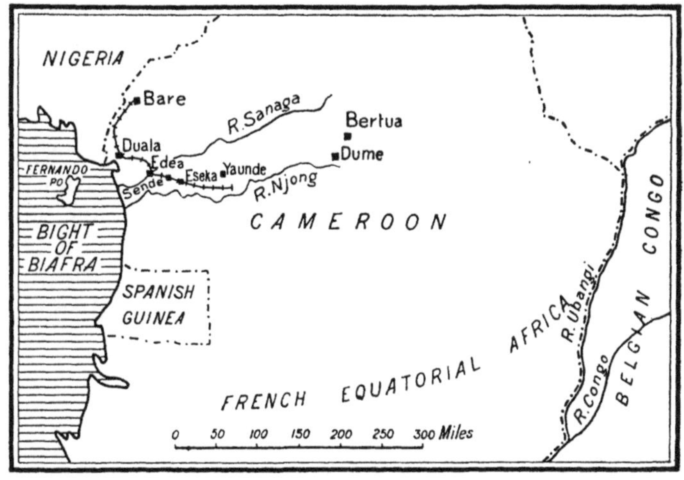

CAMEROON.

line to the Bight of Biafra of 200 miles, extends inland for an average distance of about 400 miles and has an area of nearly 200,000 square miles, with a population of about 3½ millions of whom only a few thousand are Europeans. Along the coast is a belt, 150 miles wide, of almost impenetrable forest, fringed by mangrove swamps; the interior is higher and more open. Incessant tropical rains, the absence of roads, and the dense undergrowth made active service very trying, and caused much of the fighting to be along the railways. Of these there were two, both running from Duala, the capital, one towards the east and the other towards the north. British Nigeria lies to the north-west, French Congo to the east and the latter and Spanish Guinea to the south.

Duala was occupied on 27th September, 1914, and by the end of the year the districts along the northern railway and towards Edea, which was attacked along the partly navigable rivers Sanaga and Njong, were subdued by the British and French respectively. Early in 1915 an attack on Yaunde, to which the Germans had transferred their administration, failed, and a counter-attack upon our lines of communication forced us back. Heavy rains put an end to further fighting until August when a second attack on Yaunde was organised. Allied troops captured Sende on 25th and Eseka on 30th October. French troops at Bertua and Dume and Belgian troops from the south-east co-operated, and on 1st January, 1916, Yaunde fell. Many of the enemy made their way to Spanish territory, isolated districts in the north were cleared, and by the middle of February all fighting had ended.

CHAPTER XVI.

Deaths from Disease.

In previous wars those dying from disease have usually outnumbered those killed in action. Thus, as recently as the Crimean War, the proportion was four or five to one, in the American Civil War and in the South African War it was about two to one. On the Prussian side in the Franco-German War in 1870 and on the Japanese side in the Russo-Japanese War, 1904–5, the latter proportion was reversed, but this was secured only as the result of much careful attention to the cleanliness and habits of each soldier. It was not until the Great War that, on most of the fronts, deaths from disease became negligible in comparison with those of men killed in action. This was partly due to the greater destructiveness of modern weapons, but still more to the increased skill of medical men in preventing disease. This particularly applies to the troops in western Europe. Those elsewhere were not so fortunate, and suffered from malaria in Salonica, Palestine and Mesopotamia, dysentery in Gallipoli, and various tropical diseases in Africa. Some deaths directly due to the conditions of active service abroad have been dealt with already under the different campaigns. Others occurred as follows:—

In 1914, G. V. Cross (4th Oxf. and Bucks L.I., Educ.) died at Oxford on 9th November of blood poisoning and meningitis, C. Smith (Nat. Res., Asylums) at Croydon on the 29th of ptomaine poisoning, J. A. Lund (R.F.A., Arch.) at Fulham on 12th December of blood poisoning, and F. Woodward (3rd Somer. L.I., Tram.) at Plymouth on the 14th, Lance-Corp. C. M. W. Erwood (7th Beds, Educ.) at Aldershot on the 17th, and W. Rathall (R.F.A., Tram.) on the 29th, all of pneumonia.

In 1915, G. W. Brown (9th Midx., Parks) died at Neasden on 27th January of heart failure induced by a chill, J. W. Horrigan (R.F.A., Tram.) on 7th February as the result of an accident at Mere, Wilts, M. Dacey (R.A.S.C., Tram.) on 1st May at Bexhill of pneumonia, Q.-M.-Sergt. W. H. Cox (R.E., Housing) on 26th at Camberwell of cancer, H. C. Rice (R.W. Surr., Asylums) on 14th July at Merstham of an aneurism, H. W. Turner (R.G.A., Asylums) on 24th September at Epsom of nephritis, H. J. Doughty (R.A.M.C., Educ.) at Wandsworth on 12th October after an operation, Lance-Corp. C. J. Dawes (Nat. Reserve, Tram.) at Lewisham on the 27th of pneumonia, A. Joy (24th R. Fus., Parks) at Brentwood on 21st November of liver trouble, and T. J. Middlemiss (Gren. Gds., Parks) at Belmont, Surrey, on 4th December, of consumption.

In 1916 H. J. Smith (R.M.L.I., Educ.) died of appendicitis on 12th January, J. W. S. Lowe, D.C.M. (R.F.R., L.F.B.) died at Grimsby on the 16th as the result of an accident on H.M.S. *Amphitrite*, and on the

18th W. S. Richardson (8th Essex, Tram.) died at Edmonton of heart disease. Lieut. J. Steel, B.Sc., B.A. (R.N.V.R., Educ.) on 7th February was suffocated by a fire on the ship on which he was serving, on the 14th Regt.-Sergt.-Maj. W. Rubley (Reserve Cavalry, Educ.) died of cerebro-hæmorrhage following paralysis, and on the 23rd Sergt F. Gordon (R.M.L.I., Educ.) died at Plymouth of appendicitis. C. J. Andrews (6th Lond., Tram.) died at Cambridge on 3rd April of peritonitis, Lance-Corp. G. Horsler (5th Beds, Educ.) at Lowestoft on 3rd May of phthisis, J. Cromarty (R.D.C., Tram.) on the 6th of accidental suffocation, Lieut. J. H. Aitken (7th Black Watch, Arch.) was killed at Ripon on 2nd June in a bomb accident, E. J. Coleman (R.F.C., Educ.) on the 10th in a motor cycle accident near Sunbury, W. C. Haward (R.F.A., Tram.) on the 16th in a boating accident near Stratford-on-Avon, A. Russell (4th R.W. Surr., Asylums) died at Croydon on the 17th of dropsy, W. S. Lavender (5th Lancers, Educ.) on the 24th of an aneurism, A. L. J. Hills (10th Lond., Parks) at Salisbury Plain on the 27th of cerebro-spinal meningitis, D. Johnson (15th Lond., Compr.) near Winchester on 5th August of appendicitis, W. H. Radley (19th K.R.R., Parks) at the London Hospital on the 24th of dysentery and peritonitis, F. C. Pantling (9th Midx., Parks) at Murree, India, on 6th September of appendicitis, D. A. Frame (R.F.R., Tram.) on the 9th of general debility following malaria, A. Williams (Tram.) on the 13th of pulmonary hæmorrhage, Staff Sister A. M. Russell (Q.A.A.N.R., Pub. H.) at Millbank on 5th October of septic glands following diphtheria, S. Harries (24th K.R.R., Educ.) at Ashington, Northumberland, on 30th November of pneumonia, P. L. Thorn (5th Oxf. and Bucks L.I., Tram.) in France on 11th December of ear trouble, P. J. Taylor (2nd Lond., Educ.) on the 13th at Aldeburgh of pneumonia, and Lance-Corp. W. K. Gossop (3rd Northd. Fus., Tram.) on the 27th at Sunderland of pneumonia.

In 1917 W. J. F. Day (R.E., Tram.) died at Chatham on 19th February of pneumonia, Sergt. G. G. Treacher (R. Fus., L.F.B.) was accidentally killed at Dover on 4th March, F. R. White (R.F.R., Tram.) died at Portsmouth on 21st April of pneumonia, R. J. Jobling (R.D.C., Ch. Engr.) near Weymouth on 20th July of cerebral hæmorrhage, T. S. Chaplin (R.E., Tram.) at Colchester on the 30th of paralysis, Sergt. A. E. Durban (10th Midx., Educ.) in India on 22nd August, Corp. A. Longhurst (R.E., Ch. Engr.) on 7th September of cancer, and Sergt. W. A. Stanfield (R.A.M C., Educ.) in Egypt on 1st October as the result of a motor cycle accident.

In 1918, Sergt. J. E. Bailey, M.M. (1st R. Welch Fus., Asylums) died at Manchester on 9th January of pneumonia, A. G. Poffley (R.A.M.C., Asylums) died on the 17th of duodenal ulcer, C. E. Allen (R.N.R., Tram.) on the 25th of blood poisoning, T. Davis (R.H.A., Parks) died at Meerut, India, on 5th March, Corp. H. Brown, B.Sc. (7th Midx., Educ.) in London on the 7th of cancer, A. F. Tarry (R.F.A., Tram.) on 6th April of septic poisoning, E. A. Maidment (R.G.A., Educ.) on the 16th as the result of an operation, H. W. Porter (8th E. Surr., Tram.) died in Germany on 3rd May, as the result of an accident, Sergt. E. Skingle (R.G.A., Tram.) on the 18th of heart disease, Regt. Q.-M.-S. A. H. Traylen (Labour Corps., Educ.) at Homerton on 11th June, as the result of an accident, Sergt. H. J. Carrington (10th Midx., Educ.) on 19th July as the result of a bomb accident, Lance-Corp. T. B. Tingay (R.E., Tram.) at Walton on 23rd August as the result of an explosion, J. H. Cummins (4th R. Scots Fus., Tram.) at Edinburgh on 3rd November of bronchitis, Sergt. A. J. Barringer (2/1st Surrey Yeo., Educ.) at Gort, co. Galway on 25th December, as the result of an accident.

This year was marked by two severe influenza epidemics, one in the summer (June–July) and the other in the autumn (Oct.–Nov.); a third followed in 1919 (Feb.–Mar.).[1] Those who died in 1918 included Lieut. E. R. Free (R.G.A., Educ.) at Winchester on 16th July, C. B. Horn (R.A.M.C., Educ.) at Brighton on the 17th, J. Fisher (R.E., Educ.) at Monmouth on 16th August, E. B. Clements (R.G.A., Tram.) at Tooting on 10th October, Lieut. C. G. Pearse (R.F.A., Educ.) at Luton on the 20th, J. E. Edwards (R.A.F., Educ.) on the 22nd, J. Crow (R.F.A., Ch. Engr.) at Mile End on the 25th, F. Winter (6th E. Surr., Tram.) at Agra, India, on the 31st, A. J. Gilchrist (37th Northd. Fus., Housing) at Margate on 3rd November, H. Collier (R.E., Tram.) at Kingston on the 6th, Lance-Corp. H. W. C. Davenport (25th Lond., Tram.) at Jutogh, India, on the 13th, A. G. Billson (R.N.A.S., Parks) at Queensferry on the 16th, I. H. Bonshor (R.G.A., Educ.) near Grantham on 11th December, W. H. Godfrey (3rd Essex, Parks) on the 24th, and Lieut. H. E. Shepherd (R.F.A., Educ.) at Dover on the 30th.

The deaths in 1919 from the same disease included C. Bennett (16th Manch., Stores) at Homerton on 21st January, J. M. Mace (R.E., Asylums) at Dunkirk on the 26th, Corp. J. Opie (R.A.S.C., Educ.) near Cologne, Capt. G. J. Bradley (Labour Corps, Educ.) at Camiers on 17th February, Armourer Staff-Sergt. E. J. Weall (R.A.O.C., Asylums) at Queenstown on the 18th, Capt. W. H. Swallow, O.B.E. (R.A.O.C., Educ.) at St. Omer on the 21st, B. W. F. Starling (R.N.A.S., Comp.) and H. C. Chapman (A.P.C., Solr.) on the 24th, Hon. Maj. W. A. Miller (R.A.M.C., Educ.) at Farnborough on 2nd March, A. A. Bennett (34th Lond., Ch. Engr.) at Dunkirk on the 11th, J. Cahill (R.A.M.C., Tram.) at Gibraltar on the 16th, and Corp J. S. Jones (R.A.M.C., Educ.) on 5th April.

Other deaths in 1919 from different causes included W. G. Burningham (19th Midx., Tram.) at Denmark

[1] The Council has published an account of these in *Influenza, Report by the County Medical Officer of Health* (No. 1963), price 6d.

Hill on 5th January of paralysis, Sergt. H. J. Wilcox (9th Midx., Clerk) in Mesopotamia on 10th March from the effects of an operation, Lieut. W. E. Foale (R.G.A., Arch.) at Newcastle on 1st May of erysipelas and pneumonia, W. F. D. Peters (R.A.M.C., Arch.) near Bonn on the 2nd from cerebral hæmorrhage, Sub.-Lieut. B. P. O'Hara (R.N.R., Comp.) at Malta on 14th October of pneumonia, and Capt. S. Cohen (Egyp. Labour Corps, Clerk) murdered at Cairo on 23rd November.

CHAPTER XVII.

SUMMARY.

THE numbers of the Council's staff who served in the Great War were as follows:

Department	Enlisted	Lost their lives.
Clerk of the Council	101	12
Comptroller of the Council	290	36
Chief Engineer	284	25
Architect	437	40
Solicitor	70	10
London Fire Brigade	345	27
Public Health	136	12
Estates and Valuation	87	9
Public Control	94	7
Parks	424	61
Tramways	3,507	334
Housing	100	9
Education Officer:		
Central Administrative Staff	377	39
Industrial and Special Schools	40	6
Secondary Schools and Training Colleges	28	7
Technical Institutes and Schools of Art	37	4
School Attendance Officers	117	6
Botany Scheme	5	3
Stocktakers, etc.	8	—
Schoolkeepers	235	23
Teachers	2,353	273
Stores	138	24
Parliamentary	4	1
Asylums and Mental Deficiency	943	97
Asylums Engineer	4	—
Total	10,164	1,065

The decorations won were: C.B.E. 5, D.S.O. 5, O.B.E. 14, D.S.C. 1, M.C. and two bars 1, M.C. and bar 7, M.C. 68, M.B.E. 7, Royal Red Cross 10, D.C.M. and bar 2, D.C.M. 39, D.S.M. 5, M.M. and bar 10, M.M. 125, M.S.M. 100, Medal of Military Merit 2, mentioned in despatches 313, mentioned for valuable services, etc., 11, R. Humane Socy. Cert. 1, Certificate of Merit 1, French decorations 21, Croix de Guerre (Belgian) 9, other foreign decorations 16.

In the preceding chapters it has rarely been possible to state the numbers engaged, or the losses sustained, in the different battles and campaigns. The following figures, too vast for the mind to realise in any detail, may help the reader to form some vague impression of the immensity of the conflict. The numbers of those who served from the British Empire alone were as follows: [1]

Strength of Regular Army, Reserve and Territorials on 4th August, 1914 .	733,514
England recruited during the war . .	4,006,158
Scotland	557,618
Wales	272,924
Ireland	134,202
Dominions: Canada (628,964), Australia (416,809), New Zealand (220,099), Africa (136,070), Newfoundland, etc. (23,922).	1,425,864
	7,130,280
Coloured troops: India (1,401,350, *i.e.* pre-war 239,561 and during war 1,161,789), S. Africa (92,837), W. Indies (10,000), other colonies (20,000) . . .	1,524,187
Total	8,654,467

[1] *The War Cabinet*, 1918 [Comd. 235], p. 95.

There were also Chinese and other labour units which served in France, Egypt, Mesopotamia and elsewhere.

The casualties amongst all the belligerents were as follows: [1]

Country.	Killed, including missing unless separately stated.	Missing, presumed dead.	Wounded.	Total.
Allies				
Russia	1,700,000	—	3,500,000	5,200,000
France	1,358,872	361,654	2,750,000	4,470,526
British Empire	765,483	108,346	2,090,989	2,964,818
Italy	507,169	—	*1,000,000*	1,507,169
Roumania	300,000	—	*300,000*	600,000
Serbia	300,000	—	*300,000*	600,000
Belgium	102,382	—	*200,000*	302,382
United States	53,160	1,160	179,625	233,945
Portugal	8,367	—	*16,000*	24,367
Total	5,095,433	471,160	10,336,614	15,903,207
Central Powers				
Germany	1,600,000	103,000	4,064,000	5,767,000
Austria	800,000	—	3,200,000	4,000,000
Turkey	250,000	—	*500,000*	750,000
Bulgaria	100,000	—	*200,000*	300,000
Total	2,750,000	103,000	7,964,000	10,817,000
TOTAL	7,845,433	574,160	18,300,614	26,720,207

The combined death-roll was therefore over 8,000,000, or several hundred thousand beyond the present entire population of Greater London.[2] The

[1] Exact figures are impossible as different numbers have been published at different times. The table is based on estimates prepared by the United States Army (*Times*, 4th March, 1919) as amended by other authoritative figures (*Times*, 30th Nov., 23rd and 28th December, 1918; 9th April, 6th May, 2nd Sept. and 6th Nov., 1919; 26th March, 20th April and 18th June, 1920). The figures in italics are round numbers calculated by allowing two wounded for each man killed or missing. This is a conservative estimate as the usual proportion is 2½ or even 3 to 1. The conditions in Serbia and Roumania were exceptional and a still lower estimate of the proportion of wounded to killed has been adopted.

[2] This in 1921 was 7,476,168.

total casualties approached 27,000,000, and quite probably may have been nearly 30,000,000, or about two-thirds of the population of the United Kingdom.

Only those campaigns in which the British were concerned and those incidents in which they shared have been described. Most of the main features have thus been dealt with, for, except on the eastern front in Europe, they had a part, and often an important part, in all the fighting. It is natural and right that our interest should centre in them, but the events of the war and the final victory must be regarded as a whole, not singly, nor even in relation to one country. The British Empire did not win the war, nor did France, nor Italy, nor the United States, although, if any of these had been absent, the result might have been far different; nor was any country alone in her endurance and in her sacrifices. So, when the final reckoning comes to be made, let it be remembered that Russia's losses were the heaviest, and that, but for her efforts, prolonged over two years in the face of every difficulty, the position of the Allies on the other fronts would have been most dangerous, if not impossible. For more than four years Belgium, a narrow strip excepted, was under the sway of a foreign despotism, her people were liable at any moment to heavy fines, to imprisonment and to deportation, and her industries were being impaired or even ruined. The like misfortunes befell Roumania but for a shorter time. The fate of Serbia was more terrible. After her army had been crushed by overwhelming numbers, disease and starvation swept through the country carrying off one-third of the population.[1] The sufferings of France are known, by sight or by hearsay, to all. It was on the western front that men and guns were accumulated in the greatest profusion, and it was there that the struggle was fiercest and most obstinate. For a year or more she bore the brunt of

[1] M. Savoitch, a former Serbian minister, in *Times*, 28th Dec., 1918.

the attack along a front of several hundred miles; throughout the war the fighting on the greater part fell to her lot. Her casualties, most of them incurred in this noble task, amounted to 4,470,526.[1] In the early days the enemy approached to within twenty miles of the capital, and, when driven back, lay encamped during nearly four years little more than twice that distance away. In the spring of 1918 he again closed in upon the city, which for some months was under artillery fire at long range. A belt of country, 250 miles long and twenty or thirty wide, was reduced to a desert, 1,659 communes or townships were blotted out, 2,363 others were wrecked, and 630,000 houses were destroyed or seriously damaged.[2] So many mines were ruined that the output of coal was reduced by a half, 21,000 factories were gutted, and great manufacturing centres like Lille and the Longwy district were systematically despoiled of the machinery vital to their prosperity. Deaths among civilians, by artillery in the battle zone or by aeroplanes in the back areas, were frequent.

* * * * * *

This sketch has been written so that the memory of the part taken by the Council's staff in events which called for much bravery, much endurance, much self-sacrifice, might not pass away without record, however slight. The task is now completed. On so many memorials, up and down the country, of those who fell in the Great War, it is truly written: "They died that we might live." For that example and that sacrifice no return can be adequate, but it is for each of us who survive to determine that the example and the sacrifice shall not have been wholly in vain.

[1] The British casualties on the western front were 2,719,652 (*Times*, 28th Dec., 1918).

[2] This is about the number of houses in London.

INDEX

OF NAMES OF MEMBERS OF THE COUNCIL'S STAFF MENTIONED IN THE FOREGOING PAGES

ADAM, J. G. S., 109
Adams, C. G., 53
Adams, F. W., 10
Aitken, J. H., 194
Alderton, A., 41
Allan, W., 25
Allen, C. E., 195
Allen, J. D., 179
Allender, J. H., 49
Allison, W., 26
Allum, G. A. B., 136
Almeroth, C. W., 66
Ament, E. V., 88
Ames, A. J., 49
Ames, G., M.C., 117
Amos, H., 69
Amos, J. V., 54
Andrews, C. J., 194
Andrews, E., 17
Andrews, S., 9
Angel, A. A., M.C., 124
Angus, D., 19
Aplin, C. R. S., 31
Archdeacon, T., D.C.M., 117
Archer, C., 44
Archer, F. J., 50
Archer, P. F., 102
Armes, J. G., 47
Arnold, H., 135
Ash, H. J., 44
Ashby, F., 30
Ashdown, H. G., 34
Ashley, H., 48
Aubury, J. L., 25
Auker, J. F., 127
Austin, J. R., M.M., 100
Ayles, G., 78
Ayton, W. H., 17

Babington, H. W., 35
Bailey, F., 53
Bailey, H. E., 26
Bailey, J., 24
Bailey, J. E., M.M., 41, 195
Bailey, T., 106
Bain, A. J., 66
Baker, B. R., 34
Baker, G., 7
Baker, H. W., 74
Baker, J. R., 101
Baker, S. J., 31
Baker, T. H., 158
Baldwin, E. W., 23
Barber, A. G., 101
Barker, C. T., 65
Barker, R. H., 86
Barklamb, E. C., 30
Barnard, A. H. B., 163
Barnard, E., 158
Barnes, A. D., M.C., 86
Barnes, C. H., 52
Barnes, F., 87
Barnes, S. G., 42
Barrett, J. F. B., 101
Barringer, A. J., 195
Bartram, H. F., 179
Bass, W. L., M.C., 121
Basterfield, W. J., 16
Bastian, C. J. C., 139
Batchelor, A. C., M.M., 61, 66
Batchelor, H. J., 123
Bateman, C. J., 180
Baxter, K. L., 101
Bayliss, T., 123
Beale, R. C., 25
Beardmore, H. O., 48
Beattie, E. A., M.B.E., 180
Beaumont, A. T. F., 158
Beaumont-Edmonds, W. G., 48
Beavis, A. G., 117
Bedwell, T. W., 66
Belben, H. J., 170
Belcher, D. C., 180
Bell, G. F., M.M., 69
Bell, W., 16
Bence, S. R., M.M., 53
Bennett, A. A., 196
Bennett, A. E., 73

Bennett, C., 196
Benson, E. T., 17
Bentley, H. F., 51
Bernard, P. C., 163
Berridge, P., 180
Best, S. J., 49
Bevan, M. W., 41
Beverley, W. W., 48
Bick, P. A., 45
Bickmore, A., 25
Bilcliffe, B. L., 30
Billson, A. G., 196
Birch, H., 76
Bird, W. F., D.C.M., 157
Bishop, C. W., 54
Bishop, H. E., 109
Bishop, W., 88
Bissley, W. H., 44
Blake, C. S., 157
Blake, F. S., 41
Blake, J. E., 137
Blanchard, F., 157
Blay, S. G., 90
Blunt, E. L., 127
Boden, S. S., 50
Bolt, A., 139
Bonfield, S. M. C., 87
Bonshor, I. H., 196
Boot, S. H., 51
Boucher, S. J., 127
Boughton, W. C. R., 23
Bown, V., 73
Boxall, G. T., 25
Boyes, R. T., M.C., 107
Boys, C. H., 135
Bradbury, A., 62
Bradford, I. W., 10
Bradley, G. J., 196
Braham, R. W., M.M., 34
Brawn, W., D.C.M., 43
Braybrooke, J. A., 33
Brazil, H. C., 89
Brereton, A. E., M.M., 34
Brewer, R. E., 49
Brice, H. G., 54
Briggs, F. H. W., M.M., 100
Bright, A. J., 88
Brill, W. P., 87
Brinklow, W. J., 101
Bristow, R., M.M., 65
Bristowe, A. E., 44
Broad, A. E., 106
Brook, F. C., 74
Brooker, F. N., 66
Brooker, G., 74
Brooker, W. J., 137
Broom, T. H., 16
Brown, A. I., 72
Brown, C., M.M., 86
Brown, E. C., 74
Brown, G. W., 193
Brown, H., 195
Brown, L. F., 107
Brown, S. N., 117
Brownsword, A. H., 65
Brunning, C. J., 62
Bryant, B. T., 62
Bryce, M. S., 16
Buck, A. G., M.M., 72
Buckby, H. F., 25
Buckley, J. C., M.M., 85
Bulcraig, F. J., M.M., 29
Bull, F. G., M.C., 50, 64
Bull, G., 44
Bull, G. A., 123
Burford, W. J., 57
Burgess, A., 35
Burnett, A. W. K., M.C., 116
Burnett, G., M.M., 184
Burningham, W. G., 196
Burrows, W. A., 48
Burton, H. S., 25
Burton, T. W., 66
Burwood, H. W., 101
Butcher, R. V., 101
Butland, R., 109
Butler, J. E., 26
Butler, S. H., 158
Butler, T. B., 45
Butler, W., 107
Butlin, W. A., 34
Buxton, R. P., 184

Cahill, J., 196
Cairns, J. C., D.C.M., 74, 99
Cameron, H. S., 45
Campion, E., M.M., 87
Campion, W. J., M.C., 126
Canivet, A. F., 34
Cannard, H. E., 30
Cappleman, W., 48
Carben, H., 184
Carey, E., 25
Carey, J., 16
Carne, J. R., 88
Carpenter, E. S., 19
Carpenter, H., 139
Carr, W. H., 76
Carrington, H. J., 195
Carritt, W. E., 101
Carson, F. M., 25
Carter, H. A., 129
Cater, C. D., 17
Challen, F., D.C.M., 180

Challice, C., 30
Challis, W., 135
Chalmers, J. C., M.M., 53
Chamberlain, C. J., 78
Chaney, A., 74
Channel, W., 88
Chaplin, H. H., M.M., 70
Chaplin, T. S., 195
Chapman, F. C., 135
Chapman, H. C., 196
Chappell, A. E. W., 25
Chauvin, E., 180
Chesterman, W. T., 50
Chick, A. G., 62
Chick, T. P., 35
Childs, J., 157
Chitty, H. H., 10
Chorley, P., 66
Christiansen, H. L. J., 23
Church, A. G., D.S.O., M.C., 186
Churcher, E., 147
Churchill, M. W., 73
Clark, A., 49
Clark, A., 129
Clark, C. W., 106
Clark, G., M.C., 91
Clark, P., 111
Clark, S., 23
Clark, W., 78
Clarke, B. E., 47
Clarke, C., 17
Clarke, F. W., 19
Clarke, J. A., 48
Clarkson, G. A. J., 74
Cleall, P. C., 114
Clements, A. A., 165
Clements, E. B., 196
Clifford, W., 88
Clifton, H. C. J., 66
Cohen, J. I., 73
Cohen, S., 197
Colborne, A. C., 66
Cole, D. A., 44
Cole, H. A., 42
Cole, W. H. D., 117
Coleman, C. M., 49
Coleman, E. J., 194
Collier, H., 196
Collins, A. H., M.C., 116
Colverd, W. J., 73
Comyns, A. P., M.C., 99
Conley, D., 179
Connolly, V. L., M.C., 87
Cook, A., 41
Coombes, G. W., 66
Coombes, H. F., 101
Cooper, A., 31
Cooper, H. W., 53
Cope, A. B., 44
Cope, J. H. B., 44
Cordery, H. T., 19
Corkett, G. E., 45
Coster, A. E., 21
Cotter, C. J., 47
Counter, J. H., M.M., 43, 81
Coventry, A. E., 31
Cowan, W. H., 17
Coward, L. G., 30
Cox, A., 157
Cox, E., 78
Cox, G., 25
Cox, W. H., 193
Cracknell, W. W., M.M., 65
Crane, H., 45
Crawley, A., 87
Cresswell, T. E., M.C., 44
Cripps, A. D., 180
Cromarty, J., 194
Cronyn, E. M., D.C.M., 52
Cross, G. V., 193
Crow, J., 196
Cummins, J. H., 195
Curry, J. W., 135
Curtis, W., 16
Curtis, W. S., 25
Cutler, M., 34

Dacey, M., 193
Dainty, E. J. P., D.C.M., 64, 89
Daly, D., 49
Daly, R. W., 49
Dancer, A. C., M.C., 46, 77
Daniel, W. G., 88
Dare, E. C., D.C.M., 114
Darkens, C. R., 54
Davenport, H. W. C., 196
Davey, W. A. G., 30
Davies, D. J., M.C., 99
Davies, E. J., 42
Davis, E., 42
Davis, G. D., 135
Davis, H. G., 9
Davis, J. G., 78
Davis, L. A., 88
Davis, T., 195
Davis, W., 50
Davis, W. H., 88
Davis, W. W., 27
Dawes, A. E., D.C.M., 178
Dawes, C. J., 193
Dawson, O. S., 19
Day, C. S., 106
Day, W. J. F., 195
Daysh, F. A. G., 9

Dean, H. H., 109
Dearing, C. A., M.M., 85, 102
Denly, C. J., 45
Despicht, L. T., M.C., 55
Devis, A. S., M.M., 41, 123
Diamond, F., 87
Dibble, T. H., 25
Dickens, C. A., 9
Dickens, W. G., 24
Dimond, L., 76
Dixon, F. C., 27
Dobson, G. M., 179
Dobson, W., 180
Dockett, C. J. F., 163
Dodman, A. G., D.S.C., 140
Doherty, E. H., 179
Dolan, F., 101
Dolan, F. A., 157
Doling, G., 138
Doolin, M., 34
Dormon, G., 52
Doughty, H. J., 193
Downes, B., 108
Downham, G. E., 62
Downie, G. H., 33
Drewett, F. F., 101
Drewett, H. W., 111
Drury, S. C. P., D.C.M., 31, 99
Duck, L. S., 35
Duggan, C., 88
Duncton, S. V., 108
Dunford, H. J., 51
Dunning, B. A. M., 173
Duprès, E. C., 117
Durban, A. E., 195
Dussauze, H. W., 30
Dyer, T. E., 87

Earl, F. W., 109
Eason, H., 30
Eaves, T., M.M., 55, 78
Ebbetts, S. A., 41
Ediker, H., 89
Edlin, B. A., 11
Edwards, C. H., 42
Edwards, J. E., 196
Edwards, J. P., 49
Edwards, P. H., 45
Edwards, T. A., M.C., 126
Elliott, B., 57
Elliott, F. E., 127
Elliott, R., 42
Elliott, V. M., 34
Elliott, W. L., 53
Ellner, W. T., 23
Entwistle, W. S., 139
Erwood, C. M. W., 193
Etherington, J., M.M., 65
Eton, E., D.S.O., 29
Evans, J., M.C., 119
Everett, J. G., 157
Everitt, W., 23

Fairley, P. E., D.C.M., 29, 34
Falcon, F., 157
Farley, S. J., 30
Farley, W. A., 10
Farrow, M., 107
Fasham, S. L., 67
Faulks, E., 30
Favell, A., 35
Fell, W. J., 52
Ferguson, H. H. E., 89
Ferry, W. H., 24
Field, F. H., 137
Field, H. N., 81
Field, W. J., M.C., 69, 73
Filbee, W. J., 158
Findon, R., 106
Finnessy, E. P., 45
Fish, W. F., 179
Fisher, H. W., M.C., 74
Fisher, J., 196
Fisher, J. W., D.C.M., 29
Fitzgerald, P., 74
Foale, W. E., 197
Foley, J., 41
Ford, P., 100
Forse, A., 25
Forse, W. F., 10
Foss, T., 16
Fox, C. J., 44
Fox, T. E., 91
Fox, W., 31
Foy, L., 21
Frame, D. A., 194
Free, E. R., 196
Freeman, F. B., 41
French, S. A., 100
Friday, L. J., 66
Froome, C. W., D.C.M., 34, 42
Fuller, H., 26

Gaiger, A. A., 135
Gaskell, A. J., 127
Gatehouse, H. C., 129
Gaunt, G., 78
Gaywood, G. A., 49
Gebbett, J., 101
Geis, B. A., 47
George, J. A., 54
Gethin, P. F., 34
Gilchrist, A. J., 196
Gilroy, J. J., 78

Gimble, E., 31
Gleadall, J., 47
Goddard, W. E., 73
Godfrey, W. H., 196
Golding, F. G., 52
Golle, C. V., 89
Good, S. C., 7
Goodwin, D. F., 54
Goodwin, J. A., 7
Gordon, F., 194
Gordon, G. H., 49
Gosford, W. G., 179
Goss, S., 108
Gossop, W. K., 194
Gostling, H., 21
Gould, P. J., 30
Gray, A. A. W., D.C.M., 29
Gray, G. E. F., 65
Gray, J., 25
Green, L., 52
Green, W. H., 109
Greenstreet, T. W., M.C., 178
Greenwood, A. G., 62
Greygoose, F., 16
Griffin, F. G., 23
Griffiths, E., D.S.M., 157
Griffiths, W., 86
Grist, R. G., 135
Gristwood, C., 184
Groombridge, F. W., 53
Groves, L., 88
Gunter, T. J., M.M., 81
Guy, H. C., 88
Guyver, G., 23

Haggis, P., 10
Hale, J. D., 21
Hale, R. A., 109
Hales, B. C., D.C.M., 164
Hall, J. S., 124
Halliday, F. A., 138
Hambly, B., 23
Hamer, W. H., 66
Hammond, A. J., 25
Hampton, A. H., 106
Hancock, A. C., M.C., 40, 54, 64
Hancock, E. T. G., M.C., 126
Hancock, J. L., 66
Handley, H. E., 25
Hannaford, W. G. N., 48
Hard, W. T. S., 101
Harden, W. F., 140
Harland, G., 66
Harling, A. T., 48
Harries, S., 194
Harris, C. T., 54
Harris, F. V., M.C., 164
Harris, H. C., 42
Harrison, E. S., 9
Hart, A. R., 54
Hart, E., 30
Harvey, H. V., M.M., 127
Haselden, E. A., 42
Haslum, D., 45
Hatcher, E. W., 41
Hattam, H. C., 76
Hatton, F. J., 102
Havell, E. T., 30
Haward, A. E., 49
Haward, W. C., 194
Haycraft, L. C., 49
Hayes, E. W. C., 118
Haynes, H. H., 88
Hayward, H. E., M.M., 81
Head, E. A., 45
Head, W. A., 48
Healey, C. F., M.C., 43
Heard, E. H., 124
Heatly, H. F., 19
Helps, J. W., 139
Helyar, S. E., 76
Hemming, F. T., 136
Hems, E., 101
Henderson, A. W., 191
Henderson, W. R., 16
Henstridge, C. L., M.C., 116
Hentsch, A. E., 47
Hepworth, P. W., 136
Herd, C., 106
Heritage, J., M.M., 106
Herriott, A., 25
Heskett, J., 124
Hicks, J. G., 17
Higginson, G. N., 53
Hill, J., 101
Hill, S. E., 35
Hills, A. L. J., 194
Hills, F., M.M., 47, 99
Hird, W. H., 47
Hitchcock, C. J., 162
Hoare, H. J., 158
Hodges, H. S., 78
Hodgkinson, C., 33
Hogg, G. A., D.S.M., 191
Hollingsworth, F. E., 147
Hollins, H. J., 65
Holloway, F., 67
Holmes, P. W. T., 91
Holt, G. W. J., 45
Hood, G., 23
Hook, E., 109
Horn, C. B., 196
Hornsby, W., 74
Horrigan, J. W., 193

Horsler, G., 194
Horwood, H. R., 52
Howard, S. F., 86
Howes, R. A., 101
Howes, W. J., 162
Huddart, A., 101
Huggins, J., 19
Hughes, H. G., 147
Hughes, J. E., 69
Humphrey, M., 42
Humphreys, M. M., 16
Humphreys, W. A., M.M., 74
Huntley, E. E., M.M., 127
Hutchings, C. E., 157
Hutchins, M. B., 129
Hutson, F. W., 89
Hyde, F. C., 13
Hygate, W. C., 162
Hymans, L. H., 76

Ingram, A., 30
Ireland, A., 86

Jackaman, T. T., 109
Jackson, A., 27
Jackson, F. W., D.S.O., 87
Jackson, H., 26
Jackson, T. W., 136
Jackson, W., 166
Jacobs, W. T. G., M.S.M., 123
Jago, G. F., 173
James, G., 30
James, S. W., 147
Jarman, W., M.M., 81
Jarratt, H. W. E., 19
Jeanes, J. V., M.M., 29, 52
Jefcoate, F., M.B.E., 147
Jeffery, C. J., 48
Jeffries, H. H., 16
Jenkins, G. A., 23
Jennings, S. J., 101
Jessop, R., 45
Jewell, C. J. L., 51
Jewers, W. F., 101
Jeynes, T. G., 41
Jibb, A. H., 106
Jobling, R. J., 195
Johnson, D., 194
Johnson, E. R., 78
Johnson, H. C., 125
Johnson, J. W., 86
Johnston, H., M.M., 77
Johnston, W., 65
Jolly, E. R., 76
Jones, A. C., 139
Jones, G. H., 106
Jones, H. F. C., 66
Jones, J. G., 31
Jones, J. S., 196
Jones, R., 101
Jones, S. W., 26
Joy, A., 193
Joyce, H. G., 76
Juniper, C. W. H., 23

Keane, F. J., 89
Keeler, A. S., 135
Keeler, F. W., 76
Keeling, A. E., 25
Keenan, D., M.M., 65
Kelcey, H., 49
Kelly, J., 88
Kelsey, H. C., 88
Kemp, R. E., 89
Kenchatt, C. R., 17
Kennedy, W., 101
Kenny, L. H., 34
Kenyon, H. T. J., 74
Ketcher, P. T., 34
Key, G. W., 78
Keys, W., 24
Keyworth, J. G., 66
King, A. J., 30
King, C. W., 53
King, D. G., 158
King, F., D.C.M., 52
King, G. O., 107
King, H. A., 174
King, W. E., 130
Kingham, F. A., 108
Kirby, E., 35
Kirk, R., 7
Kirkby, G., D.C.M., 162
Kirkcaldy, D., 41
Kirkwood, J., 23
Kitchen, A. E., M.M., 29
Klein, G., 25
Knight, H. A. W., 48
Knights, J. P., 11
Knowles, E. H., M.M., 100
Knowles, J., 11

Laird, W. J., 81
Lait, F., 7
Lambe, F. W., 53
Lambert, F. C., 44
Lamont, J., 91
Lane, H. V., 101
Lang, S. D., 55
Lassetter, A. E., 55
Laurence, N., 49
Lavender, W. S., 194
Laver, E. C., 34
Law, C. W., 87

Lawrance, H. E., 57
Lawrance, H. W., 49
Lawrence, W., 135
Lediard, F. S. N., 109
Lee, C. J., 78
Legg, W. A., 86
Leighton, H. E., 89
Lenney, G. K., 74
Lever, J., M.C., 41
Leverington, J., 41
Lewin, H. G., 106
Lewis, E., 54
Lewis, S. A., 101
Lewis, W. B., 73
Licence, R. E., 105
Liddle, W. S., 17
Lilburn, H., 81
Lingwood, J. A., M.M., 77
Livingstone, W., 135
Lloyd, R., 180
Lock, H. J., 24
Long, E. D., 157
Long, S. F., 87
Long, W. E., 102
Longhurst, A., 195
Longley, E. J. P., 50
Lord, E. W., 33
Lowe, J. W. S., D.C.M., 193
Lower, S., 42
Lowes, W. A., 45
Lucas, M. T., 160
Luckhurst, W. A. V., 25
Luker, A., 9
Lund, J. A., 193
Lunn, R. H., 160
Lynes, N., 48

McAlister, H. P., 73
Macartney, V. J., 24
McBean, J. R., 107
Mace, J. M., 196
McGrath, J., 162
McKimmie, A. I., 147
McMillan, R. A., 49
Macrae, F. M., 24
McShane, H., 17
Madden, A. J., 74
Maddocks, H. T., M.C., 98
Maidment, E. A., 195
Maidment, H. G., 47
Makeham, E. N., 69
Malcolm, G., 17
Maley, R. J. H., 25
Mallpress, V. K., 25
Malone, T. J., M.C., 124
Mapham, N., D.C.M., 26
Marks, L. M., 50
Marsh, H., 30
Marshall, J. R., 27
Marshall, P. S. T., 7
Marson, H. J. R., 158
Martin, A., 44
Martin, A. G., 11
Martin, C. E. J., 17
Martin, E. W., M.M., 114
Martin, P., 129
Martin, P. J., 65
Martin, S. E., 107
Martin, W. E., 102
Mason, H. W. K., 102
Matthews, J. E., 26
Maxim, W., 19
May, A. W., 106
May, W. J., 88
Mayer, L. J., 35
Mears, A. E., 19
Medhurst, R. W., 135
Meredith, E. S., 31
Middlemiss, T. J., 193
Miles, F. J., 162
Miller, A. E., 101
Miller, C., 76
Miller, E. S., 158
Miller, H., 44
Miller, I. J., 138
Miller, W. A., 196
Mills, J. C., 48
Mills, W. T., M.M., 65
Minchin, W. C., D.C.M., 20
Mitchell, A. G., 7
Mitchell, C. J., 49
Monkhouse, J. A., 53
Moody, T., 41
Moore, E., 23
Moore, E. C., 129
Moore, E. W., 11
Moore, G., 23
Morgan, E. T., 33
Morgan, F., M.C., 105
Morgan, G. H., 157
Morley, C. J., 10
Morris, A. E., 172
Morris, C. C. B., M.C., 41
Morton, C., 31
Moss, R. C., 129
Moth, E. S., 16
Mott, W. J., 19
Moxley, G. A. C., 41
Murrell, F., 158
Muscutt, B. W., 127

Nash, W. H., M.M., 34
Neate, F. B., 163
Nevey, F., 127

New, J., 139
Newbold, R. H., 45
Newton, A. E., 62
Newton, W. E., 62
Nicholl, R. A., M.C., 75
Norby, C. P., 74

Oates, H. P., 76
Obendorf, H. P., M.M., 123
O'Flynn, D. T., 108
O'Hara, B. P., 197
Olney, A., 158
O'Meara, A. T., 30
Opie, J., 196
Ore, J. F., 49
Orrin, J., M.M., 72
Osborn, H., 165
Oswald, H. R., M.C., 126
Otton, J. W., D.C.M., 13
Overton, H. A., 48
Owen, F. J., 135
Owens, J. B., 44

Page, A., 48
Page, H., 89
Page, H. T., 87
Pain, C. L., 140
Palmer, C. E., 53
Palmer, E. H., 19
Palmer, L., 48
Pantling, F. C., 194
Pardew, J. R., 66
Pardoe, C. H., 88
Parker, G. W., 88
Parker, H., 25
Parkes, W., D.S.O., M.C., 43, 105, 126
Parkington, S. A., 33
Parks, H., 78
Parry, D., M.S.M., 130
Parry, T. E., 50
Parsons, T., 101
Partridge, W. I., 179
Pascoe, J. T., 23
Patterson, G. O., 48
Patterson, J. F., 73
Paveley, A. P., M.M., 184
Pavitt, G., 89
Payne, H. J., 160
Payne, R., 26
Peake, W. J., 100
Pearce, F., 42
Pearce, J., 23
Pearse, C. G., 196
Pearson, C. E., 25
Pearson, G. F., 48
Pearson, J., 88
Pearson, W., 26
Peel, T. W., 47
Penfold, G., 73
Percival, G. A., 117
Perriman, W., 157
Perry, E. J., 34
Perry, H. H., 124
Perryman, A. G., 16
Pert, L. H., 66
Peters, A., 173
Peters, O. H., 44
Peters, W., 53
Peters, W. F. D., 197
Peterson, F. W., 49
Petherick, J. E., 25
Petrie, H. L., 44
Phenix, A. P., 53
Philips, A. M., 158
Philpott, S. J. F., M.C., 57
Pike, E. C., 127
Pikett, O. J., 100
Pitt, T. G., 19
Plater, W. J., 10
Plumb, A. S., 31
Plummer, C. H., 62
Plumridge, W. J., 101
Poate, H. J., 129
Pocock, F. C., 45
Poffley, A. G., 195
Pollard, P. J. W., M.M., 100
Pollock, W., 107
Ponting, E. W., 138
Ponton, H. F., 65
Poole, F., M.C., 75
Pope, T. C., 49
Porter, E. R., 49
Porter, H. W., 195
Potter, G. F., 129
Potter, S. H., 49
Potter, W. J., 74
Power, W. J., 54
Powlesland, J. W. W., M.M., 48
Pragnell, A. E., 163
Prentice, A., M.M., 34
Price, W. E., 124
Priest, S., 44
Prior, F., 55
Proctor, A. D. G., 42
Prophet, C., 78
Pugh, H. G., 25

Quick, H. M. F., 34
Quilter, F. W., 27
Quinlan, E., 101

Radley, W. H., 194
Raffle, A. B., M.C., 47

Rafter, J., 17
Rammage, F. B., 101
Rapson, H. T., 100
Rathall, W., 193
Rawlings, J. E., 135
Raymond, C. A., 49
Reardon, L. A., 117
Reed, W. J., 81
Rees, H. G., 48
Reeve, A., 48
Reeve, W. R., M.C., 180
Reilly, D., 16
Relf, W. J., 74
Reynolds, J., 109
Rice, H. C., 193
Rice, W. C., 42
Richards, A., 88
Richards, A. E., 109
Richards, J., 139
Richardson, F., 101
Richardson, H. B., 30
Richardson, W. S., 194
Ridgewell, A., 42
Ridlington, A. A., 23
Riley, A. A., M.C., 64
Rivers, P. H., 31
Rixon, I. C., 86
Rizzi, C. L., 23
Roake, A., D.S.M., 139, 157
Roberts, A. W., 34
Roberts, C. H. H., M.C., 48
Roberts, T., 23
Robinson, J., 45
Robson, H. C., 77
Rolfe, G. E., 33
Romer, G. E., 19
Rose, A. G., 33
Rose, E. A., D.C.M., 76
Rose, T., 44
Rosen, J., 129
Rotenberg, B., 62
Rowe, J. H., 26
Rowland, W. G., 41
Rowson, T. H., 48
Rubley, W., 194
Rushton, F., 25
Rushworth, T. S., 48
Russell, A., 194
Russell, A. H., 35
Russell, A. M., 194
Russell, C. E., 21
Russell, F., 48
Russell, S., 157
Ryan, J., 10

Salmon, H. J., 129
Salmon, V. E. T., 184
Sampford, F. M., 42
Samuels, A. F., 21
Sanders, H. J., 101
Sanderson, C. A., 57
Sapsworth, G. W., 54
Sarll, A. B. C., 16
Saunders, F. J. B., 52
Saunders, G., 57
Savage, B. A., 62
Scarf, A. W., 88
Scott, F. S., 89
Scowcroft, J., 62
Scutt, S. V., 44
Seal, A., 19
Seaman, S., M.M., 105
Searle, G. A. E., 27
Selman, P. St. C., 48
Sevier, T. J., M.M., 51
Shea, W. D., 81
Shearing, A. R., 16
Shears, R., 41
Shepherd, A. J., 23
Shepherd, H. E., 196
Sherard, P., 100
Shipton, C. W., 42
Shrewsbury, J., 31
Shrimpton, C. W., M.M., 117
Shrimpton, J. J., 26
Sibbitt, B., 107
Siebert, S. P., 76
Simmonds, W., 17
Simmons, R. E., 89
Simons, H. J., 30
Simons, J. E., 41
Simons, L., M.C., 55
Simpson, S., M.M., 47
Sizeland, C., 49
Skeggs, J., 33
Skingle, E., 195
Skipp, W. J., 74
Smith, C., 193
Smith, F. W. A., 76
Smith, G. G., 180
Smith, H. J., 193
Smith, O. J. T., 13
Smith, W. H., 87
Smithers, W. J., 89
Smythe, J., 34
Snelgar, J. T., M.B.E., 173
Spencer, L. K., M.C., 98
Spencley, F., 66
Spicer, G. H., 108
Spowage, P. H., M.M., 100
Springbett, G. T., 48
Squires, W. G., 26
Stacey, F. C., M.C., 87
Stagnell, H., 62

Stainton, R. M., 41
Stanbrough, E. G., 55
Standerwick, E. W., 106
Stanfield, W. A., 195
Stannard, G. W., 47
Stanton, F. H., 22
Starling, B. W. F., 196
Steadman, A. C., 87
Steel, J., 194
Sterry, A. W., 45
Steven, A., 50
Stevens, A. E., 52
Stevens, H. J., 20
Stevens, R. W., 107
Stevenson, J. C., 117
Stiff, W. T. F., M.M., 111
Stiller, E. M., 166
Stockdale, E. L. J., 42
Stokes, J. H., M.C., 19
Stone, F. N., M.C., 86
Stower, W. E., 50
Stretton, E. W., 7
Strugnell, E., M.M., 100
Sturtridge, F., 34
Suckling, A. J., 109
Summers, R. R., 66
Sutton, P. T., 117
Swainsbury, W., 34
Swallow, W. H., O.B.E., 196
Swanson, E., 74
Swindells, S., 180
Symons, A., 165

Tagg, C. W., 89
Tarry, A. F., 195
Taylor, F. H. H., 54
Taylor, J. H., 44
Taylor, J. H., D.C.M., 46
Taylor, L. T., 35
Taylor, P. J., 194
Taylor, T. H., 101
Templeman, W. J., 163
Terrell, V. J., 41
Terrett, J. C., 25
Tester, H., M.M., 123
Thomas, A. J., 106
Thomas, E. G., 89
Thomas, J. G., 88
Thomas, T., 87
Thompson, J., M.M., 48
Thorn, H., D.C.M., 88
Thorn, P. L., 194
Thornton, H. V., 147
Thorpe, T. V., 66
Thynne, W. J., 7
Tichener, H. O., 123
Tigg, T. H., 76
Tilney, A. J., D.C.M., 7, 31
Timpson, W. M., 87
Tingay, T. B., 195
Tinniswood, A., 123
Titcomb, E. J., 49
Toby, J., 101
Todd, J. W., 147
Todman, C. V., 147
Tongue, A. L., 108
Tonkin, T. S., 180
Toole, A. J., 16
Toseland, F. A., 160
Tott, J., 24
Tovey, R. C., 109
Townsend, F. T., 74
Townsend, S. H., 30
Traylen, A. H., 195
Treacher, G. G., 195
Treadwell, G. R., 172
Tremeer, S. C., 66
Trevett, F., M.M., 55
Trew, E. A., 49
Troke, A. J., 101
Trotman, F. W., 49
Truman, T. C., 106
Trumble, W. A., D.C.M., 160, 166
Tuffey, W., 158
Turk, G. D., 67
Turner, B. G., 30
Turner, H. C., 25
Turner, H. D., 88
Turner, H. W., 193
Turner, T. W., 76
Tysoe, H., 88

Udall, W. G., 65

Vale, A., 78
Vaughan, R. W. W., 87
Veaser, H. W., 45
Veasey, A. V., 117
Vellensworth, H. J. A., 129
Vince, E. W., 54
Voak, F. H., 108

Waddingham, J., 139
Wade, E. H., M.C., 164 *n.*
Waite, C. W., 136
Waite, J. G. J., 33
Wakeford, S. T., 66
Wale, S. J., 66
Walker, A., 172
Walker, C., 16
Walker, J., 9
Walker, J. A., 53
Walker, J. S., 30
Walpole, C. A. W., 42

Walsh, S. B., 27
Walton, P., 44
Wardley, M. E., 65
Wareham, F. W., 41
Warren, A., 52
Warren, A. F., 47
Warren, H., 88
Warry, J. L., 87
Waterhouse, T. S., 25
Waterland, D., 25
Watkins, F., 127
Watkins, T. F., M.M., 46
Watson, S. T., 164
Watts, P. F., M.C., 80
Weall, E. J., 196
Webb, A. J., 17
Webb, H., 89
West, C. E., 163
West, W., 157
West, W. F., 23
Weston, A. V., 48
Weston, F. G., 117
Wheatcroft, F. G., 86
White, C., 27
White, E. V., 135
White, F. R., 195
White, G. T., 129
White, H. E. L., 33
White, H. J. F., 16
White, J., 73
White, W. G., 66
Whiteley, F. J., 44
Whitfield, W. P., 89
Whitlock, E. W., 138
Whittam, J., 24
Whitwell, H. C. C., 24
Wholey, F., 48
Whybrow, E., 101
Wilby, A. C., 109
Wilcox, H. J., 197
Wild, J., D.C.M., 99
Wilkinson, W. A., 89
Willcock, T. H. G., 180
Willcocks, G. J., M.M., 117
Willey, L., M.M., 47
Williams, A., 194
Williams, D. J., 76
Williams, H., 41
Williams, L. H. T., 31
Williams, P. T., 66
Williams, R. B., M.M., 114
Williams, S. M., 66
Williams, V., 65
Williams, W. A., 57
Willis, W. F. B., 44
Willmer, R. A. P., M.M., 100
Wills, R. D., M.M., 65
Wilson, C. F., 111
Wilson, W., 158
Wilton, A. E., 19
Winbush, E. T., 76
Winter, F., 196
Winter, J. F., 129
Wiscombe, F., 107
Withey, A. A., 90
Wood, H. O., 47
Wood, R. A., 86
Wood, R. T., 106
Woodcock, J., 48
Woodhead, M. H., 23
Woodhouse, F., 49
Woods, A. W., 136
Woods, J. W., M.C., 55, 87
Woodward, F., 193
Woodward, J. W. H., 165
Woolley, H. E., 88
Worner, P. S., 45
Wright, A., 130
Wright, A. S. T., 66
Wright, E. A., 66
Wright, G., 33
Wright, L. N., 100
Wrigley, J., 76
Wybrow, G. E., 109
Wyllie, R. T. M., 16
Wynn, J., 78
Wynne, J. A., 35

Yalden, E. C., M.C., 117
Yates, J., 7
Yeldham, E. C., 127
York, T., 10
Young, G., 89

Zoller, H. S., 69
Zoller, V., 106

APPENDIX

RECORD OF WAR SERVICE

NOTE.—*The names of those who died while on active service are marked* *

DEPARTMENT OF THE CLERK OF THE COUNCIL

Alexander, Sydney George (1914–19); Lieutenant, R.A.O.C.; France 19 months, Salonica 2 years 3 months.

Alliston, Henry Richard James (1914–16); Bombardier, R.G.A.

Arkell, William Orace Richard Wickens (1914–19); Private, Middlesex Rgt.; India and Mesopotamia 4 years 6 months.

Attwooll, Arthur Edward (1914–19); Corporal, R. W. Kent Rgt. and 54th Light Trench Mortar Battery; India 3 years, Mesopotamia 15 months.

Auty, Harold Ainsworth (1916–19); M.M.; Corporal, 15th Bn. London Rgt.; France 1 year 7 months, Germany, prisoner of war, 9 months.

Barrett, Frederick Titlow (1915–19); Private, R.A.M.C.; France 2 years 3 months.

Barringer, Edward George (1914–19); Lance-Corporal, Royal Fusiliers; France 2 years 6 months.

Bartle, Archibald Leonard (1916–19); Aircraftsman (1st Class), R.N.A.S. and R.A.F.

***Beaumont - Edmonds, William George** (1914–16); Sec.-Lieutenant, 22nd Bn. London Rgt.; France 10 months; Killed in action, 17th September, 1916.

Bedwell, Albert Edward (1915–16); Private, London Rgt.

Bissell, Walter Henry (1914–19); Sergeant, R.G.A.

Braines, Thomas Frederick (1915–19); Lieutenant, 28th Bn. London Rgt., R.F.C. and R.A.F.

Branscombe, Percy (1914–19); Private, 13th Bn. London Rgt.; France 4 months, Germany and Switzerland, prisoner of war, 3 years 6 months.

Braun, Percy Ernest (1916–18); Company Sergeant-Major, School of Musketry.

Brockett, Henry Edwin (1914–19); Lance-Corporal, 15th Bn. London Rgt.; France 4 years.

Brownrigg, John Henry (1915–19); Corporal, 12th and 5th Bns. London Rgt.; France 1 year 7 months, Germany, prisoner of war, 8 months.

Bull, Francis George (1914–19); M.C. and bar; Captain, Royal Fusiliers; France and Germany 3 years 3 months.

Burbidge, Basil Edmund (1914–19); Lance-Corporal, Middlesex Rgt.; India and Mesopotamia 4 years 4 months.

Burge, Edward Thomas (1914–16); Corporal of Horse, R. Horse Guards; France 18 months.

Chase, Heber Lawson (1915–19); M.M.; Private, R.A.M.C.; France 3 years 2 months.

Clark, Richard Ernest (1914–19); Sergeant, 15th Bn. London Rgt.; France, Salonica and Palestine, 2 years 8 months.

***Cohen, Simon** (1914–19); Sergeant, R.A.M.C. (Sanitary Coy.), and Captain, Egyptian Labour Corps; France 12 months, Egypt 2 years 9 months; Killed by natives in Cairo, 23rd November, 1919.

Comyns, Arthur Patrick (1915–19); M.C.; Lieutenant, R. Welch Fusiliers; France and Belgium 2 years.

Cox, Maurice James (1916–19); Sapper, Rifle Brigade and R.E.; France 2 years.

Crawforth, William James Kenyon (1916–19); Lieutenant, 16th Bn. London and Middlesex Rgts.; Palestine and Syria 1 year 10 months.

Crick, Edward Clifton (1914–18); M.S.M., Mentioned in despatches for bravery; Quartermaster-Sergeant, London Regiment; France 2 years 6 months.

Cruttenden, Reginald (1914–19): Captain, London Rgt. and Machine Gun Corps; France 3 years 5 months.

Davies, William Percival (1915–19); Sergeant, R.A.M.C.; France 12 months, Italy 3 months.

Edwards, John Ambrose (1918–19); Private, R. Marine Light Infantry; France 11 months.

Evans, George Ernest (1916–19); Private, R.A.S.C.; Salonica 1 year 9 months.

Evans, Joseph (1915–19); Sergeant, E. Yorkshire Rgt., Northern Cyclists and Labour Corps; France 6 weeks.

Everingham, Charles Maxwell Ainge (1915–19); Sergeant, R.A.M.C.; Macedonia, Bulgaria and Serbia, 2 years 4 months.

***Farley, William Alfred** (1914); Private, S. Lancashire Rgt.; France about 6 weeks; Killed in action, 20th September, 1914.

Farrant, Walter Charles (1915–20); Lieutenant, R.A.S.C.; France 2 years.

FitzGerald, Thomas David (1916–19); Corporal, A.P.C.

***French, Sidney Arthur** (1914–18); Captain, London Rgt. and R. W. Kent Rgt.; France about 2 years; Missing, 20th March, 1918.

Gould, Harry Price (1916–19); Sergeant, E. Surrey Rgt.

Granger, Charles (1914–17); Corporal, Royal Fusiliers, Army Cyclist Corps and Labour Corps.

Griffiths, Henry John (1915–19); Lance-Corporal, London Rgt.; France 2 years, Germany, prisoner of war, 8 months.

Ham, Charles (1916–19); Sec.-Lieutenant, R.N.A.S. and R.A.F.

Harding, Arthur George (1915–19); O.B.E., twice mentioned in despatches; Captain, R.A.O.C.; France 3 years.

Harding, William Henry (1916–19); Sergeant, R.N.A.S. and R.A.F.

Hartman, Andrew Robert (1914–19); Sergeant, County of London Yeomanry; Egypt 17 months, Gallipoli 3 months, Salonica 6 months, Palestine and Egypt 10 months.

Harvey, Douglas Moore (1915–19); Sec.-Lieutenant, R.N.A.S. and R.A.F.; Mediterranean 10 months.

Hatton, Albert Alfred (1915–18); Gunner, R.G.A.; France 7 months.

Head, Arthur Edwin (1915–19); Lance-Corporal, London Rgt. and R.A.O.C.; France 4 months, Salonica 8 months, Palestine 2 years.

Heys, Harold James (1915–19); Sergeant, R.A.O.C.; France 18 months, Italy 2 years 3 months.

***Hoare, Henry Joseph** (1914–15); Sec.-Lieutenant, 10th Bn. London Rgt.; Gallipoli 5 days; Killed in action, 15th August, 1915.

Hobday, Henry Lynwood (1918–19); Private, Rifle Brigade and A.P.C.

Hooke, Henry Martyn (1914–19); Captain, Royal Fusiliers; France 14 months.

Hookham, John Edward (1916–19); Private, 15th Bn. London Rgt.; France 13 months.

Horsler, Percy Guy (1914–19); M.C.; Captain, Bedfordshire Rgt., Tank Corps and Lancashire Fusiliers; France 15 months.

Irwin, Reginald Montague (1915–19); Warrant Officer (1st Class), R.A.O.C.; France 2 years 9 months.

Jarvis, George Herbert (1916–19); Corporal, R.N.A.S. and R.A.F.

Jones, Alfred Ynyr Douglas (1914–19); M.S.M.; Staff Sergeant-Major, R.A.S.C.; France 3 years 3 months.

Jones, Percy James (1915–19); Sergeant, R.A.V.C.; Egypt 12 months, France 1 year 9 months.

***Keane, Frederick John** (1916–17); Private, Rifle Brigade; France 12 months; Killed in action, 2nd December, 1917.

Knight, Percy George (1917–19); Sapper, R.E.; France 2 years 2 months.

Leggett, John (1915–19); Gunner, R. Marine Artillery; Grand Fleet, North Sea 3 years.

Luxon, Charles (1915–19); Sergeant (Assistant Master Cook), R.F.A.

***Makeham, Eric Noel** (1915–17); Sec.-Lieutenant, Middlesex Rgt.; France 6 months; Died of wounds while prisoner of war, June, 1917.

Maxted, William Henry (1914–19); Corporal, R.F.A.; France about 6 months.

***McBean, James Ross** (1917–18); Sapper, R.E.; France 14 months; Accidentally killed, 22nd April, 1918.

McDowell, Robert John Blain (1915–19); Staff-Sergeant, R.A.M.C.

Moxley, Douglas John (1914–19); Corporal, Royal Fusiliers; France 2 years 10 months.

Nava, Leo Maurice (1914–19); Captain, Honourable Artillery Company, R.F.C. and R.A.F.; France 3 years 4 months.

Norton, Herbert John (1916–19); Corporal, R.E.; France 3 years.

Oliver, Laurence Herbert (1915–19); Sec.-Lieutenant, R.A.S.C.; East Africa 3 years.

O'Loghlen, Martin (1916–19); Private, Northamptonshire Rgt. and Somerset Light Infantry; France 9 months.

Parsons, Thomas John (1915–19); Private, R.A.O.C. and Northumberland Fusiliers; France 1 year 7 months, Germany, prisoner of war, 7 months.

Pippard, John (1914–19); Mentioned in despatches (Gallipoli); Boatswain, R.N.

Poole, Louis (1914–19); Corporal, London Rgt.; France 5 months, Salonica 2 years 2 months, Palestine 14 months.

***Porter, Edgar Rowland** (1916); Private, 5th Bn. London Rgt.; France 3 months; Missing, presumed killed in action, 8th October, 1916.

***Potter, George Frederick** (1917–18); Private, Rifle Brigade and Shropshire Light Infantry; France 6 months; Died, 15th November, 1918.

Rayner, George Edwin (1916–19); Clerk (2nd Class); R.N.A.S. and R.A.F.; France 10 months.

Robinson, George Henry (1914–19); Sergeant, R.A.M.C.

Sandberg, Julian (1916–19); Sec.-Lieutenant, R.G.A.

Sanders, Frank Cecil (1914–19); Captain, R.E.; France 12 months.

Sentance, Frank Stanley (1916–19); Sergeant, R.N.A.S. and R.A.F.

***Simmonds, William** (1914); Private, Royal Fusiliers; France 3 months; Missing, presumed killed in action, 11th November, 1914.

Sims, Henry George (1914–19); Corporal, London Rgt., Devonshire Rgt. and Duke of Cornwall's Light Infantry; India 12 months, Palestine 18 months, Egypt 5 months.

Smith, Alfred Edward (1916–19); Corporal, Middlesex Rgt.

Smith, David Hart Wilkins (1914–19); Sergeant, 5th Bn. London Rgt.; France 6 months.

Smyth, Edwin Hooper (1917–19); Clerk (1st Class), R.A.F.

Stead, Bertram John (1914–19); Lieutenant, London Rgt.; France 1 year 9 months.

Stuart, Alexander George (1914–19); Bombardier, R.F.A.; France 4 years.

Sutherland, William Forbes (1916–19); Private, Labour Corps, Middlesex Rgt., Sussex Rgt. and Somerset Light Infantry; France 2 years.

Tetley, John (1916–19); Lieutenant, R.A.O.C.; Malta 1 year 8 months.

Tilney, Alfred John (1914–19); D.C.M., Croix de Guerre (with palms); Sergeant, 4th Dragoon Guards; France 4 years.

Tully, James Patrick (1915–19); Corporal, R.A.O.C.

Tyler, Frank Reuben (1916–19); Aircraftsman (1st Class), R.N.A.S. and R.A.F.

Waddington, Thomas (1915–19); Private, R.A.S.C. (M.T.); France 16 months.

Warren, Herbert Charles (1915–19); Corporal, R.A.O.C., Duke of Cornwall's Light Infantry and Dorsetshire Rgt.; France 14 months.

Weeks, Vincent Augustine (1915–19); Lieutenant, R. W. Kent Rgt. and Machine Gun Corps; France 15 months.

Wheeler, Harry John (1915–19); Staff-Sergeant, R.A.O.C.; France 2 years 6 months, Italy 18 months.

***Wilcox, Herbert James** (1914–19); Sergeant, Middlesex Rgt.; India and Mesopotamia 4 years 4 months; Died, 10th March, 1919.

Willcox, Richard Walter (1917–19); Corporal, R.N.A.S. and R.A.F.

Williams, Albert Edward (1915–19); M.S.M., Mentioned in despatches; Quartermaster-Sergeant, R.A.V.C.; France 4 years 3 months.

Wise, John Hawkins (1916–19); Gunner, R.G.A.; France 12 months.

Wright, Arthur (1918–19); Private, R.A.F.

Yeoman, Maurice Hart (1916–19); Private, R.N.A.S. and R.A.F.

Department of the Comptroller of the Council

Adams, Robert (1916–19); Private, 2/6th Bn. Norfolk (Cyclist) Rgt.; Yorkshire Coast Defences.

Adamson, Joseph Edgar (1915–19); M.S.M., Mentioned in despatches; Corporal (acting Sergeant), 26th Bn. Royal Fusiliers; France 1 year 10 months.

Alison, Sidney Herbert (1915–19); Private, R.A.S.C.; Palestine 17 months.

Allcock, Christopher Ridley (1917–19); Corporal, R.A.O.C.; Mesopotamia 2 years 6 months.

Allen, Hubert James (1914–19); Company Sergeant-Major-Instructor, School of Musketry.

***Allender, John Harold** (1914–16); Sec.-Lieutenant, 4/1st Bn. London Rgt.; France 2 months; Killed in action, 7th October, 1916.

Anderson, Herbert Baylis (1918–19); Private, R. Marine Artillery.

Ashby, Edward George (1915–19); Private, 2/9th Bn. Middlesex Rgt., 13th and 12th Bns. E. Surrey Rgt.; France 18 months.

Avis, Frank Milton (1916–19); Lieutenant, R.G.A.

Bacon, George James (1915–19); Croix de Guerre (Belgian); Corporal-Signaller, R.F.A.; France 3 years 3 months.

Bailey, Joseph (1915–19); Sergeant, 7th Bn. Middlesex Rgt. and 11th Bn. Royal Fusiliers; France 6 months.

Baker, Lionel James (1916–19); Lance-Corporal, R.A.S.C. (M.T.); France 2 years 6 months.

Baldon, Edwin Victor Stanley (1915–19); Rifleman, 1/16th Bn. London Rgt.; France 2 years.

Balls, Harry Kent (1917–19); Acting Corporal, R.G.A.

Barber, Charles Henry (1917–18); Private, R.A.O.C.

Barber, Ernest John (1915–19); Lieutenant, 30th, 17th, 5th and 38/40th Bns. Royal Fusiliers, 10th Bn. R.W. Kent Rgt., and 20th Cadet Bn.; France 15 months.

Barlow, Walter Mallison (1914–19); Lieutenant, E. Yorkshire and W. Yorkshire Rgts., and Durham Light Infantry; Egypt 4 months, France 1 year 9 months, Germany 2 months.

Barnes, Alfred Douglas (1916–19); M.C.; Lieutenant, 28th and 23rd Bns. London Rgt., 15th Officer Cadet Bn.; France 8 months.

Barratt, Ralph Diamond (1916–20); Driver, Honourable Artillery Company; France 17 months, Germany 12 months.

***Barrett, John Francis Burney** (1916–18); Rifleman, 3/16th, 12th and 5th Bns. London Rgt.; France 1 year 9 months; Missing, believed killed, 28th March, 1918.

***Bartram, Harold Frank** (1914–17); Sec.-Lieutenant, 7th Bn. Wiltshire Rgt.; Salonica; Killed in action, 24th April, 1917.

***Batchelor, Arthur Charles** (1914–17); Lance-Corporal, 10th Bn. London Rgt.; France 1 year 10 months; Died of wounds, 4th May, 1917.

***Baxter, Kenneth Leslie** (1917–18); Private, Suffolk Rgt.; France 2 months; Missing, believed killed, 23rd August, 1918.

Bayliss, Ernest Edward (1915–16); Private, R.A.S.C. (M.T.).

Beal, James Ralph Gerald Ward (1915–16); Sergeant-Major-Instructor, 23rd Bn. London Rgt.

Beazley, Percy Henry (1916–19); Private, 9th Bn. R.W. Surrey Rgt., 2/5th Bn. Bedfordshire Rgt. and Labour Corps.

Bennett, William Arthur (1914–19); Lance-Corporal, 15th and 10th Bns. London Rgt.; France, Salonica and Palestine, 2 years 8 months.

Billingham, Frederick Arthur (1915–19); Private, 15th Bn. London Rgt., 6th and 46th Bns., Machine Gun Corps, Sergeant-Instructor under Army Educational Scheme; France 16 months.

Bishop, Richard John Daynes (1914–19); Pay Lieutenant-Commander, R.N.R. Various active service stations and ships.

***Blake, Francis Seymour** (1914–16); Captain, King's Liverpool Rgt., attached S. Wales Borderers; Gallipoli and France 12 months; Missing, believed killed, 2nd July, 1916.

Blicq, Herbert (1915–19); Company Quartermaster-Sergeant, R.A.S.C.; France 3 years 2 months.

Bligh, Thomas Aloysius (1914–19); Corporal, R.F.A.; France 1 year 8 months.

Blows, Walter Charles (1914–19); Acting Battery Sergeant-Major, R.F.A.; France 2 years.

Boreham, Wilfrid (1914–19); Private, 5th Bn. London Rgt., 56th Bn. Machine Gun Corps; France 3 years 4 months.

Bowley, Herbert Charles (1916–19); M.S.M.; Sergeant, R.A.F.; France 2 years 5 months.

Brading, Sebert Eccles (1915–16); Corporal, R.E.; France 9 months.

Bricknell, Stanley Mortimore (1915–19); Sergeant, R.A.S.C.; Egypt 8 months, Salonica 3 years, Constantinople 3 months.

Brooks, George Palmer (1916–19); Corporal, King's R. Rifle Corps and A.P.C.

Brown, Arthur Tom John (1916–19); Mentioned in despatches, Medal of Military Merit, 3rd Class, by H.M. the King of the Hellenes; Captain, R.A.S.C.; Egypt 3 months, Salonica, Serbia and Bulgaria 2 years 6 months, Black Sea, Caucasus, Persia and Constantinople 8 months.

Bullivant, Albert William (1914–19); Sergeant, 2/19th Bn. London Rgt.; France 9 months, Salonica 7 months, Egypt 1 year 8 months.

Bush, William Henry (1915–19); Corporal, R.F.C. and R.A.F.

Butler, John (1916–19); Corporal, 3rd and 8th Bns. R.W. Surrey Rgt., and A.P.C.; France 2 months.

Carey, Michael John (1916–19); Leading Writer, R.N.A.S. and R.A.F.; France, 8 months.

Carrée, Clovis William Octave (1918–19); Heavy Motor Driver, R.A.S.C.

Caseley, Alfred Philip (1916–19); Staff-Sergeant-Major, R.A.S.C.; Egypt and Palestine 3 years 3 months, Greece 3 months.

Catto, Leonard (1915–19); Corporal, R.E.; France 2 years 10 months.

Chadwick, Cyril Henry (1916–19); Mentioned in despatches; Lieutenant, 28th Bn. London Rgt., R.F.C. and R.A.F.; France 17 months.

Chance, Walter George (1915–19); Sergeant, R.E.; France 3 years.

Charman, Matthew Frank (1915–19); Mentioned in despatches; Acting Corporal, R.E.; France 10 months.

***Chick, Trevor Phillips** (1914–16); Sergeant, 15th Bn. London Rgt.; France 14 months; Killed in action, 22nd May, 1916.

Clegg, James Alfred (1916–19); Sergeant, R.N.A.S. and R.A.F.

Clifton, John Hall (1916–19); Corporal, Royal Fusiliers and A.P.C.

Codling, Percy Thomas (1916–19); Private, R.A.M.C.; Salonica 4 months, Egypt, Palestine and Syria, 1 year 8 months.

***Coombes, George Wilson** (1914–17); Corporal, 9th Bn. London Rgt., Sec.-Lieutenant, 1st Bn. R. Lancaster Rgt.; Killed in action, 3rd May, 1917.

Coombs, Albert John (1914–20); Lieutenant, R.A.S.C.; France 4 years 10 months.

***Cope, Albert Bertram** (1914–16); Mentioned in despatches; Driver, R.F.A.; France 12 months; Killed in action, 20th August, 1916.

Cosens, Henry George (1915–20); Private, 25th Bn. London Rgt.; India 3 years 9 months.

***Coward, Leslie Graham** (1914–15); Captain, 5th Bn. Middlesex Rgt.; France 12 months; Killed in action, 27th September, 1915.

Cowdery, Frederick Charles (1916–19); Flight-Sergeant, R.A.F.

Cracknell, Walter Willis (1916–19); M.M.; Lance-Corporal, R.F.A. and 1st Bn. Border Rgt.; France 15 months.

Craigen, John Fraser (1914–19); Sec.-Lieutenant, 12th Bn. London Rgt., Machine Gun Corps and Tank Corps; France 2 years 6 months.

Crampton, John Edward (1915–19); Lieutenant, Honourable Artillery Company, 5th Officers' Cadet Bn. and 8th Bn. London Rgt.; France 3 months.

Cridland, Alfred John (1914–19); Signaller, 10th Bn. Royal Fusiliers; France 3 years 7 months.

Cutting, Frederick (1915–19); Sergeant, 16th Bn. London Rgt.; France 4 months.

Cutts, Leonard Henry (1915–19); Staff-Sergeant, R.A.O.C.; France 3 years 4 months.

Daly, Michael Lea J. (1914–19); Lance-Sergeant, 4th Bn. London Rgt. and Lieutenant, R.A.F.

Davidson, Arthur Cyril (1915–19); Corporal, 15th Bn. London Rgt.

Davis, Frederick James (1917–19); Paymaster Sub-Lieutenant, R.N.R., North Sea Fleet.

Dines, Frederick William George (1915–19); Corporal, R.F.C. and R.A.F.; Macedonia 2 years 6 months.

Doble, Edward John (1917–19); Private, R.A.O.C.; Salonica 16 months.

***Dockett, Cyril James Fry** (1915–18); Private, 2/15th Bn. London Rgt.; France 5 months, Salonica 8 months, Palestine 5 months; Died of wounds, 21st February, 1918.

Douglas, Gordon (1915–17); Private, 3/15th and 1/15th Bns. London Rgt.; France 10 months.

Duncombe, Hedley Percy (1914–19); Private, 2/5th and 8th Bns. Bedfordshire Rgt.; France 2 years 2 months.

Dunman, Percival Edwin (1914–19); Sergeant, R.A.M.C.; Gibraltar, Malta and Macedonia, 4 years 9 months.

Dunn, George Stanley (1916–19); Driver and Gunner, R.F.A.; France 12 months.

Dunton, George Corbet (1916–19); Lance-Corporal, R.A.S.C.; France 2 years 6 months.

Dupère, Claude Atto (1917–19); Corporal, Bedfordshire and Hertfordshire Rgt. and A.P.C.

Dutton, George William (1915–19); Private, R.A.M.C.

Easton, Malcolm Henry (1914–19); Major, 25th Bn. London Rgt.; India 2 years 6 months.

Edwards, Thomas Baker (1916–19); Private, 15th Bn. London Rgt., Sergeant, No. 2 Area Gas School, and Sapper, R.E.

Eldridge, William Stanley (1916–19); Private, E. Surrey and 13th Bn. Middlesex Rgts.; France 2 years 7 months.

Eley, Arthur Lionel (1915–19); Private, Honourable Artillery Company.

Ell, William George (1916–19); Gunner, R.G.A.; France 12 months.

Ennis, Philip Francis (1918–19); Able Seaman, R.N.V.R.

Fair, Guy Oswald (1916–19); Acting Sergeant, Reserve Garrison Bn., Suffolk Rgt., R.A.O.C. and 12th Bn. Rifle Brigade; France 2 years 5 months.

Fair, Herbert Robert (1916–19); Private, 1st Reserve Bn. Suffolk Rgt., and Lieutenant, R.A.O.C.; France 2 years 7 months.

Faulks, William Dixey (1914–16); Rifleman, 11th Bn. London Rgt.; Gallipoli, 2 months.

Franklin, John Moore (1916–19); Private, Army Cyclist Corps and Dorsetshire Rgt.; France 18 months.

French, Albert Edward (1917–19); Sergeant, R.G.A. (Anti-Aircraft); France 1 year 10 months, Germany 4 months.

Frith, George Lionel (1916–19); Rifleman, Rifle Brigade; France 8 months.

Frogley, Alexander John (1915–19); Sergeant, R.A.M.C. and R.A.O.C.; France 4 months.

Goddard, Sydney Herbert Charles (1916–20); Private (acting Sergeant), R.A.M.C.; India 2 years 2 months.

Gould, Charles Alfred (1914–19); M.C., Mentioned in despatches; Lieutenant, 1st Bn. Somersetshire Light Infantry, and Captain, 11th Brigade Trench Mortar Battery; France 2 years 7 months.

Grant, Robert William (1916–18); Private, 14th Bn. London Rgt.; France, 4 months.

Greer, John Stanley (1914–19); Captain, Bedfordshire Rgt. and General Staff; France 3 years 9 months.

Griffin, Donald Arthur (1915–19); Air Mechanic (2nd Class), R.N.A.S.; German East Africa, Adriatic and South Russia, 3 years.

Gurney, William Henry (1915–19); Corporal-Signaller, R.F.A.; France 13 months.

Haggith, George Arthur (1916–17); Private, Middlesex and R.W. Kent Rgts.; France 9 months.

Haley, Gordon (1916–19); Lance-Bombardier, R.A., and Pioneer, Meteorological Observer, R.E.

Hall, Percy Henry (1914–19); Lieutenant, 15th Bn. London Rgt., 4th Bn. R. Inniskilling Fusiliers and Machine Gun Corps; France 13 months.

Hampshire, George William (1915–19); Leading Aircraftsman, R.F.C. and R.A.F.; France 14 months.

Handford, Oliver James (1914–18); Rifleman, 12th Bn. London Rgt.; France 11 months.

Hanson, Harold Ernest (1915–19); Mentioned in despatches; Quartermaster-Sergeant, E. Kent Rgt.

Harding, Reginald (1915–19); Lieutenant, R.A.O.C.

Hare, Albert (1914–19); Private, 15th Bn. London Rgt. and Sapper, R.E. (Signal Service); France 3 years 5 months.

Hare, Robert Percy (1915–19); Leading Victualling Assistant, R.N.; Mediterranean 12 months, North Russia 12 months, and North Sea Fleet.

Harman, Roland James (1916–19); Lieutenant, R.G.A.; France 1 year 8 months.

Harris, Thomas William (1915–16); Private, 15th Bn. London Rgt.

Hart, John (1917–19); Private, R.A.S.C.; Egypt and Italy 2 years 2 months.

Hawkins, Thomas (1914–19); Corporal, 7th Bn. London Rgt., and Lieutenant (Acting Adjutant), 3rd and 7th Bns. Suffolk Rgt.; France 2 years, Prisoner of War (Germany) 12 months.

Hazeldine, Alfred George (1916–19); Corporal, 5th and 21st Bns. Nottinghamshire and Derbyshire Rgt., and 2/6th Bn. Durham Light Infantry; France 8 months.

Heald, Ernest (1916–19); Signalman, R.N.V.R.; Mediterranean 2 years.

Hedger, George Arthur Wellesley (1915–20); Private, R.A.M.C.; Mesopotamia 8 months, India 15 months.

Hefford, Frank (1915–19); Corporal, 7th Bn. Middlesex Rgt.; Sec.-Lieutenant, 3rd Bn. Northamptonshire Rgt.; France 9 months.

Hennings, Lionel Brian (1914–19); Sec.-Lieutenant, 2/15th Bn. London Rgt., 6th Bn. Essex Rgt. and Cadet School, Cairo; France 5 months, Salonica 8 months, Egypt 11 months, Palestine and Syria 13 months.

***Heskett, John** (1915–18); Private, Royal Fusiliers; France 2 years 3 months; Killed in action, 14th October, 1918.

Hicks, Ernest John (1914–19); Regimental Sergeant-Major, 15th and 31st Bns. London Rgt.

Hill, Axel Charles Fischer (1914–19); Sergeant, R.E. (Signal Service); France 17 months.

Hill, Charles Percy (1916–19); Lieutenant, R.G.A.

Hilling, Edward (1914–19); Lieutenant, A.P.C., Highland Light Infantry and R.A.S.C. (M.T.); Salonica 12 months, Constantinople 9 months.

Hills, Charles Frank Clare (1914–19); Private, 19th Bn. London Rgt.; France 13 months, Salonica 7 months, Egypt and Palestine 15 months.

Hobbs, Alfred Cecil (1916–19); Qualified Signalman, R.N.V.R.; China Station 2 years 6 months.

Hockley, Joseph Thomas (1915–19); Private (acting Corporal), R.A.M.C.; France 6 months, Italy 9 months.

Holman, Ernest Albert (1916–19); Bombardier, R.G.A.; France 9 months.

Hopley, Charles William (1917–19); Corporal, E. Surrey Rgt.; Lance-Sergeant, A.P.C.

Horsler, William Edward (1915–19); Writer (2nd Class), R.N.

Hoskin, Herbert Joseph (1915–19); Private, 15th Bn. London Rgt.; France 17 months, Prisoner of war 10 months.

Howard, Frederick Percival (1916–19); Lance-Corporal, 3rd Bn. E. Surrey Rgt.

Howell, Tom (1916–19); Rifleman, 6th Bn. London Rgt., Sec.-Lieutenant, R.G.A.; France.

Hurley, Robert Cowan (1915–16); Private, 3/4th Bn. London Rgt. and 101st Provisional Bn.

Idle, Allan Duncan (1914–19); Sapper, 23rd Bn. London Rgt. and R.E.; France and Germany 4 months.

Ingle, Henry Sergeant (1914–19); Company Quartermaster-Sergeant, 2/4th Bn. Oxfordshire and Buckinghamshire Light Infantry; France 2 years 11 months.

Inkersole, Harry Theodore (1916–19); Paymaster Lieutenant, R.N.R., H.M.S. Royal Oak, Grand Fleet.

Jackson, Arthur (1914–19); Lieutenant, 18th Bn. Royal Fusiliers and R.A.F.; France 10 months.

Jackson, Leonard Scott (1917–19); Private, R.G.A. and 125th Labour Co.; France 1 year 11 months.

***Jewers, William Francis** (1917–18); Rifleman, 10th Bn. King's R. Rifle Corps; France 10 months; Killed in action, 23rd March, 1918.

Johns, Samuel (1917–19); Paymaster Lieutenant, R.N.R.; Various active service ships, West Coast of Africa 15 months.

***Johnson, Douglas** (1915–16); Rifleman, 15th Bn. London Rgt.; Died, 5th August, 1916.

***Johnson, Harry Clifford** (1915–18); Corporal, Loyal N. Lancashire Rgt.; France 2 years 9 months; Killed in action, 22nd October, 1918.

Johnson, John William (1914–16); Sergeant, M.M.P.; France 11 months.

Johnson, William Russell (1914–19); Regimental Quartermaster-Sergeant, 53rd Bn. R.W. Surrey Rgt.

Johnstone, Sidney (1914-16 and 1917); Private, 16th Bn. London Rgt.; France 1 year 10 months.

Jones, Edward Hugh (1914–19); Mentioned in despatches; Company Quartermaster-Sergeant, R. Welch Fusiliers; France 3 years 2 months.

Joyce, Joseph Edwin (1916–19); Rifleman, King's R. Rifle Corps and 4th Bn. Rifle Brigade; Salonica 1 year 7 months.

Keeler, George (1914–19); Lieutenant, 15th Bn. London Rgt., 3rd Bn. Durham Light Infantry, attached 2nd Bn. Cheshire Rgt.; France 3 months, Salonica 18 months.

Kidd, Sidney Cecil (1914–19); Signaller, 2/9th and 2/10th Bns. Middlesex Rgt., and R.F.A.; Gallipoli 4 months, Egypt and Palestine 3 years 2 months.

Kingett, Henry Frederick (1915–19); Driver, R.F.A.; France 12 months, Salonica 6 months, Palestine 18 months.

Kirkman, Alfred Henry (1915–19); M.S.M.; Company Sergeant-Major, 9th and 21st Lancers, Intelligence Corps and 10th Bn. Royal Fusiliers; France 2 years 7 months.

Kirton, Frederick John (1915–19); Sergeant, R.A.S.C. (M.T.).

Lakey, Stanley Ernest (1916–19); Aircraftsman (1st Class), R.N.A.S. and R.A.F.; East Africa 7 months.

Langford, William Henry (1916–19); Private, Royal Fusiliers.

Layen, Luther Edward (1916–19); M.S.M., Mentioned in despatches; Acting Staff Sergeant-Major, R.A.S.C.; Egypt 3 months, Mesopotamia 3 years.

Leonard, Edward (1914–19); Regimental Quartermaster-Sergeant, 8th and 6th Bns. E. Kent Rgt.; France 3 years 6 months.

Levy, Jacob (1918–20); Company Quartermaster-Sergeant, 39th Bn. Royal Fusiliers; Egypt 1 year 7 months.

Lewis, Harold Whittle (1914–19); Corporal, 15th Bn. London Rgt.; France 4 months.

Logsdail, Kenneth Wells (1914–19); Private, A.P.C., 1st Reserve Garrison Bn. Yorkshire Light Infantry, and 13th Bn. Yorkshire Rgt.; North Russia 10 months.

Logsdon, William James (1915–19); Sergeant, R.E.

Lucas, George Francis (1915–19); Lance-Corporal, Honourable Artillery Company; France 9 months, Italy 11 months.

***Macartney, Vivian John** (1914–15); Private, 13th Bn. London Rgt.; France 3 months; Wounded and missing, 9th May, 1915.

MacKenzie, Alex (1916–19); Private, 10th and 13th Bns. Welch Rgt.; France 1 year 11 months.

MacMillan, John Ross (1915–19); Sergeant, Royal Fusiliers and 36th Bn. Northumberland Fusiliers; France 12 months.

Maddocks, Hopkin Thomas (1914–19); M.C.; Private, Royal Fusiliers, and Lieutenant, Machine Gun Corps; France 2 years 6 months.

Maggs, William (1915–19): Twice mentioned in despatches; Lieutenant, 2nd County of London Yeomanry, 6th Bn. Essex Rgt., 1st Buckinghamshire Bn. Oxfordshire and Buckinghamshire Light Infantry; France 14 months, Italy 15 months.

Mahood, Samuel (1916–19); Corporal, R.A.M.C.; Italy 5 months.

Maitland, Pelham Douglas (1916–19); Corporal, A.P.C.

Malkinson, Charles Herbert (1914–19); M.M.; Sergeant, 19th Bn. London Rgt., Lieutenant, Lincolnshire Rgt. and Machine Gun Corps; France 2 years 7 months.

Manning, Ernest Henry (1916–19); Private, 2/15th Bn. London Rgt.; France 10 months, Salonica 5 months, Palestine 12 months.

Mansfield, Ernest (1916–19); Corporal, R.A.S.C.

Marsh, Sydney George (1916–19); Clerk, R.N.A.S., Lieutenant, R.A.F.

Mason, Ernest Joseph (1915-19); Sec.-Lieutenant, R.A.S.C.; Salonica 1 year 11 months, Egypt 12 months.

***Mears, Alfred Edward** (1914–15); Driver, R.F.A.; France 2 weeks; Died, 28th March, 1915.

Messenger, George Augustine (1916–19); Clerk (1st Class), R.N.A.S. and R.A.F.

Michell, Albert Francis (1916–19); Private, 25th, 7th and 19th Bns. London Rgt.; France 17 months, Prisoner of war 9 months.

Midlane, George Henry (1916–19); Sergeant, R.A.O.C.; France 2 years 8 months.

Moore, Joseph Scott (1915–19); Private, Inns of Court O.T.C., and Lieutenant, R.A.O.C.

Moore, Thomas Charles (1914–18); Mentioned in despatches; Corporal, A.P.C., and Flight Cadet, R.A.F.; France 3 years.

Moss, Albert (1918–19); Private, 29th Bn. Royal Fusiliers, 32nd Bn. Middlesex Rgt. and R.A.S.C.

Mountifield, Frederick William (1916–19); Battery Quartermaster-Sergeant, R.G.A.; France 1 year 8 months.

Muncey, Thomas Francis (1914, 1916–19); Corporal, R.A.S.C.; Mesopotamia 15 months.

Murray, John (1915–19); Bombardier, R.H.A.; India and Mesopotamia 3 years 9 months.

Nash, Herbert James (1916–19); Gunner, R.G.A.; Gibraltar 5 months.

Needham, Frank Allen (1914–19); Sec.-Lieutenant, 2/2nd County of London Yeomanry, Tank Corps, 3rd Bn. R. Lancaster Rgt., and R.A.F.; France 16 months.

Newell, George Edward (1916–19); Corporal, R.G.A.; France 10 months.

Nodes, George Leonard (1915–20); Private, R.A.M.C.; India and Mesopotamia 2 years 3 months.

***O'Hara, Bernard Patrick** (1916–19); Paymaster Lieutenant, R.N.R.; Service at sea; Died at Malta, 14th October, 1919.

Ottaway, Philip Herbert (1914–20); Sergeant, 5th Bn. London Rgt.; France 1 month.

Palmer, Albert Henry Edward (1916); Private, London Rgt.

***Partridge, Wilfred Issell** (1914–17); Lieutenant, 10th Bn. Devonshire Rgt.; France 2 months, Salonica and Egypt 16 months; Missing, believed killed, 24th April, 1917.

***Payne, Henry James** (1914–17); Sec.-Lieutenant, R. Sussex Rgt.; France 14 months; Drowned at sea, 4th May, 1917.

***Pearce, John** (1914–15); Rifleman, Rifle Brigade; France 1 month; Killed in action, 13th May, 1915.

Pearce, Wilfrid (1916–19); Gunner, R.G.A.; France 1 year 11 months, Germany 10 months.

Peck, Arthur Alan (1917–19); Gunner, R.F.A., Aircraftsman (1st Class), R.F.C. and R.A.F.

Peirson, George Frederick (1914–19); Mentioned in despatches; Sergeant, Wiltshire Rgt., and Lieutenant, R.A.F.; France 2 months.

Pendry, Ernest William (1914–16); Private, 15th Bn. London Rgt.; France.

Perring, Douglas Myrton (1915–16); Private, 2/5th Bn. R.W. Kent Rgt.

***Petherick, John Edward** (1914–15); Private, 13th Bn. London Rgt.; France 2 months; Died of wounds, 17th May, 1915.

Plumbly, Laurence David (1914–19); Sergeant, 9th and Private, 7th and 8th Bns. Middlesex Rgt.; France 3 months.

Potter, Arthur (1914–16 and 1916–19); Corporal, 15th Bn. London Rgt., 2/1st Bn. Cambridgeshire Rgt. and R.E.; France 18 months.

Potter, Harry Edwin (1916–19); Company Quartermaster-Sergeant, 2/6th and 2/7th Bns. Northumberland Fusiliers; Egypt 9 months, Palestine 18 months.

***Prophet, Cecil** (1915–17); Sec.-Lieutenant, 15th Bn. London Rgt.; France 10 months; Killed in action, 9th October, 1917.

Pugh, George Wilfred (1915–19); O.B.E., Medal (3rd Class) for Military Merit (Greek), Mentioned in despatches, Major, R.A.S.C. and R.A.O.C.; France 2 months, Salonica 1 year 5 months, Athens (Inter-allied Mission) 9 months.

***Quilter, Frederick Walter** (1915); Sec.-Lieutenant, 6th Bn. London Rgt.; France 4 months; Killed in action, 1st September, 1915.

Quinton, Leonard (1915–19); Lieutenant, R.A.S.C. (M.T.); France 3 years 7 months.

Rayment, Bertram Charles (1915–19); Private, R.A.S.C. (M.T.); France 3 years 2 months.

***Reardon, Leonard Andrew** (1914–18); Acting Lance-Corporal, 31st Bn. London Rgt.; France 6 months; Killed in action, 1st September, 1918.

Reed, Percy Alfred (1914–19); Corporal, 2/15th Bn. London Rgt., R.F.C. and R.A.F.

Reid, John William Joseph (1914–16); Rifleman, 16th Bn. London Rgt.; France 7 months.

Rhead, Albert Willie (1914–18); Sec.-Lieutenant, 22nd Bn. Manchester Rgt.; France.

***Richards, Albert Ernest** (1915–18); Private, 23rd Bn. Machine Gun Corps; France 12 months; Died of wounds, 28th August, 1918.

Richards, Frank Harold (1915–19); Aircraftsman (1st Class), 15th Bn. London Rgt. and R.A.F.; France 5 months, Salonica 10 months, Palestine 15 months, Red Sea Aerial Survey 3 months and Egypt 3 months.

Riley, Alfred Arnold (1915–19); M.C.; Captain, Inns of Court O.T.C., 7th Bn. Middlesex Rgt.; France 1 year 8 months.

Rivers, Amos (1916–19); Private, R.F.A.; France 4 months.

Roberts, Harold (1915–19); Flight-Sergeant, R.N.A.S. and R.A.F.

Robinson, George Frank (1916–19): Corporal, Royal Fusiliers and A.P.C.

Robinson, Thomas William James (1915–19); Gunner, R.F.A., and Lance-Corporal, R.A.M.C.; Salonica 17 months, Italy 4 months.

Rogers, George David (1916–19); Staff-Sergeant, R.A.O.C.

Rose, Arthur Petril (1915–19); Mentioned in despatches; Lance-Corporal, 14th Bn. King's R. Rifle Corps, 19th Bn. Hampshire Rgt.; France 2 years 8 months.

Rosenberg, Isaac Mark (1917–19); Acting Sergeant, Royal Fusiliers and A.P.C.

***Rowland, William George** (1914–16); Rifleman, 9th Bn. London Rgt.; France 1 year 8 months; Missing, presumed killed, 1st July, 1916.

Sale, John Colbourne (1914–19); Company Quartermaster-Sergeant, 15th Bn. London Rgt.; France 11 months, Salonica and Greece 7 months, Palestine 12 months.

***Scarf, Albert William** (1915–17); Private, Honourable Artillery Company; France 9 months; Killed in action, 26th July, 1917.

Scears, Lupus (1914–19); Battery Sergeant-Major, 5th London Brigade, R.F.A., Administrative Depot, and Sergeant, Reserve Battery, R.F.A.

Sedgwick, Douglas Webb (1917–19); Private, 28th Bn. London Rgt., Lieutenant, R.F.C. and R.A.F.; France (liaison officer).

Selleck, Ernest (1914–19); Private, 13th Bn. London Rgt. and Machine Gun Corps; France 4 years.

Shaddick, Charles Herbert (1915–19); M.S.M., Twice mentioned in despatches; Staff Sergeant-Major, R.A.S.C.; Mesopotamia 1 year 11 months, India 1 month.

Sharratt, Thomas Harry (1914–19); Captain, 15th Bn. London Rgt., 18th Bn. Yorkshire Rgt. and Tank Corps; France 2 years 11 months.

***Sibbitt, Bernard** (1916–18); Private, R.A.M.C.; France and Mediterranean about 2 years; Killed in action, 27th May, 1918.

Sibson, Thomas (1914–16); Private, 7th Bn. London Rgt; France 8 months.

Smith, Henry (1916–19); Writer (3rd Class), R.N.; Baltic Sea 3 months, Grand Fleet 9 months.

Snelling, Walter Carbery (1915–19); Lieutenant, 2nd and 7th Bns. Wiltshire Rgt., and 2nd Bn. R. Berkshire Rgt.; France 18 months.

Solkhon, Arthur Norris (1915–19); Lieutenant, R.A.S.C. (M.T.); Italy 4 months.

Sollis, William Powell (1915–19); Private, 2/3rd South Midland Field Ambulance, R.A.M.C.; France 3 years 8 months.

Squire, Frank Reginald (1914–19); Corporal, 1st County of London Yeomanry, Lieutenant, 1st Garrison Bn. Suffolk Rgt., 1st Garrison Bn. Yorkshire Rgt., and Acting Captain and Adjutant, 256th Company (Indian) Machine Gun Corps; France 1 month, Egypt 7 months, Gallipoli 3 months, Italy 3 months, India 2 years 1 month.

***Starling, Bertram Walter Filer** (1916–19); Aircraftsman (2nd Class), R.N.A.S. and R.A.F.; France 15 months; Died, 24th February, 1919.

Staunton, Harry Laurence (1915–19); Corporal, 1st Bn. London Rgt. and A.P.C.; France 11 months.

Stedeford, William Arthur Peardon (1917–19); Paymaster Sub-Lieutenant, R.N.R.

Stietencron, Gustav Adolph (1915–19); Acting Sergeant, 3/8th Bn. London Rgt., R.F.A. and Labour Corps.

Stillwell, Frank (1914–19); Sergeant, 6th Bn. London Rgt.; France 12 months.

Sullivan, Bernard Sidney (1917–19); Acting Staff Sergeant-Major, R.A.S.C.

Summers, Charles Alfred George (1917–19); Corporal, 265th Area Employment Co., attached V. Corps, Headquarters; France 17 months.

***Sutton, Percy Turner** (1916–18); Sec.-Lieutenant, R.G.A.; France 17 months; Killed in action, 24th August, 1918.

Tate, Charles Harold (1915–19); Air Mechanic (1st Class), R.A.F.: France 2 years 2 months, Germany 3 months.

Templeman, Stanley Grey (1915–19); Lance-Corporal, 2nd Bn. E. Kent Rgt.; Salonica 2 years 1 month.

Thomas, Bertram Charles (1914–19); Sub-Lieutenant, R.N.V.R., 1st Naval Brigade R. Naval Division; Gallipoli 8 months.

Thomas, Cyril Oliver Alexander (1914–18); Sergeant, 15th Bn. R. Welch Fusiliers; France about 2 years.

Thompson, Frederick William (1916–19); Private, R.F.C. and Lance-Corporal, R.A.S.C. (M.T.).

Thompson, Ralph (1916–19); Private, 14th Bn. Royal Fusiliers, 20th Bn. London Rgt. and R.A.M.C.; France 12 months.

Thurman, George Edward (1916–19); Corporal, Army Cyclists' Corps and A.P.C.

Thurston, Henry Atherton (1918); Labourer, R.A.F.

Tippetts, Richard Alexander Ferguson (1916–19); Lieutenant, R.G.A.; France 2 years 1 month.

Tomlinson, John George (1915–16); Air Mechanic (2nd Class), R.F.C.

Trace, George Frederic (1915–19); Corporal, R.A.S.C., and Captain, R.A.O.C.; France 3 years 2 months.

Triggle, Herbert William Tom (1917–18): Corporal, R.G.A.; France 14 months.

Trodd, Walter Charles (1916–19); Lance-Corporal, 25th Bn. London Rgt. (Cyclists) and 16th Bn. R. Irish Rifles; France 2 years 1 month.

***Trotman, Frank William** (1915–16); Private, 3/15th Bn. London Rgt.; France 3 months; Missing, believed killed, 7th October, 1916.

***Turk, George Deane** (1914–17); Sec.-Lieutenant, 1st Bn. Essex Rgt.; France and Salonica 1 year 11 months; Died as prisoner of war in Germany, 23rd June, 1917.

Turner, Albert Richard (1916–19); Private, 6th, 7th, 5th and 3rd Bns. Royal Fusiliers and 10th Bn. Devonshire Rgt.; Salonica 13 months, Bulgaria (prisoner of war) 12 months.

Turner, Frank (1914–19); Quartermaster-Sergeant, 15th Bn. London Rgt., and Lieutenant, R. North Devon Hussars.

Tutt, James Herbert (1917–19); Sergeant, R.F.C. and R.A.F.

***Vellensworth, Henry John Anthony** (1916–18); Gunner, R.G.A.; France 2 years; Died, 1st November, 1918.

Venn, Henry (1916–19); Private, 4/7th Bn. Middlesex and 13th Bn. London Rgts., and Sapper, R.E.; France 2 years 11 months.

Wakely, Leslie Day (1916–19); Private, 4th Bn. Essex Rgt., and Corporal, R.A.O.C.; France 3 years.

Walker, Frederick Thomas (1915–19); Lance-Corporal, 4th and 2nd Bns., E. Surrey Rgt., attached R.A.S.C.; Salonica 2 years 3 months, Dardanelles 5 months.

Walton, Alfred William Foster (1915–16); Corporal, Honourable Artillery Company.

Waters, Taliesin (1915); Private, Welsh Guards.

Watts, Clive (1915–19); Mentioned in despatches; Captain, 15th Bn. London Rgt. and Northumberland Fusiliers; France 2 years.

Watts, Frederick Pemberton (1917–19); Private, Honourable Artillery Company and R.A.M.C.

Watts-Fraser, John Frederick (1914–18); Lieutenant, 13th Bn. London Rgt.; Recruiting, registration, etc., work in England and work for Ministry of Munitions; France 3 months.

Weatherhead, Herbert Davenport (1916–19); Squadron Quartermaster-Sergeant, 52nd Squadron Remounts and R.A.S.C.

Webb, Alfred Walter (1914–19); M.S.M.: Quartermaster-Sergeant, 4th Bn. London Rgt.; France 2 years.

Wellsteed, Percy Thomas (1914–19); Lance-Corporal, 15th Bn. London Rgt., and Lieutenant, 1st Bn. Monmouthshire Rgt.; France 2 years 3 months.

Whildon, Walter Charles (1916–19); Private, R.N.A.S. and R.A.F.

White, Albert Alonzo (1917–19); Ordinary Seaman (acting Schoolmaster), R.N. (afloat).

White, Philip Steven (1916–19); Staff-Sergeant, R.A.S.C. and 1st Bn. Cheshire Rgt.; France 3 years 1 month.

Whitman, John Edward Alfred (1914–19); Captain, R.F.A. and R.G.A.; France 2 years.

Whitney, George Francis (1915–19); Rifleman, 6th Bn. London Rgt. and 1st Bn. King's R. Rifle Corps; France 2 years 1 month.

Williams, Bruce (1915–19); Sec.-Lieutenant, R.N.A.S. and R.A.F.

Williams, Edward Ormonde (1916–19); Leading Aircraftsman, R.N.A.S. and R.A.F.

Williamson, William Edwin (1914–15); Trooper, 2/2nd County of London Yeomanry.

Willis, Frederick George (1915–19); Sergeant, R.E. and Anti-Aircraft Service.

Wilmot, Herbert Henry (1915–19); Royal Humane Society Certificate for saving life in the sea at Ramleh, Egypt; Sergeant, R.A.M.C.; Gallipoli and Egypt 3 years 7 months.

Wilson, Robert Charles (1916–19); Lance-Corporal, 24th Bn. London Rgt., 12th Officer Cadet Bn., and Lieutenant, 5th Bn. Bedfordshire Rgt.; France 1 month, Salonica 2 months, Egypt and Palestine 16 months.

***Wood, Richard Thomas** (1914–18); Sec.-Lieutenant, 9th Bn. Machine Gun Corps; France 2 years 6 months; Died of wounds, 20th April, 1918.

***Woodward, John William Halford** (1915–18); Private, R.A.M.C. and 2/20th Bn. London Rgt.; France 12 months, Palestine 10 months; Wounded and missing, 30th April, 1918.

Worsell, Lewis James (1914–19): Private, 2/7th Bn. London Rgt., and Sapper, R.E.; France 2 years 1 month.

Wyett, William Richard (1915–19); Corporal, 8th and 7th Bns. Middlesex Rgt.

Temporary Staff

Aldcroft, Arthur James (1914–19); Squadron Quartermaster-Sergeant, 10th Royal Hussars and 11th Reserve Cavalry Rgt.

Nicholas, Hubert James (1915–18); Private, R.A.M.C.; Mesopotamia 12 months.

Rickwood, Edward (1915–19); Sergeant, R.E.

Salt, Henry Thomas (1915–19); Lance-Corporal, 2nd Reserve Cavalry Rgt.

Chief Engineer's Department

Central Offices

Barr, Arthur (1914–19); Gunner, R.F.A.; France 4 years 9 months.

Bartlett, John (1916–19); Sec.-Corporal, R.E.

Baxter, George (1915–19); Private, R.A.M.C.; Egypt and Salonica 3 years 5 months.

Best, William Howard (1916–19); Captain, R.A.O.C., Inspector of Ordnance Machinery; France 8 months, Egypt and Palestine 17 months.

Cairns, Albert Henry (1914–19); Corporal, R.E.; France 12 months.

Campbell, Archibald Sidney (1915–19); O.B.E., Mentioned in despatches; Major, General List, 3rd Army, 17th Corps, and Eastern Command Bombing School; France 2 years 1 month.

Carrington, Sidney John Ness (1916–19); M.B.E. (Military), Mentioned in despatches; Major, R.E.

Carroll, Frederick (1915–19); Private, R.A.S.C.; France 3 years.

Chapman, James (1915–17); Company Sergeant-Major, 19th Bn. Middlesex Rgt.; France 1 year 8 months.

Christy, George Daniel (1915–19); Corporal, R.G.A.; France 2 years 5 months.

Clift, Alexander Robertson (1915–19); Lance-Corporal, R.A.S.C. and Labour Corps; France 3 years.

Cook, Joseph Batterham (1918–19); Lieutenant, Inspector of Ordnance Machinery, R.A.O.C.

Cook, Percy Richard (1915–19); Lieutenant, R.E.; France 6 months.

Coveney, Henry Percival Reginald (1914–19); Lieutenant, R.F.A.; France 10 months, Balkans and Egypt 14 months.

Crush, Hugo Philip (1915–20); Captain, Inspector of Ordnance Machinery, R.A.O.C.; France, Salonica, Russia and Turkey 3 years 6 months.

Currie, William (1918–19); Lieutenant, R. Marine Engineers.

Danks, Ernest Thomas (1916–19); Sapper, 23rd and 10th Bns. London Rgt. and R.E.; Salonica 8 months, Egypt 1 year 8 months.

Davie, Percival Blomfield (1915–19); Company Sergeant-Major, Instructor in Musketry, 21st Bn. London Rgt., 107th Provisional Bn. and Corps of the School of Musketry.

Dixon, William Thomas (1915–19); Private and Aircraft hand, 2nd Bn. London Rgt., Royal Fusiliers, R.D.C. and R.A.F.

***Dolan, Frank** (1914–18); Sapper, R.E.; France; Killed in action, 28th March, 1918.

***Dolan, Frederick Albert** (1914–15); Sapper, R.E.; Gallipoli 1 month; Killed in action, 28th April, 1915.

East, George (1915–19); Lance-Corporal, R.A.M.C.; France 1 year 8 months, Italy 15 months.

Faber, Edward Gray (1915–19); Lieutenant, 28th Bn. London Rgt., Loyal N. Lancashire Rgt., and Divisional Officer, R.E., Northern Command; France 4 months.

***Falcon, Francis** (1915); Captain, 13th Bn. Worcestershire Rgt.; Gallipoli 1 month; Killed in action, 6th August, 1915.

Finch, Walter (1917–19); Pioneer, R.E.

Furnell, Charles Warwick (1915–19); Bombardier, R.G.A.; France 3 years 4 months.

Gazeley, Sidney Albert (1916–19); Private, R.W. Kent Rgt.; India and Mesopotamia 3 years.

***Golle, Claude Victor** (1915–17); Corporal, London Rgt.; France 1 month; Killed in action, 27th December, 1917.

Graham, Donald Charles (1916–19); Mentioned in despatches; Captain, R.E.; France 1 year 10 months.

Grennan, James (1916–19); Private, 1st Bn. London Rgt., R.W. Surrey and Northamptonshire Rgts. and Labour Corps; France 1 year 11 months.

Harris, Robert (1914–19); Corporal, County of London Yeomanry, Middlesex Rgt., Northumberland Fusiliers and Labour Corps; Egypt 11 months, Balkans 2 years 6 months.

Hennessey, John (1915–19); Air Mechanic (2nd Class), Essex Rgt. and R.A.F.; Egypt 4 months, France 2 years 10 months.

Hill, Frank Augustus (1914–19); Lieutenant, R.E.

Holliday, Thomas (1915–19); Mentioned in despatches; Captain, Inspector of Ordnance Machinery, R.A.O.C.; France 4 months.

***Holt, George William John** (1915–16); Corporal, King's R. Rifle Corps; France 6 months; Killed in action, 3rd September, 1916.

Hughes, George (1916–19); Rifleman, Rifle Brigade; France 2 years.

Jeffs, Alfred Horace (1914–16); Company Quartermaster-Sergeant, 12th Bn. London Rgt.; France 14 months.

Jones, Harry (1917–19); Sergeant, R.A.S.C.

Jones, Henry (1914–19); Private, Rifle Brigade and Seaforth Highlanders; France 12 months, Salonica 3 years 6 months.

Knowles, Clifford Cyril (1915–19); Private, London Rgt.; France 13 months, Salonica 6 months, Palestine 13 months.

Lee, Henry (1915–19); Corporal, R.A.M.C.; France 9 months, North Russia 9 months.

Longman, Frank Shaw (1916–19); Sapper, R.E.; Egypt 1 year 9 months.

Lyne, James Frank (1916–19); Lance-Sergeant, R.A.O.C.; France 1 year 11 months.

March, Frederick Charles (1916–19); Private, R.A.S.C.; Mesopotamia 2 years 10 months.

Mason, Charles Stephen (1914–18); Sergeant, Rifle Brigade, Oxfordshire and Buckinghamshire Light Infantry and Labour Corps; France 2 months, India 18 months.

Merritt, George Lubbock (1916–19); Private, E. Surrey Rgt., R. Inniskilling Fusiliers and R.A.O.C.; France 2 years 4 months.

Mosscrop, Gilbert Williams (1915–19); Mentioned in despatches (British and Italian); Captain, Inspector of Ordnance Machinery, R.A.O.C.; France 8 months, Italy 2 years.

Overton, Ralph (1916–19); Sergeant-Mechanic, R.N.A.S. and R.A.F.; France 2 years 5 months.

Paris, Henry Adolf (1914–19); Company Sergeant-Major, R.E.

Payne, Walter Herbert (1917–19); Wireman (2nd Class), H.M.S. Vernon.

Poynter, Charles Robert (1918–19); Private, Essex Rgt.

Reed, Frank (1915–19); Company Quartermaster-Sergeant, R.E.

Richardson, Ernest James (1914–19); Sergeant, R. Sussex and E. Surrey Rgts., and Labour Corps; France 3 years 2 months.

Robinson, William John (1915–19); Sapper, R.E.; France 2 years 11 months.

Rogers, Tom Hugh Goddard (1915–19); Lieutenant, R.E.

Rossiter, Charles William (1916–19); Corporal, 51st Bn. Middlesex Rgt.

Salmon, Thomas William (1916–19); Sapper, R.E.

Sears, Arthur Holroyd (1917–19); Lieutenant, R.A.O.C.

Sewell, Charles William (1914–19); Farrier, 9th Lancers.

Smith, George Walter (1914–17); Sergeant, 3rd Bn. Hampshire Rgt.; Convoy duty, Southampton to France.

Smith, Henry Herbert (1914–19); Private, E. Surrey and R.W. Surrey Rgts.; India 2 years, Mesopotamia 2 years 5 months.

Southby, Arthur (1914–19); Mentioned in despatches; Sergeant, R.E.; France 2 years 4 months.

Symons, James Francis (1915–19); Captain, Inspector of Ordnance Machinery, R.A.O.C.; France 3 years.

Terry, Alfred (1916–19); Sergeant, London Rgt.; France 2 years 8 months.

Thorpe, Edgar (1915–19); Gunner, R.F.A.; France 2 years 4 months.

Thurston, Ernest (1916–19); Private, R.A.M.C.

Tisman, Morris (1914); Private, 15th Bn. London Rgt.

Took, Leonard James (1914–19); Mentioned in despatches; Captain, R.F.A.; France 3 months, Egypt 8 months, Palestine 2 years 5 months.

Venn, Frederick (1915–19); Lance-Corporal, R.E.; France 2 years.

Weaving, Harold Acton (1914–19); Sapper, R.E.; France 11 months.

***White, John** (1916–17); Rifleman, London Rgt.; France 7 months; Killed in action, 6th August, 1917.

Whitehouse, William Shaw (1915–19); Sergeant, R.A.M.C.; Mesopotamia 3 years 1 month, India 5 months.

Williams, James Richard (1914–19); Private, E. Yorkshire Rgt. and R.A.O.C.; France 2 years 3 months, Gallipoli 5 months, Egypt 5 months.

Willis, Frederick George (1915–19); Sergeant, R.E.

***Woodhead, Mark Henry** (1915); Private, Middlesex Rgt.; France 1 month; Died of wounds, 29th April, 1915.

Wright, Frank Edward (1914–19); Lance-Corporal, 3rd Bn. Rifle Brigade; France 4 years 7 months.

Bridges and Embankments

Atkinson, Frederick (1917–19); Private, R.W. Surrey Rgt. and Labour Corps; France 8 months.

Glasspool, William (1914–17); Farrier-Sergeant, W. Kent Yeomanry and Dorsetshire Rgt.

Harding, Benjamin William (1916–19); Private, 18th Bn. London Rgt. and Rifle Brigade; Salonica 4 months, Egypt and Palestine 1 year 8 months.

Hubbock, Moses Benjamin (1918–19); Private, Labour Corps.

Mansell, Thomas (1914–17); Private, 3rd Bn. E. Kent Rgt.

Sargeant, John William (1915–19); Driver, R.F.A.; France 3 years.

Simmons, Henry (1914–19); Private, R.A.O.C.; France 4 years 1 month.

White, William (1914–18); Lance-Corporal, R. Welch Fusiliers.

Blackwall Tunnel

Dingle, Joseph (1917–19); Private, Labour Company, R.W. Surrey Rgt.; France 2 years 7 months.

Dukelow, John (1915–19); Gunner, R.F.A.; France 3 years.

Shead, Ernest George (1914–19); Corporal, R.E.; France 5 months.

Greenwich Tunnel

Allen, George Henry (1914–19); Mentioned in despatches; Farrier-Sergeant, R.F.A.; France 2 years 6 months.

***Clark, William** (1917); Gunner, R.F.A.; France 4 months; Died of wounds, 24th October, 1917.

Luxton, John William (1914–19); Mentioned in despatches; Petty Officer (1st Class), R.N.; Battle of Heligoland, Dardanelles and Persian Gulf.

Plant, Herbert Cornelius (1914–19); Able Seaman, R.N.; Falkland Islands, Zeebrugge and convoy duty.

Radburn, George (1915–19); Bombardier, R.F.A.; France 3 years.

Rotherhithe Tunnel

Spicer, William Alfred (1915–19); Lance-Corporal, London Rgt.; France 12 months, Salonica 6 months, Palestine 15 months.

Turner, Albert Francis (1916–19); Sec.-Corporal, 2nd Bn. London Rgt. and R.E.; France 3 years 2 months.

Woolwich Ferry and Tunnel

Allen, John Lewis (1915–19); Able Seaman, R.N. Division; France 3 years 5 months.

Ansett, Samuel (1914–16); Stoker, R.N.

Dray, George Henry (1915–17); Private, Northamptonshire Rgt.; France 16 months.

Gray, Robert Charles (1914–19); Chief Stoker, R.N.

Harber, Daniel Joseph (1914–19); Farrier-Sergeant, R.F.A.; France 2 years 3 months.

Hill, Rowland (1914–19); Stoker (1st Class), R.N.; Nore defences and Belgian coast.

Hudson, Samuel Charles (1915–19); Able Seaman, R. Naval Division; France 2 years 6 months.

Jenkins, William (1914–15); Lance-Corporal, London Rgt.

Longhurst, Arthur (1915–17); Corporal, R.E.

Margetson, Stanley (1918–19); Sapper, R.E.

Neilson, Christian Martin (1914–19); Gunner, R.F.A.; France 2 months.

Oates, Henry Frederick Powell (1914–19); Corporal, R.E.

Skinner, Edward George (1914–19); Lance-Corporal, R. Lancaster Rgt.; France 4 years 4 months.

Stephens, Arthur (1915–19); Corporal, King's R. Rifle Corps.

West, William Thomas (1915–19); Sapper, R.E. and R.F.A.; France 3 years 4 months.

Sewerage and Drainage

Banyard, Stephen Charles (1915–19); Gunner, R.G.A.; Egypt 3 years 3 months.

***Bennett, Arthur Albert** (1916–19); Rifleman, London Rgt.; France 15 months; Died, 11th March, 1919.

Bishop, Francis James (1915–19); Private, London and Suffolk Rgts., 304th Labour Company and R.A.V.C.

Bones, John Frederick (1914–18); Sergeant, Essex and Northamptonshire Rgts.; France and Gallipoli.

Brewer, John Thomas (1915–19); Private, Middlesex Rgt. and Labour Corps; France 2 years 9 months.

Burley, Walter James (1916–19); Private, Rifle Brigade and London and Middlesex Rgts.; India 9 months, Mesopotamia 18 months.

Camper, William George (1917–19); Private, R.F.A. and R.A.S.C.

Clark, Albert Arthur (1915–19); Sapper, R.E.; Salonica 14 months.

Clements, Frederick Joseph (1916–18); Lance-Corporal, Middlesex Rgt.; France 16 months.

Clench, Robert (1916–19); Private, E. Surrey Rgt., Highland Light Infantry and Agricultural Corps.

***Conley, Daniel** (1915–17); Private, London Rgt.; France and Salonica 9 months; Missing, 25th April, 1917.

Cook, Henry Charles (1916–19); Rifleman, London Rgt.; France 17 months.

Coote, Charles John (1914–19); Corporal, R.A.V.C.; France 4 years 1 month.

De Winter, Pascal Joseph (1916–19); Private, R.W. Surrey Rgt.

Eustace, William (1917–19); Private, Norfolk Rgt.; France 2 years.

Flinders, William (1915–19); Private, R.N.A.S. and R.A.F.

Foster, Reuben Edward (1916–19); Private, Rifle Brigade, Training Reserve and R.W. Kent Rgt.; Mesopotamia 2 years 1 month.

Freak, William (1915–19); Sapper, R.E. and R.F.A.; France 3 years 2 months.

Fuller, Sydney George (1914–18); Private, R.A.S.C. and Worcestershire Rgt.; France 3 years 3 months.

Fuller, William Arthur (1915–19); Sergeant, London Rgt.; France 16 months, Salonica 6 months, Palestine 1 year.

Garrett, Albert Edward (1916–19); Corporal, King's R. Rifle Corps and Machine Gun Corps; France 2 years 8 months.

Gazeley, Frederick William (1916–19); Rifleman, London Rgt.; France 1 month, Egypt 16 months, Salonica 4 months.

Grainger, Charles Edward (1915–19); Acting Sergeant, London Rgt.; France 2 years 9 months.

Gray, Henry (1916–19); Private, N. Staffordshire Rgt. and R.A.M.C.; France 6 months.

Green, Albert (1916–19); Driver, R.A.S.C. and R.F.A.; France 2 years 6 months.

Gregory, Henry Charles (1915–19); Private, R.A.S.C.; France 3 years 3 months.

Grover, Bertram James (1916–19); Private, Welch Rgt. and R. Welch Fusiliers; France 2 years 5 months.

Harper, Richard (1917–19); Private, R.A.S.C.; France.

Harvey, Benjamin (1918–19); Gunner, R.F.A.; France 9 months.

Hills, Alfred (1917–19); Air Mechanic (2nd Class), R.A.F.; Palestine 9 months, India 14 months.

***Howes, Robert** (1915–18); Corporal, R.E.; France 9 months; Killed in action, 21st March, 1918.

Hurst, Alfred (1917–19); Air Mechanic (2nd Class), R.A.F.

Ironside, Alfred William (1914–19); Company Sergeant-Major, Essex and R.W. Surrey Rgts., and R.E.; Gallipoli 2 months.

Jackson, Christopher Thomas (1915–19); Shoeing-Smith, R.A.V.C.; France 2 years 5 months.

Kenning, Arthur Ernest (1917–19); Private, Labour Corps.

Ling, William (1916–19); Private, London Rgt.; Salonica 6 months, Palestine 12 months, France 6 months.

Maloney, John (1915–19); Sergeant, R.N.A.S. and R.A.F.

Maxim, Herbert George (1916–19); Private, S. Staffordshire Rgt.; France 1 year 10 months.

Morle, Walter Sydney (1915–19); Lance-Corporal, R.E.; France 1 year 11 months.

O'Brien, John (1916–19); Sapper, R.E.

Pearson, Alfred Thomas (1915–19); Lance-Corporal, R.A.S.C.; France 4 years.

Pitt, Jabez Stephen (1915–17); Driver, R.F.A.; France 2 years.

Pollard, George (1916–19); Private, Leicestershire Rgt.; France 1 year 9 months.

Rivett, Richard (1915–19); Lance-Corporal, London Rgt.

Robertson, Frederick Joseph (1916–19); Private, E. Surrey Rgt.; France 2 years 8 months.

Robson, Henry Augustus (1914–19); Farrier-Sergeant and Carriage Smith, R.E.; France 3 years 5 months.

Ruffles, Alfred (1916–20); Private, R.W. Kent Rgt.; India 3 months, Mesopotamia 2 years 9 months.

Scotchford, Harry (1915–19); Private, E. Surrey and Middlesex Rgts., Highland Light Infantry and Gordon Highlanders.

Sheppard, James (1915–19); Sergeant, London Rgt.; France 17 months.

***Shipton, Charles** (1915–16); Corporal, R.E.; France 5 months; Accidentally killed, 1st July, 1916.

Silcock, Walter George (1915–18); M.M.; Sergeant, R.E.; France 18 months.

Sloper, Alfred Henry (1917–19); Gunner, R.G.A.; France 16 months.

Smith, John (1914–17); Private, Grenadier Guards; France 1 year 7 months.

***Spenceley, Frederick** (1916–17); Private, London Rgt.; France 5 months; Killed in action, 16th June, 1917.

Spicer, George Edward (1916–19); Private, Rifle Brigade and R.E.; France 2 years 3 months.

Stephens, William Henry (1918–19); Private, Essex Rgt.

Taylor, Edwin Charles Wilfred (1915–19); Sapper, R.E.; France 2 years.

Waldron, Thomas (1915–19); Private, Labour Corps and R.A.S.C.; France 3 years 7 months.

Whitlock, Joseph Thomas (1917–19); Gunner, R.G.A.; France 4 months.

Young, Harry (1916–19); Sapper, R.E.

Abbey Mills Pumping Station

Balcombe, Frederick Henry (1915–19); Private, Essex and Bedfordshire Rgts. and A.P.C.; France 14 months.

Cleary, Thomas (1914–19); Private, 20th Hussars; France 2 years.

Gale, George James (1917–19); Private, R.A.M.C.; Salonica 11 months.

Hall, Thomas Forster (1914–19); Fitter Staff-Sergeant, R.F.A. and R.G.A.; France 1 year 9 months, Salonica 2 years 3 months.

Jefferson, Maddison (1916–17); Private, E. Surrey Rgt.

Kennard, Arthur (1915–20); Gunner, R.F.A.; France 2 years.

Lane, Edmund (1914–19); Mentioned in despatches; Leading Stoker, R. Fleet Reserve; Dardanelles and Grand Fleet.

Nason, William John (1915–19); Driver, R.E.; France 3 years 7 months.

Perrott, Herbert Frederick (1915–19); Sec.-Corporal, R.E.; France 2 years 10 months.

***Quinlan, Edward** (1915–18); Private, London Rgt.; France 3 years 3 months; Missing, 21st March, 1918.

Quinton, Arthur George (1918–19); Private, R.F.A.

Sallnow, Charles Edward (1915–19); Private, R.A.O.C.; France 3 years.

Tanter, Frederick (1915–19); Corporal, R.A.M.C. and Essex Rgt.; Egypt 3 years 9 months.

Whitbread, Walter James (1914–19); Sapper, Essex Rgt. and R.E.; France 3 years 7 months.

Wiffen, Walter Frederick (1916–19); Private, R.A.S.C. and Hampshire Rgt.; India 18 months, Salonica 4 months, Dardanelles 6 months.

Deptford Pumping Station

***Allum, George Alfred Bertie** (1914); Stoker (1st Class), R.N.; H.M.S. Hawke; Drowned at sea, 15th October, 1914.

***Medhurst, Richard William** (1914); Leading Stoker, R.N.; H.M.S. Cressy; Drowned at sea, 22nd September, 1914.

Neville, James George (1914–16); Bandsman, London Rgt.

Packer, Ernest James (1916–19); Private, Lincolnshire Rgt.; France 3 months.

Symes, Edward George (1915–19); Sapper, R.E.; France 3 years 3 months.

North Woolwich Pumping Station

Kellam, Frederick (1916–19); Private, Rifle Brigade and Labour Corps; France 5 months.

Murray, John (1915–17); Gunner, R.F.A.; France 17 months.

Western Pumping Station

Adams, Thomas Henry (1914); Stoker (1st Class), R.N.

Denington, Thomas Philip (1915–18); Private, Essex Rgt. and Labour Corps; France 18 months.

***Jackson, Thomas William** (1914); Private, R. Marine Light Infantry; H.M.S. Hawke; Drowned at sea, 15th October, 1914.

Keough, Henry John (1916–19); Private, R. E. Kent Mounted Rifles and Labour Corps; France 16 months.

Lester, Frederick George (1916–19); Sapper, R.E.; France 2 years 2 months.

Smith, William Edward (1916–19); Sergeant, R. E. Kent Mounted Rifles, Bedfordshire Rgt. and Scottish Rifles.

Barking Outfall Works

Barker, Arthur Albert (1915–19); Private, R.A.S.C.; France 3 years 10 months.

Barnard, George Archibald Loveland (1914–19); Corporal, R.A.S.C.; Egypt 18 months.

Bass, William Patrick (1914–18); Private, Duke of Cornwall's Light Infantry; Salonica 2 years 9 months, France 6 months.

Bones, Alfred Henry (1914–16); Lance-Sergeant, Essex Rgt.

Bones, Charles William (1914–16); Sergeant, Essex Rgt.

Bones, James William (1914); Private, Essex Rgt.

Bones, Samuel George (1914); Private, Essex Rgt.

Bones, William Thomas (1914–19); Company Sergeant-Major, Essex Rgt.

Brooks, George Robert (1915–19); Private, R.A.S.C.; France 4 years.

Byers, William James Curno (1914–19); Private, Middlesex Rgt.; France 3 months, Russia 18 months, Prisoner of war (Germany) 2 years 9 months.

Chambers, Alfred (1914–19); Private, E. Surrey and Norfolk Rgts.; India 2 years 4 months, Egypt 3 months.

Clark, Frederick (1914–19); Private, R.A.S.C.; Mesopotamia 18 months, India 2 months, Persia 2 months, France 1 month.

Claydon, Charles Edward (1915–19); Corporal, Middlesex Rgt.; Salonica 2 years 5 months, Russia 5 months.

Cooper, George William (1915–19); Private, R.A.O.C.; France 3 years.

Cooper, Harry (1915–19); Private, R.A.O.C.; France 3 years.

***Crow, Joseph** (1917–18); Gunner, R.F.A.; France 13 months; Died, 25th October, 1918.

Ellison, Andrew Brown (1914–19); Shoeing-Smith, Essex Rgt. and R.F.A.; France 18 months.

Fox, George (1915–16); Private, Labour Corps.

Gaff, Harry George (1914–19); Corporal, Labour Corps; France.

Goadby, Thomas (1914–19); Company Sergeant-Major, R.A.S.C.; France 9 days.

Griffiths, Owen Martin (1915–18); Private, R.A.S.C.; France 3 years 2 months.

Gudgin, Thomas Isaac (1914–19); Corporal, R.A.S.C.; France 16 months.

Kimpton, Percival Arthur (1914–19); Lance-Corporal, Essex Rgt.; France 4 years 8 months.

Kittridge, Thomas (1916–19); Private, Rifle Brigade and King's R. Rifle Corps; France 2 years.

Luxford, James Henry (1915–17); Private, R.A.S.C.; France 1 year 10 months.

Merchant, Thomas James (1915–19); Corporal, R.A.S.C. and W. Yorkshire Rgt.; Italy 12 months, France 2 years 6 months.

Norris, Alfred James (1915–16); Private, R.A.S.C.

***Perriman, William** (1914–15); Able Seaman, R.N.; H.M.S. Bacchante 9 months; Died of wounds, 4th June, 1915.

Pridmore, William Alfred (1914–19); Stoker (1st Class), R.N.; H.M.S. Magnificent and Cyclops.

Randall, Thomas James (1914–19); Stoker, R.N.; Grand Fleet and Minesweeping.

Rayment, William John (1915–19); Private, R.A.S.C.; France 4 years.

Springett, Edward William (1915–19); Private, Duke of Cornwall's Light Infantry and Machine Gun Corps; France 2 years 6 months, Italy 5 months, Germany 5 months.

Studley, Henry Charles (1915–19); Private, Duke of Cornwall's Light Infantry, Essex Rgt., Machine Gun Corps and Labour Corps; France 17 months.

Taylor, Henry Edwin (1915–19); Private, Devonshire Rgt.; France 2 years 3 months.

Watson, James (1915–19); Gunner, R.G.A.; France 10 months, East Africa 1 year 9 months.

Wheal, Charley (1914–19); Corporal, R.A.S.C.; France 13 months.

Willis, Arthur (1914–16); Private, Essex Rgt.; France 15 months.

Wright, Horace James (1914–19); Sergeant, Grenadier Guards; France 3 years.

Crossness Outfall Works

Beadle, Herbert Walter (1915–19); Gunner, R.F.A.; France 1 year 8 months.

***Best, Sydney James** (1914–16); Private, London Rgt.; France 2 months; Killed in action, 1st October, 1916.

Blackman, John Alfred (1914–17); Private, R.A.O.C.; France 2 years 6 months.

Blundell, John (1916–19); Private, London Rgt. and County of London Yeomanry; France 7 months.

Buck, Alfred George (1914–19); M.M.; Corporal, R.F.A. and R.E.; France 3 years 8 months.

Cottenden, Ernest Harold (1914–16); Stoker, R.N.; North Sea patrol.

Cretchley, William Robert (1914–19); Battery Sergeant-Major, R.F.A.

Fryer, William (1914–16); Sergeant, R.F.A.; France 3 months.

Gibson, James (1914–19); Stoker, R.N.; North Sea patrol and convoy duty.

Howarth, Albert Edward (1914); Corporal-Fitter, R.F.A.

Hudson, Alfred (1915–17); Private, King's R. Rifle Corps; France 9 months.

Jarman, William (1914–19); M.M.; Petty Officer, R.N.V.R.; Gallipoli 4 months, France 2 years 4 months.

***Jobling, Ralph** (1914–17); Private, London Rgt. and R.D.C.; Died, 20th July, 1917.

Newbold, Robert (1914–19); Corporal, E. Lancashire and Devonshire Rgts., and Labour Corps; France 4 months.

***Page, Herbert** (1916–17); Gunner, R.F.A. and R.A.V.C.; France 1 year 4 months; Killed in action, 12th November, 1917.

Page, Mark (1917); Private, Labour Corps.

Powell, Arthur (1914–19); Private, R.D.C.

Powers, John (1914–19); Lance-Corporal, 19th Hussars; France 3 years 8 months.

Prescott, Arthur Henry (1916); Private, R.A.V.C.; France 3 months.

Pynn, Herbert John (1914–19); Able Seaman, R.N.; North Sea patrol and convoy duty.

Thompson, Albert (1914–17); Saddler, R.F.A. and R.A.S.C.

Waterman, Lewis (1914–19); Lance-Corporal, R.D.C.

West, George Thomas (1914–15); Armament Staff-Sergeant, R.A.O.C.

Sludge Vessels

Castle, Alfred John (1914–19); Leading Stoker, R.N.R.; H.M.S. Audacious and Queen Elizabeth.

Coulson, Charles (1914–19); Leading Seaman, R.N.; H.M.S. Victorious and armed merchant ships.

***Counter, John** (1914–17); M.M.; Private, Devonshire Rgt.; France 2 years 6 months; Killed in action, 6th November, 1917.

Creasey, Robert (1914–19); Leading Seaman, R.N.

***Dobson, George Morrison** (1914–17); Farrier-Sergeant, R.A.S.C.; Salonica 13 months; Died, 16th October, 1917.

Dodman, Alfred George (1914–19); D.S.C.; Lieutenant, R.N.R.; Eastern Mediterranean, 3 years 4 months.

Frost, Albert (1914–16); Able Seaman, R.N.; Grand Fleet.

Hedgman, Henry (1914–19); Driver, R.A.S.C. and R.E.; France 4 years 8 months.

Hill, Rowland (1914–19); Able Seaman, R.N.; North Sea, Dardanelles, and Persian Gulf.

Horrex, Sidney Edward (1916–20); Private, R.A.S.C.; France 3 years.

Jones, John Walker (1914–19); D.S.M.; Chief Petty Officer, R.N.; H.M.S. Carmania.

Keogh, William James (1914–19); Leading Seaman, R.N.; H.M.S. Magnificent, Royal Arthur, Dunscombe, Vale and Pembroke.

McCombie, Frederick William (1914–19); Able Seaman, R.N.R.

***Mitchell, Arthur George** (1914); Private, Lincolnshire Rgt.; France; Died of wounds, August, 1914.

Parsons, Edward James (1914–19); Stoker, R.N.; H.M.S. Sirius.

Phillips, Richard (1914–19); Stoker, R. Fleet Reserve; H.M.S. Baron Ardrossan and Alouette.

Piche, Justin George (1915–19); Admiralty Pilot.

Pitt, William (1914–19); Private, R. Marine Light Infantry and R. Fleet Reserve.

Ross, Walter (1916–20); Engineer Lieutenant, R.N.R.; Mediterranean 9 months.

Skingle, George (1914–19); Petty Officer (1st Class), R.N.; South Atlantic and Northern patrol.

Storey, Alfred Dodds (1916–19); Mentioned in Marine Orders; Lieutenant (Hon. Captain), R. Indian Marine; Mesopotamia 2 years, India 15 months.

Verner, Claude Henry (1917–19); Lieutenant-Commander, R.N.R.

Webb, Henry David (1914–19); Leading Seaman, R.N.; South Pacific and South Atlantic.

Webb, John Richard (1914–19); Chief Petty Officer, R.N.; North Atlantic.

Wilkinson, George Ezra (1914–19); Admiralty Pilot.

Wood, Thomas (1914–19); Able Seaman, R.N.

ARCHITECT'S DEPARTMENT

***Aitken, James Hunter** (1914–16); Sec.-Lieutenant, 14th Bn. London Rgt. and 2/7th Bn. Royal Highlanders; France 14 months; Accidentally killed, 2nd June, 1916.

Allum, Stanley Charles (1914–19); Mentioned in despatches; Lieut.-Colonel, 12th Bn. London Rgt., Army Printing and Stationery Services, and Imperial War Graves Commission; France, Italy and Salonica, 4 years 6 months.

Alston, Joseph William (1914–19); Aircraftsman (2nd Class), 12th Bn. London Rgt. and R.A.F.; France 8 months, Mesopotamia 12 months, India 5 months.

Anderton, William Guy (1914–19); Lance-Corporal, 4th Bn. Middlesex Rgt.; France 4 years.

Armstrong, William Henry (1915–19); Private, R.E.; France 9 months.

Atkinson, Walter Edward (1917–19); Mentioned for valuable services rendered in connection with the War; Private, R.A.S.C.

Austin, William Ernest (1914–19); Corporal, R.E.; France 5 months.

Avely, James Arthur (1915–19); Officers' Steward, R.N.; Afloat 1 year 8 months.

Bailey, Charles Joseph (1914–19); Corporal, 12th Bn. London Rgt.; France 13 months.

***Bailey, Herbert Edwin** (1914–15); Private, 5th Bn. Seaforth Highlanders; France 2 months; Killed in action, 15th June, 1915.

Baker, William (1917–19); Private, 12th Bn. R. W. Surrey Rgt. and Labour Corps; France 2 years.

Ball, Robert Henry (1914); Gunner, R.F.A.

Balls, John Alan (1914–19); Croix de Guerre (Belgian); Company Sergeant-Major, 2/11th Bn. London Rgt.; France 16 months.

Bamford, William Hubert (1915–19); Mentioned in despatches; Corporal, R.A.M.C.; Egypt, Palestine and Syria, 2 years 10 months.

Bankhead, Frank (1915–19); Gunner, R.F.A.; Salonica and Palestine 2 years 4 months.

Barks, Edward Ernest (1916–18); Sec.-Lieutenant, R.E.

Barlow-Smith, John (1917–19); Air Mechanic (2nd Class), R.N.A.S. and R.A.F.

Barnard, Charles Downing (1914–19); Able Seaman, London Division, R.N.V.R.; Belgium and Holland (interned) 4 years 2 months.

***Barnard, Edwin** (1915); Sapper, R.E.; Dardanelles 3 months; Killed in action, 27th November, 1915.

Barnes, Alfred Henry (1915–19); Petty Officer, R.N.V.R.

Barry, John Francis (1915–19); Sergeant, R.G.A.; France 2 years.

Bartholomew, Charles Frederick (1916–19); Sapper, R.E.

Bartlett, Ernest Albert (1914–19); Gunner, R.F.A.; France 3 years.

Bartlett, Percy James (1915–19); Able Seaman, R.N.V.R.; Dardanelles, Salonica and Eastern Mediterranean, 2 years 4 months.

Bartlett, Reginald Douglas (1914–19); Corporal, 1st R. Bucks Hussars and R.E.; Egypt 4 months, Gallipoli 1 month, France 11 months.

Batty, John (1914–19); Private, 24th Bn. London Rgt. and Machine Gun Corps; France 2 years 7 months.

Bax, Edwin George Goodson (1914–19); Mentioned in despatches; Major, 28th Bn. London Rgt. and Machine Gun Corps; France and Germany 4 years 6 months.

Bayley, Benjamin Charles Ernest (1915–19); Lance-Corporal, R.E.; France 2 years 8 months.

Beckett, Percy Wilfred (1915–19); Company Sergeant-Major, Musketry Instructor, 15th and 23rd Bns. London Rgt.

Beech, Thomas (1915–19); Sapper, Royal Fusiliers and R.E.; France 3 years.

Benjamin, Frederick George (1916–19); Gunner, R.G.A.; France 1 year 8 months.

Berkholz, Frederick Charles William (1915–19); Private, 18th Bn. London Rgt. and R. Irish Fusiliers; France 6 months, Salonica 7 months, Palestine 8 months.

Besant, Hubert Saxton (1915–); R.E.

***Bick, Percy Arthur** (1916); Sec.-Lieut., R. Irish Rgt.; France 3 months; Killed in action, 3rd September, 1916.

Blair, Kenneth Archibald (1915–19); Air Mechanic (1st Class); 2nd County of London Yeomanry and R.A.F.; Libya, Egypt and Palestine, 3 years 2 months.

***Blake, Charles Stanley** (1914–15); Captain, 10th Bn. S. Lancashire Rgt. and 6th Bn. Lancashire Fusiliers; Gallipoli 3 months; Killed in action, 7th August, 1915.

Blanc, Louis David (1915 19); Lieutenant, 28th Bn. London Rgt. and R.E.

Blanks, Arthur Albert (1916–19); Company Quartermaster-Sergeant, R.E.

Blyth, Charles Kydd (1915–19); Sapper, 15th Bn. London Rgt. and R.E.; France 1 year 10 months.

Bobbett, Arthur James (1915–19); Sapper, R.E.; France 3 years 6 months.

Boden, Harrold Casswell (1915–19); Lieutenant, R.E.

Bond, George Hawkins (1915–19); Private, R.A.M.C.; Egypt 3 years 6 months.

Bond, Harold Henry (1916–19); Mentioned for valuable services in connection with the War; Lance-Corporal, R.A.O.C.; Salonica 3 months.

Boniface, Philip James (1916–19); Corporal, R.F.A.

Boon, Herbert Frederick (1915–19); Rifleman, 21st Bn. London Rgt.; France 8 months.

***Boot, Stanley Horace** (1914–16); Private, 5th Bn. Seaforth Highlanders; France 8 months; Killed in action, 13th November, 1916.

Bracken, Charles Leo (1916–19); Gunner, R.G.A.

Bradford, Alfred (1915–19); Private; R.A.S.C.; France and Germany 4 years.

Bray, Alfred George (1914–19); Quartermaster-Sergeant, Middlesex Rgt.

Bray, Herbert Arthur (1915–19); Company Quartermaster-Sergeant, 3/10th Bn. Middlesex Rgt.; France 18 months.

Bricknell, Thomas Mortimore (1914–19); Signalman, R.N.V.R.

Briggs, Alfred Denbigh (1915–19); Gunner, R.N.A.S., R.H.A. and R.G.A.; Egypt, Palestine and Syria, 2 years 6 months.

Brookes, Samuel (1914–19); Corporal, 8th Mounted Brigade Field Ambulance and 2/13th Bn. London Rgt.; Gallipoli 9 months, Salonica 9 months, Egypt 10 months, Palestine 18 months.

Brooks, John Sidney (1916–18); Sapper, R.E. and Sherwood Foresters; France 9 months.

Brooks, William Edward (1916–19); Air Mechanic (Grade 2), R.N.A.S. and R.A.F.

Brooks, William Edward (1914–19); Sergeant, R.A.M.C.; France and Germany 2 years 6 months.

Broomfield, Robert Henry (1916–19); Sergeant, Royal Fusiliers, 3rd Bn. Norfolk Rgt., 29th Bn. Middlesex Rgt. and Labour Corps.

Broughton, Alfred John Leslie (1916–19); Aircraftsman (1st Class), R.A.F.

Brown, Ernest William (1915–18); Driver, R.A.S.C.; Dardanelles 7 months, Egypt 1 year 9 months.

Brown, John William (1915–19); Lance-Corporal, 15th Bn. London Rgt.; France 2 years 8 months.

Brustmeyer, Albert William (1914–19); Private, R.A.M.C.; France 2 years.

Bryan, George Albert (1916–19); Air Mechanic (2nd Class), R.N.A.S. and R.A.F.

***Bryce, Maurice Steel** (1914); Bugler, 14th Bn. London Rgt.; France 6 weeks; Killed in action, 31st October, 1914.

Bull, Walter (1915–19); Private, R.A.M.C.; France 3 years 9 months.

Butcher, John Edward (1914–19); Sergeant, 10th Bn. Somerset Light Infantry.

***Butcher, Reginald Victor** (1914–18); Rifleman, 12th Bn. London Rgt.; France 18 months; Missing, 28th March, 1918.

Capel, George Watkin (1914–19); Regimental Sergeant-Major, 11th Bn. Welch Rgt.; France 2 months; Salonica 3 years 2 months.

Carey, Ernest Edward (1917–19); Paymaster Sub-Lieutenant, R.N.V.R.; Malta 9 months.

***Carey, James** (1914); Lance-Corporal Piper, 14th Bn. London Rgt.; France 6 weeks; Died of wounds, November, 1914.

Carment, James Maxwell (1915–19); Sergeant, R.A.M.C.; France 7 months Macedonia 7 months, Egypt and Palestine 18 months.

Carter, George Albert (1915–19); Gunner, R.G.A.; France 1 year 10 months.

Carter, William Henry (1915–19); Private, R.A.M.C.; France 2 years 10 months.

Catt, Alfred Edward (1915–19); Lance-Corporal, R.G.A. and R.E.; France 2 years 3 months.

Chalmers, Frank Runcie (1915–19); Staff-Sergeant, R.A.M.C.; Egypt and Balkans 3 years 6 months.

Chamberlain, Charles (1915–19); Staff-Sergeant, R.E.

Chambers, John Wesley (1915–19); Company Sergeant-Major, R.E.; France 3 years 3 months.

***Chappell, Alfred Ernest William** (1914–15); Lance-Corporal, 24th Bn. London Rgt.; France 2 months; Killed in action, 26th May, 1915.

Chew, Richard (1914–19); Major, 15th Bn. London Rgt.; France 6 months.

Chubb, James Arthur (1918–19); Private R.A.M.C.; Russia 10 months.

Clark, Henry Stanley (1914–19); Sergeant, R.A.S.C.; Russia 11 months.

Clarke, Harold William (1915–19); Lance-Corporal, R. W. Surrey Rgt. and R.E.; France 3 years 4 months, Italy 3 months.

Clothier, William Henry (1915–19); Corporal, Royal Fusiliers; France 1 year 7 months.

Clutterbuck, Herbert Charles (1915–19); Sapper, R.E.

Coe, Robert (1915–19); Sergeant, R.E.; France 1 year 10 months, Italy 12 months.

Cole, Frank Henry (1915–19); Lance-Bombardier, R.F.A.; France 2 years 6 months.

Collett, Edward Bartlett (1914–19); Private, London Defence Corps.

Coney, Harold Robert Harvey (1914–17); M.S.M., mentioned in despatches; Private, 15th Bn. London Rgt.; France 2 years 1 month.

Cooke, Isaac (1915–19); Lieutenant, 6th Bn. Essex Rgt. and R.D.C.

Cooksey, Harold Thoresby (1914–16); Corporal, R.G.A.

Coombes, Francis John (1914–19); M.S.M., mentioned in despatches; Staff-Sergeant, R.E.; France 2 years 6 months, Italy 15 months.

Coram, Cyril Frederick (1914–18); Private, R.A.M.C.; Malta 17 months, Salonica 1 year 11 months.

Cornwell, Aubrey William (1914–19); Staff-Sergeant, Middlesex Rgt.

Cousins, Herbert Hoy (1914–19); Private, R.A.M.C.; France 18 months.

Cowper, James Bertie Francis (1914–19); Major, 14th Bn. London Rgt. and R.E.; France 3 years.

Cox, Bertram Manfred (1915–19); Corporal, A.P.C.

Coxon, James Edgar (1917–19); Private, R.A.S.C. (M.T.); France 2 years.

Creighton, Harry Richard (1915–19); Private, 28th Bn. London Rgt.

Cresswell, Thomas Edwin (1914–19); M.C.; Lieutenant, R.N.V.R. and R. Naval Division.; Afloat 12 months, France 14 months.

Crockett, George Alfred (1915–19); Private, A.P.C.

Crome, John Stanley (1914–19); Sergeant, Essex Rgt. and R.E.; France 2 years 7 months.

Cronin, Daniel Patrick (1916–19); Private, R.F.A. and Labour Corps.

Cullen, David Shearer (1915–19); Sergeant, R.A.M.C.; France 3 years 9 months.

Curling, Robert Francis (1918); Sapper, R.E.

Dalby, Harold Scott (1914–16); Trooper, 1st County of London Yeomanry; Egypt and Gallipoli 6 months.

Dawn, Herbert Cecil (1915–19); Lieutenant, 28th Bn. London Rgt. and 8th Bn. W. Yorkshire Rgt.; France and Germany 2 years 10 months.

Derbyshire, John Shirley (1916–19); Gunner, R.G.A.; France 6 months.

Dinneen, Louis Barom (1915–19); Leading Aircraftsman; 5th Bn. London Rgt. and R.A.F.; France 8 months.

Dolbear, Albert (1915–19); Sec.-Lieutenant, 2/28th Bn. London Rgt. and R.E.; France 15 months.

Douglas, Arthur Alan (1915–19); Corporal, W. Riding Rgt.

Downes, Harry Stretton (1915–17); Rifleman, A.P.C. and Rifle Brigade.

Drew, Sidney Vernon (1915–19); Sapper, 5th Bn. London Rgt. and R.E.; France and Germany 12 months.

Durant, Frederick Henry (1915–19); Private, R.A.M.C.; France 2 years 11 months.

Durden, John Henry (1914–19); Corporal, A.P.C. and Royal Fusiliers.

Durden, Stanley John (1916–19); Sapper, R.E.

Durnford, William John (1914–19); Lieutenant, R.A.M.C. and Wiltshire Rgt.; France 1 year 9 months, Salonica 3 months, Egypt 2 months.

Earl, Albert Bertram Harold (1915–19); Private, R.A.M.C.; France 7 months, Salonica 7 months, Egypt and Palestine 1 year 8 months.

Earl, William Henry (1915–19); Able Seaman, R.N.V.R.; Afloat 12 months.

Earle, Leslie Marriot (1914–19); Lance-Corporal, 24th Bn. London Rgt.; France 2 years 10 months.

Edwards, Harry Brett (1915–19); Private, R.A.M.C.; France 2 years.

***Edwards, John Percival** (1915–16); Company Sergeant-Major, Royal Fusiliers; France 5 months; Died of wounds, 7th October, 1916.

Elliott, Edward William Savery (1915–19); Private, R.A.M.C.; France 2 years 2 months, Salonica 10 months.

Evans, Reginald George Llewellyn (1914–18); Captain, S. Wales Borderers and Essex Rgt.; Gallipoli and Egypt 4 months, France 1 week.

Excell, William Isaac (1916–19); Gunner, R.E. and R.G.A.

Falconer, Herbert John (1915–19); Sergeant, W. Riding Rgt.

Faulkner, Frank (1915–19); Private, R.A.M.C.; France 3 years 7 months.

Fennell, Michael (1914–16); Private, R.E.

***Field, Herbert Noel** (1917); Private, 4th Bn. Bedfordshire Rgt.; France 9 months; Killed in action, 30th October, 1917.

Filkins, Edwin William (1915–19); Private, R.A.M.C.; France 2 years.

Fisher, Frederick (1915–20); Sergeant, R.A.F.

***Foale, William Ernest** (1916–19); Lieutenant, 28th Bn. London Rgt. and R.G.A.; Died, 1st May, 1919.

Foreman, Ernest John (1914–19); Wheeler Staff-Sergeant, R.A.S.C.; France 2 years 3 months.

Foster, Gaius (1915–19); Captain, R.A.M.C. and R.E.; France 3 years 1 month.

Foster, Herbert (1914–16); M.M. and mentioned in despatches; Private, 15th Bn. London Rgt.; France 10 months.

Francis, George Eric (1915–19); Lieutenant, R.E. and R.A.F.

Francis, John Linton (1915–19); Sapper, R.E.; France 2 years 11 months.

Franklin, Francis Evans (1915–19); Corporal, R.A.M.C.

Franklin, Herbert John (1915–19); Staff-Sergeant, R.A.M.C.; France 5 months, Macedonia 7 months, Palestine 15 months, Egypt 8 months.

Franks, Herbert William (1915-19); Mentioned in despatches; Sergeant, R.A.M.C.; Egypt and Palestine 4 years.

French, Cecil George (1915–19); Mentioned in despatches; Major, R.E.; Macedonia 4 years.

Fullbrook, Charles William Ernest (1916–19); Private, R.A.M.C.; Salonica 6 months, Palestine 17 months, Egypt 10 months, France 1 month.

Funnell, Horace Frederick (1916–19); Lieutenant, R.A.S.C.; France 12 months.

Gage, Ernest James Empleton (1915–19); Able Seaman, R.N.V.R.; Afloat 5 months.

Gamble, Arthur Ernest (1914–19); Private, 2nd Bn. E. Surrey Rgt.

Gardner, Herbert (1914–19); Private, 14th Bn. London Rgt.; France 2 years 10 months.

Geary, Frank George (1916–19); Corporal, R.A.M.C.; Salonica 2 years 5 months.

Gerrard, George (1915–17); Mentioned for valuable services rendered in connection with the War; Sergeant, A.P.C.

Gibbs, Stanley George (1914–17); Private, 24th Bn. London Rgt.; France 14 months.

Gibson, George Paterson (1914–15); Private, Middlesex Rgt.

Gilpin, William Alfred (1916–19); Sapper, King's Royal Rifle Corps and R.E.; France 12 months.

Glass, John Guthrie Lornie (1914–19); Sec.-Lieutenant, 14th Bn. London Rgt. and R.E.

Godfrey, Horace John (1915–17); Private, R.A.M.C.; Egypt and Balkans 1 year 9 months.

Godwin, Charles Samuel (1916–19); Rifleman, King's Royal Rifle Corps; France 1 month.

Goffin, Thomas James (1915–19); Sergeant, R.E.; France 3 years 2 months.

***Golding, Frederick George** (1914–16); Sergeant, 6th Bn. London Rgt.; France 17 months; Died of wounds, 21st August, 1916.

***Goodwin, Dudley Fletcher** (1914–17); Captain, 15th Bn. London Rgt. and R.F.A.; France 2 years; Died of wounds, 7th March, 1917.

Gooding, William Hines (1918–19); Air Mechanic, R.A.F.

Gordon, Charles (1915–19); Second Writer, R.N.; Afloat 3 years 1 month.

Gostling, Wilfred Bernard (1914–19); M.C.; Captain, 1st County of London Yeomanry and 11th Bn. London Rgt.; Gallipoli, Egypt and Palestine, 3 years 10 months.

Gough, Lawrence Ardeley Wyndham (1915–19); Lieutenant, Middlesex Rgt.; France 2 years 9 months.

Graeme, Alan Vincent Sutherland (1914–20); Mentioned in despatches; Captain, 14th Bn. London Rgt. and 4th Bn. Seaforth Highlanders; France 3 years 10 months.

Gray, Charles George (1914–17); Private, 15th Bn. London Rgt.; France 8 months.

Gray, Walter (1916–19); Air Mechanic (1st Class), R.N.A.S. and R.A.F.

Green, Arthur Edward (1915–19); Private, R.A.M.C.; Egypt and Palestine 3 years 4 months.

Grieve, William Holt Lacey (1914–19); Captain, 14th Bn. London Rgt. and R.A.O.C.; Afloat 4 months, France 5 months.

Grinsted, Henry Arthur (1914–19); Corporal, R.A.M.C.; France 5 months, Salonica 7 months, Palestine 2 years 1 month.

Habermehl, William Maximilian (1918–19); Rifleman, 25th Bn. Rifle Brigade.

***Haggis, Percy** (1914); Leading Seaman, R. Naval Brigade and R.N.V.R.; Belgium; Killed in action, 7th October, 1914.

Hale, Ernest (1915–19); Staff-Sergeant, R.A.V.C.

Hall, Albert Huband (1914–19); Lieutenant, R.G.A.; France 9 months.

Hall, George Langley Desmond (1914–19); Captain, 13th Bn. London Rgt.; Belgium 3 months.

Hall, William Thomas (1914–19); Corporal, 15th Bn. London Rgt. and Machine Gun Corps; France 2 years 8 months.

***Hannaford, William George Nott** (1915–16); Sapper, R.E.; France 12 months; Died of wounds, 23rd September, 1916.

***Harling, Arthur Thomas** (1915–16); Private, 15th Bn. London Rgt.; France 6 months; Killed in action, 15th September, 1916.

Harlock, Harold (1915–19); Lieutenant, R.N.V.R.; Afloat 3 years 8 months.

Harrington, John Stephen (1915–19); D.C.M.; Sergeant, R.A.M.C.; France 13 months.

Harris, Alfred Henry (1915–19); Gunner, R.F.A.; France 2 years.

Harris, Walter George (1914–19); Lieutenant, 9th Bn. London Rgt. and 1st Huntingdonshire Cyclist Bn. attached Bedfordshire Rgt.; France 5 months.

Harris, Wilfred Henry (1914–19); Sapper, 28th and 2/13th Bns. London Rgt. and R.E.; France 7 months, Salonica 8 months, Palestine 4 months.

Hart, Charles Wesley Limmer (1914–19); Leading Seaman, R.N.V.R.; Afloat 4 years 5 months.

Hayes, John Henry (1914–19); Lance-Corporal, R.E.; France 3 years 6 months.

Hayward, Arthur Edwin (1916–19); Private, Middlesex Rgt.; France 12 months.

Heiden, Charles Arthur (1915–19); Sergeant, W. Riding Rgt. and R.A.F.

Henderson, John Alexander (1914–19); Mentioned in despatches; Lieutenant, W. Kent Yeomanry and R.E.; France and Italy 2 years 9 months.

Henly, Thomas Charles Edward (1915–19); Corporal, R.F.C.; France 3 years 6 months.

Hensby, George Henry Thompson (1915–19); Private, R.A.M.C.; France 6 months, Macedonia 6 months, Egypt and Palestine 1 year 7 months.

Hepburn, James William (1915–19); M.S.M.; Private, 14th Bn. London Rgt.; France 3 years.

Hill, Alfred (1915–19); Rifleman, 6th Bn. London Rgt.; France 2 years 1 month.

Hill, Arthur Robert (1915–19); Private, R.A.M.C.; France 6 months, Salonica 12 months, Egypt and Palestine 2 years 1 month.

Hodgkinson, Edward Dunthorne (1915–19); Corporal, 15th Bn. London Rgt.

Home, Geoffrey Wyville (1914–19); Lieutenant, 28th Bn. London Rgt. and R.G.A.

Hooper, William Doughty (1914–19); Lieutenant, 15th Bn. London Rgt. and R.A.; France 15 months.

Howard, Harry Thomson (1915–19); Corporal, R.A.S.C.; France 3 years 1 month.

Howell, Edward Arthur (1914–19); Lieutenant, 19th Bn. London Rgt.; France 3 years 1 month.

Howse, Owen Charles (1915–19); Lance-Corporal, Honourable Artillery Company (Infantry); France 8 months.

Hubert, Ernest Frank (1917–19); Sapper, R.E.

Huggins, Harry (1914–17); Sapper, 24th Bn. London Rgt. and R.E.; France 10 months.

Huggins, William Edward (1915–19); Private, R.A.M.C.; France and Germany 2 years 8 months.

Hughes, Thomas Francis Collier (1914–19); Corporal, R.A.M.C.; France 4 years.

Hurcomb, Harold Francis (1915–20); Lieutenant, R.E.; France 12 months.

Hyder, Cyril (1914–16); Corporal, 15th Bn. London Rgt.; France 3 months.

Irvin, George William (1916–19); Corporal, R.A.M.C.; Italy 2 years 3 months.

Isaacs, William Charles (1916–19); Corporal, R.F.A. and R.A.F.

Jaggers, Frederick Arthur (1915–19); Corporal, R.N.V.R. and R.G.A.

James, Albert Edward (1915–19); Lance-Corporal, R.E.; France 2 years 8 months.

James, Harry Gordon (1915–19); Private, R.A.M.C.; Egypt 13 months, Palestine 12 months, France 13 months.

Jardine, Alexander (1914–19); Sergeant, 20th Bn. London Rgt., R.D.C. and King's Liverpool Rgt.

Jardine, Henry Stringer (1915–19); Lieutenant, 14th Bn. London Rgt. and R.E.; France 10 months.

Jay, Harold John Syrett (1918–19); Private, R.A.F.

Jessep, Edward Archibald (1914–19); Able Seaman, R.N.V.R.; Belgium 3 weeks, afloat 4 years.

Johnson, Frank Leslie (1914–19); Lieutenant, Argyll and Sutherland Highlanders, 2/41st Dogras, attached 3/154 Indian Infantry; India 5 months, Egypt and Palestine 11 months, France 14 months.

Jones, Alcwyn Arnold (1916); Gunner, R.F.A.

Jones, Charles Thomas (1915–19); Mentioned in despatches; Sapper, 15th Bn. London Rgt. and R.E.; France 2 years 9 months.

Jones, Launcelot Cyril Clark (1915–19); Air Mechanic, R.N.A.S.; Afloat 2 years.

Kaul, Douglas (1915–19); Corporal, R.A.S.C.; France 4 years.

Keele, John Daniel (1914–20); Lieutenant, 5th Bn. London Rgt. and Labour Corps; France 4 months.

Keen, Arthur Auger (1916–19); M.S.M.; Corporal, R.E.; France 2 years.

***Kemp, Robert Ernest** (1915–17); Private, 7th Bn. Bedfordshire Rgt., Royal Fusiliers and 4th Bn. Northamptonshire Rgt.; Dardanelles and Egypt 8 months, France 16 months; Died of wounds, 31st October, 1917.

Kendall, John David (1914–18); Assistant Paymaster, 1st London Yeomanry and R.N.R.

Kerr, Walter Matthew (1914–19); M.M.; Sergeant, 2/7th Bn. London Rgt. and Machine Gun Corps; France 14 months.

Kibblewhite, Henry James Treleaven (1914–19); Mentioned in despatches; Company Quartermaster-Sergeant, 17th Bn. Royal Fusiliers and R.E.; France 3 years 2 months.

Kingsnorth, Horace Andrew (1914–19); Able Seaman, R.N.V.R.; France 2 months, afloat 4 years 1 month.

Kirby, Harold Arthur (1917–19); Sapper, R. W. Surrey, Middlesex, and Suffolk Rgts., and R.E.

Kitchenside, Thomas (1915–19); Gunner, R.F.A.; France and Italy, 1 year 11 months.

Lambert, Edward Montague (1914–19); Staff-Sergeant, 3rd Bn. Gloucestershire Rgt.; France 12 months.

Lauder, Frederick Worthy (1916–19); Private, R.A.M.C.; France and Germany, 2 years 2 months.

***Lawrance, Herbert Ewart** (1915–17); Private, Honourable Artillery Company; France 6 months; Killed in action, 1st April, 1917.

***Lawrence, Horace Wilfred** (1915–16); Private, 15th Bn. London Rgt.; France 11 months; Killed in action, 7th October, 1916.

Leatherdale, Francis Harold (1914–19); mentioned in despatches; Cadet, R.A.M.C. and R.E.; France 12 months, Salonika 2 years 9 months.

Lewcock, George (1914–19); Private, R.A.M.C.; France 6 months, Balkans 1 year 11 months.

Lewis, Harold Henry Graham (1917–19); Lance-Corporal, R.E.

Ling, Richard Bertram (1916–19); Mentioned in despatches; Private, R.A.M.C.; Italy 2 years 6 months.

Lingard, Alfred (1916–19); Private, R.A.M.C.; France 2 years 7 months.

Linnell, Henry John (1914–19); M.M., Mentioned in despatches; Lieutenant, 15th Bn. London Rgt. and R.A.O.C.; France and Germany 4 years 5 months.

Linnett, Raymund Patrick (1914–19); Driver, R.F.A.; France 3 years 7 months.

Love, Edward Frederick (1915–19); Lance-Corporal, R.E.; France 3 years 2 months.

Love, Robert Samuel Booth (1914–19); Lieutenant, 12th Bn. London Rgt. and 1st Bn. Worcestershire Rgt.

Loweth, Sidney Harold (1916–19); Staff-Sergeant, R.E.

Lucas, Frederick James (1914–19); Captain, Inns of Court O.T.C. and W. Riding Rgt.; France 18 months.

Lucas, Walter Berwick (1914–19); Private, 10th Bn. London Rgt. and 18th Bn. Rifle Brigade; Burma 4 years.

***Lund, John Alfred** (1914); Gunner, R.F.A.; Died, 12th December, 1914.

Lythgoe, Ernest (1914–19); Private, E. Kent Yeomanry.

Machattie, John Macintosh (1914–19); Sergeant, 14th Bn. London Rgt.; France and Germany, 2 years 7 months.

Mackenzie, Henry Blinman (1917–19); Lieutenant, R.E.

Macrae, James (1917–18); Air Mechanic (2nd Class), R.A.F.

Maggs, William James Charles (1915–19); Rifleman, King's Royal Rifle Corps; France 2 years 6 months.

Maguire, Herbert William (1915–19); Sec.-Lieutenant, R.E. and 28th Bn. London Rgt.

Malvisi, Sidney Alfred (1915–19); Lance-Corporal, 5th Bn. London Rgt.; France 7 months.

Mann, Stanley Darter (1915–19); Mentioned in despatches; Sec.-Lieutenant, 5th Bn. London Rgt. and Royal Fusiliers; France 13 months.

Marks, Charles Arthur (1916); Private, 2/1st Kent Cyclists.

Marks, Charles George (1914–17); Sergeant, 12th Bn. London Rgt.; France 1 year 10 months.

Martin, Herbert William (1915–19); Lieutenant, R.F.A.; France 1 year 11 months.

Martin, Moritz Richard (1915–19); Sec.-Lieutenant, R.A.M.C. and R.E.; France 3 years 4 months.

McLachlan, Charles (1914–15); Rifleman, 12th Bn. London Rgt.; France 5 months.

Mercer, Francis Howard (1917–19); Lieutenant, R.A.S.C.

Mercer, Lionel Douglas (1915–18); Sergeant, R.E.; France 2 years 2 months.

Merriman, Percival Harry (1914–19); Private, 15th Bn. London Rgt.; Salonica 9 months, Palestine and Egypt 18 months.

Merrison, Charles Redford (1916–19); Private, 2/5th Bn. Bedfordshire Rgt. and 15th Bn. Essex Rgt.; France 10 months.

Miller, Charles (1914–19); Private; 18th Bn. London Rgt.

Mills, Harold (1914–19); Colour-Sergeant, 23rd Bn. London Rgt.; France 18 months, Salonica 7 months, Egypt 12 months.

Mills, Henry Graham Hunt (1914–19); Captain, 28th Bn. London Rgt. and R.E.; France 4 years 7 months.

Minchin, William Clayton (1914–19); D.C.M.; Staff-Sergeant, 4th Bn. Seaforth Highlanders; France 10 months.

Montgomery, George (1915–19); Gunner, R.G.A.; France and Germany 2 years 9 months.

Moody, Rowland Granville (1915–19); Able Seaman, R.N.V.R.

Moore, Alfred William (1916–19); Mentioned for valuable service; Rifleman, King's Royal Rifle Corps; France 2 years 1 month.

Moore, Thomas William (1915–19); Mentioned for valuable services in connection with the War; Corporal, W. Riding Rgt.

Morgan, Thomas George (1915–17); Corporal, R.E.; France 16 months.

Mullens, Charles Arthur (1915–19); Sergeant, Royal Fusiliers; Palestine, Egypt and Syria, 12 months.

Mumford, Albert James Whiffin (1914–19); Sapper, Essex Rgt. and R.E.; Gallipoli 6 months, Egypt, Palestine and Syria 3 years 3 months.

Murché, Percy Douglas (1916–18); Air Mechanic (2nd Class), R.F.C.

Nathan, Percy Phineas (1917–19); Private, 15th Bn. London Rgt.; France 18 months.

Neat, Robert Chalmers (1917–19); Mentioned for valuable services in connection with the War; Private, R.A.S.C.

Newman, Henry Cecil (1915–19); Sapper, 16th Bn. London Rgt. and R.E.; France 2 years 6 months.

Nicholas, Reginald Ernest (1914–19); M.M.; Corporal, 15th Bn. London Rgt.; France 8 months.

Nicoll, Alfred Doig (1914–19); Sapper, Seaforth Highlanders and R.E.; France 4 years.

Nisbet, Edgar Charley (1916–19); Lieutenant, 28th Bn. London Rgt., R.F.A. and R.G.A.; Malta 1 year 11 months.

Nott, Frederick Osmond Webber (1915–19); Private, R.A.M.C.; France 2 years 11 months.

Oakey, John George (1914–18); Private, 9th Bn. London Rgt. and Labour Corps.

Oram, Charles (1914–19); Sergeant Piper, 14th Bn. London Rgt.; France 12 months, Salonica 6 months, Palestine 12 months.

Oram, Emmanuel Joseph (1914–17); Corporal, Middlesex Rgt. and R.D.C.

Page, Charles Percy (1914–19); Private, R.A.S.C.; France 2 years 11 months, Italy 15 months.

Palser, Charles John (1914–19); Lieutenant, 15th Bn. London Rgt. and 1st Bn. E. Surrey Rgt.; France 3 years 4 months.

Parker, Alfred Thomas Hobman (1915–18); Sec.-Lieutenant, Honourable Artillery Company and 10th Bn. R. Inniskilling Fusiliers.

Parker, Ernest John Canning (1914–17); Superior Sapper, R.E.; France 2 years.

Parker, Victor (1915–17); Rifleman, 5th Bn. London Rgt.; France 10 months.

Parkin, William Gordon (1914–19); Sec.-Lieutenant, Royal Fusiliers and Northumberland Fusiliers; France 2 years 7 months.

Parnell, George Routley (1915–19); Private, R.A.M.C.; France 2 years 9 months.

Parr, Sydney Hosking (1915–19); Private, R.A.S.C.; France 4 years.

***Parry, David** (1917–18); M.S.M.; Clerk (1st Class), R.A.F. and 6th Bn. Rifle Brigade; France 9 months; Died, 25th December, 1918.

Parsons, Leonard Rudolph Charles (1916–19); Aircraftsman (1st Class), R.N.A.S. and R.A.F.; France 2 years 8 months.

Payne, Henry (1914–17); Private, R.D.C.

Peach, Edward Lionel Joseph (1914–19); Trooper, City of London Yeomanry and 20th Cavalry Machine Gun Squadron attached to Indian Cavalry; Egypt, Palestine and Syria, 2 years 7 months.

Pearson, Frederick George (1914–19); Lieutenant, 1st R. East Kent Mounted Rifles and British W. Indies Rgt.; Gallipoli 5 months, Egypt 15 months, Palestine 2 years.

Pentlow, John Harry (1914–19); Private, 2/4th R. W. Kent Rgt.; Gallipoli, Egypt and Palestine, 3 years 8 months.

Perkins, Charles Fearnall (1915–18); Private, R.A.M.C.; France 5 months.

Perrin, Henry Charles (1914, 1915–18); Private, King's Own R. Lancaster Rgt., 10th Bn. London Rgt. and London Defence Corps.

Perry, George Edward (1914–16); Able Seaman, R.N.; Afloat 2 years 3 months.

***Peters, William Frederick Daniel** (1915–19); Lance-Corporal, R.A.M.C.; France and Germany 2 years 3 months; Died, 2nd May, 1919.

Petts, Alfred William (1914–19); Private, 5th Bn. London Rgt.; France 2 years 9 months.

Peyto, Alfred James (1916–19); Air Mechanic (2nd Class), R.N.A.S. and R.A.F.

***Philips, Arthur Maxwell** (1914–15); Captain, 11th and 13th Bns. King's Own Yorkshire Light Infantry; Gallipoli 2½ months; Killed in action, 11th November, 1915.

Philp, Arthur Thomas (1916–18); Sapper, 3/18th and 20th Bns. London Rgt. and R.E.; France 1 year 8 months.

Philpott, Bertram Homersham (1916–19); Lance-Corporal, R.E.; France 18 months.

Picknell, Leonard (1915–19); Private, 28th Bn. London Rgt.; France 12 months.

Pinfold, Stanley (1916–19); Petty Officer (1st Class), R.N.A.S. and R.A.F.

Pitt, Herbert William Matthew Ovenden (1916–19); Private, R.A.M.C.; France 12 months, Italy 12 months.

Player, William John (1915–17, 1918–19); Air Mechanic (2nd Class), R.N.V.R. and R.A.F.

Plim, Harold (1914–19); D.C.M., Belgian Croix de Guerre and Mentioned in despatches; Sergeant, 2/23rd Bn. London Rgt.; France 15 months, Salonica 6 months, Palestine 12 months.

***Ponton, Harold Frederick** (1915–17); Private, 17th and 18th Bns. Royal Fusiliers; France 17 months; Killed in action, 29th April, 1917.

Pope, Thomas Campbell (1915–19); Lieutenant, R.E.

Power, Charles (1915–19); Corporal, R.E.; France 12 months.

Pratt, Frederick William (1917–19); Sapper, R.E.

Quirke, William Dathy (1914–19); Captain, 5th Bn. London Rgt. and R.E.; France 4 years.

***Rammage, Frederick Bant** (1915–18); Gunner, R.F.A.; France about 2 years; Killed in action, 28th March, 1918.

Ranger, John Samuel (1915–19); Private, R.A.M.C.; Egypt and Palestine 3 years 4 months.

Ransley, John (1914–19); Private, 1st Bn. E. Surrey Rgt.; France 4 years 3 months.

Rashleigh, Edward George (1915–19); Private, R.A.M.C.; Egypt 3 years 5 months.

Rayner, Leslie Stanley Paul Holmes (1914–20); Lieutenant, 15th Bn. London Rgt. and Machine Gun Corps; France and Germany 3 years 9 months.

Reddy, Vernon Sydney Frederick (1915–19); Private, 2/15th Bn. London Rgt.; France 13 months, Egypt and Palestine 13 months, Salonica 7 months.

Reed, Percival John (1914–19); Sergeant, 20th Bn. London Rgt.; France 9 months.

Rees, Alvine Edward (1915–19); Mentioned in despatches, Médaille d'Honneur avec Glaives (en Bronze); Private, R.A.S.C.; France 3 years 11 months.

Rich, Ernest John (1915–19); Sapper, R.E.; France and Germany 2 years 10 months.

Richards, Charles (1915–19); 2nd Corporal, R.E.; France 3 years.

***Richardson Frank** (1917–18); Private, E. Surrey Rgt.; France 1 month; Killed in action, 23rd March, 1918.

Richardson, John Ernest (1914–19); Sec.-Lieutenant, Honourable Artillery Company and R.A.S.C.; Egypt, Palestine and Syria, 4 years 6 months.

***Rizzi, Cyril Luigi** (1914–15); Rifleman, 12th Bn. London Rgt.; France 6 months; Missing, 8th May, 1915.

Robertson, Robert (1914–16); Sergeant, 14th Bn. London Rgt.

Roche, Cecil Stuart (1914–19); Captain, Middlesex Rgt.; France 8 months.

Rossiter, William Clarke (1914–19); Temporary Flight-Sergeant; 1st County of London Yeomanry, R.N.A.S. and R.A.F.

Rotherham, Douglas George (1914–19); Mentioned for valuable service; Staff-Sergeant, 14th Bn. London Rgt. and R.A.S.C.; Egypt and Palestine 3 years 2 months.

Routh, Horace (1915–16); Private, 2/3rd County of London Yeomanry.

Rowdon, William Henry (1915–19); Corporal, A.P.C.

Rowlinson, Mortimer (1914–19); Sergeant, 28th Bn. London Rgt.; France 4 years 4 months.

Ruffle, Hugh William Ellis (1915–19); Lieutenant, R.N.V.R. and Army Printing and Stationery Services; France 1 year 7 months.

Rule, John Frederick (1914–18); Corporal, R.A.M.C.

Russell, Albert Edward (1915–19); Sapper, R.E.; France and Germany 3 years 5 months.

***Russell, Archibald Henry** (1914–16); Private, 15th Bn. London Rgt.; France 12 months; Killed in action, 22nd May, 1916.

Sands, Hubert Covell (1915–19); Captain, R.A.M.C.; France 2 years 1 month.

Scott, James Maxwell (1914–19); Lieutenant, 14th Bn. London Rgt. and R.A.S.C.; France 2 years.

Scott, John Mailler (1914–19); Lieutenant, R.G.A.; France 15 months.

Shackell, William (1915–19); Private, R.A.S.C.; France 2 years 1 month.

Sharpe, Ernest Walter (1915–19); Private, R.A.M.C.; France 6 months, Salonica 7 months, Palestine 2 years.

Sharpington, Thomas James (1917–19); Sapper, R.E.; France 1 year 10 months.

Shaw, Edmund Charles Henry (1916–19); Private, 15th, 12th and 6th Bns. London Rgt.; France 16 months.

***Shears, Reginald** (1914–16); Rifleman, 9th Bn. London Rgt.; France 7 months; Missing, 1st July, 1916.

Sheasby, Harry (1914–19); Sergeant, 5th Bn. London Rgt. and R.F.C.

Shipway, George Frederick (1914–19); M.S.M.; Sergeant, 28th Bn. London Rgt. and R.E.; France 3 years 9 months.

Shipwright, William George (1915–19); Sec.-Lieutenant, R.N.V.R. and R.N.A.S.; France 3 months.

Shorrock, Maurice Stanley Booth (1915–19); Private, 20th Bn. London Rgt.; France 2 years 3 months.

Simms, William (1915–19); Corporal, R.E.; France 12 months.

Simpson, Charles Henry (1916–19); Sergeant, R.A.S.C.; France 3 years 1 month.

Singleton, Richard Harold (1915–19); M.S.M., twice mentioned in despatches; Warrant Officer (Class II.), R.A.S.C.; Gallipoli, Egypt and Palestine, 4 years.

Slight, Edward (1915–17); Able Seaman, R.N.V.R.

Smith, Arthur (1915–19); Lance-Corporal, R.E.

Smith, Frederick Thomas (1915–19); Private, R.A.M.C.; France 10 months.

Smith, George Thow (1914–19); Sergeant, Honourable Artillery Company; France 10 months.

Smith, Stanley William (1915–18); Sergeant, Honourable Artillery Company.

Smith, William Harry (1915–19); Sergeant Mechanic, R.E. and R.A.F.; Egypt 2 years 5 months.

Southgate, Charles Crouch (1914–19); Corporal, R.E.; France 4 years 2 months.

Spence, Andrew Tebbutt (1914–19); Private, 23rd Bn. London Rgt., and Sapper, R.E.; France 4 years.

Spencer, Thomas (1915–19); Lieutenant, R.F.C. and R.A.F.

Staig, John Percy (1914–19); Mentioned in despatches; Private, R.A.M.C., and Aircraftsman (1st Class), R.A.F.; France 9 months, Balkans 3 years 1 month, South Russia 3 months.

***Stanbrough, Ernest Gilbert** (1914–17); Sergeant, Royal Fusiliers; France 12 months; Missing, 17th February, 1917.

***Stanton, Frederick Henry** (1914–15); Private, 12th Bn. London Rgt.; France 5 months; Killed in action, 24th April, 1915.

Stedeford, John Britton (1915–16); Corporal, R.E.; France 2 months.

Stevens, Robert George (1914–19); Captain, R. W. Kent Rgt. and R.E.; India 16 months, France 8 months, Mesopotamia 2 years 4 months.

Stewart, William (1915–19); Lance-Corporal, 2/3rd Bn. London Rgt.; France 2 years 10 months.

Stransom, Walter Ronald (1914–16); Private, 15th Bn. London Rgt.; France 9 months.

Strudwick, Francis John (1916–19); Sergeant Mechanic, R.N.A.S. and R.A.F.

Stump, Albert Edward (1915–19); Private, Royal Fusiliers; France, Germany and Italy, 2 years 10 months.

Sturges, Herbert John (1916–19); Private, R.A.M.C.; Balkans 7 months, Egypt 1 year, Palestine 14 months.

Swain, George Henry (1917–19); Sapper, R.A.M.C. and R.E.; France and Germany 2 years 4 months.

Tarrant, Charles George (1914–17); Lance-Sergeant, 11th Bn. R. W. Kent Rgt.; France 7 months.

Taylor, James William (1915); Private, R.A.S.C.

***Taylor, Joseph Henry** (1915–16); Private, R.A.S.C.; France 16 months; Killed in action, 28th July, 1916.

Taylor, Reginald Minton (1914–19); Lieutenant, Middlesex Rgt. and R.D.C.; France 5 months.

Thirtle, Tom Owen (1915–19); Private, R.A.M.C.; France 2 years 11 months.

Thomas, Edward Albert (1917–19); Pioneer, R.E.; France 1 year 10 months.

Thomas, Frederick Charles (1915–19); Private, R.A.S.C.; Egypt 3 years 5 months.

Thomas, Noel (1915–19); Sapper, R.E.; France 3 years, Italy 4 months.

Thomas, William Albert (1915–18); Private, 23rd Bn. London Rgt.; France 18 months.

Thomason, William (1915–19); Private, R.A.M.C. and 2/13th Bn. London Rgt.; Egypt and Palestine 3 years 3 months.

***Tinniswood, Alfred** (1915–18); Sec.-Lieutenant, 28th Bn. London Rgt. and R.E.; France 3 months; Killed in action, 1st October, 1918.

Tiplady, Frederick Chester (1914–19); Mentioned in despatches; Company Quartermaster-Sergeant, 15th Bn. London Rgt., 47th Division Cyclists and Tank Corps; France 3 years 4 months.

Tippetts, Alfred William (1915–19); Sergeant, R.A.S.C. and R.E.; France 3 years 5 months.

Tisdale, Percy Charles Eardley (1915–19); Sergeant, W. Riding Rgt. and Sherwood Foresters; France 7 months.

Tomalin, Frederick William (1915–19); Sec.-Lieutenant, 25th and 10th Bns. London Rgt. and Middlesex Rgt.; France 12 months.

Toms, Bertram Henry (1915–19); Mentioned in despatches; Sergeant, R.A.M.C.; Egypt 13 months, Macedonia 2 years 10 months, Malta 4 months.

Townshend, John (1914–19); Gunner, R.F.A.; France 18 months, Salonica 6 months, Palestine 1 year 9 months.

Treadwell, Albert William Richard (1914–19); Private, 15th Bn. London Rgt.; Egypt and Palestine 1 year 8 months.

***Trumble, William Acton** (1914–18); D.C.M.; Sec.-Lieutenant, 7th and 6th Bns. Essex Rgt.; Egypt 2 years 1 month; Died, 9th October, 1918.

Turney, Walter Cecil (1914–19); Sergeant-Major, R.A.M.C.; France 3 years 9 months.

Turpin, Herbert Edward (1914–19); Signaller, R.F.A.; France 6 months, Salonica 4 months, Egypt and Palestine 8 months.

Ungar, Isidore Isaac (1914–19); M.S.M., Mentioned in despatches; Staff-Sergeant, R.A.M.C.; France 4 years 1 month.

Urquhart, Reginald Buchanan (1915–19); Corporal Mechanic, R.A.F.; Afloat 2 years 3 months.

Venn, Arthur Richard (1915–19); Leading Aircraftsman, R.F.C. and R.A.F.; France 2 years 9 months.

Vernon, Karl (1915–19); M.M.; Sergeant, R.A.M.C.; France and Germany, 2 years.

Vincent, George Edward (1915–19); Staff-Sergeant, R.E.; France 2 years 5 months.

Waight, Thomas Henry (1915–19); Private, Honourable Artillery Company.

Wakely, Albert Edward (1915–19); Private, 2/15th and 19th Bns. London Rgt.; France 1 year 10 months.

Walker, George Craufurd (1916–19); Private, R.A.M.C.; France 2 years 1 month.

Waller, Harry Bertie (1916–19); Corporal, Norfolk Rgt. and A.P.C.

Walmsley, Reginald Bertram (1915–19); Private, 15th Bn. London Rgt.; France 2 months.

Walton, Edward (1914–17); Private, R.D.C.

Ward, Benjamin Ebenezer (1915–19); Writer, R.N.V.R. and R.N.

Ward, Jesse William (1914–19); Sergeant, Royal Fusiliers.

***Warry, John Lucas** (1915–17); Sec.-Lieutenant, 28th Bn. London Rgt. and Sherwood Foresters; France 2 months; Died of wounds, 27th April, 1917.

Waters, Alexander Arthur (1915–18); Sergeant, W. Kent Yeomanry and Machine Gun Corps.

Watkins, Herbert Richard Washington (1915–19); Lieutenant, R.E.

Watson, Victor (1914–19); Corporal, City of London Yeomanry, 15th Bn. London Rgt. and Tank Corps; Egypt and Gallipoli 7 months; France 2 years 3 months.

Weald, George (1915–19); Lieutenant, R.E.; France 3 years 7 months.

Webb, Ernest Alfred (1916–19); Private, Middlesex Rgt.

Webber, Sidney Joseph (1915–19); Sapper, R.E. and R.A.M.C.; Egypt 3 years.

Wells, William Frank (1917–20); Private, R.E. and R.A.O.C.

Weeks, William (1914–16); Private, 24th Bn. London Rgt. and R.D.C.

West, Reginald John Franklin (1914–19); Lieutenant, City of London Yeomanry and Middlesex Rgt.; Palestine 2 years 8 months.

Wheeler, Edwin Paul (1916–19); Captain, R.A.M.C.; France 7 months.

Whincop, Walter George (1916–19); Lieutenant, R.G.A. and R.E.; France 17 months.

White, Percy Gordon (1914–19); Sec.-Lieutenant, 28th Bn. London Rgt. and R.F.C.; France 3 months, India 12 months.

Whitney, Eustace Scott (1914–19); Lieutenant, 11th Bn. London and 7th Bn. Worcestershire Rgts.; France 12 months.

Whittington, Harold Norman (1914–19); Sapper, R.F.A. and R.E.; France 4 years.

Wickens, Edwin James (1915–19); Private, R.A.S.C.; Salonica 1 year 9 months.

Wildish, Herbert Charles (1915–19); Lieutenant, R.E.

Williams, Frederick George (1914–19); M.S.M.; Sergeant, 15th Bn. London Rgt.; France 9 months.

Williamson, John (1914–19); Mentioned in despatches; Lieutenant, Duke of Cornwall's Light Infantry and Bedfordshire Rgt.; India 2 years 9 months, Mesopotamia 15 months.

Williamson, John Rhynd Gunn (1916–19); Sergeant, E. Kent Rgt.; Egypt 3 months, Palestine 12 months, France 10 months.

***Wills, Robert Dixon** (1914–17); M.M.; Sec.-Lieutenant, 13th Bn. London Rgt. and 5th Bn. Border Rgt.; France 10 months; Killed in action, 23rd April, 1917.

Wilson, Edwin James (1915–19); Flight-Sergeant, R.A.F.; France 18 months.

Wilson, Frank (1915–19); Corporal, A.P.C.

Wilson, Herbert David (1915–19); Able Seaman, R.N.V.R.

Wilson, Ralph (1915–19); Captain, Honourable Artillery Company and Rifle Brigade; France 15 months.

Wrampling, Elijah Justus (1914–19); Corporal, R.A.M.C.; France 2 years 11 months, Italy 16 months.

Wright, Henry (1914–19); Corporal, A.P.C., Rifle Brigade and R.A.S.C.; France 16 months.

Wright, Henry James (1915–19); Private, 23rd Bn. London Rgt.; France 3 years 1 month.

Wyatt, Cyril Edwin Aubrey (1915–19); Air Mechanic (2nd Class), R.N., R.N.A.S. and R.A.F.; Afloat 2 years 5 months.

***Wybrow, George Edward** (1914–18); Lance-Corporal, R.A.M.C.; France 13 months; Killed in action, 5th September, 1918.

Wylde, Frederick Charles (1916–19); Corporal, A.P.C. and Middlesex Rgt.

***Wyllie, Robert Theodore Morrison** (1914); Private, 14th Bn. London Rgt.; France 6 weeks; Wounded and missing, 31st October, 1914.

Solicitor's Department

Allum, Alfred John (1916–19); Private (Provl. Sergeant), Royal Fusiliers.

Arnold, Nathaniel Edmunds (1914–19); Corporal, 15th Bn. London Rgt.; France 13 months.

Bailey, George (1916–19); Sergeant, R. W. Surrey Rgt.

Bardgett, Frederick (1916–19); Private, R. W. Surrey Rgt.; France 2 years 6 months.

Bidwell, William (1915–19); Mentioned in despatches; Leading Seaman, R.N.A.S.; Dardanelles and Salonica 2 years 4 months.

Bird, James Percy (1915–19); Gunner (Able Seaman), R.N.; Served on defensively armed ships 1 year 9 months.

***Bradbury, Arthur** (1915–17); Sergeant, 16th Bn. London Rgt.; France 4 months; Killed in action, 14th April, 1917.

***Chapman, Herbert Carter** (1916 – 19); Private, Manchester Rgt. and Army Pay Corps; France 3 months; Died, 24th February, 1919.

Churchill, William Henry (1915–19); Able Seaman, R.N.V.R.

Clegg, Alfred Robert (1915–19); Private, R.A.M.C.; Egypt and Palestine 3 years 9 months.

Cooper, John James (1915–19); Signaller, R.H.A.; France 6 months.

Coulter, Harry (1915–19); Private, R.A.M.C.; France 2 years 6 months.

Cramp, William James (1914–17); Rifleman, King's Royal Rifle Corps; France 17 months.

Cummins, Charles Oswald (1914–20); Mentioned in despatches; Captain, E. Surrey Rgt.; Eastern theatre of war 5 years.

Dickson, Arthur Lorimer (1914–19); M.C., Mentioned in despatches; Captain, R.A.O.C.; France and Italy 2 years 11 months.

Dimes, Percy Etty (1915–19); Private, 28th Bn. London Rgt., Sergeant, R.A.F.

Dorken, Henry George (1914–16); Lance-Sergeant, 15th Bn. London Rgt.; France 18 months.

Douthwaite, Frederick (1916–19); Rifleman, 5th Bn. London Rgt.; France 3 months.

***Duck, Leslie Sidney** (1914–16); Sergeant, 21st Bn. London Rgt.; France 8 months; Killed in action, 23rd May, 1916.

Eborall, Henry Charles (1915–19); Able Seaman, R.N.V.R.

FitzGerald, Martin (1914–19); Lieutenant, R. Welch Fusiliers and Machine Gun Corps; France 8 months.

Forde, John Joseph (1915–17); Corporal, R.D.C.

Godfrey, William Arthur (1916–19); Lieutenant, R.A.S.C.; Palestine and Turkey 2 years 10 months.

Goldberg, Joseph (1916–19); Corporal, R. West Kent Rgt., Army Pay Corps.

Gordon, John (1914–18); Lance-Sergeant, London Rgt.

Hall, Frederick William (1917–19); Private (1st Class), R.N.A.S.; Eastern Mediterranean 16 months.

Halstead, Henry Lionel (1915–19); Lance-Sergeant, 15th Bn. London Rgt.

Hammond, Frederick Edward (1916–19); Sergeant, R.A.S.C. (M.T.).

Handy, George William (1914–19); Lance-Corporal, 15th Bn. London Rgt.; France, Salonica, Egypt and Palestine 2 years 8 months.

Harman, Percival Brooks (1915–19); Private, R.A.M.C.; Salonica 2 years 9 months.

Harris, Frederic Vivian (1914–19); M.C.; Captain, Royal Fusiliers, attached 10th Bn. London Rgt.; Egypt, Palestine and Syria 3 years 1 month.

Hart, Bernard Leslie (1915–17); Sec.-Lieutenant, E. Surrey Rgt.; France 3 months.

Henton, William Hiram (1916–19); Corporal, 15th Bn. London Rgt.

Hinman, George Ernest (1916–19); Lieutenant, R.G.A.

Hutchins, John Abberley (1914–19); Sergeant, 12th Bn. London Rgt.; France 4 years 2 months.

Jones, William John Anthoine (1915–19); Lieutenant, R.A.S.C.; Italy 10 months.

Keast, William John (1916–19); 2nd Air Mechanic, R.F.C.; France 12 months.

Kennedy, Douglas Wyburn (1915–17); Lieutenant, R.A.S.C.; France 6 months.

Layen, Norman David (1916–19); Sergeant, R.A.V.C.; France 3 years 6 months.

Lewis, Stuart Hermon (1914–19); Mentioned in despatches; Staff Captain; France.

Logsdon, Edward Charles (1915–19); Corporal, R.E.; France 1 year 8 months.

Lowman, William Lewis (1915–18); Corporal, 28th Bn. London Rgt.; France 2 years 5 months.

McDonald, John Alexander (1914–19); Sergeant, Seaforth Highlanders; France 2 months.

Norman, James Robert (1915–19); Mentioned in War Office List; 2nd Corporal, R.E.

Owen, Hugh John (1915–18); Captain, R.A.O.C.; Salonica 2 years 6 months.

***Page, Alfred** (1914–16); Private, 15th Bn. London Rgt.; Killed in France, 16th September, 1916.

Pawlyn, James Hawkins (1916–19); Sergeant, R.A.O.C.; Egypt and Palestine 3 years.

***Pearson, Clarence Ernest** (1914–15); Private, 15th Bn. London Rgt.; Died of wounds in France, 23rd May, 1915.

Peirson, Reginald (1914–19); Sergeant, 13th Bn. London Rgt.

Pierson, Alan Roach (1914–19); Major, R.A.O.C.; France 4 years 4 months.

Real, Reginald Walter (1914–19); Sergeant, 12th County of London Yeomanry, Company Quartermaster-Sergeant, 4th Bn. Liverpool Rgt.; France 11 months.

***Richards, Arthur Brindley** (1915–17); Sec.-Lieutenant, Monmouthshire Rgt.; France 10 months; Died of wounds, 27th June, 1917.

Rivers, George William (1914–19); Private, 13th Bn. London Rgt. and Machine Gun Corps; France 2 years.

Scrase, Charles Martin (1917–19); Aircraftsman (2nd Class), R.A.S.C., R.A.F.

Sherwin-White, Herbert Nicholas (1915–19); Able Seaman, R.N.V.R. (Anti-Aircraft Corps).

Stevens, William Charles James (1914–20); Private, 13th Bn. London Rgt.; India 2 years 1 month.

Stolte, Henry Joseph (1916–19); Private, 31st Bn. Middlesex Rgt.; France 2 years 7 months.

Strugnell, Eric (1915–19); M.M.; Sergeant, 15th Bn. London Rgt.; France 2 years 8 months.

Tarrant, William Henry (1915–16, 1917–19); Twice mentioned in despatches; Sergeant, 15th Bn. London Rgt., Flight Sergeant, R.A.F.

Thompson, Thomas James Edward (1914–19); Acting Sergeant, E. Surrey Rgt.; India and Mesopotamia 4 years 9 months.

Tiffen, Edgar James (1916–19); Signaller, Royal Artillery; France 1 year 8 months.

***Tonkin, Thomas Skewes** (1915–18); Private, R.A.M.C.; Salonica 1 year 10 months; Died of malaria, 17th October, 1918.

Turner, Horace (1916–19); Acting Sergeant, R.G.A.; France 1 year 7 months.

Walker, Edward Louis Haviland (1915–19); Lieutenant, R.G.A.; France 2 years 2 months.

Walsh, John (1914–19); Private 23rd Bn. London Rgt.; France, Salonica and Palestine, 2 years 2 months.

***Whittam, John** (1914–15); Private, 4th Bn. Seaforth Highlanders; France 6 months; Killed in action, 9th May, 1915.

***Whitwell, Harold Cuthbert Carlyle** (1914–15); Private, 13th Bn. London Rgt.; France 3 months; Killed in action, 9th May, 1915.

Williams, Harold Beck (1915–19); Lieutenant, Hampshire Rgt.; France 1 month.

***Williams, Lionel Henry Thomas** (1914–15); Private, 15th Bn. London Rgt.; France 6 months; Killed in action, 2nd November, 1915.

Wright, Henry Edward (1916–19); Acting Sergeant, R.A.F.

London Fire Brigade and Ambulance Service

Administrative Staff

Balcombe, Alfred Henry (1916–19); Sergeant, Acting Company Sergeant-Major, R.A.S.C., attached R.G.A.; France 1 year 7 months, Germany 7 months.

Barton, Montague Downe (1914–18); N.C.O., 23rd Bn. Royal Fusiliers, 5th Bn. Royal Fusiliers, 10th Bn. R. W. Kent Rgt.; France 1 year 8 months.

Clark, Arthur (1916–19); Engine Room Artificer, 3rd Class H.O., H.M.S. Vivid, H.M.S. Cambrian; North Sea 1 year 10 months.

Coles, Walter George (1915–18); Chief Petty Officer, R.N.V.R.; Anti-aircraft.

Cook, Ernest John (1918–19); Private, 28th Bn. London Regt., Lieutenant, R.A.F.; France and Germany 9 months.

Cornelius, Victor Ambrose (1915–19); Sec.-Lieutenant, R.E.; France 2 years 10 months.

Crump, Ernest Frank (1915–19); Sergeant, London Rgt., King's Royal Rifle Corps, Royal Fusiliers; France 17 months, Italy 4 months.

Cutbush, Bertram Mayhew (1915–19); Captain, 10th Bn. R. Welch Fusiliers; France 7 months.

Darling, Robert Reuben (1916–17); Aircraftsman, R.N.A.S.

Eddowes, John (1914–19); 1st Class Stoker, R.N.; Cameroons and German East Africa.

Evans, John Henry (1915–19); Corporal, R.N.A.S. and R.A.F.; France 12 months.

***Farley, Sidney James** (1914–15); Private, 20th Bn. London Rgt.; France 6 months; Killed in action, 25th September, 1915.

Frethey, Charles James (1915–19); Staff Quartermaster-Sergeant, R.A.O.C.

Gooding, George Walter (1915–19); Private, R.A.O.C. and 19th Bn. London Rgt.; Dardanelles 6 months, Egypt 1 year 10 months and Palestine 12 months.

Gordon (Hamilton-Gordon), Ernest Arthur (1914–18); Mentioned in despatches; Quartermaster, Hon. Major, 14th Bn. London Rgt., Captain, R.A.S.C., Captain, R.E., Major on retirement; France 2 years 8 months.

Griffin, Amos Tabor (1915); Private, R.A.M.C.

Jones, Thomas James (1915–19); M.S.M. (Naval); Second Writer, H.M.S. Europa and H.M.S. Egmont; Dardanelles 6 months, Egypt 3 years 6 months.

***Kelcey, Harry** (1914–16); Acting Quartermaster-Sergeant, R.F.A.; France 1 year 7 months; Died of wounds, 10th October, 1916.

Lingwood, John Arthur (1915–19); M.M.; Sergeant, Honourable Artillery Company; France 2 years.

Lister, Sidney Albert (1915–19); Corporal, 2nd London Sanitary Co.; Egypt 3 years 3 months.

***Lowe, John William Sibley, D.C.M.** (1914–16); Able Seaman, H.M.S. Europa and H.M.S. Buttercup; Atlantic and Mediterranean 17 months; Accidentally killed, 16th January, 1916.

Morris, Cyril Clarke Boville (1914–17); M.C., Mentioned in despatches; Major, R.A.S.C.; France 2 years 9 months.

Moss, Rupert Douglas (1915–18); Chief Petty Officer, R.N.A.S.

Nye, William Edward (1914–19); Sergeant, R.E.

Oakham, Frank Edward (1918–19); 3rd Clerk, R.A.F.; France 5 months.

Olden, John Arthur (1916–19); Private, 11th Bn. Norfolk Rgt., Labour Corps, No. 9 Co., R.A.M.C.

Page, Albert Edward (1915–19); Sergeant, R.A.O.C.; France 4 years.

Rampton, Frederick (1914–19); Company Quartermaster-Sergeant, R.E., Sec.-Lieutenant, 1st Bn. Shropshire Light Infantry; France 5 months, Germany 4 months.

Reed, Arthur Ernest (1916–19); Mentioned in despatches; Captain, R.N.A.S. and R.A.F.

Rossiter, Edward Thomas (1915–19): Lance-Corporal, 2nd London Sanitary Co.; Egypt and Palestine 3 years 4 months.

Spencer, Henry (1914–17); Commander, H.M.S. Arrogant, Dover Patrol 3 years.

Swingland, Charles (1916–19); Petty Officer, R.N.A.S., Sergeant, R.A.F.; France 2 years 6 months.

***Turner, Bernard George** (1914–15); Private, Coldstream Guards; France 8 months; Killed in action, 26th September, 1915.

Wells, Leslie Stuart Dean (1916–19); Sec.-Lieutenant, R.G.A.; France 2 years.

Yeaxlee, Archibald Henry (1915–16); Private, 4th Bn. London Rgt.

Workshops Staff

Abercrombie, William (1915–19); Driver, R.A.S.C.; France 2 years 6 months.

Bullard, Steven (1916–19); Private, 1st Bn. Oxfordshire and Buckinghamshire Light Infantry; Mesopotamia 3 years 2 months.

Carter, Charles (1914–19); Private, W. Yorkshire Rgt.; France 4 years 6 months.

Chapman, Edwin (1914–19); Sergeant, 17th Bn. London Rgt.; France 2 years 1 month.

Chester, Albert Charles (1917–18); Private, 1st Bn. Middlesex Regt.; France 4 months.

Clarke, Frederick William (1915–18); Wheeler-Sergeant, R.F.A.; France 6 months.

Donaldson, Archibald Joseph (1914–18); Able Seaman, R.N.

Fisher, Joseph William (1914–20); M.C. and D.C.M.; Regimental Sergeant-Major, 22nd Bn. London Regt.; France 3 years 1 month.

Gill, Henry Charles (1918–19); Sapper, R.E.

Lines, Aubrey William (1915–19); Chancellerie de l'ordre Danilo (1st and 2nd Order); Chief Motor Mechanic, R.N.M.B.R.; Montenegro 9 months, France 3 years 5 months.

Morant, Alfred George (1914–19); Sergeant, R.A.S.C.; France 4 years 8 months.

Nanson, John Frederick (1915–19); Lance-Corporal, Scottish Rifles and M.F.P.; France 2 years.

Nanson, William Henry (1914–16); Able Seaman, R.N.; North American Patrol 9 months, Dardanelles 14 months.

Richards, John George (1914–19); Driver, R.H.A.; France 4 years 2 months, Germany 6 months.

Salmon, William Arthur (1915–17); 2nd Air Mechanic, R.F.C.; France 15 months.

Smith, Albert Edward (1918–19); Private, R.A.F.; France 5 months, Germany 1 month.

Snowsill, William Frederick (1915–19); 2nd Air Mechanic, R.A.F.. Corporal, 16th Bn. R. Sussex Rgt.; Mesopotamia 2 years, India 1 year 11 months.

Timms, Herbert William (1918–19); Private, 5th Bn. R. Sussex Rgt.; Italy 5 months.

Uniformed Staff

Abbott, George Ernest (1914–15); Mentioned in despatches; Corporal, Royal Fusiliers; France 14 months.

Abrahams, George (1914–17); Able Seaman, R.N.; H.M.S. Hogue and H.M.S. Titania; Cruiser Squadron, 1st Division Submarine Division.

***Adams, Frederick William** (1914); Private, 3rd Bn. Worcestershire Rgt.; France 1 month; Killed in action, 21st September, 1914.

Adamson, Frederick (1914–17); Chief Petty Officer, R.N.; H.M.S. Princess Royal, H.M.S. Greyhound, and H.M.S. Erin's Isle, 2 years 8 months.

Akers, William (1918–19); Cadet, R.A.F.

Alldridge, Albert James Marsden (1914–17); Able Seaman, R.N. Afloat, 3 years 2 months.

Allen, Bertie Thomas (1914–17); Bombardier, R.G.A.; France 16 months.

Ansell, Joseph Henry (1918–19); Cadet, R.A.F.

Armstrong, Albert Victor (1914–17); Able Seaman, R.N.; North Sea and Atlantic Patrol 18 months.

Aselby, Richard (1914–17); Leading Seaman, R.N.; North Sea 3 months, Grand Fleet 2 months, and Mediterranean 2 years 9 months.

Ash, Samuel William (1914–17); Able Seaman, R.N.; Cameroons 12 months, German East Africa 15 months and Grand Fleet 9 months.

Bacon, Walter (1915–19); Private, Essex and Cheshire Rgts.; France 8 months, Salonica 2 years 5 months.

Baker, Ernest (1914–17); Able Seaman, R.N.; Patrol Boats, Sheerness Depot.

Bailes, Harry Richard (1914–17); Corporal, Royal Marines, attached R.N.A.S.; Armed Merchant Ship; France 3 months, Mediterranean, Atlantic, Pacific and Irish Sea 2 years 5 months.

Baker, Ernest Charles (1914–17); Able Seaman, R.N.; H.M.S. Juno, Atlantic, 12 months, Persian Gulf 2 years.

Banyard, Edgar (1914–17); Corporal, R.A.S.C.; France.

Bard, Arthur (1914–16); Corporal, R.F.A.; France 1 year 7 months.

Barnes, John Leonard (1914–17); Able Seaman, R.N.; H.M.S. Victorious and H.M.S. Vulcan 2 years 8 months.

Baron, Tom Lambert (1914–17); Stoker (1st Class), R.N.; H.M.S. Mars and H.M.S. Prince Rupert, 2 years 7 months.

Barton, William Henry (1914–17); Able Seaman, R.N.; Patrolling North Sea.

Baxter, Walter Edward (1914–17); Leading Seaman, R.F.R.; 10th Cruiser Squadron 2 years 4 months.

Beale, Herbert Samuel (1914–17); Able Seaman, R.F.R.; H.M.S. King Alfred and H.M.S. Montague, 10th Cruiser Squadron; 3 years' sea service.

Beatty, John (1914–19); Private, 1st and 2nd Bns. N. Staffordshire Rgt.; France 8 months, India 2 years 8 months; Afghanistan 5 months.

Belcher, Harry (1914–17); Able Seaman, R.F.R.; North Sea 2 years 8 months.

Bennett, Robert (1914–19); Leading Seaman, R.N.; H.M.S. Egmont, Egypt 3 years 2 months.

Bent, Henry (1914-19); Leading Seaman, R.N., H.M.S. Hogue, H.M.S. Arrogant, and H.M.S. Lancaster; 10th Cruiser Squadron, 2 months, Dover Patrol 12 months, Pacific Patrol 3 years.

Best, Alfred (1914–17); Able Seaman, R.F.R.; Mediterranean 2 months, Atlantic 8 months, North Sea 1 year 11 months.

Best, Bertram Stanley Leopold (1914–17); Sergeant, Manchester Rgt.; France 5 months.

***Bevan, Morgan William** (1914–16); Private, 1st Bn. Dorsetshire Rgt.; France 1 year 11 months; Died of wounds, 2nd July, 1916.

Bishop, Frederick George (1914–17); Petty Officer (1st Class), R.F.R., H.M.S. Princess Royal and H.M.S. Gibraltar; Grand Fleet 2 years 8 months.

Blackwell, William (1915); Gunner, R.F.A.

Blamey, George Albert (1914–17); Able Seaman, R.F.R.

Bloomfield, Alfred John (1914–17); Able Seaman, R.F.R., H.M.S. Glory and H.M.S. Raven; Mediterranean Squadron and Special Service.

Bluck, Samuel William (1918–19); 2nd Private, R.A.F.

Boddington, Frederick William (1914–17); Able Seaman, R.N.; West Coast of Africa 2 years, North Sea 3 years.

Bonwick, Henry Thomas (1914–18); Able Seaman, R.F.R.; Dardanelles 14 months, Egypt 12 months, Mesopotamia 18 months.

Bottrill, Edwin James (1914–17); Able Seaman, R.N.; North Sea Patrol 3 months, Western Patrol 3 months, Gallipoli 12 months, Egypt 6 months, Indian Ocean 6 months, Mesopotamia 3 months, North Coast of Africa 2 months.

Bowles, John Charles (1915–19); Petty Officer (1st Class), R.N.R.; North Sea, minesweeping, 4 years 8 months.

Brand, William Charles (1914–18); Able Seaman, H.M.S. Cæsar; West Indies 3 years 4 months.

Bridger, William Lawrence (1914–17); Able Seaman, R.N., H.M.S. Canada; Grand Fleet.

Brooks, Henry Tom (1914–17); Leading Seaman, R.N., H.M.S. Sappho; North Sea Patrol 2 years.

***Broom, Thomas Henry** (1914); Trooper, 1st Life Guards; France 1 month; Missing, 30th October, 1914.

Burton, Robert Montague (1914–17); Leading Signalman, R.N., H.M.S. St. Seiriol; Minesweeping, Dover Patrol 2 years 11 months.

Burton, William Henry (1914–17); Able Seaman, R.N.; H.M.S. Cressy 6 weeks, H.M.S. Spey 6 months.

Capper, Herbert Charles (1914–17); Able Seaman, R.N.; H.M.S. Bacchante and H.M.S. Repulse; Dardanelles 16 months, Egypt 8 months, and Grand Fleet 12 months.

***Carpenter, Henry** (1914–17); Able Seaman, R.N.; at sea 2 years 11 months; Drowned, 30th June, 1917.

Carter, Lewis Adolphus (1914–18); Able Seaman, R.F.R.; North Atlantic Fleet 2 years 10 months.

Chandler, Thomas Roland (1914–17); Able Seaman, R.F.R.; Eastern Mediterranean Squadron 12 months, East Indies Squadron 1 year 7 months.

Chapman, John Thomas (1914–17); Able Seaman, R.N.; H.M.S. Mars, H.M.S. Campania, H.M.S. Spry and H.M.S. Victorious, 2 years 9 months.

Chesmett, Thomas (1914–17); Able Seaman, R.N.; H.M.S. Glory, Atlantic Station 14 months, Dardanelles 5 months, Q3 12 months.

Chittenden, Howard Leslie (1918–19); 2nd Private, R.A.F.

Christopher, Walter Thomas (1914–17); Able Seaman, R.N.; H.M.S. Glory; 1 year 8 months.

Clarke, John William Preston (1914–19); Private, 2nd Bn. Sherwood Foresters; France 2 months, Germany, prisoner of war, 4 years 1 month.

Claydon, Edward George (1914–17); Sergeant, R.F.A.; France 3 years 2 months.

Clements, Frederick James (1914–18); Stoker, R.N.; West Coast of Africa 3 years, Belgium 6 months.

Clive, Frank (1914–17); Able Seaman, R.N., H.M.S. Glory and H.M.S. Vernon; Gallipoli 6 months.

Coe, Thomas (1914–17); Able Seaman, R.N., H.M.S. Diana; East Indies 3 years 3 months.

Coggan, Thomas Harry (1914–18); Private, R. Marine Light Infantry; 11th Cruiser Squadron 2 years 4 months, Defensive Armed Merchant Ships 12 months.

Cole, Edgar (1914–17); Leading Seaman, R.N.; North America and West Indies, Gallipoli, Egypt, North Sea, H.M.S. Glory 1 year 9 months, H.M.S. Royal Sovereign 15 months.

Coleman, Alfred Henry (1914–17); Able Seaman, H.M.S. Royal Arthur, 10th Cruiser Squadron; H.M.S. Trident and H.M.S. Osiris, Battle Cruiser Squadron; H.M. Trawler John G. Watson, Grand Fleet.

Collins, George Joseph (1914–18); Leading Stoker, R.N.; afloat 4 years.

Connell, Thomas (1914–19); Able Seaman, R.N.; Pacific Station 4 years.

Cook, Frederick (1914–17); Private, R. Sussex Rgt.; France 3 years.

Cook, Rowland John (1914–17); Driver, R.H.A.; France 3 years 1 month.

Cotton, Robert George (1914–17); Able Seaman, R.F.R.; North Atlantic 10 months, Dardanelles 10 months, Grand Fleet 14 months.

Coysh, Charles William Joseph Henry (1914–18); Able Seaman, R.N.; Belgian Coast 4 months, German East Africa 3 years.

Cregeen, James Samuel (1914–17); Leading Seaman, R.F.R.; H.M.S. Actæon, H.M.S. Brentwick Island and H.M.S. Eastchurch.

Crosby, Charles Alfred (1917–19); Deck Hand, R.N.R.T. Trawlers; H.M.T. Marloes, Dover Patrol, 18 months.

Cullen, Charles James Zachariah Young (1914–17); Private, R. Marine Light Infantry; H.M. Armed Liners, Empress of Britain, 10th Cruiser Squadron.

Curson, Thomas William (1914–17); Sergeant, R.F.A.; France 1 year 2 months, Salonica 1 year 10 months.

Dalgetty, Duncan McCowan (1914–17); Driver, R.H.A.; France 3 years 1 month.

Darby, Charles James (1916–19); Chief Officer, Royal Fleet Auxiliary, H.M.S. Ebonol; 2 years 11 months.

Davies, George Edward (1914–17); Petty Officer (1st Class), R.F.R.; North Sea Patrol 2 years 11 months.

Dean, William Henry (1914–17); Able Seaman, R.F.R.; East Indies Squadron 18 months, River Gunboat Service, Mesopotamia, 15 months.

Delamare, Joseph Walter (1914–18); Sergeant, R.F.A.; France.

Delbridge, Frederick (1914–17); 2nd Corporal, R.E.; France 18 months, Egypt 18 months.

Dell, Arthur Ernest Edward (1914–17); Stoker (1st Class), Royal Naval Division; France 3 months, Gallipoli 6 months.

Desborough, Ernest Edward Charles (1914–15); Sergeant, 18th Hussars.

Diehl, Alfred John Henry (1914–17); Gunner, R.F.A.; France 3 years.

***Doling, George** (1914–16); Able Seaman, R.N.; H.M.S. Glory and H.M.S. Queen Mary 1 year 9 months; Killed in action, 31st May, 1916.

Duffing, William Ernest (1914–17); Leading Seaman, R.N., H.M.S. Grafton, H.M. Monitor 21; 10th Cruiser Squadron 5 months, Dardanelles 5 months, Egypt and Palestine 1 year 8 months.

Dunkinson, Ernest Christopher (1914–17); Private, R. Marine Light Infantry; Dardanelles.

Ebsworth, Thomas Patteson (1914–17); Driver, R.F.A.; France 3 years.

Edwards, George Neville (1914–17); Leading Seaman, R.N.; Belgian Coast 6 months and Harwich Light Cruiser Patrol 18 months.

***Entwistle, Walter Sidney** (1914–15); Leading Seaman, R.F.R.; H.M.S. Clan McNaughton, 10th Cruiser Squadron; Drowned at sea, February, 1915.

Fawcett, Joseph Walter (1916–19); Leading Seaman, Fleet Auxiliaries 3 years.

Fay, James Edward (1914–17); Driver, R.H.A.; France 3 years 2 months.

Ferrell, Edward Charles (1918–19); Private, R.A.F.

Fitch, John Edward (1914–17); Private, R. Marine Light Infantry; North Atlantic Patrol 1 year 11 months, North America and West Indies 8 months.

Flatt, Frederick Job (1914–17); Able Seaman, R.F.R.; Mediterranean 16 months, North Sea 10 months, German East Africa 6 months.

Forrow, Thomas (1918–19); Aircraftsman (2nd Class), R.A.F.

Fowler, Charles Jackson (1914–17); Corporal, Royal Fusiliers; France 2 years 10 months.

Frost, John Lewis (1918–19); 2nd Private, R.A.F.

Fulker, Frederick (1914–17); Leading Stoker, R.N.; Belgian Coast and North Sea 3 years.

Garner, Walter James (1914–17); Corporal, 11th Hussars; France 1 year 9 months.

Gellatley, Andrew William (1914–17); Able Seaman, R.N.; North Sea 2 years 9 months.

Gibbs, Alfred Eustace (1915–19); Private, R.A.S.C. (M.T.); German South-West Africa 4 months, Balkans 3 years 6 months.

Goodwin, James Joseph (1914–19); Trooper, 18th Hussars; France 2 months, Germany, prisoner of war, 4 years 2 months.

Gore, Joseph (1914–17); Able Seaman, R.F.R.; River Gunboat Service, Mesopotamia, 2 years, North Sea Fleet 6 months.

Gray, Alfred (1914–17); Private, R. Marine Light Infantry; Belgium 1 month, Gallipoli 5 months.

Green, Harry Joshua (1914–17); Corporal, R.H.A.; France 3 years 1 month.

Griffiths, Edward (1914–17); D.S.M.; Signalman, R.F.R.; Dardanelles 10 months, North Atlantic Fleet 10 months.

Halley, George Edmund (1914–17); Acting Corporal, R.A.S.C.; France 3 years.

Halsey, Henry George (1914–17); Able Seaman, R.N., H.M.S. Bacchante; West Coast of Africa.

Hamilton, Frederick C. (1914–17); Able Seaman, R.N.

Hardiman, Alfred Ernest (1914–17); Able Seaman, R.N., H.M.S. Penelope; Light Cruiser Squadron 2 years 10 months.

Hardy, Edward Egmorie (1914–17); Able Seaman, R.F.R.; 9th Cruiser Force 7 months.

Harris, James (1914–17); Leading Seaman, H.M.S. Raglan Castle; Dover Patrol 2 years 11 months.

Harvey, James Levi (1914–17); Able Seaman, R.N.; Mesopotamia 2 years.

Hawkins, Charles Henry (1914–17); Bombardier, R.F.A. and R.G.A.; France 2 years 10 months.

Hawtin, William Sidney (1914–19); Sergeant, R. Marine Artillery; France 4 years 6 months.

Hazel, Albert Seymour (1914–18); Sergeant, R.G.A.; France 3 years 6 months.

Hazel, Allen Percy (1914–17); Gunner, R.G.A.; France 15 months.

Heffer, Albert (1914–17); Able Seaman, R.N.; Western Patrol 12 months, Persian Gulf 2 years.

Heitzer, Henry Joseph (1914–17); Able Seaman, R.N., H.M.S. King Alfred and H.M.S. Virginian; North Sea and North Atlantic 3 years.

Helyer, Richard Fletcher (1914–18); Stoker, R.F.R.; Gallipoli 6 months, Mediterranean 3 years.

***Hemming, Frederick Thomas** (1914); Private, R. Marine Light Infantry; North Sea 2 months; Drowned at sea, 15th October, 1914.

Hemming, Joseph Neal (1914–17); Private, R. Marine Light Infantry, R.F.R.; Channel 8 months, North Sea 6 months.

***Henderson, Alexander William** (1914–15); Able Seaman, R.F.R.; Belgium 4 months, German East Africa 7 months; Died of wounds, 7th July, 1915.

Herbert, William Henry Thomas (1914–16); Private, 4th Bn. Royal Fusiliers; France 18 months.

Heywood, Francis Henry (1914–17); Mentioned in despatches; Sergeant, R.G.A.; France 2 years 6 months, Egypt 4 months.

Hill, Albert Arthur (1914–19); Leading Seaman, R.N., H.M.S. Glory; North America and West Indies, Gallipoli, Egypt, North Sea and Archangel, 2 years 11 months.

Hitchcock, Arthur George (1918–19); Petty Officer (1st Class), Mercantile Marine Reserve; Mediterranean 2 months.

Hoare, Alfred Harry (1914–17); Driver, R.H.A.; France 2 years.

Holloway, Percy Augustus Harold (1914–19); Private, R. Marine Light Infantry; France 2 months, Germany, prisoner of war, 4 years 3 months.

Holmes, William Baglow (1918–19); Air Mechanic (3rd Class), R.A.F.; France 3 months.

Honey, Albert Edwin (1914–17); Able Seaman, R.N.; East Indies 2 years 9 months.

Hoskins, Alfred Henry (1914–17); Able Seaman, R.N.; H.M.S. Champion 2 years.

Hooper, Sidney (1914–17); Stoker Petty Officer, R.F.R., H.M.S. Europa; East Mediterranean 2 years 11 months.

Horsford, Reginald Percival Perrett (1914–17); Sapper, R.E.; France 2 months, Salonica 1 year 10 months.

Hughes, Daniel John (1914–18); Petty Officer (1st Class), R.N.; East and West Coasts of Africa 3 years 10 months.

Huish, Frederick (1914–17); Able Seaman, R.N.; H.M.S. Canopus, H.M.S. Doncaster, H.M S. Mahronda and H.M.S. Marwarri, 2 years 11 months.

Hurcombe, Alfred George (1914–19); Bombardier, R.F.A.; France 15 months, Germany, prisoner of war, 2 years 6 months.

***Hutchings, Charles Edward** (1914–15); Lance-Corporal, R. Marine Light Infantry; Belgium and Dardanelles 9 months; Died of wounds, 6th May, 1915.

Iddenden, George Henry (1914–17); Able Seaman, R.N.; Grand Fleet 18 months and Dover Patrol 7 months.

Jackson, Matthew (1914–17); Able Seaman, R.F.R.; North Atlantic 10 months, Dardanelles 10 months, White Sea 15 months.

Jarvis, Henry (1914–17); Able Seaman, R.N.; North Sea 3 years.

Jasper, Albert Samuel (1914–17); Able Seaman, R.N.; Northern Flotilla of Trawlers.

Jerome, Charles Francis (1914–18); Able Seaman, R.F.R.; Atlantic 7 months, East Indies 18 months, China 18 months.

***Jones, Alfred Crewdson** (1914–17); Private, R. Marine Light Infantry; At sea 2 years 11 months; Drowned, 29th July, 1917.

Jones, Arthur (1914–17); Stoker Petty Officer (1st Class), R.N., H.M.S. Europa and H.M.S. Broke; 9th Cruiser Squadron and Dover Patrol 2 years 11 months.

Jones, Percy Clement (1914–17); Able Seaman, R.N.; North Sea 16 months, Nore Defence 13 months, and West Coast 3 months.

Keeble, Frederick (1915–19); Private, R.A.S.C.; Egypt 2 years 6 months, Palestine 6 months.

Kent, Frederick John (1914–17); Able Seaman, R.N.; H.M.S. Edgar, H.M.S. Venerable, H.M.S. Marshal Ney and H.M.S. Furious, 2 years 8 months.

Kettle, Ernest Edward (1914–17); Able Seaman, R.N., H.M.S. Glory and H.M.S. Barham; North Atlantic 10 months, Dardanelles 7 months, Egypt 3 months, Grand Fleet 15 months.

King, Frederick (1914–17); D.C.M.; Sergeant, R.F.A.; France 2 years.

King, Thomas (1914–18); Able Seaman, R.F.R.; Atlantic Fleet 4 months, Dardanelles 2 years 9 months.

Knight, John Joseph (1914–17); Leading Seaman, R.N.; Grand Fleet 13 months.

***Knowles, Joseph** (1914); Private, Border Rgt.; France 2 months; Missing, presumed killed, 26th October, 1914.

Lambert, John Samuel (1914–17); Able Seaman, R.F.R.; Grand Fleet 15 months, North Atlantic 10 months, Dardanelles 10 months.

Landes, Arthur (1914–17); Able Seaman, R.N., H.M.S. Aboukir and H.M.S. Termagant; Dunkirk Patrol 6 months, North Sea 1 year 10 months.

Lane, Frederick Ernest (1914–18); Order of St. Stanislaus (Russia); Leading Seaman, R.N.; White Sea 3 months and Dardanelles 2 years 9 months.

Lane, Wallace Ralph (1914–18); Stoker Petty Officer (1st Class), R.N.; H.M.S. Sapphire, Dardanelles, 4 months, Italy 18 months, East Indies 18 months.

Leach, Sydney Joseph (1914–17); Able Seaman, R.F.R.; Mediterranean 2 months, North Sea 2 years 9 months.

Leatherbarrow, Thomas Albert (1914–17); Sergeant-Major, R.F.A.; France 3 years 2 months.

Lester, George Henry (1914–17); Able Seaman, R.N., H.M.S. Laverock; Grand Fleet.

Levey, Elisha (1914–17); Private, 2nd Bn. York and Lancaster Rgt., and R.A.S.C.; France 3 years 4 months.

Liles, Frank (1914–17); 2nd Yeoman of Signals, R.N., H.M.S. King Alfred and H.M.S. Barham; North Sea 3 years.

Lind, Willie (1914–17); Leading Seaman, R.N., H.M.S. Glory and H.M.S. Greenwich; North Atlantic 10 months, Dardanelles 6 months, Egypt 3 months, North Sea 14 months.

Lister, Linley (1914–17); Able Seaman, R.F.R.; Atlantic 10 months, Mediterranean 10 months, Grand Fleet 13 months.

Littleboy, Frederick James (1914–17); Lance-Corporal, York and Lancaster Rgt.; France 2 years 9 months.

Livings, Charles Henry (1914–16); Able Seaman, R.N.; North and South Atlantic, and Dardanelles, 1 year 8 months.

***Livingstone, Westly** (1914); Able Seaman, R.F.R.; North Sea Fleet 2 months; Drowned at sea, 22nd September, 1914.

Lloyd, William Ernest (1914–17); Acting Corporal, 7th Dragoon Guards; Egypt 1 month, Dardanelles 3 months.

McDuell, Charles Phillip (1918–19); Air Mechanic (3rd Class), R.A.F.; France 3 months.

Mansford, Joseph (1914–18); Stoker, R.N.; H.M.S. Europa and H.M.S. Foresight 3 years 9 months.

Marney, Edward John (1914–17); Able Seaman, R.N., H.M.S. Havelock (monitor); Dardanelles 2 years 11 months.

Martin, Edwin (1914–19); Able Seaman, R.N.

Martin, Sidney Herbert (1914–17); Able Seaman, R.F.R.; North Sea 18 months, Atlantic 16 months.

Matthews, Robert (1914–17); Able Seaman, R.N.; H.M.S. Brilliant 7 months, Boom Defence, Dover 2 years 4 months.

May, Augustus Ra (1914–18); Able Seaman, R.N.; Egypt 15 months and H.M.S. Venus 2 years.

Meadows, William Horace (1914–19); Bombardier, R.G.A.; France 7 months, Salonica 3 years 3 months.

Merrett, Frank (1914–17); Able Seaman, R.N.; North Atlantic 9 months, Dardanelles 8 months, Egypt 5 months, North Russia 15 months.

***Miller, Isaac John** (1914–15); Able Seaman, R.N.; Drowned at sea, January, 1915.

Mills, William Thomas (1914–17); M.M.; Bombardier, R.F.A.; France 3 years 1 month.

Morris, Archibald Thomas (1914–17); Private, R. Marine Light Infantry; France.

Morris, Ernest John (1914–17); Able Seaman, R.N.; Grand Fleet.

***Murrell, Frank** (1914–15); Able Seaman, R.N.; Naval Service 12 months; Died 15th August, 1915.

Nash, George Peter (1914–17); Corporal, R.G.A.; France 2 years 11 months.

Naylor, Francis William (1914–17); Able Seaman, R.N., H.M.S. King Alfred; Cruiser Squadron, Grand Fleet 2 years 11 months.

Neill, John (1914–17); Leading Seaman, R.N.; Minelaying 18 months and Convoy Service 18 months.

Nevill, James Samuel (1914–17); Acting Staff-Sergeant, R.A.O.C.; France 3 years 1 month.

Newberry, Walter James (1914–18); Able Seaman, R.N., H.M.S. Kent; West Indies, South Coast of Africa and South Pacific Ocean, 4 years.

Newbury, William Sear (1914–17); Able Seaman, R.F.R.; North Atlantic and Dardanelles 1 year 8 months, North Sea, minesweeping, 15 months.

Norman, Alfred William (1914–17); Able Seaman, R.N., H.M.S. Sutlej and H.M.S. Blazen, 595 Patrol Boat; Home Fleet, Dover Patrol 2 years 11 months.

Norman, George Edward (1914–17); Company Quartermaster-Sergeant, 2nd Bn. Essex Rgt., 1st Bn. Northamptonshire Rgt.; France 12 months, Dardanelles 12 months, Salonica 4 months, Egypt 8 months.

Norman, Harold James (1914–17); Gunner, R.H.A.; France 3 years.

Norris, George Henry (1914–17); Able Seaman, R.F.R.; North Sea 3 months.

Nurse, Richard Ernest Harry (1914–17); Able Seaman, R.F.R.; North Atlantic and Dardanelles 1 year 8 months.

O'Donnell, Patrick George (1914–17); Able Seaman, R.N.; Gallipoli 5 months, Egypt 4 months.

O'Leary, Daniel John (1914–16); Private, Middlesex Rgt.; France 1 year 7 months.

Oliver, Richard (1914–18); Able Seaman, R.N.; North Russia 18 months.

***Owen, Frank James** (1914); Private, R. Marine Light Infantry; North Sea Patrol 2 months; Drowned at sea, 22nd September, 1914.

Page, Edward George (1914–17); Bombardier, R.F.A.; France 3 years 2 months.

Palmer, George (1914–17); Leading Seaman, R.N.; H.M.S. Cressy 6 weeks.

Palmer, Robert (1914–17); Yeoman of Signals, R.N.; H.M.S. King Alfred, H.M.S. Surly, H.M.S. Patuca and Grand Fleet, 2 years 11 months.

Palethorpe, Harold Leslie (1918–19); Private, R.A.F. (Airship Wing).

Parker, Frederick Ives (1914–17); Able Seaman, R.N.; H.M.S. Royal Arthur 2 years 10 months.

Parrington, John (1914–17); Stoker (1st Class), R.F.R.; 7th Cruiser Squadron 2 years 10 months.

Parslow, Harry Alfred (1914–17); Corporal, 3rd Dragoon Guards; France 2 years 6 months.

Patterson, Harry (1914–17); Able Seaman, R.F.R.: H.M.S. Edgar 3 months, and H.M.S. Myrtle 2 years.

Pearcey, Albert Frederick (1914–17); Private, R. Marine Light Infantry; H.M.S. Royal Arthur, H.M.S. Cumberland and H.M.S. Crescent, 2 years 11 months.

Penfold, Harry (1914–17); Able Seaman, R.N., H.M.S. Europa and H.M.S. Royal Sovereign; 10th Cruiser Squadron, Grand Fleet 2 years 11 months.

Perrin, Henry Bruce (1914–17); Able Seaman, R.N.; American Coast 11 months, Dardanelles 7 months, Suez Canal 3 months, North Sea 10 months.

Pickard, Arthur (1914–17); Able Seaman, R.N.; Egypt 12 months, Greece 3 months, Dardanelles 7 months, East Indies 1 month, Persian Gulf 2 months, Mesopotamia 4 months, India 3 months, South Africa 4 months, German East Africa 2 months, France 1 month.

Piggott, George (1914–17); Company Quartermaster-Sergeant, 10th Bn. Seaforth Highlanders.

Pink, Philip Hermann Edward (1914–17); Stoker, R.F.R., H.M. Torpedo Boat destroyers, H.M.S. Brisk, H.M.S. Mounsey; Grand Fleet 3 years.

Pocock, George (1914–17); Able Seaman, R.N.; North Sea Patrol 2 years 1 month.

Pollard, James Aaron Frederick (1914–17); Stoker (1st Class), R.F.R.; 10th Cruiser Squadron 2 years 4 months.

***Ponting, Ernest Walter** (1914–16); Leading Stoker, R.N.; North Sea 1 year 10 months; Killed in action, 31st May, 1916.

Porter, George Thomas (1914–18); Able Seaman, R.N., H.M.S. Royal Arthur; Grand Fleet 3 years.

Preston, John Thomas (1914–17); Driver, R.F.A.; France 2 years 8 months.

Price, Phillip (1914–17); Stoker, Naval Brigade; Gallipoli 9 months, France 1 year 8 months.

Pritchard, John David (1914–17); Corporal, R.F.A.; France 2 years 11 months.

Protheroe, Ernest Robert (1914–17); Able Seaman, R.N.; South Atlantic 7 months, and North Sea 3 months.

Radford, Joseph Thomas (1914–19); Petty Officer (1st Class), 1st R. Naval Brigade; Belgium 1 month, Holland, prisoner of war, 4 years 3 months.

Record, Ernest Henry (1914–17); Able Seaman, R.N.; H.M.S. Magnificent, H.M.S. Royal Arthur, Torpedo Boat No. 23, 2 years 11 months.

Richard, Aubrey (1914–18); Able Seaman, R.F.R.; South Atlantic, West of Ireland, North Russia.

Ridden, James William (1918–19); 3rd Air Mechanic, R.A.F.

Ridgeway, Arthur Thomas (1914–17); M.M.; Mech. Sergeant-Major, R.F.A. and R.A.S.C.; France 2 years.

***Roake, Arthur** (1914–17); D.S.M.; Able Seaman, R.N.; H.M.S. Audacious, H.M.S. Cornwallis and H.M.S. Foyle, Dardanelles 12 months; Presumed drowned, 15th March, 1917.

Robinson, Alfred John Edward (1914–17); Private, R. Marine Light Infantry; East India Station, 2 years 11 months.

Robinson, Oswald Ide (1914–17); Shoeing Smith, R.A.S.C.; France 2 years.

Roffey, Charles Sidney (1914–17); Private, R. Marine Light Infantry; Dardanelles 4½ months, Egypt 10 months, France 7 months.

Rogerson, Percy Smith (1914–17); Driver, R.F.A.; France 3 years 1 month.

Rolfe, Arthur Walter (1914–15); Private, 2nd Bn. Hampshire Rgt.; France 13 months.

Root, Charles Robert (1914–17); Able Seaman, R.N., H.M.S. Juno; Persian Gulf 2 years 2 months.

Royce, William Stanley (1914–17); Able Seaman, R.N.; Grand Fleet 8 months, Gallipoli 11 months, Egypt 6 months, Mesopotamia 11 months.

Samme, William (1918–19); 3rd Air Mechanic, R.A.F.

Sandaver, Henry William (1914–17); Able Seaman, R.N., H.M.S. Glory and H.M.S. Sandown; North Atlantic 10 months, Dardanelles 7 months, Egypt 3 months, Dover Patrol Minesweepers 11 months.

Servant, Walter Frederick (1914–17); Gunner, R.F.R., R.M.A.; France 2 years 11 months.

Shawyer, Frederick Nelson (1914–17); Acting Corporal, R.E.; France 3 years.

***Shearing, Arthur** (1914); Private, Highland Light Infantry; France 3 months; Killed in action, 1st November, 1914.

Shearman, Leonard Alfred (1914–17); Leading Seaman, R.N., H.M.S. Arrogant and H.M.S. King Alfred, Minesweeper Eglinton; Atlantic Patrol 2 years 6 months, Dover Patrol, minesweeping 6 months.

Sheldrick, William Henry (1914–17). Able Seaman, R.N., H.M.S. Virginian and H.M.S. King Alfred; 10th Cruiser Squadron 2 years 11 months.

Shine, William (1914–19); Leading Stoker, R.F.R., 63rd R.N.D.; Belgium; Holland, prisoner of war, 4 years 3 months.

Sibsey, Ernest (1914–17); Stoker, R.N.; Dardanelles 12 months, Canada 10 months.

Simmons, Thomas Stafford (1918–19). Able Seaman, R.N., H.M. Tug Deluge; Special Service, Home Waters, 3 months.

Simpson, Edward J. (1914–18); Leading Signaller, R.N.; Dardanelles 6 months, Adriatic 7 months, South Atlantic 2 years, North Sea 4 months.

Sinnett, William Arthur (1914–17); Signalman, R.N., H.M.S. Glory; Atlantic 10 months, Gallipoli 7 months, Egypt 3 months.

Smith, Arthur Herbert (1917); Gunner, R.G.A.

Smith, Charles William (1914–15); Private, 5th R. Irish Lancers; France 10 months.

Smith, Charles William (1914–17); Private, 2nd Bn. Durham Light Infantry; France, 3 years.

Smith, John Henry (1914–17); Able Seaman, R.N., H.M.S. Glory; North Atlantic 10 months, Dardanelles 7 months, Egypt 3 months, North Russia 17 months.

***Smith, Oliver John Thomas** (1914–15); Corporal, 2nd Bn. King's Own Yorkshire Light Infantry; France 4 months; Died, 7th January, 1915.

Smith, Percy (1914–19); Sergeant, Royal Fusiliers and Labour Corps; Gallipoli 7 months.

Southgate, Douglas Roland York (1914–17); Bombardier, R.F.A.; France 2 years 10 months.

Southgate, Edmund William (1914–17); Russian Medal of Saint George (4th Class); Leading Seaman, R.N., H.M.S. Engadine; Special Service and Grand Fleet 2 years 11 months.

Splatt, Charles Henry (1914–17); Leading Seaman, R.N., H.M.S. Calyx, H.M.S. Alcantara and H.M.S. Royal Sovereign; 10th Cruiser Squadron 2 years 11 months.

Stent, Henry Hermes (1914–17); Private, R.A.S.C.; France 3 years.

Sterrett, Frederick Josiah (1914–17); Sergeant, R.F.A.; France 3 years 1 month.

Stone, Harry Edmund (1918–19); Stoker, Trawler Section, R.N., 4 months.

Summers, Henry Burbidge (1914–17); Able Seaman, R.N., H.M.S. Cressy and H.M.S. Brilliant; 10th Cruiser Squadron.

Sumner, Frederick Sydney (1914–17); Private, R. Marine Brigade, France and Belgium 2 months, Gallipoli 9 months; H.M.S. Swiftsure, West Coast of Africa 9 months; Merchant Seaman, Ship's Gunner, S.S. Mortlake, Middlesbrough to Dunkirk, general cargo.

Sumner, Henry William (1914–18); Acting Sergeant, R. Marine Light Infantry; Flanders 1 month, Gallipoli 6 months, Eastern Mediterranean 12 months, Adriatic 7 months.

Sumner, Walter (1914–17); Able Seaman, R.N., H.M.S. New Zealand; Battle Cruiser Squadron 2 years 11 months.

Sweeney, John James (1914–17); Able Seaman, R.N.; Persian Gulf 2 years 2 months.

Tall, William (1914–17); Bombardier, R.F.A.; France 2 years 11 months.

Thew, Charles Alfred (1914–17); Able Seaman, R.F.R., H.M.S. Sapphire, afterwards attached to R.N.A.S.; Grand Fleet 12 months.

Thomas, Alonzo Frederick (1918–19); Air Mechanic (3rd Class), R.A.F.

Thomas, William (1914–17); Able Seaman, R.F.R., H.M.S. Gibraltar and H.M.S. Cordelia; Grand Fleet 2 years 11 months.

Tobias, Joseph Leonard (1916–19); Lance-Corporal, R.G.A., R.A.S.C.; France 2 years 3 months.

Tomlin, George (1914–17); Able Seaman, R.N.; North Sea 3 months, Western Ocean Patrol 4 months, Dardanelles 11 months, Suez Canal, Egypt, 6 months, Red Sea, Persian Gulf, Indian Ocean 12 months.

Travis, Ellis (1914–17); Corporal, R.F.A.; France 3 years 1 month.

***Treacher, George Gilbert** (1914–17); Sergeant, Royal Fusiliers and 32nd Training Reserve Bn.; France 2 years 1 month; Died of injuries, 4th March, 1917.

Turner, Charles James (1914–19); Leading Seaman, R.N., H.M.S. Glory and H.M.S. Valhalla II.; Eastern Mediterranean 4 years 6 months.

Turner, Joseph William Henry (1914–17); Signalman, R.F.R.; Atlantic Patrol 2 years, Grand Fleet 11 months.

Turrell, John Samuel (1918–19); Deck Hand, R.N.R.; Minesweeper, North Sea 3 months.

***Waddingham, James** (1914–16); Private, R. Marine Light Infantry; 10th Cruiser Squadron 18 months; Killed in action, 29th February, 1916.

***Waite, Charles William** (1914); 2nd Yeoman of Signals, R.F.R.; North Sea Patrol 2 months; Drowned at sea, 15th October, 1914.

Wall, George Caton (1914–18); Able Seaman, R.N.; Merchant Cruiser (patrolling) 3 years.

Warner, Francis Charles (1914–17); Gunner, R.G.A. and R.A.M.C.; France 3 years 1 month.

Watkins, Frederick William (1914–17); Able Seaman, R.N., H.M.S. King Alfred, H.M. Monitor 15, H.M.S. Amphitrite; North Sea 3 months, Dardanelles 12 months.

Watkins, Trevor Frank (1914–17); M.M. and mentioned in despatches; Sergeant, R.F.A.; France 3 years 1 month.

Webb, Henry George (1914–18); Able Seaman, R.F.R.; Battle Cruiser Squadron, Grand Fleet, 3 years 9 months.

Welch, Joseph (1914–17); Leading Seaman, R.N.; North Atlantic 10 months, Dardanelles 6 months, Egypt 3 months.

Wells, Sydney John William (1914–17); Stoker Petty Officer, R.F.R.; Grand Fleet 2 years 10 months.

Wheeler, Alfred Ernest (1914–17); Private, 2nd Bn. Middlesex Rgt.; France 1 year 8 months, Salonica 8 months.

Wheeler, Percy (1914–17); Private, 20th Hussars; France 3 years.

White, Basil (1914–17); Able Seaman, R.F.R.; Grand Fleet 2 years 11 months.

***White, Edward Valentine** (1914); Stoker, R.N., H.M.S. Hogue; North Sea 2 months; Drowned, 22nd September, 1914.

Whittle, Henry Edward (1918–19); Mechanic, R.A.F.; France 4 months.

Wilcocks, Charles Henry Duncombe (1914–19); Able Seaman, R.N., H.M. Patrol Boat No. 1, H.M.S. Juno; Dover Patrol and East India Station 2 years.

Williams, David James (1914–17); Able Seaman, R.N.; Cameroons 12 months.

Williams, David Morgan (1914–17); Able Seaman, R.N., H.M.S. Aboukir and H.M.S. Chester; Cruiser Squadron and Grand Fleet 2 years 2 months.

Williams, Ralph Henry James (1914–17); Able Seaman, R.N.; H.M.S. Glory 1 year 9 months, and H.M.S. Minotaur 10 months.

Williams, Robert Joseph (1914–17); Able Seaman, R.N., H.M.S. Sutlej; North Atlantic 11 months, Submarine Flotilla 2 years.

Willmott, Bertie Harold (1914–17); Gunner, R.F.A.; France 12 months, Egypt 9 months, Balkans 9 months, Italy 1 month.

Windle, Alec George (1918–19); Able Seaman, Mercantile Marine Reserve.

Wisdom, James Pattison (1914–17); Able Seaman, R.F.R.; H.M.S. Juno 3 years.

Woodard, George (1914–17); Sergeant, R.A.S.C.; France 3 years 3 months.

Youngman, Harry (1918–19); Deck Hand, R.N.R., H.M.S. Pembroke 4 months.

Public Health Department

Abrey, Percy Robert (1914–19); Private, 12th Bn. London Rgt., R.A.S.C.; France 2 years.

***Adams, Cornelius George** (1914–17); Private, 5th Bn. London Rgt.; France 6 months; Died of wounds, 6th February, 1917.

Ainsworth, David James (1915–19); Sec.-Lieutenant, 15th Bn. London Rgt., R.G.A.; France 12 months, Italy 15 months.

Anderson, John Watson (June–September, 1916); Private, Royal Fusiliers; (1917–19); Labour Corps; France 12 months.

Armstrong, Richard Robins (1914–19); Private, Honourable Artillery Company, and Captain, R.A.M.C.; France 5 months, Gallipoli 5 months, Egypt 3 months, Mesopotamia 3 years.

Ash, Douglas Victor (1917–19); Private, 6th Bn. S. Staffs Rgt.; France 11 months.

Ash, Frank Walter (1917–19); Sergeant, E. Surrey Rgt., Labour Corps.

Balmer, Ruth (1918–19); O.B.E.; Hon. Capt., R.A.F., Women's Medical Service.

Barnes, Jesse (1915–19); Corporal, R.A.M.C., R.A.S.C.; France 1 year 10 months.

Beck, Frank William (1914–19); Sergeant, 2/16th Bn. London Rgt.; France 12 months, Salonica 6 months, Palestine 12 months.

***Belcher, Douglas Charles** (1915–18); Lance-Corporal, R.A.M.C.; Salonica 2 years 1 month, Egypt 3 months; Died, 5th July, 1918.

Bendrey, Henry Bezant (1916–20); Private, 8th (Cyclists) Bn. Essex Rgt., 10th Bn. R. Scots Regt.; North Russia 1 year 9 months, Prisoner of war (Russia) 18 months.

Bennett, Charles Henry (1916–19); Rifleman, 2/10th Bn. Royal Scots, 12th Bn. King's Royal Rifle Corps.; France 2 years 2 months.

Birmingham, Charles Leo (1917–19); Captain, R.A.F. (Medical Section).

Blade, Douglas Harold (1915–19); Private, R.A.M.C.; France 6 months.

Bolton, Cyril Dodd (1914–19); Mentioned in despatches; Company Sergeant-Major, 2nd and 29th Bns. London Rgt.; Malta 4½ months.

Boome, Edward James (1914–19); Mentioned in despatches; Captain, R.A.M.C.; France 4 years 1 month.

Botting, Beatrice Sarah (1914–19); Staff Nurse, T.F.N.S.; France 1 year 8 months.

Burrows, Cresswell (1914–19); Captain (Acting Major), R.A.M.C.; France 2 years 9 months.

Butler, William (1915–19); Brevet Lieut.-Colonel, R.A.M.C.; Egypt and Palestine 10 months.

Calver, Agnes Eliza Mary (1914–18); Sister, T.F.N.S.; France 17 months.

Cazalet, Charlotte Travers (1914–19); Sister, T.F.N.S.; France 2 years 1 month.

Chater, Eric (1914–19); Lieutenant, Machine Gun Corps; France 3 months, Mesopotamia 18 months.

Clark, Harold Francis (1914–19); Sergeant, 2/10th Bn. Middlesex Rgt.; Gallipoli 4½ months, Palestine 2 years, Egypt 1 year 7 months.

Clarke, Ellen Josephine (1915–17); Sister, T.F.N.S.

***Clarke James Alfred** (1916); Rifleman Rifle Brigade; France 1 month; Killed in action, 15th September, 1916.

Clarkson, Frances Mary Annette (1915–19); Staff Nurse, Q.A.I.M.N.S.R.; Salonica 1 year 9 months, Egypt 3 months, Italy 15 months.

Cooper, Samuel Douglas (1914–19); Lieutenant, 1st County of London Yeomanry, R.F.A., and Trench Mortar Battery; France 6 months.

Coppin, Dorothy Elsie (1915–19); (1) Médaille d'honneur (silver), (2) Médaille de la Reconnaisance Française (silver), two citations, (3) L'Insigné des Blessés, (4) L'Insigné spécial (in gold); Sister in Charge of Surgical Service, Hospital 22, French Army Nursing Service, Croix Rouge Française, Comité Britannique (36th Corps); France 4 years.

Cowell, Eva Victoria (1916–19); Mentioned in despatches; Sister, attached Southwark Military Hospital.

***Cripps, Arthur David** (1916–18); Gunner, 180th Heavy Battery R.G.A.; Salonica 1 year 10 months, Italy 1 month; Died, 17th December, 1918.

Crookshank, Francis Graham (1914–19); Captain, Croix Rouge Française, R.A.M.C., France 1 year 10 months.

Crowe, Margaret Mary (1915–17); Staff Nurse, T.F.N.S.

Daly, Daniel (1916–18); Private, 4th Bn. Royal Fusiliers; France 6 months.

Downing, Rosetta Bessie (1914–19); Sister, T.F.N.S.; France 15 months, Malta 10 months.

Dunn, Amelia Ellen (1915–17); Staff Sister, T.F.N.S.

Eccles, Oreste (1918–19); Lieutenant, R.A.M.C.

Fairfield, Josephine Letitia Denny (1917–20); C.B.E.; Honorary Lieut.-Colonel, R.A.M.C., attached W.A.A.C., W.R.A.F.

Fisher, Samuel Sidney (1915–18); Rifleman, Rifle Brigade; France 1 year 11 months.

Flack, Gordon Ernest (1916–19); Mentioned in Air Force List for valuable services rendered; Leading Aircraftsman, R.A.F. 6th Wing, H.Q.

Forbes, James Graham (1916–19); Mentioned in despatches; Captain, R.A.M.C.; Macedonia 2 years.

Fowler, Thomas Edward (1915–19); Sergeant R.A.M.C., R.A.S.C.; Salonica 2 years 10 months.

Fry, Francis Edward (1915–19); Sergeant, R.A.M.C.; Macedonia and Turkey 3 years 2 months.

Goldwater, Leopold (1914–19); Twice mentioned in despatches; Private, 2/15th Bn. London Rgt.; Egypt and Palestine 2 years 4 months.

Griffin, Zoe (1914–18); Staff Nurse, T.F.N.S.

Hale, Amy Marion (1914–19); Mentioned in despatches; Sister, T.F.N S.

Hanson, Helen Beatrice (1914–15 and 1916–20); Order of St. Sava (4th class) and Serbian Red Cross; Hon. Captain, R.A.M.C.; Belgian and French Red Cross Societies, Antwerp, 1 month, France 5 months, Serbia 6 months, Malta 12 months, Salonica 1 year 8 months, Turkey 13 months.

Harrington, William Jack (1914–19); Private, 1st City of London Sanitary Co., R.A.M.C.; France 4 years 1 month.

Higgs, Frederick William (1914–19); C.B.E. (Mil.), three times mentioned in despatches; Lieut.-Colonel, R.A.M.C.; France 2 years 9 months.

High, Albert Walter (1914–19); Sergeant, 2/6th Bn. E. Surrey Rgt., R.D.C.

Holland, Frank (1917–19); Private, 16th Bn. York and Lancaster Rgt.

***Hughes, John Edward** (1914–17); Sergeant, 1st County of London Yeomanry, 12th Bn. Royal Fusiliers; France 9 months; Killed in action, 16th June, 1917.

Huntley, Ernest Edward (1914–19); M.M.; Corporal, Grenadier Guards; France 3 years 9 months.

Jones, William Edward (1914–18); Sergeant, R.H.A. and R.F.A.; France 6 months, Macedonia 2 years 4 months.

Kerr, James (1917); Major, R.A.M.C.

Keville, Stanley Charles (1914–19); Corporal, 1st County of London Yeomanry; Gallipoli, Egypt and Palestine 4 years.

Kirby, Bernard Burrows (1915–19); M.C., mentioned in despatches; Captain, 12th Bn. Gloucestershire Rgt.; France 2 years 8 months, Italy 5 months.

Langmead, Frederick Samuel (1917–19); Major, R.A.M.C.; Salonica 18 months.

Layton, Annie Gertrude (1914–19); Sister, T.F.N.S.; France 3 years 8 months.

Lea, Edmund Thomas Howard (1914–20); R.A.M.C.; India and Mesopotamia 4 years 4 months.

Leach, Rosemary (1914–15); Nurse, T.F.N.S.; France 3 months.

Lewis, Harold James (1915–19); Private, R.A.M.C., and Sec.-Lieutenant, R.G.A.; France 2 years 8 months.

Low, Christina (1914–19); Staff Nurse, B.R.C.S., Q.A.I.M.N.S.R.; France 4 years 1 month.

Lush, Rowena Jeans (1914–19); Royal Red Cross; Sister, T.F.N.S.; France 2 years.

McCallum, Rosa Helen (1915–19); Royal Red Cross, Mentioned in despatches; Sister, T.F.N.S.

Macewen, William (1914–19); Captain, R.A.M.C.; Malta 4 months, France 2 years 9 months.

McHattie, Thomas John Tyndale (1914–19); Major, R.A.M.C.; France 2 years 11 months.

McIlwrath, Mary Jane Agnes (1915–19); Mentioned in despatches; Sister, T.F.N.S.; Salonica 15 months, Italy 13 months.

***McMillan, Robert Alfred** (1914–16); Private, 15th Bn. London Rgt.; France 12 months; Wounded and missing, 7th October, 1916.

McVail, Elizabeth Maud (1918–19); Hon. Major, R.A.F. (Medical Service).

Marris, Henry Fairley (1914–19); Mentioned in despatches; Major, R.A.M.C.

Marsland, Hilda (1914–19); Mentioned in despatches; Sister, T.F.N.S.; France 12 months.

Mason, Beatrice Burgess (1915–19); Sister, T.F.N.S.

Mayman, Amy Gertrude (1914–18); Staff Nurse, T.F.N.S.

Mayo, Louis Frederick (1914–15); Lance-Corporal, 6th Bn. Gordon Highlanders; France 2 months.

Mercer, Ellen Eliza (1914–19); Sister-in-Charge, T.F.N.S.

Montague, Lilian Anne (1915–17); Staff Nurse, Q.A.I.M.N.S.R.; France 14 months, H.M. Hospital Ship Asturias 10 months.

Morrish, William John (1916–17); Lieutenant, R.A.M.C.; Salonica 10 months.

Morton, Edward John (1915–18); Captain, R.A.M.C.

Mossman, Florence Mary (1914–19); Staff Nurse, T.F.N.S.

Mulcahy, Timothy (1916–20); Lance-Corporal, R.A.S.C.; Turkey 8 months.

Murray, Laura (1915–18); Sister, Q.A.I.M.N.S.R.; Salonica 2 years.

O'Connell, Kathleen (1915–19); Royal Red Cross; Sister, Brook War Hospital, Woolwich.

Orme, Archibald George (1916–19); Sergeant, R.F.A. and R.G.A.

Orr, Robina Moonie (1914–19); Royal Red Cross; Sister-in-Charge, T.F.N.S.

Osborn, William James (1915–19); Sapper, R.E.; France 1 year 8 months.

Ottaway, George (1917–19); Private, 20th Bn. R. W. Surrey Rgt., 128th Labour Co.; France 18 months.

Padbury, Caroline Augusta (1914–19); Royal Red Cross; Sister, T.F.N.S.

Palgrave, Edward Francis (1914–15); Lieutenant, R.A.M.C.; France 11 months.

Parker, Reginald Charles Christopher (1915–19); 1st Air Mechanic, R.A.C. (Wireless Section), R.A.F.; France 1 year 7 months, Germany, prisoner of war 8 months.

Pearce, Frank (1914–19); Gunner, 9th Bn. London Rgt., 25th Bn. Royal Fusiliers, Motor Machine Gun Squadron; France 16 months, German East Africa 16 months.

Pepper, William Richard (1915–19); Mentioned in despatches; Lance-Sergeant, London Sanitary Co. R.A.M.C.; France 9 months.

***Peters, Owen Herbert** (1915–16); Captain, R.A.M.C.; France; Died of wounds, 4th August, 1916.

Pfeiffer, Alois Friedrich (1916–19); Private, 30/31st Bn. Middlesex Rgt., attached R.A.F.

Pinchin, Arthur John Scott (1916–17, 1918); Lieutenant, R.A.M.C. and Ministry National Service Medical Board.

Platt, Jessie (1915 – 18); Sister, Q.A.I.M.N.S.R.; Salonica 2 years.

Pooley, Lizzie Beatrice (1915–19); Staff Nurse, T.F.N.S.

Poulden, Emma Elizabeth (1914–16); Staff Nurse, T.F.N.S.

Pulman, Ethel (1915–18); Twice mentioned in despatches; Staff Nurse, T.F.N.S.

Putt, George Harold (1915–19); Flight-Cadet, R.N.A.S. and R.A.F.

Raffle, Andrew Banks (1914–19); M.C.; Captain, R.A.M.C.; France 4 years 1 month.

Rangecroft, Lucy (1914–19); Royal Red Cross, mentioned in despatches; Sister, T.F.N.S.

Reade, Arthur George Lawrence (1914–19); O.B.E. (Mil.); Surgeon-Lieutenant, London Division R.N.V.R. and Royal Navy; South Atlantic Squadron 2 months, Grand Fleet 14 months.

Regan, Colston James (1915–20); Captain, 2nd London Sanitary Co. R.A.M.C.; France 20 months.

Roberts, Ellis James (1916–17); Lieutenant, R.A.M.C.

Rose, William Joseph (1914–19); Corporal, 16th Bn. London Rgt.; France 4 years 1 month.

***Russell, Alice Maud** (1915–16); Staff Sister, Q.A.I.M.N.S.R.; Malta 10 months; Died, 5th October, 1916.

***Sanders, Herbert Joseph** (1915–18); Rifleman, 2/5th Bn. London Rgt.; France 15 months; Killed in action, 24th March, 1918.

Saunders, Lilian Annie (1914–19); Sister, T.F.N.S.; Salonica 2 years, Malta 2 months.

Scrivener, Eleanor (1914–19); Sister, T.F.N.S.; France 2 years 6 months.

Searle, Sophie (1915–19); Mentioned in despatches; Staff Nurse, Q.A.I.M.N.S.R.; Malta 12 months, France 2 years 4 months.

***Selman, Percy St. Clair** (1916); Private, 17th Bn. London Rgt.; France 2 months; Died of wounds, 18th September, 1916.

Sikes, Alfred Walter (1914–15); Surgeon, Ambulance Train, B.R.C.S.; France 8 months.

Slowan, Wm. John More (1914–19); O.B.E. (Mil.); Captain, R.A.M.C.

Smith, Eric Bellingham (1915–19). Mentioned in despatches; Captain, R.A.M.C.; Serbia 7 months, Egypt 3 years 5 months.

Solomon, Joseph William (1915–19); Sergeant, R.A.M.C.; Salonica 3 years 7 months.

Spencer, Bernard James (1916–18); Private, E. Surrey Rgt.

Stacey, Frederick Charles (1914–20); M.C.; Sub-Lieutenant, Royal Naval Division, Anson Bn.; Gallipoli 6 months, France 2 years.

Steele, Leonard William (1914–19); Gunner, R.F.A., R.G.A.; Egypt 7 months, France 11 months.

Stiff, Philip William Henry (1914–19); Corporal, 2/1st County of London Yeomanry; France and Italy 2 years 5 months.

Stiff, William Thomas Francis (1914–19); M.M.; Private, 62nd Bn., Machine Gun Corps; France 12 months.

***Stockdale, Edward Leslie Johnson** (1914–16); Lieutenant, 10th Bn. Lancashire Fus.; France 16 months; Killed in action, 7th July, 1916.

Summerson, Samuel (1916–19); Captain, R.A.M.C.; Salonica 2 years 5 months, N. Russia 4 months.

Taylor, Henry Oswald (1916–19); Corporal, R.G.A.; France 3 years.

Tilley, John Richard (1917–19); Private, 2/1st W. Somerset Yeomanry.

Tosswill, Leonard Robert (1914–19); O.B.E. (Mil.), twice mentioned in despatches; Major, R.A.M.C.; France 2 years 4 months.

Train, Herbert James (1916–19); Private, R.A.M.C.; Salonica 2 years 8 months.

Verdon-Roe, Spencer (1916–17); Lieutenant, R.A.M.C.; Salonica 11 months.

Waite, Ruth Hannah (1914–19); Royal Red Cross, mentioned in despatches; Sister, T.F.N.S.

Walker, Mary Anable (1915–19); Royal Red Cross; Sister, T.F.N.S.; Salonica 1 year 9 months.

***Walsh, Stephen Barry** (1914–15); Lieutenant, R.A.M.C.; France 9 months; Died of wounds, 8th September, 1915.

Wanklyn, William McConnel (1914–19); Captain, R.A.M.C.; France 18 months.

Watson, James (1916–19); 2nd London Sanitary Co., R.A.M.C.; France 10 months, Italy 18 months.

While, Rose (1915–19); Staff Nurse, T.F.N.S.; France 1 year 11 months.

Williams, Alfred Carleton (1915–19); Captain, R.A.M.C.

Young, Emily Hopwood (1914–19); Sister, Q.A.I.M.N.S.R.

Estates and Valuation Department

Amies, Herbert William (1915–19); Lieutenant, Middlesex Rgt.; Belgium 3 months.

Beck, Herbert Edgar (1914–19); Acting Staff-Sergeant, R.A.M.C.; France 4 years 4 months.

Biggs, William Robert (1916–19); Private, E. Surrey Rgt.; France 2 years 4 months.

Brennan, Frederick James (1917–19); Private, R.A.S.C. (M.T.).

Brown, Leonard John (1916–19); Corporal, A.P.C. and E. Surrey Rgt.

*** Brownsword, Arthur Henry** (1915–17); Gunner, R.G.A.; France 16 months; Died of wounds, 30th April, 1917.

Carter, Charles (1914–19); Gunner, R.F.A. and R.E.; France 6 months, Salonica 7 months, Palestine 2 years.

Carter, George (1918–19); Private, Suffolk, Essex and E. Yorkshire Rgts.

Cecil, Augustus (1916–19); Private, 7th Bn. Norfolk Rgt.; France 1 year 8 months.

Clarke, Edward Baron (1915–19); Sapper, R.E.; France 2 years 7 months.

Coath, Edward Hawking (1916–19); Corporal, R.N.A.S. and R.A.F.

Creasy, Oswald Ross (1916–19); Gunner, R.G.A.; France 3 years 1 month.

Cressy, Sydney Vallentin (1917–19); Private, R.N.A.S. and R.A.F.

Davis, Frederick (1914–1917); Private, 18th Bn. London Rgt.

Davis, Joseph James (1916–18); Gunner, R.G.A., and Sapper, R.E.; France 12 months.

Dunkley, Thomas Edward (1917–19); Private, R.A.M.C.; Salonica 1 year 8 months.

Ede, George Noel (1914–19); Private, R.A.M.C.

Elford, E. J. (1914–1919); Lance-Corporal, 18th Bn. London Rgt.; Mediterranean 4 years 1 month.

*** Findon, Robert** (1914–1918); Sapper, R.E.; France 1 year 7 months; Killed in action, 18th April, 1918.

Ford, George Frederick Charles (1916–19); Corporal, Cambridgeshire Rgt.; France 2 years 5 months.

*** Geis, Bertram Alfred** (1914–16); Corporal, 7th Bn. London Rgt.; France 12 months; Killed in action, 15th September, 1916.

Gregory, George (1917–19); Private, 100th Provisional Bn. London Rgt.

Hannon, John Michael (1916–18); Bombardier, R.G.A.; France 16 months.

Harmer, Philip Stephen (1914–19); M.S.M., and twice mentioned in despatches; Sergeant, 13th Bn. London Rgt.; France and Germany 3 years 11 months.

Harrington, William Wilfrid (1915–19); Armourer Staff-Sergeant, R.A.O.C. and Loyal N. Lancashire Rgt.; France 2 years 7 months.

Hawes, Joseph James (1914–19); Regimental Sergeant-Major, 7th Bn. London Rgt.

Hendra, Albert John (1916–19); Sapper, R.E.; Egypt 2 years 4 months.

Higgs, Fred Albert (1918–19); Gunner, R.G.A.

James, Daniel (1914–19); Corporal, R.A.M.C.; France 4 years 2 months.

Jamison, Henry Arthur (1916–19); Private, E. Kent Rgt.; France 2 years 8 months.

Jones, Henry (1915–19); Battery Quartermaster Sergeant, R.F.A.

Jury, Stephen Walter (1916–19); Sergeant, R.A.M.C.; France and Germany 2 years 3 months.

Kilvington, John Henry (1916–18); Acting Corporal, R.F.C. and R.A.F.

King, Herbert Walter (1914–19); Corporal, R.A.M.C.; France 4 years.

King, John (1916–19); Private, 15th Bn. R. Fusiliers and Durham Light Infantry; France 7 months.

Ladd, Walter Willoughby (1916–19); Sapper, R.E.; Salonica 5 months, Palestine 1 year 10 months.

Lake, William Frederick (1915–19); Sapper, R.E.; France 3 years 3 months.

Lanning, Frederick Charles (1916–19); Sergeant, R. Fusiliers, Eastern Command Labour Corps.

Legge, W. Thomas (1915–19); Private, R.W. Kent Rgt.; France 12 months.

Liberty, Walter James (1916–19); Private, 13th Bn. Lincolnshire Rgt.

***Longley, Edward James Percy** (1916); Private, 6th Bn. Rifle Brigade; France; Killed in action, 23rd October, 1916.

Luffingham, William John (1914–19); Captain, R.A.S.C.

McCormach, James H. (1914–19); Private, 7th Bn. E. Surrey Rgt.; France 18 months.

***McGrath, John** (1915–17); Private, 15th Bn. London Rgt.; Egypt and Palestine 4 months; Killed in action, 31st October, 1917.

McShee, George (1914–19); Regimental Quartermaster-Sergeant, 7th Bn. London Rgt.

Maher, Michael Joseph (1918–19); Pioneer, R.E.

Martin, Henry (1916–19); Private, 23rd Bn. London Rgt., 1st Bn. Somersetshire Light Infantry, and 6th Bn. Durham Light Infantry; France 15 months.

Mason, Stephen Charles (1918–19); Aircraftsman, 2nd Class, R.A.F.

Matthews, Stanley Arthur (1914–19); Mentioned in despatches; Sergeant, E. Surrey Rgt. and R.A.S.C.; France 11 months.

***Maxim, William** (1914 – 15); Driver, R.F.A.; France 1 month; Died, 25th January, 1915.

***Meredith, Edgar Stuart** (1914 – 15); Private, 15th Bn. London Rgt.; France 8 months; Killed in action, 1st November, 1915.

Miller, Algernon Richard Rabone Augustus (1915–19); M.S.M., Mentioned in despatches; Colour-Sergeant, 14th Bn. London Rgt. and Rifle Brigade.

Morland, Thomas Wilfrid Raisbeck (1916–19); 2nd Corporal, R.E.; Palestine 18 months.

O'Callaghan, Vincent Michael (1915–19); Sapper, R.E., and Private, E. Kent Rgt. and R. Munster Fusiliers; France 1 year 9 months.

O'Connell, Patrick Joseph (1916–19); Flight Sergeant, R.A.F.

O'Connor, Michael (1916); Private, Irish Guards.

Palmer, Charles (1916–19); Private, 18th Bn. London Rgt.; France 2 years.

Parker, Charles Goode (1915–19); Sapper, R.E.; France.

Payne, Frederick George (1915–19); Lance-Corporal, R.E.; France, 3 years 1 month.

Pearce, Edmund (1914–19); Lance-Corporal, Middlesex Yeomanry and R.E.; Egypt and Palestine, 3 years 8 months.

Percival, Joseph Archer (1914–19); Company Quartermaster-Sergeant, 7th Bn. Middlesex Rgt.; Gibraltar 5 months, France 3 years 6 months.

Porter, James William Richard (1914-16); Lance-Corporal, 7th Bn. London Rgt.

Reed, Stanley Gordon (1914–19); Captain, R.A.M.C.; Gallipoli 10 months, France 3 years 9 months.

Roberts, Edmund Bertie (1914–19); Private, 12th Bn. R. Fusiliers; France and prisoner of war (Germany) 3 years 5 months.

Rollin, Percy William (1914–19); Private, R.A.M.C.; France.

Rose, James Luke (1915–17); Private, R.A.M.C.

Ruddle, Frank Joseph (1914–19); Chinese Order of Wen Hu, 4th Class, Mentioned in despatches; Major, Lancashire Fusiliers; France 2 years 3 months.

Rushworth, Harold Montagu (1914–19); Captain, London Rgt. and R.F.C.; France.

Rye, William Robert (1916–19); Flight Sergeant, R.A.F.

Sanders, Percy Thomas (1916–19); Private, 1st Huntingdonshire Cyclists Bn.

Saunders, Alexander Henry (1915–19); Corporal, R.A.M.C.; Egypt 12 months, Palestine 1 year 10 months.

Sheppard, George Henry (1915–19); Acting Staff-Sergeant, 14th Bn. London Rgt.

Shrimpton, Charles William (1914–19); M.M.; Driver, R.F.A.; France 4 years 9 months.

Smith, Ernest Disraeli (1915–19); Private, R. Marine Light Infantry.

Smith, Horace Albert (1914–19); Gunner, R.F.A.; France 13 months, Salonica 2 years 10 months.

Smith, Robert (1916–19); Sapper, R.E., and Private, R.A.S.C., Manchester Rgt. and Labour Corps.

Strachan, Herbert Edward (1915–19); M.S.M.; Sergeant, R.A.M.C.; France 3 years 1 month.

Taylor, Leonard Charles (1915–19); Lance-Corporal, R. Marine Light Infantry; Gallipoli 4 months, Salonica 4 months, France 1 year 7 months.

Taylor, Thomas Osborne (1915–19); Corporal, R.A.M.C.; Salonica 2 years 1 month.

***Thomas, Thomas** (1915–17); Private, 15th Bn. London Rgt.; France 10 months; Died of wounds, 2nd December, 1917.

***Turner, Henry Coventon** (1914–15); Private, 23rd Bn. London Rgt.; France 2 months; Killed in action, 25th May, 1915.

Walker, Albert Henry (1917–19); Private, R.A.S.C.; France 1 year 11 months.

Walker, Arthur Sydney (1914–19); 2nd Corporal, R.E.; France 5 months.

Westwood, Herbert (1915–19); Private, Honourable Artillery Company; France 3 years.

White, Harold Cedric (1914–19); Corporal, 15th Bn. London Rgt. and Labour Corps; France 7 months.

Willett, George (1914–19); Sapper, R.E.; France 4 years 5 months.

Woollett, William Alfred (1915–18); 2nd Lieutenant, R.N.V.R. and R.G.A.

Public Control Department

Allen, John Bedford (1915–16); Private, E. Kent Rgt.; France 10 months.

Aylett, Earengey Maurice Percy (1915–19); M.S.M.; Sergeant, Army Cyclist Corps, E. Yorkshire Rgt. and Labour Corps; France 2 years 8 months.

Baker, Frederick Charles (1915–19); Corporal, E. Surrey Rgt. and Northamptonshire Rgt.; Gallipoli 5 months, Palestine 5 months, Egypt 2 years, Macedonia 3 months.

***Baldwin, Ernest Wilfred** (1914–15); 5th Bn. London Rgt.; France 7 months; Killed in action, 3rd May, 1915.

Bateman, Thomas (1914–19); Private, 7th Bn. London Rgt. and Labour Corps; France 4 years 1 month.

Bentall, William Grinham (1916–19); Sapper, R.E.; France and Italy 2 years 9 months.

Bew, Arnold Frederick (1916–19); Private, 13th and 20th Bns. London Rgt.; France 12 months.

Bond, Alfred (1915–18); Private, E. Surrey Rgt. and Labour Corps; France 13 months.

Bow, D'Albert Randolf Francis Douglas (1914–19); M.S.M.; Lance-Sergeant, R.G.A., R.A.S.C., R.A.M.C.; France 4 years 7 months.

Brewer, Sydney Harold (1914–19); Mentioned in despatches; Regimental Quartermaster-Sergeant, Middlesex and Suffolk Rgts.; France 2 years 9 months.

Brimble, Arthur Stenner (1914–19); Bombardier, R.F.A.; France 3 years 4 months.

Bryden, Robert, F.R.C.V.S. (1914–19); Captain, R.A.V.C.; France 3 years 5 months.

***Burgess, Albert** (1914–16); Lance-Corporal, 21st Bn. London Rgt.; France 13 months; Killed in action, 23rd May, 1916.

Burr, Walter John (1915–19); Lance-Corporal, 10th Bn. London Rgt. and R.D.C.

Card, Stanley (1915–19); Corporal, R.A.S.C.

Cavalier, Arthur (1915–18); Private, 18th Bn. London Rgt. and R.D.C.

***Clifton, Herbert Charles Joseph** (1916–17); Private, R.G.A.; France 9 months; Died of wounds, 3rd May, 1917.

Cole, Howard Norman (1914–19); Order of Wen-Hu; Captain, Wiltshire Yeomanry and Labour Corps; France 1 year 10 months.

Corrie, Archibald John (1914–19); Sec.-Lieutenant, Norfolk Rgt. and 3rd Bn. London Rgt.; France 2 years 10 months.

Crabb, Henry (1916–19); Sergeant, R. Sussex Rgt., Hertfordshire Rgt. and Essex Cyclists.

***Curry, John William** (1914); R. Marine Light Infantry, Grand Fleet; Drowned, H.M.S. Cressy, 22nd September, 1914.

Dakin, Charles John (1916–17); Private, Labour Corps.

Dean, Horace Harry (1916–19); Lieutenant, 14th Bn. London Rgt. and Somersetshire Light Infantry; France 1 year 9 months.

Dennison, Frank Rolfe (1916–19); Gunner, R.F.A.; France 1 year 9 months.

***Downham, George Edward** (1916–17); Private, Rifle Brigade; France 4 months; Killed in action, 9th April, 1917.

Emmerson, George (1915–19); Gunner, R.F.A.; France 3 years.

Gibbins, Percy Hedon (1914–19); M.C.; Major, R.F.A.; France 2 years 5 months.

Godsell, Herbert Alfred (1916–19); Lance-Corporal, 4th and 29th Bns. London Rgt.

Goodwill, Maud Bessie (1918–19); Forewoman Clerk, Q.M.A.A.C.

Graham, Alfred (1915–19); Private, R.A.M.C.; France 2 years 9 months.

Gunstone, Frank (1914–19); Corporal, R.A.M.C.; France 4 years 2 months.

Hamilton, James Eastwood (1915–19); Sergeant Mechanic, R.N.A.S., R.A.F.; Grand Fleet, 2 years 2 months.

Hartrup, Ernest John (1917–20); Private, R.A.V.C.; Mesopotamia and Persia 16 months.

Hawley, William Joseph (1916–17); Private, R.A.S.C.

Hayes, Garrett James (1915–19); Private, 2nd Bn. London Rgt.; France 2 years 1 month.

Haywood, William Henry (1916–19); Private, Middlesex Rgt.; France 2 years 11 months.

Hepworth, Joseph (1914–19); Private, 7th Bn. London Rgt.; France 3 years 11 months.

Hewson, Charles Chambers (1918–19); Private, 29th Bn. London Rgt. and Middlesex Rgt.

Higgins, Alfred William (1915–19); Private, R.A.S.C.

Higgins, Henry Patrick (1918–19); 2nd Air Mechanic, R.A.F.

Holden, George Herbert (1915–19); Private, R.A.O.C.

Holmes, Lionel Robert (1915–19); Bombardier, R.G.A.; France 2 years 10 months.

Hughes, David Thomas (1914–19); Private, R.D.C.

Jacobs, Walter Thomas George (1917–19); M.S.M.; Sergeant, Labour Corps; France 1 year 11 months.

James, Benjamin Richard (1917–19); Petty Officer, R.N., Experimental Service.

Jessup, Bernard James (1914–19); Corporal, 21st Bn. London Rgt. and R.E.; France 7 months, Salonica 8 months, Egypt and Palestine 1 year 9 months.

Jewell, Harry (1916–19); Gunner, R.G.A.; France 16 months.

Jones, Charles Henry (1918–19); Private, R.D.C. and R.A.S.C.

Jones, William (1915–19); Sergeant, R.F.A.; France 17 months.

Keevil, James (1916–17); Lance-Corporal, Essex Rgt.; France 3 months.

***Kingham, Frederick Albert** (1915–18); Company Sergeant-Major, 15th Bn. London Rgt.; France 16 months; Killed in action, 17th June, 1918.

Knight, Henry William (1916–19); Shoeing-Smith, R.A.S.C.; Salonica 2 years, Russia 9 months.

Lawrence, Joseph Henry Hughes (1914–19); Driver, R.F.A.; France 2 months.

Lewis, William Henry (1914–19); Mentioned in despatches; Corporal, R.A.M.C.; France 2 years 4 months, Italy 17 months.

Lock, Edward (1914–19); Mentioned in despatches; Captain, R. Marine Light Infantry, R.N.V.R., York and Lancaster Rgt.

Lucas, James Beresford (1916–19); Private, 15th Bn. London Rgt. and Somersetshire Light Infantry; India 2 years 1 month.

Mackness, Frederick William (1915–19); Corporal, R.N.A.S. and R.A.F.

Maguire, Charles (1915–19); Private, 2nd London Yeomanry and Machine Gun Corps; Egypt, Palestine, etc., 17 months, France 10 months.

Manning, John (1915–19); Sergeant, Royal Fusiliers and Bedfordshire Rgt.; France 6 months.

Matkin, Charles (1914–19); Lieutenant, 3rd London Yeomanry and R.A.S.C.; France 1 year 11 months.

McKenzie, Frank Ernest Pocock Halifax (1915–19); Sergeant, 25th and 10th Bns. London Rgt., and R.A.F.

McLean, John (1915–19); Russian Order of St. Anne; Lieutenant, Honourable Artillery Company and R.A.O.C.; France 3 years, Russia 16 months.

***Mayer, Leonard Joseph** (1914–16); Lance-Corporal, 20th Bn. London Rgt.; France 14 months; Died of wounds, 31st May, 1916.

Medcalf, William Rutter (1915–19); Private, R.A.M.C.; France 12 months.

Merry, Ralph Clement (1916–19); Gunner, R.G.A.; France 12 months.

Mullin, Patrick Daniel (1915–19); Sergeant, R.N.A.S. and R.A.F.

Neale, George Harry (1914–18); Corporal, R.F.A.; France 3 years 1 month.

Newlands, Donald Richard (1916–17); Private, R.A.S.C. (M.T.).

Ockenden, Albert Charles (1915–19); Lance-Corporal, A.P.C., Northumberland Fusiliers, and R. Warwickshire Rgt.; France 6 months.

Orpin, Charles (1916–19); Private, R.A.V.C.

Paul, Stanley George (1917–18); Private, Rifle Brigade.

Pickering, John (1914–19); Lieutenant, 15th Bn. London Rgt. and Lancashire Fusiliers; France 6 months.

Preston, Frederick Alfred (1916–19); 2nd Corporal, R.E.; France 3 years.

Puryer, Charles (1914–18); Gunner, R.G.A.; Gallipoli 2 months, Egypt 3 months, France 14 months.

Radburn, James (1914–19); Company Sergeant-Major Instructor, Middlesex Rgt., and School of Musketry.

Reid, Ernest (1914–19); Air Mechanic (2nd Class); 7th Bn. London Rgt. and R.A.F.; France 1 year 7 months.

Root, Samuel (1914–19); Private, Middlesex Rgt.; France 3 years 11 months.

Saunders, Joseph William (1918–19); Corporal, R.A.S.C. and R.A.F.

Seppings, George Edward (1916–19); Air Mechanic (1st Class), E. Surrey Rgt., R. Sussex Rgt., Royal Fusiliers and R.A.F.; France 1 month.

Shorto, Leslie Eugene (1916–19); Corporal, R.N.A.S. and R.A.F.; France 2 years 5 months.

Skempton, Ernest John (1916–19); Private, E. Surrey Rgt. and Loyal N. Lancashire Rgt.; France, Salonica and Palestine, 2 years 4 months.

Smith, Charles Thomas (1914–19); Corporal, 24th Bn. London Rgt. and R.D.C.

Smith, Frederick Richards (1916–19); Sec.-Lieutenant, R.G.A.; France 1 month.

Sprules, Arthur Henry (1915–16); Able Seaman, R.N.D.

Stone, William Edward (1916–19); Sapper, R.E.; France 2 years 5 months.

Stubbs, Henry James (1915–19); Mentioned twice in despatches; Private, 22nd Bn. London Rgt.; France 5 months, Salonica 5 months, Egypt 1 year 8 months.

Stubbs, William (1915–19); Private, R.A.V.C.; France 3 years 2 months.

Talbot, George (1917–19); Lance-Corporal, R. Scots Fusiliers and Scottish Rifles; France 7 months, prisoner of war 8 months.

Taylor, James (1918–19); Private, R.A.S.C.

Taylor, William (1914–19); Private, Grenadier Guards; France 2 years.

Walton, Frank Reginald (1915–19); Company Sergeant-Major, S. Wales Borderers; Salonica 15 months.

Ware, Joseph Henry (1914–19); M.C., mentioned in despatches; Regimental Sergeant-Major, R.F.A.; France 4 years 10 months.

Wood, Arthur William (1914–19); Private, 7th Bn. London Rgt.; France 3 years 10 months.

Wood, Richard Alfred (1914–19); Regimental Sergeant-Major, 10th Bn. London Rgt.; Gallipoli 5 months.

Parks Department

Adams, George (1915–19); Gunner, R. Marine Artillery.

Adams, Henry Ernest (1916–19); Private, 21st Bn. London Rgt.; France 2 years.

Allchin, George William (1915–19); Private, 2nd Bn. Rifle Brigade and Labour Corps; France 3 years 9 months.

***Amos, John Vince** (1914–17); Lieutenant, 31st Battery R.F.A.; France 2 years 6 months; Died, 13th February, 1917.

Andrews, Charles (1914); Gunner, R.F.A., 24th Reserve Batty.

Andrews, Richard Ernest (1915–19); Driver, R.A.S.C. (M.T.).

***Andrews, Sydney** (1914); Lance-Corporal, R. W. Surrey Rgt.; France 1 month; Killed in action, 14th September, 1914.

***Ashdown, Harry George** (1915–16); Private, Royal Fusiliers; France 3 months; Missing, 27th March, 1916.

Ashman, William Arthur (1914–18); Horsekeeper, R.A.V.C.

Austin, Harry Charles Edward (1914–19); D.C.M.; Sergeant, R.G.A. School of Gunnery; France 4 months.

Austin, Joseph Richard (1915–19); M.M.; Sergeant, 138th Heavy Battery, R.G.A.; France 3 years.

Avery, John William (1918–19); Private, 30th Bn. London and 32nd Bn. Middlesex Rgts.

Baker, Henry John (1914–19); Lance-Corporal, 2nd Bn. Essex Rgt. and Military Police; France 17 months.

***Baker, Henry William** (1914–17); Rifleman, King's Royal Rifle Corps; France 2 months; Missing, 16th September, 1917.

Baker, William Frank (1915–19); Private, R.A.O.C.; France 4 years 2 months.

***Barker, Christopher Theodore** (1915–17); Ordinary Seaman, Royal Naval Division; France 1 month; Missing, 23rd April, 1917.

Barrett, James (1917–19); Private, R.D.C.

Bartlett, George William (1914–18); Private, 10th Bn. London Rgt. and R.D.C.

***Basterfield, William Joseph** (1914); Private, R. W. Surrey Rgt.; Missing, 31st October, 1914.

Bateman, John Baker (1914–16); Private, City of London Defence Corps.

Bennett, Roland Day (1916–19); Staff-Sergeant, R.A.S.C.; Egypt and Palestine 3 years.

Betts, Thomas (1914–19); Gunner, R.F.A.

Betts, William (1914–19); Private, R. Marine Light Infantry; France 6 months, Egypt 18 months.

***Billson, Arthur George** (1917–18); Aircraftsman, R.N.A.S., Kite Balloon Section; Died, 16th November, 1918.

Bird, Henry William (1915–19); Driver, 513th Field Co. R.E.; France 3 years 2 months.

Birkin, William (1915–19); Private, R.D.C.; France 2 days.

Black, Ronald Roderick (1916–18); Private, 7th and 29th Bns. London Rgt., and 16th Bn. York and Lancaster Rgt.

Blain, Albert (1916–19); Private, R.A.O.C.; France 2 years.

***Blake, John Edward** (1914); Able Seaman, R.F.R.; Lost in H.M.S. Good Hope, 1st November, 1914.

Bland, William (1916–19); Private, R.A.M.C. and 2/19th Bn. London Rgt.; Egypt 12 months.

Blane, William Thomas (1914–18); Private, London Rgt.

Bloor, Percy (1916–19); Gunner, R.G.A.; India 2 years 4 months.

Blunden, Alfred James (1918–19); Private, R.A.F.

Boughen, Robert (1918–19); Private, 1st City of London Yeomanry.

Boyle, Robert Wilson (1916–18); Private, 20th Bn. Middlesex Rgt. and 469th Employment Company; France 3 months.

Boys, James (1914–19); Company Quartermaster-Sergeant, 163rd Protection Company, R.D.C.

Braybrook, William Charles (1914, 1915–18); Sergeant, 10th Bn. R. W. Surrey Rgt.; France 2 years.

Briant, Frank Leonard (1916–19); Company Sergeant-Major, R.A.S.C.; France 3 years, Germany 2 months.

Bridges, Henry Edward Mays (1914–19); Gunner, R.G.A.

***Brinklow, William James** (1915–18); Rifleman, 16th Bn. Rifle Brigade; France 2 years 1 month; Missing, 4th April, 1918.

Britton, Andrew Bertie (1914–20); Captain, General List and King's R. Rifle Corps; France 13 months.

***Broad, Albert Ernest** (1917–18); Private, 4th Bn. Royal Fusiliers; France; Killed in action, 24th April, 1918.

Broadway, Charles Phillip (1914–19); Corporal, Machine Gun Corps; France 1 year 9 months.

***Brooker, Frederick Nott** (1916–17); Private, 14th Bn. Essex Rgt.; France 6 months; Died, 20th May, 1917.

Brooks, David Green (1914–19); Squadron Corporal-Major, 1st Life Guards.

Brooks, George (1914–19); Sergeant, 2nd Dragoon Guards and 1/3rd King's African Rifles; East Africa 1 year 8 months.

Brooks, George Burnell (1914–19); Private, Middlesex Rgt., 3rd Reserve.

***Brown, Charles** (1915–17); M.M.; Sergeant, 4th Bn. Grenadier Guards; France 2 years 4 months; Killed in action, 1st December, 1917.

Brown, Charles Thomas (1914–19); Sergeant, E. Surrey and R. W. Surrey Rgts., and Labour Corps; France 2 years 2 months.

***Brown, Ernest Cornwall** (1914–17); Sergeant, R.H.A.; France 3 years; Killed in action, 16th August, 1917.

***Brown, George William** (1914–15); Private, 9th Bn. Middlesex Rgt.; Died, 27th January, 1915.

Browning, Albert Edward (1918–19); Private, 32nd Bn. Middlesex Rgt.

Bryant, Charles (1918–19); Pioneer, R. M. Engineers.

Buckle, Henry (1914–18); Trooper, R. Horse Guards.

Bull, Edward (1914–19); Sapper, R.E.

Bullen, Edward John (1915–17); Private, Duke of Cornwall's Light Infantry; France 2 months.

Butcher, Percy George (1914–19); Private, R.A.M.C. (1st City of London Sanitary Co.); France 8 months, Egypt 1 month, Macedonia 3 years, Turkey 4 months.

Butler, Bartholomew Bevan (1914–19); Private, Machine Gun Corps (Cavalry), 2nd Life Guards, 5th and 12th Lancers; France 4 years 7 months.

Butler, Charles (1916–17); Private, R.A.V.C.; France 16 months.

Butler, George Henry (1914–16); Private, 5th Bn. Middlesex Rgt.

Camp, Lewis (1915–19); Lance-Corporal, M.F.P.; France 2 years 9 months.

***Carritt, William Edwin** (1916–18); Rifleman, Rifle Brigade; France 9 months; Missing, 23rd March, 1918.

Carter, Thomas John (1915–19); Private, 184th Labour Corps; France 4 years.

Carvell, William Albert (1914–19); Private, Royal Fusiliers; France 3 years.

Cates, Charlie Walter (1914–19); Lance-Sergeant, 1st Reserve Cavalry and Lancers.

***Chaney, Alfred** (1916–17); Private, London Rgt.; France 10 months; Missing, 16th August, 1917.

Chapman, John (1915–19); Corporal, R.A.S.C. and R.A.F.; France 12 months.

Cheek, John (1918–19); Private, Labour Corps; France 10 months.

Chenery, Frederick William (1915–19); Private, 2/20th Bn. London Rgt.; Salonica, Egypt, Palestine and Germany, 3 years.

Cheshire, Sidney John (1918–19); Stoker (2nd Class), Dover Auxiliary Patrol; Patrol work to and from France and Belgium.

Chipperfield, Alfred (1918–19); Air Mechanic (2nd Class), R.A.F.

***Chitty, Herbert Henry** (1914); Private, Royal Fusiliers; France 1 month; Died of wounds, 22nd September, 1914.

***Christianson, Hans Leonard Johan** (1914–15); Corporal, 10th Royal Hussars; France 9 months; Killed in action, 13th May, 1915.

Church, Percy Edwin Leonard (1917–19); Stoker (1st Class), R.N.; Escorting and minesweeping.

Clarke, Bertie (1916–19); Gunner, R.F.A.

***Clarke, Charles** (1914); Private, 3rd Bn. Northumberland Fusiliers; France 3 months; Killed in action 19th November, 1914.

Clarke, George (1914–19); Gunner, 65th Siege Battery R.G.A.; France 2 years 9 months.

Clarke, Thomas Ernest (1916–19); Gunner, R.G.A.; France 2 years 8 months.

Clifford, Stanley Albert (1914–19); Private, 4th Bn. Royal Fusiliers; France 3 years 4 months.

Clover, Henry Arthur (1916–19); Rifleman, Rifle Brigade.

Cobby, Charles Matthew (1918–19); Private, R. Marine Engineers.

Cockram, Vincent (1916–19); Corporal, Army Cyclist Corps and R.A.M.C.

Coffey, Daniel (1915–19); Lance-Corporal, 11th Bn. London Rgt., R.A.O.D. and King's Royal Rifle Corps; Gallipoli 4 months, Egypt 2 years, Palestine 10 months, Syria 2 months.

Collett, William Thomas (1914–19); Private, R.A.V.C.

Collins, Charles Stewart (1914–19); Corporal, 24th Bn. London Rgt.

Cooke, Herbert Vincent (1914–19); Drum-Major, R. Irish Fusiliers; Gallipoli, Serbia, Egypt and Salonica, 2 years 6 months.

Coombes, James (1916–19); Private, Durham Light Infantry; Salonica 2 years 4 months.

Cooper, William Albert (1916–19); Private, R.A.O.C.; France 1 year 9 months.

Cordock, John William (1914–19); Private, R. Marine Light Infantry; Ascension Island 3 years 7 months.

Corfield, Thomas William (1914–19); Rifleman, 18th Bn. Rifle Brigade; Burma 4 years.

Cornish, Henry Robert (1914–19); Sergeant, 10th Bn. London Rgt. and Provost Staff R.D.C.

Cornwell, Frederick Samuel (1916–19); Private, R.A.M.C.

Cornwell, William (1916–19); Private, 19th Bn. London Rgt.; Salonica 2 years, Palestine 11 months.

Cosham, Charles Ide (1917–19); Private, 6th Bn. Middlesex Rgt., Labour Corps, and 16th Bn. Scottish Rifles; France 13 months.

Cotterell, Alfred Harry (1916–18); Gunner, R.G.A.

Cotton, Harry (1916–18); Gunner, R.G.A.; France 7 months.

***Cox, Edward** (1915–17); Gunner, 103rd and 123rd Bdes. R.F.A.; France 1 year 9 months; Killed in action, 21st October, 1917.

Cox, Edwin Walter (1914–19); Private, Bedfordshire and Northamptonshire Rgts., and R.A.M.C.; France 3 months, Egypt 2 years 2 months, Salonica 10 months.

Cox, William Henry (1914–18); Sergeant, Royal Fusiliers.

Crampton, Ernest (1915–19); Private, Norfolk Yeomanry and Labour Corps; Egypt and Palestine 3 years 4 months.

***Crane, Henry** (1914–16); Private, 8th Bn. Rifle Brigade; France 7 months; Killed in action, 29th August, 1916.

Crannis, Philip Griffin (1916–19); Staff-Sergeant, R.A.S.C.; France 3 years.

Creasey, Sidney Joseph (1916–19); Gunner, R.F.A.; France 7 months, Italy 13 months.

Creed, Arthur Ernest (1914–19); Private, 9th Lancers (1st Reserve Cavalry); France 4 months, Salonica 13 months.

Currie, James Edward Thomas (1915–19); M.M.; Sergeant, R.E.; France 2 years.

Curry, Arthur (1916–19); Rifleman, 24th Bn. Rifle Brigade; India 2 years 8 months.

***Curtis, William** (1914); Private, R.W. Surrey Rgt.; Missing, 31st October, 1914.

Daines, Arthur John (1914–19); Private, 15th Hussars; France 3 years.

***Daly, Robert William** (1916); Private, 6th Bn. R.W. Kent Rgt.; France 1 month; Missing, 7th October, 1916.

Darken, Arthur (1915–19); Private, 13th and 2nd Bns. Essex Rgt.; France 3 years 6 months.

Darvill, Albert Edward (1916–19); Private, Labour Corps; France 2 years 4 months.

Davies, John (1914–19); Gunner, R.G.A.; France 3 months.

Davis, Albert Edward (1914–19); 2nd Yeoman of Signals, R.F.R.

***Davis, T.** (1914–18); Driver, R.H.A.; India; Died, 5th March, 1918.

Day, Henry (1915–19); Private, R.A.V.C.; France 4 years.

Deedman, William John (1916–18); Private, Nottinghamshire and Derbyshire Rgt.; France 13 months.

Denham, Herbert Frank (1914–19); Private, 10th Bn. London Rgt.; Gallipoli, Egypt and Palestine, 3 years 7 months.

Denny, George Philip (1914–19); Stoker (1st Class), R.N., H.M.S. Newcastle, etc.; North Sea, Egypt, Dardanelles, Pacific, East Indies, Adriatic, South Atlantic, 4 years 6 months.

Dexter, Alfred Edward (1918–19); Private, 11th Bn. Bedfordshire Rgt.

Dinmore, Edward Richard (1915–19); Private, E. Kent Rgt. and Agricultural Co.

Dixon, Francis Walter (1914–19); Sergeant, R.F.A.; France 4 years 1 month.

***Dixon, Frederick Charles** (1914–15); Sergeant, 12th Bn. Rifle Brigade; France 2 months; Died of wounds, 9th September, 1915.

***Dobson, William** (1915–19); Sergeant, R.A.O.C.; Salonica 3 years 3 months; Died, 16th January, 1919.

Dossett, Moses (1914–19); Sergeant, 1st Bn. R. W. Surrey Rgt.; France 2 years 3 months, prisoner of war 15 months.

Douglas, Joseph (1916–19); Private, King's Royal Rifle Corps and Machine Gun Corps; France 7 months, Russia 10 months.

Dove, Albert Benjamin (1917–18); Private, Machine Gun Corps; France 8 months.

Drage, Edward George (1917–19); Private, 11th Bn. Essex Rgt.; France 4 months.

Duly, William (1914–16); Gunner, R.M.A.; France 1 year 7 months.

Dykes, Edward John (1914–17); Driver, R.H.A. and R.A.S.C. (M.T.).

***Earl, Frederick William** (1914–18); Private, R.G.A.; Egypt, Gallipoli and France, 3 years 3 months; Died of gas poisoning, 20th October, 1918.

Eaton, Charles Albert (1914–19); Private, R.A.M.C. and R.A.F.; France 3 years 5 months.

Edney, George Thomas (1916–19); Private, R.A.M.C.

Edwards, Cecil (1914–19); Sergeant Drill Instructor, R. Sussex Rgt.

Eldridge, Leslie George (1915–19); Private, R.A.S.C. (M.T.); France 3 years 3 months.

Ellott, Ambrose Harry Frederick (1915–19); Sergeant, 165th and 156th Bdes. R.F.A.; France 3 years 2 months.

Elmer, Joseph (1918–19); Private, 32nd Bn. Middlesex Rgt.

Elphick, George John (1914–19); Sergeant, R.D.C., 150th Co. Reserve.

Emmett, Robert (1915–19); Horsekeeper, R.A.V.C.

Fagan, Michael (1915–19); Private, Leinster Rgt., and Sapper, R.E.; France 10 months, Egypt and Palestine 1 year 9 months.

Farey, Leonard James (1915–19); Air Mechanic (2nd Class), R.A.F.

Farey, William Thomas (1916–19); Air Mechanic (1st Class), R.A.F.

Farrow, Percy William (1914–15); Private, Royal Fusiliers.

Faulkner, Charles Albert (1914–19); Gunner, R.F.A.; France 4 years.

Featherstone, Alfred (1918–19); Private, R.E.

Fitzpatrick, Patrick (1917–19); Private, 29th Bn. R. W. Surrey Rgt.; France 1 year 11 months.

Fletcher, Thomas Ernest (1914–19); Private, R.A.S.C.; France 3 years 9 months.

Foot, Percy Cedric (1915–19); Bombardier Signaller, R.F.A.; France 3 years 3 months.

Foot, Reginald Stewart (1915–18); Private, Royal Fusiliers, Middlesex Rgt. and R.D.C.; France 3 months.

Fosdyke, Albert Henry (1914–19); Sergeant, 1st Bn. Lincolnshire Rgt.; France 1 year 8 months.

Foster, Henry (1915–17); Private, E. Kent Rgt.

Foster, Herbert George Riches (1915–19); Private, 7th Bn. Wiltshire Rgt. and Labour Corps; Salonica 2 years 5 months.

Fox, George Henry (1915–17); Lance-Corporal, R.A.O.C.; Egypt 3 months.

***Fox, William** (1914–15); Private, 3rd Bn. E. Kent Rgt.; France 7 months; Killed in action, 17th October, 1915.

Free, Charles Thomas (1915–19); Private, R.G.A. and 11th Bn. Cameron Highlanders; France 1 year 11 months.

Freeborough, Leonard (1915–19); Mentioned in despatches; Staff-Sergeant, R.A.M.C.; Dardanelles 2 months, Egypt 2 years 2 months, Palestine 12 months.

Frost, Herbert (1914–20); Regimental Sergeant-Major, 5th Bn. R. W. Kent Rgt.; India 3 years, Mesopotamia 2 years 4 months.

Frost, Walter William (1915–19); Private, 12th Bn. Suffolk Rgt.; France 13 months.

Fuller, Charles Frederick Henry (1916–19); Gunner, R.G.A.; Egypt 1 year 8 months.

Fuller, Isaac Robert (1916–19); Pioneer, R.E.; France 11 months.

Gibbons, Christopher Daniel (1914–20); Regimental Sergeant-Major, 4th Bn. London Rgt.; France 13 months.

Gilbey, Cyril Charles (1915–19); Private, R.F.A.

Gilder, Albert James (1916–19); Private, R.A.V.C. and R.F.A.

Gillies, John Jeffries (1915–19); Major, R.E.; France 4 years 2 months.

Gillson, George William (1918–19); Private, Essex Rgt. and Labour Corps; France 3 months.

Glasscock, Walter Herbert (1914–15); Private, 10th Bn. London Rgt.

Gleed, Albert Victor (1914–17); Guardsman, 3rd Bn. Coldstream Guards; France 2 months.

***Godfrey, William Henry** (1918); Private, 17th Bn. Essex Rgt.; Died, 24th December, 1918.

Golding, George Bertram (1914–19); Corporal, R.G.A.

Goldsmith, William (1914–19); Private, 2nd Dragoon Guards; France 4 years 4 months.

Goloboff, Albert James (1915–19); Corporal, M.M.P.; France 3 years 7 months.

Gordon, Albert John (1915–19); Corporal, Seaforth Highlanders; France 14 months.

***Gray, George Edmund Frank** (1916–17); Private, 19th Bn. Manchester Rgt.; France 3 months; Killed in action, 23rd April, 1917.

Green, Alfred (1916–19); Sapper, R.E. Signals; France 2 years 10 months.

Green, Herbert (1914–19); Battery Sergeant-Major, R.F.A.; France 2 years 7 months.

***Green, William Henry** (1916–18); Rifleman, 18th Bn. London Rgt.; France 10 months; Killed in action, 20th July, 1918.

Griffin, Alfred (1916–18); Rifleman, 19th Bn. London Rgt.; France 6 months.

Grimes, Frederick Charles Sidney (1915–19); Rifleman, Rifle Brigade; France 3 years 4 months.

Guy, Alfred John Harold (1914–20); Sergeant, R.G.A.; Singapore 3 years 10 months.

Hagger, Thomas Joseph (1914–19); Private, 2nd Coldstream Guards; France 1 year 10 months.

Hambelton, Joseph George (1914–19); Corporal, E. Surrey Rgt.; France 2 years 10 months.

Hammill, Herbert William (1916–19); Private, R.A.S.C., Headquarters Staff.

Harber, Henry Patey (1915–19); Private, Middlesex Rgt.; China 1 year 8 months, Siberia 12 months.

Hardaway, William (1914–19); Company Sergeant-Major, M.F.P. and R. Irish Fusiliers.

Harding, Albert Edward (1915-19); Corporal, R.A.S.C. (M.T.); France 3 years 11 months.

Harding, Frederick John (1914–18); Private, 4th Bn. Middlesex Rgt.; France 1 year 8 months.

Harling, Thomas Robert (1914–19); Sergeant, R.F.A.; France 2 years 8 months.

Harrap, Charles Reginald (1914–19); Corporal, 1st Bn. Royal Fusiliers; France 4 years 4 months.

***Harris, Cecil Tom** (1916–17); Private, Coldstream Guards; France 2 months; Killed in action, 22nd February, 1917.

Harvey, Alfred Henry (1916–19); Private, Duke of Cornwall's Light Infantry; Salonica 2 years 2 months.

Harvey, Thomas Henry (1914–19); Gunner, R.G.A.; France 3 years.

Hayes, Benjamin John (1914–17); Private, 13th Hussars.

Hayes, Frederick Charles (1914–19); Sergeant, 4th Hussars.

Haynes, George Henry (1915–18); Corporal, Grenadier Guards; France 1 year 7 months.

Haysom, Harry Frederick (1914); Gunner, R.F.A.

***Head, Ernest Augustus** (1915–16); Corporal, King's Royal Rifle Corps; France 6 months; Killed in action, 3rd September, 1916.

***Hentsch, Alfred Edward** (1915–16); Private, 10th Bn. R. W. Surrey Rgt.; France 4 months; Killed in action, 15th September, 1916.

Heywood, Alfred (1916–19); Private, R.A.S.C. (Remounts); Salonica 2 years 3 months.

Hill, George (1916–19); Private, Grenadier Guards; France 2 years 2 months.

***Hills, Albert Leopold John** (1916); Private, 10th Bn. London Rgt.; Died, 27th June, 1916.

Hinch, Frederick (1916–19); Private, 2/5th, 2/4th and 1/4th Bns. Leicestershire Rgt.; France 2 years.

Holt, Albert George (1915–19); Bombardier, R.G.A.; France 2 years 4 months.

Honychurch, William James (1914–19); Private, 2nd Bn. York and Lancaster Rgt.

Horslen, Percy Charles (1916–19); Lance-Sergeant, 17th Bn. London Rgt., King's African Rifles, and 3rd Bn. Rifle Brigade; East Africa 1 year 7 months.

Howard, Thomas (1914–18); Lance-Corporal, 16th Lancers and M.M.P.; France 3 years 3 months, Italy 4 months.

Hudgell, Frederick (1914–19); Sergeant, 385th Labour Co.; India 2 years.

Humphreys, John James (1917–19); 1st Private, R.A.F.

Hunt, Sidney George (1915–19); Private, R.A.S.C. (M.T.); Belgium and Germany 3 years.

Hunter, Harry (1918–19); Private, Labour Corps; France 7 months.

***Hutchins, Maurice Basil** (1917–18); Private, 8th Bn. R. W. Surrey Rgt.; France; Died, 25th November, 1918.

Hyde, George Alexander (1918–19); 2nd Private, R.A.F.

Hyde, Jabez (1917–19); Private, R.A.S.C.

***Ireland, Arthur** (1916–17); Private, London Rgt.; France 8 months; Missing, 22nd November, 1917.

***Jackaman, Thomas Theobald** (1917–18); Private, Devonshire Rgt.; France 16 months; Killed in action, 27th September, 1918.

Jackson, William (1915–19); Rifleman, 13th Bn. King's Royal Rifle Corps; France 2 years 4 months.

James, Henry Charles (1914–19); Bombardier, 290th Bde. R.F.A.; France 2 years.

Jauncey, Thomas Henry (1918–19); 2nd Private, R.A.F. (Salvage Section).

***Jeffries, Henry Herbert** (1914); Lance-Corporal, Northumberland Fusiliers; France 3 months; Missing, 8th November, 1914.

Jenkins, Charles Thomas (1914–19); Regimental Sergeant-Major, Argyle and Sutherland Highlanders.

Jepps, John (1917–19); Private, Labour Corps; France 2 years.

Johnson, A. E. (1914–19); Gunner, R.F.A.

Johnson, Leonard (1916); Private, 2/5th Bn. R. W. Kent Rgt.

Johnson, Lionel (1918–19); 2nd Private, 66th Wing, R.A.F.; Italy 4 months.

Johnson, Walter (1914–19); Gunner, 61st Siege Batty. R.G.A.; France 3 years 4 months.

Joiner, George Thomas (1915–18); Private, 2/5th London Field Ambulance, R.A.M.C.; France 5 months, Macedonia 7 months, Palestine 15 months.

***Joy, Albert** (1914–15); Bugler, 24th Bn. Royal Fusiliers; Died, 21st November, 1915.

Joyce, Randall Victor (1915–19); Signaller, 1096th Batty. R.F.A.; India 3 years 6 months.

Keen, George William (1914–15); Private, Rifle Brigade.

***Kenchatt, Charles Reading** (1914); Private, 2nd Bn. W. Riding Rgt.; France 3 months; Killed in action, 10th November, 1914.

Kennett, Thomas Joseph (1914–19); Corporal, R.D.C.

Kett, Robert (1914–19); Rifleman, 16th Bn. London Rgt.

Kimsey, Alfred (1916–19); Private, 24th Bn. Royal Fusiliers; France 2 years 3 months.

Knight, Stephen (1914–18); Lance-Corporal, R.D.C.

Lambert, Thomas (1918–19); Private, R.A.M.C. and Labour Corps, 421st Agricultural Co.

Lambourne, Caleb Victor (1914–17); Corporal, E. Surrey Rgt.

Langford, George Henry (1916–19); Private, N. Staffordshire Rgt.; France 13 months, prisoner in Germany 9 months.

***Law, Charles William** (1915–17); Private, 20th Bn. London Rgt.; France 12 months; Died of wounds, 25th April, 1917.

Lawrence, John (1914–16); Private, 24th Bn. London Rgt.

Layton, Charles Frederick (1914–19); Sergeant, 3rd Bn. Royal Fusiliers, 1st Bn. E. Kent Rgt. and 17th Bn. Essex Rgt.; France 16 months, Egypt 4 months.

Leatt, Alfred Edward (1914–19); Private, R. Marine Light Infantry and R.N.; France 3 weeks, Belgium 3 months, Germany, prisoner of war, 4 years.

Lee, William Robert (1916–19); Private, King's Royal Rifle Corps; France 8 months.

***Lenney, George Knight** (1916–17); Private, 10th Bn. Suffolk Rgt.; France 8 months; Missing, 16th August, 1917.

***Liddle, William Seale** (1914); Private, 14th Bn. London Rgt.; France 3 months; Killed in action, 24th December, 1914.

Littleboy, Arthur Edward (1916–19); Driver, R.A.S.C.; France 2 years 4 months.

Long, Frank (1916–19); Private, 2/7th Bn. Northumberland Fusiliers; Egypt 1 year, Sudan 14 months.

Love, Frederick Charles (1916–19); Private, Royal Fusiliers; France 2 years 3 months.

Loveday, George Arthur (1915–17); Rifleman, King's Royal Rifle Corps; France 2 months.

Lovett, James William (1914–19); Leading Stoker, Navy Engine Room; Egypt 3 years.

McCall, Daniel Thomas (1914–19); Sapper, R.E.; France 15 months.

McConkey, John (1918–19); Corporal, R.A.F.

Mack, Frederick Cecil (1916–19); Private, 3rd Bn. London Rgt.; France 2 years 1 month.

***McShane, Hubert** (1914); Lance-Sergeant, 1st Bn. Scots Guards; France 3 months; Missing, 11th November, 1914.

Maddox, Arthur (1914–17); Private, R.D.C.

Maile, Samuel (1915–19); Private, London Rgt.

Mann, Thomas James (1915); Private, 3rd Bn. R. Sussex Rgt.

Manser, Thomas Edward (1914–19); Gunner, R.G.A.

Marsh, Walter Charles (1918–19); Private, 2/1st Herts Yeomanry.

***Martin, Percival James** (1916–17); Private, 7th Bn. Royal Fusiliers; France 8 months; Died of wounds, 28th April, 1917.

Mason, Charles Stephen (1914–18); Sergeant, Rifle Brigade, and Oxfordshire and Buckinghamshire Light Infantry; France 3 months, India 1 year 7 months.

Masser, Harry Marden (1917–19); Gunner (1st Class), R.G.A.; France 2 years, Germany 6 months.

Matthews, Victor Henry (1916–19); Private, Middlesex Rgt.; France 2 years 1 month.

Matthieu, Charles Louis (1916–19); Corporal, R.G.A.; France 1 year 8 months.

Maud, Philip (1914–19); C.M.G., C.B.E.; Brigadier-General, General Staff, and commanding Northern Air Defences.

Maythorn, Robert Frederick (1916–19); Private, Nottinghamshire and Derbyshire Rgt. and 23rd Bn. Lancashire Fusiliers; France 1 year 9 months.

Meadows, William Henry (1915–19); Private, R.A.S.C.; France 3 years 5 months.

***Middlemiss, Thomas James** (1915); Private, Grenadier Guards; Died, 4th December, 1915.

Mitchell, Charles (1916–18); Lance-Corporal, 17th Bn. Scottish Rifles.

Mitchell, Henry Ernest (1916–19); Lance-Corporal, N. Staffordshire Rgt. and R.E. Transportation; France 6 months.

Montague, Samuel Sutton (1915–19); Warrant Officer (2nd Class), Reserve Cavalry and S. Lancashire Rgt.; France 12 months.

Moore, Reginald Robert (1915–19); Corporal, M.M.P.; France 3 years 9 months.

Moreton, George (1916–19); Private, 8th Welsh Pioneers; Mesopotamia and Persia 2 years 6 months.

Morgan, Herbert William (1914–19); Mentioned in despatches; Battery Quartermaster-Sergeant, R.F.A. and R.G.A.; France 14 months.

Morley, Alfred (1915–19); Private, R.A.M.C.; France 2 years 1 month.

Morris, Albert Edmund (1917–19); Private, R.A.S.C. (M.T.); France 1 year 8 months.

Morris, James (1915–16); Lance-Corporal, R.E.

Morton, William Henry (1914–19); Sergeant Instructor of Signalling, 3rd Bn. E. Kent Rgt., 29th Bn. Middlesex Rgt., and Bedfordshire and Hertfordshire Rgts.; France 15 months.

Mott, William (1914–17); Sergeant (Asst. Prov. H.Q.S.), R.D.C.

Mouser, William Harry (1915–19); Private, R.A.O.C.; France 3 years.

Musk, William John (1918–19); Private, Oxfordshire Hussars.

Narraway, Leonard Augustus (1916–19); Private, R.A.M.C.

***Neate, Frederick Bertie** (1916–18); Private, 24th Bn. London Rgt.; Salonica, Egypt and Palestine, 1 year 9 months; Killed in action, 9th March, 1918.

Neate, Robert (1918–19); Lance-Corporal, Rifle Brigade; France 10 months.

Needham, John (1915–19); Lance-Corporal, M.F.P. and M.M.P.; Egypt and Palestine 2 years 8 months.

***Newton, Walter Ernest** (1916–17); Sergeant, R.G.A.; France 3 months; Killed in action, 9th April, 1917.

Noble, Walter (1914–17); Lance-Corporal, Coldstream Guards.

Norman, Henry Aldis (1915–19); Private, 3rd Bn. Middlesex Rgt.; France 6 months, Salonica 3 years 4 months, Turkey 4 months.

Nye, Frederick James (1916–19); Rifleman, King's Royal Rifle Corps; France 2 years 1 month.

Olliver, Frederick Henry (1914–19); Bombardier, R.G.A.; France 3 years 4 months.

Orton, Walter (1914–17); Private, King's Royal Rifle Corps.

Ottley, George (1916–19); Private, Essex Rgt.; France 6 months.

Pales, Ernest Albert (1918–19); Private, R.A.S.C.

Palmer, William Charles (1914–16); Private, 1st Royal Dragoons; France 2 years 2 months.

Palmer, William Stevens (1916–19); French Médaille de Vermeil; Lance-Corporal, R.A.O.C. and King's Royal Rifle Corps; France 2 years 4 months.

***Pantling, Frederick Charles** (1915–16); Private, 9th Bn. Middlesex Rgt.; India 4 months; Died, 6th September, 1916.

Parker, Robert George (1918–19); Air Mechanic (3rd Class), R.A.F.

***Patterson, George Oudney** (1915–16); Sergeant, 3/7th Bn. London Rgt.; France 11 months; Killed in action, 15th September, 1916.

Payne, George Thomas Harold (1917–18); Private, R. Sussex Rgt. and Labour Corps.

***Payne, R.** (1914–15); Private, E. Surrey Rgt.; Missing, 25th April, 1915.

Payne, Thomas (1915–19); Private, 2/22nd Bn. London Rgt.; France 6 months, Salonica 6 months, Egypt and Palestine 2 years 2 months.

Peacock, Francis Edgar (1917–19); Rifleman, 6th Bn. London Rgt.; France 13 months.

Pears, Arthur James (1916–17); Private, R. W. Surrey Labour Bn.; France 10 months.

Pearson, Albert Edward (1917–19); Pioneer, R.E.; France 1 year 9 months.

Pearson, Walter (1917–19); Private, 21st Bn. London Rgt.; France 5 months.

Penfold, Ernest Edward (1916–19); Rifleman, Rifle Brigade; France 2 years.

Perrin, William (1916–19); Private, Nottinghamshire and Derbyshire Rgt. and Labour Corps; France 2 years.

Perry, Robert (1914–19); Corporal, 12th Lancers and Labour Corps.

Peters, James (1915–19); Sergeant, R.H.A.

Phillips, Walter Ashley (1915–18); Corporal, R.A.S.C.; France 3 years 4 months.

Pike, Robert Thomas (1916–19); Gunner, R.G.A.; France 6 months.

Plummer, Robert (1915–19); Corporal, R.A.S.C. and Royal Marine Labour Corps; France 3 years 4 months.

***Poate, Harry Joseph** (1915–18); Corporal, R.A.S.C.; France 2 years 11 months; Died, 25th November, 1918.

Porter, William Arthur (1916–18); Private, R.G.A.; France 3 months.

Powel, Evan Thomas (1917–19); Corporal (Gunnery Instructor), 28th Bn. London Rgt. and R.A.F.

Prangell, William Henry (1914–19); Private, Coldstream Guards; France 4 years 5 months.

Pratley, Richard (1916–19); Private, Bedfordshire Rgt.

Pratt, Henry Marshall (1916–19); Private, King's Own Yorkshire Light Infantry.

Purland, Walter (1914–19); Gunner, R.G.A.; France 3 years 7 months.

Pursglove, Robert Walter (1915–19); Private, Grenadier Guards; France 11 months.

Radley, Wilfrid Harold (1916); Rifleman, 19th Bn. King's Royal Rifle Corps.

Read, Charles (1918–19); Pioneer, R.O.D. and R.E.; Salonica 5 months.

Reader, Walter Edward (1916–17); Private, 2/6th Bn. Nottinghamshire and Derbyshire Rgt.

Reid, George (1915–19); Private, R. W. Kent Rgt.; France 2 years 6 months.

Rhoades, William Dufton (1914–19); Company Sergeant-Major, 2nd Bn. Leinster Rgt.; France 2 years 3 months.

Richards, Herbert John (1915–19); Private, 10th Bn. London Rgt.; France, Egypt and Palestine, 3 years 4 months.

Richardson, Alfred James (1914–19); Lance-Bombardier, R.F.A.; France 2 years 2 months, Mesopotamia 2 years 6 months.

Ricketts, William Henry (1915–16); Private, 24th Bn. London Rgt.

Ritchie, Frederick William (1914–19); Company Sergeant-Major, R.G.A.; France 6 months.

Roach, Arthur Richard (1916–19); Corporal, R.A.M.C.

***Robinson, Jacob** (1914–16); Sergeant, 5th Bn. E. Surrey Rgt.; India 1 year 7 months, France 1 month; Killed in action, 3rd September, 1916.

Rodway, Arthur Louis (1915–19); Driver, R.A.S.C.; France 6 months, Salonica 9 months, Egypt and Palestine 1 year 9 months.

Rogers, John (1914–16); Corporal, R. Welch Fusiliers, Private, R.A.S.C.; France 4 months.

Rooks, William Arthur Ernest (1914–19); Driver, R.F.A.; France 3 years 3 months, Italy 6 months.

Rowbotham, Harry Arnold (1916–19); Lance-Corporal, Intelligence Police.

Rowling, Frederick (1914–19); Private, 6th Bn. R. W. Surrey Rgt.; France 4 years.

Rule, George John (1914–19); Bombardier, R.F.A.; France 2 years 10 months.

Russell, James Enos (1916–17); Private, R.A.S.C.; France 14 months.

Salway, Walter Morris (1916–19); Private, R.A.M.C.; France 1 year 9 months.

Saunders, Alfred (1914–19); Corporal, 10th Bn. Rifle Brigade; India 4 years 1 month.

Saunders, Ernest (1914–19); Sergeant-Instructor, Rifle Brigade; India 4 years 1 month.

Saunders, Robert William (1916–19); Gunner, R.G.A. and A.A.

***Savage, Bertie Arthur** (1915–17); Private, 6th Bn. Middlesex Rgt.; France 12 months; Died of wounds, 12th April, 1917.

Savin, Walter (1914–16); Private, R. Berkshire Rgt.

Sawer, Frederick (1914–16); Lance-Corporal, 12th Bn. Royal Fusiliers; France 1 month.

Scott, Thomas (1916–19); Sergeant, 52nd Bn. Rifle Brigade.

Scott, Thomas Nathaniel (1915–19); Sergeant i/c prison; R.A.S.C. and Labour Corps; France 3 years 9 months.

Scullion, James (1914–19); Guardsman, Scots Guards.

Seldon, Archie (1914–19); Sergeant, Devonshire Rgt.; France 3 years 6 months.

Self, Reginald Hugh (1914–19); Sapper, 9th Bn. E. Surrey Rgt., King's Own Yorkshire Light Infantry and R.E.; France 4 years.

Shackcloth, Eli (1917–19); Driver, R.A.S.C. (H.T.) and Labour Corps.

Shakespeare, Tom Rodway (1917–19); Private, 2/10th Bn. London Rgt.; France 9 months.

Shirvill, William (1914–19); Rifleman, King's Royal Rifle Corps; France 3 years 8 months.

Shrubsall, David William (1916–19); Private, 14th Bn. Argyle and Sutherland Highlanders; France 8 months.

Silvester, Henry (1915–19); Corporal, Middlesex Rgt.

Silvester, Henry George Buller (1918–19); Drummer, R. W. Surrey Rgt.; Germany 10 months.

Simmonds, Robert William (1914–19); Gunner, R.F.A.; France 3 years 8 months.

Sinden, William Horace (1914–19); Driver, R.F.A.; France 3 years 2 months, Italy 15 months.

Sleight, Frederick (1915–19); Private, 9th Bn. Middlesex Rgt.; India 15 months, Mesopotamia 17 months.

Smart, George Albert (1914–19); Driver, R.F.A.; France 3 years 4 months.

Smith, David (1914–15); Private, Royal Fusiliers; France 12 months.

Smith, James (1914–19); Sergeant, 2nd Bn. R. Inniskilling Fusiliers and Machine Gun Corps; France 11 months.

Smith, Thomas Martin (1914–19); Sergeant, Royal Scots; Gallipoli 3 months, Egypt 3 years 4 months.

Smith, William Job (1916–19); Gunner, R.F.A. and R.G.A.

Smith, William Thomas (1914–19); Sergeant, R.A.V.C.; France 4 years 2 months.

Snare, Albert Edward (1915–19); Able Seaman, R.N.; Belgian Coast Patrol; 2 years 8 months.

Spender, William John (1914–19); Sapper, R.E.; France 4 years 7 months.

Squibb, Charles (1918–19); Rifleman, King's Royal Rifle Corps; France and Germany 9 months.

Staples, Ernest (1915–16, 1917); Lance-Corporal, 2/5th Bn. E. Surrey Rgt. and Labour Corps.

Stevens, Frederick (1915–19); Private, R.A.M.C., 1st London Sanitary Co.; France 3 years 8 months.

Stokes, Charles (1914–18); Private, Suffolk Rgt.; France; Prisoner of war in Germany 4 years 4 months.

Styan, Harry (1915–19); Private, R.A.V.C.; France 3 years 9 months.

Suggate, Reginald William (1915–19); Mentioned in despatches; Warrant Officer (1st Class), R.A.S.C.; France 12 months.

***Swainsbury, William** (1914–16); Gunner, R.F.A.; France 1 year 9 months; Killed in action, 7th May, 1916.

Swallow, William Henry (1914–18); Sergeant, Scots Guards; France 3 years 3 months.

Syms, Henry William (1917–19); Driver, R.A.S.C.; France 17 months.

***Tagg, Charles William** (1917); Private, R. W. Surrey Rgt.; France 9 months; Died, 28th November, 1917.

Taylor, Edwin Joseph Thomas (1915–19); Private, Rifle Brigade and Devonshire Rgt., Officer Cadet, 9th Scottish Officer Cadet Bn.

Taylor, George Joseph (1914–19); Lance-Corporal, 2/7th Bn. London Rgt., R.D.C. and Prisoners of War Camp.

Taylor, Joseph (1916–19); Bombardier, R.G.A., R.F.A., Tank Corps and R.H.A.

Taylor, Joseph Harry (1915–17); D.C.M.; Sergeant, R. W. Surrey Rgt.

Terry, Frederick (1918–19); Private, R.A.F.; France 5 months.

Tester, Henry (1914–19); M.M.; Sergeant, R.F.A.; France 2 years 6 months, Gallipoli 6 months.

Thomas, Henry William (1915–19); Lieutenant, R.E.

Thorndycraft, Edward (1914–19); Signaller, R.H.A.; France 3 years 4 months.

Thurston, Elliott Henry (1914–18); Sergeant, 24th Bn. London Rgt.; France 3 years 2 months.

Tidd, Henry (1914–16); Private, Coldstream Guards.

Todd, William Ernest (1918–19); Private, R.N.A.S.

***Troke, Andrew James** (1917–18); Rifleman, King's Royal Rifle Corps; Missing, 21st March, 1918.

Trolley, Archibald Watson (1914–19); Private, National Reserve, R.D.C. and 17th Bn. Essex Rgt.

Troughton, John Henry (1914–19); Staff-Sergeant, M.P.

Tubb, Harry (1914–19); Mentioned in despatches; Company Sergeant-Major, R. Lancaster Rgt.; France 12 months, Mesopotamia 2 years 4 months.

Valentine, George Frederick (1915–19); Rifleman, Rifle Brigade; France 2 years 4 months.

***Veaser, Herbert Walter** (1915–16); Corporal, 17th Bn. King's Royal Rifle Corps; France 12 months; Killed in action, 3rd September, 1916.

***Vince, Edmund William** (1916–17); Private, London Rgt.; France 3 months; Killed in action, 14th March, 1917.

Waldon, Walter William (1915–19); Pioneer, 271st Railway Labour Company, R.E.; France 3 years 1 month.

Warner, John David (1915–19); Driver, R.F.A.; France 6 months, Salonica 6 months, Palestine 1 year 8 months.

Warren, George Robert Charles (1914–19); Sergeant, R.A.

Webb, Herbert William (1916–19); Private, 13th Bn. Devonshire Rgt., 4th Bn. R. Berkshire Rgt. and 161st Labour Co.; France 2 years 1 month.

Webb, John William (1914–17); Private, Rifle Brigade and Oxfordshire and Buckinghamshire Light Infantry; France 12 months.

Welch, Archibald Major James (1916–19); Corporal, R.H.A.; France 5 months.

Welham, Albert Henry (1915–19); Private, 10th Bn. E. Surrey Rgt.

Werndley, Arthur (1914–19); Corporal, Middlesex Rgt.; France 4 years 7 months.

West, Charles William (1914–19); Lance-Corporal, 18th Bn. Rifle Brigade; India 4 years 1 month.

Whitaker, Arthur Edgar (1914–19); Aircraftsman (1st Class), R.A.F., 21st Bn. London Rgt.; France 5 months.

White, George Roberts (1918–19); Private, 13th Bn. London Rgt.

White, James Cornell (1917–19); 1st Aircraft Hand, 49th Balloon Section, R.A.F.; Egypt, Palestine, Syria, 1 year 11 months.

White, Reginald Alfred (1917–19); Private, Labour Corps.

White, William James (1917–19); Private, R.A.M.C. 6th London Field Ambulance; German East Africa 1 year 11 months.

Whittome, Josiah Jabez (1917–19); Corporal, Royal Marines (Labour Co.); France 1 year 9 months.

Wicks, Edwin Frank (1916–19); Private, R.A.V.C.; France 2 years 4 months.

***Willcock, Thomas Henry George** (1915–18); Private, R.A.M.C. (1st City of London Sanitary Co.); France and Salonica 3 years 6 months; Died, 28th November, 1918.

Williams, Francis (1916–19); Gunlayer, R.G.A.; France 17 months, Gibraltar 9 months.

Williams, Frederick (1918–19); Private, Labour Corps; France 3 months.

Wilson, James John (1915–17); Corporal, 19th Hussars.

Wilson, John William (1914–19); Private, Grenadier Guards; France 18 months.

Wilson, William James (1916–19); Sapper, R.E. (Inland Water Transport), and Private, Gordon Highlanders; France 2 years 8 months.

Wiltshire, George Thomas (1915–19); Private, R.A.M.C.

Winterhalder, Alois Alfred (1914–16); Lance-Corporal, Oxfordshire and Buckinghamshire Light Infantry and 2nd Bn. Hampshire Rgt.

Winter, Henry William (1914–19); Private, R. W. Surrey Rgt.; Germany, prisoner of war, 4 years.

Winters, George William (1914–19); Private, 24th Bn. London Rgt. and R.D.C.

Wood, Samuel William (1914–19); Sergeant, R.A.M.C.; France 4 years 6 months.

Woodward, Frederick William (1914–19); Private, Oxfordshire and Buckinghamshire Light Infantry; France 2 months, Balkans 3 years 6 months.

Wright, Charles (1914–15); Gunner, R.G.A.; France 3 months.

Wright, Leonard Nathaniel (1918–19); Private, R. Marine Engineers and R.N.

Wyatt, George Benjamin (1915–19); Sergeant, R.A.S.C. and Labour Corps; France 12 months, Egypt 2 months, Salonica 2 years 2 months.

Yeoman, Charles William (1914–19); Corporal, R.D.C.

Tramways Department

Abberline, Edward (1914–16 and 1916–18); Private, R.A.M.C.; France 12 months.

Abbiss, Edwin (1914–19); Leading Signalman, R.N.; Naval Service 4 years 6 months.

Abbott, Sidney Ernest (1917); Private, Labour Corps.

Abell, Richard (1914–19); Corporal, R. W. Surrey Rgt.; France 2½ months, prisoner of war 4 years 6 months.

Abra, Samuel (1916–19); Private, Norfolk Rgt.; Egypt 11 months.

Ackland, Henry James (1914–19); M.M.; Sergeant, R.G.A.; France 2 years 5 months.

Acott, Charles George (1914); Private, R. Sussex Rgt.

Acourt, Francis Henry (1917–19); Driver, R.F.A.; India, Egypt and Palestine, 1 year 11 months.

A'Court, William Charles (1915–19); Wireman, R.N.; Naval Service, 3 years 10 months.

Adams, Albert George (1914–19); Corporal, R.A.S.C.; France and Salonica 4 years 6 months.

Adams, Albert William (1915–19); Private, R.A.M.C.; France 3 years 6 months.

Adams, Edward William (1914–19); Lance-Corporal, R.E.; France 4 years 3 months.

Adams, Frank (1914–19); Driver, R.A.S.C. (H.T.); France 2 years 3 months.

Adams, Henry Frederick William (1914–18); Sergeant, London Rgt.; France, Salonica, Egypt and Palestine, 1 year 10 months.

Adams, Reginald Augustus (1914–19); Staff-Sergeant, R.E.; India 2 years, Mesopotamia 2 years 4 months.

Adams, Thomas (1914–19); Leading Stoker, R.N.; Naval Service 4 years 6 months.

Adams, Walter Frank (1914–19); Private, Northamptonshire Rgt.; France 2 years, Germany 10 months.

Adams, William Albert (1914–18); M.M.; Private, Border Rgt.; France 2 years 7 months.

Adaway, Charles (1914–19); Stoker, Petty Officer, R.N.; Naval Service 4 years 3 months.

Adcock, Albert Victor (1915–19); 2nd Writer, R.N.: Naval Service 2 years 4 months.

Addington, George Lawrence (1914–19); Sapper, R.E.; France 3 years 8 months.

Addis, James Bawn (1915); Rifleman, King's Royal Rifle Corps.

Addison, Joseph William (1915–19); Sergeant, R.E.; France 2 years.

Adkins, Christopher (1914–19); Acting Sergeant, R.F.A.; France 3 years 7 months.

Adshead, Samuel (1914–19); Wheeler-Sergeant, R.A.S.C.; France 2 years 10 months.

Aggersberg, George Charles (1914–16); Sergeant, R.D.C.; France 4 years.

Agombar, Samuel (1917–19); Private, R.A.M.C.

Ainge, Edwin Alban (1916–19); Private, Machine Gun Corps; Salonica 2 years, Russia 4 months.

Ainsworth, Edward (1917–19); Air Mechanic (1st Class), R.A.F.

Akerman, James (1914); Private, R.A.S.C.

Akerman, Sidney Kingston (1914–18); Sapper, R.E.; France 3 years.

Alaway, Sidney Charles (1916–19); Private, E. Surrey Rgt.; France 1 year 10 months.

Albon, George Frederick (1915–19); Private, R.A.S.C.; France 3 years 10 months.

Alcock, Thomas William (1915–19); Signaller, Machine Gun Corps; Palestine and France 2 years 9 months.

Alderman, Frederick Walter (1914–19); Gunner, R.F.A.; France, Salonica and Palestine, 2 years 11 months.

Aldridge, Robert (1914–19); Corporal, Dragoon Guards; France 3 years 6 months.

Aldridge, William Hugh Goodland (1914–18); Sergeant, R.A.F.

Alexander, Hubert Victor (1918–19); Guardsman, Grenadier Guards.

Alford, Sydney Herbert (1915–19); Driver, R.F.A.; France 3 years 1 month.

Allan, Arthur (1914–19); Private, Dorsetshire Rgt.; France 3 years 2 months.

Allan, George (1916–19); Mechanic (1st Class), Tank Corps; France 1 year 8 months.

Allan, Reuben (1916–18); Private, Royal Fusiliers; France 6 months.

***Allan, William** (1914–15); Private, R. W. Surrey Rgt.; France 5 months; Died of wounds, 27th May, 1915.

Allaway, Arthur Richard Henry (1918–19); Private, R. Sussex Rgt.; France and Germany 6 months.

Allaway, Ernest Alliester (1916–19); Signaller, R.F.A.; France 5 months.

Alleeson, William Charles (1915–19); Signaller, R.F.A.; France 2 years 11 months.

Allen, Alfred Charles (1915–19); Corporal, Labour Corps; France 2 years.

Allen, Arthur (1917–19); Rifleman, King's Royal Rifle Corps.

Allen, Charles (1914–18); Rifleman, King's Royal Rifle Corps; France 4 years 5 months.

***Allen, Charles Edwin** (1914–18); Junior Reserve Attendant, R.N.; Died, 25th January, 1918.

Allen, Edward Richard (1914–19); Gunner, R.F.A.; France 2 years.

Allen, Ernest (1914–19); Acting Sergeant, R.A.S.C.; France, Mesopotamia and India, 4 years 5 months.

Allen, Frederick George (1918–19); Gunner, R. Marine Artillery; Naval Service.

Allen, Harry Henry (1914–19); Private, Devonshire Rgt.; France 2 years 8 months, Italy 10 months.

Allen, Stanley Abbott (1914–19); Gunner, R.F.A.; France 4 years.

Allen, Walter Henry (1914–18); Corporal Shoeing-Smith, R.F.A.; France 3 years.

Allison, Alfred Thomas (1916–19); Private, R.A.M.C.; France 2 years 3 months.

Allison, George Douglas (1914–17); Lance-Corporal, Labour Corps; France 6 months.

***Allison, William** (1914–15); Private, Middlesex Rgt.; France 10 months; Died of wounds, 20th June, 1915.

Allwright, Philip Frederick (1915–19); Private, London Rgt.; France, Salonica and Palestine, 2 years 10 months.

***Almeroth, Charles Wrede** (1914–17); Private, R. Berkshire Rgt.; France 2 years; Died of wounds while prisoner of war, 5th May, 1917.

Almond, Richard (1916–19); Corporal, R.A.S.C.; France 2 years 9 months.

Almond, William (1915–19); Private, R.A.S.C. (M.T.); France, Salonica and Palestine, 3 years 10 months.

Alsop, Charles Edward (1916–19); Rifleman, London Rgt.; Salonica and Palestine 2 years 2 months.

Alston, Albert Thomas (1915–17); Private, Hampshire Rgt.; France 14 months.

Ambridge, Walter Ernest (1916–19); Gunner, R.F.A.

***Ament, Ernest Victor** (1916–17); Rifleman, Rifle Brigade; France 6 months; Killed in action, 23rd June, 1917.

Amey, Alfred (1915–19); Sapper, R.E.; France 4 years.

Amey, William Henry (1914–19); Stoker, R.N.; Naval Service 3 years 4 months.

Amies, Henry Frederick (1914–19); Driver, R.E.; France and Germany 3 years 6 months.

Amies, James Frederick (1914–17); Gunner, R.F.A.

***Amos, Harry** (1917); Rifleman, London Rgt.; France 1 month; Missing, 7th June, 1917.

Anderson, Bruce Thomas (1916–19); Acting Corporal, R.A.S.C.

Anderson, Ernest William (1914–16); Rifleman, London Rgt.

Andrews, Andrew Oliver (1916–17); Gunner, R.G.A.

Andrews, Charles Alfred (1915–19); Private, R.A.M.C.; France 10 months.

Andrews, Charles Henry (1918–19); Lance-Corporal, Suffolk Rgt.

***Andrews, Charles John** (1914–16); Rifleman, London Rgt.; Died, 3rd April, 1916.

Andrews, James John (1914–19); Gunner, R.F.A.; France 4 years 1 month.

Andrews, Job (1916–18); Private, Labour Corps.

Andrews, John Hector (1914–19); Lieutenant, R.F.A.; Egypt, Dardanelles, Mesopotamia and France, 4 years 3 months.

Andrews, John William (1916–17); Gunner, R.G.A.

Andrews, William Henry (1915–19); Pioneer, R.E.; France 3 years.

Andrews, William Latham (1915–19); Lance-Corporal, R.A.S.C. (M.T.); France 3 years 8 months.

Angelinetta, Onorata James (1916–19); Private, Machine Gun Corps; France 1 year 8 months.

***Angus, David** (1914–15); Private, R. Warwickshire Rgt.; France 6 months; Missing, 25th April, 1915.

Anness, Alfred Burgess (1914–19); Gunner, R.F.A.; Dardanelles 6 months, Mesopotamia 2 years 6 months.

Ansell, Harry (1915–19); Driver, R.E.; France 3 years 4 months.

Ansell, James (1914–19); Regimental Quartermaster-Sergeant, Wiltshire Rgt.; France and Salonica 3 years 3 months.

Anstey, Henry Robert (1918–19); Private, R. Sussex Rgt.; France and Germany 6 months.

Anstey, Herbert William (1914–19); Battery Quartermaster-Sergeant, R.H.A.; France 4 years 6 months.

Antebring, Francis Charles (1915–17); Private, Dragoon Guards.

Anthony, George (1916–19); Private, Labour Corps; France 6 weeks.

***Aplin, Charles Richard Simeon** (1914–15); Private, London Rgt.; France 9 months; Killed in action, 30th December, 1915.

Appelman, Frederick Herbert (1915–19); 2nd Corporal, R.E.; France 2 years 5 months.

Appleby, Thomas (1914–19); Corporal, R.H.A.; France 4 years 4 months.

Appleton, John Henry (1917–19); Sapper, R.E.

Archer, Frederick Henry (1914–19); Corporal, R.F.A.: France 3 years 8 months.

***Archer, Frederick Joseph** (1915–16); Bombardier, R.F.A.; France 11 months; Died of wounds, 2nd November, 1916.

***Archer, Percy Frederick** (1914–18); Driver, R.H.A.; France 3 years 7 months; Died of wounds, 1st September, 1918.

Archer, Thomas (1915); Private, R.A.O.C.

Argent, Henry (1915–19); Private, Labour Corps; France 16 months.

Arman, William (1915–19); Gunner, R.F.A.; France 3 years 3 months.

***Armes, James George** (1914–16); Private, Royal Fusiliers; Malta, Egypt and France, 18 months; Killed in action, 12th September, 1916.

Armfield, John Arthur (1917–19); Private, Labour Corps; France 6 months.

Armitage, Samuel (1916–19); Private, Royal Fusiliers; France 2 years, prisoner of war 10 months.

Armstrong, George (1914–19); Driver, R.F.A.; France 2 years, Italy 18 months.

***Arnold, Henry** (1914); Stoker (1st Class), R.N.; Killed at sea, 22nd September, 1914.

Arnold, Joseph Reginald (1914–19); Corporal, R.E.; France 7 months.

Arnold, Mark (1914–19); Sick Berth Reserve Attendant, R.N.; Naval Service 2 years 4 months.

Arnold, Sydney (1914–19); Sergeant, R.E.; France and Burmah 4 years.

Arnold, Walter Harold (1918–19); Private, R. W. Kent Rgt.

Arnold, William (1914–16); Private, London Rgt.

Arnott, Augustus (1916–19); Sergeant, London Rgt.; Draft Conductor, France.

Ashburn, George (1914–19); Sergeant, R.F.A.; France 3 years 7 months.

Ashby, Charles Albert (1915–19); Gunner, R.F.A.; France 2 years 7 months.

***Ashby, Frank** (1915); Mentioned in despatches; Private, R.A.M.C.; France 1 month; Died of wounds, 30th September, 1915.

Ashby, Frederick (1915–16); Private, Middlesex Rgt.

Ashby, George Joseph (1914–19); Battery Sergeant-Major, R.F.A.; France 2 years 6 months.

Ashby, Walter William (1914–19); Lance-Corporal, R. W. Surrey Rgt.; Soudan and Dardanelles 2 years.

Ashley, Alfred William (1914–19); Private, Middlesex Rgt.; France 1 month, prisoner of war 3 years 6 months, interned in Holland 8 months.

***Ashley, Harry** (1914–16); Driver, R.F.A.; France 2 years; Killed in action, 15th September, 1916.

Aspin, Richard George (1915–19); M.M.; Private, R. W. Surrey Rgt.; France and Italy 2 years 3 months.

Asser, William (1917–19): Private, R.A.S.C.

Aston, Frederick Charles (1916–19); Private, Middlesex Rgt.; France 8 months.

Aston, Thomas James (1915–19); Private, Oxfordshire and Buckinghamshire Light Infantry; France 15 months, prisoner of war 9 months.

Atkins, Charles Stanley (1917–18); Rifleman, London Rgt.; France 2 months.

Atkins, James (1918–19); Gunner, R.F.A.; France 2 months.

Atkins, James William (1914–19); Private, Duke of Cornwall's Light Infantry; France 4 years 1 month.

Atkins, Joseph (1915–17); Private, R.A.V.C.; France 1 year 11 months.

***Aubury, John Leitch** (1914–15); Private, London Rgt.; France 2 months; Killed in action, 26th May, 1915.

***Auker, John Frederick** (1916–18); Private, W. Riding Rgt.; France 1 year 9 months; Killed in action, 12th October, 1918.

Austen, Ernest Henry (1916–19); Rifleman, Rifle Brigade; France 6 months, Salonica and South Russia 1 year 8 months.

Austin, Frank (1915–19); Company Sergeant-Major, Cameron Highlanders; France 18 months.

Austin, Frederick Charles (1917–19); Gunner, R.F.A.; France 18 months.

Austin, Frederick William (1914–19); Gunner, R.F.A.

Austin, Henry (1914–18); Chief Petty Officer, R.N.; Naval Service.

Austin, William (1914–19); Sergeant, Hampshire Rgt.; France 2 years.

Avant, Albert (1914–19); Private, Middlesex Rgt.; France 4 years 4 months.

Avis, Robert Charles (1914–19); Gunner, R.F.A.; France and Germany 4 years 7 months.

Aylen, Walter Davey (1917–19); Private, R.A.M.C.; France 12 months.

Aylmer, Alfred (1914–19); Private, R.D.C.

***Ayton, William** (1914); Private, R. W. Surrey Rgt.; France 2 months; Killed in action, 17th December, 1914.

Bacon, Benjamin (1914–19); Private, Northamptonshire Rgt.; India 3 years 6 months.

Bacon, Jabez (1914–19); Rifleman, Rifle Brigade; Burmah 4 years.

Badcock, Edward (1914–15 and 1917–19); Guardsman, Coldstream Guards; France 14 months.

Bagwell, Albert Edwin (1917–19); Sapper, R.E.; France 15 months.

***Bailey, Frank** (1914–15 and 1915–17); Private, Middlesex Rgt.; France 5 months; Killed in action, 4th February, 1917.

Bailey, Henry (1914–16); Corporal, London Rgt.; France 11 months.

Bailey, Walter Edwin (1917–19); Sapper, R.E.; France 2 years 7 months.

Baillie, Alexander (1914–19); Sapper, R.E.; France 3 years 11 months.

Baines, Thomas (1914–19); Private, Middlesex Rgt.; France 4 years 5 months.

Baker, Frank Thomas Cawson (1914); Private, E. Surrey Rgt.

Baker, Frederick Thomas (1914–15); Private, Essex Rgt.

Baker, Harold Olney (1914–15); Trooper, Dragoon Guards.

Baker, James Gregory (1918–19); Ordinary Seaman, R.N.; Naval Service 7 months.

***Baker, Sidney James** (1915); Private, London Rgt.; France 2 months; Died of wounds, 28th October, 1915.

Baker, William David (1918–19); Private, Middlesex Rgt.; France and Germany 12 months.

Baker, William Henry (1914–15 and 1917–18); Gunner, R.G.A., Lance-Corporal, R.A.S.C.; France 16 months.

Balcombe, Charles William (1914–19); Chief Petty Officer, R.N.; Naval Service 2 years 3 months.

Baldock, Richard Henry (1915–18); Corporal, M.F.P.; France 3 months.

Baldock, Thomas (1917–19); Private, Labour Corps.

Baldry, Edward Cecil (1915–16); Driver, R.F.A.

Baldwin, Frederick (1914–19); Leading Seaman, R.N.; Naval Service 3 years.

Ball, Frank Ernest (1915–18); Driver, R.A.S.C.; Salonica 2 years.

Ball, Frederick John (1914–18); Rifleman, London Rgt.; France 3 months.

Ball, James (1914–19); Corporal, R.A.M.C.; France 4 years 6 months.

Ball, Thomas (1914–17); Private, R.A.M.C.; France 2 years 7 months.

Balls, Albert Edward (1914–19); M.M.; Battery Sergeant-Major, R.F.A.; France 3 years 4 months.

Balls, Frederick (1916–19); Driver, R.A.S.C.; France 2 years 6 months.

Balls, George William (1914–17); Sergeant, R.F.A.

Balsom, Edward (1915–17); Pioneer, R.E.

Bamforth, Alfred (1917–19); Rifleman, King's Royal Rifle Corps; France, Italy and Germany, 1 year 9 months.

Bance, William Charles (1914–19); Gunner, R.H.A.; France 4 years.

Banfield, Walter George (1916–19); Gunner, R.G.A.; East Africa 10 months.

Banford, Favell (1915–19); Private, R.A.S.C.; France and Salonica 3 years 9 months.

Banham, Alfred Edward (1915–19); Private, Labour Corps; France 3 years 3 months.

Banham, Ernest (1914–19); Sergeant, Labour Corps; France 2 years 10 months.

Banham, George Harry (1914–19); Corporal, Labour Corps; France 4 years.

Banham, John Frederick (1914–19); Gunner, R.G.A.; France 17 months.

Banks, Ernest Harry (1915–16); Driver, R.A.S.C.

Banner, John (1914–19); Sergeant, R.F.A.; France 2 years 8 months.

***Barber, Albert George** (1915–18); Sapper, R.E.; France 2 years 11 months; Killed in action, 27th March, 1918.

Barber, Arthur Edward (1917–19); Driver, R.A.S.C.

Barber, Sydney Charles (1914–19); Private, Dragoon Guards.

Barefoot, Charles (1914–18); Private, R.D.C.

Barham, Harmond Elliss (1914–19); Bombardier, R.F.A.; France, Salonica and Egypt, 2 years 8 months.

Barker, Albert (1916–19); Private, Labour Corps; Salonica 4 months.

Barker, Frederick Tim (1915–17); Private, R.A.S.C.; France 2 years 2 months.

***Barker, Robert Harris** (1915–17); Private, R. W. Surrey Rgt.; France 12 months; Killed in action, 20th November, 1917.

Barnard, Frederick Charles (1915–19); Gunner, R.F.A.; France and Salonica 3 years 9 months.

Barnard, George Roach (1916–19); Leading Aircraftsman, R.A.F.

***Barnes, Charles Henry** (1914–16); Private, E. Surrey Rgt.; France 11 months; Killed in action, 21st August, 1916.

Barnes, James Albert (1914–16); Lance-Corporal, E. Surrey Rgt.; France 3 months.

Barnes, Stanley (1916–18); Private, Labour Corps.

Barnett, Alfred John (1915); Air Mechanic (2nd Class), R.F.C.

Barrett, Alfred (1917); Private, Training Reserve.

Barrett, Charles Richard (1914–19); Sergeant, W. Kent Yeomanry.

Barrett, Edward Frank (1916–19); Private, Machine Gun Corps; France 2 months, Salonica 8 months, Egypt 1 year 8 months.

Barrett, Harold Karl (1914–17); Sergeant, Royal Fusiliers; France 15 months.

Barrett, James Henry (1914–19); Lance-Corporal, Scottish Rifles; France 3 years 8 months.

Barrett, John Thomas (1915–19); Gunner, R.G.A.; Palestine 18 months.

Barriball, Louis Stanley (1916–17); Private, Middlesex Rgt.

Barrow, Aaron Robert (1914–19); Gunner, R.F.A.; Gallipoli and France 4 years.

Barry, Richard (1915–19); Private, Middlesex Rgt.; France 3 years 6 months.

Bartle, Augustus Evered (1917–18); Aircraftsman (1st Class), R.A.F.

Bartler, Ernest (1916–19); Rifleman, King's Royal Rifle Corps; France 10 months.

Bartlett, Arthur Edward (1915–19); Private, R.A.S.C.; France 3 years 4 months.

Bartlett, Frederick William (1914–18); Private, R.D.C.

Barton, Harold (1914–19); Private, Somersetshire Light Infantry; Egypt 18 months.

Bassett, Charles Henry (1914–19); Corporal Fitter, R.F.A.; France 3 years 4 months.

Bassett, Ernest John (1915–19); Lance-Corporal, Surrey Yeomanry; Salonica and Egypt 3 years 2 months.

Bassett, Harry Horton (1914–19); Private, Norfolk Rgt.; France 2 years 11 months, Italy 5 months.

Batchelor, Thomas George (1917–19); Driver, R.E.

Bateman, Elisha Thomas (1914–19); Lance-Sergeant, Rifle Brigade; Burmah 4 years.

Bateman, Thomas Charles (1915–17); Gunner, R.F.A.; France 7 months.

Bates, Alfred (1914–19); Gunner, R.G.A.; France 4 years 3 months.

Bates, Alfred Henry Monument (1916–17); Private, Durham Light Infantry.

Bates, Jesse George (1915–19); Corporal, R.F.A.; France 2 years.

Bates, Thomas Arthur (1915–19); Corporal, Middlesex Rgt.; France 3 years 3 months.

Batty, William John (1914–19); Acting Sergeant, R. Sussex Rgt.; France 3 years 4 months.

Baulch, Cecil Alfred (1915–19); Private, Labour Corps; France 12 months.

Baulch, James Walter (1915–19); Shoeing-Smith, R.A.V.C.; France 3 years 6 months.

Baulch, Lawrence William (1915–19); Gunner, R.F.A.; France 6 months, Salonica 6 months, Egypt 2 years 6 months.

Baxter, Edward John (1915–19); Driver, R.F.A.; France 4 months, Salonica 2 years 6 months.

Bayford, Walter Charles (1914–19); Sapper, R.E.; France, Salonica and Egypt, 2 years 9 months.

Bayne, George Alexander (1915–19); Sergeant, R.A.O.C.; France and Salonica 3 years 6 months.

Baynes, Alfred George (1916–19); Private, Yorkshire Rgt.; France 3 months.

Beacham, Thomas Henry Philip (1918–19); Private, London Rgt.; France 4 months.

Beadle, Edward (1915–19); Private, Labour Corps.

Beadle, Frederick Ernest (1914–19); Private, Labour Corps; France 4 years 9 months.

Beagley, Henry Cecil (1914–18); Corporal, A.P.C.

Beak, Alfred James (1916–19); Private, London Rgt.; France 2 years 5 months.

Beal, Albert (1917–19); Ordinary Seaman, R.N.V.R.; Naval Service 9 months.

Beal, Ernest Heathcote (1916–19); Mentioned in despatches; Captain, R.A.S.C.; German East Africa 3 years.

Beal, George (1914–18); Private, R.A.M.C.; France 15 months.

Beales, Albert James (1917–19); Rifleman, London Rgt.; France 12 months.

Beamish, Henry Frederick (1914–19); Sergeant, London Rgt.; France 10 months.

Bean, James (1915–19); Private, Hampshire Rgt.; India, Salonica and Mesopotamia, 2 years 10 months.

Bean, Sidney Valentine (1914–19); Sapper, R.E.; Mediterranean 9 months, Egypt 2 years 10 months.

Beard, Ernest (1914–19); Gunner, R.G.A.; France 4 years 7 months.

Beardsall, Thomas Langley (1914–18); Gunner, R.F.A., Corporal, Labour Corps; France.

Beare, Augustine Edwin (1914); Driver, R.F.A.

Bearman, Frederick (1916–19); Private, London Rgt.; Salonica 4 months, Egypt 2 years 3 months.

Beart, Arthur Walter Charles (1915–19); Private, County of London Yeomanry; Egypt and Salonica 16 months.

Beasley, William (1916–19); Lance-Corporal, Wiltshire Rgt.; France 7 months.

Beatlin, Edward (1914–19); Sergeant, R.E.; France 5 months.

***Beaumont, Arthur Thomas Freeman** (1914–15); Sergeant, London Rgt.; Dardanelles 1 month; Killed in action, 15th August, 1915.

***Beavis, Arthur George** (1914–18); Sergeant, King's Own Yorkshire Light Infantry; France 2 years 2 months Killed in action, 19th August, 1918.

Beazleigh, Arthur Alfred (1915–19; Private, R.A.M.C.; Palestine 3 years 8 months.

Beckford, Benjamin Frederick (1916–17); Private, Derbyshire Yeomanry.

Beckford, Charles Stacey (1914–19); Lance-Corporal, R.E.; France 3 years 3 months.

Beckford, Walter (1914–17); Shoeing-Smith, R.F.A.; France.

Becroft, Henry (1914–16); Stoker (1st Class), R.N.; Naval Service 8 months.

Bedford, William Richard (1914–19); Lance-Corporal, 5th Lancers; France 3 years 6 months.

***Bedwell, Thomas William** (1914–17); Lance-Sergeant, Middlesex Rgt.; France; Missing, 31st May, 1917.

Beedle, James (1914–19); Able Seaman, R.N.; Egypt 4 years.

Beer, Edmund Richard (1914–19); Driver, R.F.A.; France 3 years 11 months.

Beetles, George Frederick (1915–19); Gunner, R.F.A.; France, Salonica and Egypt, 3 years.

Beeton, Charles William (1916–19); Sergeant, Rifle Brigade; France 12 months.

Begg, Hamilton James (1914–19); Company Sergeant-Major, London Rgt.

Begley, Thomas James (1914–18); Private, R.D.C.

Begley, William George (1914–19); Private, Royal Fusiliers; France 2 years, East 18 months.

Behr, Richard (1915–19); Private, Labour Corps; Dardanelles, Egypt and France, 3 years 5 months.

Belcher, George Alfred (1914–16); Gunner, R.G.A.; France 1 year 7 months.

Bell, Arthur Baxter (1915–19); Driver, R.E.; France 12 months.

Bell, Arthur William (1916–19); Private, Labour Corps; France 2 years 9 months.

Bell, George (1914–18); Private, E. Kent Rgt.; France and Germany (prisoner of war) 3 years.

Bell, George (1914–19); Private, R.D.C.

Bell, Thomas (1916–19); Private, York and Lancaster Rgt.; France and Italy 2 years.

Bell, Thomas Herbert (1918–19); Corporal, R.A.F.

Bell, Walter Harvey (1916–19); Bombardier, R.F.A.; France and Germany 3 years.

Belson, Walter (1915–19); Lance-Corporal, R.A.S.C.; France 4 years.

Bennett, Charles Edward (1915–19); Pioneer, R.E.; France 8 months.

Bennett, Stanley Charles Frederick (1916–19); Private, Sherwood Foresters; France and Germany 8 months.

Benson, George William (1915–19); Corporal, R.A.S.C.; Salonica 3 years 1 month.

Benson, Leonard (1915–19); Gunner, R.F.A.; France 3 years 8 months.

Benstead, Frederick William (1918–19); Rifleman, Rifle Brigade; France 5 months.

Bentall, Anthony Frank (1914–19); Sec.-Lieutenant, R.E.; Dardanelles 9 months, Salonica 4 months, France 6 months, Palestine 10 months.

Bentley, Henry (1914–19); Corporal, Bedfordshire Rgt.; France 12 months.

***Bentley, Horace Frederick** (1914–16); Able Seaman, R.N.V.R.; Killed in action, 13th November, 1916.

***Bernard, Percy Clements** (1916–18); Private, Essex Rgt.; Dardanelles and France 1 year 7 months; Died of wounds, 5th March, 1918.

Berry, James (1914–16); Private, Northamptonshire Rgt.

Best, Arthur Frederick (1914–19); D.C.M.; Corporal, R.H.A.; France 4 years 3 months.

Best, Ernest (1914–18); Private, London Rgt.

Best, Thomas (1916–19); Private, R.A.M.C.

Best, Walter (1916–19); Private, Labour Corps; Malta 5 months, France 6 months.

Betchley, Robert Langdon (1914–19); Gunner, R.G.A.; France 8 months.

Bethroy, Thomas Albert Francis (1915–19); Mentioned in despatches; Sergeant, R.E.; France 3 years 4 months.

Betteridge, James William (1915–19); Private, Middlesex Rgt.; France 2 years 9 months.

Betterton, Rupert (1915–18); Gunner, R.H.A.; France 2 years 7 months.

***Beverley, Walter William** (1914–16); Private, Middlesex Rgt.; Egypt and France 1 year 8 months; Missing, 16th September, 1916.

Bezodis, Arthur Bertrand (1915–19); Lance-Sergeant, London Rgt.

Bianchi, Rinaldo Natale (1916–19); Corporal, London Rgt.

Bibbing, Harry Ruby (1916–19); Private, Machine Gun Corps; France 2 years.

Bibbings, Ernest James (1918–19); Gunner, R.G.A.; France 3 months.

Bibby, Thomas Alexander (1914–15); Private, London Rgt.

Bicker, Leslie James (1914–19); Lieutenant, Gurkha Rifles; India 5 years.

***Bickmore, Arthur** (1914–15); Private, London Rgt.; France 2 months; Killed in action, 26th May, 1915.

Bidwell, Frederick Charles (1916–19); Sapper, R.E.; France 1 year 9 months.

Biggerstaff, Daniel (1914–15); Private, Dragoon Guards.

Bigglestone, Howard Ernest (1917–19); Private, Honourable Artillery Company; France 1 month, Italy 16 months.

Bignell, James (1914–19); Private, R.A.V.C.; France 3 years 6 months.

Bilby, William Robert (1915–19); Private, Labour Corps; France 3 years 6 months.

Biller, Frank Ernest (1917–19); Gunner, R.G.A.

Billing, George Edward (1914–19); Driver, R. Marine Artillery; France 3 years 6 months.

Billings, Sidney George (1915–19); Pioneer, R.E.; France 2 years 9 months.

Billington, George Albert (1916–18); Rifleman, King's Royal Rifle Corps; France.

Bilyard, Walter Samuel (1916–19); Driver, R.A.S.C.

Bilyard, William (1915–19); Private, Labour Corps; France 2 years 3 months.

Binge, Albert David (1917–19); Private, Labour Corps; France 10 months.

Bingham, Harry Roland (1915–19); Bombardier, R.F.A.; India 14 months, France 7 months.

Bird, Ernest John (1915–18); 2nd Corporal, R.A.O.C.

Bird, Frank (1914–19); Company Sergeant-Major, R.E.; East Africa 9 months.

Bird, George (1915–18); Driver, R.F.A.; France 17 months.

Bird, Thomas (1915–18); Sapper, R.E.; France 3 years 3 months.

Birt, Albert Henry Thomas (1917–19); Private, N. Staffordshire Rgt.; France 2 years 6 months.

***Bishop, Charles William** (1915–17); Private, R. Berkshire Rgt.; France 1 year 7 months; Killed in action, 4th March, 1917.

***Bishop, Henry Embleton** (1914–18); Corporal, Rifle Brigade; France 3 years; Died while prisoner of war, 29th June, 1918.

Bishop, William Henry (1914–19); Croix de Guerre (Belgian); Corporal, Dorsetshire Rgt.; France 3 years 4 months.

Bissill, Joseph Wright (1917–19); Sergeant, King's Royal Rifle Corps; France 12 months.

Blackman, Alfred (1914–19); Shoeing-Smith, R.F.A.; France, Salonica and Egypt, 3 years.

Blackman, Arthur (1914–19); Private, R.D.C.

Blackmore, William James (1915 and 1915–19); Leading Mechanic, R.A.F.

Blackwood, George (1915–19); Corporal, Shoeing-Smith, R.F.A.; France 2 years 2 months.

Blades, Joseph Percy (1915–19); Sergeant, R.E.; France 2 years 10 months.

Blake, Frederick (1914–18); Lance-Corporal, R.A.S.C.; France 3 years 5 months.

Blake, Harry William (1916–19); Private, R. Sussex Rgt.; France 3 months.

Blakeley, Joseph Edward (1914–19); Stoker, R.N.; Naval Service 1 year 7 months.

Bland, John (1914–19); Sergeant, R.F.A.; France 2 years 6 months.

Blandford, Henry Walter (1916–19); Gunner, R.G.A.; France 12 months.

Blay, Charles James (1915–19); Gunner, R.F.A.; France 2 years.

***Blay, Stephen George** (1914–18); Private, E. Kent Rgt.; France 2 years 6 months; Killed in action, 19th January, 1918.

Bleach, Patrick (1916–18); Private, Highland Light Infantry.

Bleasby, Frederick (1916–19); Private, London Rgt.; France 8 months, Russia 12 months.

Bliss, Albert Edward (1914); Private, Essex Rgt.

Blizard, Rupert Joseph (1914–15); Private, Oxfordshire and Buckinghamshire Light Infantry.

Bloomfield, Harry (1916–19); Pioneer, R.E.; France 2 years 3 months.

Blow, Percy Frederick (1916–19); Private, Royal Scots; France 2 years 2 months.

Bloxham, James Thomas (1914–16); Private, London Rgt.

Blyth, Alfred Stanley (1916–19); Private, Labour Corps.

Boatwright, Thomas (1914–17); Guardsman, Grenadier Guards; France 5 months.

Boggis, William James (1914–19); Pioneer, R.E.; France 16 months.

***Bolt, Alfred** (1914–16); Able Seaman, R.F.R.; Naval Service; Killed at sea, 7th March, 1916.

Bolton, Frederick John (1917–19); Driver, R.A.S.C.

Bolton, Henry Joshua (1914–19); Driver, R.A.S.C.; France 17 months, Salonica 12 months, East Africa 1 year 10 months.

Bolton, John Alfred (1914–19); Serbian Cross; Sergeant, R.A.S.C.; France and Serbia 3 years 5 months.

Bond, Alfred Ernest (1915–19); Corporal, Labour Corps; France 14 months.

Bond, Archibald Cameron (1916–19); Private, Loyal N. Lancashire Rgt.; France 7 months.

Bond, Edwin Henry (1914–17); Guardsman, Coldstream Guards; France 14 months.

Bond, Thomas (1915–19); Private, R. Sussex Rgt.

Bone, Arthur (1914–18); Sergeant, R.G.A.; France 12 months.

Bone, George Frederick (1914–19); Lance-Corporal, Welch Rgt.; France 14 months.

Boner, Frederick James (1918–19); Private, R.A.S.C.

Booker, Charles (1914–19); Private, Rifle Brigade and R.D.C.; Burmah 12 months.

Booley, Walter William (1914–19); Attendant, Sick Berth Reserve; France 1 year 11 months, Ægean Sea 1 year 9 months.

Booth, George Henry (1914–19); Petty Officer (1st Class), R.N.; Naval Service 4 years 4 months.

Booth, Henry Isaac (1914–19); Lance-Corporal, R.E.; Gallipoli 14 months, France 18 months.

Booth, James Alfred (1914–19); Private, Labour Corps; France 2 years 2 months.

Borley, Robert (1914–15); Shoeing-Smith, Dragoon Guards.

Bosomworth, Frank (1918–19); Private, R. Sussex Rgt.; Germany 3 months.

Bottcher, John (1914–19); Regimental Sergeant-Major, Essex Rgt.; Egypt 2 years 11 months.

Boucher, Frederick Thomas (1916–19); Private, Surrey Yeomanry; France 5 months.

Bough, Henry Herbert (1916–19); Private, Labour Corps; France 2 years 4 months.

Boulden, William John (1918–19); Private, R. Sussex Rgt.; Italy 3 months.

Boulter, Richard Robert Mark (1916–19); Gunner, R.G.A.; France 18 months.

Bounds, Albert Jesse (1915–19); Driver, R.E.; France 2 years 7 months.

Bourlet, Henry Thomas (1918–19); Private, R. Sussex Rgt.; France and Germany 6 months.

Bovingdon, Henry (1915–19); Driver, R.E.; France, Salonica and Egypt, 3 years.

Bowers, John (1914–19); Driver, R.A.S.C.; France, Salonica and Palestine, 3 years 2 months.

Bowers, William Alfred (1915–19); Driver, R.A.S.C.; Salonica 3 years 3 months.

Bowker, Frederick Henry (1915–19); Driver, R.E.; Egypt 3 years 10 months.

Bowles, Frederick John (1915–19); Private, Labour Corps; France 2 years 8 months.

Bowles, George Arthur (1916–19); Lance-Corporal, R. Irish Rgt.; France 2 years 11 months.

Box, Harry (1914–19); M.S.M.; Battery Sergeant-Major, R.F.A.; France 4 years 5 months.

Boyce, Henry John (1915–19); Private, E. Surrey Rgt.; France 3 years 2 months.

Boyce, Thomas Joseph (1914–19); Corporal, R.F.A.; France 3 years 5 months.

Boyd, George Robert (1918–19); Air Mechanic (3rd Class), R.A.F.

Boydon, Howard William (1914–19); Guardsman, Grenadier Guards.

Boyer, William John (1915–19); Gunner, R.F.A.; France, Salonica and Egypt, 3 years 1 month.

Boyle, John (1915–19); Private, Labour Corps; Gallipoli, Egypt and France, 2 years 3 months.

***Boys, Charles Henry** (1914); Able Seaman, R.F.R.; Naval Service; Killed in action, 22nd September, 1914.

Bradbury, Frederick Arthur (1918); Private, Middlesex Rgt.; France 2 months.

Bradbury, Frederick Joseph (1914–16); Lance-Corporal, Royal Fusiliers; France 6 months.

Bradbury, John Edward Hall (1915–19); Corporal, R.F.A.; Palestine and Egypt 2 years 6 months.

Braddick, Charles William (1914–19); Private, E. Surrey Rgt.; France and Germany (prisoner of war) 3 years.

Braddick, George James (1914–19); Sergeant, London Rgt.; France 3 years 11 months.

Braddick, Victor Edward (1915–16); Private, London Rgt.

Braddick, William John Stephen (1914–19); Sergeant, London Rgt.; France and Egypt 2 years 8 months.

Bradford, Albert George (1915–19); Sapper, R.E.; Dardanelles, Egypt and France, 3 years 11 months.

Bradford, Edward (1915–17); Sergeant, R.F.A.; France 2 years 4 months.

Bradley, George (1915–19); Bombardier, R.F.A.; France, Salonica and Egypt, 2 years 6 months.

Bradley, Joseph Clarence (1916–19); Private, R. Scots Fusiliers; Palestine 18 months, France 9 months.

Bradshaw, Alfred Charles (1918–19); Aircraftsman (1st Class), R.A.F.

Bradshaw, Arthur Walter Henry (1914–19); Trooper, R. Horse Guards.

Bradshaw, George (1917–18); Private, Labour Corps.

Bradshaw, Harold (1918–19); Private, Royal Dragoons.

Bradstreet, Ernest Frank (1915–19); Private, R.A.S.C.; France 2 years.

Braisher, Arthur (1914–19); Saddler Sergeant, R.A.S.C.; Egypt 18 months.

Brake, William John (1917–19); Sapper, R.E.; France 1 year 8 months.

***Braybrooke, Joseph Albert** (1915–16); Private, Middlesex Rgt.; France 3 months; Died of wounds, 29th February, 1916.

Braybrooke, Oliver Edward (1914–19); Private, Royal Marine Light Infantry; France 1 year 8 months.

Brazier, William (1916–19); Private, Royal Fusiliers; France 2 years 3 months.

***Brazil, Horace Charles** (1916–17); Rifleman, King's Royal Rifle Corps; France 12 months; Missing, 26th December, 1917.

Breavington, Joseph Edward (1915); Private, E. Kent Rgt.

Brett, Charles Russell (1914 and 1915–19); Private, Bedfordshire Rgt.; France and Italy 3 years 8 months.

Brett, Charles Stewart (1914–18); Private, London Rgt.; Malta and France.

Brett, John Allen (1914–15); Lance-Corporal, King's Shropshire Light Infantry.

Brett, Joseph Bertram (1914–16 and 1917); Gunner, R.G.A.

Brewer, Charles John (1918–19); Private, R. W. Kent Rgt.; France 3 months.

Brewer, Frederick Charles Ernest (1916–19); Private, R.A.M.C.; France 2 years 2 months.

Brewer, George Thomas (1915–19); Sergeant Cadet, R.F.A.; France 18 months.

Brewer, Henry Herbert (1914–19); Private, R.A.F.; France 2 years 8 months.

Brewer, Henry James (1915–19); Gunner, R.G.A.; France 2 years 2 months.

Brewer, William (1914–19); Sec.-Lieutenant, R.H.A.; France 2 years 10 months.

Brewster, Herbert Charles (1918–19); Air Mechanic (3rd Class), R.A.F.

Brianse, William Frederick (1914–19); Corporal, London Rgt.; Egypt and Palestine 3 years.

Briant, Edward (1914–19); Gunner, R.F.A.; France 3 years 11 months.

***Brice, Horace Garnham** (1916–17); Rifleman, London Rgt.; France 2 months; Died of wounds, 7th March, 1917.

Brickwood, George (1915–19); M.M.; Staff-Sergeant, R.E.; France 3 years 3 months.

Bridge, Herbert (1914–19); Corporal, R.H.A.; France 4 years 3 months.

Bridge, Philip Alexander (1915–19); Gunner, R.G.A.; France 2 years.

Bridger, Albert Henry (1918–19); Private, R.A.S.C.

Bridges, Alfred (1916–19); Sapper, R.E.

Bridson, William Ernest (1914–15); Sergeant, Lincolnshire Rgt.; France 8 months.

Briffitt, Josiah (1914–18); Private, E. Surrey Rgt.

Bright, Charles (1916–19); Private, Loyal N. Lancashire Rgt.; France 2 years.

Brightwell, William Percy (1917–19); Private, Labour Corps; France 2 years.

Brimblecombe, Frederick John (1915–17); Private, 18th Hussars; France 6 months.

Brimer, Henry (1914–19); Private, Royal Fusiliers; France 3 years 4 months.

Bristo, Frederick (1914–19); Driver, R.H.A.; France and Germany 4 years.

Bristow, James Alfred (1914–17); Sergeant, Devonshire Rgt.

Bristow, John Reuben (1915–19); Driver, R.F.A.; France, Italy and Germany, 3 years.

Britt, Richard (1914–19); Private, Border Rgt.; France 8 months, Egypt 3 years 6 months.

Brittain, Henry Thomas (1916–18); Private, R.D.C.

Britton, James Samuel (1915–19); Gunner, R.F.A.; Salonica, Palestine and France, 3 years.

Britton, Vincent (1916–18); Gunner, R.G.A.

Broad, Alfred (1914–19); Driver, R.A.S.C.; France 3 years.

Broad, Charles Ernest (1914–19); Bombardier, R.F.A.; France 2 years 7 months.

Broad, John Williams (1914–19); Sergeant, Labour Corps; Gallipoli and France 2 years 2 months.

Brobyn, Frederick Robert (1915–17); Sapper, R.E.; France 1 year 10 months.

Brockhurst, Frederick (1915–19); Sapper, R.E.; France 7 months, German East Africa 1 year 11 months.

Brockwell, Thomas Clifton (1915–19); Battery Quartermaster-Sergeant, R.F.A.; France 2 years 11 months.

Brodie, William (1915–19); Driver, R.F.A.; France 3 years 3 months.

Brookbank, George (1915); Private, Dorsetshire Rgt.

Brooker, Reuben (1914–19); M.M.; Sergeant, Coldstream Guards; France 3 years 9 months.

***Brooker, William** (1914); Able Seaman, R.F.R.; Naval Service; Drowned at sea, 1st November, 1914.

Brooks, Arthur (1915–19); Driver, R.E.; France 2 years 2 months, Italy 5 months.

Brooks, Charles (1914–19); M.S.M., mentioned in despatches; Staff Sergeant-Major, London Rgt.

Brooks, George Henry (1915–19); Lieutenant, Machine Gun Corps; France 1 year 9 months.

Brooks, Thomas Colston (1914–19); Private, Royal Marine Light Infantry; Naval Service 4 years 6 months.

Broom, Ernest Edgar (1915–19); Lance-Bombardier, R.F.A.; France, Salonica and Egypt, 2 years 9 months.

Broom, John (1916–19); Private, Yorkshire Rgt.; France 3 months, Italy 1 year.

Broome, Ernest Frederick (1914–18); Lance-Corporal, Labour Corps; Gallipoli and France 2 years 11 months.

Broome, William (1914–19); Private, R.A.S.C.; France 3 years.

Broomfield, Frederick (1915–19); Private, R.A.S.C.; France 3 years 8 months.

Brouder, Michael (1917–19); Private, Labour Corps; France 14 months.

Brown, Albert Edward (1914–15); Gunner, R.F.A.

Brown, Albert Edward (1914–19); Corporal, Coldstream Guards; France 4 years 4 months.

***Brown, Alexander Irvine** (1915–17); Rifleman, King's Royal Rifle Corps; France 14 months; Killed in action, 31st July, 1917.

Brown, David Baxter (1917–19); Leading Aircraftsman, R.A.F.

Brown, David Charles (1915–19); Driver, R.A.S.C.; France 1 year 8 months.

Brown, Edward James (1914–17); Sergeant, Royal Fusiliers.

Brown, Ernest Edgar (1916–17); Rifleman, Rifle Brigade.

Brown, Frederick (1916–19); Private, Labour Corps; Salonica 2 years 2 months.

Brown, Harry (1914–19); Private, King's Own Yorkshire Light Infantry; France and Germany (prisoner of war) 4 years.

Brown, Herbert Arthur (1918–20); Private, R. Sussex Rgt.; France and Egypt 16 months.

Brown, Herbert William (1914–19); Private, R.D.C.

Brown, James (1914–19); Private, R.D.C.

Brown, James (1916–17); Private, Royal Fusiliers; France 1 month.

Brown, James (1914); Private, London Rgt.

Brown, John Benjamin (1914–19); Private, R. Welch Fusiliers.

Brown, John Edgar (1915–19); Corporal, R. W. Surrey Rgt.; France 1 year 9 months.

Brown, John Leonard (1915–19); Private, R.A.M.C.; France 2 years 7 months.

Brown, Ralph Harris (1914–19); Lance-Corporal, R.A.S.C.; France 2 years 8 months.

Brown, Thomas (1915–19); Private, R.A.S.C.; France 3 years 8 months.

Brown, Thomas (1914–19); Sergeant, R. Dublin Fusiliers; Gallipoli and Salonica 3 years 8 months.

Brown, Thomas Weston (1914–19); Private, R.A.S.C.; France 4 years 5 months.

Brown, William James (1914–17); Private, Dragoon Guards.

Brumby, Frederick (1914–19); Driver, R.F.A.; France 3 years 5 months.

***Brunning, Charles James** (1916–17); Corporal, London Rgt.; France 10 months; Killed in action, 14th April, 1917.

Bryan, Frank (1916–19); Private, Highland Light Infantry; France 7 months.

Bryant, Albert Edward (1917–19); Private, R.A.V.C.; France 18 months.

Bryant, Alfred (1914–16); Sergeant, R. Sussex Rgt.; France 8 months.

Bryant, William (1915–19); Stoker, R.N.; Naval Service 3 years 3 months.

Bryen, William (1917–19); Gunner, R.G.A.; France 11 months.

Buck, Edward (1914–19); Driver, R.F.A.; France 2 years 2 months.

Buck, Frank Albert (1914–19); Driver, R.A.S.C.; France and Salonica 4 years 2 months.

Buck, John William (1915–19); Gunner, R.F.A.; France 3 years.

Buckingham, Frederick (1914–19); Lance-Corporal, London Rgt.; France, Salonica, Egypt and Palestine, 2 years 10 months.

Buckingham, Walter (1916–18); Private, London Rgt.; France 5 months.

Buckland, Herbert (1918–19); Private, R. W. Surrey Rgt.

Buckland, Sidney Lawrence (1914–16); Driver, R.F.A.; France.

Buckman, Kelsham John (1915–19); Gunner, R.F.A.; France 3 years.

Budd, Ernest Henry (1915–19); Mentioned in despatches; Sec.-Lieutenant, R.A.S.C.; France 2 years 10 months.

Budds, Ernest Valentine (1916–19); Private, Labour Corps.

Buen, Percy (1917–18); Private, R.A.M.C.

***Bull, George** (1914–16); Corporal, E. Surrey Rgt.; France 1 year 11 months; Killed in action, 26th July, 1916.

***Bull, George Adolphus** (1915–18); Gunner, R.F.A.; France 1 year 10 months; Died of wounds, 15th November, 1918.

Bull, James (1916–19); Private, Somersetshire Light Infantry; France 11 months.

Bull, William James (1917–19); Private, Labour Corps; France 1 year 9 months.

Bullimore, William (1916–19); Gunner, R.F.A.; France 6 months, Salonica 7 months, Egypt 2 years.

Bullock, John Henry (1914–19); Rifleman, London Rgt., and Private, Labour Corps; France 10 months.

Bullock, William Charles (1914–19); Sergeant, R.A.V.C.; France, Mesopotamia and Egypt, 4 years.

Bunce, William Stanley (1914–19); Private, Durham Light Infantry; France 3 years.

Bunkall, Walter (1915–19); Corporal, R.A.F.; Mudros, Egypt, Aden and Salonica, 3 years 5 months.

Bunker, Albert William (1917); Private, Labour Corps.

Bunker, William Joseph (1915–17); Gunner, R.F.A.; France and Salonica 18 months.

Bunting, Arthur Edward (1915–17); Driver, R.F.A.; France and Salonica 16 months.

Burbridge, William (1914–19); Sergeant, Suffolk Rgt.

Burcham, Arthur Robert (1917–19); 1st Private, R.A.F.; France 1 month.

Burchett, Harry (1916–19); Gunner, R.G.A.

Burden, Harry (1916–19); Private, Middlesex Rgt.; France 7 months.

Burden, John Louis (1917–19); Private, London Rgt.; France 11 months.

Burden, William Lewis John (1914–19); Sergeant, Machine Gun Corps; Malta 4 months, France 3 years 3 months, Germany (prisoner of war) 10 months.

Burgess, George (1914–19); Able Seaman, R.N.; Naval Service 3 years 9 months.

Burgoyne, Albert Edgar (1916–19); Private, R.A.S.C.; Salonica 1 year 11 months.

Burk, John (1914–19); Mentioned in despatches; Regimental Sergeant-Major, R. Sussex Rgt.; France 8 months, Egypt 3 years 6 months.

Burkin, George William (1918–19); Private, E. Surrey Rgt.; France 4 months.

Burls, Richard George (1914–19); Staff-Sergeant Instructor, Army Gymnastic Staff; France 6 months.

Burnage, Arthur Charles (1914–19); Rifleman, Rifle Brigade; France 3 years 6 months.

Burnell, Arthur Michael (1918–19); Private, R. Sussex Rgt.

Burnett, Francis Samuel (1916–19); Gunner, R.F.A.

Burnett, Morris Samuel (1915–19); Driver, R.F.A.

***Burningham, Walter George** (1914–19); Private, Middlesex Rgt.; France 2 years; Died, 5th January, 1919.

Burnley, Richard Edward (1914–19); Rifleman, Rifle Brigade; Burmah 4 years.

Burr, Albert Henry (1917–19); Pioneer, R.E.

Burree, Arthur George (1916–19); Rifleman, R. Irish Rifles; France and Germany 1 year 11 months.

Burrell, Alfred Ernest (1914–19); Bombardier, R.F.A.; France 4 years 6 months.

Burrell, David (1914–19); Private, Royal Fusiliers; France 6 months.

Burrell, Thomas (1914–17); Private, London Rgt.

Burry, John Jacob (1914–19); Battery Sergeant-Major, R.F.A.

Burt, Thomas Christopher (1915–19); Lance-Corporal, R. Warwickshire Rgt.; France 3 years.

Burt, William (1915–18); Squadron Sergeant-Major, Shropshire Yeomanry.

Burton, George Charles (1914–19); Gunner, R.F.A.; France 4 years 4 months, Italy 2 months.

***Burton, Thomas William** (1914–17); Private, E. Surrey Rgt.; France 1 year 10 months; Killed in action, 1st May, 1917.

Burton, Walter Frederick (1917–19); Private, Labour Corps; France 17 months.

Burville, William Henry (1914–17); Sergeant, 100th Provisional Bn.

Bush, Alfred Thomas (1917–20); Private, Labour Corps; France and Germany 2 years 8 months.

Bush, Arthur (1914–19); Petty Officer, R.N.; Naval Service 4 years 3 months.

Bush, James Thomas (1917–19); 3rd Air Mechanic, R.A.F.

Bush, Reuben Frederick (1914–19); Driver, R.A.S.C.; Malta 15 months, France 2 years 3 months.

Bushell, Edwin (1915–19); Driver, R.F.A.; France 3 years 2 months.

Buss, Alfred Richard (1915–19); Corporal, R.A.M.C.; France 2 years.

Butcher, Charles Walter (1914–17); Private, Dragoon Guards; France 2 years 7 months.

Butcher, Edward (1914–19); Gunner, R.F.A.; France 3 months, Salonica 3 years.

Butcher, Walter (1915–19); Guardsman, Guards Machine Gun Rgt.; France 12 months.

Butler, Edward George (1914–18); Private, Yorkshire Light Infantry and Lance-Corporal, R.D.C.; France 2 years.

***Butler, James Ernest** (1914–15); Corporal, Rifle Brigade; France 3 months; Missing, 6th July, 1915.

Butler, William Richard Alfred (1914–19); Leading Seaman, R.N.; Naval Service.

Butlin, Harry (1914–19); Bombardier, R.F.A.; France 6 months, Italy 2 months.

***Butlin, William Arthur** (1915–16); Private, R. Berkshire Rgt.; France 1 month; Killed in action, 19th April, 1916.

Buttle, Reuben (1914–18); Private, Labour Corps.

Button, Thomas Arthur (1915–19); Driver, R.F.A.; France 3 years 1 month.

Bynoth, Henry (1914–19); Sergeant, R.A.V.C.; France, Egypt and Salonica, 4 years.

Byrne, Richard Thomas (1915–19); Corporal, R.A.S.C.

***Cahill, James** (1914–19); Private, R.A.M.C.; Gibraltar 4 years; Died, 16th March, 1919.

Caiger, Walter Joseph (1914–19); Sapper, R.E.; France and Salonica 3 years.

Calaz, John Joseph (1915–16); Private, Middlesex Rgt.

Cale, William John (1915–19); Gunner, R.F.A.; France 3 years 9 months.

Callaghan, Dennis (1914–19); Sapper, R.E.; France, Belgium and Mesopotamia, 3 years 6 months.

Calver, Charles Ronald (1918–19); Private, Essex Rgt.

Calver, George Ernest (1918–19); Private, Machine Gun Corps.

Calver, William Henry (1914–19); Bombardier, R.G.A.; France 3 years 8 months.

Calvert, Edward (1915–18); Sapper, R.E.

Cameron, St. John Digby Coutts (1914–19); Private, Dragoon Guards; France 10 months.

Camp, William George (1914–19); Corporal, R.A.S.C.; France and Germany 4 years 7 months.

Cann, Frederick Charles (1914–19); Able Seaman, R.N.; Naval Service.

Cann, George Richard (1914–19); Gunner, R.F.A.; France 4 years 5 months.

***Cannard, Henry Ernest** (1914–15); Private, Middlesex Rgt.; France 13 months; Killed in action, 25th September, 1915.

Cannon, Frederick (1915–19); Driver, R.F.A.; France 13 months.

Cannon, Thomas William (1914–19); Sergeant, Labour Corps; Gallipoli and France 14 months.

Cant, Arthur Frederick (1915–19); Private, R.A.S.C. (M.T.); France 2 years 10 months.

Canter, Thomas William (1914–19); Gunner, R.H.A.; France 4 years 6 months.

Canton, John (1914–19); Lance-Corporal, R.A.S.C.; France 4 months.

Capel, George (1914–17); Private, R.D.C.

***Cappleman, Walter** (1916); Rifleman, Rifle Brigade; France 1 month; Missing, 15th September, 1916.

***Carben, Henry** (1917); Private, R.A.M.C.; France and Italy 2 months; Died, 20th July, 1917.

Card, George (1915–19); Gunner, R.H.A.; France 4 years.

Cardy, William Arnold (1914–19); Private, Middlesex Rgt.; France and Germany (prisoner of war) 4 years 5 months.

Carlton, Thomas (1914–16); Private, London Rgt.

Carmichael, Finlay (1914–19); Gunner, R.F.A.; Egypt and Salonica 3 years 3 months.

Carpenter, Harry Thomas (1916–19); Gunner, R.F.A.; France, Italy and Egypt, 2 years 9 months.

Carr, Joseph James (1918–19); Air Mechanic (3rd Class), R.A.F.

Carstairs, James Lockhart (1915–19); M.M.; Corporal, R.F.A.; France 9 months.

Carter, Arthur John (1914–19); Lance-Corporal, London Rgt.

***Carter, Edward William** (1914–19); Corporal, R.F.A.; France, Salonica and Egypt, 2 years 7 months.

Carter, Edwin Thomas (1914–19); Private, Middlesex Rgt.; France 3 years 6 months.

Carter, Ernest Charles (1914–19); Lance-Sergeant, Dragoon Guards; France 4 years 1 month.

Carter, Henry Arthur (1916–18); Driver, R.A.S.C.; France 2 years; Died, 3rd December, 1918.

Carter, James (1914–15); Private, Scots Guards.

Carter, James Alfred (1916–17); Cyclist, Norfolk Rgt.

Carter, James Frederick (1916–19); Corporal, R.A.O.C.; Egypt, Palestine and Syria, 2 years 2 months.

Carter, William (1915–19); Corporal, R.E.; France 2 years.

Cartwright, John (1918–19); Private, R.A.O.C.; France and Germany 11 months.

Carver, Arthur George (1916–19); Gunner, R.F.A.

Carver, Frederick James Daniel (1914–19); Air Mechanic, R.A.F.; France 2 years 10 months.

Case, James (1916–17); Gunner, R.F.A.

Casey, Charles Percy (1916); Private, London Rgt.

Castell, Henry Edwin (1915–17); Corporal, R.F.A.; France and Salonica 13 months.

Castle, Ernest Albert (1916–19); Private, Labour Corps.

Castle, Ernest Arthur (1914–19); Sergeant, Royal Fusiliers; France 2 years 8 months.

Castle, Frank George (1917–19); Lance-Corporal, Military Police.

Castle, George Charles (1916–19); Private, Cameron Highlanders and Labour Corps; France 1 year 9 months.

Castle, John Dennis (1914–19); Stoker, R.N.; Naval Service, 3 years 2 months.

Castle, William Bannon (1914–19); M.M.; Company Quartermaster-Sergeant, W. Yorkshire Rgt.; Dardanelles, Egypt and France, 3 years 5 months.

Catmull, Walter Robert (1915–19); Corporal, R.A.M.C.

Catt, Arthur (1915–19); Wheeler, R.F.A.; France 2 years 3 months.

Catt, Richard (1918–19); Private, London Rgt.

Cawson, Richard Pearse (1915–19); Driver, R.A.M.C.; France 4 years 1 month.

Chalfont, Frederick William (1916–20); Private, R. W. Kent Rgt.; India and Afghanistan 3 years 5 months.

***Challis, Walter** (1914); Leading Signalman, R.N.; Killed at sea, 22nd September, 1914.

Chamberlain, Henry James (1915–19); Driver, R.A.S.C.; France 3 years 7 months.

Chambers, Herbert Thomas (1914–19); Lance-Sergeant, Rifle Brigade; Burmah 4 years.

Champney, William (1914–19); Able Seaman, R.N.; Naval Service 4 years 7 months.

Chance, Frederick Lewer (1914–19); Sapper, R.E.

Chandler, Thomas Gerald (1916–19); Private, Labour Corps; France 2 years.

Channing, Alderman Joseph Charles (1917); Private, Northamptonshire Rgt.

Channing, Herbert Samuel (1916–19); Sapper, R.E.

***Chaplin, Thomas Sidney** (1917); Sapper, R.E.; France 2 months; Died, 30th July, 1917.

Chapman, Alfred James (1915–16); Guardsman, Coldstream Guards; France 6 months.

Chapman, Edgar Charles (1914–15); Private, London Rgt.

Chapman, Ernest Edward (1916–18); Private, Cheshire Rgt.; France 11 months.

Charles, Horace Frank (1914–19); Private, Labour Corps; France 4 years.

Charlwood, Ernest James (1916–19); Private, R.A.O.C.; France 3 years 6 months.

Charman, Henry George (1914–19); Private, Duke of Wellington's Rgt.; France 3 years 6 months.

Charrott, James (1914-19); Bombardier, R.F.A.; France and India 3 years 9 months.

Charsley, Louis Albert (1914); Bombardier, R.F.A.

Chase, Thomas Hackett (1918–19); Gunner, R.F.A.; France 4 months.

Chastney, Frank William (1917–19); Gunner, R.F.A.; France 1 year 7 months.

Chatman, Alfred (1914–19); Gunner, R.H.A.; France 2 years 10 months.

Cherry, Sidney Thomas (1914–19); Lance-Corporal, Labour Corps; France 2 years 3 months.

Cheshire, Albert Edward (1916–19); Sergeant, Military Police.

Cheshire, Thomas (1914–19); Lance-Sergeant, Oxfordshire and Buckinghamshire Light Infantry; France 18 months.

Chessun, Thomas (1914–19); Rifleman, Rifle Brigade; France and prisoner of war 4 years 6 months.

***Chesterman, William Thomas** (1916); Private, R.W. Surrey Rgt.; France 2 months; Killed in action, 3rd November 1916.

Chilcott, George Henry (1916–19); Lance-Corporal, Labour Corps; Salonica 2 years 10 months.

Chilcott, Thomas Edwin (1914–19); M.M.; Lance-Corporal, R.E.; Germany and France 4 years 4 months.

Childs, Arthur John Kent (1917–18); Private, London Rgt.; France 4 months.

Chilvers, Joseph Ernest (1916–19); Private, S. Staffordshire Rgt.; France 16 months.

Chinn, Louis John (1918–19); Private, Middlesex Rgt.

Chinnock, John Henry (1916–19); M.M.; Private, E. Surrey Rgt.; France 2 years 4 months.

Chipling, William Edward (1914–19); Gunner, R.F.A.; France 12 months, Mesopotamia 1 year 8 months.

Chipperfield, Robert George (1915–19); Private, R. Warwickshire Rgt.; France and Italy 3 years 8 months.

Chipperfield, William Charles (1915–19); Gunner, R.F.A.; France 3 years 1 month.

Chorley, Robert Percival Thomas (1916–19); Private, R.A.S.C.; France 2 years 4 months.

Christian, George Edward (1914–18); Pioneer, R.E.; France 15 months.

Christopher, Charles Henry (1914–19); Driver, R.F.A.; France 3 years, Italy 14 months.

Church, Stanley George (1914–15); Auxiliary Sick Berth Reserve, R.N.; Naval Service 8 months.

Church, William James (1916–19); Corporal, Machine Gun Corps; France and Germany 2 years 5 months.

***Churchill, Mark William** (1914–17); Private, Royal Fusiliers; France 2 years; Killed in action, August, 1917.

Chymist, James Samuel (1918–19); Private, R.A.S.C. (M.T.).

Clare, George Henry John (1916–19); Able Seaman, R.N.; Naval Service 2 years 4 months.

Clark, Albert Ernest (1916–19); Leading Aircraftsman, R.A.F.; France 2 years 2 months.

Clark, Albert Henry (1914–17); Driver, R.D.C.

Clark, Alfred (1915–19); Private, R.A.S.C.; France 3 years 10 months.

Clark, Bertie William (1915–19); Driver, R.F.A.; France 2 years, India 2 years.

Clark, Charles Edwin (1916–19); Private, R.A.M.C.

Clark, Charles Lever (1915–18); Private, York and Lancaster Rgt.; France 1 year 5 months.

Clark, David (1914–19); Croix de Guerre (French); Sergeant, R.A.S.C. (M.T.); France and Germany 3 years.

Clark, Ernest Richard (1914–19); Lance-Corporal, Essex Rgt.; Egypt and Salonica 4 years.

Clark, Frederick (1917–19); Private, Labour Corps.

Clark, Frederick George (1916–18); Private, Middlesex Rgt.; France 13 months.

Clark, James George (1915–19); Driver, R.E.; France 2 years 11 months.

Clark, Jesse William (1914–19); Leading Seaman, R.N.; Naval Service.

Clark, John (1914–19); Cadet (Petty Officer), R.N.D.; Egypt, Gallipoli, Salonica and France, 3 years.

Clark, John William (1916–19); Private, R.A.S.C.; France 2 years 9 months.

Clark, Oswald Drew (1917–19); Private, R.A.S.C. (M.T.).

Clark, Percy Le Brun (1918–19); Private, R.A.S.C. (M.T.).

Clark, Samuel John (1914–19); Driver, R.F.A.; France 3 years 6 months.

***Clark, Sidney** (1914–15); Lance-Corporal, Royal Fusiliers; France 1 month; Died of wounds, 28th May, 1915.

Clark, William (1914–18); Private, R.D.C.

Clark, William Charles (1915–19); Lance-Corporal, R.E.; France 17 months.

Clark, William Edward (1914–19); Pioneer, R.E.; France 3 years.

Clarke, Albert Herbert (1917–19); Gunner, R.G.A.; France 4 months.

Clarke, Arthur (1918–19); Private, Essex Rgt.; France 3 months.

Clarke, Arthur John (1916–19); Private, Labour Corps.

Clarke, George (1914–19); Able Seaman, R.N.

Clarke, Henry Edwin (1915–19); Bombardier, R.F.A.; France 3 years 3 months.

Clarke, Joseph George (1914–17); Private, R.A.S.C.

Clarke, Leonard Henry (1916–17); Private, R. Scots Fusiliers.

***Clarkson, George Alfred** (1916–17); Corporal, King's Own Yorkshire Light Infantry; France 1 year; Killed in action, 16th August, 1917.

Clarry, Frederick Alfred (1916–19); Private, Worcestershire Rgt.; France 3 months.

Clay, George (1914–19); Gunner, R.F.A.; France, Salonica and Egypt, 3 years.

Clayton, Frederick Harry (1914–19); Sergeant, R.F.A.; France and Salonica 3 years 6 months.

***Clements, Edgar Bletsoe** (1918); Gunner, R.G.A.; Died, 10th October 1918.

Clements, Martin James (1917–18); Signaller, R.F.A.; France 3 months.

Clibbon, Joseph Henry (1915–19); Driver, R.A.S.C.; France 2 years 10 months, Egypt 2 months.

Clifford, Henry Arthur Butcher (1915–19); Pioneer, R.E.; Salonica 2 years.

Clover, Allan (1915–19); Signaller, R.E.; France 2 years 10 months.

Coates, Charles Albert (1916–19); Lance-Corporal, R. Sussex Rgt.

Coates, Harry (1915–19); Private, R.A.S.C. (M.T.); France 3 years 8 months.

Coates, Robert Skelton (1914–19); Rifleman, London Rgt.; France 3 years 10 months.

Cobb, Joseph George (1914–19); Private, Dragoon Guards; France 6 months.

Cockrill, Arthur Edward (1914–16); Sergeant, Essex Rgt.

Cogger, Walter (1914–19); Sergeant, R.F.A.; Palestine 2 years, France 18 months.

Cohen, Gerald Maurice (1917–19); Private, R.A.S.C. (M.T.); France 18 months.

Coke, Charles Stuart (1915–19); Private, R.A.S.C.; France 3 years 10 months.

***Colborne, Alfred Charles** (1915–17); Bombardier, R.F.A.; France 17 months; Died of wounds, 24th May, 1917.

Colbran, Henry Horace (1915–19); Sapper, R.E.; Salonica 18 months, France 7 months.

Coldrick, Joseph (1915–19); Private, R.A.V.C.; France 3 years.

***Cole, Henry Alfred** (1914–16); Lance-Corporal, Dorsetshire Rgt.; France 1 year; Died of wounds, 12th July, 1916.

Cole, Horace Albert (1914–19); Gunner, R.F.A.; France 14 months.

Cole, John Francis (1915–19); Gunner, R.F.A.; France 2 years 4 months.

Cole, Robert Charles Patrick (1917–19); Private, R.A.F.

***Cole, William Henry Davis** (1914–18); Private, Bedfordshire Rgt.; France 3 years; Died of wounds, 25th August, 1918.

***Coleman, Charles** (1914–16); Private, Royal Fusiliers; France 2 years 2 months; Missing, 7th October, 1916.

Coleman, Harry Albert (1916–19); Private, London Rgt.; Salonica 6 months, Egypt 18 months.

Coleman, Henry Douglas (1917–19); Lance-Corporal, London Rgt.; France 1 year 7 months.

Coleman, John (1916–19); Private, R. Sussex Rgt.; France 6 months.

Coles, William (1916–19); Lance-Corporal, London Rgt.; Salonica 6 months, Egypt 18 months.

Collard, Edwin (1914–19); D.C.M.; Company Quartermaster-Sergeant, Lincolnshire and Nottinghamshire and Derbyshire Rgts. and Labour Corps; France, Greece and Egypt, 4 years 2 months.

Collett, Ernest Hiram (1914–17); Private, Middlesex Rgt.; France 18 months.

Collett, William (1915–19); Private, R.A.V.C.; France 4 years.

Colley, Charles Stratton (1915–19); Private, R.A.S.C. (M.T.); Salonica and Egypt 3 years 5 months.

Colley, John Richard (1916–19); Private, S. Nottinghamshire Hussars.

***Collier, Harry** (1915–18); Sapper, R.E.; France 1 year 8 months; Died, 6th November, 1918.

Collier, John Albert (1914–17); M.M.; Lance-Corporal, London Rgt.; France 1 year 7 months.

Collins, John (1914–19); M.M.; Sergeant, R.E.; France 3 years 6 months.

Collins, John (1916–17); Private, Northumberland Fusiliers.

Collins, Leonard Ernest Percy (1914–19); Sergeant, R.A.M.C.; France 4 years 6 months.

Collins, William John (1915–19); Private, R.A.S.C. (M.T.); France 2 years.

***Colverd, William James** (1915–17); Gunner, R.F.A.; France 14 months; Died of wounds, 16th August, 1917.

Compton, Thomas Joseph (1914–19); Driver, R.F.A.; France 3 years 10 months.

Conaron, William (1917); Air Mechanic (2nd Class), R.A.F.

Conie, Harry (1914–19); Bombardier, R.H.A.; France 2 years 10 months.

Connor, George Herbert (1918–19); Private, Machine Gun Corps.

Connor, Reginald Edmund Clement (1914–19); Corporal, London Rgt.; France 2 years.

Constable, George (1916–19); Private, Northumberland Fusiliers; France 2 years 2 months.

Constable, William Henry (1914–19); Sergeant, R.F.A.; Russia 6 months, France 3 months, Salonica 3 years.

Conway, John William (1918–19); Gunner, R.G.A.; France 3 months.

Cook, Albert Victor (1914–17); Private, Middlesex Rgt.; France 3 months.

Cook, Alfred Arthur (1914–19); Sergeant, London Rgt.; Egypt 13 months, France 10 months, Salonica 8 months.

Cook, Charles Herbert (1914–16); Private, 9th Lancers; France 2 years.

Cook, Herbert (1914–19); Sergeant, Essex Rgt.; France 3 months.

Cook, Herbert Eli (1914–19); Lance-Corporal, London Rgt.; Burmah 4 years.

Cook, Robert William (1917–19); Battery Quartermaster - Sergeant, R.G.A.; France and Germany 18 months.

Cook, Stanley John (1916–19); Private, R.A.O.C.; France 15 months.

Cook, William (1914–19); Driver, R.F.A.; France 3 years 6 months.

Cook, William James (1916–19); Private, Dorsetshire Rgt.; France 1 year.

Coole, John Henry (1914–19); Sergeant, Wiltshire Rgt.

Coombes, Stanley George (1914–19); Gunner, R.F.A.; France 4 years 6 months.

***Cooper, Arthur** (1914–15); Private, Essex Rgt.; France 4 months; Died of wounds, 19th December, 1915.

Cooper, Charles Leonard (1915–19); Sapper, R.E.; France 3 years 3 months.

Cooper, Edward (1914–19); Driver, R.F.A.; France and Italy 3 years 6 months.

Cooper, Edward Henry (1915–19); Sergeant, R.A.V.C.; France 2 years 8 months.

Cooper, Frederick Walter (1918–19); Private, R.A.S.C. (M.T.); Mesopotamia 4 months.

***Cooper, Harold William** (1915–17); Private, London Rgt.; France 1 month; Died of wounds, 6th January, 1917.

Cooper, John Verdon (1915–19); Rifleman, King's Royal Rifle Corps; France 2 years 2 months.

Cooper, Sidney Raikes (1915–19); Fitter, R.G.A.; France 3 years.

Cooper, Thomas George (1915–19); Gunner, R.F.A.; India 1 year 8 months, France 1 year 7 months.

Cooter, William Christopher (1914–19); 2nd Corporal, R.E.; France 4 years 5 months.

Copeland, Albert James (1914–19); Rifleman, Rifle Brigade; India 3 years 1 month.

Copeland, Frederick William (1915–17); Bombardier, R.F.A.; France 9 months.

Copeman, Henry John (1914–19); Wheeler Corporal, R.A.S.C.; France 4 years 1 month.

Copping, William (1915–16); Driver, R.F.A.; France 6 months.

Copsey, Charles George (1915–19); Corporal, R.A.S.C. (M.T.); Balkans 2 years 6 months.

Copsey, Henry John (1917–20); Pioneer, R.E.; France and Germany 2 years 3 months.

Copus, George William (1914–17); Private, R.D.C.; Mediterranean Expeditionary Force 15 months.

Cordell, James Samuel (1914–19); Rifleman, Rifle Brigade; India 3 years 9 months.

Cork, Herbert William (1914–19); Able Seaman, R.N.; Naval Service 4 years 6 months.

***Corkett, George Ernest** (1915–16); Sergeant, Rifle Brigade; France 6 months; Missing, 3rd September, 1916.

Corlett, Percy (1915–19); Staff Quartermaster-Sergeant, R.A.S.C.

Corne, Leonard (1916–19); Private, R. Welch Fusiliers; Salonica and Turkey 2 years 11 months.

Cornelius, Dick (1914–19); Lance-Corporal, R.E.; Egypt, Gallipoli and Malta, 4 years.

Cornford, William Henry (1914–19); Bombardier, R.G.A.

Cornish, Frederick (1915–18); Private, Middlesex Rgt.; France 17 months, Italy 3 months.

Cosgrove, Martin (1917); Private, Labour Corps.

Cossey, Theophilus (1917–19); Driver, R.A.S.C.; France 13 months.

Costello, Robert Joseph (1917–19); Corporal, Labour Corps.

***Coster, Arthur Edward** (1914–15); Corporal, Border Rgt.; France 5 months; Missing, 12th March, 1915.

Cotton, Charles Frederick William (1916–19); Private, R.A.M.C.

Counter, Sydney (1914–19); Chief Petty Officer, R.N.; Naval Service 3 years.

Court, Frederick Ernest (1918–19); Rifleman, Rifle Brigade; France 3 months.

Cousins, Alfred (1915–18); Lance-Corporal, R.E.; France 1 year 7 months.

Cousins, Edward Emanuel (1915–19); Sergeant, R.E.; France 3 years 8 months.

Cousins, William (1914–19); Private, R.D.C.

Coventon, Henry James (1914–17); Private, Middlesex Rgt.

***Coventry, Albert Edward** (1914–15); Private, R. Berkshire Rgt.; France 4 months; Killed in action, 27th November, 1915.

Coventry, Arthur Charles (1914–19); Private, Machine Gun Corps; France 3 years 3 months.

Covill, Frederick William (1915–19); Gunner, R.F.A.; France 2 years 2 months.

Cowdray, Stanley (1917–19); Corporal, R.A.F.

Cowland, Charles (1914–17); Sergeant, London Rgt.

Cowley, Arthur James (1918–19); Private, R. Sussex Rgt.; Germany 5 months.

Cox, Adrian George (1916–19); Private, Labour Corps; France 2 years 5 months.

***Cox, Albert** (1914–15); Private, Essex Rgt.; Dardanelles 1 month; Missing, 28th June, 1915.

Cox, Albert Bastow (1918–19); Private, Royal Fusiliers.

Cox, Alfred Robert (1917–19); Gunner, R.G.A.; France 14 months.

Cox, Arthur (1916–19); Private, King's Own Yorkshire Light Infantry; France 2 years.

Cox, Edward James (1915–19); Private, R.A.V.C.; France 3 years 5 months.

Cox, George (1914–16); Driver, R.F.A.; France 5 months.

***Cox, George** (1914–15); Lance-Corporal, R.W. Surrey Rgt.; France 4 months; Killed in action, 16th May, 1915.

Cox, Maurice (1918–19); Driver, R.F.A.

Cox, Reginald George (1916–19); Private, Worcestershire Rgt.; France 2 months.

Cox, Thomas (1914–18); M.C., Mentioned in despatches; Regimental Sergeant-Major, London Rgt.; France 2 years 6 months.

Cox, William Edward (1914–19); Sec.-Lieutenant, Tank Corps; France 1 year.

Crabb, John (1918–19); Lance-Corporal, R. Sussex Rgt.; France, Egypt and Palestine, 17 months.

Cradock, Henry John (1916–18); Rifleman, London Rgt.; France 6 months.

Cradock, Joseph John (1916–19); Private, S. Staffordshire Rgt.; France 13 months, prisoner of war 8 months.

Craker, Richard Frederick Joseph (1914–17); Private, 12th Lancers.

Cramer, George Richard (1915–19); Private, R.A.S.C. (M.T.); France 3 years 9 months.

Crane, William George (1914–15); Corporal, R. Irish Rgt.

Cranfield, Oliver (1915–19); Private, London Rgt.; Egypt 1 year, France 13 months, Salonica 6 months.

Craske, Edward Ernest (1916–19); Sapper, R.E.; Salonica 5 months, Egypt and Palestine 2 years 3 months.

Crawley, Daniel (1914–19); Gunner, R.H.A.; France and Salonica 4 years 2 months.

Crawley, William (1914–19); Private, W. Yorkshire Rgt.; France 3 years 5 months.

Creasey, Sydney John (1914–19); Lance-Corporal, Middlesex Rgt.; India and Mesopotamia 4 years 6 months.

Cressell, George (1916–18); Private, R.D.C.

Cresswell, Albert Edward (1915–19); Private, R.A.S.C. (M.T.); France 4 years 6 months.

Cresswell, William George Henry (1914–19); Sergeant, Machine Gun Corps; France 2 years 10 months.

Cripps, George (1914–19); Corporal, R.G.A.; Gallipoli, Salonica and Palestine, 3 years 9 months.

Crisp, Edwin (1914–19); Air Mechanic (1st Class), R.F.C.; France 1 year 9 months.

Crocker, Thomas Henry (1914–19); Private, E. Kent Rgt.; France 9 months, Egypt and Palestine 2 years 6 months.

***Cromarty, John** (1914–16); Private, R.D.C.; Accidentally killed, 6th May, 1916.

Crone, Edward (1917–19); Private, Labour Corps; France 1 year.

Crook, Charles William (1914–19); Private, London Rgt.; France 3 years 11 months.

Crook, David Martin (1915–19); Sapper, R.E.; Salonica 2 years 2 months.

Cross, Albert Edward Robert (1916–19); Driver, R.A.S.C.; France 17 months.

Cross, James Alfred (1918–19); Rifleman, Rifle Brigade; France 5 months.

Cross, William (1915–19); Private, R.A.S.C. (M.T.); France 3 years 9 months.

Crossley, George Henry (1915–19); 2nd Corporal, R.E.; France 3 months; Salonica 3 years 1 month.

Crossley, Robert Joshua Francis (1916–19): Corporal, R.E.; France 2 years 5 months.

Crossman, George Edward (1914–19); Gunner, R.F.A.; France 2 years 4 months, Salonica 16 months.

Crossman, John Charles (1914–19); Gunner, R.G.A.; France 4 years.

Crouch, Sydney Alfred (1914–19); Private, E. Surrey Rgt.; France 2 weeks, prisoner of war 4 years 4 months.

Crow, Arthur George (1914–19); Able Seaman, R.N.; Naval Service 4 years 7 months.

Crowe, Frederick Walter (1914–19); Lance-Corporal, Northumberland Fusiliers; France 2 weeks, prisoner of war 4 years 6 months.

Crowther, Robert (1915–19); Private, Yorkshire Rgt.; Dardanelles and France 4 years.

Crozier, James William (1915–18); Gunner, R.F.A.

Crumpler, George Victor (1914–19); Company Sergeant-Major, Dorsetshire Rgt.; France 3 years 7 months.

Cruse, George Thomas (1915–19); Bombardier, R.F.A.; Egypt 1 year 9 months, France 6 months, Salonica 6 months.

Cullen, Edwin Thomas (1916–18); Private, Labour Corps.

Cullen, Thomas (1918–20); Gunner, R.G.A.; Malta 17 months.

Cullender, Alfred John (1915–16); Rifleman, Rifle Brigade; France 5 months.

Culling, Albert Frederick (1914–19); Gunner, R.F.A.; France 3 months, Salonica 3 years 3 months.

Culmore, John Richard (1914–19); Private, 20th Hussars; France 2 years.

Culver, James Edward (1917–19); Private, R.A.M.C.; Salonica 11 months.

***Cummins, James Henry** (1915–18); Private, R. Scots Fusiliers; France 2 years 10 months; Died, 3rd November, 1918.

Curnick, Arthur Ernest (1917–19); Private, R.A.M.C.; Egypt 18 months.

Curry, Denis Patrick (1916–17); Private, Middlesex Rgt.

Curtis, William John (1917–19); Signaller, R.G.A.; France 2 months.

Curtis, William John (1917–19): Private, R.A.S.C. (M.T.); France and Germany 2 years 5 months.

Cusack, George Paul (1917–19); Blacksmith, R.N.

Cutbill, George Andrew (1915–19); Gunner, R.F.A.; France 3 years 6 months.

Cuthbert, William (1914–19); Sergeant, Middlesex Rgt.

***Cutler, Mark** (1914–16); Sergeant, Grenadier Guards; France 1 year 9 months; Killed in action, 6th May, 1916.

Cutting, James Alfred (1914–19); Private, London Rgt. and M.M.P.; Egypt 3 years 11 months.

Cutts, Edward D'Arcy (1915–19); Driver R.E.; France 3 years.

***Dacey, Michael** (1914–15); Driver, R.A.S.C.; Died, 1st May, 1915.

Dale, Henry John (1917–19); Private, R.A.M.C.

Dalton, Arthur Knowsley (1915–19); Company Quartermaster-Sergeant, R.E.

Dalton, William (1914–19); Sapper, R.E.; France 9 months.

Daly, Henry James (1916–19); Private, W. Yorkshire Rgt.; France 3 months, Malta 17 months.

Daly, James Francis (1914–19); Lance-Corporal, Royal Fusiliers; France 3 years 4 months.

Dance, Frank John (1914–19); Private, London Rgt.; France 1 year 10 months.

Daniels, Henry George (1914–19); Leading Stoker, R.N.; Naval Service.

Daniels, John William (1918–19); Signaller, R.F.A.

Daniels, Thomas John (1916–19); Private, R. Scots Fusiliers; France and Egypt 2 years 2 months.

Daniels, William (1918–19); Private, Royal Fusiliers; France 2 months.

Daniels, William Arthur Cook (1914–16); Rifleman, London Rgt.; France 18 months.

Dapling, Herbert Hawkins (1914–19); Private, E. Surrey Rgt.; India and Mesopotamia 3 years.

Darby, Arthur Thomas (1915–18); Gunner, R.F.A.; France 3 years 6 months.

Darch, Edward Isaac (1914–19); Guardsman, Coldstream Guards; France 3 years 5 months.

Dark, Albert Francis Martin (1914–19); Sergeant, Bedfordshire Rgt., and Officer Cadet; France 2 years.

***Darkens, Cecil Robert** (1916–17); Private, E. Surrey Rgt.; France 5 months; Killed in action, 14th March, 1917.

Darling, Clement Henry (1914–19); Staff-Sergeant, R.E.

Darwood, Ernest (1914–19); Private, R.A.S.C.; France 1 year 9 months.

Dauncey, William Joseph (1914–19); Sapper, R.E.; France 3 years 3 months, Italy 4 months.

***Davenport, Henry William Charles** (1914–18); Lance-Corporal, London Rgt.; India 2 years 9 months; Died, 13th November, 1918.

Davenport, Philip Sanders (1915–19); Corporal, R.A.S.C.

Davey, Arthur Edward William (1914–19); 2nd Corporal, R.E.; France and Salonica 4 years.

Davey, Henry (1914–18); Gunner, R.G.A.; France 1 year 8 months.

Davey, Sidney Alfred (1914–19); Private, R.A.F.

Davies, Albert Edward (1915–19); Private, R.A.M.C.; France 8 months.

Davies, Bertram (1916–19); Leading Aircraftsman, R.A.F.; France 2 months.

Davies, Charles John (1914–19); Sergeant, London Rgt.; France 4 years.

Davies, Ernest Haydn (1914–19); Mentioned in despatches; Sergeant, R.G.A.; Macedonia 2 years 4 months, Egypt 5 months, Gallipoli 3 months.

***Davies, Evan Joseph** (1915–16); Private, R. Welch Fusiliers; France 7 months; Killed in action, 10th July, 1916.

Davies, Leyston (1914–19); Lance-Corporal, M.F.P.; France 2 years 1 month.

Davis, Albert Henry (1915–19); Corporal, R.F.A.; France 2 years 1 month.

Davis, Alfred (1914); Private, Loyal N. Lancashire Rgt.

Davis, Benjamin Isaac (1915–18); Sergeant, Middlesex Rgt.; France 2 years 7 months.

Davis, Clifford (1915–16); Rifleman, 16th Bn. London Rgt.

Davis, Ernest Bell (1915–18); Private, Royal Fusiliers; German East Africa 3 years 3 months.

Davis, Frank (1915–19); Gunner, R.G.A.; France 2 years 4 months.

Davis, Gordon Frederick (1916–19); Aircraftsman (1st Class), R.A.F.; France 2 years 6 months.

Davis, James (1914–17); Gunner, R.F.A.; France and Salonica 1 year.

Davis, Joseph Henry (1914–19); Regimental Sergeant-Major, R. Berkshire Rgt.; France 5 months.

Davis, Wyndham (1916–19); Private, E. Yorkshire Rgt.; France 1 year.

Davis, William John Thomas (1918–19); Private, R.A.S.C. (M.T.); France 16 months.

***Davis, William Warren** (1914–15); Corporal, R.E.; France 5 months; Killed in action, 30th August, 1915.

Davy, Thomas William (1914–19); Private, Labour Corps; France and Dardanelles 4 years.

Dawe, Francis Frederick (1915–19); Corporal, R.A.S.C.; France 3 years 5 months.

Dawe, Percy Edward (1917–18); Private, Labour Corps.

Dawe, Walter (1915–19); Driver, R.A.S.C.; France 3 years 11 months.

***Dawes, Charles John** (1914–15); Private, National Reserve; Died, 27th October, 1915.

Dawes, Charles Walter (1915–19); Sergeant, R.G.A.; France 3 years 1 month.

Dawes, Sydney William (1914–19); Lance-Corporal, M.F.P.; France 3 years 5 months.

***Day, Frank** (1916–17); Sapper, R.E.; Died, 19th February, 1917.

Day, John Arthur (1915–19); Private, S. Staffordshire Rgt.; France 1 year.

Deacon, George Anthony (1915–19); Gunner, R.F.A.; France 3 years 3 months.

Deamer, George (1915–19); Private, Labour Corps; France 3 years 2 months.

Dean, Ernest Arney (1914–19); Sick Berth Reserve, R.N.; Naval Service 3 years 5 months.

Dean, George William (1918–19); Private, Machine Gun Corps Training Bn.

***Dean, Harry Hewer** (1917–18); Private, Machine Gun Corps; France 6 months; Died of wounds, 10th September, 1918.

Dean, John Aburrow (1918–19); Private, Royal Marine Light Infantry.

Dean, Thomas Abraham (1915–19); Private, London Rgt.

Deas, William (1914–19); Gunner, R.G.A.; France 2 years.

Deason, Ambrose Berry (1917–19); Private, King's Own Yorkshire Light Infantry; France 1 year 8 months.

Deavin, John Walter (1916–19); Rifleman, Rifle Brigade; France 1 year 8 months.

Deegan, Peter (1915–19); Private, R. Irish Rgt.; France, Salonica, Palestine and Egypt, 2 years 9 months.

Defer, Charles Edward (1914–19); D.C.M.; Sergeant, R.F.A.; France 3 years 6 months.

Delay, John Oliver (1914–19); Bombardier, R.F.A.; France, Italy and Germany, 3 years.

Deller, William James (1916–19); Sapper, R.E.; France 2 years 8 months.

Dempsey, John (1914–18); Private, Labour Corps; France 17 months.

Dench, Edwin George (1914–19); Private, Essex Rgt.; France 2 years 3 months.

Denison, Frederick Charles (1914–19); Driver, R.F.A.; France, Egypt and Palestine, 3 years 4 months.

Dennant, Albert Edward (1915–18); Private, Royal Fusiliers; France 11 months.

Dennant, Walter (1916–19); Gunner, R.G.A.; France 2 years 3 months.

Denney, William George (1914–16); Private, 18th Hussars.

Denning, William (1917–19); Private, Labour Corps; France and Germany 2 years 9 months.

Dennis, Frederick John (1916–19); Private, Durham Light Infantry; France 3 months.

Dennison, Harwood (1914–19); Corporal, Loyal N. Lancashire Rgt.; France 3 months, Prisoner of war 4 years.

Dent, William George (1914–19); Private, R.A.S.C. (M.T.): France 2 years.

Denton, Frederick Henry (1915–19); Lance-Corporal, R.E.; France and Mesopotamia 2 years 8 months.

Derry, Cornelius Philip (1914–16); Lance-Corporal, Royal Fusiliers; France 3 months.

Devereux, John (1914–19); Gunner, R.H.A.; France 3 years 6 months.

***Devis, Arthur Stanley** (1914–18); M.M.; Sergeant, Tank Corps; France 3 years 6 months; Missing, 29th September, 1918.

Dewar, Albert Edward (1914–19); Squadron Sergeant-Major, R.A.S.C. (Remounts): Palestine 7 months, Egypt 9 months, Salonica 1 year 8 months.

De Witt, Ferdinand (1914–19); Captain, R.F.A.; France 2 years.

Dibbs, John Edward (1914–19); Stoker (1st Class), R.N.; Naval Service.

Dick, John (1915–19); Private, King's Own R. Lancaster Rgt.; France 3 years 10 months.

***Dickens, William George** (1914–15); Private, London Rgt.; France 2 months; Killed in action, 9th May, 1915.

Dickenson, George Noel (1915–18); Sergeant-Mechanic, R.N.A.S. and R.A.F.; Naval Service 17 months.

Dickenson, James Alfred (1916–19); Gunner, R.F.A.; Mesopotamia 1 year 8 months.

Dickson, James (1914–18); M.M.; Lance-Sergeant, Coldstream Guards; France.

Diggens, Albert Edward (1914); Driver, R.F.A.

Dimon, Harold Vincent William (1915–19); M.M.; Corporal, R.F.A.; France 2 years 1 month.

Dingley, Henry James (1917–19); Corporal, Labour Corps; France 2 years.

Dinsdale, William (1915–19); Private, Bedfordshire Rgt.; France 3 years 4 months.

Diplock, David (1914–19); Staff-Sergeant, R.F.A.; France 2 years 5 months.

Diplock, John Henry (1914–19); Sergeant, R.A.S.C. (M.T.); France 3 years 4 months.

Dipper, James (1914–19); Gunner, R.F.A.; France 10 months.

Dobby, Ernest (1914–19); Able Seaman, R.N.; Naval Service 4 years.

Doble, Evan Frederick (1914–19); Corporal, R.E.; France 3 years 5 months.

Dobson, Austin Wilsdon (1914–19); Driver, R.A.S.C.; Palestine, France and Salonica, 3 years.

Dobson, William (1918–19); Rifleman, Rifle Brigade; France 5 months.

Dodson, Charles William (1916–19); Driver, R.F.A.; Mesopotamia 2 years 8 months.

Doe, Alfred John (1916–18); Private, Labour Corps; France 15 months.

***Doherty, Edward Henry** (1916–17); Private, Durham Light Infantry; Salonica 8 months; Died, 25th August, 1917.

Doidge, Edwin (1915–19); Gunner, R.F.A.; France 2 years.

Dolling, Charles Samuel (1916–19); Private, Hertfordshire Rgt.; France 1 year.

Dolling, James Frederick (1915–19); Sergeant-Wheeler, R. Naval Division; Greece 3 months, France 2 years 10 months.

Dolton, Wilfred Charles (1915–19); Bombardier, R.F.A.; France 3 years 3 months.

Donohoe, James (1914–18); Private, Irish Guards; France 1 year 10 months.

***Doolin, Michael** (1915–16); Private, R. Munster Fusiliers; Dardanelles and France 8 months; Missing, 25th June, 1916.

Doolin, Stephen (1914–19); Driver, R.F.A.; France 3 years 6 months.

Dorman, Fred (1915–19); Gunner, R.G.A.; France 2 years 5 months.

***Dormon, George** (1915–16); Corporal, Hampshire Rgt.; Dardanelles and France 13 months; Killed in action, 9th August, 1916.

Dorset, Albert William (1916–19); Private, Labour Corps; France 2 years.

Dorsett, Stanley William (1917–19); Private, Royal Fusiliers; France 1 year 7 months.

Dossett, Ralph Ernest (1915–19); Private, R.A.S.C.; France 3 years 9 months.

Doughty, Frederick Augustus (1914–19); Company Quartermaster-Sergeant, R.E.; France 11 months.

Dove, Thomas (1914–19); Able Seaman, R.N.; Naval Service 4 years 6 months.

Dowling, Harry Thomas (1914–15); Driver, R.H.A.; France 13 months.

Dowling, James (1914–19); Sergeant, Oxfordshire and Buckinghamshire Light Infantry; France 3 years 6 months.

Dowse, Alfred Thomas (1915–19); Private, Middlesex Rgt.; France 2 months, Salonica 3 years 4 months.

Doyle, John (1915–19); Private, R.A.S.C.

Doyle, Patrick (1916–19); Private, R.F.C.

Doyle, Thomas (1915–19); Sapper, R.E.; France and Macedonia 3 years 9 months.

Drain, William John (1915–19); Lance-Sergeant, Royal Fusiliers; France 1 year 7 months.

Drake, Charles William Henry (1915–17); Private, R.D.C.

Drane, James (1914–19); Private, Essex Rgt.; France 1 year, India 4 years.

Drew, Howard Willis (1916–19); Rifleman, London Rgt.; France 7 months.

***Drewett, Frank Frederick** (1916–18); Private, R.W. Surrey Rgt.; France 6 months; Killed in action, 23rd March, 1918.

***Drewett, Henry William** (1916–18); Private, Hampshire Rgt.; France 7 months; Killed in action, 20th July, 1918.

Drewry, Harry Smith (1915–19); Staff-Sergeant, R.A.S.C.

Driscoll, James (1914–19); Private, Duke of Cornwall's Light Infantry; France 4 years 2 months.

Driver, William Lawrence (1915–17); Lance-Corporal, London Rgt.

Duce, George Alfred (1916–19); Corporal, R.A.O.C.

Ducker, Albert James (1914–19); Private, E. Surrey Rgt.; France and Italy 1 year 8 months.

Ducker, William George (1914–19); Private, Lincolnshire Rgt.; France 3 months, prisoner of war (Germany) 4 years.

Dudley, Christopher George (1914–19); Driver, R.G.A.; France 3 years.

Duffell, George Walter Herbert (1914–16); Gunner, R.F.A.; India and Burmah 17 months.

***Duggan, Cornelius** (1915–17); Lance-Corporal, Rifle Brigade; France 7 months; Killed in action, 28th July, 1917.

Dulieu, William (1914–19); Gunner, R.G.A.; France 2 years.

Dummer, William (1916–19); Private, Middlesex Rgt.; France 16 months.

Dunbar, Samuel Stuart (1914–19); Sergeant, Labour Corps.

Duncan, John Henry (1914–19); Private, Royal Fusiliers; France 4 years.

***Duncton, Sidney Valentine** (1915–18); Private, Royal Fusiliers; France 18 months; Killed in action, 15th June, 1918.

Dunford, Frederick Charles (1915–19); Driver, R.F.A.; France 3 years 1 month.

Dunlop, William Robert (1914–19); Sergeant, Rifle Brigade; India 3 years 2 months.

Dunn, Amos (1914–19); Sick Berth Steward, R.N.; Naval Service 2 years 10 months.

Dunn, Edward George (1914–19); Private, Northamptonshire Rgt.; France and Germany 4 years 6 months.

Dunn, James (1914–16); Driver, R.A.S.C. (M.T.).

***Dunning, Bernard Allen Miller** (1914–18); Driver, R.E.; France 9 months, Mesopotamia 13 months; Died, 6th December, 1918.

Dunsdon, William John (1915–19); Driver, R.F.A.; Italy, France and Germany, 2 years 8 months.

Durant, Edwin Charles (1914–19); Private, R.A.S.C. (M.T.); France 4 years 2 months.

Durnsford, William James (1915–19); Lance-Corporal, R.A.S.C.

Dutch, George William (1914–19); Private, Royal Fusiliers; France 4 years 1 month.

Dyer, Edward (1915–19); Fitter, Wiltshire Rgt.

***Dyer, Thomas Edward** (1914–17); Rifleman, King's Royal Rifle Corps; France 2 years; Killed in action, 1st June, 1917.

Eades, Alfred (1918); Private, R.A.S.C. (M.T.); France 4 months.

Eades, Edwin (1917–18); Private, Labour Corps; France 16 months.

Eagle, Charles Alfred George (1915–19); Driver, R.F.A.; France 3 years 5 months.

Eagle, James (1917–19); Leading Aircraftsman, R.A.F.; France and Germany 2 years 5 months.

Earwaker, Robert (1918–19); Private, R. Sussex Rgt.; France and Germany 6 months.

Eastaugh, Henry George (1914–19); Lance-Corporal, London Rgt.; France 1 year 9 months.

Easterbrook, Edward (1914–19); Rifleman, Rifle Brigade; France 2 years 11 months.

Eastlake, Frederick (1914–19); Sergeant, R.F.A.; France 4 years 4 months.

Eaton, Alfred (1918–19); Private, R.A.S.C. (M.T.); France 5 months.

Eaton, George Thurner (1916–19); Private, Labour Corps; France 2 years 6 months.

***Eaves, Thomas** (1914–17); M.M.; Sergeant, Suffolk Rgt.; France 2 years; Killed in action, 12th October, 1917.

Edis, Joseph Edward (1914–19); Private, Royal Dragoons; France 4 years 6 months.

Edward, Harold Arthur (1915–19); Gunner, R.F.A.; France, Salonica and Egypt, 3 years.

Edwards, Cecil Frederick (1918–19); Lance-Corporal, Rifle Brigade.

***Edwards, Charles Horace** (1915–16); Private, Royal Fusiliers; Dardanelles 2 months, France 5 months; Missing, 7th July, 1916.

Edwards, Ernest Albert (1915–19); Lance-Corporal, R. Welch Fusiliers; France 4 years.

Edwards, Harold John (1915–19); Gunner, R.F.A.; France 3 years 8 months.

Edwards, Horace (1915–19); Corporal, Lancashire Fusiliers; France 3 months.

Edwards, Joseph (1916–19); Private, Royal Fusiliers; France 1 year.

***Edwards, Philip Henry** (1916); Rifleman, Rifle Brigade; France 4 months; Killed in action, 3rd September, 1916.

Edwards, Thomas Llewellyn (1917–19); Signaller, Scottish Horse.

Edwards, Warwick Henry (1914–18); Rifleman, London Rgt.; France.

Edwards, William John (1916–19); Private, Bedfordshire Rgt.; India 2 years.

Egan, Edward (1914–19); Private, R.A.S.C.; France 3 years 8 months.

Egan, Frank Herbert (1917–20); Private, R.A.O.C.; Salonica 4 months, Constantinople 1 year.

Eldridge, John William (1914–19); Private, Dorsetshire Rgt.; France 1 month, Prisoner of war (Germany) 4 years 2 months.

Element, Alfred George (1914–17); Private, Labour Corps; France 1 year 10 months.

Ellen, Michael Edward (1915–19); Gunner R.F.A.; Egypt, Palestine, France and Salonica, 3 years.

Ellicott, Herbert Edward (1915–19); Lance-Corporal, R.A.S.C.; France 3 years 10 months.

***Elliott, Frederick Edward** (1918); Private, Middlesex Rgt.; France 1 month; Died of wounds, 6th November, 1918.

Elliott, Gerald (1915–19); Quartermaster-Sergeant, R.A.M.C.; India and Mesopotamia 2 years 4 months.

***Elliott, Richard** (1914–16); Lance-Corporal, Royal Fusiliers; France 13 months; Missing, 7th July, 1916.

Ellis, Alfred Edwin (1914–17); Sergeant, Royal Scots; France 2 years 9 months.

Ellis, Edwin William (1915–19); Saddler, R.F.A.; France and Germany 3 years 10 months.

Ellis, Henry William (1915–19); Lance-Corporal, R.A.S.C. (M.T.); France 3 years 9 months.

Ellis, Lawrence Alfred (1914–19); Gunner, R.F.A.; France 3 months, Salonica 3 years 6 months.

Ellis, Leslie Charles (1917–19); Able Seaman, R.N.; Naval Service 1 year 6 months.

Ellis, Thomas (1914–19); Private, R. Naval Division; France 2 years.

Ellis, Thomas Walter (1914–19); Corporal, Royal Fusiliers; France 3 years 8 months.

Ellis, William (1914–19); Lance-Corporal, Labour Corps; France 10 months.

Ellis, William John (1914–19); Sergeant, A.P.C.

Ellmers, Joseph Albert (1914–19); Bombardier, R.H.A.; Egypt and France 3 years.

***Ellner, William Thomas** (1914–15); Private, Royal Fusiliers; France 1 month; Missing, 24th May, 1915.

Elsey, William (1914–19); Sergeant, Middlesex Rgt.; France 8 months.

Ely, William (1914–19); Driver, R.A.S.C.; France 4 years 6 months.

Emery, Albert Edward (1914–19); Gunner, R.G.A.; France 2 years 10 months, India 15 months.

Emmett, George (1914–15); Private, S. Lancashire Rgt.; France 18 months.

Emons, Albert Thomas (1914–19); Private, Royal Fusiliers; France 3 years 6 months.

Emons, Walter (1914–18); Private, Cambridgeshire Rgt.

Englefield, Charles Frederick (1916–19); Rifleman, Rifle Brigade; France 2 years 6 months.

English, Albert (1914–19); Gunner, R.G.A.; German East Africa 1 year 9 months, France 13 months.

English, Robert Edward (1914–16); Horsekeeper, R.A.V.C.

English, Walter Charles (1914–19); Bombardier, R.F.A.; France and Salonica 4 years 7 months.

Enness, William (1915–19); Private, R.A.S.C.; France 3 years 6 months.

Epps, Henry William (1914–18); Blacksmith, R.E.; Dardanelles and Egypt 1 year.

Evans, Albert (1915–17); Private, Lincolnshire Rgt.

Evans, Albert Douglas (1917–19); Sapper, R.E.; France 2 years 1 month.

Evans, Charles Edward (1916–19); Driver, R.A.S.C.

Evans, Claude George (1916–18); Gunner, R.F.A.

Evans, Ernest George (1915–17); Bombardier, R.F.A.

Evans, Frank (1916–18); Rifleman, London Rgt.; France 8 months.

Evans, George William (1917–18); Rifleman, London Rgt.; France 9 months.

Evans, Oliver Samuel Harold (1915–17); Sapper, R.E.

Everett, Harold (1914–19); M.M.; Sergeant, Surrey Yeomanry; France and Salonica 4 years 2 months.

***Everett, John George** (1914–15); Able Seaman, R.N.; Naval Service; Killed in action, 25th April, 1915.

Everitt, James (1914–19); Lance-Sergeant, Leicestershire Rgt.; France 6 months.

***Everitt, Walter** (1914–15); Private, Dragoon Guards; France 9 months; Killed in action, 24th May, 1915.

Ewen, John (1914–19); Sergeant, R.A.S.C. (M.T.); Malta, France and Italy, 3 years 6 months.

Fairall, Herbert James (1914–19); Sergeant, Oxfordshire and Buckinghamshire Light Infantry; India 3 years 3 months.

Fairey, Walter Charles (1915–17); Guardsman, Coldstream Guards.

Fairhead, Henry (1914–15); Private, R.W. Surrey Rgt.

Fairhead, William (1915–19); Sergeant, R. Welch Fusiliers; France 6 months.

Fallaize, Ernest Alfred (1917–19); Private, Labour Corps.

Farebrother, Walter George (1914–15); Gunner, R.F.A.

Farmer, Albert (1914–16); Private, Essex Rgt.; France.

Farmer, Alfred Ernest (1915–19); Sapper, R.E.; Gallipoli 6 months, Mesopotamia 3 years.

Farmer, William Arthur (1914–18); Private, R.D.C.

Farmer, William Joseph (1915–19); Gunner, R.F.A.; France, Salonica and Palestine, 2 years 9 months.

Farr, Frederick (1916–19); Private, Lancashire Fusiliers; France 14 months.

Farrell, John Isaac (1914–18); Rifleman, Rifle Brigade; France.

Farrell, William (1914–15); Private, Essex Rgt.

Farrell, William Henry (1916–19); Private, Middlesex Rgt.; France 2 years 5 months.

Farrington, James Gregory (1915–19); Private, Essex Rgt.; France 15 months, Prisoner of war (Germany) 8 months.

Farrow, William (1916–17); Private, Labour Corps.

***Fasham, Stephen Leonard** (1916–17); Private, London Rgt.; France 4 months; Killed in action, 16th June, 1917.

Faulkner, William Henry (1914–15); Driver, R.A.S.C.

Feldwick, Albert Ernest (1914–19); Private, London Rgt.

Fellingham, Ernest Henry (1914–19); Corporal, R.F.A.; France 13 months.

Felton, Thomas Albert (1915–19); Private, R.A.S.C.; France 4 years.

Felton, William Henry (1915–19); Corporal, R.A.F.

Fenney, Henry James (1914–18); Leading Seaman, R.N.; Naval Service 3 years 11 months.

Fentiman, Frank Latter (1914–19); Gunner, R.F.A.; France 3 years 6 months.

***Ferry, William Henry** (1914–15); Private, Northamptonshire Rgt.; France 8 months; Killed in action, 9th May, 1915.

Feuell, Alfred Ernest (1917–19); Gunner, R.G.A.; France 15 months.

Few, Thomas (1915–19); Private, R.A.M.C.; France 7 months.

Fewkes, Frederick William (1917–19); Gunner, R.G.A.

Fewtrell, John Charles (1914–19); Sergeant, R.D.C.

Field, Albert Edward (1915–18); Private, Royal Fusiliers; France 11 months.

***Field, Frederick Henry** (1914); Able Seaman, R.F.R.; Naval Service; Killed at sea, 1st November, 1914.

Field, William (1916–19); Private, Nottinghamshire and Derbyshire Rgt.; Egypt 1 year.

Fielder, Edward Joseph (1915–19); Pioneer, R.E.; German East Africa 2 years.

Fielding, Arthur James (1915–17); Rifleman, Rifle Brigade; France 8 months.

***Filbee, William John** (1914–15); Private, Royal Fusiliers; Dardanelles 4 months; Died of wounds, 4th November, 1915.

Fillery, Eldred George (1914–19); Battery Quartermaster - Sergeant, R.F.A.; France 3 years 9 months.

Fillis, James (1914–19); Private, R.W. Surrey Rgt.; France and India 4 years 5 months.

Filmer, Stanley Josiah Corti (1916–19); Private, London Rgt.; France.

Finch, Frank (1914–19); Private, R.A.S.C.; France 4 years 4 months.

Finch, George (1914–19); Lance-Corporal, Labour Corps.

Finch, Henry Victor (1918–19); Rifleman, King's Royal Rifle Corps.

***Finnessy, Edward Peter** (1914–16); Bombardier, R.H.A.; France 2 years; Killed in action, 7th September, 1916.

Finnis, Henry (1914–19); Driver, R.E.; France 2 years 6 months.

Fisher, Albert Edward (1915–19); Driver, R.F.A.

Fisher, Arthur William (1914–19); Sergeant, E. Kent Rgt.; France 3 years 6 months.

Fisher, George Henry (1914–15); Driver, R.A.S.C.; France 7 months.

Fisher, Tom (1914–19); Private, Royal Marine Light Infantry; Naval Service 3 years 9 months.

Fisk, George Edward (1915–19); Sergeant, R.F.A.; France 2 years 1 month.

Fisk, Herbert Arthur (1918–19); Private, R. Sussex Rgt.; France and Germany 5 months.

Fiske, James (1915–19); Driver, R.E.

Fitch, Charles Hardwick (1916–19); Private, Nottinghamshire and Derbyshire Rgt.; Egypt 1 year.

Fitzpatrick, Francis Joseph (1918–19); Ordinary Seaman, R.N.V.R.

Flack, Edwin (1918–19); Private, R. Sussex Rgt.; France 5 months.

Fleck, Ronald Frederick (1914–19); Bombardier, R.F.A.; France and Salonica 3 years 10 months.

Fleming, Edgar John (1914–15); Private, Border Rgt.; France 6 months.

Flemming James (1914–15); Gunner, R.G.A.

Fletcher, Harvey Harold (1916–19); Private, Derbyshire Yeomanry.

Fletcher, William John (1914–19); Petty Officer, R.N.; Naval Service 3 years 8 months.

Flood, Arthur Frederick (1914–19); Gunner, R.F.A.; France and Salonica 3 years.

Flynn, William (1916–19); Rifleman, Rifle Brigade; France 2 years 8 months.

Foale, Charles Edward (1915–19); Private, R.A.S.C.; France 4 years.

Foden, Albert Charles (1914–19); Sergeant, M.M.P.; France 3 years, Italy 1 year.

Fogarty, Patrick (1915–19); Private, R. Irish Rgt.; France, Salonica and Palestine, 2 years 9 months.

Fogg, Harry (1914–19); Driver, R.F.A.; France and Salonica 3 years 6 months.

Foord, George Edmund (1914–17); Private, R.D.C.

Foote, Walter George (1916–19); Private, Labour Corps; France 2 years 6 months.

Ford, Albert Francis (1916–19); Private, Labour Corps.

Ford, Benjamin (1917–19); Pioneer, R.E.; France and Germany 2 years 4 months.

Ford, John (1914–19); Corporal, Machine Gun Corps; France 4 years.

***Ford, Patrick** (1914–18); Lance-Corporal, R. Dublin Fusiliers; Gallipoli 3 months, France 11 months; Missing, 21st–29th March, 1918.

Ford, Percy William (1915–19); Gunner, R.F.A.; France and Germany 3 years 8 months.

Forde, James (1914–19); Sergeant, Bedfordshire Rgt.; France 2 years, Prisoner of war (Germany) 18 months.

Fordyce, Stewart Melville (1916–18); Officers' Steward (2nd Class), R.N.; Naval Service 1 year 8 months.

Foreman, Thomas (1914–19); Rifleman, Rifle Brigade; Burmah 3 years 4 months.

Forester, Ernest (1915–19); Private, R.A.S.C.; France 3 years 6 months.

Forman, Francis James (1915–19); Private, Essex Rgt.; France, Salonica and Egypt, 2 years 8 months.

***Forse, Albert** (1914–15); Private, London Rgt.; France 2 months; Died of wounds, 10th May, 1915.

***Forse, William Frederick John** (1914); Private, R. Marine Reserve; Belgium; Killed in action, 9th October, 1914.

Forster, Richard Stanley (1917–19); Aircraftsman (1st Class), R.A.F.; France 17 months.

Forster, William (1915–19); Private, R.A.M.C.; France and Germany 3 years 9 months.

Forward, Richard French (1918–19); Aircraftsman (2nd Class), R.A.F.

Forward, Robert George (1915–19); Private, Tank Corps; France 2 years 7 months.

Foskett, Frederick (1917–19); Private, R.A.V.C.; France 1 year 9 months.

***Foss, Thomas** (1914); Private, R. Inniskilling Fusiliers; France 2 months; Killed in action, 7th November, 1914.

Fossey, Augustus Frederick (1915–19); Private, Gordon Highlanders; France 4 years.

Foster, Frederick (1915–19); Gunner, R.F.A.; Salonica 2 years 11 months.

Foster, William (1914–19); Private, London Rgt.; Gallipoli 8 days, Egypt 3 years 1 month.

Fountain, Charles William (1915–17); Private, E. Kent Rgt.; France and Prisoner of war (Germany) 2 years 5 months.

Fovarque, Frederick (1914–19); Private, R.A.S.C.; France and Germany 4 years 6 months.

Fowler, Frank Lionel (1916–19); Driver, R.A.S.C.

Fowler, William Joseph (1918–19); Private, R. Sussex Rgt.; France 3 months.

Fowles, William (1914–16 and 1917–18); Driver, R.F.A. and R.H.A.; France 10 months.

Fox, Edward James (1914–17); Rifleman, London Rgt.

Fox, John (1915–19); Sapper, R.E.; France 3 years 4 months.

***Fox, Thomas Edward** (1914–18); Lance-Corporal, Cameronians; France 3 years 7 months; Died of wounds, 13th March, 1918.

Foxwell, William John (1914–17); Private, E. Surrey Rgt. and Labour Corps.

***Foy, Leonard** (1914–15); Private, London Rgt.; France 4 months; Died of wounds, 5th April, 1915.

***Frame, Douglas Alexander** (1914–16); Gunner, Royal Marine Artillery; Naval Service; Died, 9th September, 1916.

Francis, Thomas Henry (1914–17); Private, Labour Corps; France 1 year.

Francis, William Hammond (1914–19); Stoker, R.N.; Egypt 3 years.

Franklin, Albert (1915–19); Corporal, R.A.S.C.; France 3 years 7 months.

Franklin, Edward George (1914–19); D.C.M.; Company Sergeant-Major, Bedfordshire Rgt.; France 2 years 8 months.

Franklin, Henry (1914–19); Private, Labour Corps; France 2 years 4 months.

Franklin, Sidney John (1915–19); 2nd Corporal, R.E.; Egypt, France, Italy and Germany, 4 years.

Franks, Bertram (1914–19); Corporal, R.E.; France 18 months.

Fraser, Donald George (1916–19); Private, R.A.S.C.; Egypt and Palestine 3 years.

Fraser, Frederick Charles (1915–19); Sergeant, R.A.M.C.; France 3 years 10 months.

Freeman, Charles Edward (1914–18); Private, Labour Corps; France and Prisoner of war (Germany) 2 years 6 months.

Freeman, Edwin James (1914); Private, R.W. Kent Rgt.

Freeman, William Dudley (1915–19); Private, R.A.V.C.; France 3 years 9 months.

French, Albert (1915–19); Sapper, R.E.; France 3 years 4 months.

French, Charles George William (1915–19); Driver, R.A.S.C.; France 3 years 6 months.

French, Edward (1916–17); Rifleman, Rifle Brigade; France 7 months.

French, Frederick (1915–19); Private, R.A.M.C.; France and Germany 2 years.

French, William Ernest Alexander (1914–15); Private, R.A.M.C.

Freshwater, Henry John (1916–19); Sapper, R.E.; France 2 years 5 months.

Frith, George Ernest (1914–17); Lance-Corporal, Training Reserve Bn.

Frost, George Henry (1915–19); Private, Labour Corps; France 2 years 9 months.

Fry, Alexander Edwin (1916–19); Sergeant, Labour Corps; France 3 years 3 months.

Fry, Frederick James (1914–16); Private, London Rgt.

Fry, Henry (1914–19); Shoeing-Smith, R.F.A.; France 3 years 6 months.

Fuller, Charles (1914–19); Corporal, Rifle Brigade; Mediterranean Expeditionary Force 1 year 11 months.

Fuller, Ernest Harry (1916–19); Private, Labour Corps; France 9 months.

***Fuller, Harry** (1914–15); Private, N. Staffordshire Rgt.; France 8 months; Died of wounds, 30th July, 1915.

Fuller, Harry (1914–19); Corporal, Rifle Brigade; Egypt 2 years 1 month.

Fuller, Harry Richard (1916–19); Sergeant, R.G.A.; France 2 years 2 months.

Fuller, Walter (1914–19); Lance-Corporal, R.A.M.C.; France and Malta 4 years.

Furzman, James (1914–19); Sergeant, R.A.V.C.; France 4 years 5 months.

Gabbitas, Albert Palmer (1915–19); Private, Machine Gun Corps; France 2 years 10 months.

***Gaiger, Arthur Alfred** (1914); Able Seaman, R.F.R.; Killed at sea, 22nd September, 1914.

Gailer, Albert Ernest (1915–19); Private, Royal Fusiliers; France and Germany 16 months.

Gains, Charles (1918–19); Gunner, R.G.A.; France 1 month.

Gallard, Henry Thomas George (1914–19); Bombardier, R.F.A.; France 2 years 9 months.

Gallo, Frederick John (1914–19); Corporal, Dragoon Guards; France 1 year.

Galvin, George (1918–19); Private, R.W. Surrey Rgt.; Italy 4 months.

Galvin, John St. Valentine (1914–19); Private, London Rgt.; France 1 year 9 months.

Gambie, William Harold (1918–19); Telegraphist, R.N.V.R.; Naval Service 11 months.

Game, Charles Henry (1917–19); Private, R.A.M.C.; France 1 year 8 months.

Ganney, Herbert Christian (1915–19); Driver, Tank Corps; France 3 years.

Gant, Frederick Herbert (1917–19); Private, Norfolk Rgt.; France 6 months.

Gardner, Alfred (1915–19); Lance-Corporal, M.F.P.; France 3 years 6 months.

Gardner, Percy Lawrance (1916–19); Corporal, E. Surrey Rgt.; France 5 months.

Gardner, Thomas (1914 and 1915–16); Private, Middlesex Rgt. and R.W. Kent Rgt.; France 3 months.

Garnham, Ernest Richard (1916–19); Private, R.A.M.C.; Egypt 1 year 10 months.

Garnsey, Herbert (1915–19); Corporal, R.E.; France 3 years 3 months.

Garwood, John Powley (1914–19); Lance-Corporal, King's Royal Rifle Corps; France 3 months, Prisoner of war (Germany) 3 years 4 months.

Gascoyne, John David (1914–19); Chief Boatswain, R.N.; Naval Service 3 years 9 months.

Gasworthy, Albert Victor (1918–20); Private, County of London Yeomanry; Palestine 11 months.

Gatti, Joseph (1916); Private, R.D.C.

Gatward, George William (1915–19); Gunner, R.F.A.; France 18 months.

Gay, Frank (1918–19); Private, R. Sussex Rgt.; France and Germany 6 months.

Gay, John Roberts Redvers (1918); Cadet, R.A.F.

Gaymer, John (1914–19); Guardsman, Grenadier Guards; France 4 years.

***Gaywood, George Albert** (1914–16); Private, Machine Gun Corps; France 17 months; Killed in action, 8th October, 1916.

Geary, Francis John (1917–19); Sergeant, R.G.A.

***Gebbett, Jesse** (1916–18); Private, Northumberland Fusiliers; France 1 year; Killed in action, 29th March, 1918.

George, James John (1915–19); Private, Labour Corps.

George, Maurice Arthur (1916–19); Sergeant, Labour Corps; France 2 years 6 months.

Gibbons, Harry James Harold (1915–17); Gunner, R.F.A.

Giggins, Frederick John (1915–19); Private, London Rgt.; France 10 months, Salonica 6 months, Egypt and Palestine 14 months.

Gilbert, Percy Wilfred (1914); Rifleman, London Rgt.

Gilder, Alfred Edward (1914–19); Sergeant, Dragoon Guards.

Giles, Herbert John (1914–17); Private, R.D.C.

Giles, Herbert William (1918–19); Rifleman, Rifle Brigade; France 8 months.

Gilks, George Henry (1914–19); Corporal, R.F.A.; France 3 years 6 months.

Gillanders, David (1914–19); Private, R. Sussex Rgt.; France 2 years.

Gillard, Albert Francis (1917–19); Private, Labour Corps; France 2 years.

Gillett, Arthur Herbert (1917–18); Private, Labour Corps.

Gillett, Charles Alfred (1917–19); Private, R.A.S.C.

Gillingham, George (1916–19); Private, Royal Fusiliers; France 2 years 9 months.

Gillson, Bernard (1914–19); Lance-Bombardier, R.F.A.; France 5 months, Salonica 7 months, Egypt 2 years.

Gilmour, Albert (1914–19); Sergeant, 19th Hussars; France 4 years 5 months.

Gilmour, James (1914–19); Lance-Corporal, London Rgt.; France 4 years.

Gilroy, Horace Harding (1916–19); Private, Labour Corps; France 2 years.

***Gilroy, John James** (1914–17); Private, R.A.M.C.; France 3 years 1 month; Died of wounds, 19th October, 1917.

Gimble, Edward (1914–17); Albert Medal (2nd Class); Private, Middlesex Rgt.; France.

Gimson, Stanley George (1914–17); Lance-Corporal, Royal Fusiliers.

Gipson, William George (1917–19); Private, Worcestershire Rgt.

Gladdy, Charles William (1915–19); Lance-Corporal, King's Liverpool Rgt.; France and Germany 3 years 2 months.

Glass, Henry Sidney (1916–19); Private, Labour Corps; France 2 years 5 months.

Glasscock, Albert William (1918–19); Private, E. Surrey Rgt.; France 1 month.

Glazebrook, Alfred Ellis (1915–19); Gunner, R.F.A.; France 3 years 1 month.

Glen, George (1914–19); Private, Royal Scots; France, Italy and Salonica, 3 years 8 months.

Glen, William John (1915–18); Gunner, R.F.A.; France 2 years 1 month.

Glennon, Matthew (1914 and 1915–19); Private, R.A.S.C.; France and Germany 4 years.

Glover, Alfred Leonard (1915–19); Driver, R.A.S.C.; France 2 years 3 months.

Glue, William Theodore (1915–19); Company Quartermaster-Sergeant, London Rgt.; France 2 years.

Gobey, Edward Joel (1914–19); Private, Labour Corps; Gallipoli and France 15 months.

Goddard, Charles Richard (1914–19); M.M.; Sergeant, R.E.; France 4 years 2 months.

Goddard, Ernest William (1915–17); Gunner, R.G.A.

Goddard, Frederick James (1915–19); Corporal, R.F.A.; France 3 years 4 months.

Goddard, George (1915–19); Lance-Corporal, R.A.S.C.; France 3 years.

***Goddard, William Edward** (1915–17); Gunner, R.F.A.; France 17 months; Died of wounds, 29th August, 1917.

Goddard, William James (1915–19); Private, Royal Fusiliers; France 2 years.

Godden, Charles William (1916–19); Private, Labour Corps.

Godfrey, James Henry (1914–19); Bandsman, London Rgt.; France, Salonica and Egypt, 3 years.

Godfrey, Reginald Jack (1915–19); Sergeant, R.A.F.; France 3 years 1 month.

Godfrey, Sidney James (1918–19); Private, R. Sussex Rgt.; France 6 months.

Godsiff, Albert Victor (1915–19); Stoker, R.N.; Naval Service 3 years.

Godsmark, Edward Stephen (1915–19); Battery Quartermaster-Sergeant, R.F.A.; France 2 years 6 months.

Godwin, Frederick Charles (1914–17); Private, 16th Lancers; France 2 years 5 months.

Godwin, Herbert (1915–17); Trooper, Surrey Yeomanry.

Goff, Bartholomew (1916–19); Gunner, R.G.A.; France 2 years 8 months.

Golden, John (1915–19); M.M. and bar; Sergeant, R.A.M.C.; France 4 years.

Goldsmith, William (1916–19); Private, Labour Corps.

Goldspink, Bert Frank (1917–19); Private, Royal Scots; Russia 10 months.

Gooch, Alfred James (1918–19); Private, R. Sussex Rgt.; France 6 months.

Gooch, Maurice Alfred (1918–19); Private, R.W. Surrey Rgt.

***Good, Sidney Charles** (1914); Private, Dragoon Guards; France; Died of wounds, 2nd October, 1914.

Good, Walter Henry (1915–19); Private, Welsh Rgt.; Egypt 3 months, Salonica 2 years 9 months.

Goodchild, John Alfred (1914–19); Private, M.M.P.; France 4 years 8 months.

Goode, Isaac (1915–17); Private, R.A.S.C.; France 2 years.

Goodridge, Thomas (1914–16); Able Seaman, R.F.R.; Naval Service 18 months.

Goodsell, Walter William (1914–17); Stoker, R.N.; Naval Service 3 years 2 months.

Goodwin, Arthur Edward (1915–19); Sergeant, R.E.; France 16 months.

Goodwin, Edward (1915–19); M.M.; Sergeant, R.G.A.; France 3 years.

***Goodwin, John Alfred** (1914); Driver, R.F.A.; France; Killed in action, 26th August, 1914.

Goody, John (1915–19); Corporal, R.F.A.; France and Germany 3 years 3 months.

Goodyer, Frank (1914–19); Sergeant, R.A.S.C.; France 4 years.

Gorton, William Bristowe (1914–19); Lance-Corporal, R. W. Kent Rgt., and Cadet (Acting Sergeant), XII Officer Cadet Bn.; France 15 months, Italy 4 months.

***Gossop, William Kelita** (1914–16); Lance-Corporal, Northumberland Fusiliers; France 1 year 8 months; Died, 27th December, 1916.

***Gostling, Henry** (1914–15); Private, Middlesex Rgt.; France 2 months; Killed in action, March, 1915.

Gostling, William (1914–19); Private, London Rgt.; France 8 months, Prisoner of war (Germany) 9 months.

Gotts, William (1917–19); Private, R.A.S.C.; France 2 years.

Gould, Michael Henry (1915–16); Gunner, R.F.A.

Gould, William James (1914–19); Sergeant, R.F.A.; France 2 years.

Graham, William Marcus (1914–19); D.C.M.; Battery Quartermaster-Sergeant, R.G.A.; France 2 years 6 months.

Granger, Harry (1915–19); Sergeant, R.A.O.C.; France 3 years 5 months.

Granger, Thomas (1917–19); Private, R.A.M.C.; Egypt 2 years 1 month.

Grant, Arthur Henry (1915–19); Driver, R.E.; France 2 years 3 months, Italy 6 months.

Grant, Robert (1914–16); Gunner, R.F.A.; France.

Graves, Walter Thomas (1916–19); Private, Labour Corps.

Gray, Albert Ernest (1916–19); Private, R.A.M.C.; France 1 year 10 months.

Gray, Alfred Alexander William (1914–17); D.C.M.; Sergeant, Machine Gun Corps; France 2 years.

***Gray, Joseph** (1914–15); Private, Royal Fusiliers; Malta 5 months, France 2 months; Killed in action, 10th May, 1915.

Gray, William (1914); Private, London Rgt.

Gray, William Gerard (1916–19); Rifleman, Rifle Brigade; India 2 years 6 months.

Greef, Edgar (1915–19); Corporal, R.A.V.C.; France and Italy 3 years 11 months.

Green, Charles Edward (1916–19); Private, Labour Corps; France 2 years.

Green, Frederick (1914–19); Leading Seaman, R.N.; Naval Service 4 years 6 months.

Green, Frederick George (1916–19); Gunner, R.G.A.; France 1 year 7 months.

Green, George (1915–19); Corporal, R.E.; France and Italy 3 years 6 months.

Green, George Burt (1914–19); Battery Sergeant-Major, R.G.A.; Gallipoli, Egypt and France, 4 years.

Green, Thomas Charles William (1915–19); Corporal, R.E.; France and Germany 3 years 2 months.

Green, William (1914–19); Gunner, R.H.A.; France 4 years 1 month.

Green, William Alec (1914–19); Private, Duke of Cornwall's Light Infantry; France 3 years 6 months.

Greenfield, Edmund (1915–16); Private, 6th Reserve Rgt. of Cavalry.

Greenfield, Frederick Oscar (1914–19); Corporal, R.A.S.C.

Greenwood, Frederick (1917–19); Gunner, R.G.A.; France 3 months.

Greenwood, George Charles (1914–19); Gunner, R.F.A.; France 4 months, Salonica 2 years 11 months, Russia 3 months.

Greetham, James Arthur (1915–19); Gunner, R.F.A.; France 3 years 4 months.

Gregory, Sidney John (1915–19); Gunner, R.F.A.; France 2 years.

Grey, Ernest (1914–19); Private, Labour Corps; France 6 months.

***Greygoose, Francis** (1914); Rifleman, King's Royal Rifle Corps; France 2 months; Died of wounds, 23rd October, 1914.

Grice, Frederick James (1916–19); Private, Middlesex Rgt.

Grice, George Francis (1914–18); Corporal, R.F.A.; France 2 years 9 months.

***Griffin, Frederick George** (1914–15); Lance-Corporal, Royal Fusiliers; France 1 month; Missing, 24th May, 1915.

Griffin, George Love (1914–19); Gunner, R.G.A.; France 3 years 5 months.

Griffin, William John (1916–17); Private, Essex Rgt.

Griffiths, Henry William (1915–19); Sapper, R.E.; France 3 years 7 months.

Griffiths, Joseph Henry (1916–19); Lance-Corporal, Nottinghamshire and Derbyshire Rgt.; Egypt 1 year.

Griffiths, Thomas James (1914–16); Sapper, R.E.; France 1 year 5 months.

***Griffiths, William** (1914–17); Private, Middlesex Rgt.; France 1 year 10 months; Killed in action, 1st December, 1917.

Grigg, Henry James (1914–19); Corporal, R.F.A.; France, Salonica and Palestine, 3 years.

Griggs, Frederick John (1916–19); Private, E. Surrey Rgt.; India 1 year, Mesopotamia 18 months.

Griggs, Joseph William (1916–19); Gunner, R.G.A.; Salonica 2 years.

Griggs, William (1914–18); Private, Norfolk Rgt.; India 2 years.

Grimes, Douglas Frederick (1914–19); 2nd Corporal, R.A.O.C.; France 3 years 8 months.

***Grist, Robert George** (1914); Able Seaman, R.F.R.; Naval Service; Killed at sea, 22nd September, 1914.

***Gristwood, Charles** (1915–18); Driver, R.F.A.; France and Italy 2 years 1 month; Died, 24th January, 1918.

Gritt, William John (1916–19); Private, Labour Corps.

Grokes, George Frederick (1914–19); Private, R.D.C.

Groom, James Charles (1917–19); Private, R.A.F.

***Groombridge, Frederick William** (1914–17); Cyclist, Army Cyclist Corps; France 9 months; Died of wounds, 26th January, 1917.

Grose, Wilfred John (1914–15); Private, Royal Fusiliers.

Grout, Alfred (1915–19); Bombardier, R.F.A.; France 2 years 8 months.

Groves, Charles (1914–19); Rifleman, Rifle Brigade; Egypt 3 years 4 months.

Groves, Edward (1917–19); Air Mechanic (2nd Class), R.A.F.

Grubb, William George Henry (1914–19); M.M.; Corporal, R.E.; Egypt, Dardanelles and France, 2 years 4 months.

Guerin, James (1914–19); Sapper, R.E.; France 3 years 8 months.

Gunner, William (1917–19); Guardsman, Grenadier Guards; France 2 months.

Gunning, Frank (1914–19); Private, Suffolk Rgt.; France 4 years.

Guntley, Edward William (1915–19); Private, Labour Corps; France 2 years.

Gurden, Edward (1916–19); Private, R.A.M.C.; France 8 months.

Guyott, Frank Horace (1914–19); Sergeant, R.F.A.; France 2 years.

***Guyver, George** (1914–15); Lance-Corporal, 11th Reserve Rgt. of Cavalry; France 8 months; Killed in action, 13th May, 1915.

Gyseman, John Albert (1916–19); Private, E. Riding of Yorkshire Yeomanry.

Hack, Herbert (1914–19); Able Seaman, R.N.; Naval Service.

Hackett, Albert Sidney (1915–19); Corporal, R.A.S.C.; France 1 year.

Hackett, Cecil Stephen (1914–19); M.S.M., mentioned in despatches; Staff Sergeant-Major, R.A.S.C.; France 3 years 6 months.

Hackett, Francis Ernest (1914–19); Private, M.F.P.

Haddrell, Stanley Lewis (1914–19); Private, London Rgt.; France 3 years 9 months.

Haddrill, Frederick George (1914–15); Corporal, M.M.P.

Haden, Charles Henry (1918–19); Private, R. W. Kent Rgt.; France 3 months.

Hadrill, Valentine Thomas Charles (1915–16); Gunner, R.F.A.

Haines, Alfred James (1914–19); Air Mechanic (1st Class), R.A.F.; France 7 months.

Halden, Ernest Joseph (1914–19); Sergeant, R.A.M.C.; France 4 years 6 months.

Hale, Andrew James (1914–17); Private, R.D.C.

Hale, Arthur Thomas (1915–19); Gunner, R.F.A.; France 2 years 5 months.

Hale, Matthew Joseph (1915–18); Gunner, R.F.A.; France 2 years 6 months.

Hale, William Edward (1915–19); Driver, R.F.A.; France 3 years 5 months.

Hall, Albert (1914–19); Lance-Corporal, Essex Rgt.; Egypt, Salonica, Dardanelles and Palestine, 3 years 6 months.

Hall, Arthur (1917–19); Rifleman, King's Royal Rifle Corps; France 16 months.

Hall, Ernest John (1917–19); Gunner, R.G.A.; France 13 months.

Hall, Frank Richard (1914–19); Corporal, Lincolnshire Rgt.; France 1 year 7 months.

Hall, Herbert Stanley (1916–19); Gunner, R.G.A.; France and Germany 2 years 1 month.

***Hall, James Sidney** (1914–18); Corporal, London Rgt.; France and Palestine 2 years 2 months; Killed in action, 28th September, 1918.

Hall, Leonard (1916–17); Private, Labour Corps.

Hall, Richard (1914–19); Private, R.A.S.C. (M.T.); France 5 months.

Hall, William Daniel (1918–19); Private, R. Sussex Rgt.; France and Germany 3 months.

Hall, William Orchard (1914–16); Private, Wiltshire Rgt.; France 1 year.

Hallett, William John (1916–19); Sergeant Clerk, R.A.F.; France 2 years 9 months.

Halliwell, Walter Nimrod (1914–19); Sergeant, Argyle and Sutherland Highlanders; France 3 years 11 months.

Hammond, Harry Charles (1914–19); Gunner, R.H.A.; France 4 years.

Hammond, Henry Samuel (1914–19); M.M.; Corporal, R.E.; France 3 years 8 months.

Hampshire, John (1914–19); Lance-Corporal, M.F.P.; France 4 years 6 months.

Hamshere, James Barlow (1916–19); Private, Middlesex Rgt.: France 1 year 8 months.

Hancock, Alfred (1914–19); Private, Tank Corps; France 8 months.

Hancock, Robert Samuel (1916–19); Leading Aircraftsman, R.A.F.

Hand, Walter Thomas (1915–19); Driver, R.E.; France 3 years.

Handel, George Frederick (1918–19); Private, E. Surrey Rgt.; France 11 months.

Hankins, Francis Henry (1914–19); M.S.M.; Regimental Sergeant-Major, R.A.M.C.: France 4 years.

Hann, Thomas William (1914–19); Signaller, E. Surrey Rgt.; India 5 years.

Hanson, Charles Henry (1914–19); Private, Royal Marine Light Infantry; Naval Service 2 years 3 months.

Harden, Edward Ernest (1914–19); Private, Manchester Rgt.; Gallipoli 3 months, Hong-Kong 6 months, India 2 years 6 months.

Harding, Albert Henry (1917–19); Signaller, R.G.A.; France 1 year.

Harding, Harry (1917–19); Acting 2nd Corporal, R.E.

Harding, Henry Alfred (1914–16); Private, R.A.S.C. (M.T.).

Harding, James Joseph (1914–19); Ship's Corporal (1st Class), R.N.; Naval Service 4 years 7 months.

Hardy, Ernest William (1915–17); Gunner, R.F.A.

Hardy, John James (1914–19); Private, London Rgt.; Palestine and Balkans 4 years.

Hardy, William Charles (1914–17); Private, R.D.C.

Harley, Edward Samuel (1914–15); Private, Oxfordshire and Buckinghamshire Light Infantry; France 3 months.

Harley, James (1916–19); Private, Labour Corps; France 2 years 10 months.

Harlow, Frederick (1914–17); Corporal, R.F.A.

Harmack, Albert Thomas (1918–19); Private, E. Surrey Rgt.

Harman, George Arthur (1915–19); Bombardier, R.F.A.; France 4 months.

Harper, William James (1914–19); Sergeant, 11th Hussars; France 2 years 6 months.

Harrington, Edward (1915–19); Flight-Sergeant, R.A.F.; France 1 year 8 months.

Harriott, Frederick (1914–17); Lance-Corporal, Middlesex Rgt.; France 5 months.

Harris, Arthur Charles (1914–19); Rifleman, Rifle Brigade; France 2 years 1 month.

Harris, George Henry (1914–16); Private, 9th Lancers; France 9 months.

Harris, Harry (1914–19); Private, R.A.S.C. (M.T.); France 4 years 5 months.

Harris, John (1915–19); Driver, R.F.A.; France 2 years 6 months.

Harris, John (1917–19); Private, R.A.M.C.; Egypt and Palestine 1 year 10 months.

Harris, Percy Stanley (1914–19); Sergeant, R.F.A., and Sergeant Cadet, Cadet School; France and Italy 4 years.

Harris, Samuel Hickman (1914–19); Private, R.A.S.C. (M.T.); France 3 years 3 months.

Harris, Thomas (1914–19); M.S.M.; Corporal, R.F.A.; France 3 years 8 months.

Harris, William Elijah (1918–19); Private, Middlesex Rgt.; Russia 6 months.

Harris, William James (1915–19); Leading Aircraftsman Wireless Operator, R.A.F.; France 2 years 6 months.

***Harrison, Ernest Sidney** (1914); Private, R.W. Kent Rgt.; France; Killed in action, 13th September, 1914.

Harrison, William John (1915–19); Driver, R.F.A.; France 3 years 10 months.

Hart, Albert Edward (1914–19); Private, London Rgt.

Hart, Albert George (1914–19); Private, Labour Corps; France 2 years 6 months.

Hart, James Henry (1914–19); Private, Middlesex Rgt.; France 4 years 5 months.

Hart, Michael (1915–19); M.M.; Corporal, R.E.; Dardanelles and France 2 years.

Hart, Tom (1915–18); Corporal, Labour Corps; France 3 years.

Hartley, Edward George (1916–17); Private, Northamptonshire Rgt.; Egypt and Palestine 18 months.

Harvest, Richard Ernest (1917–19); 1st Aircraft Hand, R.A.F.; France 10 months.

Harvey, Christopher Robert (1914–19); 2nd Corporal, R.E.; Egypt 18 months, France 8 months, Salonica 6 months.

Harvey, Daniel Thomas (1914–19); Private, R. Sussex Rgt.; France 2 years 2 months.

Harvey, George William (1914–19); Sergeant, Middlesex Rgt.; India 4 years 6 months.

Harvey, Haydn Augustine (1914); Driver, R.F.A.

***Harvey, Henry Valentine** (1914–18); M.M.; Corporal, R.F.A.; France 2 years 11 months; Killed in action, 1st November, 1918.

Harvey, Henry Walter (1914–17); Corporal, R.F.A.

Harvey, William (1914–19); Private, R. Berkshire Rgt.; France 2 months, Salonica 3 years 4 months.

Harvey, William James (1914–19); Sapper, R.E.; France 3 years.

Hase, Leonard Algernon (1914–17); Lance-Corporal, Royal Fusiliers; France 6 months.

Hasleham, John (1914); Private, Cavalry Reserve.

Haslum, Christopher John (1914–17); Private, R. Sussex Rgt.

***Haslum, David** (1915–16); Gunner, R.F.A.; France 8 months; Killed in action, 31st August, 1916.

Hatcher, George (1915); Driver, R.E.

Hatcher, John William (1914–19); Private, R.D.C.

Hatcher, William Walter (1915–18); Gunner, R.F.A.; France 8 months.

Hatton, Benjamin Brett (1914–19); Private, London Rgt.

Hatwell, William James (1915–16); Pioneer, R.E.

Haustead, John Henry (1915–19); Gunner, R.F.A.; France 3 years.

Haviland, Alfred (1914–19); Private, Royal Fusiliers; France 3 years 5 months.

***Haward, William Cressweller** (1914–16); Gunner, R.F.A.; France 7 months; Accidentally drowned, 16th June, 1916.

Hawkes, Herbert (1917–19); Signaller, R.G.A.: France and Germany 1 year.

Hawkins, Albert Edward (1916–19); Private, Labour Corps.

Hawkins, Arthur Albert (1915–19); Driver, R.F.A.; France 3 years 1 month.

Hawkins, Frederick (1914–19); Driver, R.F.A.; France 4 years 6 months.

Hawkins, Henry Thomas (1914–16); Private, 16th Bn. London Rgt.

Hawkins, James (1915–19); M.M.; Private, R.A.M.C.; Malta and France 3 years 6 months.

Hawkins, John Edward (1915–19); Driver, R.E.; Gallipoli, Italy and France, 4 years.

Hawkins, Richard Stanope (1916–19); Lance-Corporal, Rifle Brigade; France 2 years 6 months.

Hayden, Albert William (1914–19); Gunner, R.F.A.; France 3 years 5 months.

Haydon, Frederick Albert (1914–19); Private, R.A.M.C.; Malta 2 years 8 months.

***Hayes, Edward William Charles** (1916–18); Corporal, London Rgt.; France 1 year 7 months; Killed in action, 2nd September, 1918.

Hayes, James (1915–16); Driver, R.E.

Hayhoe, George (1916–19); Private, R.A.V.C.; France 2 years 7 months.

Haylor, William (1914–19); Private, Scots Guards; France 3 years 8 months.

Haynes, Albert Charles (1916–19); Corporal, Bedfordshire Rgt.

Hayward, Charles Frederick (1918–20); Private, R.A.M.C.; France 16 months.

Hayward, William James (1915–19); Corporal, R.E.; France 1 year 7 months, Italy 4 months.

Head, Herbert (1914–19); Rifleman, Rifle Brigade; France 4 years.

Head, Richard (1914–19); Stoker (1st Class), R.N.; Naval Service 2 years 10 months.

Healey, William George (1917–19); Guardsman, Grenadier Guards; France 5 months.

Heard, Edward (1915–19); Driver, R.A.S.C.; France 1 year 10 months.

Hearn, Henry Joseph (1916–19); Gunner, R.G.A.; Palestine 14 months.

Hearn, Thomas (1915–18); Private, R.A.M.C.

Heath, Frederick William Francis (1915–19); Driver, R.F.A.; France 2 years 9 months.

Heath, Valentine (1916–19); Private, Labour Corps.

Hedges, George (1915–19); Gunner, R.G.A.; France 1 year.

Hedges, George Henry (1915–19); M.S.M.; Regimental Quartermaster-Sergeant, Royal Fusiliers.

Heffer, George (1916–19); Private, R.A.M.C.; Salonica 9 months.

Helps, Joseph (1914–19); Private, Bedfordshire Rgt.; India 2 years 2 months.

Hemmings, Richard (1917–19); Private, R.A.M.C.

***Hems, Edward** (1917–18); Private, London Rgt.; France 3 months; Killed in action, 5th April, 1918.

Henderson, Alexander (1914–19); Driver, R.F.A.; France 3 years 5 months.

Hensby, John (1915–19); Private, Labour Corps; Egypt and Salonica 3 years 6 months.

Henshaw, Albert (1916–19); Rifleman, London Rgt.; France 10 months.

Hepper, Richard George (1914–19); M.M.; Private, York and Lancaster Rgt.; France and Italy 4 years 5 months.

Herbert, Albert Edward (1914–19); Private, R.A.S.C. (M.T.); Salonica 2 years, Egypt 2 years.

***Herd, Charles** (1914–16 and 1917–18); Gunner, R.F.A.; France 1 year 7 months; Died of wounds, 19th April, 1918.

***Heritage, Jack** (1914–18); M.M.; Sergeant, R.G.A.; France 2 years 6 months; Killed in action, 21st April, 1918.

Heron, Arthur Wilfred (1914–19); Sapper, R.E.; France 4 years 5 months.

Herrick, Henry John (1918–19); Rifleman, King's Royal Rifle Corps; France 2 months, Germany 3 months.

Herring, Albert Sydney (1914–17); Lance-Corporal, R.D.C.

Herring, Robert Henry (1916–19); Corporal, Essex Rgt.

***Herriott, Archibald** (1914–15); Private, London Rgt.; France 2 months; Killed in action, 25th May, 1915.

Heskett, John (1914–19); Private, Manchester Rgt.; France.

Hewett, Alfred (1915–19); Private, R.A.S.C.; France and Italy 4 years 4 months.

Hewett, William George (1917–19); Gunner, R.G.A.; France 3 months.

Hewitt, Jesse Benjamin (1914–15); Private, London Rgt.

Hewitt, Thomas (1914–19); Sergeant, R.F.A.; France 2 years 4 months.

Hickman, Jesse James (1917–18); Private, Labour Corps; France 4 months.

Hickman, Richard (1915–19); Private, Labour Corps; France 1 year 8 months.

Hierons, Reuben Henry (1914–19); Private, R.A.S.C. (M.T.); France 1 year 7 months.

High, John George (1915–19); Private, R.A.M.C.; Salonica 3 years 1 month.

Hiley, John Edward (1914–17); Private, E. Surrey Rgt.; France 16 months.

Hill, Arthur (1914–18); Gunner, R.H.A. France 4 years.

Hill, Frederick George (1915–19); Gunner, R.F.A.; France 3 years 9 months.

Hill, Harold Bligh (1914–19); Mentioned in despatches; Sergeant, Labour Corps; France 3 years 6 months.

Hill, Louis (1914–16); Corporal, Middlesex Rgt.

Hill, Robert John (1915–19); Lance-Corporal, Cheshire Rgt.; France, Salonica and Egypt, 3 years 8 months.

Hill, William Thomas (1915–19); Private, Labour Corps; France 1 year 10 months.

Hillary, Robert George (1914–19); Private, R.A.S.C. (M.T.); France 3 years.

Hilliard, Charles Alfred (1916–19); Private, Yorkshire Light Infantry.

Hilliard, Edwin Frederick (1915–19); Private, Labour Corps; France 2 years.

Hills, George Ernest (1914–19); 2nd Corporal, R.E.; Egypt and Palestine 3 years 6 months.

Hills, Reginald James (1914–19); Gunner, R.F.A.; France 3 years 6 months.

Hills, Walter (1918–19); Air Mechanic, R.A.F.

Hillyer, Albert Edward (1916–17); Private, London Rgt.

Hilton, Alfred James (1915–19); Gunner, R.F.A.; France 3 years.

Hinton, Henry Arthur (1915–19); Private, London Rgt.; France, Egypt, Salonica and Palestine, 3 years 6 months.

Hipgrave, Bertie (1915–19); Gunner, R.F.A.; France, Salonica and Palestine, 2 years 6 months.

Hipgrave, George (1914–16); Sergeant, S. Wales Borderers; France 2 months.

Hirst, Alfred Ernest (1916–19); Private, Suffolk Rgt.

Hiscott, Ralph Walter James (1918–20); Sapper, R.E.; Germany 10 months.

Hitchcock, Bertram Albert (1916–19); Private, Middlesex Rgt.; France 2 years 2 months.

Hoad, Edwin Lewis (1914–19); Sergeant, R.W. Kent Rgt.; France 3 years 6 months.

Hoadley, Clarence Howard (1917–19); Pioneer, R.E.; France 2 years.

Hoadley, John Joseph (1917–19); Lance-Corporal, R.E.; France 2 years 8 months.

Hobbs, Thomas (1917–18); Private, Labour Corps.

Hobbs, Thomas James Rutter (1914–19); Sergeant, R.F.A.; France, Palestine, Gallipoli and Balkans, 3 years 11 months.

Hobbs, William Henry (1914–19); Private, Cyclists Bn.; France 3 years 6 months.

Hobday, Edward Theodore (1914–19); Petty Officer, R.N.; Naval Service 10 months.

Hocking, Henry (1914–19); Gunner, R.F.A.; France 3 years 6 months.

Hodge, Albert (1915–19); Driver. R.A.S.C. (M.T.); France 17 months.

***Hodgkinson, Cecil** (1915–16); Sapper, R.E.; France 8 months; Killed in action, 25th March, 1916.

Hodgkinson, William (1914–19); Sergeant, R.E.; France 3 years 10 months.

Hodgson, Zebulon (1916–19); Private, R.A.S.C.; France 2 months.

Hogg, George Alfred (1914–19); D.S.M.; Leading Seaman, R.N.; Naval Service 3 years 4 months.

Holden, Albert John (1914–19); Rifleman, Rifle Brigade; India 6 months, Burmah 3 years 4 months.

Holden, George Llewellyn (1916–19); Private, Lancashire Fusiliers; France 3 months.

Holdom, Alfred (1914–19); Able Seaman, R.N.; Naval Service 4 years 6 months.

Holladay, Albert (1918–19); Private, R.W. Kent Rgt.; France 3 months.

Hollaman, Arthur John (1915–19); Gunner, R.F.A.; France 3 years 1 month.

Holland, Alfred Henry (1914–19); Private, 13th Hussars; France 1 year 8 months, Mesopotamia 2 years 7 months.

Holland, Joseph Henry (1914–19); Corporal, Royal Marine Light Infantry; Naval Service 3 years 7 months.

Holland, Sydney Critcher (1915–19); Private, R.A.M.C.; Mesopotamia 2 years.

Holland, Walter (1914–19); Bombardier, R.F.A.; France and Salonica 4 years 1 month.

Hollands, William (1915–19); Wheeler, R.F.A.; France, Salonica and Palestine, 2 years 9 months.

Holley, Frederick James (1914–19); Private, Lancashire Fusiliers; France 8 months, Salonica 18 months.

***Hollins, Henry James** (1914–17); Sergeant, E. Surrey Rgt.; France 8 months; Killed in action, 17th April, 1917.

Holloman, George Walter (1914–19); Leading Seaman, R.N.; Naval Service 4 years 6 months.

Holman, Arthur James (1915–17); Bombardier, R.G.A.; France 5 months.

Holman, Edwin (1914–16); Lance-Corporal, R.W. Surrey Rgt.

Holman, Henry (1915–17); Driver, R.H.A.

Holmes, Albert (1914–19); Lance-Corporal, R.E.; France 4 years 4 months.

Holmes, Francis (1914–19); Driver, R.F.A.; France 2 years 6 months.

Holmes, James William (1914–19); Private, Gloucestershire Rgt.; France 1 year, Salonica 2 years.

Holmes, Walter (1915–19); Private, R.A.S.C. (M.T.); France 3 years 9 months.

Holt, Alfred James (1915–19); Driver, R.A.S.C., and Gunner, R.G.A.; France 2 years 5 months.

Holt, Percy (1918–19); Private, Labour Corps.

Holt, Robert Henry (1914–19); Able Seaman, R.N.; Naval Service 4 years 6 months.

Holtham, Ernest (1917–19); Gunner, R.G.A.; France and Germany 1 year 9 months.

Honeyball, Arthur Charles (1914–19); Company Quartermaster-Sergeant, Highland Light Infantry; France 2 years 11 months.

***Hood, George** (1914–15); Private, Duke of Cornwall's Light Infantry; France 1 month; Killed in action, 28th April, 1915.

Hooper, George (1915–17); Lance-Corporal, R.E.

Hooper, Robert Alfred (1916–19); Private, London Rgt.; France, Salonica and Egypt, 1 year 11 months.

Hooper, Thomas William (1918–19); Private, Machine Gun Corps.

Hooton, Arthur Ernest (1916–19); Corporal, R.A.V.C.; France 2 years 7 months.

Hopkins, Albert John (1914–19); Private, Northumberland Fusiliers; India and Mesopotamia 2 years 8 months.

Hopkins, Frederick William (1914–19); Gunner, R.F.A.; Salonica and Egypt 3 years 6 months.

Hopper, Albert Edward (1914–19); Stoker (1st Class), R.N.; Naval Service 4 years 6 months.

Hopwood, James (1914–19); D.C.M.; Corporal, London Rgt.; Palestine, Dardanelles and Egypt, 3 years 7 months.

Hopwood, William (1914–19); Private, R.A.S.C. (M.T.); Egypt, Gallipoli and Salonica, 3 years 7 months.

Horan, James Joseph (1915–19); Stoker, R.N.; Naval Service 3 years 3 months.

Horn, Frederick Charles (1917–19); Corporal Clerk, R.A.F.

Horn, Frederick William (1917–19); Private, Labour Corps; France 2 years.

Horn, Percy James (1917–19); Gunner, R.G.A.; France 2 months.

Horne, Edwin Albert (1915–19); Private, E. Surrey Rgt.; France 2 years 6 months.

Horne, George (1914–17); Corporal, Cheshire Rgt.; France 3 years 1 month.

Horner, Henry George (1914–19); Lance-Corporal, M.F.P.

Horner, William Thomas (1914); Private, Royal Fusiliers.

***Horrigan, John William** (1914–15); Gunner, R.F.A.; Accidentally killed, 7th February, 1915.

Horscroft, Frederick (1914–17); Lance-Corporal, London Rgt.

Horsey, Thomas Henry (1914–19); Shoeing-Smith, R.F.A.; Egypt 8 months, France 5 months, Salonica 6 months.

Horsnell, Frederick Charles (1918–19); Private, R. Sussex Rgt.; France 4 months.

Horton, Charles Edward (1914–19); Sergeant, R.F.A.; France 4 years 8 months.

Horwood, Ernest Alfred (1914–19); Corporal, Worcestershire Rgt.; Salonica 3 years 6 months.

***Horwood, Harold Ralph** (1914–16); Lance-Corporal, London Rgt.; France 10 months; Died of wounds, 15th September, 1916.

Hosier, Henry James (1916–18); Private, Labour Corps; France 5 months.

Houchin, Harry (1916–18); 2nd Corporal, R.E.; France 5 months.

Hoverd, John (1914–19); Corporal, Essex Rgt.

Howard, Arthur Percy (1914–19); Driver, London Rgt.; France 2 years 6 months.

Howard, Jasper Harry (1914–19); Sergeant-Major, R.A.F.

Howard, Sidney Alfred (1917–19); Lance-Corporal, R.A.S.C.

Howard, William (1914–19); Private, 15th Hussars; France 4 years 6 months.

Howard, William White Henry (1915–19); Staff-Sergeant, A.P.C.

Howcutt, Mark (1914–19); Driver, R.F.A.; France 3 years 9 months.

Howe, William Frederick (1915–19); Gunner, R.F.A.; Egypt, France and Salonica, 2 years 9 months.

Howell, Alfred (1914–19); Private, Royal Marine Light Infantry; Naval Service 4 years 2 months.

Howells, Edward John Robert (1914–19); Lieutenant, Loyal N. Lancashire Rgt.; France 3 years.

Howells, Frank Cecil (1914–19); Battery Fitter, R.F.A.; France 3 years 3 months.

***Howes, William Joseph** (1917); Private, London Rgt.; Egypt and Palestine, 4 months; Killed in action, 2nd November, 1917.

Howland, Robert Alfred (1915–19); Lance-Corporal, R.A.S.C. (M.T.); France 3 years 3 months.

Hoy, Frederick George (1917–19); Gunner, R.G.A.; France 6 months.

Hoyle, Robert Joseph (1918–19); Pioneer, R.E.; France 7 months.

Hubbard, Frederick William (1916–19); Air Mechanic (1st Class), R.A.F.; France 5 months.

Hubbard, William George (1917–19); Air Mechanic (2nd Class), R.A.F.

Hudgell, William Thomas (1914–19); Shoeing-Smith, R.G.A.

Hudson, Alfred Andrew (1918–19); Private, Royal Fusiliers.

***Huggins, Joseph** (1914–15); Private, Royal Fusiliers; France 1 month; Missing, 8th February, 1915.

Hughes, Alfred William (1916–19); Private, Machine Gun Corps; France 17 months, Prisoner of war 10 months.

Hughes, George William (1914–19); Corporal, E. Surrey Rgt.; Salonica 3 years.

***Hughes, Henry Grey** (1915); Air Mechanic, R.A.F.; Accidentally drowned, 26th April, 1915.

Hughes, James Edward (1916–17); Sergeant, Middlesex Rgt.

Hughes, Joseph Robert (1914–19); Gunner, R.G.A.; France 3 years 8 months.

Hughes, Myles Patrick (1914–19); Corporal, R.F.A.; France 4 years.

Hulcoop, Horace Frederick (1917–19); Private, R.A.S.C.; France 11 months.

Humbles, Ernest (1915–17); Gunner, R.G.A.

Hume, Edward Charles (1914–19); Leading Seaman, R.N.; Naval Service 4 years.

Hume, James (1915–19); Corporal, R.A.S.C.; France 2 years 9 months.

Humm, William James (1915–19); Sergeant, R.F.A.; France 3 years.

Humphrey, Charles Albert (1915–17); Driver, R.E.; France 2 years 6 months.

Humphrey, Henry Charles (1915–18); Lance-Corporal, Labour Corps.

***Humphrey, Mark** (1915–16); Driver, R.F.A.; France 8 months; Died of wounds, 15th July, 1916.

Humphrey, Thomas William (1917–18); Private, Labour Corps; France 8 months.

Humphrey, William Charles (1918–19); Private, R.W. Kent Rgt.

Humphrey, William James (1915–19); Private, London Rgt.; France 3 years 3 months.

Humphries, James (1918–19); Private, E. Surrey Rgt.

Hunt, Herbert James (1914–19); Private, Leicestershire Rgt.; France 3 years 3 months.

Hunt, Robert (1917–19); Private, Bedfordshire Rgt.

Hunter, Charles William (1914–19); Sergeant, London Rgt.; France 2 years 9 months.

Hunwick, William (1917–19); Private, Labour Corps; France 2 years.

Hursey, Sidney George (1917–19); 2nd Aircraftsman, R.A.F.; France 6 months.

Hutcheson, Robert John (1914–19); Private, 7th Hussars; Palestine, France and Salonica, 4 years.

Hutchings, James Harris (1916–19); Private, Highland Light Infantry; France 7 months.

Hutchinson, Frederick John (1917–19); Pioneer, R.E.

Hutchinson, Robert (1914–19); Sapper, R.E.; France 3 years 5 months.

Hutt, Percy Charles (1917–19); Driver, R.F.A.; Belgium 5 months.

Huzzey, George Victor (1914–19); M.M.; Sergeant, Worcestershire Rgt.; France 3 years, Prisoner of war 7 months.

Hyams, Sidney (1916–19); Private, Labour Corps; France 13 months.

Hyatt, Alfred (1914–19); Private, Highland Light Infantry; France 2 years 3 months.

Hyatt, John William (1914–19); Driver, R.F.A.; France 3 years 9 months.

Hyde, Alfred James (1915–19); Private, Machine Gun Corps; France 5 months.

Hyde, Ernest Charles (1915–19); Private, R.A.M.C.; Palestine, France and Salonica, 2 years 9 months.

***Hyde, Frederick Charles** (1914); Private, Wiltshire Rgt.; France 2 months; Missing, 31st October, 1914.

***Hygate, William Charles** (1915–17); Gunner, R.F.A.; France 6 months, Salonica 8 months, Egypt 3 months; Died of wounds, 7th November, 1917.

Igglesden, George (1916–18); Private, Northumberland Fusiliers.

Imison, Montague (1915–19); Lance-Bombardier, R.F.A.; France 1 year 11 months, Italy 4 months.

Imlach, James (1914–19); Private, R.D.C.

Impey, Rodney William (1915–19); Able Seaman, R.N.; Naval Service 3 years.

Ing, Robert Ralph (1914–19); Gunner, R.F.A.; France 3 years.

Ingram, Robert John (1916–19); Gunner, R.G.A.

Ingrams, William (1914–19); 2nd Corporal, R.E.; Italy and France 1 year.

Ingrey, Charles David (1914–16); Private, Middlesex Rgt.; France 1 year 10 months.

Ings, Harry (1916–19); Lance-Sergeant, London Rgt.; France 2 years.

Innalls, Alfred Ernest (1914–19); Driver, R.A.S.C.; France and Prisoner of war (Germany) 4 years.

Inns, Charles Henry (1917–19); Rifleman, Rifle Brigade; France 9 months, Prisoner of war (Germany) 9 months.

Ireland, Arthur William (1915–19); Shoeing-Smith, R.F.A.; France, Salonica and Egypt, 2 years 9 months.

Irvine, Albert Charles (1914–19); Private, Dragoon Guards; France 3 years 8 months.

Irving, James William (1915–18); Private, Labour Corps; France 18 months.

Isaacs, Samuel (1914–19); Sapper, R.E.; France 2 years 8 months.

Isted, George Henry (1916–18); Rifleman, London Rgt.; France 14 months.

Jackaman, George Edward (1914–19); Private, R.A.S.C.

Jackman, William George (1918–19); Stoker, R.N.; Naval Service.

Jackson, Arthur James (1915–19); Sergeant, Bedfordshire Rgt.; France 1 year 8 months.

***Jackson, Harry** (1914–15); Private, R. Scots Fusiliers; France 10 months; Missing, 16th June, 1915.

Jackson, Richard John (1915–19); Sapper, R.E.; Dardanelles, France and Germany, 3 years 10 months.

Jackson, Thomas Charles (1914–19); Private, Bedfordshire Rgt.; Egypt and Palestine, 3 years 6 months.

Jackson, William (1914–19); M.S.M.; Sergeant, R.E.; Gallipoli 8 months, France 3 years 2 months.

Jackson, William James (1918–19); Sergeant, R. Sussex Rgt.; France 1 year.

Jacob, Alfred John (1915–19); Private, Welch Rgt.; Dardanelles and Mesopotamia 4 years 3 months.

Jacobs, Frederick (1917–19); Private, R.A.S.C.; France 17 months.

Jagger, Henry Francis (1914–19); Gunner, R.G.A.; France 3 years.

Jago, Alfred Edward (1918–19); Rifleman, Rifle Brigade; France 5 months.

James, Albert Clifford (1915–19); Corporal, R.E.

James, Albert Edward (1914–15); Gunner, R.F.A.

James, Albert Edward Webber (1915–19); Private, R.A.S.C.; France and Egypt 3 years 10 months.

***James, George** (1914–15); Private, R.W. Surrey Rgt.; France 9 months; Missing, 25th September, 1915.

James, William Alfred Leverson (1916–19); Lance-Corporal, R.W. Surrey Rgt.; France 1 year 9 months.

James, William Henry (1915–18); Private, R.A.S.C.; France 2 years 8 months.

James, William Thomas (1914–19); Regimental Sergeant-Major, R.A.S.C.; Malta and France 3 years 6 months.

Jamieson, Edward Dalley (1914–19); Chief Petty Officer, R.N.; Naval Service 5 years.

Jarvis, Charles William (1914–18); Corporal, R.F.A.; France 2 years.

Jarvis, Clapton Charles (1915–17); Private, Training Reserve Bn.; France 6 months.

Jarvis, Ernest Thomas (1914–19); Private, R. Welch Fusiliers; France, Salonica and Russia, 3 years 5 months.

Jarvis, William (1914–19); Sergeant, R.E.; France, Salonica and Palestine, 4 years.

Jaynes, Henry William (1914–18); Sergeant, R.F.A.; Dardanelles and Egypt 2 years 9 months.

Jaynes, Herbert (1914–18); Gunner, R.F.A.; France.

Jeffery, John (1915–17); Sapper, R.E.; France, Salonica, Malta and Egypt.

***Jeffrey, Charles James** (1914–16); Corporal, E. Kent Rgt.; France 1 year 7 months; Killed in action, 30th September, 1916.

Jeffrey, Henry (1915–19); Sergeant, London Rgt.

Jeffries, Walter (1916–19); Private, W. Kent Yeomanry.

Jenkin, Percy Alfred (1914–15); Private, London Rgt.; France 3 months.

Jenkins, Edmund George (1914–19); M.M., Mentioned in despatches; Corporal, Royal Fusiliers; France 3 years 9 months.

Jenkins, Harry Benjamin (1918–20); Private, Manchester Rgt.; Italy and Egypt 16 months.

Jenkins, Henry (1915–19); Corporal, R.F.A.; France 2 years 7 months.

Jennings, William James (1916–20); Private, Royal Fusiliers.

Jennings, William John (1916–19); Private, Welch Rgt.; France 2 years.

***Jewell, Charles John Louis** (1915–16); Gunner, R.G.A.; France 8 months; Died of wounds, 14th November, 1916.

Jewell, John Henry (1914–19); Saddler Corporal, R.A.S.C.; France 4 years 6 months.

Jex, Leonard (1914–19); Corporal, R.F.A.; France and Italy 4 years.

Johncock, William Henry (1915–19); 2nd Corporal, R.E.; Egypt and Palestine 4 years.

Johns, Arthur Ernest (1915–19); Rifleman, Rifle Brigade; France 6 months, Egypt 2 years 8 months.

Johnson, Albert (1916–20); Private, Labour Corps; France 2 years 2 months.

Johnson, Archer Alexander (1914–17); Lance-Corporal, Royal Fusiliers; France 17 months.

Johnson, Arthur Henry (1914–17) Sergeant, R. Sussex Rgt.

Johnson, Charles (1914–19); Gunner, R.F.A.; France 3 years 11 months.

Johnson, Charles (1915); Platelayer, R.E.

Johnson, Charles Henry (1914–19); Stoker, R.N.; Naval Service 4 years 8 months.

Johnson, Charles James (1915–19); Private, Labour Corps; France 3 years.

Johnson, Frank (1917–19); Private, Labour Corps; France 1 year 11 months.

Johnson, Frederick (1916–17); Private, E. Kent Rgt.

Johnson, George Alfred (1918–19); Private, R.A.S.C.; France 3 months, Germany 8 months.

Johnson, Harold (1915–19); Gunner, R.F.A.; France 1 month, Salonica 7 months, Egypt and Palestine 1 year 7 months.

Johnson, Herbert William (1916–18); Private, Middlesex Rgt.

Johnson, Jesse Harry (1917); Driver, R.F.A.

Johnson, John (1914–18); Guardsman, Coldstream Guards; France 2 years 4 months.

Johnson, Saville (1916–19); Private, R.A.V.C.; France 2 years 8 months.

Johnson, Sydney (1915–19); Private, Middlesex Rgt.; France 3 years.

Johnson, William (1915–19); Private, R.A.S.C.; France 2 years, Italy 1 year.

Johnson-Steele, Thomas Edward (1914–18); Trooper, 12th Lancers.

Jones, Albert Edward (1918–19); Private, R. Sussex Rgt.

Jones, Alfred Ernest (1914–16); Rifleman, London Rgt.

Jones, Edward (1914–19); Private, R.A.S.C.; Salonica 2 years 6 months.

Jones, Edward Walter (1914–19); Lieutenant, R.E.

Jones, Frederick Arthur (1914–19); Corporal, Machine Gun Corps; France 14 months, Mesopotamia 15 months, India 6 months.

Jones, Frederick William Cecil (1914–19); Senior Reserve Attendant, R. Naval Sick Berth Reserve; Naval Service 7 months.

***Jones, George Henry** (1915–18); Driver, R.F.A.; Died while prisoner of war, 15th July–15th October, 1918.

Jones, Henry William (1914–19); Private, Bedfordshire Rgt.

Jones, John Charles (1916–19); Lance-Corporal, Cambridgeshire and Suffolk Rgts.; France 9 months.

***Jones, John George** (1914–15); Sergeant, London Rgt.; France 9 months; Killed in action, 31st October, 1915.

***Jones, Richard** (1914–18); Trooper, Dragoon Guards; France 3 years; Killed in action, 25th March, 1918.

***Jones, Samuel William** (1914–15); Private, London Rgt.; France 5 months; Died of wounds, 30th July, 1915.

Jones, Stephen George (1914–19); Private, E. Surrey Rgt.; France and Prisoner of war (Germany) 4 years 4 months.

Jones, Thomas William (1915–19); Gunner, R.F.A.

Jones, Wallace Henry (1915–19); Gunner, R.F.A.; France 1 year 8 months, Italy 14 months.

Jones, Walter Leonard (1914–19); Private, London Rgt.; France, Salonica, Egypt and Palestine, 3 years.

Jones, William Alfred (1914–19); Bombardier, R.F.A.; France 2 years 1 month.

Jones, William Anthony (1914–19); Regimental Quartermaster-Sergeant, Northumberland Fusiliers.

Jones, William Henry (1914–19); Private, Labour Corps; France 3 years 7 months.

Jones, William Joseph (1918–19); Private, R.A.S.C.; Mesopotamia and India 10 months.

Jordan, Charles Ernest (1915–18); Sergeant, London Rgt.

Jordan, Ernest John (1914–19); Guardsman, Grenadier Guards; France 4 years.

Jordan, Frank (1916–19); Sergeant, Northumberland Fusiliers; Malta 15 months.

Jordan, George Edward (1915–19); Driver, R.E.; Gallipoli, Egypt and France, 3 years 7 months.

Jordan, Herbert Francis (1914–19); Private, R.D.C.

Jordan, Sydney (1917–19); Air Mechanic (3rd Class), R.A.F.

Joyce, John Robert (1914–15); Private, London Rgt.

Judd, Ernest Gilbert (1917–19); Gunner, R.G.A.

Judd, Thomas James (1914–19); Corporal, R.F.A.; France 3 years 9 months.

Judge, Roland Charles (1914–19); Petty Officer, R.N.; Naval Service 4 years 4 months.

Jump, Charles Richard (1914–19); Private, Machine Gun Corps; France 4 years 4 months.

***Juniper, Charles William Henry** (1914–15); Private, Essex Rgt.; France 3 months; Killed in action, 4th May, 1915.

Jupp, Henry Charles (1914–19); Leading Seaman, R.N.; Naval Service 4 years 6 months.

Kadwill, George Edward (1914–19); Rifleman, Rifle Brigade; Burmah 3 years 5 months.

Kaley, Joshua Percy (1915–19); Sapper, R.E.; Salonica 2 years 9 months, Egypt 3 months.

Kane, Charles (1915–19); Private, London Rgt.

Kane, James Thomas (1914–19); Private, Royal Marine Light Infantry; Naval Service 3 years 7 months.

Karley, Walter Frederick (1917–19); Private, Labour Corps; France 18 months.

Kear, Thomas David (1914–18); Private, R.A.S.C.; France.

***Keeler, Albert Sydney** (1914); Stoker (1st Class), R.F.R.; Naval Service; Lost in H.M.S. Aboukir, 22nd September, 1914.

***Keeler, Frederick William** (1916–17); Rifleman, King's Royal Rifle Corps; France 1 year; Killed in action, 1st October, 1917.

Keen, Arthur John (1917–19); Private, R.A.M.C.; Egypt and Palestine 2 years 1 month.

Keene, Ernest Frederick (1914–19); Rifleman, London Rgt.; France 3 years 10 months.

Keene, George Arthur (1915–18); Corporal, Grenadier Guards; France 1 year 10 months.

Keene, John Patrick (1914–19); Sergeant, Fife and Forfar Yeomanry.

Kelly, Edward (1915–18); Lance-Corporal, R.E.

***Kelsey, Herbert Charles** (1916–17); Gunner, R.F.A.; France 1 month; Killed in action, 29th July, 1917.

Kelson, George Charles (1916–19); Sapper, R.E.; France 18 months.

Kemp, Horace (1914–19); Bombardier, R.F.A.; France 2 years.

Kemp, Lawrence Smeed (1914–19); Corporal, R.F.A.; France 4 years.

Kemp, Robert Samuel (1914–18); Gunner, R.F.A.

Kempton, Sidney (1915–19); Pioneer, R.E.; France 5 months, Salonica 7 months, Palestine 1 year 10 months.

Kendrick, Edward (1915–19); Gunner, R.F.A.; France 2 years 10 months.

Kenealy, Michael John (1914–18); Driver, R.F.A.; France 3 years 1 month.

Kennard, Ernest William (1917–19); 2nd Corporal, R.E.

Kennett, Edward Francis (1914–19); Private, R.A.S.C.; France 2 years 4 months.

Kenney, Edward (1914–19); Lance-Corporal, M.M.P.; France 4 years 6 months.

Kentsbeer, John Samuel (1916–19); Driver, R.A.S.C.; France and Germany 2 years 6 months.

Keogh, Patrick (1914–16); Gunner, R.F.A.; France.

Kerr, Francis John (1917–19); Private, Labour Corps; France 10 months.

Kewell, Henry James (1914–18); Leading Seaman, R.F.R.; Naval Service 3 years 6 months.

***Keyworth, James George** (1915–17); Private, E. Surrey Rgt.; France 15 months; Missing, 3rd May, 1917.

Kiddy, George (1917–19); Private, Essex Rgt.; France 15 months.

Kiely, Patrick (1915–19); Corporal, R.E.; France 3 years 3 months.

Killick, John (1914–18); Private, Northumberland Fusiliers; France 3 years 9 months.

Killingray, Philip John (1915–19); Private, Essex Rgt.; Egypt 3 years 6 months.

Kimber, William Joseph (1915–18); Sapper, R.E.; Egypt and France 3 years 8 months.

***King, Alfred John** (1914–15); Lance-Corporal, R. Berkshire Rgt.; France 5 months; Killed in action, 13th October, 1915.

King, Charles Augustus (1914–19); Private, R.A.F.

King, Ernest (1914–19); Private, Royal Fusiliers; France 4 months, Prisoner of war (Germany) 3 years 6 months.

King, Frederick Charles (1915–19); Flight-Sergeant, R.A.F.

King, James Edwin (1917); Private, R.A.M.C.

King, John Herbert (1914–19); Private, R.A.M.C.; France 2 years.

King, Thomas William (1914–19); Sergeant, R.F.A.; France 2 years 6 months.

***King, William Eugene** (1916–18); Driver, R.A.S.C.; France 18 months; Died of wounds, 11th December, 1918.

Kingham, George Edward (1916–19); Sapper, R.E.; France 2 years.

Kingsley, Frederick (1914–19); M.M.; Private, 2nd Dragoons; France 4 years 5 months.

Kington, William (1914–16); Petty Officer (2nd Class), R.N.

Kinsey, George Henry (1915–19); Gunner, R.F.A.; France 3 years.

Kinsey, William Stephen (1916–18); Private, Machine Gun Corps; France 1 year.

Kinton, Walter William (1915–19); Mentioned in despatches; Driver, R.A.S.C.; France 2 years 6 months.

***Kirby, Ebenezer** (1915–16); Corporal, R.F.A.; France 5 months; Died of wounds, 24th May, 1916.

Kislingbury, Alfred James (1915–19); Driver, R.F.A.; France, Salonica, Egypt and Palestine, 2 years 9 months.

Kite, Walter George (1914–18); Private, Machine Gun Corps; France 2 months.

***Klein, George** (1914–15); Corporal, London Rgt.; France 2 months; Killed in action, 25th May, 1915.

Knapp, Albert Thomas (1914–19); Regimental Quartermaster-Sergeant, Border Rgt.; France 2 months, Salonica 3 years 4 months.

Knight, George (1914–19); Trooper, 20th Hussars; France 4 months.

Knight, Herbert (1914–19); Mentioned in despatches; Sergeant-Major, R.A.F.

Knight, Percy (1915–18); Sapper, R.E.; France.

Knight, Richard Herbert (1915–19); Sergeant, R.A.S.C.; France, Salonica and Egypt, 2 years 9 months.

Knightley, Phillip (1915–19); D.C.M.; Sergeant, R.F.A.; France 3 years 6 months.

Knights, Ernest (1914–19); Driver, R.A.S.C.; France 1 month, Salonica 6 months, Egypt 2 years.

Knivett, Albert John (1914–19); Corporal, London Rgt.; France 6 months.

Knopp, Nathaniel (1915–19); Driver, R.E.; France and Mesopotamia 3 years 6 months.

Knopp, William (1914–18); Private, R.D.C.

Kyne, Thomas James (1914); Private, W. Kent Yeomanry.

Lafferty, Frederick Arthur (1914–19); Signaller, E. Kent Rgt.; France 3 years 7 months.

***Laird, William Joseph** (1914–17); Sergeant, London Rgt.; France 2 years 8 months; Killed in action, 4th November, 1917.

Lake, Albert Ernest (1914–19); Mentioned in despatches; Chief Petty Officer, R.N.

Lake, Alfred Henry (1916–19); M.M.; Private, Royal Fusiliers; France 2 years.

Lake, John Patrick (1914–19); Private, Durham Light Infantry; France 4 years 4 months.

Lamb, James Charles (1916–18); Rifleman, London Rgt.; France and Salonica 14 months.

Lambert, George (1914–19); Driver, R.E.; France 3 years 11 months.

Lambert, James Walter (1914–19); Private, R.A.M.C.; France 3 years 11 months.

Lambert, Joseph Claude (1918–19); Private, Machine Gun Corps.

Lambert, Thomas (1914–19); Private, Middlesex Rgt., and Corporal, Labour Corps; France 4 years 2 months.

Lambourne, William (1916–17); Private, Essex Rgt.

Laming, Frederick Charles (1914–19); Sergeant, R.F.A.; France, Mesopotamia and India, 3 years 6 months.

Lane, George (1914–19); Private, Middlesex Rgt.

Langdon, William Charles (1914–19); Driver, R.A.S.C.; France 8 months, Mesopotamia 1 year 10 months.

Langdon, William Ernest (1915–19); Private, R.A.M.C.; France 3 years 6 months, Germany 3 months.

Langford, Thomas Henry (1914–19); Sergeant, London Rgt.; France 3 years 10 months.

Langrish, Henry John (1914–17); Driver, R.F.A.

Lansdell, Harry (1916–19); Private, R.A.M.C.

Lapworth, Walter Osborne (1914–16); Gunner, R.F.A.; France 11 months.

Lardge, James William (1915–18); Corporal, A.P.C.

Last, Frank James (1917–19); Sapper, R.E.; France 15 months.

***Laver, Edward Cyril** (1914–16); Gunner, R.F.A.; France 7 months; Died of wounds, 19th June, 1916.

Lavers, Frank (1915–19); Driver, R.A.S.C.; France 1 year 9 months.

Law, George (1914–16); Rifleman, London Rgt.

Law, John Alfred (1915–19); Private, London Rgt.; France 1 year 10 months, Prisoner of war (Germany) 8 months.

Lawes, William (1914–17); Trooper, 15th Hussars; France 2 years 2 months.

Lawrence, Henry George (1914–19); Sergeant, Middlesex Rgt.

Lawrence, Herbert (1915–18); Sergeant, R.A.V.C.; France 2 years 7 months.

Lawrence, Walter George (1917–19); Sapper, R.E.; France and Germany 1 year 8 months.

Laws, William Charles (1914–19); Corporal, R.F.A.; France 3 years.

Lawson, Norman (1914–16); Private, Argyll and Sutherland Highlanders; France 3 months.

Leach, Edward Archibald (1914); Private, London Rgt.

Leader, George (1918–19); Driver, R.A.S.C.; France 2 months.

Leamon, Frederick Ellis (1917–19); Gunner, R.F.A.; France 10 months.

Leaney, Walter Daniel (1915–19); Pioneer, R.E.; France 3 years.

Lear, Alfred James (1914–19); Gunner, R.F.A.; France 3 years.

Leavey, Edward (1916–19); Private, Leicestershire Rgt.; France 7 months.

Lee, Arthur James (1915–17); Private, S. Wales Borderers; France 1 year.

Lee, William Charles (1915–19); Sergeant, R.F.A.; France 3 years 6 months.

Leeder, Robert (1916–19); Private, Tank Corps; France 2 years 9 months.

Leeves, Thomas Albert (1914–19); Sergeant, Loyal N. Lancashire Rgt.; France 3 months.

Legge, Charles John (1916–19); Corporal, Labour Corps; France 2 years 6 months.

Leggett, Arthur Percy (1915–18); Private, Middlesex Rgt.; France 15 months.

Leighton, George Albert (1914); Petty Officer (1st Class), R.F.R.

***Leighton, Harry Ethelbert** (1916–17); Rifleman, King's Royal Rifle Corps; France 1 year; Killed in action, 26th December, 1917.

Lelliott, Herbert Luke (1915–18); Sapper, R.E.; France 2 years 3 months.

Lemage, Sidney Charles (1916–19); Gunner, R.G.A.

Leonard, Charles Peter (1914–17); Driver, R.F.A.; France 3 years 8 months.

Lever, Arthur William (1915–19); Driver, R.F.A.; France 4 years.

***Leverington, James** (1915–16); Rifleman, London Rgt.; France 5 months; Missing, 1st July, 1916.

Levett, Alfred Henry (1915–19); Driver Wheeler, R.A.S.C.; France 3 years 10 months.

Levy, Henry Thomas (1914–16); Corporal, R. Berkshire Rgt.; France 7 months.

Lewington, George John (1916–17 and 1917–19); Private, R.A.M.C.; France and Germany 18 months.

Lewis, Arthur Thomas (1914–18); Sergeant, R.G.A.; France 2 years.

Lewis, Charles Samuel (1916–17); Private, London Rgt.

Lewis, George William (1914–19); Chief Petty Officer, R.N.; Naval Service.

Lewis, Horatio Montague (1914–19); Lance-Sergeant, London Rgt.; France 9 months.

Lewis, John William (1915–19); Private, Essex Rgt.; France 1 year 7 months, Egypt 17 months.

Lewis, Mark Owen (1916–19); Private, Labour Corps; France 2 years.

***Lewis, Samuel Arthur** (1914–18); Gunner, R.F.A.; France 2 years 5 months; Missing, 27th March, 1918.

Lewis, Thomas Henry (1914–19); Gunner, R.F.A.; France 15 months.

Lewis, Thomas William (1915–18); Gunner, R.G.A.; France 2 years 1 month.

Lewis, Thomas William (1916–19); Air Mechanic (3rd Class), R.A.F.; France 7 months.

***Lewis, William Benjamin** (1916–17); Private, Royal Fusiliers; France 7 months; Missing, 31st July, 1917.

Leys, Charles (1914–19); Private, Labour Corps; France and Salonica 3 years.

Lias, William James (1914–19); Sergeant, R.W. Surrey Rgt. and Labour Corps; France 2 years.

Licence, Henry Francis (1915–19); Private, R.A.S.C.; France 3 years 7 months.

Liddard, John (1915–19); Private, R.A.S.C.; Palestine and Egypt 3 years 9 months.

Lightfoot, William (1915–19); Private, R.A.O.C.; France 3 years 11 months.

***Lilburn, Henry** (1915–17); Bombardier, R.F.A.; France 1 year 9 months; Killed in action, 8th November, 1917.

Liles, George Charles (1918); Private, R.A.M.C.

Lilley, Harry (1914–17); Lance-Corporal, London Rgt.

Lillie, Henry Benjamin (1917–19); 1st Aircraftsman, R.A.F.; France 18 months.

Lilly, Joseph Douglas (1914–19); Corporal, M.F.P.; Malta 8 months.

Ling, Claude (1917–19); Private, Northamptonshire Rgt.; France 1 month, Prisoner of war (Germany) 7 months.

Ling, George Robert (1915–19); Sergeant, R.A.S.C.; Mesopotamia 2 years 9 months.

Ling, William Gordon (1915–19); Bombardier, R.G.A.; France 2 years.

Ling, William Sidney (1915–17); M.M.; Sergeant, R.A.V.C.; France 2 years 6 months.

Lingard, Frank Howard (1914–16); Gunner, R.F.A.; France and Salonica 15 months.

Lingham, Charles (1915–18); Private, Royal Fusiliers; East Africa 3 years.

Lingwood, Frederick (1915–19); Sapper, R.E.; France 6 months.

Linklater, George (1916–19); Corporal, Suffolk Rgt.; France 2 months.

Linnington, Alfred George (1918–19); Rifleman, Rifle Brigade.

Lisney, James Thomas (1914–17); Corporal, E. Surrey Rgt.; France 5 months, Salonica 14 months.

Little, Arthur (1918–19); Private, Machine Gun Corps.

Little, George James (1915–19); Private, R.D.C.

Livermore, Edward Harry Graham (1917–18); Private, Cheshire Rgt.; France 1 month.

Livett, William Thomas (1914–19); Private, R.A.O.C.; Egypt and France 3 years.

Lloyd, Alfred Ernest (1914–19); Private, R. Marine Light Infantry; Naval Service 4 years 6 months.

Lloyd, William (1915–19); Private, R.A.M.C.; Salonica 2 years 7 months.

Loader, Albert (1914–17); Private, Labour Corps; France 1 year.

Lock, Charles (1914–18); Lance-Corporal, M.M.P.; France 3 years 7 months.

***Lock, Henry John** (1914–15); Sergeant, Middlesex Rgt.; France 5 months; Killed in action, 9th May, 1915.

Lock, Joseph William (1914–19); Driver, R.F.A.; France 3 years 10 months.

Lock, Percy John (1914–16); Trooper, 3rd Reserve Cavalry Rgt.; France 13 months.

Locke, Edgar James (1915–19); Private, R.A.S.C.; France 3 years 11 months.

Locke, Henry George (1914–19); Bombardier, R.F.A.; France and Salonica 2 years 10 months.

Lockwood, Thomas Frederick (1918–19); Private, R. Sussex Rgt.

Lockyer, Henry Walter (1915–19); Corporal, R.W. Surrey Rgt.; France 2 years 2 months.

Lodge, James (1914–15); Corporal, Essex Rgt.

***Long, Evan David** (1914–15); Sergeant, Wiltshire Rgt.; Dardanelles 2 months; Missing, 10th August, 1915.

Long, George (1914–19); Gunner, R.G.A.; France 3 years 8 months.

Long, Hugh (1914–19); Corporal, E. Yorkshire Rgt.

***Long, Sydney Frederick** (1915–17); Lance-Corporal, London Rgt.; France 16 months; Died of wounds, 9th December, 1917.

Lopez, Thomas (1915–19); Private, R.A.S.C.; France 4 years.

Lord, William Frederick (1914–19); Sergeant, Dorsetshire Rgt.; France 2 years 1 month.

Loscombe, Alexander Frederick (1914–19); Signaller, R.F.A.; France, Salonica and Egypt.

Loveday, Charles Thomas (1918–19); Flight-Sergeant, R.A.F.; France 1 month.

Loveless, Reginald Thomas (1918–19); Air Mechanic (3rd Class), R.A.F.

Lovell, Henry Robert (1915–18); Corporal, Machine Gun Corps; Egypt 7 months, France 4 months.

Lovell, William (1915–19); Corporal, R.A.S.C.; Egypt 3 years 4 months.

Lovett, Walter David (1914–19); Sergeant, Labour Corps; France and Germany 2 years 9 months.

Lowdell, James (1914–19); Private, E. Kent Rgt.; France 3 years 6 months.

Lowe, Leonard (1915–19); Lance-Corporal, Suffolk Rgt.; Salonica and Dardanelles 1 year 9 months.

***Lower, Samuel** (1915–16); Private, Royal Fusiliers; France 1 year; Killed in action, 7th July, 1916.

Lower, William Walter (1914–19); Able Seaman, R.N.; Naval Service 4 years.

Lown, Victor (1915–19); Driver, R.A.S.C.; France 2 years 3 months.

Lowry, Walter Alexander (1917–18); Rifleman, London Rgt.; France 5 months.

Lowson, William (1915–19); Rifleman, London Rgt.; France 3 years.

Lowther, John Christopher (1917–18); Gunner, Honourable Artillery Company; France 3 months.

Lucas, William Thomas (1918–19); Private, R. Sussex Rgt.; France 18 days.

Luck, William Frederick (1915–19); Shoeing-Smith, R.E.; France 2 years 4 months.

Lucker, George Edmonds (1915–19); Private, Bedfordshire Rgt.; India 3 years 2 months.

Luckhurst, Edward William Charles (1915–19); Corporal, R.A.S.C.; France 3 years.

Luckhurst, Henry Edward Joseph (1916–19); Private, R.A.S.C.; France 13 months.

***Luckhurst, William Albert Victor** (1914–15); Private, London Rgt.; France 2 months; Killed in action, 18th May, 1915.

Ludbrook, Charles Henry (1914–19); Sec.-Lieutenant, R.F.A.; France and Germany 4 years 10 months.

Luetchford, Christopher Jonathan (1915–19); Gunner, R.F.A.; France, Salonica and Egypt, 2 years 9 months.

Luff, John Francis (1914–19); Corporal, London Rgt.; Malta and France 4 years 4 months.

Lungley, Robert William Benjamin (1918–19); Stoker (1st Class), R.N.; Naval Service.

Lunney, James (1915–19); Corporal Shoeing-Smith, R.F.A.; Salonica 14 months.

Lupton, Charles Arnold (1917–19); Pioneer, R.E.

Luther, Frederick Charles (1916–19); D.C.M.; Private, Wiltshire Rgt.; France 2 years 7 months.

Luther, Martin (1915–19); Driver, R.F.A.; France 3 years 1 month.

Lutter, George (1915–19); Gunner, R.F.A.; France, Salonica and Egypt, 2 years 10 months.

Luttridge, Charles Henry (1918–19); Private, R. W. Kent Rgt.

Lye, William (1916–19); Private, Machine Gun Corps; France and Prisoner of war (Germany) 18 months.

Lynch, Charles Edward (1915–19); Rifleman, Rifle Brigade; Burmah 3 years 11 months.

Lynch, Edward Alexander (1914–18); Company Sergeant-Major, Royal Fusiliers and Labour Corps; France 3 months.

Lynch, John Joseph Aloysius (1916–17); Driver, R.F.A.

Lynch, Michael (1915–18); Private, Machine Gun Corps; Palestine and France 2 years 8 months.

Lyne, George (1914–19); Air Mechanic (2nd Class), R.A.F.; France 1 year 7 months.

Lyne, John Frederick Charles (1914–19); Driver, R.F.A.; Egypt and Palestine 3 years 9 months.

Mable, Benjamin (1914–20); Regimental Quartermaster-Sergeant, London Rgt.; Gallipoli, Egypt and Syria, 4 years 7 months.

Macclesworth, Henry (1915–19); Private, R.A.S.C. (M.T.); France 3 years 6 months.

MacDonald, Alexander James (1914–19); M.M.; Corporal, Cyclist Corps; France 3 years 4 months.

Mace, John (1914–17); Private, E. Kent Rgt.

Macintyre, Robert Edward (1914–19); M.M.; Corporal, London Rgt. and Labour Corps; France, Salonica and Egypt, 2 years 9 months.

Macmaster, Hugh Archibald (1915–19); Corporal, R.A.M.C.; France 2 years 6 months.

***Madden, Albert John** (1916–17); Private, Northumberland Fusiliers; France 6 months; Missing, 16th August, 1917.

Madkins, Thomas Albert (1916–19); Private, R.A.O.C.; France 2 months.

Maides, Albert James (1918–19); Lance-Corporal, Royal Fusiliers; France 13 months.

Mainwaring, Julius Thomas (1914–15); Gunner, R.F.A.

Major, Percy Norman (1915–19); Corporal, R.A.M.C.; Egypt 2 years 10 months, Gibraltar 15 months.

Malyan, William Henry (1915–19); Sapper, R.E.; Palestine and Egypt 3 years 4 months.

Manby, Arthur (1914–19); Corporal, Machine Gun Corps; France 1 year 9 months.

Mancey, Alfred John (1915–18); Sapper, R.E.; France and Greece 2 years 3 months.

Manester, William Leslie (1915–19); Private, Machine Gun Corps; France 1 year 9 months.

Manfield, Frederick Ernest (1915–19); Fitter, R.F.A.; France 3 years.

Mann, Charles (1914–17); Private, R.D.C.

Mann, Harry James (1914); Private, Hertfordshire Yeomanry.

Mann, James (1916–19); Gunner, R.G.A.; France 2 years 1 month.

Manning, Frederick George (1915–19); Sergeant, London Rgt. and Labour Corps; France 3 months.

Manning, Timothy (1915–17); Private, R. Munster Fusiliers; France.

Manning, Walter (1916–18); Private, Norfolk Rgt.; France 8 months.

Manning, William (1915–19); Private, R.A.S.C.; France 4 years.

Mansfield, Charles Philip (1915–16); Private, London Rgt.

Manwaring, Charles Alfred (1916–19); Gunner, R.F.A.; Egypt, Palestine, France and Salonica, 2 years 9 months.

March, Henry Charles (1914–18); Private, Welch Rgt.; France and Gibraltar 3 years 4 months.

March, William John (1914–18); Corporal, Labour Corps; France 1 year.

Marchant, John (1914–19); Corporal, Middlesex Rgt.; France 1 year 11 months.

Marchment, Albert Edward (1914–19); Leading Seaman, R.N.; Naval Service 3 years 7 months.

Marfleet, Walter Robert (1915–19); Lance-Corporal, R.E.; France 3 years 6 months.

Margerum, Walter (1917–19); Private, Somersetshire Light Infantry.

Mariner, James (1914–19); Private, Labour Corps; France 10 months.

***Marks, Leonard Martin** (1914–16); Corporal, Essex Rgt.; France 1 year, Egypt 6 months; Killed in action, 15th October, 1916.

Markwick, Thomas Alfred David (1917–19); Private, Worcestershire Rgt.

Marley, Clarence George (1915–19); Bombardier, R.F.A.; France 3 years.

Marley, Richard Miles (1914–19); Lance-Corporal, R.D.C.

Marney, Thomas (1916–19); Private, Labour Corps.

Marrion, William John (1915–19); Driver, R.E.; France 13 months.

Marriott, John (1918–19); Gunner, R.F.A.

Marsh, Edgar Robert (1915–19); Driver, R.E.; France 3 years.

***Marsh, Harold** (1914–15); Rifleman, London Rgt.; France 6 months; Killed in action, 25th September, 1915.

Marsh, James Frederick (1915–19); Private, R.A.S.C.; France 14 months.

Marsh, Stephen John Thomas (1914–19); Private, 9th Lancers; France 7 months.

Marshall, Albert Arthur (1914–17); Sergeant, R.A.V.C.; France 2 years 7 months.

Marshall, Alfred William (1914–15); Trooper, County of London Yeomanry.

Marshall, George Frederick (1915–19); Gunner, R.F.A.; France 3 years 6 months.

Marshall, Herbert James (1915–19); Lance-Corporal, R.A.M.C.; France and Germany 3 years 8 months.

Marshall, Herbert James (1915–19); Private, London Rgt.; France 1 year 8 months.

***Marshall, James Richard** (1914 15); Private, Worcestershire Rgt.; France 1 year; Died of wounds, 26th August, 1915.

Marshall, Leonard William Edward (1916–19); Private, Durham Light Infantry; France 16 months.

***Marshall, Percy** (1914); Private, Lincolnshire Rgt.; France 1 month; Died of wounds, 11th September, 1914.

***Marson, Herbert John Richard** (1914–15); Private, Essex Rgt.; Dardanelles 3 months: Died of dysentery, 24th November, 1915.

Marston, Arthur (1915–19); Gunner, R.G.A.; France 3 years.

***Martin, Albert** (1914–16); Private, E. Surrey Rgt.; France 11 months; Killed in action, 12th August, 1916.

***Martin, Albert George** (1914); Private, Wiltshire Rgt.; France 2 months; Died of wounds, 24th October, 1914.

Martin, Albert James (1914–19); Leading Seaman, R.N.; Naval Service 2 years 10 months.

Martin, Alfred (1914–19); Corporal, R.A.S.C.; France 4 years 5 months.

Martin, Alfred Ernest (1914–19); Private, 4th Hussars; France 2 years 10 months, Prisoner of war (Germany) 9 months.

Martin, Arthur (1916–17); Rifleman, King's Royal Rifle Corps; France 7 months.

Martin, Charles Alfred (1915–19); Gunner, R.F.A.

***Martin, Charles Edward John** (1914); Lance - Corporal, R.W. Surrey Rgt.; France 3 months; Died of wounds, 4th December, 1914.

Martin, Conway (1916–19); Private, Labour Corps; France 3 years 3 months.

Martin, Francis Edward (1917–19); Private, R.A.M.C.; France 11 months.

Martin, James (1914–19); Corporal, R.A.S.C. (M.T.); France 4 years.

Martin, Leonard (1917–19); Rifleman, Rifle Brigade; France 1 year 8 months.

***Martin, Patrick** (1914–18); Lance-Corporal, Royal Fusiliers; France 3 years 8 months; Died, 20th November, 1918.

***Martin, Stanley Edward** (1916–18); Guardsman, Grenadier Guards; France 1 year; Died of wounds, 27th May, 1918.

Martin, Sydney William (1915–19); Corporal, R.F.A.; France 16 months.

Martin, William (1914–19); Private, 12th Lancers; France 4 years 5 months.

Martingell, Russell George (1914–19); Hon. Lieutenant, R.A.F.; France 16 months.

Mash, William Joseph (1915–19); Private, E. Surrey Rgt.; France 6 weeks, Prisoner of war (Germany) 3 years 6 months.

Maskell, William Ernest (1914–19); Able Seaman, R.N.; Naval Service 4 years 6 months.

Maslin, Jesse (1915–19); M.M. and bar; Sergeant, R.E.; France 2 years 9 months.

Mason, Alfred (1914–16); Private, Royal Fusiliers; France and Dardanelles 7 months.

Mason, Alfred (1914–19); Corporal Shoeing-Smith, 3rd Reserve Hussars; France 6 months.

Mason, Charles Edward (1916–18); Private, London Rgt.; France 2 years 10 months.

Mason, Harry (1914–19); Company Quartermaster-Sergeant, E. Kent Rgt.; Mesopotamia 1 year 8 months.

Mason, Henry (1914–19); Private, 15th Hussars; France and Egypt 3 years 4 months.

Masters, Frederick (1918–19); Private, E. Surrey Rgt.; France and Germany 1 year.

Masters, Percy Richard (1918–19); Sapper, R.E.

Mather, Walter Patrick (1914–17); Private, R.D.C.

Maton, Frank (1915–17); Corporal, R.F.A.

Matthews, Albert Edward (1915–19); Driver, R.F.A.; France 3 years 6 months.

Matthews, Alfred James (1914–16); Private, Training Bn.

Matthews, Frank Maurice (1915); Private, Grenadier Guards.

Matthews, George (1916–19); Private, R. Guernsey Light Infantry; France 15 months.

***Matthews, James Ellis** (1914–15); Mentioned in despatches; Private, Middlesex Rgt.; France 8 months; Killed in action, 19th July, 1915.

Mattick, William Charles (1916–18); Private, Oxfordshire and Buckinghamshire Light Infantry; France and Salonica 10 months.

***May, Archibald William** (1916–18); Private, R.W. Surrey Rgt.; France 1 year; Killed in action, 13th April, 1918.

Maycock, Alfred Charles Herbert (1916–19); Corporal, R.A.S.C.; France 1 year.

Mayers, George (1915–19); Bombardier, R.F.A.; France 3 years 2 months.

Mayes, John William (1914–19); Corporal, R.A.S.C.; France 4 years 7 months.

Mayo, Thomas Richard (1916–18); Rifleman, Rifle Brigade; France 13 months.

Mayze, Henry (1914–19); Private, Argyle and Sutherland Highlanders.

McCarthy, Daniel (1916–19); Driver, R.H.A.; France 2 years 3 months.

McCarthy, Denis Jeremiah (1914–19); Shoeing-Smith, R.A.S.C.; France, Salonica and Egypt, 3 years.

McCarthy, Patrick (1915–18); Private, R. Munster Fusiliers.

McCarthy, William Alfred (1917–19); Private, Norfolk Rgt.; France 3 months.

McCartney, Arthur George (1914–19); Leading Seaman, R.N.; Naval Service 4 years 8 months.

McColl, John (1914–19); M.M.; Sergeant, E. Surrey Rgt.; France 3 years 4 months.

McCrossan, Thomas (1915–19); Mentioned in despatches; Corporal, R.E.; Dardanelles 5 months, Macedonia 3 years 2 months.

McDermott, Charles John (1914–19); Lance-Corporal, London Rgt.; Egypt 1 year 8 months, France 6 months, Salonica 7 months.

McDonald, Albert William (1915–19); Driver, R.A.S.C.; Salonica 2 years 8 months.

McDonnell, Richard (1915–19); Sergeant, Royal Fusiliers; France 2 years.

McDougall, Frederick James (1914–19); Gunner Signaller, R.F.A.; Italy and France 3 years 6 months.

McEwen, Thomas (1914–18); Private, R.D.C.

McGowan, Herbert George (1914–18); Corporal, R.E.; Mesopotamia 1 year 9 months, India 2 years 8 months.

McGrail, John (1914–19); M.S.M.; Company Sergeant-Major, R.A.S.C.; France, Egypt and Palestine 3 years.

McGuirk, James Patrick (1916–19); Private, R.A.S.C. (M.T.).

McIntosh, Alfred (1915–19); Private, R.W. Surrey Rgt.; France 2 months, Prisoner of war (Germany) 3 years 3 months.

McKee, Charles Alfred (1915–19); Lance-Corporal, R.E.; France 5 months.

McKenna, Robert William (1917–18); Private, R.A.V.C.

McLaren, Le Roy (1914–19); Private, London Rgt.; France 2 years.

McMahon, William Matthew (1914); Private, Nottinghamshire and Derbyshire Rgt.

McQuade, Frank James (1914–19); Bombardier, R.F.A.; France and Salonica 3 years 7 months.

Mead, Albert de Montpied (1914–19); Sec.-Lieutenant, R.A.F.

Mead, George James (1914–19); Driver, R.F.A.; France 4 years 1 month.

Mead, John (1915–19); Private, R.D.C.

Meagher, Michael Joseph Patrick (1915–16); Sergeant, R. Irish Fusiliers.

Meakins, Henry Thomas (1914–19); Corporal, R.A.S.C.; France 2 years 11 months.

Mears, Harry Martin (1914–17); Bandsman, Reserve Cavalry.

Meatyard, Robert Edward (1917); Private, Labour Corps.

Mee, Charles Arthur (1918–19); Gunner, R.G.A.; Italy 9 months.

Mellars, Sydney Paul (1915–19); Gunner, R.F.A.; France, Salonica, Egypt and Palestine, 2 years 9 months.

Mells, Edmund Arthur (1914–19); Private, R.A.S.C.; France 4 years.

Melton, Albert George (1916–19); Private, R.A.F.

Menday, Robert Charles (1918–19); Private, R. Sussex Rgt.; France 3 months.

Mercer, Douglas William Yates (1917–19); Lance-Corporal, Duke of Cornwall's Light Infantry; France 5 months.

Merrington, William Henry (1917–18): Acting 1st Mechanic, R.A.F.

Merry, Henry John (1915–19); Gunner, R.G.A.; France 2 years 8 months.

Merryweather, William George (1915–19); Driver, R.A.S.C.; France, Italy and Germany, 3 years 11 months.

Meteyard, Leslie (1914-19); Corporal, R.A.S.C. (M.T.); France, Salonica and Egypt, 18 months.

Metson, James (1916–19); Sergeant, Hampshire Rgt.; Egypt and Sudan 2 years 8 months.

Meyer, Frederick John (1914–19); Sergeant, Essex Rgt.; Gallipoli and Egypt 3 years 11 months.

Middleton, George (1915–19); M.M.; Battery Quartermaster-Sergeant, R.F.A.; France 2 years 3 months.

Miell, Frederick James Charles (1916–17); Private, R.W. Surrey Rgt.

Miles, Charles William (1917–18); Sapper, R.E.

Miles, Sidney Herbert (1915–19); Sapper, R.E.; France 3 years 8 months.

Millard, Armagle William (1916–19); Lance-Corporal, E. Surrey Rgt.; France 2 years 9 months.

Miller, Albert Arthur (1915–19); Pioneer, R.E.; Dardanelles and France 1 year 9 months.

Miller, Arthur George (1918–19); Air Mechanic (3rd Class), R.A.F.

***Miller, Charles** (1915–17); Private, E. Surrey Rgt.; France 18 months; Missing, 21st September, 1917.

Miller, George (1914–17); Private, Training Reserve.

Miller, Henry Leonard (1914–19); Pioneer, R.E.

***Miller, Herbert** (1914–16); Private, Middlesex Rgt.; France 11 months; Killed in action, 18th August, 1916.

Miller, Jacob Albert (1917–19); Sapper, R.E.; Egypt 1 year 8 months.

Miller, John Frank (1915-19); Bombardier, R.G.A.; France 3 years 3 months.

Miller, Reginald William (1914–19); Sergeant, Wiltshire Rgt.; Gallipoli and Mesopotamia 3 years 8 months.

Miller, William (1916–19); Private, Royal Fusiliers; Egypt 2 years 7 months.

Millgate, Albert Edward (1916–18); Rifleman, London Rgt.

Millgate, George John (1915–19); Driver, R.F.A.; France 4 years 3 months.

Milling, William (1914–18); Shoeing-Smith, 3rd Hussars; France 3 years 11 months.

Millo, Sidney George (1917–19); Corporal Mechanic, R.A.F.

Mills, Charles (1914–19); Gunner, R.F.A.; France 3 years 9 months.

Mills, George (1915–19); Battery Sergeant-Major, R.F.A.; France, Egypt, Salonica and Palestine, 2 years 8 months.

Mills, George Edwin (1915–19); Sapper, R.E.; France 3 years 4 months.

Mills, George Henry (1916–19); Gunner, R.G.A.; France 14 months, Salonica 13 months.

Mills, Harry William (1914–17); Sergeant, King's Royal Rifle Corps; France.

Mills, Herbert Valence (1916–19); Private, R.A.O.C.

***Mills, James Charles** (1914–16): Sergeant, London Rgt.; France 16 months; Killed in action, 15th September, 1916.

Mills, John Alexander (1914–19); Corporal, R.D.C.

Mills, Sidney Samuel (1914–16); Sapper, R. Marine Light Infantry; Naval Service.

Mills, Thomas William (1914–19); Driver, R.F.A.; France 14 months, Salonica 3 years.

Milne, Henry Malcolm (1914–15); Lance-Corporal, King's Royal Rifle Corps; France 5 months.

Milne, William John (1915–18); Driver, R.F.A.; France 6 months.

Milner, Walker Arthur Joseph (1916–18); Gunner, R.G.A.; France 13 months.

Milo, John (1915–19); Driver, R.E.; France 3 years 4 months.

Milton, Alfred Thomas (1914–19); Driver, R.E.; France 3 years 7 months.

Milton, Thomas Frederick (1914–19); Lieutenant, County of London Yeomanry; Egypt and Palestine 13 months, France and Germany 17 months.

Minahan, William Albert (1917–20); Private, R.A.S.C. (M.T.); Egypt 2 years 3 months.

Minson, Albert Joseph (1918–19); Air Mechanic (2nd Class), R.A.F.

Mirams, Louis Stephen (1915–19); M.S.M.; Staff Sergeant-Major, R.A.S.C.; France 3 years 4 months.

Mitchell, Alfred Osborne (1914–19); Driver, R.H.A.; France 4 years 3 months.

Mitchell, Cyril James Dudley (1915–19); Gunner, R.G.A.; Egypt 1 year 9 months.

Mitchell, Francis (1915–19); Signaller, R.F.A.; France 3 years 2 months.

Mitchell, Herbert (1914–19); Able Seaman, R.N.; Naval Service 4 years 6 months.

Mockford, Hubert Vivian Claude (1916–19); Gunner, R.G.A.; France 2 years.

Moir, Horace Edwin (1915–19); Driver, R.A.S.C.; France 2 years 3 months.

Monk, Charles Thomas (1914–19); Private, E. Surrey Rgt.: France and Salonica 3 years, Prisoner of war 9 months.

Monk, Henry Lewis (1915–20); Acting Sergeant, R.F.A.; Mesopotamia 2 years 6 months.

Monk, James Henry (1914–18); Private, R.D.C.

Moodie, Albert Herbert (1915–19); Private, E. Surrey Rgt.; France and Russia 3 years.

Moody, Charles Frederick (1914–19); D.C.M., M.M., Mentioned in despatches; Sergeant, R. Sussex Rgt.; France 18 months.

Moody, William (1914); Private, Essex Rgt.

Moody, William James (1914–19); Gunner, R. Marine Artillery; Naval Service 4 years 3 months.

Moore, Alfred John (1914–19); Private, Suffolk Rgt.; France 6 months.

Moore, Bert (1914–19); Shoeing-Smith, R.F.A.; France 2 years.

***Moore, Edward** (1914–16); Private, Reserve Cavalry Rgt.; France 8 months; Died, 10th January, 1916.

***Moore, Edwin Walter** (1914); Private, Royal Fusiliers; France 2 months; Missing, 26th October, 1914.

***Moore, George** (1914–15); Private, E. Surrey Rgt.; France 1 month; Killed in action, 28th May, 1915.

Moore, George Henry (1915–19); Lance-Corporal, R.A.S.C.

Moore, John Leslie (1915–19); Private, R.A.M.C.; France 2 years.

Moore, William John (1918–19); Private, Suffolk Rgt.

Moran, Michael (1917–18); Pioneer, R.E.

Morbin, John Henry (1914–16); Driver, R.F.A.; France.

Moreton, Frank (1914–19); Sergeant, R.E.; France 4 months.

***Morgan, George Henry** (1914–15); Private, R. Marine Light Infantry; Belgium and Egypt 7 months; Missing, 29th April, 1915.

Morgan, Harry (1916–19); Pioneer, R.E.; Salonica 2 years 8 months.

Morgan, Stanley Frank (1914–19); Signaller, R.W. Kent Rgt.; France 3 years.

Moriarty, John (1916–19); Private, Northumberland Fusiliers; France 14 months.

Morley, Alfred Robert (1914–19); Private, 20th Hussars; France 4 years 5 months.

Morris, Frederick (1914–19); Private, Duke of Cornwall's Light Infantry; France 1 year.

Morris, George John Bernard (1914–19); Saddler, Essex Rgt.; Gallipoli, Egypt and Syria, 4 years.

Morris, William George (1917–19); Private, Labour Corps; France and Germany 2 years 4 months.

Morris, William James (1915–19); Bombardier, R.F.A.; France 8 months, Salonica 2 years 10 months.

Morrish, Charles William (1917–19); Private, Labour Corps; France 9 months.

Mortimer, Albert Victor (1914–17); Private, Gloucestershire Rgt.

Morton, Arthur (1914–18); Gunner, R.F.A.; France 9 months, Salonica 15 months.

Moseley, William (1915–19); Private, Labour Corps; France 1 year, Italy 15 months.

Moss, Albert Henry (1915–19); Driver, R.F.A.; France 3 years 4 months.

***Moss, Robert Charles** (1914–18); Private, R.A.S.C. (M.T.); France 4 years; Died, 2nd December, 1918.

Moss, Thomas Henry (1916–17); Private, Devonshire Rgt.

Moss, William Byford (1914–19); Private, Royal Fusiliers.

Moth, Walter William (1915–19); Private, London Rgt.; Egypt and France 2 years 9 months.

Mott, Alfred (1914–19); Lance-Bombardier, R.F.A.; France 3 years 5 months.

***Mott, Walter James** (1914–15); Private, R.W. Kent Rgt.; France 6 months; Killed in action, 9th March, 1915.

Mould, Oscar Charles (1915–17); Private, Honourable Artillery Company.

Moulds, Sidney Arthur (1914–19); Driver, R.A.S.C.; France 4 years 6 months.

Moule, Alfred Frank (1915–19); Gunner, R.F.A.; France, Salonica and Egypt, 2 years 10 months.

Mudd, Thomas Henry (1916–19); Driver, R.F.A.; France 2 years.

Mullett, George (1914–17); Private, Devonshire Rgt.

Mullin, Patrick (1915–19); Sapper, R.E.; France, Egypt, Salonica and Mesopotamia, 3 years 9 months.

Mulloy, Michael (1914–16); Private, Irish Guards; France.

Mulvany, James (1915–19); Private, Somersetshire Light Infantry; France 7 months.

Mumford, Henry James (1914–18); Sergeant, R.G.A.; France 3 years.

Muncey, Frederick George (1916–19); Private, Labour Corps; Salonica 2 years 3 months.

Munday, Philip (1914–19); Chief Petty Officer, R.N.; Naval Service 1 year 7 months.

Munford, Albert Edwin (1915–19); Private, R.A.S.C. (M.T.); France 3 years 11 months.

Munro, Charles (1916–19); Shoeing-Smith and Bombardier, R.F.A.; France 11 months.

Munyard, Arthur Edward (1915–19); Sergeant, R.G.A.; France and Germany 3 years.

Murphy, Daniel (1914–19); Private, York and Lancaster Rgt.

Murphy, Daniel Hubert (1914–19); Guardsman, Irish Guards; France 2 months.

Murphy, Francis (1914–16); Private, Essex Rgt.; France 1 year 7 months.

Murphy, George (1914–19); Sergeant, E. Lancashire Rgt.; France 2 months, Salonica 5 months.

Murphy, Henry (1915–17); Driver, R.F.A.

Murphy, John (1914–15); Corporal, Reserve Cavalry.

Murray, Alfred George (1914–19); Battery Quartermaster-Sergeant, R.F.A.; France 2 years 10 months.

Murray, Joseph (1915–19); Signaller, R.E.; France 3 years.

Murray, Stephen Joseph (1914–19); Gunner, R.F.A.; France 4 years 2 months.

Murray, William Arthur Edward (1914 19); M.M., Mentioned in despatches; Sergeant, R.F.A.; France 2 years.

Murrell, George (1916–18); Private, Labour Corps; France 15 months.

Murrell, James Stanley (1915–19); Private, Welch Rgt.; Dardanelles 3 months, Salonica 2 years 9 months.

Murrell, Walter Tudor (1915–19); Private, Machine Gun Corps; France 5 months.

***Muscutt, Benjamin William** (1917–18); Private, York and Lancaster Rgt.; France 5 months; Missing, 13th October, 1918.

Musgrove, Arthur James (1915–19); Gunner, R.F.A.; France 2 years.

Musgrove, Herbert Charles (1915–19); Private, Hampshire Rgt.; France 10 months, Mesopotamia 1 year 7 months.

Musk, Arthur Edward (1915–19); Sergeant, R.A.S.C. (M.T.); France 2 years 8 months.

Myall, William John (1917–19); Lance-Corporal, M.F.P.

Naldrett, Edwin Jesse (1917–19); Air Mechanic, R.A.F.

Nash, George William (1916–19); Private, R. Scots Fusiliers; France and Egypt 2 years 6 months.

Nason, George Henry (1914–15); Private, R.W. Surrey Rgt.; France.

Neale, George Thomas (1916–19); Private, Labour Corps; France 1 year 8 months.

Neate, Herbert Henry (1916–19); Private, Lancashire Fusiliers; France 2 years.

Neate, William Henry (1914–16); Private, Middlesex Rgt.; France 1 year 7 months.

Neech, Percy Walter (1918–19); Private, R.A.M.C.

Neill, Thomas (1914–19); Corporal, 3rd Hussars; France 2 years 8 months.

Nelson, Arthur George (1915–19); Lance-Corporal, R.E.; France and Egypt 2 years 4 months.

Nelson, William Thomas (1914–19); Private, R.A.S.C.; France 3 years 7 months.

***New, James** (1914–17); Stoker (1st Class), R.N.: Naval Service; Killed at sea, 7th July, 1917.

Newman, Arthur William (1914–19); Private, E. Kent Rgt.; France 4 years 4 months.

Newman, Frederick Malcolm (1916–19); Driver, R.A.S.C.; France 2 years 8 months.

Newman, Maurice Jeptha (1914–19); Company Sergeant-Major, Labour Corps; France 4 years 6 months.

Newman, Robert Charles Adams (1914–19); Staff Sergeant, R.A.M.C.; Dardanelles 8 months, Egypt 3 years 3 months.

Newman, William Augustus (1914–19); D.S.M.; Petty Officer (1st Class), R.N.; Naval Service 4 years 6 months.

Newport, Charles Semple (1915–19); Gunner, R.F.A.; France 3 years.

Newport, Thomas William (1914–19); Petty Officer, R.N.; Naval Service 4 years 9 months.

Newsom, Henry (1914–19); Rifleman, Rifle Brigade; France 10 months.

Newson, Benjamin Thomas (1916–19); Private, Argyle and Sutherland Highlanders.

Newson, Henry Joseph (1915–17); Private, Labour Corps.

Newson, Stephen (1914–19); Sergeant, Royal Fusiliers.

Newton, Frederick William (1914–17); Private, London Rgt.

Newton, William (1915–19); Gunner, R.F.A.; France 3 years.

Newton, William John (1914–19); Sergeant, R.F.A.; France 4 years.

Nicholls, Alfred (1915–19); Private, Oxfordshire and Buckinghamshire Light Infantry; France 1 year 7 months.

Nicholls, Henry (1915–19); Corporal Fitter, R.F.A.; France 2 years 9 months.

Nicholls, John William (1914); Private, E. Surrey Rgt.

Nicholls Thomas (1915–18); Private, Labour Corps; Dardanelles and Salonica 2 years 6 months.

Nicholls, William James (1914–19); Lance-Corporal, London Rgt.

Nichols, Ernest George (1914–17); Lance-Corporal, S. Wales Borderers; France.

Nichols, John Charles (1914–19); Able Seaman, R.N.; Naval Service 4 years 7 months.

Nichols, Richard Arthur (1915–19); Lance-Corporal, R.A.S.C.; France 2 years 3 months.

Nichols, Ronald Alvan (1914–19); Electrical Artificer, R.N.; Naval Service 4 years 7 months.

Nichols, William (1918–19); Private, R. Sussex Rgt.; France and Germany 6 months.

Nightingale, Percival Daniel (1914–17); Lance-Corporal, Labour Corps; Dardanelles and Egypt 4 months.

Noakes, Douglas Angus (1914–19); Sergeant, M.F.P.

Noble, Thomas David (1914–18); Sergeant, R.F.A.; France 3 years 3 months.

Nokes, Edward Albert (1916–19); Supply Staff-Sergeant, R.A.S.C.; France and Germany 2 years 10 months.

***Norby, Charles Phillips** (1914–17); Rifleman, R. Irish Rifles; France 9 months; Missing, 16th August, 1917.

Norman, Frederick (1914–16); Private, E. Surrey Rgt.; France.

Norman, George Henry (1914–19); Gunner, R.F.A.; France 2 years.

Norman, Harry (1914–19); Driver, R.A.S.C.; France 4 years 6 months.

Norman, John Greville (1916–19); Private, R. Scots Fusiliers; France 6 months.

North, Albert North (1914–19); Bombardier, R.F.A.; France 3 years 3 months.

North, William Charles (1915–19); Gunner, R.F.A; France 1 year 10 months.

Northcott, Elias Herbert (1915–19); Sergeant, R. Sussex Rgt.; India 3 years 6 months.

Norton, Arthur (1914–19); Private, London Rgt.; France, Salonica and Palestine, 2 years 8 months.

Norton, Henry Charles (1918–19); Rifleman, Rifle Brigade.

Noton, Arthur Robert (1914–19); Sergeant, R.W. Surrey Rgt.; France 3 years.

Nottingham, Charles Frederick (1915–19); Company Sergeant-Major, School of Musketry.

Noyce, Charles Edward (1914–17); Private, Cavalry Reserve.

Nunn, Arthur Thomas (1918–19); Lance-Corporal, R. Marine Engineers.

Nunn, George (1917–19); Private, R.A.V.C.; France 1 year 11 months.

Nunn, Henry William (1915–19); Private, Labour Corps; France 2 years 6 months.

Nunn, Samuel (1917–20); Private, London Rgt.; Egypt 2 years 3 months.

Nunn, Walter James (1915–19); Private, R.A.M.C.; Mesopotamia 2 years 8 months.

Nunn, William Henry (1917–19); Private, Essex Rgt.; France 2 years.

Nye, Thomas Edward (1915–19); Lance-Corporal, R.E.; France 3 years 2 months.

Oakeley, John Loncelo (1916–19); Private, Labour Corps; France 1 year.

Oakham, Charles William (1918–19); Lance-Corporal, Coldstream Guards.

Oakley, Frank Henry (1915–19); Private, R.A.S.C. (M.T.); Salonica 3 years 2 months.

Oakley, William (1915–19); Private, London Rgt.; France, Salonica, Egypt and Palestine, 2 years 4 months.

Oatley, Albert (1915–19); Lance-Corporal, London Rgt.; France, Salonica, Egypt and Palestine, 2 years 9 months.

O'Brien, Matthew (1915–19); Private, Labour Corps; France 3 years 7 months.

O'Brien, Michael (1915–19); Private, Royal Fusiliers; Gibraltar and Egypt 3 years 11 months.

Ockendon, George (1916–19); Sergeant, R.A.F.

O'Connell, Dennis (1915); Gunner, R.F.A.

O'Donnell, Thomas Francis (1914–19); Private, Worcestershire Rgt.

O'Keefe, John Frederick (1914–19); Sergeant, Reserve Cavalry; France 6 months.

Oliver, Arthur (1915–19); Corporal, R.E.; France 3 years.

Oliver, Harold Charles (1917–19); Private, R.A.M.C.; Egypt 14 months.

Oliver, Herbert (1914–19); Private, R.D.C.

***Olney, Arthur** (1915); Private, R.A.S.C.; Killed at sea, 14th August, 1915.

Ong, Arthur (1917–19); Private, R.A.M.C.; Salonica, Russia and Turkey, 1 year 10 months.

Orchard, John Harrison (1916–19); Private, Royal Highlanders; France 9 months.

Order, John William (1915–17); Private, R.A.S.C.; France 1 year 9 months.

Orman, Charles George (1915–19); Wheeler-Sergeant, R.A.S.C.

Orme, Thomas John (1916–19); Leading Mechanic, R.A.F.; Italy, Greece and Malta, 17 months.

Orritt, Charles William (1916–19); Private, E. Surrey Rgt.; France 2 years.

Orwin, Bernard John (1917–19); Telegraphist, R.N.V.R.

Osborn, Albert William (1917–19); Sapper, R.E.

Osborn, Thomas William (1915–19); Private, R.E.; France and Germany 3 years 2 months.

Osborn, William John (1915–17); Private, Devonshire Rgt.

Osborne, John (1915–19); Private, Labour Corps; France 3 years 8 months.

Osborne, John Frost (1914–19); Leading Stoker, R.N.; Naval Service 4 years 7 months.

Osborne, William James (1914–19); Gunner, R.F.A.; France 3 years 6 months.

Osborne, William Timothy Herbert (1915–19); Private, Labour Corps; France 3 years 6 months.

Osmond, Charles Richard Ernest (1916–18); Private, R.A.S.C. (M.T.).

Otley, William John (1918–19); Guardsman, Coldstream Guards.

Otten, Alfred Edward (1914–19); Corporal, London Rgt.; France 13 months.

Otton, Horatio Edmund (1915–19); Lance-Bombardier, R.F.A.; France 3 years 6 months.

***Otton, John William** (1914); D.C.M.; Private, Middlesex Rgt.; France 1 month; Killed in action, 5th November, 1914.

Ottway, James Joseph (1917–19); Private, R.A.F.

Outhwaite, Charles Alfred (1914–19); Private, Dragoon Guards; France 4 years 6 months.

Ovendon, Frederick Thomas (1914–19); Guardsman, Grenadier Guards; France 2 years 3 months.

Overy, James Frederick (1916–19); Company Quartermaster-Sergeant, Labour Corps; France 3 years 2 months.

Owen, Arthur William (1914–19); Sergeant, R.E.; Egypt and Gallipoli 1 year, France 2 years 8 months.

Owen, Ernest Louis (1916–19); Private (2nd Class), R.A.F.; France 11 months.

Owen, George James (1916–18); Private, R. Lancaster Rgt.; Salonica 18 months.

Owen, Henry Milner (1915–19); Driver, R.A.S.C.; France and Germany 3 years 4 months.

***Owens, Joseph Bertie** (1914–16); Private, Royal Fusiliers; Dardanelles 7 months, France 5 months; Died of wounds, 11th August, 1916.

Oxley, Graham Burrell (1914–19); Corporal, London Rgt.; Salonica and Egypt 2 years 5 months, France 12 months.

Pace, Ernest (1915–19); Gunner, R.F.A.; India 18 months.

Packham, Albert Henry (1917–19); Private, London Rgt.; France 13 months.

Page, John (1914–19); Stoker, Petty Officer, R.N.; Naval Service 4 years 6 months.

Page, John (1914–19); Able Seaman, R.N.; Naval Service 3 years 1 month.

Page, Percy Spencer (1914–19); Shoeing-Smith, R.A.V.C.; France 3 years 8 months.

Page, Robert Walter (1916–19); Gunner, R.G.A.; France and India 2 years.

***Pain, Cyril Leonard** (1914–18); Able Seaman, R.N.; Naval Service; Killed at sea, 12th February, 1918.

Paine, David (1914–19); Corporal, Grenadier Guards; France 4 years.

Paine, John Christopher (1914–15); Cyclist, London Rgt.

Palmer, Albert Edward (1915–19); Gunner, R.G.A.; India 3 years 6 months.

Palmer, Alfred (1916–19); Corporal, Welsh Rgt.; France 6 months.

Palmer, Charles (1915–19); Private, R.F.A.; France 2 years 6 months.

***Palmer, Charles Ernest** (1916); Private, Royal Fusiliers; France 4 months; Died of wounds, 6th November, 1916.

***Palmer, Edward Henry** (1914–15); Private, Essex Rgt.; France 2 months; Killed in action, 8th February, 1915.

Palmer, Frank (1916–19); Rifleman, King's Royal Rifle Corps; France 1 year, Germany 1 year.

Palmer, Richard George (1914–19); Sergeant, W. Kent Yeomanry; France 3 years 5 months.

Pankhurst, Arthur Philip (1914–19); M.M.; Private, R.A.S.C. (M.T.); France 4 years 4 months.

Pannell, Alfred William (1914); Private, Dragoon Guards.

Papworth, George (1914–19); Private, R.A.M.C.; France 4 years.

Papworth, Robinson (1915–20); Private, Middlesex Rgt.; France 2 years 3 months.

***Pardew, John Roger** (1916–17); Corporal, Royal Fusiliers; France 9 months; Killed in action, 3rd May, 1917.

***Pardoe, Charles Henry** (1915–17): Sergeant, London Rgt.; France 4 months; Killed in action, 4th July, 1917.

Parish, Sydney (1915–16); Gunner, R.F.A.

Park, James (1917-19); Gunner, R.F.A.; France 1 year.

Parker, Charles Ernest (1914–17); Private, Labour Corps; France 2 months.

Parker, Charles Thomas (1914–19); M.M.; Sergeant, London Rgt.; Palestine, France and Salonica, 2 years 7 months.

Parker, Charles Thomas (1915–19); Sapper, R.E.; France 3 years 11 months.

Parker, Edward William (1916–19); Bombardier, R.G.A.; France 8 months.

Parker, Frederick Benjamin (1917–19); Private, Norfolk Rgt.; Egypt and Palestine 1 year 10 months.

Parker, George Henry (1916–19); Private, Nottinghamshire and Derbyshire Rgt.; France 2 months.

***Parker, George William** (1916–17); Gunner, R.G.A.; France 4 months; Killed in action, 4th June, 1917.

Parker, Richard Edward (1915–19); Private, R.A.M.C.; France 9 months.

Parkes, Leonard William (1916–19); Sapper, R.E.; France 1 year.

***Parkington, Sidney Arthur** (1914–16); Private, R. Welch Fusiliers; France 1 month; Killed in action, 11th January, 1916.

Parkinson, Edward (1914–19); Lance-Corporal, R.A.S.C.; France 3 years 9 months.

***Parks, Harry** (1914–17); Guardsman, Grenadier Guards; France 8 months; Killed in action, 15th October, 1917.

Parr, Charles (1915–19); Sapper, R.E.; France 3 years 5 months.

Parrett, George David (1918–19); Private, Suffolk Rgt.

Parrish, Frank (1916–19); Rifleman, King's Royal Rifle Corps; France 3 years 3 months.

Parry, Michael George (1914–18); Corporal, Gloucestershire Rgt.; France 3 years 3 months.

Parry, Richard James (1915); Private, Royal Fusiliers.

Parsons, Charles (1917–18); Driver, R.A.S.C.

Parsons, Charles Edward (1915–19); Lance-Corporal, M.M.P.; France 5 months.

Parsons, Ernest (1914–19); Corporal, Rifle Brigade; Burmah 4 years.

Parsons, Harry (1914 – 19); Driver, R.F.A.; France 4 years 7 months.

Parsons, Percival Henry (1916–19); Private, Labour Corps.

***Parsons, Thomas** (1914–18); Gunner, R.H.A.; France 2 years 8 months; Died of wounds, 29th March, 1918.

Parsons, Thomas (1914–19); Corporal, R.E.

Partleton, Frederick (1914–17); Private, R. Berkshire Rgt.

***Pascoe, John Thomas** (1914–15); Corporal, Somersetshire Light Infantry; France 4 months; Died of wounds, 29th April, 1915.

Pascoe, William (1916–17); Driver, R.F.A.

Pashley, Albert Victor (1914–19); Company Sergeant-Major, Labour Corps, and Sergeant, London Rgt.; France 4 years.

Pashley, Sidney Charles (1914–19); Driver, R.F.A.; France, Salonica and Palestine, 2 years 8 months.

Paterson, Charles Edward (1914–19); Private, E. Kent Rgt.; France and Prisoner of war 3 years.

Patey, Ben William (1914–17); Private, London Rgt.

Patey, Frank William (1914–19); Sergeant, R.F.A.; France 3 years.

***Patterson, James Frederick** (1914–17); Corporal, Machine Gun Corps; France 2 years 9 months; Killed in action, 14th August, 1917.

Patterson, John Edward (1915–19); Gunner, R.G.A.; France 1 year 10 months.

Paul, Edmund Frederick (1914–20); Private, Machine Gun Corps; Dardanelles, France and Italy, 2 years 5 months.

Paul, John Henry Richard (1916–19); Private, R.A.M.C.

Pavelin, Francis William Walter (1917–19); Private, York and Lancaster Rgt.; France 15 months.

***Pavitt, George** (1914–17); Gunner, R.F.A.; France 3 years 1 month; Accidentally killed, 13th December, 1917.

Pay, Reginald (1915–19); Private, London Rgt.; Egypt 2 years 3 months.

Payne, Arthur Bertie (1918–19); Private, Machine Gun Corps.

Payne, Arthur Joseph (1915–18); Private, E. Surrey Rgt.; France 1 year 7 months.

Payne, Charles (1914–19); Driver, R.E.; France and Italy 4 years 6 months.

Payne, Charles Frederick (1917–19); Sapper, R.E.; France 13 months.

Payne, Harry (1915–18); Gunner, R.F.A.; France 1 year 8 months.

Payne, Henry (1915–19); Staff-Sergeant, R.A.O.C.; France 2 years 7 months.

Payne, Herbert Lewis (1914–19); Private, Middlesex Rgt.; France 1 year 8 months, Prisoner of war 1 year 8 months.

Payne, Joseph (1916–19); Private, Essex Rgt.

Payne, Ralph Burgoyne (1914–19); Sapper, R.E.; France 3 years 4 months.

Payne, Simeon Henry (1918–19); Corporal, Rifle Brigade.

Pays, Arthur Frederick (1914–19); Sapper, R.E.; France 16 months.

Peabody, Joseph Henry (1917–19); Private, R.A.S.C. (M.T.); Mesopotamia 2 years 2 months.

***Peake, William John** (1915–18); Private, Royal Fusiliers; France 2 years 10 months; Missing, 20th March, 1918.

Pearce, Alfred John (1915–18); Driver, R.A.S.C.; France 18 months.

Pearce, Archibald (1914–19); Company Sergeant-Major, R.E.; France 4 years.

***Pearce, Frank** (1915–16); Private, R. Welch Fusiliers; France 2 months; Killed in action, 10th July, 1916.

Pearce, Frederick James Courton (1915–19); Corporal, R.F.A.; France 3 years.

Pearce, William James George (1915–19); Driver, R.F.A.; France, Salonica and Palestine, 3 years.

***Pearson, James** (1915–17); Driver, R.F.A.; France 1 year 7 months; Killed in action, 30th June, 1917.

Pearson, John Edward (1914–19); Sub-Conductor, R.A.O.C.; Dardanelles, Egypt and Palestine, 3 years 10 months.

Pearson, Robert James (1914–16); Driver, R.F.A.

Pearson, William (1916–19); Private, Royal Fusiliers; France 2 years 3 months.

Pearson, William Alfred (1914–19); Air Mechanic (2nd Class), R.A.F.; France 2 years 8 months.

Peck, Arthur (1914–19); Private, Suffolk Rgt.; Egypt 1 year, France 1 year.

Peckham, Percy John (1916–19); Lance-Corporal, King's Royal Rifle Corps; France 8 months, Prisoner of war 18 months.

Pegnall, Gerald Frank (1915–19); Driver, R.F.A.; France 2 years 6 months.

Pellatt, Sydney Ernest (1917–19); Rifleman, King's Royal Rifle Corps: France 6 months, Prisoner of war 14 months.

Penfold, Albert (1914–19); Rifleman, Rifle Brigade; Burmah 4 years.

Penfold, Herbert Bertie (1914–19); Driver, R.F.A.; France 2 years 6 months.

Pengelly, Francis John (1916–19); Private, R.G.A.; France 13 months.

Pennick, William (1918–19); Private, Essex Rgt.

Penny, Joseph (1918–19); Private, R.G.A.; Gibraltar 4 months.

Percival, Edward (1916–19); Private, W. Riding Rgt.; France and Italy 1 year 9 months.

***Percival, George Alfred** (1915–18); Bombardier, R.F.A.; France 1 year 7 months; Killed in action, 1st September, 1918.

Perkins, Harry Walter (1917–19); Private, R.A.F.; Ægean Sea, Arabia and Egypt, 18 months.

Perrin, Henry George (1918–19); Rifleman, King's Royal Rifle Corps; France 2 months.

Perring, Arthur Edward (1916–19); Private, Labour Corps; France 2 months.

Perry, George (1918–19); Private, R. Sussex Rgt.

Perry, Herbert (1914–15); Rifleman, London Rgt.

***Perryman, Arthur George** (1914); Rifleman, King's Royal Rifle Corps; France 2 months; Missing, 31st October, 1914.

***Peters, Arthur** (1914–18); Sergeant, Gloucestershire Rgt.; Mesopotamia 15 months; Died, 10th July, 1918.

Peters, Charles Herbert (1915–19); 2nd Corporal, R.E.; France 3 years 1 month.

***Peterson, Frederick William** (1915–16); Private, R.W. Kent Rgt.; France 5 months; Killed in action, 7th October, 1916.

Pett, William John (1914–19); Private, 9th Lancers; France and Germany 2 years 8 months.

Pettit, Albert Douglas (1917–19); Gunner, R.G.A.; France and Germany 1 year 7 months.

Pettit, William Henry (1914–19); Sergeant, Border Rgt.; France 3 years 3 months.

Petty, Frederick James (1918–19); Private, R.A.S.C. (M.T.); Mesopotamia 10 months.

Pheasant, William Albert (1915–19); Sergeant, R.F.A.; France 3 years 3 months.

***Phenix, Albert Price** (1916); Rifleman, King's Royal Rifle Corps; France 3 months; Died, 15th December, 1916.

Phillips, Albert Edward (1918–19); Gunner, R.G.A.; France 4 months.

Phillips, Arthur Charles (1914–18); Sergeant, London Rgt.; France 9 months.

Phillips, George (1915–19); Gunner, R.F.A.; France 2 years 8 months.

Phillips, Joseph (1915–19); Driver, R.E.; France 3 years 8 months.

Phillips, John Edward (1915–19); Sapper, R.E.; France 13 months, India 9 months, Mesopotamia 17 months.

Phillips, William (1914–19); Mentioned in despatches: Private, R.A.V.C.; France and Italy 4 years 6 months.

Phillips, William John (1915–19); Shoeing-Smith, R.E.; France and Germany 2 years 11 months.

Philpot, Bertie (1915–16); Gunner, R.F.A.

Philpot, William (1915–19); Sapper, R.E.; France 7 months, Russia 9 months.

Philpott, Charles Herbert (1917–19); Aircraftsman (1st Class), R.A.F.

Philpott, William John (1914–16); Corporal, London Rgt.; Dardanelles and Malta 15 months.

Piercy, Frederick George (1916–19); Private, Labour Corps; France 18 months.

Piggott, George Henry (1915–19); Driver, R.A.S.C.; Salonica 2 years 2 months.

Piggott, Samuel Joseph (1914–19); Corporal, R.F.A.; France and Salonica 3 years 4 months.

Pike, Albert George (1916–19): Private, Labour Corps; France 18 months.

***Pike, Ernest Campbell** (1915–18); Private, Warwickshire Rgt.; France 3 years 2 months; Died of wounds, 9th November, 1918.

Pike, Frederick Henry (1916–19); Private, Labour Corps.

Pike, George Jabez (1914–19); Mentioned in despatches; Sergeant, R.A.S.C.; Egypt and Palestine 3 years 3 months.

Pike, William Henry (1915–19); Rifleman, Rifle Brigade; France 17 months.

***Pikett, Oliver James** (1914–18); Rifleman, Rifle Brigade; France 2 years 3 months; Missing, 21st March, 1918.

Pilgrim, Alfred Edward (1914–19); Private, London Rgt. and Labour Corps; France 2 years 6 months.

Pinchen, Joseph (1914–19)· Private, R.F.A.; France 18 months.

Pipe, William Henry (1914–19); Corporal, Rifle Brigade; Burmah and Andamans 3 years 5 months.

Pitt, Arthur John William (1916–19); Private, Lincolnshire Rgt.; France 2 years.

Pitt, Frederick James (1914–19); Lance-Corporal, M.F.P.; France 3 years 2 months.

***Pitt, Thomas George** (1914–15); Private, Dragoon Guards: France 3 months; Died of wounds, 10th March, 1915.

Pitts, Frederick Thomas (1914–19); Chief Petty Officer, R.N.; Naval Service 3 years 3 months.

Pitts, James Frederick (1915–19); Private, R. Marine Light Infantry; Naval Service 4 years.

Pittuck, Isaac (1914–19); Lance-Corporal, R.D.C.

Pizzey, Leonard (1914–16); Gunner, R.F.A.

Planner, Arthur Edward (1915–19); Corporal, R.F.A.; France 1 year 11 months.

***Plater, William John** (1914); Guardsman, Coldstream Guards; France 2 months; Killed in action, 4th October, 1914.

Plowman, Henry James (1915–19); Gunner, R.F.A.; France 2 years 6 months.

Plumb, Albert George (1914); Gunner, R.F.A.

***Plumb, Arthur Samuel** (1914–15); Rifleman, Rifle Brigade; France 5 months. Died of wounds, 30th October, 1915.

Plumb, Herbert (1914–19); Lance-Corporal, Labour Corps; France 3 years 6 months.

Plumb, William Harry (1916–19); Private, R.A.S.C.; France 2 years 2 months.

Plumb, William Philip (1914–19); Private, M.M.P.; France 2 years 2 months.

Plummer, Arthur Edward (1918–19); M.M.; Private, Royal Fusiliers; France 7 months.

***Plummer, Charles Harvey** (1916–17); Private, Royal Fusiliers; France 8 months; Killed in action, 10th April, 1917.

Plummer, George Edward (1914-19); Private, Shropshire Light Infantry; France 3 years 6 months.

Plummer, Reginald Harry (1918–19); Private, R.A.S.C. (M.T.); Salonica and Russia 6 months.

Plummer, Victor Herbert (1916–19); Private, Durham Light Infantry; Salonica and Russia 11 months.

Pocock, Albert Reuben (1914–19); Private, Scots Guards; France and Prisoner of war (Germany) 4 years 2 months.

Pocock, Charles (1914–19); Sergeant, R.A.S.C.; France 2 years 5 months.

***Pocock, Frederick Charles** (1914–16); Sergeant, Worcestershire Rgt.; France 2 years; Died of wounds, 25th August, 1916.

Pointer, Eustace (1915–19); Private, London Rgt.; France, Salonica and Egypt, 3 years 6 months.

Pointer, Wilfred (1914–19); Company Quartermaster-Sergeant, R.W. Kent Rgt.

Pond, Edmund George (1918–19); Rifleman, Rifle Brigade; France and Germany 10 months.

Ponder, Edgar (1916–19); Pioneer, R.E.; France 2 years.

Poole, William John (1915–19); Private, R.A.M.C.; France 2 years 2 months.

Pope, Frederick (1914–16); Private, Leicestershire Rgt.; France 4 months.

Pope, Frederick James (1916–19); Private, Labour Corps; Salonica 2 years 1 month.

Pope, Harry Henry (1914); Private, R. Berkshire Rgt.

Pope, Joseph (1916–19); Private, R.A.M.C.

Pope, Thomas (1915–19); Driver, R.E.; Gallipoli Egypt and France, 3 years 9 months.

Poppy, Charles Arthur (1915–18); Driver, R.E.; France, Dardanelles, Egypt and Salonica, 2 years 5 months.

Porter, Albert Edward Phillip (1916–19); Sapper, R.E.; France 2 years 6 months.

Porter, Anthony Thomas (1914–19); 2nd Sick Berth Steward, R.N.; Naval Service 3 years.

Porter, Arthur Robert (1915–19); Lance-Corporal, London Rgt.; India 3 years 6 months.

***Porter, Horace William** (1914–18); Private, E. Surrey Rgt.; France 1 year 7 months, Prisoner of war (Germany) 15 months; accidentally killed while prisoner of war, 3rd May, 1918.

Portley, John (1914-19); Gunner, R.G.A.; France 2 years.

Postans, Thomas (1914–19); Private, R.D.C.

Potter, Edmond George (1914–19); Sapper, R.E.; France 3 years 9 months.

Potter, George Philip (1914–19); Corporal, E. Kent Rgt.; France 15 months.

Potter, Henry Thomas (1914–19); Sergeant, M.M.P.; France and Salonica 4 years.

***Potter, Sidney Henry** (1915–16); Private, R. W. Kent Rgt.; France 5 months; Missing, 7th October, 1916.

Potter, William (1914); Private, Northumberland Fusiliers.

Pound, Charles William (1914–19); Corporal, R.A.S.C.; France 4 years 2 months.

Pounds, Samuel (1917); Driver, R.H.A.

Powell, Albert James (1914–19); Private, Labour Corps.

Powell, George Joseph (1914–18); Private, R.E.; Mesopotamia 5 months.

***Powlesland, John William Wallington** (1915–16); M.M.; Guardsman, Grenadier Guards; France 11 months; Killed in action, 25th September, 1916.

Powley, Harry Albert (1917–19); Gunner, R.G.A.; France 14 months.

Pratt, George Edward (1917–19); Private, Labour Corps.

Pratt, Joseph James (1914–19); 1st Class Staff Sergeant-Major, R.A.S.C.; France 2 years 10 months.

Prendergast, Edward Arthur (1916–19); Private, Labour Corps; France 18 months.

Presley, William Charles (1916–19); Rifleman, King's Royal Rifle Corps; France 18 months, Italy 4 months, Prisoner of war 4 months.

Press, William George (1918–19); Private, R.A.S.C.

Preston, George (1916–19); Rifleman, King's Royal Rifle Corps; France 7 months, Prisoner of war 18 months.

Price, Colin Edward Warren (1914–19); Driver, R.F.A.; France 3 years 9 months.

Price, George (1914–17); Corporal, 5th Lancers; France 3 years.

Price, James William (1914–19); Sergeant, Rifle Brigade; France 3 years.

Price, Louis Septimus (1917–19); Company Quartermaster-Sergeant, R.E.; France 2 years.

Price, Thomas George (1914–19); Corporal, R.A.S.C. (M.T.); France 18 months.

Price, Thomas William (1914–19); Driver, R.F.A.; Italy and France 3 years 6 months.

Price, Walter (1915–19); Private, R.A.V.C.; France 3 years 11 months.

***Price, Walter Everard** (1916–18); Rifleman, Rifle Brigade; France 18 months; Killed in action, 20th August, 1918.

Prideaux, Richard Henry (1915–19); Private, R.A.S.C.; France 3 years 5 months.

Pridmore, William George (1915–19); Sapper, R.E.; France 2 years 11 months.

***Priest, Sidney** (1914–16); Lance-Corporal, E. Kent Rgt.; France 6 months; Killed in action, 13th August, 1916.

Prince, George Henry (1914–18); Corporal, R.A.S.C.; France, Egypt and Salonica, 3 years 5 months.

Prince, Walter Escott (1914–19); Gunner, R.F.A.; France and Salonica 3 years 5 months.

***Prior, Frederick** (1914–17); Sergeant, Royal Fusiliers; France 3 months; Killed in action, 18th February, 1917.

Prior, Frederick (1915–19); Driver, R.F.A.; France 3 years.

Prior, Joseph Alfred (1914–17); Private, Machine Gun Corps; France 2 months.

Pritchett, Charles Edwin Turl (1914–19); Sergeant, R.F.A.; Salonica 14 months.

Procter, William (1915–19); M.M.; Rifleman, Rifle Brigade; France 2 years 6 months.

Proops, Joseph (1915–19); Private, R.W. Surrey Rgt.; France 2 years.

Prosser, William (1915–19); Saddler, R.A.S.C.; France and Italy 4 years 1 month.

Proud, Albert Edward (1914–16); Trooper, City of London Yeomanry.

Pryor, Arundel Thomas Webster (1914–16); Gunner, R.H.A.; France.

Puddicombe, Joseph Charles William (1914–19); Private, London Rgt.; France, Salonica and Palestine, 2 years 9 months.

Pude, John Francis (1914–19); Lance-Corporal, Essex Rgt.; France, Egypt, Salonica and Palestine, 3 years 6 months.

Pugh, Frederick Peter Wilson (1915–16); Sapper, R.E.; France.

Pullen, Arthur (1916–18); Private, Labour Corps; France.

Pullen, Arthur (1916–19); Private, Durham Light Infantry; Salonica 9 months, France 10 months.

Pullen, Herbert George (1914–19); M.S.M.; Private, R.W. Kent Rgt.; France 3 years 9 months.

Pummery, Charles William (1915–19); M.M.; Sergeant, R.F.A.; France 2 years 6 months.

Purcell, Thomas (1916–19); Private, Middlesex Rgt.; France 2 years 3 months.

Purdy, John (1916–19); Rifleman, London Rgt.; France 3 years 2 months.

Purkiss, Frederick John (1918–19); Stoker, R.N.; Naval Service 4 months.

Purser, Frederick (1916–19); Private, London Rgt.; France 2 years 5 months.

Purslove, William Harold (1915–19); Sergeant, R.F.A.; France 16 months.

Purton, George James (1916–20); Private, R.A.O.C.; France 9 months, Egypt 1 year 10 months.

Pyne, George (1914–18); Guardsman, Coldstream Guards; France 2 years 6 months.

Quelch, Douglas Edwin Gerald (1914–19); Company Sergeant-Major, Rifle Brigade; Burmah 4 years 2 months.

Quick, Alfred John (1917–19); Private, Northamptonshire Rgt.; France 2 years 5 months.

***Quick, Herbert Montague Frederick** (1914–16); Private, Royal Fusiliers; France 11 months; Killed in action, 5th April, 1916.

Raggett, George Frederick (1914–19); Gunner, R.F.A.; France 13 months, Salonica 6 months, Egypt 1 year 8 months.

Ralph, Frederick Robert (1914–19); Company Quartermaster-Sergeant, R.E.; France 3 years 9 months.

Ralph, William Elias (1918–20); Private, R. Sussex Rgt.; France 9 months, Egypt 10 months.

Ramm, Frederick Thomas (1915–19); Sergeant, R.F.A.; France and Salonica 2 years.

Ramsey, William Wallace (1914–16); M.M.; Lance-Corporal, Dorsetshire Rgt.; France 7 months.

Rance, Godfrey Russell (1914–19); Able Seaman, R.N.; Naval Service 3 years 9 months.

Randall, Cyril George (1916–18); Gunner, R.F.A.

Randall, Thomas Charles (1916–19); Corporal, King's Royal Rifle Corps; France 2 years 6 months.

Ransley, Alfred (1914–19); Staff-Sergeant, R.E.; France 1 year 9 months.

Rapley, Herbert Charles (1915–19); Pioneer, R.E.

***Rathall, William** (1914); Driver, R.F.A.; Died, 29th December, 1914.

Raven, Hugh (1914–17); Sergeant, 17th Lancers.

Rawlings, Harry Edward (1914–19); Lance-Sergeant, London Rgt.; France, Salonica, Egypt and Palestine, 2 years 8 months.

***Rawlings, Joseph Eastoe** (1914); Stoker (1st Class), R.F.R.; Naval Service; Killed at sea, 22nd September, 1914.

Rawlings, Thomas Edward (1914–19); Driver, R.A.S.C.; France 4 years.

Rawson, Walter (1916–19); Corporal, R.A.V.C.; France 16 months.

Ray, Herbert John (1916–19); Rifleman, King's Royal Rifle Corps; France 13 months.

Rayner, James (1914–18); Sergeant, R. Sussex Rgt.; France 3 years.

Read, George Edward (1917–19); Private, R.A.S.C.; France 4 months.

Read, William (1914–19); Able Seaman, R.N.; Naval Service 4 years.

Reading, Ernest James (1916–19); Gunner, R.F.A.; France 1 year.

Reading, Reginald Sylvester (1915–19); Sapper, R.E.; France 1 year 8 months.

Reason, William James (1915–19); Driver, R.F.A.; France 3 years 6 months.

Reed, Charles Frederick (1918–19); Rifleman, Rifle Brigade; France 2 months.

Reed, Henry Charles (1918–19); Private, R. Sussex Rgt.

Reeman, William Samuel (1916–19); Gunner, Tank Corps; France 13 months.

Reeve, Albert (1915–19); Gunner, R.G.A.

***Reeve, Alfred** (1915–16); Private, London Rgt.; France 1 year; Killed in action, 16th September, 1916.

Reeve, Charles Edward (1916–18); Private, E. Kent Rgt.; France 2 years.

Reeve, Charles William (1915–19); Private, R.A.S.C.; France 1 year 10 months.

Reeve, Walter Francis (1916–19); Private, London Rgt.; Salonica 6 months, Egypt 1 year 8 months.

Reeves, Frederick (1914–19); Sergeant, Labour Corps; France 3 years.

Regan, James (1914 and 1915–19); Sergeant, R.A.S.C.; France 4 years.

Regester, George Benjamin (1914–19); Sergeant, R.A.F.

***Reilly, Daniel** (1914); Private, R.W. Surrey Rgt.; France 2 months; Missing, 31st October, 1914.

Reilly, Richard (1914–19); Private, R. Dublin Fusiliers; France 3 years 8 months.

***Relf, William Joseph** (1914–17); Private, R. Dublin Fusiliers; Dardanelles and Egypt 1 year, France 8 months; Killed in action, 16th August, 1917.

Reynolds, George (1916–19); Private, S. Staffordshire Rgt.; France and Germany 2 years.

Reynolds, William George (1917–19); Gunner, R.F.A.; France and Germany 1 year.

Rhodes, Henry (1915–19); Sergeant, R.A.O.C.; France 3 years 10 months.

***Rice, Walter Charles** (1914–16); Rifleman, Rifle Brigade; France 1 year; Killed in action, 11th July, 1916.

Richards, Alfred (1915–17); Private, R.A.S.C.

Richards, Alfred James (1914–19); Private, R.A.S.C.; France 2 years, Salonica and Egypt 18 months.

Richards, Charles Ernest (1914–19); Sapper, R.E.; France 4 years.

***Richards, John** (1914–17); Stoker (1st Class), R.N.; Naval Service; Killed at sea, 12th December, 1917.

Richards, William George (1914–19); Private, R.A.S.C.; France 1 year.

Richardson, Charles (1915–19); Sergeant, R.E.; France 2 years.

Richardson, Frederick (1916–17); Sapper, R.E.

Richardson, George (1918–19); Rifleman, King's Royal Rifle Corps; France 4 months.

Richardson, George Edward (1918–19); Private, London Rgt.; France 14 months.

Richardson, George Frederick (1914–17); Private, Royal Fusiliers; France 13 months.

Richardson, Richard Percy (1916–19); Rifleman, King's Royal Rifle Corps; France and Germany 2 years.

Richardson, Walter Albert (1914–19); Private, Bedfordshire Rgt.

Richardson, Walter Albert (1914–19); Gunner, R.G.A.; France 4 years 6 months.

***Richardson, Walter Sidney** (1914–16); Lance-Corporal, Essex Rgt.; Died, 18th January, 1916.

Richardson, William (1916–18); Private, Northamptonshire Rgt.; France 11 months.

Ricketts, James Henry (1914–17); Sergeant, R. Welch Fusiliers.

Ricketts, John Joseph (1916–19); Private, Labour Corps; France 18 months.

Rideout, Albert Edwin (1914–19); Driver, R.G.A.; France and Germany 3 years.

Rider, William Frederick (1917–19); Sapper, R.E.; France 2 years 4 months.

Ridley, James Henry (1914–18); Driver, R.E.

***Ridlington, Alexander Augustus** (1914–15); Private, E. Kent Rgt.; France 6 months; Missing, 3rd May, 1915.

Rigby, Frank (1915–19); Corporal, R.A.M.C.

Riordan, William John (1918–19); Rifleman, London Rgt.

Risley, George Thomas (1918–19); Private, R. Sussex Rgt.; France 3 months.

Rivers, George (1916–18); Private, Labour Corps; France 18 months.

***Rivers, Percy Hubert** (1915); Sapper, R.E.; France 3 months; Died of wounds, 4th December, 1915.

***Rixon, Ivo Charles** (1914–17); Gunner, R.F.A.; France 2 years 6 months; Died of wounds, 23rd November, 1917.

Roach, William George (1914–16); Sergeant, London Rgt.

Roan, Frederick George (1916–19) Private, Somersetshire Light Infantry; France 11 months.

Roan, George Francis (1915–19); Private, Machine Gun Corps; France 7 months, India 2 years 1 month.

Roan, Sidney Lawrence (1915–19); Private, R.A.S.C.; France and Germany 3 years 7 months.

Robbins, George (1914–18); Private, Dragoon Guards; France 2 years 2 months.

Robbins, William Edward (1917–19); Private, Scottish Rifles.

***Roberts, Alfred William** (1915–16); Private, Wiltshire Rgt.; France 4 months; Died of wounds, 8th April, 1916.

Roberts, George (1914); Private, London Rgt.

Roberts, John (1914–19); Sergeant, R.F.A.; France 3 years 1 month.

Roberts, Richard (1914–19); Private, London Rgt.; Palestine 3 years 1 month.

Robinson, Alfred James (1918–19); Private, R. Sussex Rgt.; France and Germany 8 months.

Robinson, Frederick William (1914–17); Lance-Corporal, R.W. Kent Rgt.

Robinson, Henry James (1914–17); Sergeant Master Cook, Royal Fusiliers.

Robinson, Stuart Charles (1916–19); Private, Nottinghamshire and Derbyshire Rgt.

Robinson, William Authar (1914–19); Company Quartermaster-Sergeant, R. Irish Fusiliers; Dardanelles and Salonica 18 months.

Robinson, William Edward (1914–19); Private, Devonshire Rgt.; France and Salonica 3 years 6 months.

Robson, Alfred Charles (1916–19); Sapper, R.E.; Salonica 1 year.

Robson, Arthur Charles (1916–18); Private, Nottinghamshire and Derbyshire Rgt.; France 8 months.

Robson, Forster (1914–15); Private, R.A.S.C.

Rochford, James (1914–19); D.C.M., M.M. and bar; Guardsman, Irish Guards; France 3 years.

Roe, Frank (1915–19); Corporal, R.A.S.C.; France 2 years 11 months.

Rogers, Edwin (1915–19); Lance-Corporal, R.A.S.C.; Egypt 2 years.

Rogers, Frederick (1914–19); Private, Border Rgt.; France 4 years 3 months.

Rogers, William Adolphus (1916–19); Sapper, R.E.; France 14 months.

Rogerson, John Samuel (1915–19); Private, R.A.M.C.; France 2 years 4 months.

Rolfe, Charles Thomas George (1916–17); Rifleman, Rifle Brigade.

***Rolfe, George Ernest** (1914–16); Private, Middlesex Rgt.; France 9 months; Died of wounds, 16th March, 1916.

Rolfe, James Alden (1914–18); Gunner, R.G.A.

Rollison, Arthur William (1917–19); Private, Labour Corps; France 1 year 10 months.

Rolph, Thomas (1914–19); Private, Liverpool Rgt.; France 2 years 4 months.

***Romer, George Edward** (1914–15); Private, E. Surrey Rgt.; France 1 month; Killed in action, 25th March, 1915.

Roney, Francis William (1918–19); Lance-Corporal, R. Sussex Rgt.; France 4 months.

Rook, Arthur Edward (1915–19); Gunner, R.F.A.; France 3 years 6 months.

Root, Henry George Dayley (1914–19); Sergeant, E. Surrey Rgt. and Supply and Transport Corps (Indian Army); India and Mesopotamia 4 years 4 months.

Rose, Henry (1914–17); Private, R.D.C.

Rosier, Thomas Albert James (1914–19); Driver, R.F.A.; France 2 years 11 months.

Round, Arthur (1914–17); Private, London Rgt.

Rourk, John Joseph (1915–19); Lance-Corporal, R.E.; France 3 years 6 months, Germany 2 months.

Rous, Ernest Albert (1914–15); Gunner, R.F.A.

Rousell, Joseph Henry (1916–19); Private, Oxfordshire and Buckinghamshire Light Infantry; Salonica 2 years 7 months.

***Rowe, Joseph Henry** (1914–15); Lance-Corporal, London Rgt.; France 7 months; Died of wounds, 8th June, 1915.

Rowell, George James (1916–19); Sapper, R.E.; France 2 years 7 months.

Rowland, Arthur George (1914–19); Leading Seaman, R.F.R.; Naval Service 4 years 6 months.

Rowley, Robert (1914–19); Corporal, Royal Fusiliers; France 4 years.

Rozier, Albert Louis (1914–19); M.C.; Sec.-Lieutenant, R.F.A.; France 3 years 2 months.

Rudd, Henry Herbert (1915–19); Private, Middlesex Rgt.; France 13 months.

Rudland, James (1915–19); Private, R.A.S.C.; France 3 years 8 months.

Ruffell, Francis Joseph (1915–18); Private, R. Welch Fusiliers; France 2 years 1 month.

Rugless, Stephen William (1914–19); Sergeant, London Rgt. and Labour Corps; France 1 year.

Rumfitt, Arthur William (1914–19); Private, Dragoon Guards; France 4 years.

Rundall, William (1914–19); Private, Dragoon Guards; France 3 years 6 months.

Rush, George Albert (1914–16); Private, London Rgt.

Rush, Thomas (1914–19); Bombardier, R.G.A.; France 3 years 5 months.

***Rushton, Frederick** (1914–15); Lance-Corporal, London Rgt.; France 2 months; Killed in action, 25th May, 1915.

Russell, Alfred James (1914–17); Private, E. Kent Rgt.; France 7 months.

Russell, Arthur John (1914–18); Stoker, R.F.R.; Naval Service.

Russell, Herbert James (1916–19); Private, Labour Corps; France 9 months.

***Russell, Samuel** (1914–15); Private, Hampshire Rgt.; Dardanelles 3 months; Missing, 6th August, 1915.

Russell, Stanley Arthur (1916–19); Rifleman, King's Royal Rifle Corps; France 16 months.

Russell, Thomas Charles (1917–19); Wireman, R.N.; Naval Service 1 year 1 month.

Rutherford, George Charles Alexander (1915–19); Lance-Corporal, R.E.; Egypt 13 months.

Rutherford, John Robert (1914–19); Corporal, E. Surrey Rgt.

Rutland, Charles (1914–19); M.M.; Gunner, R.F.A.; France 4 years 8 months.

Ryall, Harry (1915–17); Corporal, Berkshire Rgt.

***Ryan, John** (1914); Private, Irish Guards; France 1 month; Missing, 16th September, 1914.

Ryan, Joseph Anthony (1914–18); Private, Machine Gun Corps; France 2 years 10 months.

Rymill, William George Phillip (1914–19); M.S.M.; Brigade Quartermaster-Sergeant, Middlesex Rgt.; France 3 years 7 months.

Sadd, William Lewin (1916–19); Rifleman, London Rgt.; Salonica 5 months, Egypt 1 year, France 8 months.

Sadler, Frederick William (1916–18); Gunner, R.G.A.

Sadler, George James (1916–19); Driver, R.F.A.

Sainsbury, Thomas Golden (1914–19); Private, R.A.M.C.; France 3 years 7 months.

Sales, Ernest Walter (1915–19); Gunner Shoeing-Smith, R.F.A.; France 3 years 4 months.

Salisbury, John Thomas (1915–19); Gunner, R.G.A.; France 10 months.

Salmon, Harry John (1917–19); Driver, R.A.S.C.; France 2 years 1 month.

Salmon, Robert (1914–19); Driver, R.A.S.C.; France 1 year, Salonica 2 years 7 months.

Salter, Frederick James (1917); Private, R.A.S.C.

Salvage, Edward Henry (1917–19); Private, R.A.V.C.; France 6 months.

Sampford, Arthur George (1914–19); Private, Machine Gun Corps; France 9 months, East Africa 9 months.

***Sampford, Frank Mynott** (1914–16); Lance-Corporal, London Rgt.; Malta and Dardanelles 13 months, France 2 months; Missing, 1st July, 1916.

Sampson, William George (1914–19); Private, M.M.P.; Gallipoli 4 months, Egypt 3 years 2 months.

Sams, Robert (1917–19); Private, Labour Corps; France 3 months.

***Samuels, Albert Frederick** (1914–15); Private, Yorkshire Rgt.; France 5 months; Killed in action, 12th March, 1915.

Sandall, William George (1914); Private, Gordon Highlanders.

Sandell, Frederick Charles (1915–19); Sergeant, R.A.V.C.; France 3 years.

Sanders, John Thomas (1915–19); Private, R.A.S.C.; France 3 years 5 months.

Sanders, Percy Alfred (1916–18); Rifleman, London Rgt.; France 18 months.

Sands, Albert Richard (1915–18); Corporal, R.A.S.C.; France.

Sands, William George (1914–19); Sergeant, Royal Fusiliers; Malta 8 months, Egypt 4 months, Gallipoli 4 months, France 6 months.

Sargent, Frank Henry (1915–19); Private, R.A.S.C.; France 6 months, Salonica 7 months, Egypt 2 years 5 months.

Sasse, Edward William (1914–17); Private, Labour Corps; France 8 months.

Saul, John Henry (1916–19); Rifleman, Rifle Brigade; France 1 year 10 months.

Saunders, Alfred John (1915–19); Rifleman, London Rgt.; France 6 months, Salonica 6 months, Palestine 9 months, Prisoner of war (Turkey) 8 months.

***Saunders, George** (1914–17); Private, Royal Fusiliers; France 2 years 7 months; Killed in action, 4th April, 1917.

Saunders, George (1916–17); Private, E. Surrey Rgt.

Saunders, John William (1914–19); Private, R. Marine Light Infantry; Naval Service 4 years.

Saunders, William (1914–18); Petty Officer, R. Naval Division; Dardanelles and France 14 months.

Saunderson, Edwin (1916–17); Private, Leicestershire Rgt.; France 5 months.

Savage, James John (1915–19); Rifleman, Rifle Brigade; Burmah 3 years 5 months.

Savage, John (1914–19); Private, Royal Fusiliers; France 3 years.

Savage-Eatten, Thomas (1916–19); Private, R.A.M.C.; France 4 months.

Saxton, William George (1914–17); Gunner, R.F.A.; France 11 months.

Say, Thomas (1914–15); Guardsman, Coldstream Guards; France 3 months.

Sayer, Henry John Edgar (1915–19); Company Sergeant-Major, R.E.; France 2 years 1 month.

Sayer, Herbert Stanley (1916–19); Guardsman, Grenadier Guards; France 1 year 7 months.

Scaddan, Albert Victor (1915–19); Rifleman, London Rgt.; France, Salonica and Egypt, 3 years 11 months.

Scales, Alfred Moreton (1914–19); Lieutenant, Devonshire Rgt.; India 3 years, Mesopotamia 2 years.

Schofield, Alfred Henry (1916–19); Lance-Corporal, Machine Gun Corps; France and Italy 14 months, Prisoner of war 8 months.

Scotcher, Herbert John (1916–19); Private, Labour Corps.

Scothorne, Frederick (1914–19); Mentioned in despatches, Medaille d'Honneur avec Glaives en Argent; Private, 7th Bn. London Rgt.; France 2 years 2 months.

Scott, Alick (1914–15 and 1918–19); Gunner, R.H.A.; France 16 months.

***Scott, Frederick Sutton** (1916–17); Rifleman, King's Royal Rifle Corps France 10 months; Died of wounds, 18th August, 1917.

Scott, Walter (1918–20); Private, R.A.S.C.; France and Germany 4 months.

Scott, William Skilton (1916–19); Private, W. Riding Rgt.; France 14 months.

Scowen, Harold Victor (1915–16); Staff-Sergeant, R.A.M.C.

Scowen, Walter Sidney (1915–19); Corporal, R.A.M.C.; France 1 year 10 months, Italy 9 months.

Scratchley, Henry (1914–19); Sapper, R.E.; France 3 years 3 months.

Scrivener, Horace Percy (1915–19); Shoeing-Smith, R.F.A.; France 3 years 1 month.

Scrivens, Charles Frederick (1915–18); Private, R.A.M.C.; France 1 year.

Scuffell, Herbert Henry (1914–19); Sapper, R.E.

Scutchings, William (1914–18); Bombardier, R.H.A.; France 9 months.

Scutt, Edward (1914); Private, Norfolk Rgt.

***Scutt, Seymour Vincent** (1914–16); Private, R.W. Kent Rgt.; France 1 year 7 months; Killed in action, 22nd July, 1916.

Seagust, Edward James (1917–19); Gunner, R.G.A.; France 2 years.

Sealey, Arthur Frederick (1918–19); Rifleman, King's Royal Rifle Corps; France 5 months.

Sear, Frank William (1917–19); Gunner, R.H.A. and R.F.A.; France 16 months.

Searle, Arthur Edward (1914–16); Sergeant, R.F.A.; France 6 months.

Searle, Charles (1918–19); Lance-Corporal, R. Sussex Rgt.; France and Germany 6 months.

Searle, Joseph William (1914–19); Stoker Petty Officer, R.N.; Naval Service 4 years 3 months.

Searle, Thomas Albert (1914–19); 2nd Air Mechanic, R.A.F.; France, Salonica, Egypt and Palestine, 2 years 6 months.

Seaward, Herbert (1914–17); Private, R.W. Surrey Rgt.

Seidler, Horace Albert (1916–19); Lance-Corporal, King's Royal Rifle Corps; France and Italy 8 months, Prisoner of war (Germany) 8 months.

Seigne, Mark Albert George (1914–19); Corporal, R.A.S.C.; Egypt and Palestine 3 years.

Self, James William (1914 and 1915–19); Private, Norfolk Rgt. and R.W. Surrey Rgt.; France 2 years 1 month.

Self, Thomas Valentine (1918–19); Private, Essex Rgt.

Sewell, David George (1914–17); Sergeant, R.D.C.

Seymour, Frederick (1914); Rifleman, London Rgt.

Seymour, William (1914–18); Private, 9th Lancers.

Shannon, James William (1914–19); Sergeant, Labour Corps.

Sharp, Hubert Alfred (1917–19); Private, Labour Corps; France 2 years 7 months.

Sharp, Reginald Joseph (1915–19); Sapper, R.E.; France 2 years.

Sharp, Sidney Archibald (1914–19); Sapper, R.E.; Egypt 9 months, Salonica 2 years, France 5 months.

Sharp, William Stuart (1915–19); Corporal, 13th Hussars; France 2 months.

Sharpe, Walter Frederick (1917–18); Private, Middlesex Rgt.; France 8 months, Italy 4 months.

Shaw, Ernest (1914–19); Company Quartermaster-Sergeant, Suffolk Rgt.; France 1 year.

Shawyer, Albert Alfred (1917–19); Able Seaman, R. Naval Division; France 14 months.

Shea, William John (1914–18); Private, R.A.S.C.; France 2 years 9 months.

Sheahan, Thomas (1915–19); Fitter-Corporal, R.G.A.; Salonica 2 years 2 months.

Shearman, George William (1914–19); Sergeant, E. Surrey Rgt.; France 3 years 8 months, Germany 1 month.

Shearman, Richard Thomas (1915–19); Stoker, R.N.; Naval Service 3 years 10 months.

Sheers, Thomas Albert (1915–19); Private, Border Rgt.; France 3 years 7 months.

Sheldon, James (1917–19); Private, Labour Corps; France 18 months.

Sheldrick, George (1914–19); Driver, R.F.A.; France 4 years 5 months.

Shephard, Frederick (1916–19); Rifleman, London Rgt.; France 2 years 1 month.

Shephard, Samuel (1915–19); Driver, R.E.; France 3 years.

Shepherd, Albert Edward (1915–16); Gunner, R.F.A.; France 3 months.

***Shepherd, Alfred Joseph** (1914–15); Sergeant, Royal Fusiliers; France 3 months; Killed in action, 20th May, 1915.

Shepherd, Charles Reginald (1914–17); Private, N. Staffordshire Rgt.; France 1 month.

Shepherd, Henry James (1914–19); Driver, R.A.S.C.; France 2 years 6 months.

Sheppard, Albert Ernest (1918–19); Private, E. Kent Rgt.

Sheppard, Frederick Charles (1916–19); Private, Nottinghamshire and Derbyshire Rgt. and R.D.C.; France 8 months.

Sheppard, Henry Elias (1917–19); Rifleman, King's Royal Rifle Corps; France 16 months.

Sheppard, William Henry (1916–19); Private, Labour Corps.

Sherman, William Henry (1914–17): Bombardier, R.G.A.; France 18 months.

Sherrott, Francis Percival (1914–19); Corporal, London Rgt.; Malta and France 2 years 10 months.

Shields, William (1914–16); Private, London Rgt.

Shillum, John William (1915–19); Gunner, R.F.A.; France 6 months, Salonica 6 months, Egypt 1 year 9 months.

Shirley, Frederick Joseph (1914–17); Rifleman, London Rgt.

Shorrock, George Norman Walmsley (1915–19); Staff-Sergeant, R.A.M.C.; Egypt and France 3 years.

Short, Charles Reginald (1914–19); Able Seaman, R.N.; Naval Service 4 years 5 months.

Short, Walter James (1917–19); Private, Labour Corps; France 6 months.

Shoult, Bertram Horace (1915–19); Corporal, R.A.S.C.; France 3 years.

***Shrimpton, James John** (1914–15); Chief Petty Officer, R.F.R.; Naval Service; Killed in action, 23rd May, 1915.

Shuttleworth, Albert (1914–19); Corporal, Essex Rgt.

Shuttleworth, George (1915–19); Guardsman, Coldstream Guards; France 2 years 7 months.

Sibbons, Albert Henry (1917–19); Corporal, A.P.C.

Sibley, George Henry (1917–19); Private, Labour Corps; France 1 year 11 months.

Siequien, Frederick George (1918–19); Private, R.A.S.C.; France and Germany 14 months.

Silver, George (1914–19); Lance-Corporal, Royal Fusiliers; France 2 years 4 months.

Simmons, Edwin Alfred (1915–19); Sergeant, Cheshire Rgt.; Gallipoli 5 days, Salonica 2 years 9 months.

Simms, John Henry (1916–19); Private, Labour Corps.

***Simons, Henry Joseph** (1914–15); Lance-Corporal, E. Surrey Rgt.; France 2 months; Killed in action, 15th October, 1915.

***Simons, John Ernest** (1914–16); Sergeant, E. Surrey Rgt.; France 10 months; Killed in action, 1st July, 1916.

Simpson, Albert Edward (1917–19); Private, Labour Corps; France 1 year 8 months.

Simpson, Alfred Ernest (1915–16); Private, Labour Corps.

Simpson, Henry John (1914–18); Guardsman, Coldstream Guards; France 3 years.

Simpson, John Jordan Fletcher (1918–19); 2nd Private, R.A.F.

Sims, George Henry (1917–19); Private, R.A.M.C.; France 1 year.

Sinclair, Alexander (1914–19); Private, London Rgt.; France, Salonica and Palestine, 3 years.

Sinnett, Henry (1916–18); Private, Suffolk Rgt.

Skeggs, George Thomas (1915–19); Gunner, R.F.A.; France 2 years.

***Skeggs, James** (1914–16); Corporal, Royal Fusiliers; France 6 months; Died of wounds, 27th January, 1916.

Skerry, James (1914–18); Private, R.D.C.

Skiggs, Walter Alexander (1915–19); Lance-Bombardier, R.F.A.; France 1 year 10 months.

***Skingle, Edward** (1914–18); Sergeant-Instructor, R.G.A.; France 1 year; Died, 18th May, 1918.

Skingsley, James (1914–16 and 1917–19); Private, R.E.; France 3 years 6 months.

Skinner, George (1917–19); Lance-Corporal, R.A.M.C.; France 2 years 2 months.

Skinner, Henry Blackbourn (1915–19); Sergeant, R.F.A.; France, Salonica and Palestine, 3 years.

Skinner, James William (1914–19); Private, R.W. Kent Rgt.; France 2 years 9 months, Prisoner of war (Germany) 8 months.

***Skipp, William John** (1916–17); Private, Northumberland Fusiliers; France 1 month; Missing, 16th August, 1917.

Skippage, Charles Alfred (1918–19); Pioneer, R.E.; France 4 months.

Slade, Alfred (1914–17); Private, R.D.C.

Sloane, William James (1914–19); Gunner, R.G.A.; Italy and Egypt 18 months.

Slow, Percy John (1915–18); Gunner, R.F.A.; Salonica, Malta and France, 1 year 11 months.

Smart, Frederick Thomas (1915–19); Corporal, R.A.S.C.; France 9 months.

Smith, Albert Henry Burdett (1914–18); Private, Middlesex Rgt.; France 3 years.

Smith, Alexander Thomas (1916–19); Corporal, R.G.A.

Smith, Alfred Herbert (1914–19); Rifleman, London Rgt.; France 3 years 7 months.

Smith, Arthur (1915–19); Driver, R.F.A.; France 3 years 6 months.

Smith, Arthur (1916–19); Private, Labour Corps.

Smith, Arthur Victor (1915–19); Able Seaman, R.N.; Naval Service 3 years 3 months.

Smith, Charles Robert (1915–19); M.M.; Driver, R.E.; France 2 years 10 months.

Smith, Edward George (1914–15); Private, Dragoon Guards.

Smith, Ernest (1915–19); Corporal, R.A.S.C.; France 3 years 10 months.

Smith, Ernest Alfred (1915–19); Driver, R.A.S.C.; France 14 months.

Smith, Frank (1915–19); Private, R.A.S.C.; France 4 years 1 month.

Smith, Frank Charles (1914–19); Sergeant, Labour Corps; France 2 years 2 months.

Smith, Frederick (1914); Sergeant, R.F.A.

Smith, Frederick Charles (1915–19); Pioneer, R.E.; France 1 year.

Smith, Frederick James (1914–16); Private, Highland Light Infantry; France 1 year.

Smith, Frederick James (1916–19); Sapper, R.E.; France 2 years 2 months.

Smith, George (1915–18); Corporal, Dragoon Guards; France 5 months.

Smith, George (1916–19); Lance-Corporal, Labour Corps; France 2 years.

Smith, George (1917–19); Rifleman, London Rgt.; France 2 years 4 months.

Smith, George Charles (1917–19); Sapper, R.E.; France 1 year 6 months.

Smith, George Edward (1915–19); Driver, R.E.; France 2 years 11 months.

Smith, George Edward (1914–19); Private, Labour Corps; France 3 years 3 months.

Smith, George Henry (1914–19); Corporal, London Rgt.; France 4 months.

Smith, George Henry (1914–19); Driver, R.E.; France 4 years.

Smith, George Henry (1915–19); Sapper, R.E.; France 3 years 2 months.

Smith, George Samuel (1914–19); Private, R. Marine Light Infantry; Naval Service 3 years 3 months.

Smith, Henry (1915–19); Sapper, R.E.; France 3 years 4 months.

Smith, Henry Frederick (1915–19); Sapper, R.E.; Egypt 4 years.

Smith, Henry Samuel (1915–17); Driver, R.F.A.; France 18 months.

Smith, Henry Samuel (1914–19); Private, R.A.F.

Smith, Herbert Alfred (1914–19); M.B.E. (Mil. Div.), M.S.M.; Sergeant, Bedfordshire Rgt.

Smith, James (1914-17); Corporal, London Rgt.

Smith, James Henry (1914–19); Corporal, Royal Fusiliers; France, Italy and Germany, 2 years 10 months.

Smith, John (1915); Driver, R.E.; France.

Smith, John (1914–19); Company Quartermaster-Sergeant, King's Royal Rifle Corps; France 3 years 6 months.

Smith, John Charles (1914–19); Bombardier, R.F.A.; Gallipoli, Salonica and Palestine 3 years 6 months.

Smith, John William Ernest (1915–19); Sapper, R.E.; France 3 years 3 months.

Smith, Joseph Henry (1915–19); Private, R.A.S.C.; France and Mesopotamia 3 years 2 months.

Smith, Leonard Charles (1915–19); Driver, R.E.; France 5 months, Salonica 3 years.

Smith, Newman Sydney (1916–19); Private, Tank Corps; France 2 years.

Smith, Percy (1914–15); Private, R.A.S.C.

Smith, Percy Thomas (1916–19); Private, R. Warwickshire Rgt.; France and Italy 17 months.

Smith, Stephen Page (1914–15 and 1916–19); Gunner, R.F.A.; France 18 months, Italy 14 months.

Smith, Thomas William (1916–19); Private, Essex Rgt.; France 1 year 7 months.

Smith, William (1915–19); Private, R. Marine Labour Co.; France 4 years.

Smith, William (1915–19): 2nd Corporal, R.E.; France 4 months, Balkans 3 years 3 months.

Smith, William (1914–19); Sergeant, R.A.S.C.; France 3 years 6 months.

Smith, William (1914–19); Lance-Corporal, Rifle Brigade; Burmah 3 years 6 months.

Smith, William (1914–19); Rifleman, Rifle Brigade; Burmah 4 years.

Smith, William Frederick (1917–19); Lance-Sergeant, Suffolk Rgt.

Smith, William Granville (1915–19); Private, R.A.S.C.; France 3 years 6 months.

***Smith, William Henry** (1915–17); Gunner, R.F.A.; France 17 months; Died of wounds, 9th May, 1917.

Smith, William James (1915–19); Private, Labour Corps; Egypt 3 years 4 months.

Smith, William James (1915–19); Armourer Staff-Sergeant, R.A.O.C.; France 2 years.

Smith, William James (1916–19); Lance-Corporal, R. Lancaster Rgt.; Salonica 2 years 9 months.

Smith, William John (1915–19); Private, Labour Corps; Egypt 3 months, France 7 months.

Smith, William Thomas (1916–19); Lance-Corporal, Labour Corps; France and Germany 2 years 4 months.

Smith, William Walter (1914–19); Sergeant, R.F.A.; France 3 years 5 months.

Smithin, Benjamin John (1915–19); Sergeant, R.E.

Smy, Edgar Ernest (1914–19); Private, E. Surrey Rgt.; France 3 years 6 months.

***Smythe, James** (1915–16); Lance-Corporal, R.W. Surrey Rgt.: France 5 months; Killed in action, 20th April, 1916.

Smythe, Peter (1914–19): Sergeant, R.E.; Gibraltar 13 months.

Snare, Frederick (1916–19); Air Mechanic (3rd Class), R.A.F.

Solomon, John William (1914–15); Lance-Corporal, R.E.

Soper, Percy Charles (1915–19); Corporal, R.A.V.C.; France and Egypt 3 years 5 months.

Sorrell, Albert Joseph (1914–19); Private, Middlesex Rgt.; India and Mesopotamia 2 years 6 months.

Sorrell, Frederick Benjamin (1916–17); Private, London Rgt.

Southgate, Alfred (1917–19); Private, Labour Corps; France 2 years.

Sparkes, George Augustus (1914–19); 2nd Sick Berth Steward, R.N.; Naval Service 4 years 10 months.

Sparks, Harry (1914–19); Private, 2nd Dragoon Guards; France 4 years 1 month.

Sparksman, James (1915–19); Lance-Bombardier, R.F.A.; France 3 years 7 months.

Sparrow, Percy William George (1915–17); Gunner, R.F.A.

Spaull, Thomas Robert (1914–19); Sergeant, Royal Fusiliers; France 9 months, Salonica 2 years 9 months.

Spearing, William Philip (1915–19); Company Sergeant-Major, R.A.S.C.; France 10 months, Balkans 2 years 2 months.

Speer, William (1915–19); D.C.M.; Corporal, R.F.A.; France 3 years.

***Spicer, George Henry** (1914–18); Sec.-Lieutenant, Royal Fusiliers; Killed in action, 6th June, 1918.

Spicer, Thomas (1914–19); Private, Essex Rgt.; Gallipoli and India 4 years.

Spicer, William Henry (1917–19); Private, R.A.S.C.

Spickett, Francis Owen (1915–19); Corporal, Hertfordshire Rgt.; France 2 years.

Spittlehouse, Frederick William (1915–19); Private, R.A.O.C.; Salonica 2 years, Egypt 14 months.

Spooner, Frederick (1918–19); Rifleman, Rifle Brigade; France 5 months.

Sprague, Walter Henry (1914–19); Stoker, R.F.R.; Naval Service 4 years 6 months.

Springer, Henry James (1914–17); Sergeant, R.H.A.

Springett, Harry (1916–19); Private, Labour Corps; France 2 years 3 months.

Springett, Harry George (1915–19); Sergeant, R.F.A.; France, Salonica and Egypt, 3 years.

Springthorpe, William Frederick (1914–16); Private, Middlesex Rgt.; France 2 years.

Stace, Henry (1914–15); Wheeler-Driver, R.A.S.C.

Stacey, William Thomas (1916–19); Private, R.A.M.C.; France 6 months.

Stagg, Sydney Horace (1915–17); Private, R.A.M.C.

Staines, Harry Stephen (1918); Private, R. Marine Engineers.

Standen, Thomas Frederick (1914–17); Corporal, Devonshire Rgt.; France 10 months.

Standfield, James Charles (1915–17); Private, R.A.S.C.

Standivan, Albert Henry (1918–19); Private, Royal Fusiliers.

Stanford, Edward (1915–19); Private, Labour Corps; France 4 months.

Stanley, Leslie Ernest (1917–19); Able Seaman, R.N.; Naval Service 2 years 4 months.

Staples, Albert Victor (1915–19); Sergeant, R.A.O.C.; France 13 months, Italy 1 year 9 months.

Stares, Frank (1917–19); Private, Labour Corps; France 1 year.

Starkins, Harry (1916–19); Corporal, Labour Corps; France 5 months.

***Steadman, Arthur Charles** (1916–17); Private, Royal Fusiliers; France 6 months; Died of wounds, 13th May, 1917.

Steadman, Christopher John (1915–19); Bombardier, R.F.A.; France 3 years.

Steadman, David Alfred (1915–19); Fitter, R.F.A.; France and Germany 2 years 8 months.

Stedman, Alfred (1916–19); Driver, R.F.A.

Steel, Arthur Edwin (1915–19); Sergeant, Middlesex Rgt.

Steel, Ernest (1918–20); Private, London Rgt.; France, Germany and Egypt, 14 months.

Steel, Sydney Herbert (1916–19); Lance-Bombardier, R.G.A.; Mesopotamia 1 year 9 months.

Steer, George (1914–16); Rifleman, London Rgt.

Steer, Thomas William (1914–19); Lance-Corporal, Middlesex Rgt.; India and France 3 years.

Steggles, Walter George (1916–19); Private, Labour Corps.

Stenning, Charles Edward (1914–19); Lance-Corporal, R.E.; France, Salonica and Egypt, 2 years 8 months.

Stephens, Edwin Harry (1918–19); Private, R.A.F.

Stephens, Francis Walter (1914–19); Able Seaman, R.F.R.; Naval Service 4 years 5 months.

Stephens, Thomas Henry Bevan (1917–19); Gunner, R.G.A.; France 1 year.

***Sterry, Arthur William** (1914–16); Sergeant, Norfolk Rgt.; France 2 years; Killed in action, 4th September, 1916.

Stevens, Arthur Albert (1915–19); Sergeant, R.A.S.C.; France 4 years 3 months.

Stevens, Charles George (1916–19); Private, Labour Corps.

Stevens, Frederick (1914–19); Sergeant, Tank Corps; France 2 years.

Stevens, George (1915–19); Lance-Corporal, R.A.V.C.; Egypt, Salónica and France, 3 years 4 months.

***Stevens, Roland William** (1914–18); Sergeant, Northamptonshire Rgt.; France 10 months; Missing, 27th May, 1918.

Stevens, Sidney Thomas (1916–19); Leading Aircraftsman, R.A.F.; France 10 months.

Stevens, Thomas (1916–19); Private, London Rgt.; France 2 years.

Stevens, Walter William (1916–19); Gunner, R.G.A.: France 2 years.

Stevenson, George Ernest (1914–19); M.M.; Private, E. Kent Rgt. and Labour Corps; France 6 months.

Stevenson, Leonard William (1915–19); Sergeant, R.A.S.C.; France 8 months, Egypt and Palestine 3 years 4 months.

Stevenson, Percy Walter (1914–15); Private, Border Rgt.

Steward, Charles George (1915–19); Driver, R.F.A.; France 3 years 8 months.

Stewart, John Edward (1914–19); Private, Duke of Cornwall's Light Infantry; France and Italy 4 years 5 months.

Stickling, Frederick Charles (1914–19); Private, R.A.O.C.; France 1 year, Salonica 3 years 2 months.

Stiff, James (1915–19); Sergeant, R.F.A.; France 1 year 8 months.

Stiff, Joseph Alfred (1914–19); Sergeant, R.A.S.C.; Salonica and Egypt 2 years 7 months.

Stiff, Robert (1916–19); Lance-Corporal, Durham Light Infantry; Salonica 2 years 6 months.

Stiling, Frederick John (1915–17); Gunner, R.G.A.; France 2 years 7 months.

***Stiller, Edward Mark** (1914–18); Corporal, R.F.A.; France 6 months, Salonica and Palestine 2 years; Died, 14th December, 1918.

Stillman, Edgar John (1915–19); Private, R.W. Kent Rgt.; France and Italy 2 years 1 month.

Stimpson, Philip Brewster (1918–19); Armourers' Crew, R.N.

Stimson, Henry Samuel (1914–19); Lance-Corporal, King's Royal Rifle Corps; France 2 years.

Stirling, John Henry (1914–19); Sergeant, London Rgt.; France 1 year.

Stirrat, John George (1914–19); Sergeant, R.A.F.; France 10 months.

Stock, Charles (1917–19); Gunner, R.G.A.

Stock, George Reuben (1916–19); Corporal, Norfolk Rgt.; France 18 months.

Stock, John Charles (1915–19); Sergeant, R.A.S.C.; France 5 months.

Stock, John Edward (1915–19); Private, R.A.S.C.; France 3 years 3 months.

Stock, Sidney James (1915–19); Private, R.A.M.C.; East Africa 8 months.

Stockham, Henry Thomas (1914); Private, Royal Fusiliers.

Stocks, Maximilian (1914–17); Private, London Rgt.

Stodgell, Charles Albert (1918–19); Private, Wiltshire Rgt.; France 2 months.

Stokes, Alfred Frederick (1917–19); Private, R.A.S.C.

Stokes, John (1917–19); Rifleman, King's Royal Rifle Corps; France 5 months, Prisoner of war (Germany) 8 months.

Stokes, John Charles (1914–19); Sergeant, Royal Fusiliers; France 10 months.

Stone, Albert Henry (1916–17); Private, Labour Corps.

Stone, Walter (1917–19); Private, London Rgt.; Egypt 1 year, France 14 months.

Stone, Walter Edgar (1915–19); 2nd Corporal, R.E.; France 3 years 6 months.

Stone, William Richard (1916–19); Lance-Corporal, M.F.P.

Stopher, Edward Robert (1916–19); Private, Labour Corps; France 1 month.

Storer, Edward William (1915–19); Company Sergeant - Major, R.A.S.C.; Burmah 3 years, Mesopotamia 8 months.

Storrie, Robert (1915–18); Corporal, R.F.A.; France 2 years 2 months.

Stow, William (1914–18); Private, 11th Cavalry Reserve Rgt.

Stowell, John (1915–19); Private, R.A.S.C.; Egypt, Palestine and Arabia, 3 years 3 months.

Strange, Bertie (1916–19); Private, Worcestershire Rgt.; France 1 year.

Strange, Charles Henry (1916–17); Private, Labour Corps.

Strange, Charles Thomas (1917–20); Private, Labour Corps; France 8 months.

Strange, Frederick Arthur (1914–19); Driver R.F.A., and Private, Labour Corps; France 4 years 6 months.

Stratford, Henry James (1915–19); M.M. and bar; Company Sergeant-Major, Royal Fusiliers; France 2 years 11 months.

Straw, Alfred George (1916–19); Private, Labour Corps; Salonica and France 2 years 3 months.

Street, William Albert (1916–19); Private, Labour Corps; France 2 years 6 months.

Stribling, Branwhite Gordon (1916–17); Private, Middlesex Rgt.

Strickland, John Herbert (1917–19); Private, Labour Corps.

Stritch, Patrick (1917–19); Aircraftsman (2nd Class), R.A.F.

Strong, Albert Arthur (1915–19); Sergeant, R.A.M.C.

Strong, Roland Randall (1914–19); Lance-Corporal, R.A.S.C.; Malta and France 3 years 6 months.

Stroud, Henry (1916–19); Private, York and Lancaster Rgt.; France 8 months.

Stubbs, Robert John William (1915–19); Gunner, R.F.A.; France 1 year 8 months.

Sturgeon, Christopher (1914–19); Private, R. Marine Light Infantry; Naval Service 4 years 6 months.

Sturt, William (1918–19); Lance-Corporal, R. Sussex Rgt.; France 4 months.

Stuttart, Albert Edward (1914–17); Private, R. Berkshire Rgt.

Styles, Thomas Francis (1914–17); Rifleman, London Rgt., and Private, R.D.C.; France 2 months.

***Suckling, Alfred James** (1916–18); Rifleman, London Rgt.; France 1 year; Died of wounds, 10th August, 1918.

Suckling, Arthur (1914–19); Private, R.A.M.C.; France, Egypt and Palestine 3 years 9 months.

Suckling, John Elvy (1914–19); Private, R.A.S.C.; France 4 years 4 months.

Sullivan, John (1914–19); Private, R.D.C.

Summerhayes, Arnold (1915–19); Lance-Corporal, R.E.; France 3 years 3 months, Germany 6 months.

Sumner, Henry (1917–19); Rifleman, Rifle Brigade; France 1 year.

Sumner, John Percy (1914–19); Driver, R.E.; Gallipoli 9 months, France 1 year 11 months.

Sunnucks, Frank George (1917–19); Gunner, R.G.A.; France 11 months.

Susans, Alfred (1914); Rifleman, Rifle Brigade.

Swaby, John (1918–19); Private, R. Sussex Rgt.; France and Germany 6 months.

Swaker, William Leslie (1914–19); Private, R.A.S.C.; France 4 years 6 months.

Swann, Sidney William (1915–19); M.M.; Private, Machine Gun Corps; Egypt and France 3 years.

Swarman, Frederick John (1916–19); Gunner, R.F.A.; France 10 months.

Sweet, Hedley Arthur Thomas (1914–17 and 1918); Lance-Corporal, Labour Corps; France 2 years 4 months.

Sweeting, Alfred William (1915–19); Bombardier, R.F.A.; France 3 years 1 month.

***Swindells, Samuel** (1915–18); 1st Private, R.A.F.; Mediterranean 11 months; Died, 18th November, 1918.

Symonds, Albert Edward (1915–19); Sergeant, R.A.S.C.; France 3 years 8 months.

Symonds, Charles Robert (1915–19); Rifleman, Rifle Brigade; France 3 months.

Talbott, Edwin John (1915–19); Sapper, R.E.; France 3 years 5 months.

Tallent, Frederick James (1918); Private, R.F.A.

Tanner, Willie Harry (1918–19); Gunner, R.G.A.

Tarbutt, George Henry (1918–19); Driver, R.A.S.C.

Tarraway, George (1914–19); Chief Petty Officer, R.N.; Naval Service 3 years.

***Tarry, Arthur Frederick** (1916–18); Gunner, R.F.A.; Died, 6th April, 1918.

Tasker, Alfred Reginald (1914–19); Private, Labour Corps; France 4 years 7 months.

Tatchell, William (1914–19); Saddler Staff-Sergeant, R.A.S.C.; France 3 years 9 months.

Taylor, Albert Edward (1915–19); Saddler, R.F.A.; France 3 years.

Taylor, Alfred Henry (1915–19); Private, Labour Corps.

Taylor, Charles (1914–19); Private, Gloucestershire Rgt.; France 3 years 8 months.

Taylor, Charles William (1915–19); Gunner, R.F.A.; Italy 18 months, France 2 years.

Taylor, Edmund (1916–19); Private, Essex Rgt.

Taylor, Edwin (1914–15); Trooper, R. Horse Guards; France.

Taylor, George Ernest (1914–19); M.M.; Lance-Corporal, R.E.; France 2 years, Gallipoli 8 months.

Taylor, George James (1914–17); Private, Royal Fusiliers; France 2 years 8 months.

Taylor, Harry William (1917–19); Signaller, R.G.A.; France 1 year 9 months.

Taylor, Henry (1915–19); Private, London Rgt.; France 13 months, Salonica 6 months, Palestine 1 year.

Taylor, James Henry (1914–19); Private, Yorkshire Light Infantry; France 2 weeks, Prisoner of war (Germany) 4 years 4 months.

Taylor, James Joseph (1914–19); Battery Quartermaster-Sergeant, R.G.A.; France 2 years.

Taylor, John (1916–19); Rifleman, Rifle Brigade; France 2 years, Prisoner of war (Germany) 7 months.

Taylor, Samuel (1915–19); Driver, R.E.; France 3 years.

Taylor, Thomas (1914–19); Private, London Rgt. and Labour Corps; France 3 years 11 months.

***Taylor, Thomas Henry** (1914–18); Private, E. Yorkshire Rgt.; Mesopotamia 8 months, France 1 year 9 months; Killed in action, 27th March, 1918.

Taylor, Vincent Chatterton (1917–19); Private, London Rgt.; France 6 weeks, Prisoner of war 9 months.

Taylor, William David (1914–20); Rifleman, Rifle Brigade; India 4 years 1 month.

Taylor, William George (1914–19); Private, R.D.C.

Teall, Ernest George (1914–18); Rifleman, Rifle Brigade; India 14 months.

Tebbutt, Jim (1915–19); Lance-Corporal, R.E.; France 3 years.

Tedman, Bert Edward (1914–18); Driver, R.G.A.; France.

Tegmere, Frederick Thomas (1914–17); Private, Lincolnshire Rgt.

***Templeman, William John** (1915–17); Gunner, R.F.A.; France 5 months, Salonica 7 months, Palestine 6 months; Died, 7th December, 1917.

Tennison, George Henry (1915–19); Private, Labour Corps; Dardanelles and France 3 years 9 months.

Terry, Donald Ernest (1917–19); Cadet, R.A.F.

Terry, Herbert Charles (1914–18); Sec.-Lieutenant, R.F.A.; France 2 years 2 months.

Terry, William George (1914–19); Private, R. Warwickshire Rgt.; France and Egypt 4 years 6 months.

Tester, Francis Charles (1914–19); Sergeant, R.A.S.C. (M.T.); France 3 years 10 months.

Thomas, Albert Edward George (1916–19); Private, W. Yorkshire Rgt.; France 6 months.

***Thomas, Albert James** (1915–18); Lance-Corporal, R.E.; France 2 years 9 months; Killed in action, 14th April, 1918.

***Thomas, Edward George** (1914–17); Gunner, R.F.A.; France 8 months; Killed in action, 2nd October, 1917.

Thomas, Edward Joseph (1918); Private, R.W. Kent Rgt.; France 3 months.

Thomas, Frederick (1916–19); Aircraftsman (2nd Class), R.A.F.

Thomas, Job (1914–19); Driver, R.E.; France 3 years 6 months.

Thomas, John David Oswell (1915–19); Leading Aircraftsman, R.A.F.; Salonica 1 year 11 months.

Thomas, Melville John (1916–18); Private, Labour Corps; France 8 months.

Thomas, Mornington Henry (1916–19); Deck Hand, Motor Launch; Naval Service 2 years 6 months.

Thomas, Richard (1916–19); Driver, R.G.A.; France 2 years 3 months.

Thomas, Samuel Walter (1914–19); Company Quartermaster-Sergeant, Machine Gun Corps; France 13 months.

Thompsett, Stephen William (1914–19); Sergeant, R.E. Kent Yeomanry; France 2 months.

Thompson, Alfred (1918–19); Private, R.E.; Germany 6 months.

Thompson, Alfred Herbert (1917–19) Private, R.A.S.C.

Thompson, Frank (1915–19); Corporal, R.F.A.; France 3 years 3 months.

Thompson, Frederick Charles (1915–19); Lance-Bombardier, R.G.A.; France 3 years 3 months.

Thompson, Henry (1914–19); Mentioned in despatches; Sergeant, Guards Machine Gun Rgt.; France 2 years 6 months.

***Thompson, John** (1914–16); M.M.; Corporal, E. Kent Rgt.; France 14 months; Killed in action, 30th September, 1916.

Thompson, Joseph (1915–19); Private, R.E.; Dardanelles and Egypt 3 years 9 months.

Thompson, William Alfred (1914–19); Sergeant, E. Lancashire Rgt.; France 3 years 8 months.

Thomson, Alexander James Frank (1914–18); Bombardier, R.F.A.; France 1 year 9 months.

Thomson, Alfred Davies (1915–19); Private, R.A.S.C.; France 2 years.

***Thorn, Percy Lewis** (1915–16); Private, Oxfordshire and Buckinghamshire Light Infantry; France 18 months; Died, 11th December, 1916.

Thorne, Jeremiah (1917–19); Pioneer, R.E.; France 3 months.

Thorne, William Edwin (1915–19); Gunner, R.F.A.; France, Egypt and Palestine 3 years 3 months.

Thornton, Archibald Ernest (1914–19); Farrier-Sergeant, R.F.A.; France and Italy.

Thoroughgood, John Henry (1915–19); Lance-Corporal, R.A.S.C. (M.T.); France 3 years 10 months.

Thorp, Edwin George (1917–18); Corporal, R.E.; France and Germany 11 months.

Thrussell, Thomas Henry (1915–17); Sapper, R.E.

Thurtle, Albert George (1914–19); Sergeant, R.A.M.C.; Egypt 1 year 9 months.

Thynne, Albert Edward (1914–19); Private, Guards' Machine Gun Rgt.; France 3 years 1 month.

***Thynne, William John** (1914); Private, E. Surrey Rgt.; France; Missing, 24th August, 1914.

***Tigg, Thomas Henry** (1914–17); Private, R.A.M.C.; France 2 years 4 months; Killed in action, 20th September, 1917.

***Tingay, Thomas Burgess** (1914–18); Sapper, R.E.; Accidentally killed, 23rd August, 1918.

Tinker, Frederick George (1914–18); Corporal, R.D.C.

Tinworth, Alfred Edward (1915–19); Gunner, R.F.A.; India 4 months, Mesopotamia 1 year 10 months.

Tisdall, William George (1914–19); M.S.M.; Driver, R.H.A.; France 4 years 2 months.

***Titcomb, Ernest James** (1915–16); Rifleman, London Rgt.; France 3 months; Killed in action, 7th October, 1916.

Titmuss, Alfred Joseph (1914–19); Private, Remount Squadron; France and Italy 18 months.

***Toby, John** (1914–18); Private, Oxfordshire and Buckinghamshire Light Infantry; France 6 months; Died of wounds whilst a prisoner of war, 3rd April, 1918.

***Todd, James William** (1917); Cadet, R.A.F.; Accidentally killed, 28th September, 1917.

Todd, Robert (1916–19); Sergeant, M.F.P.

Tolhurst, Jacob Isaac (1914–17); Lance-Corporal, R.D.C.

Tolland, Thomas Edward (1914–19); Gunner, R. Marine Artillery; Naval Service 3 years.

Tombs, Edward (1915–19); Private, York and Lancaster Rgt.; France 2 years 6 months.

Tomlinson, Alfred George (1916–19); Private, Labour Corps; France 1 year 11 months.

Toon, Walter Harold (1918–19); Rifleman, Rifle Brigade; France 5 months.

Topp, Cyril (1914–18); Gunner, R.F.A.; France 2 years 2 months.

Topp, George Ernest (1914–19); Private, R.A.S.C. (M.T.); France 4 years 7 months.

Topple, George Luke (1918–19); Rifleman, Rifle Brigade; France 4 months.

Torrance, Harry Thomas (1915–19); Lance-Corporal, R.D.C.

***Tott, John** (1914–15); Private, Scottish Rifles; France 5 months; Killed in action, 9th May, 1915.

Tow, Harold James (1915); Private, London Rgt.

Townsend, Alfred William (1914–15); Gunner, R.F.A.

Townsend, James (1914–19); Gunner, R.G.A.; France 4 years 5 months.

***Townsend, Stanley Henry** (1914–15); Gunner, R.F.A.; France 1 month; Killed in action, 25th September, 1915.

Tracey, Ernest Edwin (1915–19); Private, London Rgt.; France 1 year 9 months, Salonica 6 months, Egypt and Palestine 1 year.

Tregent, William (1914–19); Rifleman, Rifle Brigade; France 3 years 8 months.

Trembath, George Henry (1915–19); Sapper, R.E.; France 1 year 11 months.

Trembath, William (1915–19); M.M.; Sergeant, R.E.; France 3 years 2 months.

Trevanna, William Thomas (1914–19); Rifleman, London Rgt.; France, Salonica and Egypt, 3 years.

***Trevett, Frank** (1914–17); M.M.; Lance-Sergeant, King's Royal Rifle Corps; France 1 year 7 months; Killed in action, 17th February, 1917.

Tring, Henry (1915–19): Gunner, R.F.A.; France 3 years 7 months.

Tripp, Ernest John (1914–19); Gunner, R.F.A.; France 2 years 6 months, Italy 14 months.

Tripp, Charles Frank (1915–19); Gunner, R.F.A.; France 3 years 3 months.

Tritton, Charles Elliott (1916–19); Private, R.A.S.C.; France 3 years 6 months.

Trodd, William Morrin (1914–19); M.M.; Sapper, R.E.; France, Mesopotamia and Italy 4 years.

Trubridge, Ernest Alfred (1918–19); Private, R.A.S.C. (M.T.).

Trudgill, Charles (1915–19); Shoeing-Smith, R.F.A.; France 3 years.

True, Ernest John Henry (1914–19); Gunner, R.F.A.; France 4 years 3 months.

Truscott, William Lawrence (1914–19); Private, Dragoon Guards; France 1 year.

Truss, Frederick (1915–18); Sapper, R.E.; Gallipoli and France 2 years.

Trussell, Alfred John (1915–19); Private, Nottinghamshire and Derbyshire Rgt.; France 1 year.

Trusson, James (1915–19); Corporal, Labour Corps; France 13 months.

Tucker, Harry (1915–19); Private, Dragoon Guards; France 2 years.

Tucker, Walter Henry (1915–19); Gunner, R.F.A.; France and Germany 3 years 6 weeks.

Tulley, Charles Thomas Edwin (1914–19); Gunner, R.F.A.; France 3 months, Salonica 2 months.

Turnbull, Robert James (1918–19); Private, R. Sussex Rgt.; France and Germany 5 months.

Turnbull, Stephen (1914–17); M.M.; Sergeant, Royal Fusiliers; France.

† **Turner, Alfred John** (1915–19); Stoker, R.N.; Naval Service 3 years 11 months.

Turner, Frederick William (1916–20); Private, London Rgt.; France 5 months, Egypt 2 years 1 month.

Turner, Herbert (1918–20); Private, R. Sussex Rgt.; France, Egypt and Palestine 16 months.

Turner, John Forwood (1915–19); Private, Labour Corps; France 6 months, Salonica 6 months, Egypt 1 year 7 months.

***Turner, Thomas William** (1915–17); Sergeant, R.F.A.; France 2 years; Missing, 21st September, 1917.

Turner, Walter (1914–19); Private, King's Hussars; India, Mesopotamia and France 4 years.

Turner, William Henry (1914–17); Sergeant, R. Berkshire Rgt.; France.

Turton, Edward Isaiah (1914–19); Corporal, R.F.A.; France 1 year, Salonica 7 months, Malta 5 months.

Turton, Joseph William (1914–19); Private, Northumberland Fusiliers; France, Mesopotamia and India 5 years.

Tustin, Arthur George John (1918–19); Private, R.A.O.C.

Tuvey, Charles William (1914–15); Private, Middlesex Rgt.

Tuvey, George (1914–19); Private, Machine Gun Corps; France 3 years.

Twichett, Alfred Ezra (1914–17); Private, Labour Corps; France 14 months.

Twiggs, Joseph Edward (1914–15); Driver, R.F.A.; France 5 months.

Twiner, Arthur Edward (1914–17); Bombardier, R.F.A.: France 2 years 7 months.

Tyler, Frederick Arthur (1914–17); Driver, R.F.A.; Italy and France 4 years 4 months.

Tyler, Herbert William (1914–19); D.C.M., Mentioned in despatches; Company Sergeant-Major, Devonshire Rgt.; France 6 months, Salonica 2 years 3 months.

Tyler, John (1914–19); Sergeant, R.A.V.C.; France 4 years 4 months.

Tyler, Richard Bernard William (1914–19); M.S.M.; Private, R.A.S.C.; France 2 years 10 months.

Tyrrell, Albert (1918–19); Private, R. Sussex Rgt.; France and Germany 6 months.

Tyrrell, Henry George (1914–19); Sapper, R.E.; German East Africa 2 years 9 months.

Tyrrell, William (1915–19); Gunner, R.H.A.; France 2 months.

***Tysoe, Harry** (1915–17); Sapper, R.E.; France 14 months; Killed in action, 20th July, 1917.

Umpelby, John Benjamin (1917–19); Lance-Corporal, R.A.S.C. (M.T.).

Underwood, William Vaughan (1915–19); Driver, R.E.; France 3 years.

Usher, Edward Joseph (1915–19); Saddler Driver, R.A.S.C.; Salonica, Egypt and Batoum, 3 years 5 months.

Usher, Henry James (1914–19); Private, Northumberland Fusiliers; France 3 years, Prisoner of war 15 months.

Vagg, Harry Stewart Montagu (1918–19); Private, R.A.S.C. (M.T.).

***Vale, Arthur** (1914–17); Gunner, R.F.A.; France 2 years; Killed in action, 10th October, 1917.

Valentine, Albert Edward (1914–19); Private, London Rgt.; Egypt 3 years 4 months.

Varney, Ernest Edward (1917–18); Gunner, R.G.A.

Varney, John (1916–19); Pioneer, R.E.; Salonica 2 years 7 months.

Varrow, Alfred George (1915–19); Private, London Rgt.; France 3 years 6 months.

Vaughan, George (1915–19); Private, Labour Corps; France 2 years 7 months.

Veal, Richard George Thomas (1915–19); Driver, R.A.S.C.; France 2 years 4 months.

***Veasey, Albert Victor** (1917–18); Gunner, R.G.A.; France 7 months; Killed in action, 21st August, 1918.

Vennard, Henry (1914–15); Private, R. Irish Fusiliers; France 3 months.

Verlander, George Walter (1915–19); Private, Devonshire Rgt. and Labour Corps; France 3 years 8 months.

Vickers, Harrison William (1915–19); Gunner, R.G.A.; France and East Africa 2 years.

Vickers, Walter (1914–19); Lance-Corporal, Suffolk Rgt.; France 1 year 9 months.

Vickers, William (1918–19); Ordinary Seaman, R.N.; Naval Service.

Vickery, Albert James (1916–19); Private, Labour Corps.

Vickery, Edgar William (1915–18); Gunner, R.F.A.; France 10 months.

Vickery, Joseph Samuel Frederick (1916–19); Lance-Sergeant, A.P.C.

Vidler, Edward (1915–19); Driver, R.F.A.; France 3 years 6 months.

Vidler, Henry Jonathon (1916–19); Private, Labour Corps; France 1 year 7 months.

Vimont, Alphonse James (1915–19); Corporal, R.A.S.C. (M.T.); France 3 years 9 months.

Vincent, George Alfred (1916–17); Private, Royal Fusiliers; France 2 months.

Vincent, James Henry (1914–19); Guardsman, Coldstream Guards; France 3 months.

Vincent, Stanley (1916–19); Private, R.A.S.C.

Vine, Charles Edward (1916–19); Pioneer, R.E.; Salonica 2 years 7 months.

Vinn, Bert Alfred (1915–19); Lance-Corporal, R.E.; France 1 year 10 months.

***Voak, Frederick Henry** (1915–18); Bombardier, R.F.A.; France and Italy 3 years; Killed in action, 9th June, 1918.

Voller, Thomas James William (1915–19); Sapper, R.E.; France 2 years 9 months.

Wackett, James (1914–19); Rifleman, Rifle Brigade; Burmah and India 3 years 5 months.

Waddell, George Frederick (1914–19); Fitter - Corporal, R.F.A.; France 8 months.

Wade, Ernest Henry (1915–19); M.C.; Lieutenant, Machine Gun Corps (Motors); France 4 months, Egypt, Arabia and Palestine 2 years 4 months.

Wade, Thomas (1914–19); Petty Officer (1st Class), R.N.; Naval Service 4 years 5 months.

Wadley, Frederick James (1916–18); Private, Royal Dragoons.

Waghorn, Walter (1917–19); Rifleman, London Rgt.; France 2 months.

***Waite, John George James** (1915–16); Rifleman, King's Royal Rifle Corps; France 1 month; Killed in action, 11th January, 1916.

Wakeford, Frederick Charles (1914–16); Private, London Rgt.; France.

Wakelin, George Thorp (1915–19); Driver, R.F.A.; France 1 year.

Walding, William Alfred (1914–19); Gunner, R.F.A.; France and Italy 2 years 3 months.

Waldron, Louis Arthur (1914–19); Wheeler-Sergeant, R.A.S.C.; Salonica 4 months.

Walker, Alfred (1914–19); Private, Royal Fusiliers; France 3 years 7 months.

***Walker, Arthur** (1914–17); Private, R. Welch Fusiliers; France 4 months, Mesopotamia 11 months; Killed in action, 15th February, 1917.

***Walker, Charles** (1914); Gunner, R.F.A.; France 2 months; Killed in action, 21st October, 1914.

Walker, Charles (1915–17); Bombardier, R.F.A.; France 7 months.

Walker, James (1914–17); Lance-Corporal, Wiltshire Rgt.; France 1 year.

***Walker, Joseph Schofield,** (1914–15); Private, R. Welch Fusiliers; France 11 months; Died of wounds, 26th September, 1915.

Walker, John Thomas (1915–19); Driver, R.A.S.C.; France 2 years 8 months.

Walker, Mark John (1914–19); Sergeant, R. Warwickshire Rgt.; France 4 years 6 months.

Walker, Willie James (1914–17); Private, R.D.C.

Walkington, Jack (1915–19); Gunner, R.G.A.; France 3 years 2 months.

Walking, Aubrey Edward Arthur (1917–18); Gunner, R.F.A.; France 5 months.

Waller, John Joseph (1916–19); Private, Labour Corps; France 2 years.

***Walpole, Charles Alfred William** (1914–16); Corporal, R.F.A.; France 2 months; Killed in action, 15th July, 1916.

Walsh, Arthur John (1918–19); Private, Machine Gun Corps.

Walsh, James (1916–19); Rifleman, King's Royal Rifle Corps; France 2 years 4 months.

Walsh, Patrick (1914–19); Sergeant, R.A.S.C.; Dardanelles and France 3 years 6 months.

Walsh, Robert Patrick (1916–19); Private, Scots Guards; France and Germany 2 years.

Walter, Arthur Ernest (1914–19); Lance-Corporal, R.W. Surrey Rgt.; India 3 years.

Walter, Frederick Victor (1915–19); Gunner, R.F.A.; France 3 years 6 months.

Waltham, James William (1914–17); Private, E. Kent Rgt.; France 5 months.

Walton, Charles Thomas (1914–19); Driver, R.A.S.C.; France 3 years 8 months.

Walton, George James (1914–19); Able Seaman, R.N.; Naval Service 4 years.

Walton, John (1918–19); Private, E. Surrey Rgt.; France 3 months.

Walton, Michael Francis (1914–19); Sergeant, R.F.A.; France, Palestine and Salonica, 3 years 9 months.

Walton, William Albert (1914–19); Stoker, R.N.; Naval Service 4 years 6 months.

Wanstall, Percy Robert Walter (1916–19); Able Seaman, R.N.; Naval Service 4 years 6 months.

Ward, Bernard (1914–19); Rifleman, Rifle Brigade; India and Burmah 4 years.

Ward, Ernest (1914–17); Guardsman, Coldstream Guards; France 18 months.

Ward, Frederick George (1918–19); Private, London Rgt.

Ward, George (1914–15); Private, Middlesex Rgt.

Ward, George Henry (1914–19); Sergeant, 21st Bn. London Rgt.

Ward, Herbert (1918–19); Gunner, R.G.A.; France and Germany 11 months.

Ward, Thomas (1914–19); M.M.; Corporal, R. Inniskilling Fusiliers; France 4 years 4 months.

Ward, William (1917–18); Private, R.A.S.C. (M.T.); German East Africa 11 months.

Ward, William (1915–19); Rifleman, Rifle Brigade; France 3 years.

Ward, William John (1914–19); Lance-Corporal, Gloucestershire Rgt.; France and Malta 4 years 4 months.

Warder, William (1914–19); Private, R.A.M.C. and Sapper, R.E.; France 4 years 1 month.

Warne, Henry Edward (1914–17); Sapper, R.E.; France.

Warnes, Horace (1918–19); Gunner, R.F.A.; France and Germany 1 year.

Warren, Alfred William (1914–19); Lance-Sergeant, R. Inniskilling Fusiliers; Dardanelles and France 2 years.

Warren, Frederick Charles (1915–19); Private, R. Irish Rifles; France 2 years.

Warren, James (1914–17); Private, R.D.C.

Warren, Joseph Thomas (1914–19); Signaller, Rifle Brigade; Burmah 4 years.

Wartnaby, George (1916–19); Private, Labour Corps; France 2 years.

Warwick, George Ernest (1916–19); Private, Northamptonshire Rgt; Salonica and France 2 years 4 months.

***Waterhouse, Thomas Samuel** (1914–15); Lance-Corporal, London Rgt.; France 2 months; Killed in action, 26th May, 1915.

Waterman, George Edward (1915–19); Corporal, R.A.S.C.; France 3 years 1 month.

Waters, George Albert (1915–19); Private, Labour Corps; France and Italy 18 months.

Waters, Leonard (1916–19); Lance-Corporal, Bedfordshire Rgt.

Watkins, Arthur Ernest (1914–18); Private, 15th Hussars; France 2 years 6 months.

Watkins, Arthur James (1917–19); Private, Labour Corps.

Watkins, John Sydney (1914–19); Corporal, W. Yorkshire Rgt.; France 10 months.

Watkins, Sydney Charles (1914–19); Sergeant, R.E.; France 1 year 11 months.

Watling, Edward (1916–18); Rifleman, Rifle Brigade; Balkans 17 months.

Watling, Henry Alfred (1915–18); Gunner, R.F.A.; France 3 years.

Watson, Edward Jasper (1914–19); Private, Loyal N. Lancashire Rgt.; France, Egypt, East Africa and Salonica, 2 years 3 months.

Watson, Ernest (1915–16); Driver, R.E.

Watson, Francis (1918–19); Rifleman, Rifle Brigade; France 5 months.

Watson, George James Charles (1915–19); Private, Surrey Yeomanry; Egypt and France 3 years 8 months.

Watson, John Nicholl McKean (1915–18); Sergeant, R.F.A.; France 2 years.

Watson, Joseph (1914–19); Sapper, R.E.; France 13 months.

Watts, Arthur Harry (1915–18); Private, R.A.M.C.

Watts, Conrad Alfred Philip (1915–19); Private, R.A.M.C.; Mesopotamia 2 years 3 months, India 6 months.

Way, Frank Edwin (1916–17); Rifleman, King's Royal Rifle Corps; France 5 months.

Weaterton, Stewart (1914–19); Sec.-Lieutenant, Northumberland Fusiliers; France 9 months.

Weaver, John Wilton (1914–19); Lance-Corporal, M.F.P.; India and Mesopotamia 4 years 8 months.

Webb, Albert John (1914–19); Sergeant, Machine Gun Corps; France 10 months.

Webb, Alfred Walter (1917–19); Air Mechanic (3rd Class), R.A.F.

Webb, David (1914–19); Lance-Corporal, Machine Gun Corps; Malta and France 3 years.

Webb, George Frederick (1915–19); Private, King's Dragoon Guards; India and Burmah 2 years 11 months.

Webb, Harold Frederick (1918–19); Rifleman, Rifle Brigade.

***Webb, Henry** (1917); Rifleman, King's Royal Rifle Corps; France 3 months; Killed in action, 19th September, 1917.

Webb, James Richard (1914–19); Acting Sergeant, Devonshire Rgt.; France, Salonica, Egypt and Palestine, 4 years 6 months.

Webb, William (1916–19); Private, Labour Corps; France 2 years 6 months.

Webb, William (1914–19); Bombardier, R.F.A.; France 3 years 4 months.

Webberson, George William (1914–19); Private, R. Sussex Rgt.; France 2 years 10 months.

Webster, Albert Edward (1916–19); Private, R.A.S.C. (M.T.); France 2 years 11 months.

Webster, George Arthur (1915–17); Fitter, R.A.O.C.

Webster, William (1915–19); Private, Royal Fusiliers and R.D.C.; France 11 months.

Webster, William Daniel (1914–19); Bombardier, R.F.A.; France 3 years 4 months.

Weeks, Edwin Joseph (1916–19); Gunner, R.F.A.; France 10 months.

Weeks, William Herbert (1914–16); Private, Middlesex Rgt.; France 3 months.

Welch, Charles Alfred (1914–16); Driver, R.E.

Welch, Frederick James (1914–19); Leading Seaman, R.N.; Naval Service 4 years 3 months.

Welch, George Clarence (1915–18); Bombardier, R.G.A.; France 2 years 7 months.

Welch, William Arthur Charles (1914–19); Sergeant, London Rgt.: Gallipoli 3 months, Egypt 3 years 10 months.

Weller, Arthur John (1915–18); Gunner, R.F.A.; France 1 year 9 months.

Weller, Reuben David (1916–19); Private, Welch Rgt.; Egypt and Palestine 1 year 11 months.

Weller, Thomas James (1915–19); Private, R.D.C.

Wellerman, Walter George (1914–19); Sergeant, R.G.A.; France 4 years.

Wellings, James (1918–19); Rifleman, King's Royal Rifle Corps; France and Germany 7 months.

Wells, Albert Ernest (1916–19); Shoeing-Smith, R.G.A.; France 9 months.

Wells, Edward (1916–19); Private, Labour Corps; Salonica 2 years.

Wells, Frank (1915–19); Pioneer, R.E.; France 3 years.

Wells, Sydney Herbert (1914–19); Sergeant, R.G.A.; France and Salonica 3 years.

Wells, William James (1914–19); Sergeant, Worcestershire Rgt.; France 3 years 7 months, Prisoner of war 6 months.

Wells, William Percy (1915–19); Driver, R.F.A.; France, Salonica and Egypt, 2 years 9 months.

Wenborne, James Edward George (1914–19); Driver, R.F.A.; France 3 years, Italy 6 months.

Wenman, William Walter (1915–19); Gunner, R.F.A.; France, Salonica and Egypt, 2 years 9 months.

West, Alfred Fred (1917–19); Stoker, R.N.; Naval Service 1 year 8 months.

West, Arthur William (1916–19); Private, Middlesex Rgt.; France 1 year.

West, Herbert James (1916–19); Gunner, R.G.A.; India 13 months.

West, John William Charles (1916–19); Rifleman, London Rgt.; France and Germany 2 years 8 months.

West, Oliver Beavis (1914–19); Sapper, R.E.; France 3 years 2 months.

West, Rupert (1914–19); Able Seaman, R.N.; Naval Service 4 years.

Westbrook, Charles Sidney (1914–19); Driver, R.F.A.; France 4 years 1 month.

Westbrook, Ernest Albert (1916–19); Corporal, Tank Corps.

Westlake, Frederick (1915–19); Private, R.A.M.C.; France 3 years 7 months.

Westley, Samuel Joseph (1914–18); Guardsman, Coldstream Guards; France 3 years 2 months.

***Weston, Alfred Vincent** (1915–16); Lance-Corporal, E. Surrey Rgt.; France 4 months; Killed in action, 17th September, 1916.

Weston, William (1914 and 1915–19); Corporal, R.A.V.C.; Egypt and Salonica 3 years 3 months.

Weston, William John (1915–19); Corporal, Middlesex Rgt.; France 2 years 8 months.

Westwood, Henry Charles (1914–19); Sergeant, R.W. Surrey Rgt.; France, Italy and Germany 3 years 1 month.

Wetherall, Fred (1914–19); Lance-Corporal, Bedfordshire Rgt.

Whale, Henry (1917–19); Private, R.A.S.C.

Wheatley, Robert (1917); Private, Labour Corps.

Wheeler, Alfred (1914–18); Private, R.A.M.C.; France and Malta 2 years 6 months.

Wheeler, Arthur Richard (1914–19); Private, Machine Gun Corps; India, France and Egypt 3 years.

Wheeler, John (1915–19); Private, Labour Corps; France 3 years.

Wheeler, Stanley Frederick John (1915); Trooper, County of London Yeomanry.

Wheller, Winford George (1915–19); Rifleman, 12th Bn. London Rgt.; France 2 years 11 months.

Whiley, William Richard (1914–19); Lance-Corporal, R.A.S.C.; France 4 years 3 months.

Whincop, Alfred Horace (1914–19); Private, London Rgt. and Labour Corps; France 11 months.

Whitbread, Ernest William (1914, 1915, and 1918–19); Private, Duke of Cornwall's Light Infantry; France 17 months.

White, Arthur (1916–18); Private, N. Staffordshire Rgt.; France 3 months.

White, Claude (1914–18); Sapper, R.E.

White, Frederick James (1915–19); Private, London Rgt.; France 2 years 5 months.

***White, Frederick Rostrevor** (1914–17); Able Seaman, R.N.; Naval Service; Died, 21st April, 1917.

***White, George Thomas** (1914–18); Private, R.A.S.C.; France 2 years 9 months; Died, 6th November, 1918.

***White, Henry Ernest Lyle** (1914–16); Rifleman, Rifle Brigade; France 7 months; Killed in action, 6th January, 1916.

***White, Henry John Francis** (1914); Guardsman, Life Guards; France 2 months; Missing, 31st October, 1914.

White, Herbert Thornton (1916–19); 2nd Corporal, R.E.; France 2 years.

White, Horace Edgar (1916–20); Corporal, R.A.S.C. (M.T.).

White, Thomas James (1915–19); Driver-Farrier, R.A.S.C.; France and Italy 3 years 4 months.

White, Walter William (1915–19); Corporal, R.F.A.; France, Salonica and Egypt 2 years.

White, William Edward (1918–19); Rifleman, Rifle Brigade; France 4 months.

***White, William Gladstone** (1914–17); Sergeant, Middlesex Rgt.; France 1 year 10 months; Killed in action, 3rd May, 1917.

White, William Henry (1914–19); Company Sergeant-Major, R.A.S.C.; France 4 years 6 months.

White, William John (1915–19); Gunner, R.F.A.; France 2 years 1 month.

Whitehead, Harold Alfred (1915–19); Sergeant, Dorsetshire Rgt.

Whiteing, Joseph John (1914–19); Company Quartermaster-Sergeant, R.W. Surrey Rgt.; France 13 months.

Whitfield, Enoch Alfred (1915–19); Guardsman, Irish Guards; France 3 years 8 months.

Whitfield, Joseph (1914–19); Company Sergeant-Major, W. Riding Rgt.; France 3 years 10 months.

Whiting, Benjamin (1915–19); Gunner, R.F.A.; France 3 years 3 months.

***Whitlock, Ernest William** (1914–16); Private, R. Marine Light Infantry; Naval Service; Killed at sea, 31st May, 1916.

Whitmore, Herbert George (1916–19); Private, Liverpool Rgt.; Russia 9 months.

Whitmore, John (1914–19); M.M; Sergeant, Rifle Brigade; France 3 years.

Whitney, Herbert Edwin (1918–19); Private, R.A.M.C.

Whitty, William Jones (1914–19); Sergeant, E. Surrey Rgt.; Mesopotamia and India 4 years 3 months.

***Whybrow, Ernest** (1917–18); Rifleman, Rifle Brigade; France 9 months; Died of wounds while prisoner of war, 5th April, 1918.

Wickham, Henry Albert (1915–19); Sergeant, Somersetshire Light Infantry; France 10 months.

Widdicks, William (1914–19); Private, R.A.S.C.; France 2 years 3 months.

Wieck, Herbert (1914–19); Sergeant, Middlesex Rgt.; India 4 years 6 months.

Wieck, Oscar (1916–19); Private, Labour Corps; France 2 years 3 months.

Wiggins, James Henry (1914–19); Private, E. Surrey Rgt.; France and Italy 4 years 6 months.

Wiggins, William Arthur (1915–19); Private, R.A.M.C.; Egypt, German East Africa, Mesopotamia and France 2 years 6 months.

Wiggs, Charles Arthur (1914–19); Sergeant, R.A.M.C.; France 4 years 5 months.

Wightman, Charles William (1917–19); Gunner, R.G.A.

***Wilby, Arthur Charles** (1914–18); Sergeant, E. Kent Rgt.; France 1 month, Prisoner of war 2 years 6 months, Holland 4 months; Died, 14th August, 1918.

Wilcock, Albert James (1917–19); Corporal, R.A.S.C. (M.T.); France and Germany 1 year 10 months.

Wiles, Leonard King (1914–19); Driver, R.A.S.C.; France 3 years 8 months.

Wilkerson, William (1915–19); Private, R.D.C.

Wilkes, Charles (1915–19); Gunner, R.F.A.; Gallipoli and Egypt 3 years 9 months.

Wilkes, William Henry (1914–19); Sergeant, R. Irish Rgt.; Salonica and Egypt 3 years 5 months.

Wilkie, William Morley (1916–19); Private, Durham Light Infantry; Macedonia 2 years, France 3 months.

Wilkins, Herbert William (1914–20); Sergeant-Major, R.A.M.C.; Egypt 5 months, Malta 4 months, Salonica 15 months, France 2 years 2 months.

Wilkins, James Thomas Morris (1915–19); Air Mechanic (1st Class), R.A.F.

Wilkinson, George Alfred (1914–19); Bombardier, R.G.A.; France 4 years 4 months.

Wilkinson, William Robert (1914–19); Private, Bedfordshire Rgt. and Labour Corps; France 11 months.

Willan, William (1915–19); Mechanic, R. Marine Artillery; France 3 years 6 months.

***Williams, Albert** (1916); Private, Middlesex Rgt.; Died, 13th September, 1916.

Williams, Arthur James (1914–19); Corporal, R.E.; Gallipoli 3 months, France 2 years 11 months.

Williams, Frederick (1914–15); Driver, R.F.A.; France.

Williams, Henry (1915); Private, R.A.S.C.

Williams, Herbert (1914–19); Gunner, R.G.A.; France 2 years 2 months.

Williams, Horace Charles (1914–19); Driver, London Rgt.; France 3 years.

Williams, John Walter (1914–19); Corporal, Rifle Brigade; Burmah 3 years 4 months.

***Williams, Percival Trevor** (1915–17); Rifleman, London Rgt.; France 1 year; Died of wounds, 27th June, 1917.

Williams, Philip (1914–19); Private, R. Marine Light Infantry; Naval Service 4 years 6 months.

Williams, Richard (1916–19); Private, Labour Corps; France 2 years.

Williams, Robert Henry (1914–19); Sergeant, R.E.; Mesopotamia 3 years.

Williams, Walter (1914–19); Private, R.D.C.

Williams, Walter (1914–19); Sergeant, R.W. Surrey Rgt. and Labour Corps; France 2 years.

Williamson, John (1918–19); Rifleman, King's Royal Rifle Corps; France 5 months.

Willicombe, William Christian (1914–19); Private, Royal Fusiliers; France 2 years 8 months.

Willicombe, William Francis (1914–19); Shoeing-Smith, Machine Gun Corps; Egypt and Salonica 3 years 10 months.

Willis, George Sherrington (1916–19); Private, Labour Corps; France 1 year 9 months.

Willis, James William Augustine (1918); Private, Reserve Cavalry.

Willis, Percy (1918–19); Aircraftsman, R.A.F.; Egypt and Palestine 16 months.

Willis, Reuben (1914–19); 2nd Corporal, R.E.; India and Mesopotamia 16 months.

Willis, Thomas Norman (1916–19); Private, Labour Corps; France 2 years 9 months.

Wills, John (1915–19); M.M.; Corporal, R.F.A.; France 2 years 5 months.

Willson, Robert (1916–19); Rifleman, King's Royal Rifle Corps; France 2 years 9 months.

Wilmott, Edward James (1915–19); Corporal, R.F.A.; France, Mesopotamia and Palestine 3 years 6 months.

Wilmshurst, Frederick Charles (1914–19); Guardsman, Guards Machine Gun Rgt.; France and Germany 3 years 6 months.

Wilshire, Henry Francis (1915–19); Private, Labour Corps; France 3 years 2 months.

Wilson, Arthur (1916–19); Private, Labour Corps; France 2 years 7 months.

Wilson, Arthur (1915–19); Private, R.A.S.C.; France and Italy 3 years.

Wilson, Arthur Thomas (1918–19); Private, Machine Gun Corps.

Wilson, Charles (1914–17); Lance-Corporal, Middlesex Rgt.; France 1 year 10 months.

Wilson, Charles Frank (1915–19); Sergeant, R.F.A.; Salonica 1 year 9 months.

Wilson, Ernest Edward (1915–19); Shoeing-Smith, R.F.A.

Wilson, Frederick Ernest (1916–19); Private, R.A.S.C.; France 2 years 11 months.

***Wilson, William** (1914–15); Private, Scottish Horse; Dardanelles 1 month; Killed in action, 27th September, 1915.

Wilson, William Henry (1917–19); Private, Labour Corps.

Wimshurst, George (1914–19); Gunner, R.F.A.; France 4 years 2 months.

Winch, John Royal (1914–19); Gunner, R.F.A.; France 4 years 4 months.

Winchester, James (1915–19); Driver, R.F.A.; France 3 years.

Windley, William Thomas (1914–19); Lance-Corporal, Essex Rgt.

Windrew, John William (1916–19); Lance-Corporal, R.A.M.C.; France 7 months, Italy 1 year 7 months.

Winslow, Walter Henry (1917–19); Private, R. Warwickshire Rgt.; France 6 months, Italy 6 months.

***Winter, Frederick** (1916–18); Private, E. Surrey Rgt.; India 2 years 5 months; Died, 1st November, 1918.

Winter, Frederick Charles (1915–19); Private, R.A.S.C.; France 2 years.

Winter, John (1914–19); Bombardier, R.F.A.; France, Salonica and Egypt, 3 years.

Winton, Alfred (1914–19); Leading Seaman, R.N.; Naval Service 4 years.

Wirtz, Albert Napoleon (1916–19); Private, Labour Corps; France 2 years.

Wisdom, William (1915–19); Gunner, R.F.A.; Mesopotamia 18 months, India 7 months.

Wiseman, Alfred (1916–19); Private, Labour Corps; France 1 year 8 months.

Wiseman, Frederick Arthur (1917–19); Lance-Corporal, Labour Corps; France 1 year 8 months.

Witherden, George (1915–18); Private, Labour Corps; France 3 years 5 months.

***Withey, Arthur Albert** (1914–18); Lance-Corporal, King's Royal Rifle Corps; France 1 year 8 months; Missing, 16th January, 1918.

Wittig, Fred (1914–19); Driver, R.F.A.; France 3 years 4 months.

Wood, Albert Edward (1914–19); Gunner, R.H.A.; France 3 years 3 months.

Wood, Bertram Alfred (1915–17); Driver, R.E.; France 10 months.

Wood, Frederick Alfred (1916–19); Gunner, R.F.A.; France 15 months.

Wood, George William (1914–18); Lance-Corporal, R. Warwickshire Rgt.; France 3 years 2 months.

Wood, Herbert James (1915–19); Driver, R.F.A.; France 3 years 4 months.

Wood, William Sidney (1914–19); Battery Quartermaster-Sergeant, R.F.A.; France 4 years 6 months.

Woodcock, Thomas (1916–19); Pioneer, R.E.; France 18 months.

Woodcock, Walter Charles (1914–19); Sergeant, Middlesex Rgt.; France 3 years 11 months.

Woodcock, William (1916–17); Private, Labour Corps.

Woodcock, William Whitby (1914–19); Corporal, R.A.M.C.; France 1 year 9 months.

Woodeson, Herbert Walter (1915–19); Private, Labour Corps; France 3 years 2 months.

Woodfine, Sidney James (1918–20); Corporal, R. Sussex Rgt.; France 9 months, Egypt 10 months.

Woodfine, William Thomas (1915–19); Sapper, R.E.; France 18 months.

Woodgate, Horace (1914–19); Lance-Corporal, R. Sussex Rgt.; India 2 years 11 months.

Woodman, Thomas James (1915–17); Driver, R.A.S.C. (M.T.); France 3 months.

Woodruff, David Henry (1914–19); Driver, R.A.S.C.; Salonica, Egypt and Palestine, 4 years.

Woods, Albert Edward (1914–19); Sec.-Lieutenant, R.F.A.; France 2 years 2 months.

Woods, Alfred Charles (1915–19); Private, R.A.S.C. (M.T.); France and Germany 2 years 3 months.

***Woods, Arthur William** (1914); Stoker, R.N.; Naval Service; Killed at sea, 15th October, 1914.

Woods, Daniel (1914–19); Gunner, R.F.A.; France 3 months, Balkans 3 years 3 months.

Woods, John Charles (1917–19); Private, Labour Corps; France 2 years.

Woods, John Henry (1914–19); Petty Officer, R.N.; Naval Service 3 years 9 months.

Woodward, Cecil Percy Lee Warner (1916–19); Private, Royal Fusiliers; France and Germany 2 years 6 months.

***Woodward, Frederick** (1914); Private, Somersetshire Light Infantry; Died, 14th December, 1914.

Woodward, George Henry (1914–19); Aircraftsman (2nd Class), R.A.F.; France 9 months, Salonica 7 months, Egypt 17 months.

Woodward, Reginald Algernon (1916–19); Private, Nottinghamshire and Derbyshire Rgt.; France 18 months.

Woodward, William (1915–19); Private, R.A.S.C.; France 2 years 7 months.

Wooler, Herbert George (1914–18); Private, Royal Fusiliers; France 1 year.

Woolfenden, Percy (1914–19); Gunner, R.G.A.; France 2 years 7 months.

***Woolley, Herbert Edward** (1914–17); Fitter, R.F.A.; France 2 years 2 months; Died of wounds, 25th June, 1917.

Woolnough, Reginald Alfred (1914–19); Lance-Corporal, London Rgt.; Malta, Egypt, Gallipoli and France 2 years 6 months.

Worboys, Edward William (1916–19); Private, R. Welch Fusiliers; France 2 years 5 months.

Worman, William (1915–19); Corporal, Labour Corps; France 3 years 3 months.

Worrow, Charles Frederick (1914–19); Driver, R.E.; France 3 months.

Worsfield, Frederick Charles (1915–19); Lance-Sergeant, E. Surrey Rgt.; France 2 years 7 months.

Wraight, James (1917–18); Rifleman, R. Irish Rifles; France 5 months.

Wraight, Sidney Arthur (1915–19); M.M.; Corporal, R.F.A.; France 3 years 3 months.

Wrangles, Samuel Joseph (1914–19); Gunner and Shoeing-Smith, R.F.A.; France 3 years 4 months.

Wright, Albert John (1914–17); Bombardier, R.F.A.

***Wright, Alfred Sidney Thomas** (1915–17); Private, Essex Rgt.; France 4 months; Missing, 3rd May, 1917.

Wright, Alfred Thomas (1917–19); Gunner, Motor Machine Gun Section; Afghanistan 1 year, India 2 years.

Wright, Charles Jesse (1916–17); Private, Middlesex Rgt.

Wright, Clifton Lionel (1915–19); Sergeant, R.A.S.C. (M.T.); France 2 years.

Wright, Edgar Leonard (1914–19); Leading Seaman, R.N.; Naval Service 6 months.

Wright, Edward (1914–17); Private, Norfolk Rgt.; France 2 years 7 months.

***Wright, Ernest Albert** (1916–17); Private, London Rgt.; France 4 months; Killed in action, 13th May, 1917.

Wright, Frederick William (1915–18); Lance-Sergeant, A.P.C.

***Wright, George** (1915–16); Lance-Corporal, Middlesex Rgt.; France 5 months; Killed in action, 18th March, 1916.

Wright, George Christopher (1914–15); Private, Yorkshire Rgt.

Wright, Harold Arthur (1918–19); Air Mechanic (3rd Class), R.A.F.

Wright, Samuel (1914–19); Sergeant, R.D.C.

Wright, William (1918–19); Private, R. Sussex Rgt.; Germany 3 months.

Wright, William (1915–19); Sapper, R.E.; France and Egypt 4 years 6 months.

Wright, William George (1915–17); Private, R.A.S.C.; France 1 year 10 months.

Wright, William James (1914–19); Sergeant, R.G.A.; France 18 months, Italy 1 year 10 months.

Wright, William John (1914–19); Gunner, R.H.A.; France 4 years 2 months.

Wright, William John (1916–19); Private, R.A.S.C.; Italy and France 1 year 7 months.

Wyatt, William (1917); Driver, R.F.A.

Wyatt, William Thomas (1914–19); Sergeant, R.A.S.C. (M.T.); France 2 years 9 months.

***Wynn, James** (1915–17); Sergeant, R.F.A.; France 9 months; Killed in action, 14th October, 1917.

Yarrow, Frederick Harold (1917–19); Corporal, R.A.O.C.

Yates, Albert Ernest (1914–18); Bombardier, R.F.A.; France 3 years 8 months.

***Yates, John** (1914); Private, R. Scots Fusiliers; France; Died of wounds, 24th August, 1914.

Yates, Joseph (1914–19); Gunner, R.F.A.; France and Germany 3 years 10 months.

Yeadon, William (1914–19); Private, R.D.C.

Yearley, Henry (1916–19); Private, Durham Light Infantry; Russia.

Yeates, William Henry (1917–19); Air Mechanic (2nd Class), R.A.F.

***Yeldham, Edgar Charles** (1916–18); Private, W. Yorkshire Rgt.; France 11 months; Killed in action, 1st November, 1918.

Yeomans, George Leonard (1915–19); Wireman (1st Class), R.N.; Naval Service 3 years 6 months.

Youde, Wilfrid (1914–19); Mentioned in despatches; Air Mechanic, R.A.F.; France 3 years 11 months.

Youldon, William John (1915–19); Driver, R.F.A.; France 3 years 1 month.

Young, Albert Francis (1915–19); Bombardier, R.F.A.; France 3 years.

Young, Alfred (1915–19); Bombardier, R.G.A.; France 13 months.

Young, Edward Arthur (1915–19); Staff-Sergeant, R.A.M.C.

Young, George Thomas Inkerman (1914–19); Sergeant, Duke of Cornwall's Light Infantry.

Young, Henry Judd (1918–19); Aircraftsman (2nd Class), R.A.F.

Young, John (1915–19); Able Seaman, R.N.; Naval Service 3 years 5 months.

Young, John Henry (1916–18); Private, R.D.C.

Young, Samuel (1914); Guardsman, Grenadier Guards.

Young, Walter John (1914–19); Corporal, R.F.A.; France 2 years 11 months.

Yuille, Albert (1914–16); Private, R. Scots Fusiliers.

Housing Department

Acton, Henry James (1917–19); Air Mechanic (1st Class), R.A.F.; France 15 months.

Adams, Charles Andrew (1915–18); Private, 60th Canadians; France 2 years 2 months.

Adby, Victor (1915–16); Corporal, R.F.A.; France 5 months.

Alexander, Harold (1917–19); Sergeant, R. Inniskilling Fusiliers; France 17 months.

Allard, George Amos (1914–19); Lance-Corporal, Oxfordshire and Buckinghamshire Light Infantry; France 3 years 6 months, Germany 9 months (prisoner of war).

Attewell, John (1914–18); Quartermaster-Sergeant, R.E.; France 1 month.

Ball, Sidney Herbert (1916–19); Private, Middlesex and R.W. Surrey Rgts., and Labour Corps.

***Barklamb, Edward Charles** (1914–15); Private, E. Surrey Rgt.; France 6 months; Killed in action, 27th September, 1915.

***Bayliss, Thomas** (1914–18); Private, 4th Bn. Grenadier Guards; France 17 months; Killed in action, 27th September, 1918.

Bell, Charles Herbert (1916–19); Private, R.A.F.; France 2 years 4 months.

Beresford, Henry Albert (1915–19); Sergeant, Middlesex Rgt.; France 15 months.

Bloomfield, Harry (1916–19); Private, R.A.S.C. (M.T.); France 16 months.

Bolger, Edward (1914–19); Sergeant, 1st Bn. Irish Guards; France 4 years 9 months.

Bouch, Arthur Charles (1915–19); Sergeant, R.F.A.

Bowtle, George Phillips (1915–19); Sergeant, R.A.S.C.; France 3 years.

***Bradford, Ivan Wilfred** (1914); Private, 1st Bn. Coldstream Guards; France 2 months; Died of wounds, 21st October, 1914.

Breeze, William Thomas (1916–19); Sergeant, R.A.F.; Palestine 2 years 10 months.

Butcher, Richard James (1914–19); Gunner, R.G.A.

***Carey, Edward** (1914–15); Lance-Corporal, Irish Guards; France 4 months; Killed in action, 18th May, 1915.

Carter, Henry (1914–19); Private, R. Irish Rifles; Gallipoli 8 months, France 3 years.

Cook, John Percy (1915–19); Private, 8th Bn. E. Surrey and 3rd Bn. E. Kent Rgts.; France 14 months.

Cooper, Arthur Henry (1916–19); Private, Royal Fusiliers; France 2 years.

***Cox, William Henry** (1914–15); Quartermaster-Sergeant, R.E.; Died, 26th May, 1915.

Cranstoun, Edward (1915–19); Lance-Corporal, R.A.S.C. (M.T.); France 3 years 6 months.

Cross, Ernest Charles (1915–19); Private, King's Royal Rifle Corps; France 1 year, Germany (prisoner of war) 18 months.

Cross, Stephen (1916–19); Corporal, 10th Bn. London Rgt., 13th Bn. Devonshire Rgt. and Labour Corps.

Cullum, William Frederick (1914–19); Quartermaster-Sergeant, E. Yorkshire Rgt., W. Riding Rgt. and Labour Corps; France 1 month.

***Daysh, Frederick Arthur George** (1914); Private, Coldstream Guards; France 1 month; Missing, believed dead, 14th September, 1914.

Deare, Alban Bertie (1917–19); Private, 13th Bn. Devonshire Rgt. and Labour Corps; France 2 years.

Doggett, Ernest Edward (1915–18); Sapper, R.W. Kent Rgt. and R.E.

Downes, Arthur (1916–19); Private, R.W. Surrey Rgt. and Labour Corps; Salonica 2 years 6 months.

Dunn, Jesse William (1916–19); Acting Corporal, R.A.O.C.; France 3 years 4 months.

Elliott, Thomas Joseph (1918–19); Private, R. Marine Engrs.

Evans, Frederick Charles (1914–19); Driver, R.A.S.C.; France 3 years 9 months.

Exall, Nelson Victor (1915–19); Private, R.A.S.C. (M.T.); France 2 years 6 months.

Flook, Lewis Paul (1915–19); Sergeant, 22nd Bn. London Rgt. and R.A.F.

French, Alfred Arthur (1915–16); Sapper, R.E.; France 7 months.

Gentry, Henry Thomas (1915–19); Lieutenant, R.N.V.R., Anti-Aircraft; France 1 month.

***Gilchrist, Amos Jeeves** (1914–18); Private, Royal Fusiliers, E. Kent and Middlesex Rgts., Labour Corps and Northumberland Fusiliers; Died, 3rd November, 1918.

Gilchrist, Oliver (1915–19); Private, R.W. Kent Rgt.

Grady, Henry Charles (1918–19); Private, R.A.F.

***Hale, Joseph Dinnin** (1914–15); Private, Yorkshire Rgt.; France 7 months; Killed in action, 10th March, 1915.

Haliday, Frank (1915–19); Private, Norfolk and Essex Rgts.; Gallipoli 6 months, France 16 months.

Harris, Harold (1916–19); Private, R.W. Surrey Rgt., Rifle Brigade, Devonshire Rgt., 29th Bn. Middlesex Rgt. and Labour Corps; France 4 months.

Haselgrove, Reginald Howard (1914–19); Lieutenant, 5th Bn. London Rgt. and R.G.A.; France 9 months.

Henfrey, Arthur William (1914–18); Sec.-Lieutenant, 16th Bn. London Rgt.; France.

Hobbs, Frederick Charles (1916–19); Private, King's Royal Rifle Corps, R.W. Kent Rgt. and Rifle Brigade; India 2 years 1 month.

Holden, John Herbert (1915–19); Sapper, R.E.; France 3 years 4 months.

Horsman, Samuel Henry (1915–19); Sec.-Lieutenant, R.F.A.; France 2 years Salonica 1 year.

Huber, Ernest Henry (1915–19); Mentioned in despatches; Quartermaster-Sergeant, R.A.M.C.; France 4 years 1 month.

Huggett, John Averest (1914–19); Private, Royal Fusiliers; France 4 years 6 months.

Hugkulstone, Albert Edward (1915–19); Sapper, R.E.; France 3 years 3 months, Germany 6 months.

Humphreys, Albert Edward (1915–19); Private, Middlesex Rgt., Argyle and Sutherland Highlanders, and R.D.C.

Jackson, Herbert Russell (1916–19); Sergeant, R.E.

Kemble, Harry (1915–19); Private, R.A.S.C.; France 3 years 8 months.

Kendall, Harry (1915–19); Sergeant, R.F.A., Royal Scots and R.A.S.C.

Keyte, John Thomas (1916–19); Lance-Corporal, York and Lancaster Rgt. and R.E.; France 5 months.

Kimberley, William Charles (1915–19); Private, R.A.S.C. and Labour Corps; France 3 years 9 months.

Knight, John Deacon (1914–18); Serjeant, Training Reserve.

Knowler, William Henry (1916–19); Private, Royal Fusiliers, Black Watch, R.D.C. Middlesex and R.W. Surrey Rgts.

Knowles, Edmund Harvey (1915–19); M.M.; 2nd Corporal, R.E.; France 3 years 10 months.

Lambert, Herbert John (1914–19); Sec.-Lieutenant, R.W. Kent and R.W. Surrey Rgts. and R.A.S.C.; Gallipoli 3 months, Egypt 2 months, France 1 week.

Lawrence, Phillip Shepherd (1917–19); Air Mechanic (3rd Class), R.A.F.

Lockwood, Ernest Hesse (1916–18); Corporal, Royal Fusiliers, Northamptonshire Rgt. and Labour Corps; France 7 months.

Marks, Alfred Henry (1914–19); Private, London Rgt., Rifle Brigade and Labour Corps; France 16 months.

Margeson, James Edward (1914–19); Private, 4th Dragoon Guards; France.

Martin, S. C. (1916–19); Private, 6th Bn. London Rgt.; France 18 months.

Mead, Samuel William (1915–19); Private, Middlesex Rgt. and Machine Gun Corps; France 16 months.

Mills, J. W. (1916–19); Air Mechanic (1st Class), R.A.F.; France 13 months.

Oliver, Walter James (1914–19); Lance-Corporal, London Rgt.; France 3 years 11 months.

Orrin, James (1914–19); M.M., Mentioned in Army Orders; Sergeant, R.E.; Gallipoli 6 months, France 1 year 9 months.

Orrin, William Alexander (1915–19); Gunner, R.F.A. and R.G.A.; France 2 years.

Osborn, Felix (1914–19); Private, R. Marine Light Infantry; Belgium 1 month, Gallipoli 8 months.

Page, Victor Lawrence (1915–19); Bombardier, R.F.A.; France 2 years 8 months.

Perkins, Stanley George (1915–18); Private, London Rgt.; France 2 years 6 months.

Pessell, Thomas Frederick (1914–19); Private, R. W. Surrey Rgt.; France 3 years 9 months.

Priest, Henry Arthur (1916–19); Private, R. W. Surrey and R. Sussex Rgts. and Somerset Light Infantry; France 17 months.

Ray, James Scott (1916–19); Private, London Rgt.; France 14 months, Salonica 6 months, Palestine 1 year, Germany 7 months.

Rees, Alfred Edward (1914–19); Major, Royal Fusiliers; Mediterranean 7 months.

Richardson, Joseph (1915–19); Sapper, R.E.; France 3 years 7 months.

Roots, Roberts Odell (1914–18); Corporal R.F.A.; France 6 weeks, Salonica 3 years.

Rouse, C. (1916–19); Private, London Rgt. and Royal Fusiliers; France 2 years 4 months.

***Rushworth, Tom Sadler** (1914–16); Captain, 7th Bn. London Rgt.; France 15 months; Killed in action, 18th September, 1916.

Smith, Alfred (1917–19); Staff-Sergeant, R.A.S.C. (M.T.).

Snook, George (1914–19); Private, 4th Grenadier Guards.

Stone-Fry, Walter William (1914–19); Sergeant, 3rd Hussars and E. Surrey Rgt.; France 1 week.

Strachan, William Hardie (1914–19); Regimental Sergeant-Major, R.E.; France 6 months, Salonica 2 years 6 months.

Suttle, Benjamin Thompson (1914–19); Private, Royal Fusiliers; Malta 5 months.

Taylor, Sidney William (1915–19); Gunner, R.G.A.; France 2 years 6 months.

Tennant, William Henry (1914–19); Lance-Bombardier, R.G.A.; France 3 years 6 months.

Tilsley, John (1918–19); Private, R.A.F.; France 5 months.

Tokins, Harry (1914–19); Sergeant, R.G.A.; France 3 years 8 months.

Townsend, Edgar Randolph (1915–19); Leading Air Mechanic, R.N.A.S. and R.A.F.; France 13 months, Greece 1 year 8 months.

Townsend, Edward Aldridge (1915–19); Lance-Corporal, R.E.; France 1 year 11 months, Germany 1 month.

Turner, Henry Charles Pettit (1915–18); Corporal, R. Marine Light Infantry.

Twilley, Herbert (1916–19); Sergeant, Northumberland Fusiliers and Tank Corps; France 13 months.

Walker, Percy Gordon (1914–19); R.D.; Paymaster Lieutenant-Commander, R.N.R.; France 18 months.

Wiles, Albert Edward (1915–19); Corporal, R.A.S.C. and R.E.; France 2 years.

Willey, Lawrence Walter (1914–19); M.M.; Sergeant, E. Surrey Rgt. and Labour Corps; France 3 years 4 months.

Williams, Christopher Edward (1916–19); Private, Royal Fusiliers and Labour Corps; France 16 months.

Education Officer's Department

Central Administrative Staff

Ackland, George Bidder (1916–18); Private, R.A.S.C. (M.T.) and Labour Corps.

Adams, Andrew Herbert Crawford (1915–19); Lieutenant, R.H.A. and R.F.A.; France 3 years.

Adams, Frederick George (1914–19); Company Quartermaster-Sergeant, Royal Fusiliers.

Adams, William Henry Peregrine (1915–19); Sergeant, Durham Light Infantry; France 2 years 4 months.

Adcock, Percy John (1915–19); 2nd Corporal, R.E. (Field Survey Bn.); France 2 years 6 months.

Albrow, Alfred Arthur (1915–19); Staff Sergeant-Major, R.A.S.C.; Mesopotamia 17 months.

Allan, John Richard (1914–19); Lance-Corporal, Middlesex Rgt.; India 3 years, Mesopotamia 16 months.

***Ames, Arthur James** (1914–16); Lance-Corporal, Middlesex Rgt.; Gibraltar 6 months, Egypt 12 months, France 3 months; Killed in action, 7th October, 1916.

Andrew, William Charles (1915–19); Corporal, R.A.M.C.; France 2 years 6 months, Italy 14 months.

Andrews, Edward Ransford (1915–19); Sergeant, R.A.M.C.

Ansell, Joseph George (1914–19); Sergeant, A.P.C. and Royal Fusiliers; France 2 years 7 months, Italy 9 months.

Anstey, Alfred John (1915–19); Sapper, London Electrical Engineers, R.E., and Anti-Aircraft Corps; France 2 years.

Arkcoll, Harold Baxter (1914–19); Lance-Corporal (Assistant Signalling Instructor), London Rgt.; France 13 months, Salonica 7 months, Palestine 12 months.

***Ash, Herbert Joseph** (1915–16); Private, Royal Fusiliers; France 9 months; Killed in action, 31st July, 1916.

Ashby, Frederick (1917–19); Corporal, R.E.; Mesopotamia 1 year 9 months.

Atkins, Albert Edwin (1915–19); Gunner, Honourable Artillery Company; Palestine 1 year 10 months.

Austin, Alfred Carson (1915–16); Private, R.A.M.C.; France 3 months.

Avis, Tallis Augustus (1917–19); Corporal, Oxfordshire and Buckinghamshire Light Infantry and A.P.C.

***Babington, Herbert William** (1915–16); Private, London Rgt.; France 7 months; Killed in action, 22nd May, 1916.

Bailey, Alfred George (1914–18); Sergeant, London Rgt. and Machine Gun Corps; France 2 years 11 months.

Bailey, Ernest Gordon (1914–19); Rifleman, London Rgt.; France 3 years 11 months.

Baker, Arthur Leopold (1914–18); Sec.-Lieutenant, Royal Fusiliers and Suffolk Rgt.; France 6 months, Macedonia 15 months.

Bark, George Henry (1914–19); Lieutenant-Commander, R.N.V.R. (Naval Transport Service); France 15 months, Egypt 13 months, Palestine 18 months.

Barker, Harry Parsons (1916–19); Lance-Corporal, R.A.O.C.; France 2 years 4 months.

***Barnard, Alfred Henry Brunker** (1916–18); Private, London Rgt.; Salonica, Egypt and Palestine, 14 months; Killed in action, 20th February, 1918.

***Barnes, Frederick** (1915–17); Corporal, R.F.A.; France 13 months; Killed in action, 4th June, 1917.

Barnes, Leslie James (1914–19); Sec.-Lieutenant, Honourable Artillery Company, Essex and London Rgts.; Draft conducting officer.

Barter, William Anthony (1915–19); Bombardier, Honourable Artillery Company and R.H.A.

Bartlett, Thomas Lewis (1914–19); Private, R.A.M.C.; France 9 months, Salonica 7 months, Palestine 18 months.

Barwood, Harry Pearce (1914–19); Mentioned in despatches; Captain, R. Irish Fusiliers, attached Machine Gun Corps and Tank Corps; France 3 years 1 month.

Bastable, George (1914–17); Private, S. Staffordshire and Lincolnshire Rgts.; France 6 months.

Bastard, Arthur Henry (1915–19); Corporal, R.A.M.C.; France 12 months, Italy 18 months.

Baxter, Ernest (1916–17); Private, N. Irish Horse and R. Irish Rifles; France 6 months.

Baylis, Albert James (1915–19); M.S.M.; Staff Sergeant-Major, R.A.S.C.; France 3 years 7 months.

Beecher, John (1915–19); Corporal, London Electrical Engineers, R.E.

Bell, Walter Percy (1914–19); Mentioned in despatches; Captain, Corps of the School of Musketry; France (Inspecting), June, 1918.

Bellsham, Horace Stafford (1916–19); Private, R. West Kent Rgt.; France 1 year 7 months.

Benford, William David (1915–19); Pioneer, 15th Bn. London Rgt. and R.E. (Signals); France 2 years 10 months.

Bennett, Neville Lefevre (1915–19); Mentioned in despatches; Captain, University of London O.T.C., R. Berkshire Rgt., and Yorkshire Light Infantry; France 3 years 3 months, Egypt 3 months.

Bennett, Stanley James (1916–19); Corporal, R.F.A.

Berger, Alfred (1915–19); Sergeant, R.G.A.; France and Germany 12 months.

Betts, Edgar Harry (1914–19); Sergeant, 15th Bn. London Rgt.; North Russia 13 months.

Birkbeck, Scott (1914–19); Captain, Middlesex Rgt.; Gibraltar 6 months, France 4 years.

***Bishop, Wilfred** (1915–17); Sec.-Lieutenant, Inns of Court O.T.C. and Border Rgt.; France 7 months; Died of wounds, 5th July, 1917.

Bispham, James Webb (1916–19); O.B.E., twice mentioned in despatches; Captain, R.E.; France 2 years 9 months.

Blackaby, Selwyn Henry (1915–19); Private, R.A.M.C.; France 17 months, Salonica 6 months, Palestine 9 months.

Blake, Frederick Henry (1916–19); Victualling Assistant, R.N.

Bloomfield, Samuel Isaiah (1916–19); Private, R.A.S.C.(M.T.); Mesopotamia and Persia 2 years.

Bodger, Ernest William (1916–19); Mentioned in despatches; Sergeant, R.G.A.

Bolke, Henry Louis (1915–19); Corporal, R.A.M.C., R.A.S.C. and Middlesex Rgt.; France 2 years.

Bolton, Thomas (1915–19); Sapper, R.E.

Bonner, Charles John (1916–19); Company Quartermaster-Sergeant, R.E.; France and Germany 2 years 11 months.

Boorman, Henry Alfred (1914–19); Corporal, Hertfordshire Rgt. and R.A.S.C.

Bostock, Herbert (1917–19); Private, R.A.O.C.; France 1 year 9 months.

Bowles, Richard George (1915–19); Private, R.A.S.C. (M.T.); Salonica 3 years.

Bradwin, Charles (1916–19); Gunner, R.G.A.; Egypt and Palestine 7 months, Balkans 7 months.

Braham, Richard William (1914–19); M.M.; Sergeant, R.F.A.; France 2 years 3 months, Italy 3 months.

Brayley, Leopold Oliver Wedlake (1917–19); Lance-Corporal, Northern Cyclist Battalion.

Brewer, William Henry (1915–19); Sergeant, R.A.M.C.; Salonica 2 years 2 months.

Brewster, Arthur Walter (1915–19); Sergeant, R.A.M.C.

Brimacombe, Augustus (1914–18); Sergeant, London Rgt.; France 6 months.

Bryant, Herbert Walter (1915–19); Corporal, R.E.; France 2 years 6 months.

Buck, Sydney Thacker (1914–19); M.C.; Major, R.A.S.C., R. Sussex Rgt. and Bedfordshire Rgt.; France 2 years 3 months.

Burgess, Walter (1916–19); Bombardier, R.G.A.; Salonica 2 years.

***Burwood, Henry Walter** (1915–18); Private, R.A.M.C.; France 2 years; Killed in action, 24th March, 1918.

Butcher, Frank Noble (1916–18); Corporal, R.A.S.C. (M.T.); France 18 months.

***Butler, Walter** (1916–18); Signaller, Westmorland and Cumberland Yeomanry and Border Rgt.; France 3 months; Died in Germany whilst a prisoner of war, 8th September, 1918.

Byron, Edmond (1915–19); Gunner, Honourable Artillery Company; France 2 years 2 months.

Callinan, Edmund John (1915–19); Telegraphist, R.N.V.R.; Sea Service 2 years 8 months.

Canning, Maurice John (1914–19); Private, R.A.M.C.; France 2 years 11 months.

Carlile, Percy (1914–19); M.S.M.; Sergeant, Honourable Artillery Company; France 4 years 3 months.

Chamings, Ernest Edmund (1914–16); Private, Oxfordshire and Buckinghamshire Light Infantry; France 9 months.

Chapman, Christopher (1915–19); Sergeant, R.A.M.C.; France 9 months.

Cherry, Alfred (1914–19); Lance-Corporal, Middlesex Rgt.; Gallipoli 5 months, India 2 years (N.W. Frontier 18 months), Mesopotamia 15 months.

Christophers, Arthur Harold (1916–19); Flight-Sergeant, R.A.F.

Coe, Lawrence Gordon (1914–18); Sergeant, Oxfordshire and Buckinghamshire Light Infantry and Lincolnshire Rgt.; France 10 months, Prisoner of war in Germany and Switzerland 14 months.

Cogman, William Frederick (1916–19); Corporal, R.A.F.; France 2 years.

Cole, Walter Laurence (1916–19); Sergeant, E. Surrey Rgt., Suffolk Rgt., and R.A.O.C.; France 2 years 6 months.

Connor, Louis Roussez (1915–19); Gunner, Machine Gun Corps; East and South Africa 18 months, Egypt and India 1 year.

Corfield, Frederick John (1915–19); Gunner, R.G.A.; Palestine 15 months.

Cousin, James (1916–19); Corporal, Suffolk Rgt. and Cambridgeshire Rgt.; France 1 year 7 months.

Cracroft, Edmund Henry (1917–19); Private, R.A.S.C.

***Crawley, Arthur** (1916–17); Pioneer, R.E.; France 10 months; Killed in action, 4th May, 1917.

Crisp, Herbert Charles (1916–19); Lance-Sergeant, Middlesex Rgt.

Cross, Albert George (1914–19); Sergeant, R.A.M.C.; France 2 years 8 months.

Cross, Nathaniel John (1916–19); Corporal, R.A.M.C.; France 6 months, Italy 15 months.

Cross, William Amos (1916–19); Mentioned in despatches; Flight-Sergeant, R.A.F., and London Rgt.

Cryer, Harold George (1918–19); Corporal, London Rgt.

Cunningham, Malcolm (1918–19); Private, Middlesex Rgt.; France 5 months.

Curd, Harold Albert (1915–19); Lieutenant, R.F.A.; France 15 months.

Curnall, Charles Alfred (1914–18); Private, Middlesex Rgt.; Gibraltar 5 months, France 1 year 7 months.

Curtis, Alfred Cecil (1915–19); M.S.M., Twice mentioned in despatches; Staff-Sergeant, R.E.; Mesopotamia 3 years 6 months.

***Daly, Daniel** (1914–16); Private, London Rgt.; France 15 months; Missing, 7th October, 1916.

Daniels, James Henry (1915–19); Company Sergeant-Major (Musketry Instructor), 15th Bn. London Rgt.; France 3 months.

Davies, Harold (1916–19); Sergeant, R. W. Surrey and Welch Rgts.; France 2 years.

***Davis, John George** (1916–17); Private, Irish Guards; France 4 months; Killed in action, 9th October, 1917.

Dawes, Albert (1915–19); Private, London Rgt. and R.E.; India 3 years.

de Mouilpied, Alfred Theophilus (1916–19); Captain, General List, attached Chemical Warfare Section; France 12 months.

Dear, George Roots (1916–19); Company Sergeant-Major (Instructor), Corps of the School of Musketry.

Dines, Herbert Sapsford (1915–19); Quartermaster-Sergeant, R.E.; France 2 years 10 months.

Dohoo, Arthur Godfrey (1916–19); Lieutenant, R.A.S.C.; France 4 months.

Doughty, Ernest (1914–19); Sergeant, Middlesex Rgt.; Gibraltar 4 months; France 2 years 8 months.

Driver, Frederick George (1914–19); Lieutenant, R.A.M.C., Loyal N. Lancashire Rgt. and R. Welch Fusiliers; France 1 year 9 months.

Duncan, Adam (1915–19); M.S.M.; Sergeant, R.A.V.C.; France 3 years 5 months.

Eames, Frank Wells (1914–19); Major, London Rgt.; France 7 months, Macedonia 6 months, Palestine 14 months.

East, Edward Samuel (1916–19); Corporal, Royal Marine Light Infantry.

Edey, Edwin Charles (1914–19); Private, R.A.M.C.; France 3 years 8 months.

Ellsmoor, Frank James Brian (1915–19); Serbian Gold Medal; Staff Sergeant-Major, R.A.S.C.; Near East 3 years 9 months.

Emary, Walter (1916–19); Corporal, London Rgt.

Eton, Ernest (1914–19); D.S.O., Twice mentioned in despatches; Lieut.-Colonel, R.F.A.; France 3 years, Egypt and Palestine 5 months.

Fageant, Henry Charles (1917–19); Corporal, A.P.C.

Farrell, Arthur Patrick Joseph (1915–19); Corporal, London Rgt.; France 6 months.

Ferguson, Thomas William (1915–19); Signaller, R.G.A., and Sapper, R.E.; France 3 years.

Field, William George (1914–19); Lieutenant, Middlesex and Wiltshire Rgts.; Gibraltar 6 months, Egypt 8 months, France 2 years 6 months.

Field, William Thomas (1914–19); Private, R. W. Surrey Rgt. and Labour Corps; France 4 years 6 months.

FitzPatrick, John (1914–20); Captain, graded D.A.Q.M.G., December 1917 to April 1918; Inns of Court O.T.C. and Manchester Rgt.; France 12 months, Mesopotamia and India 9 months, Palestine 1 year 8 months, Egypt 2 months.

Flawn, Charles Leslie (1914–19); Sec.-Lieutenant, London and N. Staffordshire Rgts., Labour Corps, and R.A.F.; Malta 4 months, France 14 months.

Fletcher, Nora Ida (1918–19); Mechanic-Driver, R.A.S.C.; France 6 months.

Flint, Joseph (1915–19); Captain, R.A.M.C.; France 2 years 11 months.

Flynn, Daniel Hender (1914–19); Sec.-Lieutenant, R. Bucks Hussars and R.F.A.; France 9 months, Palestine 7 months.

Forbes, William (1914–19); Private, London Rgt. (R.D.C.).

Fox, John (1914–15); Trooper, Surrey Yeomanry.

French, Albert Joseph (1915–19); Sapper, R.E.; France 2 years.

French, Stanley Frederick (1915–19); Private, R.A.M.C.; France 5 months.

Friedson, Nathan (1915–19); Driver, R.F.A., and Intelligence Agent, Intelligence Corps; France 2 years 6 months; Germany 6 months.

Friend, Robert Ernest (1915–19); Private, London Rgt., E. Surrey Rgt. and R.A.S.C.; France 12 months, Salonica 6 months.

Frost, James Kesterton (1915–16); Private, Home Counties Divisional Cyclist Co.

Fuller, Harry Walter (1915–19); Lieutenant, London Rgt.; France 9 months.

Furness, Harold (1915–19); Private, R.A.M.C.; France 2 years 11 months.

Gardner, Harry John (1915–19); Private, R.A.M.C.; France 2 years 7 months.

***Gaskell, Arnold Joseph** (1916–18); Sec.-Lieutenant, Middlesex and R. W. Surrey Rgts., and Norfolk Yeomanry; France 1 month; Killed in action, 2nd November, 1918.

Gaylard, Norman Samuel (1914–19); Sec.-Lieutenant, Middlesex Rgt., 15th Bn. London Rgt., and R.A.F.; Gibraltar 7 months, Egypt 8 months, France 5 months.

Gibbons, Harold (1914–17); Private, London Rgt.; France 3 months.

Gibson, Archie Leonard (1915–19); Private, R.A.M.C.; France 7 months, Salonica 7 months, Palestine 17 months, Egypt 2 months.

Gordon, Frank Allen (1915–19); Lieutenant, Machine Gun Corps; France 16 months.

Gordon, Patrick (1914–19); Sergeant, London Rgt., Rifle Brigade, and Machine Gun Corps; Malta 6 months, Gallipoli 5 months, Salonica 12 months, Egypt and Palestine 2 years 6 months.

Gould, Herbert Wadeson (1915–19); Sergeant, R.A.M.C.; France 2 years 6 months.

Gould, Sydney Albert (1915–19); Mentioned in despatches; Staff Sergeant-Major, R.A.S.C.; Mesopotamia 2 years 5 months.

Grant, Samuel Sutherland (1916–19); Private, R.A.F.; France 4 months.

Green, Frank Barnes (1914–19); Company Sergeant-Major, King's Royal Rifle Corps and Rifle Brigade; France 14 months.

Green, Walter Barnes (1914–19); M.S.M.; Sergeant, 16th Bn. London Rgt.; France 4 years 4 months.

Griffiths, Ronald Henry (1915–19); Sergeant, London Rgt and King's African Rifles; France 6 months, East Africa 10 months.

Grigs, Herbert (1916–19); Victualling Assistant, R.N.; Sea service, 3rd Battle Squadron and 7th Light Cruiser Squadron (Grand Fleet), 2 years 4 months.

Guiton, Martin Joseph (1914–18); Corporal, 15th Bn. London Rgt.; France 1 year 7 months.

Gunn, John Ballantine (1915–19); Staff Sergeant-Major, R.A.S.C.; Egypt 6 months, France 12 months, East Africa 1 year 9 months.

Hadgraft, Edwin Tidman (1917–19); Corporal, Essex Rgt. and A.P.C.

Hales, Edward Louis (1916–19); Victualling Assistant, R.N.; Light Cruiser Squadron, Grand Fleet, 12 months; Storekeeper and Engineer's Writer, East Africa 1 year 10 months.

Hall, Edwin Thomas (1915–19); Lance-Corporal, 16th Bn. London Rgt.; France 13 months, Macedonia 6 months, Palestine 12 months.

Hall, Henry Finden (1916–19); M.S.M.; Bombardier, R.G.A.

Hall, John Alfred (1915–19); Sec.-Lieutenant, R.A.M.C. and Tank Corps; France 1 year 8 months.

Hall, Norman Heaton (1916–17); Sapper, R.E.

Hamlyn, Herbert (1918–19); Clerk, R.A.F.

Harding, William Ewart (1915–19); Private, Royal Marine Light Infantry.

Hardy, Harold Ivan (1914–19); Mentioned in despatches; Captain, 5th Bn. London Rgt. and R.G.A.; France 10 months.

Hare, Edward (1915–19); Gunner, R.G.A.; France 3 years.

***Harries, Stanley** (1915–16); Rifleman, King's Royal Rifle Corps; Died, 30th November, 1916.

Harris, Frederick George (1914–19); Lieutenant, 23rd Bn. Royal Fusiliers and Middlesex Rgt.; France 12 months.

Hart, John Yealand (1916–19); 2nd Corporal, London Electrical Engineers, R.E.

Hartill, Ernest Arthur (1915–19); Staff Sergeant-Major, R.A.S.C.; Egypt 3 months, France 3 years.

***Havell, Eric Tunbridge** (1914–15); Private, R. Sussex Rgt.; France 1 month; Killed in action, 26th September, 1915.

Hawley, Henry Nathan (1916–19); Corporal, A.P.C.

***Haycraft, Leonard Courteney** (1914–16); Sec.-Lieutenant, London Rgt.; France 12 months; Killed in action, 7th October, 1916.

Hayden, Bernard Rondeau (1915–18); Lieutenant, 15th Bn. London Rgt. and Machine Gun Corps; France 2 years, Italy 4 months.

Healy, Christopher Francis (1914–19); M.C., Croix de Guerre (Belge), Mentioned in despatches; Lieut.-Colonel, R. Inniskilling Fusiliers and R. Dublin Fusiliers; Dardanelles 3 months, France 2 years 11 months.

Heddon, Percy William Selman (1915); Staff Sergeant-Major, R.A.S.C.

Henderson, Ernest Alfred (1914–19); Private, R.A.M.C.; France 4 years.

Henderson, Percival (1915–19); Captain, E. Surrey Rgt. and R.E.; France 3 years.

Henrich, Albert Sims (1915–19); Private, 15th Bn. London Rgt.; France 1 year 9 months.

Hertel, Louis (1914–19); Sergeant, Middlesex Rgt. and R.A.S.C.; Gibraltar 6 months, Egypt 3 years 6 months.

Hewkley, Stanley George (1914–17); Lance-Corporal, Middlesex Rgt. and 5th Bn. London Rgt.; Gibraltar 6 months, Egypt 11 months, France 4 months.

Hill, George John Albert (1914–16); Sec.-Lieutenant, R. Sussex Rgt.; Malta 8 months, Egypt 4 months.

***Hird, William Honour** (1914–16); Private, Middlesex Rgt. and 5th Bn. London Rgt.; Gibraltar 6 months, Egypt 8 months, France 4 months; Killed in action, 10th September, 1916.

Hirst, Hubert (1916–19); Private, R.F.A. and R.A.S.C.

***Hitchcock, Charles James** (1914–17); Private, 3rd County of London Yeomanry (Sharpshooters) and Machine Gun Corps (Cavalry); Gallipoli, Egypt and Palestine 2 years; Died of wounds, 28th October, 1917.

Hitchcock, William Henry (1916–18); Private, London and Middlesex Rgts.; France 2 years 2 months.

Hodgson, Frederick Sewell (1916–19); 2nd Writer, R.N.

Holmes, Adrian Philip (1916–19); Sergeant, E. Surrey and Bedfordshire Rgts.; India 2 years 3 months.

***Holmes, Percy William Tompsett** (1914–18); Lance-Corporal, R.A.M.C.; France 2 years; Died of wounds, 13th March, 1918.

Holyoak, Albert Henry Perkins (1915–19); Lieutenant, R.A.S.C. and Supply and Transport Corps, Indian Army; Mesopotamia 2 years 6 months, India 6 months.

Hopkins, Cecil Romboy (1916–19); Corporal, R.A.F. (Canadian Training Squadron and School of Aerial Fighting); Canada 18 months, U.S.A. 6 months.

***Horsler, Gilbert** (1914–16); Lance-Corporal, Bedfordshire Rgt.; Died, 3rd May, 1916.

Howe, Frederick Arthur (1916–19); Sergeant, King's Royal Rifle Corps; France and Germany 2 years.

Howell, Ralph Charles (1916–19); Private, E. Surrey Rgt., Gordon Highlanders and Scottish Horse.

Hummel, Philip George (1914–19); Able Seaman, R.N.V.R.; Sea service, Grand Fleet, 4 years 6 months.

Hutchins, Frank Abberly (1916–19); Private, Northamptonshire and Essex Rgts.

Hutchinson, Bertram Hugh (1915–19); Private, R.A.M.C.; France 9 months.

Hyde, Frank William (1914–19); Sergeant, Bedfordshire and Hertfordshire Rgts.; France 18 months.

Hyde, Leslie Cornelius (1914–19); Sec.-Lieutenant, Seaforth Highlanders and Middlesex Rgt.; France 2 years 10 months.

Izzard, Frank William (1916–19); Corporal, King's Royal Rifle Corps.

Jackson, Frank Whitford (1914–19); D.S.O., Thrice mentioned in despatches; Major, R.A.S.C., graded for pay as D.A.A.G., 1919; France 5 years 2 months.

Jackson, Joseph Frank (1915–19); 2nd Corporal, London Electrical Engineers, R.E.

Jacobs, Robert Tom (1917–19); Corporal, Royal Fusiliers, attached A.P.C.

Jervis, Edward Stanley (1915–19); Private, R.A.M.C.; Macedonia 2 years 3 months, Dardanelles 3 months.

Jervis, Tom Edward (1916–19); Sergeant, R.A.M.C.

Johnson, Frederick John (1916–19); Corporal, R.A.S.C.

***Johnston, William** (1916–17); Gunner, R.G.A.; France 6 months; Died of wounds, 19th April, 1917.

Jones, Margaret (1917–19); O.B.E.; Commandant, Women's Corps, Navy and Army Canteen Board.

Jordan, Edwin James (1915–19); Private, S. Staffordshire Rgt., and Sapper, R.E.; France 2 years.

Keefe, Arthur Percy (1916–19); Corporal, R.A.S.C.

Kennedy, Frederick Robert Alfred (1914–19); Private, R.A.S.C.; France 2 years 6 months.

***Kenny, Laurence Henry** (1914–16); Sec.-Lieutenant, Inns of Court O.T.C. and Suffolk Rgt.; France; Killed in action, 26th June, 1916.

Kiloh, Alfred Petrie (1915–19); Engineer Clerk Quartermaster-Sergeant, R.E. (Establishment for Engineer Services); France 2 years.

King, Herbert Walter (1915–19); Corporal, R.A.O.C.; Dardanelles 6 months, Egypt, Palestine and Red Sea, 3 years 2 months.

Kirby, Harry Richard (1918–19); Clerk, R.A.F.

Knight, Arthur Stanley (1916–19); Sergeant, R.A.F.

Knight, William Moss (1914–19); Corporal, London Rgt.; France 2 years 2 months.

Laird, Arthur Robert (1917–19); Corporal, R.A.F.

Laird, Kenneth (1917–19); 1st Air Clerk, R.A.F.

***Lambe, Frederick William** (1915–16); Sec.-Lieutenant, R.A.M.C. and Norfolk (attached R. Berkshire) Rgt.; France 2 months; Died of wounds, 10th November, 1916.

Langman, Andrew William Fenton (1914–15); Mentioned in despatches; Lieut.-Colonel, 2/7th London Brigade, R.F.A.

Lardent, George Alfred (1918–19); Air Mechanic (3rd Class), R.A.F.

Ledger, Ebenezer Frederick (1915–19); Lance-Corporal, R.E. (Field Survey Company); France 2 years.

Libby, William Percy (1915–19); Corporal, R.A.V.C.

Liddall, William James (1916–19); Staff-Sergeant, R.A.O.C.

Littlewood, Alexander Bowman (1915–19); Private, Royal Marine Light Infantry.

Loder, John Edward (1915–19); Flight-Sergeant, R.A.F.

Lomax, William Edward (1915–19); Gunner, R.F.A.; France 2 years 1 month.

Lucey, Robert Gray (1914–18); Sergeant, R. W. Surrey Rgt.; France (overseas draft-conducting N.C.O.).

McCafferty, Alexander (1917–19); Clerk, R.A.F.

McComb, Joseph (1916–19); Gunner, R. Marine Artillery.

McKechnie, James Wilson (1917–19); Leading Aircraftsman, R.A.F.

McKenna, Curtin (1915–19); Lieutenant, India Army Reserve of Officers; Mesopotamia 6 months, India 2 years 6 months.

MacKeown, Samuel Ellison (1914–19); Sec.-Lieutenant, Oxfordshire and Buckinghamshire Light Infantry, and Worcestershire Rgt.; France 12 months.

Macnamara, William Herbert (1915–19); Corporal, 18th Bn. London Rgt., and A.P.C.

Mahony, Henry Edward (1914); Private, Inns of Court O.T.C.

Manser, Herbert William Carr (1915–19); Sapper, R.E.; Palestine, Egypt and Cyprus, 2 years.

Margach, Thomas Harvey (1914–19); Sergeant, Seaforth Highlanders; France 1 year 7 months.

Marlborough, George (1914–19); Sec.-Lieutenant, R.A.M.C. and R.A.F.; France 3 years 4 months.

Marshall, Alfred William Neame (1914–16); Private, London Rgt.; France 7 months.

Mason, Edwin Alexander Young (1916–19); Lieutenant, Irish Guards and Leinster Rgt.; France and Egypt 7 months.

***Mason, Harry William Kirkland** (1914–18); Private, R. W. Kent Rgt.; France 1 year 4 months; Missing, 24th April, 1918.

Matthews, Charles (1916–19); Sergeant, R G.A.; France 5 months.

May, Charles Reginald (1917–19); Leading Aircraftsman, R.A.F.

Mellor, Samuel Hall (1914–19); Corporal, R. Berkshire Rgt.; France 2 years 4 months.

Metcalfe, Alfred Lucien Gustave (1915–19); Sapper, R.E.; France 3 years.

Metcalfe, Henry John (1917–19); Victualling Assistant, R.N.; Sea service, 4th Battle Squadron, 7 months.

Middlemiss, Philip Maclagan (1914–19); Lance-Corporal, Oxfordshire and Buckinghamshire Light Infantry and Labour Corps; France 2 years 7 months, Italy 16 months.

Miller, Percy Ellis (1915–19); M.S.M.; Colour-Sergeant, R.A.S.C. and Labour Corps; France 3 years 9 months.

***Miller, Walter Augustus** (1916–19); Civilian Radiographer (as Major), R.A.M.C.; Died of pneumonia, 2nd March, 1919.

Mitchell, William Edward (1915–19); Sergeant-Major, R.E.

Moloney, Thomas James (1915–17); Private, R.A.M.C.; France 9 months.

Momber, Hugh (1915–19); Corporal, R.F.A. and A.P.C.

Mordaunt, Henry John (1918–19); Sec.-Lieutenant, R.A.F. (Air Ministry).

Moreton, Humphrey Randle (1917–19); Victualling Assistant, R.N.

***Moxley, Gerald Archibald Charles** (1915–16); Private, R.F.A. and 14th Bn. London Rgt.; France 6 months; Killed in action, 1st July, 1916.

Mullin, John Benedict (1915–19); Sergeant-Instructor, R.A.F.

Newman, Leslie Gordon (1915–19); Corporal, 14th Bn. London Rgt.; France 2 years.

***Newton, Albert Edward** (1914–17); Private, London Rgt.; France 4 months; Died of wounds, 13th April, 1917.

Newton, William James Oliver (1916–19); Captain, R.A.F. (No. 1 School of Aeronautics).

Nichols, Harold Percy (1916–19); Lieutenant, R.F.A.; France 15 months.

Nicholson, Claude Elzear (1914–19); Captain, London Rgt. and R.A.S.C.(M.T.); France 4 years 4 months.

Nodder, Edward George (1917–19); Bombardier, R.G.A.

Nodin, Valentina Dora (1918–19); Deputy Assistant Commandant, W.R.A.F.

Norris, Ernest De La Mare (1914–19); Private, R.A.M.C.: France 11 months, Macedonia, Bulgaria and Serbia, 3 years 2 months.

Norris, Sydney Francis Gray (1917–19); Private, R. W. Surrey Rgt., Labour Corps, and Northumberland Fusiliers.

***Oates, Herbert Prudent** (1915–17); Sec.-Lieutenant, University of London O.T.C., 28th Bn. London Rgt., and King's Liverpool Rgt.; France 9 months; Killed in action, 20th September, 1917.

O'Brien, Jeremiah (1915–19); Sergeant, R.E.; France 2 years 7 months.

O'Donnell, Timothy (1914–19); Company Quartermaster-Sergeant, Rifle Brigade and Machine Gun Corps; France 3 years 7 months.

***Opie, John** (1914–19); Corporal, R.A.S.C. (M.T.); France and Germany 4 years; Died, 17th February, 1919.

***Osborn, Henry** (1914–18); Lance-Corporal, 16th Bn. London Rgt.; France 3 months, Salonica 10 months, Egypt and Palestine 10 months; Killed in action, 30th April, 1918.

Ostler, Wilfred Ewart (1914–19); M.S.M.; Sergeant, R.A.M.C.; France 4 years 2 months.

Oswald, Harold Robert (1915–19); M.C.; Lieutenant, 28th Bn. London Rgt., Welch Rgt., and King's Liverpool Rgt.; France 18 months.

Owen, Robert John (1916–19); M.S.M.; Staff-Sergeant Instructor, A.G.S.; France 11 months.

Page, Charles Henry (1915–19); Private, Royal Marine Light Infantry.

Painton, Walter (1914–19); Major, R.A.S.C.; France 3 years.

Palmer, Henry (1914–19); Private, Argyll and Sutherland Highlanders.

Parker, John Wortley (1916–19); Corporal, R.A.M.C.; France 1 year 10 months.

Parkes, Walter (1914–19); D.S.O., M.C. and Bar, Chevalier of the Legion of Honour, Thrice mentioned in despatches; Lieut.-Colonel, South Wales Borderers and Gloucestershire Rgt.; France 3 years 6 months.

Parsons, Charles Stanley (1915–19); Sergeant, R.A.M.C.; Italy 2 years 2 months.

Pashler, Percy William (1915–19); Corporal, 15th Bn. London Rgt.; France 4 months East Africa 9 months.

Pearse, Albert Thomas (1914–19); Transport Sergeant, London Rgt.; India 4 years.

Percy, John Ephraim (1915–19); Lance-Corporal, R.E.

Perry, Arthur Evenden (1916–19); Private, Essex Rgt. and R.A.O.C.; France 2 years 4 months.

***Petrie, Henry Lawson** (1915–16); Sec.-Lieutenant, R.A.M.C. and King's Own Scottish Borderers; France 1 month; Killed in action, 30th July, 1916.

Pitkin, Walter Stanley (1914–19); Sergeant, 15th Bn. London Rgt. and Machine Gun Corps; France 6 months, Salonica 18 months.

Polley, Joseph Samuel (1915–19); Staff-Sergeant-Major, R.A.S.C.; France 1 year 11 months.

Potter, Charles Gerald (1915–19); Lieutenant, London Rgt.; France 1 year 7 months.

Potter, Edmund Victor (1916–19); Rifleman, King's Royal Rifle Corps and Rifle Brigade; France 10 months, Prisoner of war in Germany 7 months.

Pratt, William Henry (1915–19); Corporal, R.A.V.C.; France 1 year, Italy 18 months.

Prickett, Harry (1915–19); Mentioned in despatches; Lieutenant, Lancashire Fusiliers; France 3 years.

Pride, Arthur John (1915–19); Sergeant, R.A.S.C.; Mesopotamia 18 months.

Pullen, Harry George (1915–19); Signalman, R.N.V.R.; Sea service, 10th Cruiser Squadron and Dover Patrol, 3 years.

Putley, Walter Meller (1916–19); Driver, R.F.A. and Labour Corps, attached R.F.A.

Putnam, Tom Clarke (1915–19); Lieutenant, London Rgt. and Indian Army; France 8 months, India 2 years 3 months.

Pye, Robert Arthur (1915–19); Sergeant, R.A.F.; France 3 years 2 months.

Rapley, Edward (1916–19); Private, London Rgt. and Labour Corps.

***Rapson, Harold Thomas** (1914–18); Captain, R. W. Kent and Manchester Rgts.; France 10 months; Died of wounds, while a prisoner of war, 23rd March, 1918.

Rayment, Alfred John (1915–19); Private, R.A.S.C. (M.T.); France 2 years 10 months.

Reader, William Henry (1916); Private, R. Sussex and Hertfordshire Rgts.

Redmond, John Raymond (1915–19); Sergeant, R.A.S.C.; France 15 months, Italy 13 months.

Reilly, Bernard Patrick (1914–18); Lieutenant, Bedfordshire and R. Berkshire Rgts.; Salonica 18 months.

Rice, Thomas Henry (1916–19); Sec.-Lieutenant, R.G.A.; France 1 year 8 months.

Richards, John Elsom (1915–19); 2nd Corporal, R.A.O.C. and London Rgt.; Egypt 2 years 4 months, Palestine and Syria 1 year.

Ridout, Edmund George (1914–19); Company Quartermaster-Sergeant, Seaforth Highlanders; France 9 months.

Ridpath, Henry Samuel (1914–19); Private, R.A.M.C.; France 11 months.

Roberts, Arthur Owen (1915–17); Sergeant, R.A.S.C.; France 1 year.

***Robson, Harry Charles** (1914–17); Company Sergeant-Major, R. W. Surrey Rgt.; France 4 months; Killed in action, 4th October, 1917.

Rose, Frederick (1915–19); Captain, commanding 19th and 46th Sanitary Sections, R.A.M.C.; Egypt and Palestine 2 years 2 months, Mesopotamia 1 year, India and South Africa 4 months.

Rowe, Edward Coe (1916–19); Writer (1st Class) R.N.

Rule, Henry Alexander (1917–19); Private, R.A.M.C.; Egypt and Palestine 18 months.

Ryder, Herbert John Spackman (1916–19); Private, Essex Rgt.; France 14 months.

Ryder, Richard Chapple (1915–17); Bombardier, R.F.A.; France 2 months.

Sargent, Alfred George (1914–19); Private, 15th Bn. London Rgt.; France 11 months.

***Scowcroft, James** (1916–17); Rifleman, 16th Bn. London Rgt.; France 3 months; Killed in action, 14th April, 1917.

Selley, Frank Oliver (1918–19); Signaller, R.F.A.

Shanly, Augustus Bernard (1916–19); Sergeant, R.A.F.; France 2 years 3 months.

Shapcott, Stanley Thiele (1914–15); Private, Seaforth Highlanders.

Sharp, Thomas (1917–18); Aircratfsman (1st Class), R.A.F.

Sharpen, Harold Alfred (1916–19); Sergeant, R.G.A.; France 8 months.

Shaw, Albert Edward (1914–19); Company Quartermaster-Sergeant, R.E.

Sheehan, James (1916); Rifleman, London Rgt.: France 2 months.

Sheridan, Patrick Joseph Malone (1916–19); Mentioned in despatches; Staff-Sergeant, R.F.A. and Intelligence Corps; France 18 months.

Sherriff, Percy William (1916–19); Private, R.A.S.C. (M.T.); France and East Prussian Expedition, 2 years 8 months.

Sherwood, Harry (1916–19); Lieutenant, R.G.A.; France 7 months.

Shiach, George William (1914–19); Private, London Rgt.; France 6 months.

Simpson, Sydney (1914–19); M.M.; Sergeant, London Rgt.; France 4 years 4 months.

Sisley, George Owen (1915–19); Private, London Rgt.; France 3 years.

Skinner, Maurice Sidney (1915–19); Private, London Rgt. and R.A.F.

Snelgar, John Thomas (1914–19); M.B.E. (Military), Mentioned in despatches; Captain, Wiltshire Rgt.: France 13 months, Mesopotamia 2 years 3 months, India 5 months.

Spratt, William Richard (1915–19); Staff Sergeant-Major, R.A.S.C.; Balkans 3 years 4 months.

***Stevens, Albert Ernest** (1914–16); Lance-Corporal, London Rgt.; France 6 weeks; Killed in action, 3rd August, 1916.

Stock, William Frederick (1915-19); Sergeant, R.A.V.C.; Egypt 3 years 1 month; Salonica 2 months.

***Stokes, John Hill** (1914–15); M.C.; Captain, R. W. Kent Rgt., attached R. Berkshire Rgt.: France 5 months; Died of wounds, 22nd March, 1915.

Stone, John (1915–19); Captain and Quartermaster, R.A.M.C.; France 3 years, Italy 3 months.

Stow, Alfred Thomas (1914–19); Corporal, Oxfordshire and Buckinghamshire Light Infantry; France 1 year 8 months.

Sturgess, Jesse Edwin (1914–19); Corporal, Middlesex Rgt., Labour Corps, and A.P.C.; Gibraltar 7 months, Egypt 6 months, France 7 months.

Sullivan, Patrick (1916–19); Private, R. W. Surrey and Bedfordshire Rgts., and Labour Corps.

***Summers, Robert Rendel** (1915–17); Corporal, Honourable Artillery Company; France 4 months; Missing, 3rd May, 1917.

***Swanson, Ernest** (1914–17); Sergeant, Middlesex Rgt. and 5th Bn. London Rgt.; Gibraltar 6 months, Egypt 8 months, France 15 months; Killed in action, 16th August, 1917.

Tate, Harry Fleetwood (1914–16); Private, E. Surrey Rgt.

Taylor, George William (1915-19); Staff-Sergeant, Essex Rgt. (attached Eastern Command Anti-Gas School).

***Taylor, Percy James** (1916); Private, London Rgt.; Died, 13th December, 1916.

Thomas, Conrad Robert (1914–19); Sec.-Lieutenant, R. Welch Fusiliers and Somersetshire Light Infantry; France 2 years 5 months.

Thompson, Percy (1914–16); Company Sergeant-Major, S. Staffordshire Rgt.; France 9 months.

Thompson, William Sturdy (1918–19); Aircraftsman (2nd Class), R.A.F.; France 5 months.

Thomsett, George William (1914–19); Chief Mechanic, R.A.F. (Motor Boat Section); Sea service 2 years, Italy 15 months.

Thorp, Sidney Armer (1915–19); Mentioned in despatches; Lieutenant, R.A.S.C.; Salonica 7 months, Egyptian Exped. Force 3 years 5 months.

***Thorpe, Thomas Vaughan** (1915–17); Private, Kent Cyclist Bn., and E. Kent Rgt.; France 5 months; Missing, 3rd May, 1917.

Thurston, Walter (1916–19); Private, Royal Fusiliers; France 1 year.

Tibble, Albert Montague (1915–19); Sergeant, R.A.V.C.

Toole, Joseph Edward James (1916–19); Corporal, London and R. W. Surrey Rgts., and Labour Corps.

Topping, Charles John Hill (1915–19); M.S.M.; Staff Sergeant-Major, R.A.S.C.; France 3 years 8 months.

Tripp, Cecil Lewis (1917–19); Private, R.A.S.C.; France 1 year 7 months.

Tucker, Harry Castledine (1916–19); Corporal, A.P.C.

Turner, Alfred Ernest (1914–19); Mentioned in despatches; Lieutenant, Middlesex Rgt. and Machine Gun Corps; Gibraltar 6 months, France 2 years, Mesopotamia 18 months, India 6 months.

Turner, George Bailly (1915–19); Staff-Sergeant, R.A.M.C.; France 3 years 6 months.

Turvey, George Sidney (1915–19); Sergeant, R.A.V.C.

Tyson, Gilbert Burrows (1916–19); Flight-Sergeant, R.A.F.

Vincent, Reginald John (1917–19); Aircraftsman (2nd Class), R.N. and R.A.F.

Vinton, William Joseph (1914–19); Private, Middlesex Rgt. and Machine Gun Corps; Gibraltar 6 months, France 1 year 9 months.

Wadey, James Edwin (1915–19); Private, R.A.M.C.; Macedonia 2 years 3 months, Gallipoli 4 months.

Walker, Frank Wilden (1916–19); Lance-Bombardier, R.F.A.; France and Germany 14 months, Italy 4 months.

Walker, Simon Robert Wensley (1914–19); Lieutenant, London Rgt.; France 14 months.

Walker, Stanley Hone (1915–19); Signaller, R.F.C. and Lancashire Fusiliers; France 2 years 2 months.

Wall, Henry John (1914–18); Able Seaman, R. Naval Division; Antwerp, October, 1914; interned in Holland 4 years 1 month.

Wallington, Albert Walter (1916–19); Russian Silver Medal (St. Stanislaus); Sergeant, R.G.A.; Russia 2 years 2 months.

Wallis, Hugh Stanley (1914–19); Private, 19th Hussars, and York and Lancaster Rgt.; France 3 years.

Wallis, John Primmer (1916–19); First Writer, R.N.; Sea service, 3rd Battle Squadron and 7th Light Cruiser Squadron (Grand Fleet), 2 years 3 months.

Warren, Frank Mountain (1914–19); Private, R.A.S.C. (H. and M.T.); India 3 months, Mesopotamia 1 year 9 months.

Watts, Albert Fred (1916–19); Air Mechanic (1st Class), R.A.F.; France 2 years 3 months.

Watts, Frank Potto (1915–19); Corporal, R.A.M.C.; France 3 years 10 months.

Weightman, Herbert (1914–19); Mentioned in despatches; Captain, Middlesex Rgt.; France 1 month, Egypt 1 month, Salonica 2 years 10 months.

Welsh, Laurence (1915–19); Mentioned in despatches; Staff Quartermaster-Sergeant, R.A.S.C.

Whiddington, John Chilvers Reginald (1916–19); Company Sergeant-Major (Instructor), Corps of the School of Musketry; France (inspecting), June, 1918.

Whitaker, Fred (1915–19); Lance-Corporal, Army Cyclist Corps, Scottish Rifles, Royal Scots and A.P.C.

Whitaker, Frederick William (1916–19); Leading Aircraftsman, R.A.F.; France 2 years 3 months.

White, Edwin Charles (1914–19); Captain, R.F.A.; France 1 year 7 months, Mesopotamia and Persia 1 year 8 months, India 2 months.

Willcocks, George James (1915–19); M.M.; Private, R.A.M.C.; France 2 years 1 month.

Willey, John Charles (1915–19); Mentioned in despatches; Quartermaster-Sergeant, Corps of the School of Musketry; France (inspecting), June, 1918.

Williams, Richard Bonner (1914–19); M.M.; Corporal, London Rgt.; France 2 years.

Willmot, William George (1916–19); Paymaster Sub-Lieutenant, R.N.V.R.; Sea service, Northern Patrol, 2 years.

Willson, Frank Edwin (1916–19); Private, R.F.A. and Middlesex Rgt.; France 10 months.

Wilson, John Williams (1915–19); Sergeant, R.A.M.C.; France 8 months, Italy 16 months.

Winter, Charles (1915–19); Corporal, R.A.S.C.; France 3 years 4 months.

Withers, Edward Henry (1915–19); Sergeant, R.A.M.C.; France 1 year 10 months.

Withers, George William (1914–19); Sergeant, Bedfordshire Rgt.; France 1 year.

Young, William Henry (1914–19); Regimental Sergeant-Major, 14th Bn. London Rgt.; France 4 months.

Industrial and Special Schools

***Archer, Charles** (1916); Private, R. Sussex Rgt.; France 7 weeks; Missing, 23rd July, 1916.

***Bailey, James** (1914–15); Private, R. Sussex Rgt.; France 6 months; Killed in action, 9th May, 1915.

***Batchelor, Henry Joseph** (1916–18); Private, Northamptonshire and York and Lancaster Rgts.; France 2 years; Killed in action, 1st October, 1918.

Boneham, Harry (1914–19); Lieutenant, General List; France 4 years 9 months.

Cheek, James Alfred (1918); Private, R. Marine Engineers.

***Chorley, Percy** (1916–17); Sapper, R.E.; France 7 months; Killed in action, 2nd May, 1917.

Christian, George Frederick (1916–19); Private, R.A.S.C.

Davies, Henry (1918–19); Private, W. Riding Rgt.; France 7 months.

Denman, Frank Charles (1914–18); Sergeant, Nottinghamshire and Derbyshire Rgt.; France 1 year.

Drew, William Henry (1914–19); Staff-Sergeant, R.A.S.C.; Gallipoli 9 months.

Evans, Edward (1914–16); Staff-Sergeant, Honourable Artillery Company; France 8 months.

Fowler, John George (1914–19); Lance-Corporal, London Rgt.; France 2 years.

Gibson, James (1915–19); M.M. and Bar; Sergeant, R.A.M.C.; France 2 years 4 months.

Griffiths, Samuel (1916–18); Private, Welsh Guards; France 14 months.

Henderson, William Louis (1918–20); Company Quartermaster-Sergeant, Bedfordshire Rgt.; France 5 months.

Hillyard, James Richard (1916–19); Trumpeter, R.E.; France 2 years 6 months.

Holder, Alfred Sidney (1916–19): Stoker (1st Class), R.N.; North Sea 2 years 8 months.

***Jarratt, Henry William Emmanuel** (1914–15); Sergeant, Coldstream Guards; France 4 months; Killed in action, 4th February, 1915.

Johnson, Leonard Charles (1914–19); Sergeant, Surrey Yeomanry; Dardanelles 8 months, Egypt 5 months.

Keep, William Henry (1914–19); Sapper, R.E.; France 4 years 5 months.

Landels, Walter (1915–19); Private, Seaforth Highlanders: Mesopotamia 2 years.

Livingstone, John Stewart (1915–20); O.B.E.; Captain, Middlesex Rgt.; France 2 years 9 months.

Lyons, William (1917–19); Driver, R.F.A.; France 2 years.

Markland, George (1916–19); Sec.-Lieutenant, R.A.S.C. (M.T.); Salonica 10 months.

Miles, Albert George (1915–19); Rifleman, King's Royal Rifle Corps; France 2 years.

Palmer, George Edward (1917–19); Bombardier, R.G.A.; France 1 year 11 months.

Parker, Albert (1914–18); Sergeant, London Rgt.; France 3 months.

Parkins, Frederick (1914–19); Company Sergeant-Major, Grenadier Guards; France 18 months.

Phillips, Walter Philpin (1914–19); Mentioned in despatches; Lieutenant, Welch Rgt.; Egypt 3 years 6 months.

Pimm, William (1915–18); Private, R.A.O.C.; France 2 years 11 months.

Prangnell, Ernest George (1914–19); Sergeant, R.W. Surrey Rgt.; India 2 years 9 months.

Pratt, Albert Edward (1915–19); Twice mentioned in despatches; Captain, King's Liverpool Rgt.; France 3 years 2 months.

Seal, John Everitt (1914–19); Squadron Quartermaster-Sergeant, 21st Lancers.

Smeeth, Herbert Percy (1914–19); Private, Durham Light Infantry; France 4 years.

***Stevens, Henry John** (1914–15); Sergeant, Durham Light Infantry; France 6 months; Killed in action, 10th March, 1915.

Taylor, Harry (1916–19); Sapper, R.E.; Salonica 2 years.

Way, William George (1915–18); Sergeant-Major, R.F.A.

Webber, William (1914–19); Sergeant, R.A.V.C.; France 4 years 7 months.

West, George Edward (1917–19); Private, R. W. Kent Rgt.; France 1 year 10 months.

Wilton, Albert Eugene (1914–19); Corporal, R.F.A.; France 3 months, Macedonia 2 years 7 months.

Secondary Schools and Training Colleges

Barnett, William (1915–19); Sergeant, R.W. Kent Rgt. and Machine Gun Corps; France and Germany 3 years 6 months.

Best, Henry William (1915–18); Company Sergeant-Major, R.E.

***Blanchard, Frank** (1914–15); Company Sergeant-Major, Royal Marine Light Infantry; Gallipoli 4 months; Killed in action, 25th May, 1915.

***Bristowe, Albert Edward** (1914–16); Sergeant, Rifle Brigade: France 1 year; Killed in action, 7th August, 1916.

***Cater, Charles** (1914); Private, Northumberland Fusiliers; France 2 months; Missing, 8th November, 1914.

Edwards, George (1916–17); Corporal, R. W. Surrey Rgt.: France 6 months.

Evans, Walter James (1915–19); Corporal, R.F.A.: France 3 years 1 month.

Gamble, Harry William James (1915–19); Lance-Corporal, London Rgt.; France 10 months, Salonica 6 months, Egypt and Palestine 13 months.

Gibson, James William (1916–19); Private, Northumberland Fusiliers; France 11 months.

***Gordon, Frank** (1914–16); Sergeant, Royal Marine Light Infantry; Died, 23rd February, 1916.

Gulliver, Arthur Charles (1914–19); Saddler, R.F.A.; France 13 months.

Jenner, Albert George (1914–17); Petty Officer, Stoker, R.N.; North Sea and Western Patrol 6 months, Mediterranean 13 months, Home Waters 2 months.

Kingston, Frank Henry (1915–19); Lance-Corporal, R.A.M.C.; Macedonia 2 years 6 months.

***Lavender, Walter Starling** (1914–16); Acting-Corporal, 5th Lancers; Died, 24th June, 1916.

Leigh, Frederick Bertram (1915–19); Private, R.A.O.C.; France 3 years 3 months.

Pass, William (1915–19); Private, 15th Bn. London Rgt.; France 7 months.

Reding, Henry Edward (1914–19); Private, London Rgt.; France 2 years.

Russell, Alfred John (1916–19); Staff Sergeant-Major (Instructor, Lancing College O.T.C.), E. Kent Rgt.

Salter, George Richard (1916); Private, London Rgt.

Seaman, John Harold (1914–19); Gunner, R. Marine Artillery; Northern Patrol 2 years 5 months, Mediterranean and West Indies 14 months, Grand Fleet 3 months.

Steadman, Alfred Frank (1916–19); Private, London Rgt.; France 15 months, Prisoner of war in Germany 8 months.

Taylor, Edwin Arthur (1915–19); Corporal, Surrey Yeomanry: France 4 months, Salonica 3 years 6 months.

Taylor, George Thomas (1916–19); Sapper, R.E.; France 1 year 8 months.

Treves, Harry (1914–19); Gunner, R.H.A.; France 4 years 2 months, Italy 4 months.

Wheeler, Walter William (1915–19); Able Seaman, R.N.; North Sea 4 years.

***Whitfield, William Peel** (1915–17); Private, R. Lancaster Rgt.; France 6 weeks; Died of wounds, 28th October, 1917.

Woods, F. J. (1914–15); Private, R.A.M.C.

***Wright, Alfred** (1914–18); Private, London Rgt.; France; Died on service, December, 1918.

Technical Institute and Schools of Art

Biggs, George Daniel (1915–19); Petty Officer, R.A.F.

Bolton, Albert (1914–19); Corporal, R.E.; France 4 years 2 months.

Bull, Henry Thomas (1914–17); Sergeant, King's Own Scottish Borderers; France 2 years.

Buswell, William Davies (1915–19); Sapper, R.E.; France 1 year.

Clark, Edward John (1918–19); Clerk (3rd Class), R.A.F.

Clark, Thomas Henry (1914–19); Stoker, R.N.; Sea service 4 years, including 3 years' special service in submarine-net laying.

Dawes, Albert Edward (1916–19); Sergeant-Farrier, R.A.O.C.

Dawson, Charles George (1914–19); Corporal, R.A.S.C.; France 4 years.

Dix, Frederick Arthur (1914–17); M.M., Twice mentioned in despatches; Sergeant, Royal Fusiliers; France 6 months.

Ellum, Sydney (1915–19); Private, 15th Bn. London Rgt.; France 5 months, Macedonia 9 months, Egypt and Palestine 16 months.

Elworthy, Albert Edward (1914–19); Acting Warrant Officer, Royal Marine Light Infantry.

Enness, Frederick Charles (1915–19); Private, Duke of Cornwall's Light Infantry; France 2 years 8 months.

Foy, William (1914–19); Colour-Sergeant, Royal Marines; Grand Fleet 2 years.

Freeman, Ralph Steven (1915–19); Sergeant, R.A.O.C.

Gazeley, Joseph Harry (1916–19); Air Mechanic (3rd Class), R.A.F.; France 2 years 6 months.

Gibson, Edward (1914–19); Staff-Sergeant, R.A.V.C.; France 2 years.

Hemington, William Henry (1915–19); Driver, R.F.A.; France 2 years 5 months.

Hilditch, Albert Arthur (1917–19); Bombardier, R.F.A.; France 1 year 8 months.

Hills, Frederick Henry (1914–19); M.M. and Bar; Sergeant, London Rgt.; France 3 years 8 months.

Hough, Herbert William (1914–19); Sapper, R.E.; Gallipoli 3 weeks.

Jackson, William George (1914–19); Leading Aircraftsman, R.A.F.; France 2 years.

Jarvis, Arthur Edgar (1914–19); Sergeant, Essex Rgt.; France 6 months.

King, Thomas (1917–19); 1st Private, R.A.F.; France 6 months.

Lane, Harry George (1916–19); Leading Aircraftsman, R.A.F.; Salonica 2 years.

Lee, Arthur Walter (1914–19); Mentioned in despatches; Squadron Sergeant-Major, M.M.P.; France 4 years 6 months.

Merrell, Robert W. (1914–19); Rifleman, Scottish Rifles.

Newton, Benjamin Arthur (1915–19); Lance-Corporal, Welch Regiment; France 2 years.

***O'Meara, Albert Thomas** (1914–15); Lance-Sergeant, Norfolk Rgt.; France 5 months; Killed in action, 13th October, 1915.

Page, Avery King (1918); Private, Middlesex Rgt.

Riley, Percy (1918–19); Private, Essex Rgt.

***Sanderson, Charles Albert** (1915–17); Private, 15th Bn. London Rgt.; France 6 weeks; Killed in action, April, 1917.

Spowage, Percy Henry (1915–19); M.M.; Sergeant, Royal Fusiliers; France 2 years 9 months.

***Stretton, Ernest William** (1914); Corporal, R. Irish Fusiliers; France 3 months; Missing, November, 1914.

Talbot, Walter (1914–19); Stoker (1st Class), R.N.; Mediterranean Squadron 12 months, Indian waters 12 months, North Sea Patrol 2 years 6 months.

Thomas, William George (1914–19); Corporal, 15th Bn. London Rgt. and R.E.; France 2 years 7 months.

***Wakeford, Sidney Thomas** (1915–17); Private, 9th Bn. London Rgt.; France 9 months; Died of wounds, 3rd May, 1917.

Woods, Albert (1914–19); Gunner, R.F.A.

School Attendance Officers

Argent, Charles Sidney Lee (1915–19); Thrice mentioned in despatches, once in King's Birthday Honours, Chevalier de mérite d'Agricole, France; Captain, R.A. and General Staff List; France 3 years.

Baker, William (1915–19); Sergeant, R.A.S.C.; France 3 years 5 months.

Ball, William Henry (1914–19); Regimental Sergeant-Major, E. Surrey Rgt.

Barrett, David James (1915–19); Private, London Rgt.; France 12 months.

Bartlett, Henry Evelyn (1916–19); Corporal, 8th Bn. Essex Rgt., and A.P.C.

Bateman, William Alfred (1914–16); Sergeant, M.M.P.

Bayliss, Arthur Ernest (1916–19); Lance-Corporal, R.E.

Bell, Ferdinand (1916–19); Corporal, 20th Bn. London Rgt. and R.E.; France 2 months, Salonica 6 months, Palestine 2 years.

Bishop, William Charles (1915–19); Staff-Sergeant, R.A.V.C.

Boreham, Albert George (1916–19); Gunner, R.G.A.; Salonica 2 years 6 months.

***Bradley, George Joseph** (1914–19); Captain, 2/2nd Bn. London Rgt., 8th Divisional Coy. Employment Corps; Malta, Egypt and Gallipoli 15 months, France 2 years; Died, 17th February, 1919.

Brunswick, Leopold Warren (1914–17); Company Sergeant-Major, Royal Fusiliers and Labour Corps.

Burrows, Percy (1914–19); Squadron Quartermaster-Sergeant, R.A.S.C. (Remounts); France 3 years 6 months.

Carpenter, Harry (1915–18); Sergeant, M.F.P.

Castle, William Henry (1917–19); Lieutenant, R.D.C.

Cates, Arthur Charles (1914–19); Sec.-Lieutenant, 2/17th Bn. London Rgt. and E. Surrey Rgt.; France 6 months, Salonica 7 months, Egypt and Palestine 9 months.

Chipperfield, George James (1916–18); Private, 15th Bn. London Rgt.

Clark, George (1915–19); M.C., Mentioned in despatches; Quartermaster and Captain, 7th Bn. Shropshire Light Infantry, 14th Bn. Devonshire Rgt. and General List.

Clarke, Herbert Frederick (1915–19); Lieutenant, R.A.V.C. and R.D.F.

Cobb, George Fincher (1916–19); Corporal, R.G.A.; France 8 months.

Collins, Martin Albert (1914–19); Sergeant, R. Naval Division and R.E.; Gallipoli and Egypt 12 months, France 2 years.

Concannon, Patrick (1914–16 and 1918–20); Mentioned in despatches; Captain, R.E. and Middlesex Rgt.; Dardanelles 7 months.

Craft, Thomas Henry (1914–19); Corporal, 2/10th Bn. Middlesex Rgt. and 4/5th Bn. Welch Rgt.; Gallipoli and Palestine 3 years 9 months.

Cribb, Harry (1916–19); Lance-Sergeant, 5th Bn. London Rgt.

Cunningham, Michael Owen (1914–19); Bombardier, R.G.A.; France 18 months, Salonica 12 months.

Davis, Frank (1914–19); Quartermaster-Sergeant Instructor, R.E.

Denney, John Michael (1916–19); Sergeant, R.G.A.

Denny, Michael Lawrence (1915–19); Twice mentioned in despatches; Sergeant, R.A.S.C. (H.T.); Salonica 2 years 3 months, Army of the Black Sea 5 months.

Dixon, John Henry (1914–18); Sergeant, London Rgt. and R.F.C.

Dowsett, Albert Edward (1916–19); Air Mechanic (1st Class), R.N.A.S. and R.A.F.; France 4 months.

Doyle, George (1914–19); Staff Sergeant-Major, Middlesex Rgt. and R.A.F. Cadets; Egypt 18 months.

Dunk, Joseph (1915–20); Mentioned in despatches; Lieutenant, R.G.A. and R.A.O.C.; France 4 years.

Fox, Henry Edward (1915–19); Bombardier, R.G.A.; France 2 years 5 months.

Ganiford, Arthur James (1914–19); Corporal, 10th Bn. London Rgt.; Mudros and Gallipoli 4 months, Egypt 1 year 8 months, Palestine 1 year 8 months.

Garrett, Herbert John (1915–19); M.S.M.; Sergeant, R.A.M.C. (Sanitary Section), Gallipoli 3 months, Egypt 2 years 7 months, Palestine 7 months.

Greenstreet, Thomas Wilfred (1914–); M.C.; Lieutenant, R. Irish Fusiliers; Salonica 3 years. Still in hospital.

Hale, Richard Dennis (1914–19); Captain, Royal Marine Light Infantry.

Hammond, Thomas Wiles (1914–19); Corporal, A.P.C., Wiltshire Rgt. and Royal Fusiliers; France 7 months.

Harby, Herbert Richard (1916–19); Bombardier, R.G.A.

Harper, Matthew James (1915–19); Private, 28th Bn. London Rgt.; France 3 months.

Harding, William (1914–16); Staff-Sergeant, Military Police.

Hassell, Edwin Samuel (1915–19); Sergeant, Royal Fusiliers and R.A.F.; France 2 years 9 months.

Hatfull, Lewis Edward (1914–19); Croix de Guerre (French), Twice mentioned in despatches; Lieutenant, R.A.S.C. and R. Irish Rifles; France and Germany 4 years 6 months.

Hawkins, George Henry (1914–19); Warrant Officer (2nd Class), 17th Bn. London Rgt. and R.A.F.

Hayes, Frederick (1914–19); Chief Master Clerk, 20th Bn. London Rgt. and R.A.F.; France 3 months, Germany 2 months.

Hayward, George Edward (1914–16); Company Quartermaster-Sergeant, 12th Bn. King's Royal Rifle Corps; France 5 months.

Hayward, Walter (1915); Trooper, Surrey Yeomanry.

Hone, Frederick William (1916–19); Leading Signalman, R.N.V.R.

Hooker, John Alexander (1916–19); Gunner, R.G.A.

Inwood, William Charles (1915–19); Private, 2/20th Bn. London Rgt. and 929th Area Employment Company; France 18 months.

Jamieson, Alexander (1915–19); Sergeant, 3rd Bn. Loyal N. Lancashire Rgt. and Tank Corps.

Jefferys, Frederick Bernard (1916–19); Sergeant, R.N.A.S. and R.A.F.

Jennings, William Frank (1914–20); Sergeant, Middlesex Rgt. and R.A.F.; India 18 months.

Jessop, William James (1914–19); Mentioned in despatches; Company Sergeant-Major, 4th Bn. Essex Rgt.; Palestine 3 years 8 months.

Johnston, James Richard (1914–17 and 1918–19); Company Sergeant-Major Instructor, Cameron Highlanders; Sergeant, R.A.F.

Kendall, George (1916–19); Lance-Corporal, 17th Bn. London Rgt. and R.A.O.C.

Kerr, Victor (1915–19); Sapper, R.E.

Kilgour, Walter Bruce (1915–19); Lance-Corporal, R.A.M.C.; Salonica 2 years 4 months.

Killeen, Bernard (1915–18); Colour-Sergeant, Border Rgt.

King, George Chelmsford (1915–19); Lieutenant and Quartermaster, Machine Gun Corps, 3rd Bn. Worcestershire Rgt. 52nd Bn. W. Yorkshire Rgt. and 51st Bn. Durham Light Infantry.

Kingwell, Thomas (1914–18); Sergeant, 5th Bn. R. W. Kent and 19th Bn. R. W. Surrey Rgts.

***Lait, Frederick** (1914); Corporal, R.G.A.; France 1 month; Killed in action, 11th September, 1914.

Lake, Herbert (1916–19); Sergeant, 5th Bn. Rifle Brigade, 2nd Bn. Northamptonshire Rgt., 29th Bn. Middlesex Rgt. and Labour Corps.

Lidstone, Frederick (1914–19); Twice mentioned in despatches; Captain, Worcestershire Rgt., and Nottinghamshire and Derbyshire Rgt.; France 18 months, Italy 6 months.

Marr, Arthur Marshall (1915–19); Signaller, R.G.A.; France 3 years.

Marshall, George Morris (1914–16 and 1916–19); D.C.M., Fourth Class Order of St. George (Russian); Company Sergeant-Major, Middlesex Rgt. and R.E.; France 2 years 9 months.

Massen, Herbert Frederick (1914–19); Sergeant, R.A.M.C.

Mepstead, Leonard Graham (1914–20); Lieutenant, 1st Bn. Worcestershire Rgt.; France 1 year.

Morgan, William Robert (1915–19); Lance-Corporal, R.A.S.C.; France 3 years 3 months.

Musto, Alfred Charles (1916–19); Air Mechanic (1st Class), R.A.F.

Nay, Thomas Henry (1916–19); Corporal, 3/7th Bn. Middlesex Rgt., 10th Wiltshire Yeomanry and R.A.O.C. Salonica 2 years.

Nicholl, Robert Alexander (1914–19); M.C., Mentioned in despatches; Captain, R.E.; France 3 years 7 months.

O'Brien, Charles John (1915–19); Company Quartermaster-Sergeant, E. Surrey Rgt.

Oliver, Arthur (1914–19); Sergeant, E. Surrey Rgt.

Parish, Charles Reginald (1914–19); Staff Quartermaster-Sergeant, R.A.S.C.; France 1 year 7 months.

***Parker, Herbert** (1914–15); Corporal, 15th Bn. London Rgt.; France 2 months; Killed in action, 16th May, 1915.

Parkes, Frederick Gray (1915–19); Sergeant, R.G.A.; France 4 months, Salonica 3 years.

Pearce, Frederick William (1916–19); Bombardier, R.G.A.; France 2 years.

Perrin, James Charles (1914–19); Sergeant, Royal Fusiliers.

Pickett, Frederick (1914–19); Company Sergeant-Major, 8th Bn. R. Berkshire Rgt.; France 12 months.

Powell, Frederick Edward (1915–19); Private, R.A.M.C.; Salonica 18 months, France 12 months.

Preston, Oswald Lewis (1916–19); Bombardier, R.G.A.; France 2 years.

Price, Edgar Henry (1915–19); Trooper, R. Buckinghamshire Hussars and R. Gloucestershire Hussars; Egypt and Palestine 1 year 9 months.

Rangecroft, George Stimson (1914–20); Twice mentioned in despatches; Major, Shropshire Light Infantry and Chinese Labour Corps; France 5 years.

Redmond, James Lorrimer (1914–19); Lieutenant, Connaught Rangers and R.A.S.C.

Richards, Clement George (1915–19); Corporal, R.A.M.C.; France 2 years, Italy 15 months.

Ross, James Edwin Ernest (1914–19); M.S.M.; Company Quartermaster-Sergeant, 21st Bn. London Rgt.

Scholey, Horace George (1916–19); Private, 20th Bn. London Rgt.; France 2 years 1 month.

Scrine, Walter (1915–19); Sergeant, Honourable Artillery Company; France 2 years.

Sheppard, Richard Henry (1915–19); M.S.M.; Regimental Sergeant-Major, 14th Bn. Royal Fusiliers and R.E.

Sillitoe, Henry William Charles (1915–19); Private, R.A.M.C.; France 6 months, Salonica 7 months, Egypt and Palestine 1 year 10 months.

Simmonds, Robert James (1916–19); Captain, R.A.O.C.; France 12 months.

Slattery, Jerome Joseph (1915–19); Captain, Special List.

Smith, George Robert (1914–19); M.S.M. and Twice mentioned in despatches; Regimental Sergeant-Major, Scottish Horse and R.A.M.C.; Gallipoli 7 months, France 2 years.

Smith, Herbert Edward (1914–19); Mentioned in despatches; Lieut.-Colonel, 4th Bn. Duke of Cornwall's Light Infantry, 7th Bn. Dorsetshire Rgt. and Labour Corps; Dardanelles 2 months, France 3 years.

Smithson, George Thomas (1915–19); Corporal, R.A.; France 3 years.

Snowden, William Edward (1914–19); Sec.-Lieutenant, R.G.A.; France 6 months.

Stallard, Lionel (1915–19); Sergeant, R.G.A.

Stammers, Francis Alfred (1914–16); Sergeant, 22nd Bn. London Rgt.

Stevens, Frederick William (1915–19); Lance-Corporal, R.A.M.C.; Salonica 2 years 5 months.

Stuchbery, Harry (1916–19); Lance-Corporal, Military Police.

Terrett, John Isaac (1916–19); Lance-Corporal, 13th Bn. Somersetshire Light Infantry.

***Terrett, Joseph Charles** (1914–15); Private, 23rd Bn. London Rgt.; France 2 months; Killed in action, 26th May, 1915.

***Toole, Arthur James** (1914); Sergeant, M.M.P.; France; Killed in action, 21st October, 1914.

***Traylen, Alfred Henry** (1914–18); Staff-Sergeant, Middlesex Rgt.; Died, 11th June, 1918.

Treloar, George Giles (1915–19); Captain, Yorkshire Light Infantry; France 1 year 8 months, Germany 11 months.

Trowbridge, William Edwin (1915–19); Private, 2nd London Yeomanry; Egypt and Palestine 2 years 7 months.

Valder, Alfred James (1915–19); Private, R.A.M.C., 2/3rd Bn. Nottinghamshire and Derbyshire Rgt., and 2/5th Bn. E. Yorkshire Rgt.

Vincent, John Herbert (1914–19); Lieutenant and Quartermaster, 6th Bn. R. W. Surrey Rgt. and Labour Corps; France 3 years 8 months.

Wall, Charles Edward (1915–19); Lance-Corporal, R.A.M.C.; France 7 months, Egypt and Palestine 2 years 4 months.

Walsh, William Edward (1915–19); Private, R.A.M.C.

Webster, John Stephen Bruce (1914–19); Mentioned in despatches; Captain, R.H.A. and R.F.A.

Wells, Leonard Arthur (1916–19); Corporal, R.G.A.; France 2 years 1 month.

Withers, Edwin Ernest (1915–19); Private, R.A.M.C.; Salonica 2 years 6 months.

Woodroffe, Sydney Horace (1914–17); Sergeant, R.F.A.; France 3 months.

Wray, Frederick (1914–19); Sergeant, R.H.A., R.F.A. and R.G.A.; France 3 years 4 months.

Wright, Arthur Frederick (1914–19); Battery Sergeant-Major, R.F.A.; France 7 months, Balkans 8 months, Palestine 2 years.

Botany Scheme

***Andrews, Ernest** (1914); Lance-Corporal, Worcestershire Rgt.; France 3 months; Killed in action, 13th November, 1914.

***Cole, David Allen** (1915–16); Private, R. Fusiliers; France 7 months; Killed in action, 27th July, 1916.

Elson, William (1917-19); Gunner, R.G.A.; France 1 year 8 months.

Hales, James (1917-19); 1st Private, R.A.F.

***Williams, Harold** (1914–16); Lance-Corporal, London Rgt.; France 17 months; Killed in action, 1st July, 1916.

Stocktakers, etc.

Castagnola, Albert (1914–19); Lance-Corporal, Essex Rgt. and Rifle Brigade; India 3 years 5 months.

Clark, David Firth (1917–19); Aircraftsman (1st Class), R.A.F.

Gillman, Percy (1916–19); Sergeant, R.G.A. and Labour Corps; France 8 months.

Hawkins, Benjamin Thomas (1916–19); Corporal, R.A.O.C. and R.A.F.

Humphries, Henry Charles (1915–19); Corporal, Honourable Artillery Company; France 14 months, Italy 14 months.

Mott, Albert George William (1917-19); Air Mechanic (3rd class), R.A.F.; France (Independent Air Force).

Stein, Herbert (1915–17); Private, E. Surrey Rgt. and Highland Light Infantry; France 6 months.

Weeks, James Charles (1916–19); Private, Durham Light Infantry; Salonica 2 years 3 months.

Schoolkeepers

Adams, William Thomas (1915–19); M.S.M. and Mentioned in despatches; Regimental Sergeant-Major, R.A.S.C.; France 2 weeks, Balkans, Russia, Italy 2 years 5 months.

Alden, Edwin (1916–19); Private, Durham Light Infantry; Salonica 2 years.

Andreoli, Cæsar Angus (1914–19); Petty Officer, R.N.; Africa (East, South and West) 2 years 2 months.

Archibald, David Andrew (1914 and 1917–18); Sergeant, Seaforth Highlanders and Suffolk Rgt.

Austen, Frederick Charles (1914–19); Yeoman of Signals, R.N.; Egypt 2 years 2 months, Arabia and Red Sea 1 year 2 months, Dover Patrol 1 year 5 months.

Baker, Valentine (1915–19); Private, Yorkshire Light Infantry and York and Lancaster Rgt.; France 1 year 8 months.

Bane, Robert Henry (1914–19); Leading Stoker, R.N.; Mediterranean 8 months, India 2 years, North Sea 1 year 10 months,

Baron, William John (1918–19); Private, R.A.F.

Bartholomew, John Edwin Meadows (1918–19); Gunner, R.G.A.

***Bastian, Charles John Crawford** (1915–17); Shipwright (2nd class), R.N.; H.M.S. Vanguard; Accidentally killed, 9th July, 1917.

Batchelor, Ernest (1914–19); Colour-Sergeant, R. Marine Light Infantry.

Beams, Arthur Edward (1914–19); Acting Sergeant-Major, R.A.M.C.; France 2 years 3 months.

Beardow, Charles John (1914–16 and 1918–19); Petty Officer, R.N., and Pilot Officer Sec.-Lieutenant, R.A.F.; H.M.S. Euryalus 2 years 3 months.

Bell, Joseph George (1914–19); Colour-Sergeant, R. Marine Light Infantry; H.M.S. Hermione 4 years 6 months.

Bilbe, Alfred Joseph (1916–19); Rifleman, King's R. Rifle Corps, and Private, Labour Corps.

Billing, William Herbert (1914–16); Battery Sergeant-Major, R.F.A.

Blackman, John (1914–19); Able Seaman, R.N.; H.M.S. Wizard 4 years 7 months.

Blake, Charles (1917–19); Driver, R.A.S.C. (M.T.) and Machine Gun Corps.

Booth, Alfred Albert (1914–19); Gunner, R.G.A.

***Boucher, Sidney James** (1914–18); Sergeant, Devonshire Rgt.; France 1 month; Killed in action, 20th October, 1918.

Bown, Sidney Rich (1916–19); Private, R.A.S.C.; France 2 years 7 months.

Brand, Oliver William (1915–19); Leading Aircraftsman, R.A.F.; France 1 year 9 months.

Brandish, Robert (1918–19); Pioneer, R.E.

Brandish, Samuel (1916–19); Staff-Sergeant, R.G.A.; France 2 years 3 months.

Braybrook, William Charles (1915–16); Wheeler, R.A.S.C. (M.T.); France 11 months.

Bridgman, William (1914–19); Colour-Sergeant, R. Marine Light Infantry; France 2 months; Grand Fleet 20 months.

Brinkworth, William (1915–19); Private, R.A.M.C.; Egypt 3 years 8 months.

Bristow, George (1915–19); Corporal, R.A.S.C. (M.T.); France 3 years 5 months.

Brooks, Albert (1918–19); Gunner, R. Marine Artillery.

Brown, Edward Thomas (1914–19); Sergeant, Middlesex Rgt.; France 1 year 9 months.

Buck, Alfred Edward (1914–18); Private, R. Marine Light Infantry; Flanders 3 months, Gallipoli 11 months and H.M.S. Collen 2 years.

Bunker, Alfred Edward (1915–19); Sapper, R.E.; France 17 months.

Bunker, Henry William (1917–19); Private, Royal Scots.

Burt, Frank (1915–19); Corporal, R.A.V.C.; Egypt 3 years 7 months.

Butcher, Frank (1914–16); Private, Rifle Brigade and R.A.M.C.; France 10 months.

Butler, Charles Martin (1918–19); Air Mechanic (1st Class), R.A.F.

Carter, Frederick George (1918–19); Air Mechanic (3rd Class), R.A.F.

Catchpole, Edwin Ansley (1916–19); Corporal, Rifle Brigade; France 2 years.

Catt, Charles Henry (1914–19); Leading Signalman, R.N.; Harwich Flotilla 5 months, 10th Cruiser Squadron 3 years 10 months, Convoying 1 month.

Challen, Frederick (1914–19); D.C.M., French Médaille Militaire and Mentioned in despatches; Company Sergeant-Major, Border Rgt.; France 4 months, Salonica 3 years 3 months.

***Chapman, Frederick Charles** (1914); Leading Stoker, H.M.S. Cressy; Killed in action, 22nd September, 1914.

Clark, Ernest Charles (1916–19); Lance-Corporal, R.A.F. and R.A.O.C.

Clark, James George (1918–19); 2nd Private, R.A.F.

Clarke, Walter (1915–19); Flight-Sergeant, R.A.F.

Clear, Frederick John (1918); Fitter-Mechanic, R.A.F.

Clegg, Ralph (1915–19); Company Sergeant-Major, Middlesex and Suffolk Rgts.; France 12 months.

***Clements, Arthur Alfred** (1915–18); Sergeant, R.A.V.C.; Egypt 2 years 5 months; Died of wounds, 2nd April, 1918.

Clinch, William George (1915–19); Fitter, Quartermaster-Sergeant, R.F.A.; France 6 months.

Childs, William John (1916–19); Corporal, R.A.S.C.; France 9 months.

Coburn, James (1915–19); Farrier Staff-Sergeant, Dragoon Guards; Egypt 2 years.

Coker, William Alfred (1917–19); Air Mechanic (1st Class), R.A.F.

Connor, James Alfred (1915–19); Petty Officer (1st Class), R.N.

Cook, Henry John (1915); Sapper, R.E.

Cooke, Morris James (1916); Private, Essex Rgt.

***Cope, John Henry Bennett** (1915–16); Sergeant, Middlesex Rgt.; France 10 months; Killed in action, 8th August, 1916.

Coules, Robert Arthur (1915–19); M.M. and Mentioned in despatches; Staff-Sergeant Fitter, R.F.A.; France 3 years 7 months.

***Cowan, William Heslop** (1914); Corporal, Scots Guards; France 1 month; Killed in action, 18th December, 1914.

Craig, William Frederick (1918–19); Sapper, R.E.

Cranfield, William James (1915–19); Armourer Staff-Sergeant, R.A.O.C.; France 2 years 2 months.

Crick, Albert (1916–19); Lance-Corporal, King's R. Rifle Corps.

Cullen, John William (1916–19); Signaller, R.G.A.; France 12 months.

Dales, William Thomas (1916–18); Private, London Rgt.

Dallimore, William Joseph (1916–17); Rifleman, King's R. Rifle Corps.

Davidson, Stephen Frederick Donald (1914–19); Sergeant, R.A.M.C.; France 4 years 6 months.

***Davis, George David** (1914); Petty Officer (1st Class), R.N.; H.M.S. Cressy; Killed in action, 22nd September, 1914.

***Davis, Henry George** (1914); Private, W. Riding Rgt.; Missing, 15th September, 1914.

***Davis, Louis Augustus** (1916–17); Private, Cyclists' Corps and R. Sussex Rgt.; France 10 months; Killed in action, 24th July, 1917.

Davis, Samuel (1914–19); Petty Officer (1st Class), R.N.; North Sea 2 years 7 months.

Dawes, John (1915–17); Private, R.A.S.C.; France 1 year 8 months.

Day, George Edwin (1915–19); Corporal, R.A.S.C. (M.T.).

Dennett, Edwin Young (1915–19); Corporal, R.A.F.; France 17 months.

Desborough, John Percy (1916–18); Private, Northumberland Fusiliers and Yorkshire Rgt.; France 5 months.

Dorey, Frederick Job (1917–18); Air Mechanic, R.A.F.

Dorey, William Frank (1917–18); Air Mechanic (2nd Class), R.A.F.

Dyer, Robert (1916–19); Lance-Corporal, Tank Corps; France 1 year 8 months.

***Ediker, Harry** (1916–17); Private, Nottinghamshire and Derbyshire Rgt.; France 8 months; Killed in action, 26th September, 1917.

Edwards, Albert William (1914–19); Mentioned in despatches; Sergeant, R.G.A.; France 3 years 9 months.

Elliott, Daniel Thomas (1916–19); Gunner, R.G.A.; France 10 months.

Ellis, Henry (1915–19); Chief Petty Officer, R.N.A.S.

England, John (1918–19); Private, Middlesex Rgt. and R.A.S.C.

Evans, William Henry (1917–19); Gunner, R.G.A.

Everitt, Edward (1914–17); Sergeant, S. Staffordshire Rgt.

Fairer, Charles Philip (1916–19); Gunner, R.G.A.; France 1 year 11 months.

Fawcett, Henry (1918–19); Air Mechanic, R.A.F.

Ferguson, George (1916–17); Private, London Rgt.

Flindall, Arthur Frank (1914–19); Sergeant, London Rgt. and R.D.C.

Franklin, Benjamin (1917–19); Private, S. Staffordshire Rgt. and R.A.S.C. (M.T.).

Gamon, Howard John (1915–19); Sergeant-Mechanic, R.A.F.; France 12 months.

Gawthorpe, John Mawson (1918–19); Pioneer, R.E.

Gifford, Cecil Henry (1914–19); Gunner, R.M.A.; France 4 years 7 months.

Gilham, Ernest (1914–15); Petty Officer (1st Class), R.N.; North Sea and Mediterranean 6 months.

Glinnan, Thomas Lorenzo (1915–17); Sergeant, Machine Gun Corps; France 5 months.

Gordon, Frederick William (1914–19); Corporal, R.F.A.; France 1 year 8 months, Salonica 2 years 9 months.

Gordon, Huntley Sizer (1914–19); Staff-Sergeant, R.A.S.C.; France 7 months, Salonica 8 months, Egypt 17 months.

***Gosford, William George** (1915–16); Private, R.A.S.C.; Died 3rd September, 1916.

Gowen, Frederick (1916–19); Private, London Rgt.; Salonica 6 months, Egypt 1 year 9 months.

Grant, Alfred Albert (1914–18); Sergeant, R. Marine Light Infantry; France 1 month, Germany (Prisoner of war) 4 years.

Grey, George Henry (1918–19); Private, A.P.C.

Griffin, George Roots (1917–19); Corporal, Life Guards.

Grover, Francis Alexander (1915–19); Able Seaman, R.N.; Falkland Islands, South America and Canada, 2 years 8 months.

Hale, Albert Joseph (1915–18); Gunner, R.G.A.; France 3 months.

***Halliday, Francis Albert** (1914–15); Chief Petty Officer, R.N.; H.M.S. Clan McNaughton; Missing at sea, 3rd February, 1915.

Hallums, Albert Ernest (1915–19); Private, R.A.M.C.; France 2 years 2 months, Italy 17 months.

Hamilton, Robert Henry (1914–19); Mentioned in despatches; Sergeant, London Rgt.; France 4 years.

Hanneman, Ernest Leopold (1914–19); Mentioned in despatches; Yeoman of Signals, R.N.; Cape Verde Islands, South-West Africa 6 months, Dardanelles 1 year 3 months.

Harding, Charles John (1918–19); Air Mechanic, R.A.F.

Hatch, William (1915–19); Sergeant, King's R. Rifle Corps; France 3 years.

Hayes, Thomas Henry (1914–16); Company Sergeant-Major, Bedfordshire and Hertfordshire Rgt.; France 4 months.

Head, Charles William (1918–19); Private, R.A.M.C.

***Helps, John William** (1914–18); Able Seaman, R.N.; Killed in action, 20th January, 1918.

Hewitt, Albert (1916–19); Lance-Sergeant, Grenadier Guards.

Hill, Albert Edward (1914–19); M.S.M. and Mentioned in despatches; Staff Sergeant-Major, R.A.S.C.; France 3 years 9 months.

Hill, George Thomas (1914–16); Lance-Corporal, R. Irish Rifles; France 6 months.

Hinton, Charles Ernest Edward (1915–19); Sergeant, R.A.V.C.; Egypt 3 years 6 months.

Hodges, Stephen Bennett Gold (1915–18); Driver, R.A.S.C.; France 8 months.

Hollington, George Edmond (1916–19); Pioneer, R.E.; France 2 years 5 months.

Holloway, Sidney Herbert (1914–19); Corporal, R.F.A.; France 2 years 6 months.

Howes, Robert Arthur (1914–18); Private, London Rgt. and R.D.C.

Hunt, John Henry (1915–19); Corporal of Horse, Life Guards.

Irving, John Henry (1915–19); Staff-Sergeant, R.F.A.

Isaac, William Jesse (1915–18); Chief Petty Officer, R.N.

Izatt, Herbert John (1914–19); Lance-Corporal, Essex Rgt.; Mesopotamia 2 years 3 months.

James, Robert John (1914–19); Sergeant, R. Marine Light Infantry; Belgium 1 month.

Johnson, James Robert (1914–19); Sergeant, R.G.A.; France 3 years 6 months.

Johnson, Harry (1917–19); Sapper, R.E.

Jones, James Samuel (1916–19); Private, Essex Rgt.; France 1 year 10 months.

Jude, Thomas (1916–18); Gunner, R.G.A.; France 10 months.

Keel, William Frank (1916–19); Company Sergeant-Major, London Rgt.

Kennedy, Ernest William John (1915–19); Private, Coldstream Guards; France 1 year 7 months.

Keys, Robert Ferguson (1914–19); Company Sergeant-Major, Middlesex Rgt.; France 8 months.

***King, George Osmond** (1914–18); Sergeant, R.G.A.; France 3 years 9 months; Died, 11th May, 1918.

Knapman, Edward George (1916–19); Air Mechanic (1st Class), R.A.F.

Lawrence, John (1914–19); Corporal, London Rgt.; France 11 months.

Lewis, Frederick (1916–19); Private, Grenadier Guards and R.A.O.C.

Lewis, William Henry (1917–19); Mentioned in despatches; Company Sergeant-Major, W. Yorkshire Rgt.

Liley, Albert (1914–19); Chief Petty Officer, R.N.

Littlewood, Percy Walter (1915–19); Mentioned in despatches; Corporal, Tank Corps; France 2 years 4 months.

Love, George (1915–16); Corporal, R.A.S.C. (M.T.); France 7 months.

Lubbock, Edwin Henry (1914–19); Company Quartermaster-Sergeant, London Rgt. and R.E.; Macedonia, Egypt and Palestine, 2 years 5 months.

Lucas, Alfred Charles (1914–19); Sergeant-Instructor, R. Fusiliers and Machine Gun Corps; France 4 years 3 months.

McLaren, Robert James Clark (1914–19); Gunner, R.F.A.; France 4 years.

Macleod, Roderick (1914–18); Chief Gunnery Instructor, R.N.; H.M.S. Orama 3 years.

Maher, Arthur John (1916–18); Private, R.A.M.C.

***Malcolm, George** (1914); Company Quartermaster-Sergeant, Grenadier Guards; France 4 months; Killed in action, 20th December, 1914.

Mallard, George (1914–19); Colour-Sergeant, R. Marine Light Infantry.

Mansfield, Alfred (1915–19); Corporal, R.F.A.; France 1 month, Salonica 2 years.

Margetson, William Louis (1915–19); Rifleman, King's R. Rifle Corps and Labour Corps; France 2 years.

Marsh, William John (1916–19); Corporal, R.A.S.C.

Martin, Wesley George (1917–19); Leading Aircraftsman, R.A.F.; France 12 months.

Meadows, John William (1915–19); Sapper, R.E.; France 15 months.

Meakins, Frederick (1914–19); Sergeant, R. Marine Light Infantry; France 3 months, Dardanelles 3 months.

Middlemiss, Ernest Thomas (1916–19); Aircraftsman, R.A.F.

Millard, John William (1918–19); Air Mechanic, R.A.F.

***Miller, Albert Edward** (1916–18); Private, London Rgt.; France 18 months; Missing, 21st March, 1918.

Miller, George Theodore (1915–19); Private, R.A.S.C. (M.T.) and Labour Corps; France 18 months.

Mills, Harry (1914–18); Gunner, R.F.A.; France 3 years, Mediterranean 5 months.

Minhall, George James (1915–19); Sergeant, R.F.A.; France 3 years 6 months.

Montgomery, James (1917–19); Air Mechanic (1st Class), R.A.F.

Morris, Herbert Vaughan (1916–17); Air Mechanic (2nd Class), R.A.F.; France 12 months.

Nash, James (1914–19); Private, R. Marine Light Infantry; H.M.S. Euryalus and S.S. Adriatic 4 years 6 months.

New, Horace Robert (1914–15); Quartermaster-Sergeant, R. Marine Light Infantry; France 4 months.

Newman, Arthur Edward (1914–20); Regimental Sergeant-Major, Durham Light Infantry; Germany 10 months.

Newman, Samuel Hugh (1915–19); Mechanic, R. Marine Artillery; France 3 years 5 months.

Nice, William George (1914–19); Leading Signalman, R.N.; Falkland Islands and South America 7 months, Dardanelles and Mediterranean 1 year 2 months, Grand Fleet 2 years 3 months.

Nichol, Adam William (1916–19); Lance-Bombardier, R.G.A.; East Africa 10 months, France 10 months, Germany 9 months.

Nichols, Arthur Demark (1914–16); Sergeant, Coldstream Guards; France 17 months.

Nicol, Alexander (1914–18); Private, E. Surrey Rgt., and Sapper, R.E.; France 12 months.

Norton, Henry George (1914–19); Squadron Sergeant-Major, 2nd Cavalry Rgt. and 4th Dragoons.

O'Brien, John (1914–17); Battery Sergeant-Major, R.F.A.

Outlaw, Arthur Samuel (1918–19); Air Mechanic (3rd Class), R.A.F.

Page, Frank (1916–19); Air Mechanic (2nd Class), R.A.F.

Parfitt, George Alexander (1914–18); Company Sergeant-Major, Northumberland Fusiliers; France 17 months.

Parry, Thomas Edward (1916–19); Private, R.A.F.

Pawley, Charles (1915–19); Acting Sergeant, R.E.; France 11 months.

Pearce, Edward Harold (1918–19); Aircraftsman, R.A.F.

Porter, Arthur Keinton (1915–19); Sergeant, Middlesex Rgt.; France 3 years.

Powell, Joseph William (1918–19); Pioneer, R. Marine Engineers.

Raison, John Edward (1915–19); Petty Officer, R.N.

***Raymond, Charles Arthur** (1915–16); Lance-Corporal, R.W. Surrey Rgt.; France 5 months; Killed in action, 8th October, 1916.

Reece, Walter (1914–18); Battery Sergeant-Major, R.F.A.; France 12 months, Salonica 2 years.

Rees, Archibald Richard (1915–20); Chief Petty Officer, R.N.A.S.; France 12 months.

Reynolds, Leonard Adams (1914–19); Colour-Sergeant, R. Marine Light Infantry; North Sea, Suez Canal and Gallipoli 1 year 9 months.

Richardson, Frank (1918–19); Air Mechanic (2nd Class), R.A.F.

Rix, Sidney William (1914–19); Able Seaman, Gunlayer, R.N.; North Sea and Mediterranean 3 years 7 months.

Rogers, George John (1915–19); Corporal, Rifle Brigade and London Rgt.; India 3 years 6 months.

Ropkins, Thomas (1915-19); Sapper, R.E.; France 3 years 4 months.

***Rubley, William** (1914–16); Squadron Sergeant-Major, Cavalry Rgt.; France 18 months; Died, 15th February, 1916.

Sainsbury, William Francis (1915–17); Private, R.A.S.C.; France 1 year 10 months.

Sanders, Ernest William (1918–19); Private, Bedfordshire and Hertfordshire and Suffolk Rgts.

***Sapsworth, George William** (1916–17); Rifleman, King's R. Rifle Corps; France 2 months; Died of wounds, 1st March, 1917.

Saunders, Thomas (1914–19); Sergeant-Major, R.A.M.C.; Egypt 1 year 8 months.

Saunders, William George (1916–19); Air Mechanic, R.A.F.; France 3 months.

Scholefield, James Edward (1914–19); Chief Petty Officer, Telegraphist, R.N.; West Indies 4 years 3 months.

Searby, George Stephen (1917–19); Private, R.A.V.C.

Sears, Nelson (1914–19); D.S.M.; Colour-Sergeant, R. Marine Light Infantry; H.M.S. Hermione, etc., 3 years 2 months.

Sewell, George Frederick (1914–16 and 1917–18); Private, R. Scots, Driver, R.A.S.C.; France 10 months.

Sheldon, Francis (1917–19); Rifleman, King's R. Rifle Corps; France 6 months.

Shepherd, George (1914–19); Colour-Sergeant, R. Marine Light Infantry; France 2 months, Germany (Prisoner of war) 4 years.

Sibley, Edward James (1915–19); Private, R.A.M.C. and R.A.F.; France 14 months.

Simmonds, Charles Thomas (1916–19); Air Mechanic, R.A.F.; France 13 months.

Skellett, Charles William (1914–19); Sec.-Lieutenant, E. Surrey Rgt.; France 2 years, Germany 3 months.

Skelsey, William Henry (1916–19); Private, R. Marine Light Infantry.

Sketcher, Frank (1915–19); Shoeing-Smith, R.F.A.; France 3 years.

Smith, Alfred John (1915–19); Sergeant, R.A.M.C.; Egypt and Palestine 2 years 9 months.

Smith, Charles Richard (1916–19); Air Mechanic (1st Class), R.A.F.

Smith, Francis Christopher (1917–19); Air Mechanic (2nd Class), R.A.F.

***Smith, Henry James** (1914–16); Private, R. Marine Light Infantry; Died, 12th January, 1916.

Spinks, William Francis (1915–19); Gunner, R.F.A.; Mesopotamia 2 years 6 months.

Stribley, John Frederick (1915–19); Sapper, R.E.; France 2 years 4 months.

Sullivan, James (1916–19); Air Mechanic (2nd Class), R.A.F.

Sullivan, Thomas (1916–19); Corporal, R.A.F.; France 2 years 9 months.

Taylor, Daniel (1914); Trooper, Life Guards.

Taylor, Joseph (1918); O.B.E.; Pioneer, R.E.; France 8 months.

***Thorn, Herbert** (1914–17); D.C.M.; Sergeant, Royal Fusiliers; France 17 months; Died of wounds, 27th June, 1917.

Thorpe, William Henry (1914–18); Sapper, R.E.; France 8 months.

Timson, John (1915–16); Air Mechanic, R.A.F.

Towill, Edward (1914–19); Corporal, R. Marine Artillery.

***Trew, Ernest Albert** (1916); Rifleman, King's R. Rifle Corps; France 6 weeks; Killed in action, 3rd October, 1916.

Trower, Albert Edward (1914–18); Sergeant, London Rgt.

Turner, Robert Alfred (1916–19); Petty Officer (1st Class), R.N.; Patrol duty, Orkney Islands and North Sea.

Turner, William (1915–18); Sergeant, Suffolk Rgt.

Watson, Edward Jasper (1917–19); Private, R.W. Surrey Rgt. and Labour Corps; France 1 year 11 months.

Webster, Henry Josiah (1916–19); Private, R.A.F.

West, Alfred Henry Walter (1914–17); Stoker (1st Class), R.N.; North Sea 1 year 9 months, Mediterranean 1 year 3 months.

West, Frederick (1916–19); Lance-Corporal, R.A.S.C. (M.T.).

Whitbread, William Thomas (1917–19); Gunner, R.F.A.

White, Frederick William (1915–19); Sapper, R.E.; France 3 years 3 months.

White, William Alfred (1914–20); Colour-Sergeant, R. Marine Light Infantry.

Williams, Thomas (1914–18); Colour-Sergeant, R. Marine Light Infantry; North Sea and St. Helena 3 years 7 months.

Willson, Henry (1916–19); Lance-Corporal, R.E.

Wing, Thomas (1914–18); Gunner, R.F.A.; Gallipoli 3 months, Egypt 4 months, Salonica 2 months.

Withey, George (1916–19); Company Sergeant-Major, R.E.

Wyborn, John (1914–19); Sergeant-Major, R. Marine Light Infantry; France 4 months, Gallipoli and Salonica 15 months.

Yates, Alfred Edward (1914–19); Colour-Sergeant, R. Marine Light Infantry; France 2 months, Gallipoli and Egypt 15 months, Dover Patrol 15 months.

***York, Thomas** (1914); Colour-Sergeant, R. Marine Light Infantry; H.M.S. Victory; Killed in action, 6th October, 1914.

Teaching Staff

Abbott, Bernard (1918–19); Private, London Rgt.

Ackery, Arthur Henry (1918–19); Air Mechanic (2nd Class), R.A.F.

Acutt, Bertie Lionel Oswald (1916–18); Sapper, R.E.

***Adam, John Gill Sampson** (1915–18); Company Sergeant-Major, London Rgt.; France 4 months; Missing, 25th July, 1918.

Adams, Alfred Sydney (1914–19); Sapper, R.E.; France 2 years.

Adams, Ewart Frank (1915–19); Lance-Corporal, London Rgt.; France 6 months, Salonica 7 months, Palestine 1 year 9 months.

Adams, Frederic George (1916–19); Air Mechanic (1st Class), Acting Corporal-Mechanic, R.A.F.; France 2 years 1 month.

Adams, George Robert (1915–19); Lance-Corporal, London Rgt. and Army Education Corps; France 6 months, Salonica 6 months, Egypt 2 years.

Adams, Philip (1914–19); Lieutenant, London Rgt.; France 9 months, Germany (Prisoner of war) 10 months.

Addison, Frank (1914–19); Lance-Sergeant, Middlesex Rgt.; India 4 years 6 months.

Adlington, John (1917); Private, Hampshire Rgt.

Alderson, John Albert (1918–19); Air Mechanic (2nd Class), R.A.F.

Allan, Alfred John (1915–19); Lance-Sergeant, London Rgt. and Labour Corps; France 6 months, Salonica 6 months, Egypt 1 year 8 months.

Allard, Edgar Gordon (1914–19); Captain, R.F.A. and R.A.O.C.; North Russia 1 year.

Allden, Henry Arthur (1916–17); Private, Bedfordshire Rgt.

Allen, Alfred Frederick (1915–19); Captain, R.N.V.R. and R.A.F.

Allen, Francesco (1916–19); Corporal, R.E.

Allen, George Frederick (1914–16); Private, Middlesex Rgt.; Gibraltar 6 months.

***Allen, James Dollman** (1914–17); Lance-Corporal, London Rgt.; France 4 months, Salonica 5 months; Died of wounds, 10th May, 1917.

Allen, Stephen George (1916–19); Lance-Corporal, Middlesex Rgt.; France 7 months.

Allison, George (1916–19); Sapper, R.E.

Allpress, Arthur Kidman (1915–18); Private, Honourable Artillery Company; France 6 months.

Alvey, Frank Henry (1914–17); Sergeant, Royal Fusiliers; Malta 6 months, Egypt 9 months, Gallipoli 2 months.

Ames, George (1914–19); M.C., Mentioned in despatches; Captain, R.H.A.; France 2 years 5 months, Germany 6 months.

Amess, Nelson Stanley (1914–19); Private, R.F.A. and Labour Corps.

Amphlett, Eustace Northcott (1914–19); Private, R.A.M.C.; France 3 years 6 months.

Amstell, Samuel (1916–19); Corporal, London Rgt. and A.P.C.; France 4 months.

Anderson, Richard (1915–19); Sec.-Lieutenant, R.A.S.C. and N. Staffordshire Rgt.; France 5 months.

Andrews, Horace (1916–19); Bombardier, R.G.A.; France 2 years 1 month.

Andrews, Walter Horace (1916–19); Private, Essex Rgt.; Palestine 16 months.

Andrews, William Thomas (1914–15); Corporal, London Rgt.; France 5 months.

Angel, Alfred Aloysius (1916–19); M.C.; Sec.-Lieutenant, London Rgt. and Machine Gun Corps; France 10 months.

Angel, Albert Heale (1914–19); Lieutenant, R.F.A.; France 2 years 5 months.

Anniss, Frank (1916–19); Sapper, R.E.; France 8 months.

Anson, Walter Charles Frederick (1918–19); Bombardier, R. Marine Artillery.

Anstead, Frank (1916–19); Private, R.N.A.S. and R.A.F.

Anthony, Charles Alfred (1916–17); Lance-Corporal, R. W. Surrey Rgt. and Northamptonshire Rgt.

Anthony, David Brynmor (1914–19); M.C. and Bar, Italian Medal for Valour, Mentioned in despatches; Captain, R. Welch Fusiliers; France 2 years, Italy 15 months.

Appleby, William Percy (1914–19); Staff-Sergeant, R.A.M.C.; France 3 years.

Appleford, Henry Maltby (1918–19); Sergeant, London, Middlesex and Manchester Rgts.

Appleton, Richard (1914–18); Lieutenant, Royal Fusiliers, Middlesex Rgt. and Machine Gun Corps; France 10 months.

Archdeacon, John (1914–19); D.C.M.; Company Sergeant-Major, London Rgt.; France 2 years.

Archibald, Thomas (1916–17); Bombardier, R.G.A.

Argue, Thomas (1918); Private, London Rgt.; France 8 months.

Argyle, Reginald Cecil Blackwall (1918–19); Private, R.A.F.

Armett, Harry Thomas (1914–19); Sergeant, R.F.A. and R.G.A.; Egypt 3 months, France 3 years.

Armitstead, John (1915–19); Lance-Corporal, Tank Corps.

Armstrong, Harold Henry Rhodes (1914–16); Sergeant, London Rgt.

Arnold, Henry James (1915–19); Lieutenant, R.A.O.C.; Gallipoli 7 months, Egypt 1 year, Salonica 15 months.

Ash, Charles Henry (1916–19); Air Mechanic (1st Class), R.F.C. and R.A.F.; France 2 years 3 months, Germany 1 month.

Ashdown, Harry (1916–19); Sapper, R.E.

Ashworth, John Wilfred Wilson (1915–19); Mentioned in despatches; Captain, R.A.F.; France 4 months; Egypt 1 month; East Africa 18 months, Mesopotamia 1 month, Italy 1 month, U.S.A. Mission (Aviation) 7 months.

Atkin, Matthew Henry (1915–19); Captain, R.A.S.C.

Atkins, William John (1914–17); Corporal, R.F.A.; France 2 years.

Atkinson, Albert William (1914–19); Sergeant, Middlesex Rgt.; Gibraltar 6 months, Egypt 6 months, India 2 years.

Atkinson, Harold (1914–19); M.S.M.; Sergeant-Instructor, R. Welch Fusiliers; France 2 years.

Atkinson, John Hartley (1914–19); Sergeant, R.F.A.: Gallipoli 3 months, Egypt 9 months, France 2 years 4 months.

Atton, Francis George (1914–19); Lance-Corporal, London Rgt. and R.E.; France 2 years 10 months.

Atwill, Harold Frederick (1916–19); Lance-Corporal, R.E.

Atwood, Charles Frederick (1914–19); Company Sergeant-Major, E. Surrey Rgt.; India 3 years, Mesopotamia 15 months.

Atwood, Hubert (1916–19); Sapper, R.E.

Attwooll, Harry (1914–19); Company Sergeant-Major, London Rgt.; France 8 months, Salonica 7 months, Palestine 1 year.

Aubrey, Francis Edward (1914–18); Private, London Rgt. and Machine Gun Corps; France 2 years 1 month.

Audus, Arthur Rohan (1916–19); Gunner, R.G.A.; France 1 year 8 months.

August, Charles George William (1914–17); Sergeant, R.F.A.; France 2 years 11 months.

Austin, Charles Frederick (1914–19); Corporal, London Rgt.; France and Germany 2 years.

Austin, Samuel Ashley (1914–19); Sergeant, R. Warwickshire Rgt., R.A.V.C. and Hampshire Rgt.; France 11 months, Germany 3 months.

Avery, Frank (1916–19); Bombardier, R.G.A.

Ayers, Dick (1914–19); Lieutenant, London Rgt.; France 6 months.

***Ayles, George** (1914–17); Staff-Sergeant, R.A.M.C., Lance-Corporal, Machine Gun Corps; France 2 years 6 months; Killed in action, 10th October, 1917.

Ayling, George Habbin (1917–19); Private, R.A.O.C.; Egypt and Palestine 13 months.

Ayres, Herbert Michael (1914–19); Mentioned in despatches; Staff Captain (flying), Middlesex Rgt., R.F.C. and R.A.F.

Badman, Charles J. (1916–19); Sapper, R.E.

Badman, Leonard Dean (1915–18); Corporal, R.E.

Badminton, James Walker (1915–18); Sec.-Lieutenant, R.G.A.; France 3 months.

Baggallay, William Ryder (1914–19); Lieutenant, London and W. Yorkshire Rgts.; France 1 month.

Baggs, Frank Henry John (1916–19); 2nd Corporal, R.E.

Bailey, Frederick William (1915–18); Lance-Corporal, Middlesex Rgt.; France 1 year.

***Bailey, James** (1914–15); Private, R. Sussex Rgt.; France 6 months; Killed in action, 9th May, 1915.

Bailey, William Edward (1915–19); Lieutenant, 28th Bn. London Rgt. and R.G.A.: France 18 months.

Baillieu, J. (1914–17); Lance-Sergeant, London Rgt. and R.D.C.

***Baker, Bertram Reginald** (1914–16); Sec.-Lieutenant, Royal Fusiliers; France 9 months; Killed in action, 3rd May, 1916.

Baker, Herbert Arthur (1915–19); Warrant Officer, R.N., R.F.C.

Baker, Harold Robert (1918–19); Private, R.A.F.

***Baker, James Robert** (1915–18); Private, London Rgt.; France 15 months; Killed in action, 23rd March, 1918.

Baldwin, Frederick (1916–19); Leading Aircraftsman, R.A.F.; France 3 years.

Ball, Arthur William (1914–17); Company Sergeant-Major, Oxfordshire and Buckinghamshire Light Infantry; France 2 months.

Ball, Reginald Harry (1916–19); Sergeant, R.G.A.; France 2 years.

Ballantine, John Herbert (1915–19); Private, R.A.M.C.; France 2 years 3 months.

Ballantyne, James Douglas (1915–19); Captain, Middlesex and W. Yorkshire Rgts.; France 2 years 4 months.

Ballisat, Reginald (1915–19); Lance-Corporal, London Rgt.

Bamford, G. H. (1916–19); Captain, R.G.A.; France 2 years 5 months.

Bamford, William Samuel (1916–19); Sapper, R.E.

Bancroft, Percy (1916–19); Sapper, R.E.

Banner, William (1916–19); Company Quartermaster-Sergeant, R.G.A.

Barham, Archibald Rowland (1918–19); Lance-Corporal, R.E.; France 14 months.

Barham, Herbert Walter (1916–19); Lance-Corporal, R.E.; Salonica 2 years 3 months.

Barker, Ernest (1916–19); Sapper, R.E.; France 2 months.

Barkway, Reginald Charles (1914–19); Sergeant, Middlesex and London Rgts.; Gallipoli 2 months, Egypt and Palestine 2 years 8 months.

Barnes, Ernest Albert (1915–19); Corporal, R.A.S.C.; Salonica 2 years 2 months.

Barnes, Frederick (1916–19); Bombardier, R.G.A.; Italy 1 year 8 months.

Barnes, Herbert Thomas (1916–19); Air Mechanic (1st Class), R.N.A.S. and R.A.F.

Barnes, James Quick (1914–19); Private, London Rgt. and King's R. Rifle Corps; France 4 years.

***Barnes, Sydney George** (1914–16); Rifleman, London Rgt.; France 18 months; Died of wounds, 4th July, 1916.

Barnes, William John (1916–19); Air Mechanic (1st Class), R.G.A. and R.A.F.; France 8 months, Italy 9 months.

Barnett, Henry Herbert (1916–19); Sergeant, Royal Fusiliers.

Barons, Percy Alfred (1914–19); Private, A.P.C. and R. Warwickshire Rgt.; France 1 year.

Barrett, Robert Malcolm (1916–19); Sapper, R.E.

Barrett, William Francis (1916–19); Flight-Sergeant, R.A.F.

***Barringer, Arthur John** (1914–18); Sergeant, London Rgt.; Accidentally killed, 25th December, 1918.

Barron, Frederick Henry (1915–18); Private, R.A.M.C.; France 3 months.

Barry, Gordon Temple (1915–19); Mentioned in despatches; Regimental Quartermaster-Sergeant, R.A.M.C.; Salonica 1 year 8 months.

Barter, Harry William (1916–19); Corporal, R.E.

Bartholomew, Benjamin (1917–19); Private, R.A.S.C.

Bartle, Thomas Richard (1915–19); Driver, R.A.S.C.; France 2 years 3 months.

Bartlett, Alec Laine (1914–19); Lance-Corporal, Hampshire Rgt.; India 3 months, Mesopotamia and Persia 2 years.

Bartlett, Ernest (1916–19); Captain, R.A.F.; Malta 18 months.

Bartlett, Herbert (1918–19); Private, Honourable Artillery Company.

Bartley, George Harry (1915–19); Air Mechanic (1st Class), R.N.A.S. and R.A.F.; France 9 months.

Barton, Charles Thomas (1916–19); Sergeant, R.A.O.C. and Intelligence Corps; France 2 years 7 months.

Bass, William Leopold (1916–19); M.C. and Mentioned in despatches; Lieutenant, Acting Captain Adjutant, Middlesex and Leicestershire Rgts.; France 3 years 2 months.

Bassett, James (1916–19); Sapper, R.E.; France 8 months.

Bastian, John (1916–19); Lance-Corporal, R.E.

Bately, Irvine (1915–19); Captain, R.G.A.; France 18 months.

Bateman, Alexander Lizars (1916–19); Leading Aircraftsman, R.N.A.S. and R.A.F.

Batho, Walter Scott (1914–19); Lance-Corporal, Middlesex Rgt.; India 4 years 2 months, Mesopotamia 5 months.

Batson, Augustus William (1916–17); Gunner, R.F.A.

Bawden, Richard Harry (1914–18); Corporal, R.F.A.; France 3 years 5 months.

Baxandall, Ernest Reginald (1915–19); M.S.M. and Mentioned in despatches; Company Sergeant-Major, R.E.

Baxandall, Victor Harold (1914–19); Sec.-Lieutenant, R.F.A.; France 2 years 4 months.

Bayley, George Steward (1917–19); Corporal, R.E.; Mesopotamia 1 year 8 months, India 2 months.

Beach, William John Henry (1914–15); Sergeant, Middlesex Rgt.

Bean, Harry Edmond (1916–19); 2nd Corporal, R.E.

Beard, Louis John (1917–19); Leading Aircraftsman, R.A.F. · France 16 months.

Beattie, Edward Allsop (1915 – 19); M.B.E.; Captain and Quartermaster, R.A.M.C.

Beck, Robert Farish (1915–20); Captain, R.A.M.C. and General List; France 2 weeks.

Beddous, Thomas Walter (1916–19); Corporal R.E.

Bedford, Wilfred (1914–19); Corporal, Middlesex and London Rgts.; Gallipoli 4 months, Egypt and Palestine 3 years 3 months.

Bee, Cecil Wilson (1915–19); Driver, R.A.S.C.; France 2 years 1 month.

Beesley, Charles (1916–18); 2nd Corporal, R.E.

Beesley, William Charles (1914–15); Trooper, R. Buckinghamshire Hussars.

***Belben, Harold Jones** (1914–16); Corporal, Hampshire Rgt.; India 10 months, Mesopotamia 4 months; Died, 19th January, 1916.

Belcher, Frederick Cecil Edmonds (1915–19); Acting Corporal, R.A.M.C.; France 2 years 9 months.

Belcher, Tom Hill (1915–19); Lance-Corporal, London Rgt.; France 18 months, Prisoner of war in Germany 9 months.

Bell, Herbert (1916–19); Private and Sapper, London Rgt., R.W. Surrey Rgt., Labour Corps and R.E.; France 2 years 2 months.

Bell, Marshall John (1916–19); Air Mechanic (1st Class), R.A.F.

Bell, Valentine Augustus (1915–19); Mentioned in despatches; Captain and Quartermaster, R.A.M.C.; France 3 years 6 months.

Bellamy, Ernest Albert (1914–19); Captain, Durham Light Infantry, W. Yorkshire Rgt. and York and Lancaster Rgt.; France 18 months.

Bellamy, Frank Edmond (1914–19); Sergeant, R.F.A.; France 2 years.

Bellamy, Joseph Nathaniel (1915–19); Lance-Corporal, R.A.O.C.; France 3 years 2 months.

Belsham, William Frederick (1914–17); Corporal, London Rgt.; Malta 8 months, Egypt 5 months, Gallipoli 4 months; France 7 months.

Benbow, Hubert (1914–19); Major, Middlesex Rgt.; Burmah 10 months, Straits Settlements 1 year 4 months.

***Bence, Sidney Robert** (1914–17); M.M.; Sergeant, London Rgt.; Malta 3 months, France 2 years 1 month; Killed in action, 17th February, 1917.

Benjamin, Joseph (1916–19); Sapper, R.E.; France 2 months.

Bennett, Fred Larat (1916–19); Lance-Corporal, Manchester Rgt.; France 9 months, Salonica 6 months.

Bennett, George Walter (1915–19); Mentioned in despatches; Sergeant, R.G.A.

Bennett, Henry Stanley (1915–18); Sec.-Lieutenant, London Rgt.; France 7 months.

Bennett, Lemuel Thomas (1916–19); Sapper, R.E.; France 7 months.

Berger, William Henry (1915–19); Lance-Corporal, London Rgt.; France 7 months.

Bernstein, Philip (1916–17); Corporal, Oxfordshire and Buckinghamshire Light Infantry.

Bertram, Arthur Knightbridge (1915–19); Corporal, R.A.M.C.; France 3 years 2 months.

Best, Norris Wellington (1915–19); Corporal, R.E.; France 13 months.

Bethell, Walter William (1915–19); Corporal, R.A.S.C.; Egypt 6 months, Salonica 18 months.

Bettess, John Pearce (1917–19); Acting Sergeant, R.N.A.S. and R.A.F.

Betts, Edgar Henry (1918–19); Private, H.A.C.; France 2 months, Germany 1 month.

Betts, William Edwin Peill (1915–18); Lieutenant, H.A.C. and Liverpool Rgt.; France 9 months.

Bevans, Herbert Ernest (1914–19); D.C.M.; Regimental Sergeant-Major, R.A.M.C.

Beverley, George Rutland (1915–19); Lieutenant, R.G.A.

Beverley, John (1914–19); Sergeant, R. Warwickshire Rgt.; France 2 years 10 months.

Bichard, Herbert Nicholas (1916–19); Acting Sergeant, R.G.A. and Intelligence Corps; France 13 months, Italy 14 months.

Bidgood, Owen Percy Lee (1918–19); Pioneer, R.E.

Bidwell, William Henry (1916–19); Lieutenant, R.E. and R.G.A.; France 8 months.

Biggs, John James (1917–19); Gunner, R.G.A.

***Bilcliffe, Basil Leonard** (1914–15); Private, London Rgt.; France 7 months; Killed in action, 14th October, 1915.

Billenness, Edward Jeremiah (1918–19); Corporal, R.A.F.

Binger, Frederick Herman Edwin (1916–19); Corporal, Middlesex Labour Company; France 1 year 11 months.

Birch, Arthur Cecil (1916–18); Gunner, R.G.A.

Birch, Edward Henry (1916–19); Gunner, R.G.A.; France 2 years 2 months.

Birch, Harold Thomas (1918–19); Aircraftsman (1st Class), R.A.F.

Birch, John Trevor (1918–19); Aircraftsman (2nd Class), R.A.F.

Bird, Bernard Aloysius (1916–19); Lieutenant (Flying Officer), King's R. Rifle Corps and R.A.F.; France 5 months, Germany (Prisoner of war) 7 months.

Bird, Francis William (1914–19); D.C.M.; Sergeant, Middlesex Yeomanry; Egypt 1 year 9 months, Gallipoli 4 months, Salonica 4 months, Palestine 18 months.

Bird, James Edward (1914–19); Sapper, London Rgt. and R.E.; France 6 months.

Birkett, Walter Snowden (1915–19); Twice mentioned in despatches; Lieutenant, R.A.F.

Bishop, Arthur Frank (1916–19); Sergeant, Northamptonshire and E. Lancashire Rgts.; France 2 months.

Bishop, Herbert Eugene (1915–19); Captain, R.E.; France 3 years 7 months.

Bishop, Leonard (1915–19); Staff-Sergeant, R.A.O.C.; France 3 years 1 month.

***Bissley, William Howe** (1915–16); Sec.-Lieutenant, R. Berkshire Rgt.; France 14 months; Killed in action, 19th August, 1916.

Black, Ernest Edwin (1914–19); Sergeant, Surrey Yeomanry; Macedonia 2 years 8 months.

Blackett, John Daly (1915–19); Sergeant, R.A.M.C.; France 2 years, Italy 14 months.

Blacklee, Josiah Henry (1915–19); Private, London Rgt. and R. Inniskilling Fusiliers; France 2 years 8 months.

Blackman, Philip (1916–19); Pioneer, R.E.; France 2 years 6 months.

Blackwell, Herbert James (1915–19); Sec.-Lieutenant, London Rgt. and R.A.F.; France 18 months.

Blake, Charles Henry (1914–19); Lieutenant, Honourable Artillery Company and Wiltshire Rgt.; France 17 months, Germany (Prisoner of war) 2 years.

Blake, Frederick William (1914–19); Tank Mechanist (1st Class), Middlesex Rgt. and Tank Corps; Gibraltar 7 months, Egypt 9 months, France 2 years 8 months.

Blewitt, Reginald Treleaven (1914–19); Trooper, Surrey Yeomanry; Egypt 1 year, Salonica 2 years.

Bloom, Alexander Abraham (1916–19); 2nd Lieutenant, Rifle Brigade; France 2 years.

Bloom, Ernest James (1914–17); Company Quartermaster-Sergeant, Middlesex Rgt.

Bloom, Percy William (1916–19); Sapper, R.E.; France 1 year 7 months.

Bloomfield, Frederick Henry (1916–19); Private, R.A.M.C.

Bloomfield, Henry Bell (1915–18); Company Sergeant-Major, London Rgt.

Blunden, Sydney Alfred William (1914–19); Sergeant, Middlesex Rgt., Rifle Brigade and Labour Corps; Gallipoli 4 months, Egypt and Palestine 3 years 1 month.

Blunsdon, Thomas (1914–19); 2nd Lieutenant, R.F.A.; France 2 years 5 months.

***Blunt, Ernest Lindsay** (1914–18); Captain, London Rgt. and R.G.A.; France 2 years 4 months; Killed in action, 2nd November, 1918.

***Boden, Samuel Standridge** (1914–16); Sec.-Lieutenant, Durham Light Infantry; France 9 months; Killed in action, 15th October, 1916.

Bolingbroke, Alfred (1916–18); Corporal, Tank Corps; France 1 year.

Bolton, John Hewlett (1914–19); M.S.M.; Regimental Quartermaster-Sergeant, London Rgt.; France 13 months, Salonica 6 months, Palestine 1 year.

Bond, Joseph Richard (1916–19); Corporal, R.N.A.S. and R.A.F.

Boneham, Harry (1914–19); Staff-Captain, Seaforth Highlanders; France 4 years 7 months.

***Bonfield, Sidney Mark Cann** (1915–17); Sergeant, London Rgt. and R.E.; France 7 months; Accidentally killed, 6th April, 1917.

Bonner, Arthur William (1914–19); Corporal, R.A.M.C.; France 3 years 3 months.

***Bonshor, Isaac Henry** (1917–18); Private, R.G.A.; Died, 11th December, 1918.

Bool, Charles John (1916–19); Sapper, R.E.

Boorman, Arthur (1914–16); Rifleman, London Rgt.; France 5 months.

Bootes, Alfred Blucher (1914–19); Major, R.G.A.; France and Germany 2 years 8 months.

Borash, Frank Harold (1917–19); Private, Middlesex Rgt.

Bosworth, Ernest (1915–19); Sergeant, London Rgt., and Army School of Musketry and Light Gunnery.

Bottomley, Alfred William (1914–17); Private, Middlesex Rgt.; Gibraltar 8 months.

***Boughton, William Charles Richard** (1914–15); Private, London Rgt.; France 3 months; Missing, 13th May, 1915.

Boughton, William John (1914–18); M.M.; Private, Machine Gun Corps (Cavalry); Egypt 2 years, Salonica 6 months.

Boulton, Charles Edmund (1916–17); Private, Essex Rgt.

Bowden, Robert Charles Ernest (1918–19); Sapper, R.E.

Bowen, Francis William (1914–19); Sergeant, London Rgt.; France 1 year 9 months.

Bowling, W. H. (1916–17); Sapper, R.E.

Bowness, George (1916–19); Sapper, R.E.

Bowyer, Arthur Ernest (1915–17); Private, R.A.M.C.; France 8 months.

Box, David (1915–19): Signaller, R.G.A.; France 1 year 9 months.

***Boxall, George Thomas** (1914–15); Lance-Corporal, London Rgt.; France 2 months; Killed in action, 25th May, 1915.

Boyes, Richard John (1914–19); M.C.; Sec.-Lieutenant, London Rgt., R. Sussex Rgt. and Machine Gun Corps; France 10 months, Salonica 7 months.

Brace, Reginald Basil (1914–19); M.C.; Lieutenant, London Rgt.; France 2 years 1 month, Germany (Prisoner of war).

Bradford, William Frederick George (1915–19); Corporal, R.A.S.C.

Bradley, W. (1914–20); Captain, E. Kent Yeomanry; Service in East.

Bradshaw, Charles Colin (1914–19); Private, London Rgt.

Bradshaw, John Archibald (1914–19); M.S.M.; Sergeant, R.A.M.C.; France 3 years 10 months.

Branford, George Richard (1914–17); Rifleman, London and Middlesex Rgts.; Gibraltar 7 months, Egypt 8 months, France 8 months.

Brangham, Harold Archibald Mansell (1916–19); Warrant Schoolmaster, R.N.

Brawn, Charles (1914–19); 2nd Corporal, London Rgt. and R.A.O.C.; France 4 years 4 months, Russia 3 months.

Brawn, James Wilfred (1916–18); Lance-Corporal, London Rgt., Worcestershire Rgt., Somersetshire Light Infantry, Devonshire Rgt. and Labour Corps.

Brawn, William (1914–19); D.C.M.; Lieutenant, R.A.O.C.; Mesopotamia 8 months, France 3 years 9 months, India 4 months.

Bray, Frederick Charles (1915–19); Sergeant, R.A.S.C.; Corfu 2 months, Salonica 2 years 8 months, Chanak 2 months.

Bray, Harold Henry (1918–19); Corporal, R.A.F.

Braybrook, Walter (1914–19); Private, A.P.C. and Royal Fusiliers; France 2 years.

Breach, Wallace George (1916–19); Private, King's R. Rifle Corps and Devonshire Rgt.; Palestine 1 year, France 18 months.

Brears, Charles (1914–19); Lieutenant (Flying), R.A.F.; India 6 months, Egypt 6 months, Mesopotamia 3 years 6 months, Persia 3 months.

Brenton, Thomas Henry Crispin (1918–19); Private, Grenadier Guards and Tank Corps.

Brereton, Albert Edward (1914–17); M.M.; Corporal, Oxfordshire and Buckinghamshire Light Infantry; France 6 months.

Brett, John Reynolds (1916–19); Lieutenant, King's R. Rifle Corps; France 4 months.

***Brewer, Reginald England** (1914–16); Mentioned in despatches; Sec.-Lieutenant, R.F.A.; France 1 year 7 months; Killed in action, 10th October, 1916.

Bride, Arthur John Robert (1918–19); Sergeant, R.A.F.

Bridle, Ernest Charles (1915–18); Corporal, Middlesex Rgt.; France 4 months.

***Bright, Alfred John** (1914–17); Sergeant, London Rgt.; France 3 months; Killed in action, 6th July, 1917.

Brightman, Frank (1915–18); Battery Sergeant-Major, R.G.A.; France 2 years 1 month.

Brightman, Percy (1915–19); Sergeant, R.G.A.; France 8 months.

Brimicombe, Martin Henry (1916–19); Sapper, R.E.; Salonica 6 months, Trans-Caucasia 2 months.

Brister, Harold William (1914–19); Company Sergeant-Major, Cameron Highlanders and Army Gymnastic Staff; France 11 months.

Bristow, Robert (1915–19); M.M.; Private, R.A.M.C.; France 3 years 4 months.

Bristow, William Percival (1916–19); Sapper, R.E.; France and Germany 8 months.

Britt, George William (1918–19); Mechanic (2nd Class), R.N.

Britton, Arthur Ernest (1916–19); Private, R.A.S.C.; East Africa 2 years.

‡ Britton, Harry (1914–19); M.C. and Mentioned in despatches; Captain, Liverpool Rgt.; France 3 years 11 months.

Broadberry, Albert Benjamin Arthur (1915–19); Corporal, R.N.A.S. and R.A.F.

Broadribb, Harry Frederick (1914–19); Mentioned in despatches; Sec.-Lieutenant, London Rgt. and R.A.F.; France 2 years 2 months.

Broad, Howard Bennicke (1915–18); Rifleman, London Rgt.; France 10 months.

Brommage, Alfred George (1915–19); Lieutenant, Royal Fusiliers, R. Welch Fusiliers, Ministry of Munitions (Aeronautical Inspection Department); France 6 months.

***Brooker, George** (1916–17); Corporal, London Rgt.; France 8 months; Killed in action, 21st August, 1917.

Brooks, Henry (1916–19); Corporal, R.F.A., R.W. Kent and R. Irish Rgts.; France 5 months.

Brookes, William Henry (1916–19); Company Quartermaster-Sergeant, E. Kent and Gloucestershire Rgts.

Broome, Walter Frederick (1916–19); Private, R.N.A.S. and R.A.F.; France 6 months.

Brosnan, Thomas (1916–19); Corporal, R.E.; France 2 years 9 months.

Broughton, Hugh (1915–19); Lance-Corporal, R.E.

Brown, Cecil Augustus (1914–19); Corporal. Middlesex Rgt.; Gibraltar 4 months, France 3 years, Germany (Prisoner of war) 7 months.

Brown, David (1914–19); Sergeant, R.A.M.C.; France 3 years 6 months.

Brown, Frank Hubert (1916–19); 2nd Corporal, R.E.

***Brown, Harold** (1914–18); Corporal, Middlesex Rgt.; Gibraltar and Egypt 1 year 3 months, France 1 year; Died, 7th March, 1918.

Brown, James Taylor (1917–19); 2nd Corporal, R.A.O.C.; France 1 year 7 months, Germany 4 months.

***Brown, Louis Foster** (1914–18); Lieutenant, Royal Fusiliers and Machine Gun Corps; France 2 years; Died of wounds, 14th May, 1918.

Brown, Percy Wilfred (1914–18); Lieutenant, London Rgt., Duke of Cornwall's Light Infantry and Machine Gun Corps; France 2 years 9 months.

Brown, Robert Anthony (1916–19); Sapper, R.E.

Brown, Rupert Clarence Cooper (1915–19); Company Sergeant-Major, London Rgt.; France 2 years.

***Brown, Stanley Newman** (1914–18); Sec.-Lieutenant, R. Welch Fusiliers and R. Berkshire Rgt.; France 1 year 11 months; Killed in action, 27th August, 1918.

Brown, William Elder (1915–19); Sergeant, Wiltshire Rgt.

Brown, William Springfield (1915–19); Company Sergeant-Major, London Rgt.

Browne, Charles Sydney (1914–19); Squadron Quartermaster-Sergeant, Bedfordshire Yeomanry and 47th Remount Squadron; Egypt 2 years 6 months.

Brunswick, Roland (1914–19); Sergeant, London Rgt. and Machine Gun Corps; France 9 months.

Bruton, James Eli (1918–19); Air Mechanic (3rd Class), R.A.F.

***Bryant, Bertram Thomas** (1914–17); Captain and Adjutant, King Edward's Horse and Yorkshire Rgt.; France 2 years; Killed in action, 11th April, 1917.

Bryant, Percy Lewin (1915–19); Private, R.A.M.C.; Egypt 3 months, Salonica 2 years 8 months.

Bubb, Lawrence George (1915–19); Lance-Corporal, R.A.M.C.; Salonica 2 years.

***Buckby, Harry Fisher** (1914–15); Private, Cameron Highlanders; France 4 months; Killed in action, 18th May, 1915.

Buckle, Archibald Walter (1914–19); D.S.O., 1st, 2nd and 3rd Bars, Five times mentioned in despatches; Commander, R.N.V.R.; France 2 years 6 months.

Buckley, Frederick James (1914–18); Sergeant, London Rgt. and R.E.; France 7 months.

Buckley, Joseph Christopher (1915–19); M.M.; Private, R.A.M.C.; France 16 months.

Buckwell, Frank James (1915–19); Battery Quartermaster-Sergeant, R.F.A.; France 6 months, Salonica 18 months.

Buesnel, Edmond Clement (1916–19); Sapper, R.E.

Bull, Alfred Henry (1915–19); Lieutenant, R.A.F.

Bull, Cyril Edward Aubrey (1914–19); Bombardier, R.F.A.; France 3 years 10 months.

Bull, George Walter (1915–19); Lance-Corporal, R.E.

Bull, William Henry (1914–17); Corporal, Essex Rgt. and R.D.C.

Bulley, Adrian Leo John (1915–19); Twice mentioned in despatches; Lieutenant, Honourable Artillery Company; France 2 years 5 months.

Burbridge, Henry (1914–19); Sergeant, Middlesex Rgt.

Burch, William Francis Thomas (1915–19); Private, R. Marine Light Infantry; H.M.S. Bellerophon, Grand Fleet, North Sea 3 years.

Burdett, Frederick Bertram (1917–19); Mentioned in despatches; Sergeant, R.G.A.

Burdon, John Hall (1914–19); Sergeant-Major, R.A.M.C.

***Burford, William James** (1914–17); Corporal, Oxfordshire and Buckinghamshire Light Infantry; France 2 years; Killed in action, 5th April, 1917.

Burgess, Harry Alwyne (1915–19); Mentioned in despatches; Lieutenant, R.G.A.; France 5 months, Italy 2 years.

Burgess, Robert (1914–19); Sec.-Lieutenant, London Rgt. and R.G.A.; France 3 years 3 months.

Burgess, Robert (1916–19); Sergeant, London Rgt. and Machine Gun Corps; France 2 years 3 months.

Burke, Edmund (1916–19); Air Mechanic (1st Class), R.A.F.; France 2 years 4 months.

Burkett, George Peter Watts (1914-19); M.S.M.; Sergeant, Royal Artillery.

Burnell, Eric Barstowe (1916–19); Sapper, R.E.

Burnett, Arthur William Kirkman (1915–19); M.C.; Captain, R.F.A.; France 1 year 9 months.

Burnett, Ernest Stanley (1914–16); Bombardier, R.F.A.

Burnett, George (1915–19); M.M.; Sergeant, Honourable Artillery Company; France 10 months, Italy 1 year, Austria 2 months.

Burr, Percy Charles (1916–19); Sapper, R.E.

Burraston, Percy James (1916–19); Sapper, R.E.; France 7 months.

***Burrows, William Arthur** (1914–16); Sec.-Lieutenant, London Rgt.; Egypt, Gallipoli and France 10 months; Killed in action, 15th September, 1916.

Burt, Walter (1914–19); Sec.-Lieutenant, Royal Fusiliers and Manchester Rgt.; Service abroad 2 years 3 months.

Burtenshaw, Alfred Charles (1915–18); Sec.-Lieutenant, R.F.A.; France.

***Burton, Harold Sidney** (1914–15); Lance-Corporal, London Rgt.; France 2 months; Killed in action, 25th May, 1915.

Burton, Joseph Ashton (1914–17); M.M.; Sergeant, London Rgt.; France.

Burton, William James (1916–19); Lance-Corporal, R.E.

Busby, Alfred Richard (1915–19); Private, R.A.S.C. (M.T.); France 2 years 9 months.

Butcher, Ernest (1915–19); Battery Quartermaster-Sergeant, R.G.A.; France 2 years 11 months.

Butcher, Sydney Frederick (1915–19); Staff-Sergeant, R.A.S.C.; France 2 years 1 month.

Butler, Charles (1914–19); M.S.M. and Mentioned in despatches; 1st Class Staff Sergeant-Major, R.A.S.C.

Butler, Frank (1914–19); Mentioned for valuable services, *London Gazette*, 1917; Staff-Sergeant, County of London Yeomanry and Army Gymnastic Staff.

Butler, Robert Franklin (1918); Private, Middlesex Rgt.

Butler, William (1914–19); Lieutenant, London Rgt. and E. Surrey Rgt.; France 2 years 6 months, Italy 6 months.

***Buxton, Richard Percy** (1914–18); Captain, Oxfordshire and Buckinghamshire Light Infantry; France and Italy 2 years; Killed in action, 15th June, 1918.

Byrne, William (1916–19); Rifleman, Rifle Brigade.

Cairns, James Campbell (1914–19); D.C.M. and Bar; Company Sergeant-Major, Oxfordshire and Buckinghamshire Light Infantry; France 2 years.

Calderbank, John (1914–19); Lieutenant, London Rgt. and Machine Gun Corps; Malta 6 months, Gallipoli 4 months, Egypt 3 months, France 6 months, Italy 1 year.

Calverley, Alfred Horace (1916–19); Lance-Corporal, R.A.M.C.; France 2 years 2 months.

Cambourn, Frederick (1916–19); Leading Aircraftsman, R.N.A.S. and R.A.F.

***Cameron, Hume Smith** (1914–16); Captain, Norfolk Rgt.; France 18 months; Killed in action, 4th September, 1916.

Cammack, Walter (1915–17); Corporal, R.E.; France 11 months.

Campbell, Charles (1915–19); Battery Quartermaster-Sergeant, London Rgt. and R.G.A.; France 2 years.

Campbell, Edward Norman (1914–19); Staff-Sergeant, London Rgt. and Rifle Brigade; India 15 months, Burmah 2 years 1 month.

Campion, Ernest (1915–19); M.M.; Private, R.A.M.C.; France 2 years 2 months.

Campion, Walter John (1914–19); M.C.; Captain, Bedfordshire Rgt.

Camps, John William (1915–16); Private, Honourable Artillery Company.

***Canivet, Auguste François** (1914–16); *Brigadier interprète*, attached to British forces in France; Killed in action, 31st May, 1916.

Canty, H. (1915–19); Major, Loyal N. Lancashire Rgt.; France 3 years.

Card, Albert Walter Dudley (1915–19); Artificer, Honourable Artillery Company; France 1 year 7 months.

Carey, Alban Frank (1916–19); Private, R.A.S.C.

Carlton, Harold Stephen (1916–19); Gunner, R.G.A.; France 2 years 2 months.

***Carne, John Reeves** (1915–17); Sec.-Lieutenant, R. Sussex Rgt.; France 8 months; Died of wounds, 25th July, 1917.

***Carpenter, Edgar Stanley** (1914–15); Corporal, London Rgt.; France 5 weeks; Killed in action, 21st April, 1915.

Carpenter, George Frederick (1916–17); Lance-Corporal, R.A.S.C. and Welch Rgt.

Carr, Ernest (1915–19); Bombardier, R.F.A.; France 9 months.

Carr, Henry George (1914–19); Company Sergeant-Major, London Rgt.; France 2 years.

Carr, Thomas (1914–19); Flight-Sergeant, Essex Rgt. and R.A.F.; France 2 years 7 months.

Carr, Thomas Frederick William (1916–19); Private, London Rgt.; Salonica 6 months, Palestine 12 months, France 7 months.

***Carr, William Herbert** (1914–17); Company Sergeant-Major, London Rgt.; France 9 months; Killed in action, 20th September, 1917.

Carr, William Threlfall (1914–18); Quartermaster - Sergeant, R.F.A. and R.G.A.; France 5 months.

***Carrington, Harry John** (1914–18); Sergeant, Middlesex Rgt.; India 3 years 10 months; Accidentally killed, 19th July, 1918.

Carrington, John Wilfred (1915–19); Lieutenant, London Rgt.; France 1 year, Germany (Prisoner of war) 9 months.

***Carson, Frank Murray** (1914–15); Private, London Rgt.; France 2 months; Killed in action, 26th May, 1915.

Carter, Frederick James (1915–19); Corporal, R.E.; France 1 year 8 months.

Carter, George Edgar (1917–19); Corporal, R.A.F.

Carter, Robert (1915–18); Sapper, R.E.

Carter, Walter George (1916–19); Bombardier, R.G.A.; France 2 years 3 months.

Carter, William (1916–19); M.S.M.; Sergeant, R.A.F. and R.E.; France 2 years 5 months, Germany 4 months.

Cartwright, Bertram (1916–19); Corporal, R.E.

Cartwright, Isaiah Harold (1915–19); Sergeant, R.N.A.S. and R.A.F.

Case, Cecil (1916–19); Corporal, R.A.F.; France 3 years 1 month.

Cass, Edward Charles (1915–19); Corporal, R.A.M.C.; Egypt and Palestine 3 years.

Cassidy, James Joseph Francis (1915–19); Sergeant-Major, London Rgt. and Army Gymnastic Staff.

Catcheside, Edward Ernest (1914–15); Lieutenant, London Rgt., Rifle Brigade and Machine Gun Corps; France 2 years.

Catesby, Percy James (1914–17); Private, Middlesex Rgt.; Gibraltar 6 months, France 3 months.

Caughey, John William (1914–19); M.M.; Sergeant, Seaforth Highlanders; France 2 years 6 months.

Caukill, Francis (1918–19); Gunner, R. Marine Artillery.

Cave, Stephen James (1914–19); Company Quartermaster-Sergeant, London Rgt. and Labour Corps; France 2 months.

Chadwick, Claude Ralpho (1916–18); Sergeant, R.G.A.

Chalk, William James (1915–19); Corporal, R.E.

***Challice, Claude** (1914–15); Private, Devonshire Rgt.; France 1 month; Missing, 25th September, 1915.

***Chalmers, John Cyril** (1914–16); M.M.; Sec.-Lieutenant, Northumberland Fusiliers; France 1 year 9 months; Killed in action, 16th October, 1916.

***Chamberlain, Cyril John** (1914–17); Lieutenant, London Rgt. and Rifle Brigade; France 2 years; Killed in action, 7th October, 1917.

Chambers, Thomas Francis (1915–19); Private, R.A.M.C.; France 9 months, Italy 13 months.

Chamings, Reginald Gordon (1914–19); M.M.; Lieutenant, Oxfordshire and Buckinghamshire Light Infantry and Indian Army Reserve of Officers; France 1 year 7 months, India 15 months.

Champion, Harold (1914–19); Staff-Sergeant, R. Sussex Rgt. and Army Gymnastic Staff.

Chandler, Edwin Albert Brookbank (1914–19); Mentioned in despatches; Captain, London Rgt.; France 2 years 9 months.

Chandler, William Frank (1914–19); Corporal, London Rgt.; France 9 months.

Chanin, William (1915–19); Sec.-Lieutenant, R.G.A.; Macedonia 13 months.

Channon, George Creasy (1915–19); Twice mentioned in despatches; Sergeant, R.A.M.C.; Salonica 2 years 8 months.

Chaperlin, Sidney (1917–19); Sergeant, Labour Corps.

Chapman, Harold Arthur (1915–19); Lance-Corporal, R.A.M.C.; Gallipoli 2 months, Egypt 3 months, India 2 months, Mesopotamia 3 years.

Chapman, Hubert John (1915–19); Sergeant, Oxfordshire and Buckinghamshire Light Infantry and R.E.; France 3 years.

Chapman, Horace Lewis (1914–19); Mentioned in despatches; Captain, Dorsetshire Rgt.; France 1 month, Egypt and Palestine 3 years.

Chapman, Samuel Bartholomew (1914–19); Lieutenant, Middlesex Rgt. and Labour Corps; France 13 months, Egypt and Palestine 4 years.

Chapman, Thomas (1914–17); Corporal, London Rgt.

Chattaway, Arthur (1916); Private, Cambridgeshire Rgt.

***Chauvin, Eugene** (1916–18); Driver, R.G.A.; Salonica 15 months; Died, 17th November, 1918.

Cheek, James Alfred (1918); Private, R. Marine Engineers.

Cheshire, Frederic Thomas George (1916–19); Sergeant, R.N.A.S. and R.A.F.

***Chick, Albert George** (1914–17); Sergeant, London Rgt.; France 2 years 3 months; Killed in action, 14th April, 1917.

Chick, Herbert George (1914–19); Sergeant, R.W. Surrey Regiment and Labour Corps; Gallipoli 3 days, France 3 months.

Chilton, Charles Elijah (1916–17); Private, Royal Fusiliers.

Chipperfield, Gordon Frederick (1914–19); Company Sergeant-Major, Middlesex Rgt.; France 1 year 7 months.

Chitty, Albert George (1916–19); Sergeant, London Rgt.

Christian, George Frederick (1916–19); Private, R.A.S.C.

Chubb, John William Henry (1915–19); Corporal, R.E.; France 2 years 2 months.

Chunn, Alfred Oscar (1914–19); Company Quartermaster-Sergeant, Middlesex Rgt.; India 1 year 10 months, France 2 years.

Chunn, John William (1914–19); M.C., Mentioned in despatches; Lieutenant (acting Captain and Adjutant), London Rgt.; France 4 years.

Church, Archibald George (1915–19); D.S.O., M.C., Order of St. Vladimir and Mentioned in despatches; Major, Royal Artillery; France 2 years 11 months, Russia 7 months.

***Churcher, Edgar** (1914–17); Sec.-Lieutenant, London Rgt.; Salonica 6 months, France 1 year 11 months; Killed in action, 14th July, 1917.

Clancey, John Henry Edwards (1915–19); Driver, R.E.

Clare, William Horatio (1916–19); Private, R.A.M.C.; Salonica 5 months, Egypt and Palestine 1 year 9 months.

Clark, Alexander John (1918–19); Sergeant, Liverpool, London, and Middlesex Rgts.

***Clark, Colbert Walter** (1916–18); Lieutenant, London Rgt.; France 15 months; Killed in action, 26th April, 1918.

Clark, George Thomas (1914–19); Regimental Sergeant-Major, R.A.M.C.; Ambulance transports on voyages to France 2 years, Gallipoli and Egypt 1 year, Italy and Mediterranean Ports 1 year.

Clark, Percival William (1916–19); Lance-Corporal, Royal Fusiliers and Machine Gun Corps; France 1 year.

***Clarke, Blandford Edward** (1914–16); Private, Middlesex Rgt.; Gibraltar 5 months, France 14 months; Killed in action, 11th September, 1916.

Clarke, Ernest William Cecil (1915–19); Sec.-Lieutenant, R.E. and R.G.A.; France 1 year 8 months, Italy 2 months.

Clarke, Harold (1915–19); Mentioned in despatches; Lieutenant, Royal Fusiliers, Norfolk Rgt. and R.A.F.; France 9 months, Coastal Patrol 9 months.

Clarke, Harold Bailey (1917); Gunner, R.F.A.

Clarke, Thomas Harold (1915–19); Rifleman, London Rgt.; France 1 year 7 months.

Clayson, Ernest William (1916–19); Sapper, R.E.

***Cleall, Percy Cawdell** (1915–18); Lieutenant, Essex Rgt.; France; Died of wounds in Germany, 28th August, 1918.

Clear, Charles Alfred (1914–19); Mentioned for valuable services; Lieutenant, R.A.S.C.

Cleary, Frank Benjamin John (1915–19); Lance-Corporal, London Rgt.

Clegg, Harold (1915–19); Company Sergeant-Major, Honourable Artillery Company; France 9 months.

Clements, Nicholas (1916–19); Sergeant, Rifle Brigade.

Click, Thomas James (1915–19); Mentioned in despatches; Lieutenant, Middlesex Rgt. and Machine Gun Corps; France 2 years 6 months, Germany 3 months.

Cliff, Frank (1915–19); Sergeant, R.F.A.; France 2 years 5 months, Italy 4 months, Germany 4 months.

Clifford, William John (1918–19); Rifleman, London Rgt.; France 5 months.

Clinch, Ernest Arthur (1915–19); Corporal, R.N.A.S. and R.A.F.

Cloake, John (1915–19); Bombardier, R.A.S.C., R.F.A. and R.G.A.; France 10 months.

Cloke, Thomas (1916–19); Sapper, R.E.

Clothier, John Owen (1914–19); Lieutenant, Honourable Artillery Company and R.G.A.; Egypt 1 year, Aden 3 months, France 2 years 3 months, Germany 9 months.

Clubb, Ernest Alfred (1914–19); Major, Essex Rgt.; France 1 year 11 months.

Cobbett, William Frank (1917–19); Air Mechanic, R.A.F.

Cobbing, William Edward (1916–19); Second Writer, R.N.

Cobbold, Felix George (1916–19); 2nd Corporal, R.E.; Mesopotamia 1 year 8 months, India 7 months.

Cockburn, Alfred Mungo (1915–19); Corporal, R.A.M.C.; Egypt 6 months, France 2 years 7 months.

Cocks, George (1917–19); Gunner, R.G.A.; France 16 months, Germany 8 months.

Cocks, George Fry Mark (1917–19); Bombardier, R.G.A.; France 4 months.

Cocks, John Herbert (1917–19); Warrant Schoolmaster, R.N.

Cocks, William Pinney (1915–19); Corporal, R.A.M.C.; France 3 years 6 months.

Coe, Charles William (1916–17); Private, R.A.O.C.

Coffin, Percy Edwin (1915–19); Private, R.A.M.C. and R.G.A.; France 18 months, Italy 10 months.

Coghlan, Joseph (1915–19); Sergeant, R.F.A.; France 7 months, Macedonia 8 months, Egypt, Palestine and Syria 1 year 9 months.

Cohen, Elias (1916–18); Rifleman, London Rgt.; France 5 months.

***Cohen, John Isaac** (1915–17); Lance-Corporal, R. Wiltshire Yeomanry; France 8 months; Killed in action, 31st July, 1917.

Cohen, Joseph (1915–19); Corporal, R.W. Surrey Rgt.; France 2 years 1 month.

Colbeck, Harry (1916–19); Sapper, R.E.; France and Germany 4 months.

Cole, Edward Joseph (1915–19); Sergeant, R.A.F.; France 3 years.

Colebrook, Alfred Henry North (1914–20); Sapper, Middlesex Rgt. and R.E.; France 3 years, Germany 14 months.

***Coleman, Ernest James** (1916); Air Mechanic (2nd Class), R.F.C.; Accidentally killed, 10th June, 1916.

Coleman, Henry (1915–19); Corporal, R.N.A.S. and R.A.F.; France 11 months, Italy 1 week.

Coleman, Howard (1916–18); Sapper, R.E.; France 3 months.

Coleman, Percy Michael (1915–19); Corporal, R.E.; France 1 year 8 months.

Collier, John Francis (1916–19); Sergeant, R.F.A.; France 1 year 10 months.

Collings, Henry James (1918–19); Sergeant, Rifle Brigade.

Collins, Harold Wynne (1915–19); M.C., Mentioned in despatches; Major, R.G.A.; France 2 years 5 months.

Collinson, Harry Massey (1916–19); Lance-Corporal, R.A.M.C.

Comeau, Alfred James (1915–19); Writer (2nd Class), R.N.

Compton, Albert Sidney (1915–19); Lieutenant, London Rgt.; France 2 years.

Compton, Sydney Harry (1914–19); Lieutenant, London Rgt., Middlesex Rgt. and Labour Corps.

Connelly, Herbert Percy (1916–19); Staff-Sergeant, R.A.M.C.

Connor, William Christie (1915–19); Corporal, R.A.M.C.; France 1 year 10 months.

Conway, George James (1918–19); Bombardier, R. Marine Artillery.

Conway, Laurence (1914–17); Private, Middlesex Rgt.; Gibraltar and France 2 years.

***Cook, Alfred** (1914–16); Private, London Rgt.; France 16 months; Killed in action, 1st July, 1916.

Cook, Arthur James (1914–19); Lieutenant, R.W. Kent Rgt. and Labour Corps; Gallipoli 2 months, Palestine and Egypt 3 years 4 months.

Cook, Eric Trayler (1918–19); Acting-Sergeant, R.A.S.C.

Cook, George Henry (1916–19); 2nd Corporal, London Rgt. and R.E.; France 2 years 5 months.

Cook, George Marriott (1915–19); Corporal, R.A.M.C.; France 3 years 6 months.

Cook, George Percy (1917–19); Air Mechanic (1st Class), R.N.A.S.

Cook, Reginald Victor (1916–19); Sapper, R.E.; France 4 months.

Cook, Thomas John (1916–19); Sec.-Lieutenant, Machine Gun Corps and Devonshire Rgt.; France and Italy 1 year 5 months.

Cook, Victor Douglas (1914–19); Acting Captain and Adjutant, Royal Fusiliers; France 3 years 1 month.

Cooke, John Joseph Oliver (1916–19); Sapper, R.E.; France 6 months.

Coombs, Lewis Newton (1915–20); Captain, R.E. and R.A.O.C.; France 2 years 6 months.

Coombs, Thomas Herbert (1916–19); Private, Loyal N. Lancashire Rgt., Liverpool Rgt. and Army Cyclist Corps; France 1 year 9 months.

Cooper, Francis Theodore (1914–19); Sergeant, R.A.M.C.; France 3 years 3 months.

Cooper, George Jonathan (1918–19); Private, R.A.F.

Cooper, Willie Thomas (1914–18); Sergeant, Royal Fusiliers; France 13 months.

Corker, Robert John (1915–19); Private, R.A.M.C.; Mesopotamia 2 years 11 months.

Corless, Arthur James (1914–19); M.S.M.; Company Sergeant-Major, Middlesex and Norfolk Rgts.; Mesopotamia 2 years 3 months.

Cornell, Phillip Robins (1915–17); Lance-Corporal, Royal Fusiliers; East Africa 1 year 10 months.

Cornes, Harold William (1916–19); Sergeant, R.A.M.C.; Macedonia, Bulgaria and Constantinople 2 years 2 months.

Cornwell, Phillip David (1914–16); Private, Oxfordshire and Buckinghamshire Light Infantry; France 4 months.

Corrin, William Henry (1918–19); Corporal, R.E.

Costard, Percival Richard (1916–19); Air Mechanic, R.N.A.S. and R.A.F.

Cotsford, Henry John (1916–19); Lance-Corporal, Middlesex and E. Surrey Rgts.; France 1 year 11 months, Italy 3 months.

***Cotter, Cecil John** (1914–16); Sergeant, Middlesex Rgt.; Gibraltar 7 months, Egypt and France 5 months; Killed in action, 15th September, 1916.

Cotterell, William Eric (1914–19); Captain, London Rgt. and Labour Corps; France 2 years 11 months.

Cottom, Arthur (1917–19); M.S.M.; Sergeant, R.F.A. and R.E.; France 2 years.

Cottrell, Walter Harold Kennett (1914–17); Lance-Sergeant, London Rgt.; France 5 months.

Coumbe, Ernest W. (1915–19); Corporal, London Rgt. and Rifle Brigade; Burmah 3 years 4 months.

Court, Arthur Frederick (1915–19); Lance-Corporal, R.A.M.C.

Couzens, Reginald Churchill (1915–19); Private and Sapper, R.A.M.C., Middlesex Rgt., Machine Gun Corps and R.E.; France 10 months.

Cowan, David Miller Watson (1917–19); Air Mechanic (2nd Class), R.A.F.

Cowland, Albert George (1917–19); Corporal, R.E.; France 1 year 11 months.

Cox, Alfred Vincent (1918–19); Clerk (3rd Class), R.A.F.

Cox, Charles Albert (1914–19); Mentioned in despatches; Regimental Quartermaster-Sergeant, London Rgt. and Royal Fusiliers; France 6 months, Salonica 7 months, Palestine 1 year 8 months.

Cox, George James (1914–18); Sergeant, Royal Fusiliers and Machine Gun Corps.

Cox, James Wolseley (1914–19); M.C., Mentioned in despatches; Major, E. Lancashire Rgt. and Machine Gun Corps; France 2 years.

Crabtree, Edward John (1914–19); Sergeant, Middlesex Rgt.; Gibraltar 6 months, France 2 years.

Cracknell, Sidney Herbert (1914–19); Corporal, R.A.M.C.

Craine, Thomas Arthur (1915–19); Gunner, Honourable Artillery Company; Egypt and Palestine 3 years 2 months.

Crapper, Stanley Barrett (1916–19); Sapper, R.E.; France 8 months, Germany 3 months.

Crawford, John Randolph (1915–19); Sergeant, R.A.M.C.; Adriatic 4 months, Salonica 2 years 9 months.

Cray, Malcolm George Alfred (1916–17); Bombardier, R.G.A.

Crew, Stanley Frank (1914–19); Lieutenant, R.A.M.C. and R. Warwickshire Rgt.; Gallipoli and Egypt 16 months, France 4 months.

Cripps, Evans Cave (1915–19); Driver, R.A.S.C.; France 3 years.

Crispin, Reginald John Charles (1915–19); Sapper, R.E.; France 16 months, Palestine 14 months.

Croal, James Anderson (1915–19); Sergeant, King's R. Rifle Corps; France 11 months.

Crockett, Thomas (1914–19); Major, Black Watch and Machine Gun Corps; France 9 months.

Croft, Cyril Benson (1915–19); Sergeant, R.A.F.; France 9 months.

Crooks, Oliver Frederick (1917–19); Naval Schoolmaster (Chief Petty Officer), R.N.

Cross, Arthur (1914–19); Lieutenant, Royal Fusiliers and Loyal N. Lancashire Rgt.; France 1 year 7 months.

***Cross, Geoffrey Verriers** (1914); Sergeant, Oxfordshire and Buckinghamshire Light Infantry; Died, 9th November, 1914.

Crowe, Ernest Edmund (1916–19); Corporal, R.E. and Tank Corps.

Crowe, Richard Henry (1918–19); Acting Sergeant, R.A.F.; France 6 months.

Crowther, Herbert James (1916–19); Private, London Rgt. and Labour Corps; France 2 years.

Croxford, George Frederick (1918–19); Corporal, R.A.F.

Crump, Robert Ralph (1916–19); Company Sergeant-Major, Instructor of Musketry, Army School of Musketry and Light Gunnery.

Cruse, Charles James (1914–19); Regimental Quartermaster-Sergeant, London Rgt.

Crutchley, William Leigh (1914–19); Quartermaster - Sergeant, London and Middlesex Rgts.; France 5 months.

Crute, John (1918–19); Sergeant, Middlesex and Welch Rgts.; Germany 5 months.

Culliford, Walter Charles (1915–19); Private, London Rgt.

Cumming, Leonard S. (1915–19); Lieutenant, R.G.A. and R.E.; France 18 months.

Cunningham, Arthur William (1914–20); Twice mentioned in despatches; Staff-Captain, R.F.A.; France 3 years 7 months.

Cunningham, Charles Alexander (1915–19); Sec.-Lieutenant, R.F.A.; France 1 year.

Cureton, Henry Albert (1917–19); 2nd Aircraftsman, R.A.F.

Curtis, Adalbert Percy (1915–18); Sec.-Lieutenant, R.A.M.C. and R.G.A.; France 2 years 11 months.

***Curtis, William Strafford** (1914–15); Private, London Rgt.; France 2 months; Killed in action, 25th May, 1915.

Cusworth, Herbert (1915–19); M.C.; Lieutenant, R.A.M.C. and R.G.A.; France 2 years 6 months.

Cutts, Percy Walter (1916–19); Driver, R.A.S.C. (M.T.); Serbia 2 years 1 month.

***Dainty, Edward Joseph Patten** (1914–17); D.C.M.; Company Sergeant-Major, Royal Fusiliers; Malta, Egypt and Gallipoli 16 months, France 1 year 8 months; Accidentally killed, 8th November, 1917.

Dakin, Harry Percy (1914–19); Lieutenant, R.A.M.C. and Suffolk Rgt.; France 9 months.

Daly, Frederick (1916–19); Sec.-Lieutenant, R.G.A.

Danbury, Albert Samuel (1915–19); Mentioned in despatches; Acting Sergeant, R.A.M.C.; France 3 years 1 month.

***Dancer, Alfred Christopher** (1914–17); M.C.; Captain, Surrey Yeomanry and Dorsetshire Rgt.; Gallipoli and France 1 year 7 months; Killed in action, 4th October, 1917.

Danson, William (1914–19); Sergeant, Middlesex Rgt.; India 4 years 6 months.

Dare, Edward Cox (1914–19); D.C.M.; Sergeant, London Rgt.: France 8 months.

Datson, Albert (1915–19); Warrant Officer, R.N.; North Sea 2 years 6 months.

Davies, David John (1914–19); M.C. and Mentioned in despatches; Lieutenant, R. Welch Fusiliers; France 2 years.

Davies, Edwin Stewart (1915–19); Private, R.A.M.C.: France 2 years.

Davies, Gomer (1916–19); Private, R. Marine Light Infantry; Ægean Sea 16 months.

Davies, Henry (1915–19); Private, R.A.M.C.; France 7 months.

Davies, John James (1915–19); Lance-Corporal, London Rgt. and R.E.; France 6 months.

Davies, Percy William (1916–19); Private, Middlesex Rgt. and Machine Gun Corps; France 1 year 10 months.

Davies, Sidney Price (1914–19); Croix de Guerre, Ordre de Corps (French), Twice mentioned in despatches; Lieutenant, London Rgt.; France 10 months, Salonica 7 months, Palestine 1 year.

Davies, Thomas (1916–19); Sapper, R.E.; France 1 year 11 months.

Davies, Thomas Osman Yorath (1916–19); Sergeant, R.E.

Davies, Thomas Robert (1916–19); Lieutenant, R.G.A.

Davies, William (1916–19); Sapper, R.E.

Davies, William Henry (1915–19); Private, R.A.V.C.; Egypt 19 months, Palestine 1 year 8 months.

Davis, Edward Gordon (1915–19); Corporal, R.E.; Egypt 2 months, Salonica 6 months, France 2 years 1 month.

Davis, Edwin Gibson (1916–19); Lieutenant, R.E. and R.A.O.C.

***Davis, Ernest** (1914–16); Private, Royal Fusiliers; France 1 year; Died of wounds, 23rd July, 1916.

Davis, Frederick William (1914–19); Lieutenant, Middlesex Rgt., Yorkshire Light Infantry and Labour Corps; France 2 years 2 months.

Davis, Oscar William (1915–19); Sergeant, R.A.V.C.

***Davis, Wallace Howard** (1914–17); Sec.-Lieutenant, London Rgt. and Nottinghamshire and Derbyshire Rgt.; France 7 months; Killed in action, 1st July, 1917.

***Davis, William** (1914–16); Sec.-Lieutenant, Essex Rgt.; France 1 year; Killed in action, 18th October, 1916.

Davis, William Henry Powell (1916–19); Private, R.N.A.S. and R.A.F.

Dawes, Arthur Ernest (1914–19); D.C.M.; Company Sergeant-Major, London Rgt.; France 9 months, Salonica 7 months, Palestine 1 year.

Dawes, Spencer Thomas (1915–19); 2nd Corporal, R.E.

Dawkins, Dalton John Nicholson (1915–19); Lieutenant, London Rgt. and R.A.S.C.; France 2 years 2 months.

***Day, Charles Spencer** (1914–18); Sec.-Lieutenant, London Yeomanry and R.F.A.; Egypt, Gallipoli and France 14 months; Died of wounds, 25th April, 1918.

Day, Frank (1916–19); Corporal, London Rgt. and Army Education Corps; Salonica 8 months, Egypt and Palestine 16 months.

Day, George Edward (1914–19): Sergeant, London Rgt. and R.A.M.C.; Gallipoli 7 months, Egypt 15 months, Palestine and Syria 1 year 10 months.

Day, John Henry (1916–17); Rifleman, London Rgt.; France 3 months.

Dean, Arthur William (1916–19): Lieutenant, R.F.A.; Salonica 1 year 9 months, Caucasus 2 months.

Dean, Edward (1914–19): Lieutenant, King's R. Rifle Corps; France 2 years 1 month.

Dear, Arthur James (1915–19); Sapper, R.E.

***Dearing, Charles Alfred** (1914–18); M.M.; Sergeant, London Rgt.; France 3 years 1 month; Died of wounds, 16th April, 1918.

Delaney, Bernard Oswald (1916–18); Private, London Rgt. and R.A.S.C.; France 5 months.

Denham, Percy Clement (1915–19); Rifleman, London Rgt.; France 16 months.

***Denly, Charles John** (1914–16); Private, R.F.A.; France 17 months; Killed in action, 23rd August, 1916.

Denmark, Reuben Alan (1914–19); Mentioned in despatches; Captain, R.A.M.C. and R.A.O.C.

Dennett, George Edwin John (1914–19); Sergeant, London Rgt.

Denning, George John Berggren (1915–19); Mentioned in despatches; Lieutenant and Inspector of Ordnance Machinery, R.A.O.C.; France 3 years.

Denny, William John (1916–17); Private, E. Surrey and Liverpool Rgts.; France 6 months.

Denoon, Walter Neil (1914–19); Sergeant, R.A.M.C.; France 5 months, Salonica 9 months, Egypt 4 months, Palestine 11 months, India 3 months.

Derrick, Roland Frank (1914–19); Private, Middlesex Rgt.; India 4 years 4 months.

***Despicht, Leonard Terry** (1914–17); M.C. and Mentioned in despatches; Lieutenant, Bedfordshire Rgt.; France 2 years 2 months; Killed in action, 11th February, 1917.

***Dibble, Thomas Herbert** (1914–15); Private, London Rgt.; France 2 months; Killed in action, 26th May, 1915.

***Dick, Percy Charles** (1918–19); Lieutenant, R.A.F.

Dickinson, Albert Edward (1914–18); Lieutenant, Middlesex and London Rgts.; France 13 months.

Dickinson, Samuel (1916–19); 2nd Corporal, R.E.

Dickinson, William Horlick (1916–19); Sergeant, R.N.A.S. and R.A.F.

Digby, Arthur Edward (1914–19); Private, London Rgt.; France 2 years 9 months.

***Dimond, Leonard** (1914–17); Sergeant-Major, London Rgt.; France 8 months; Died of wounds, 21st September, 1917.

Dinmore, Hubert Dunstan (1915–19); Sapper, R.E.

Dix, Walter James (1914–19); Private, Middlesex Rgt.

Dixon, Daniel Thomas Gilbert (1915–19); 2nd Corporal, R.E.

Dobie, Tom (1916–19); Corporal, R.E.

Dobson, Percy Harold (1914–19); Quartermaster-Sergeant, London Rgt.; France 2 years.

Dockerill, Will Harry Atkin (1915–18); Sapper, R.E.

Dodd, Charles Baker (1916–19); 2nd Corporal, R.E.

Dodge, Samuel (1914–19); Sergeant, W. Surrey Yeomanry and Machine Gun Corps.

Dodge, Sidney Christopher (1915–18); Lieutenant, R.G.A.; France 8 months.

Dodson, George Edward (1916–19); Sergeant, R.N.A.S. and R.A.F.

Donaghy, Michael (1916–19); Lieutenant, R.A.V.C. and R.F.A.; France 15 months.

Donbavand, Thomas Egerton (1918–19); Private, E. Surrey Rgt.

Dooley, Herbert (1915–19); Bombardier, R.F.A.

Dooley, James Francis (1916–19); Gunner, R.G.A.; France 1 year 8 months.

Dooley, Patrick James (1914–16); Private, London Rgt.; France 2 months.

Doran, Daniel Joseph (1915–19); Sec.-Lieutenant, Essex and Yorkshire Rgts.; France 17 months.

Doughty, Frank Herbert (1914–19); Company Quartermaster-Sergeant, London Rgt.; France 2 years.

***Doughty, Harry James** (1914–15); Private, R.A.M.C.; France 3 months; Died, 12th October, 1915.

Downham, Theodore Leslie (1914–19); Mentioned in despatches; Lieutenant, Oxfordshire and Buckinghamshire Light Infantry and R.G.A.; France 1 year, Italy 15 months.

***Downes, Benjamin** (1914–18); Sec.-Lieutenant, London Rgt.; France, 1 year; Killed in action, 2nd June, 1918.

Dowsett, George William (1916–17); Pioneer, R.E.; France 1 year.

Doyle, John James (1915–18); Private, R.A.M.C.; France 18 months.

Drage, William Mark (1916–19); Sapper, R.E.; France 11 months.

Draisey, Henry (1915–19); Corporal, R. Marine Artillery; France 2 years 2 months.

Drake, Bertram Ernest (1915–19); Private, R.A.M.C.; Egypt and Palestine 2 years 11 months.

Drake, Wallace James (1915–19); Sapper, R.E.; France 8 months.

Drayton, Frederick James (1914–19); Company Sergeant-Major, London Rgt.; France 6 months, Salonica 6 months, Egypt 14 months, Palestine 6 months.

Drew, William Henry (1914–19); Staff-Sergeant, R.A.S.C.; Gallipoli 3 months, Mudros and Lemnos 1 month, Malta 1 month.

Drew, William Percival (1915–19); Private, R.A.M.C.; Salonica 2 years 9 months.

Drinkwater, Leonard (1914–19); M.S.M.; Regimental Sergeant-Major, Middlesex Rgt.; India 3 years 1 month, Mesopotamia 16 months.

Drury, Samuel Charles Portman (1914–19); D.C.M. and Bar, Médaille Militaire (French); Company Sergeant-Major, R.E.; France 4 years.

Du Bois, John Hubert Valencia (1916–19); Gunner, R. Artillery; France 2 years 3 months.

Ducé, Frederick Rayward (1916–18); Sapper, R.E.

Dudley, William (1916–19); Sergeant, R.A.M.C.

Duffill, Miles Wilfred (1915–17); Quartermaster-Sergeant, London Rgt.

Duley, John Alfred (1916–19); 2nd Corporal, R.E.

***Dunford, Herald James** (1915–16); Private, Honourable Artillery Company; France 4 months; Missing, 14th November, 1916.

Dunger, William George Ernest (1916–19); Sapper, R.E.; France 1 year 9 months.

Dunkerley, Joseph Braithwaite (1916–18); Sec.-Lieutenant, R.G.A.; France 16 months.

Dunton, Fred Douglas (1914–18); Sergeant, London Rgt.; France 12 months.

***Duprès, Ernest Cruzick** (1914–18); Captain, Royal Fusiliers; France 18 months; Killed in action, 28th August, 1918.

***Durban, Allan Edwin** (1914–17); Sergeant, Middlesex Rgt.; India 3 years; Died, 22nd August, 1917.

Durbin, John (1916–19); Corporal, R.N.A.S. and R.A.F.

***Dussauze, Henri Willem** (1914–15); *Sergent*, 103e *régiment d'infanterie;* France 12 months; Killed in action, 25th September, 1915.

Dyball, Robert (1916–19); Senior Reserve Attendant, R.N.; Escort duty between America and England.

Dyer, Charles Edwin (1916–18); Sergeant, R.A.M.C.

Dyer, Thomas Ernest (1914–19); Acting Corporal, Middlesex Rgt.; Gibraltar 5 months, France 16 months.

Dywien, Edward (1918–19); Corporal, R.A.F.

Eames, Herbert (1918–19); Private, Middlesex Rgt.

Earl, Harold Martin (1916–19); Sapper, R.E.

Earnshaw, Percy Harold (1915–18); Sec.-Lieutenant, London Rgt. and R.G.A.

Earthrowl, Eliab George (1915–19); Armourer Staff-Sergeant, R.A.O.C.; France 2 years 9 months.

***Eason, Henry** (1914–15); Sergeant, London Rgt.; France 11 months; Killed in action, 13th October, 1915.

Easter, Henry William (1916–19); Corporal, R.A.S.C.; France 2 years 11 months.

Easton, Edwin Guy (1916–19); Sapper, R.E.; France 7 months.

Eaton, Reginald Morris (1914–19); Private, London Rgt., Rifle Brigade and R. Irish Rgt.; France 16 months.

Ebbetts, Charles Edward (1916–18); Lance-Corporal, London Rgt. and R. Irish Rifles; France 13 months.

***Ebbetts, Sidney Arthur** (1914–16); Corporal, London Rgt.; France 15 months; Killed in action, 1st July, 1916.

Ebdon, William Alan (1914–19); Captain, London Rgt.

Edden, Henry Percival (1914–16); Quartermaster-Sergeant, R.A.M.C.

Eden, Humphrey Edward (1914–19); Mentioned in despatches; Regimental Quartermaster-Sergeant, R.A.M.C.; France 13 months, Egypt 9 months, Palestine 9 months.

Eden, James Arthur (1915–19); Sapper, R.G.A. and R.E.; France 1 year.

Edwards, David Llewellyn (1914–17); Corporal, London Rgt.; France 2 months.

Edwards, George Victor (1916–18); Private, N. Staffordshire Rgt.

Edwards, Harold (1916–19); Corporal, R.A.M.C.; Italy 2 years.

***Edwards, John Evans** (1918); Private, R.A.F.; Died, 22nd October, 1918.

Edwards, James Henry (1915–19); Acting Sergeant, R.A.M.C.; Balkan States 3 years.

Edwards, Robert Reuben (1916–19); Corporal, R.E.

Edwards, Thomas Arthur (1914–19); M.C.; Lieutenant, R.N.V.R., A.P.C., R. W. Kent Rgt. and R. Naval Division.

Eggar, Alfred James (1916–19); 2nd Corporal, R.E.; France 2 years.

Elliott, Alfred (1916–19); Sec.-Lieutenant, R.F.A.; France 15 months.

***Elliott, Bertie** (1914–17); Sergeant, Oxfordshire and Buckinghamshire Light Infantry; France 1 year; Killed in action, 7th April, 1917.

Elliott, Harry Courtenay (1915–19); Mentioned in despatches; Flight-Sergeant, London Rgt. and R.A.F.

Elliott, Sidney George (1915–19); Acting Flight-Sergeant, London Rgt. and R.A.F.; Egypt 1 year 9 months.

***Elliott, Victor Maurice** (1914–16); Lance-Sergeant, Oxfordshire and Buckinghamshire Light Infantry; France 2 months; Died of wounds, 1st July, 1916.

***Elliott, Walter Leonard** (1914–16); Lieutenant, Rifle Brigade; France 17 months; Accidentally killed, 21st November, 1916.

Ellis, Albert William (1916–19); M.C.; Sec.-Lieutenant, R.G.A.

Ellis, John Procter (1916–19); 2nd Corporal, R.E.

Ellison, Gilbert Joseph (1914–19); Corporal, London Rgt.; France 1 year 8 months.

Elsey, William George (1916–18); Sapper, Royal Fusiliers, R. Sussex Rgt. and R.E.; France 5 months.

Elsom, John Arthur (1914–19); Sapper, R.E.

Endean, Frederick George (1916–19); Acting Sergeant, King's R. Rifle Corps.

England, Herbert Arthur (1918–19); Air Mechanic (2nd Class), R.A.F.

England, Walter William (1914–19); Private, London Rgt.; France 5 months, Prisoner of war 3 years 7 months.

Engledow, Frederick William (1918–19); Private, London Rgt.; France 4 months.

English, Charles Edward (1916–19); Lance-Corporal, R.E.; France 6 months.

***Erwood, Charles Malcolm Williams** (1914); Lance-Corporal, Bedfordshire Rgt.; Died, 17th December, 1914.

Erwood, Frank Charles Elliston (1917–19); Sergeant, R.E.; France 2 years, Germany 3 months.

Etherington, Herbert Maurice (1914–19); Regimental Quartermaster-Sergeant, London Rgt. and R.D.C.

Evans, Arthur Edward (1918–19); Sergeant, R.A.F.

***Evans, John** (1915–18); M.C.; Sec.-Lieutenant, Coldstream Guards and Royal Fusiliers; France 1 year; Died of wounds whilst a prisoner of war, 22nd September, 1918.

Evans, Morgan (1914–19); Sec.-Lieutenant, Royal Fusiliers and R. Welch Fusiliers.

Evans, Owen Lewis (1914–19); Sergeant, London Rgt.; France 18 months.

Evans, Richard Albert (1915–19); Corporal, R.A.M.C.; France 2 years 11 months.

Evans, Victor Stanley (1915–19); Private, Honourable Artillery Company; France 13 months, Italy 14 months.

Evans, Walter (1914–19); Lieutenant, R. Welch Fusiliers and Montgomery Yeomanry: France 3 months.

Evans, Walter Bristow (1915–19); Corporal, R.A.S.C.; France 3 years 8 months.

Evans, William (1916–19); Corporal, R.N.A.S. and R.A.F.; North Russia 10 months.

Everett, William Henry (1914–17); Corporal, Essex Rgt.

Eveson, Thomas Edward (1915–19); Mentioned in despatches; Captain, R.F.A.; France 2 years 11 months, Germany 4 months.

Evison, Charles William George (1918–19); Air Mechanic (3rd Class), R.A.F.; Italy 3 months.

Evans, Lewis James (1918–19); 3rd Clerk (General), R.A.F.

Fairbairn, Horace John (1916–19); Gunner, R.G.A.; France 15 months.

Fairclough, Frederick Stafford (1914–19); Lieutenant, Middlesex Rgt. and Queen Victoria's Own, Indian Army; India 3 years 2 months, Mesopotamia 11 months, Persia 5 months.

***Fairley, Philip Ernest** (1914–19); D.C.M.; Captain, R. Irish Rifles; France 2 years 1 month; Died of wounds, 4th February, 1919.

Farrants, Maurice Charles (1915–19); Private, R.A.M.C.; Egypt and Palestine 3 years.

Farrow, Richard Ronald Frank (1916); Private, Middlesex Rgt.; France 4 months.

***Favell, Arthur** (1914–16); Lance-Corporal, London Rgt.; France 9 months; Killed in action, 18th May, 1916.

Fay, Archibald Michael (1915–19); Private, R.A.M.C.

Fay, Arthur Farnham (1915); Private, London Rgt.

Felix, Hugh (1916–19); Corporal, R.F.C. and R.A.F.; France 1 year.

***Fell, William John** (1915–16); Private, Royal Fusiliers; France 10 months; Killed in action, 8th September, 1916.

Fenn, Henry Cuthbert (1916–19); Sapper, R.E.; France 2 years.

Fennell, Harry George (1914–16); Company Quartermaster-Sergeant, London Rgt.

Fenner, Gilbert Frank (1915–19); Armourer Staff-Sergeant, R.A.O.C.

Fenning, Robert William (1915–19); M.B.E. (military division); Lieutenant, London Rgt. and R.E.

Fennings, Alfred James (1916–19); Lance-Corporal, R.E.; France 18 months, Germany 2 months.

***Ferguson, Henry Horatio Edward** (1915–17); Captain, Highland Light Infantry; France 16 months; Died of wounds, 23rd September, 1917.

Ferguson, William V. (1915–19); Sapper, R.E.

Festorazzi, Bertram (1916–19); Corporal, R.A.M.C.

Field, Benjamin Jacob (1915–16); Corporal, R.E.

***Field, William James** (1914–17); M.C.; Sec.-Lieutenant, Royal Fusiliers; Malta, Egypt, Gallipoli and France 3 months; Killed in action, 31st July, 1917.

Filby, Leonard Charles (1915–19); Lance-Corporal, R.E.; France 2 years 4 months, Germany 8 months.

Fillis, Edgar (1915–19); Corporal, R.G.A.; France 2 years 9 months.

Finan, John Patrick (1917–19); Private, R.A.S.C.

Finerman, Louis (1916–19); Corporal, R.A.M.C.; France 2 years 5 months.

Finnie, William Stoddart (1916–19); 2nd Corporal, R.E.

Fisher, Edward Albert (1917–18); Signaller, acting Bombardier, R.F.A.

Fisher, George Harry (1914–19); M.C.; Sec.-Lieutenant, R.A.M.C. and R.F.A.; France 2 years, Egypt 2 months, Salonica 1 year 7 months.

Fisher, Hubert William (1914–19); M.C.; Lieutenant, Middlesex Rgt.; Gibraltar 6 months, France 14 months.

***Fisher, John** (1916–18); Private, R.E.; Died, 16th August, 1918.

Fisher, William Henry (1917–19); 2nd Lieutenant, London Rgt.

Fitch, Lincoln Cowell (1914–17); Corporal, Oxfordshire and Buckinghamshire Light Infantry; France 1 year 9 months.

Fitch, Stanley Henry (1914–15 and 1917–19); Private, London and Essex Rgts.; France 6 months.

Fleetcroft, John Stratford (1915–19); Lance-Corporal, Machine Gun Corps.

Fletcher, Evan (1914–19): Corporal, London Rgt.; France 4 months.

Fletcher, Ernest John (1916–19); Lieutenant, R.E.; France 10 months, Egypt 18 months.

Fletcher, Frank (1915–19); Sergeant, R.F.A.

Fletcher, Frederick (1915–19); Corporal, R.A.M.C. and R.G.A.

Flood, Thomas Arthur (1915–19): Sergeant, London Rgt.; France 10 months, Salonica 7 months, Palestine 1 year.

Flower, Frederick James (1914–18); Corporal, City of London Yeomanry and County of London Yeomanry; Egypt 2 years, Palestine 5 months.

Foden, Oliver Cornelius (1916–19); Corporal, R.G.A.

Foley, George Ernest (1914–17); Corporal, Oxfordshire and Buckinghamshire Light Infantry and R.D.C.

***Foley, John** (1914–16); Captain, Northumberland Fusiliers; France 6 months; Died of wounds, 1st July, 1916.

Foot, William Ewart (1916–19); Rifleman, London Rgt. and Rifle Brigade; Salonica 5 months, Palestine 4 months, Egypt 16 months.

Forbes, Reginald Henry (1915–19); Acting Staff-Sergeant, R.A.M.C.; Egypt 2 weeks, Balkans 3 years 2 months.

Ford, Arthur (1914–19); Mentioned in despatches; Sergeant, R.A.M.C.; France 11 months, Salonica 3 years 1 month, Russia (Caucasus) 2 months.

Ford, George William (1915–19); Corporal, R.A.M.C.; France 9 months.

Ford, Henry Charles (1914–19); M.C. and Bar; Lieutenant, R. Welch Fusiliers; France 3 years.

Ford, Leonard Charles (1916–19); Lieutenant, R.E.; France 9 months.

Ford, Mark (1914–18); Sergeant, R.E.

Fordham, Charles Howard Atkinson (1916–19); Bombardier, R.F.A.

Forrest, Edward Methuen (1914–19); Sergeant, Middlesex Rgt.; India 4 years 2 months.

Forrest, William Robert Edwin (1917–19); Air Mechanic (1st Class), R.N.A.S. and R.A.F.; France 16 months.

Forrester, Leonard Cecil (1915–19); Private, R.A.S.C. (M.T.); France 4 years 1 month.

Forsey, Wallace (1916–19); Staff-Sergeant, R.N.A.S. and R.A.F.; France 3 months.

Forsyth, William John (1914–19); Lieutenant, London Rgt.; France 4 months, Salonica and Egypt 2 years 1 month.

Foskett, Horace Walter (1915–19); Sergeant, R.A.F.

Foster, David (1914–19); M.S.M.; Sergeant-Major, Dorsetshire Rgt., R.F.A. and R.G.A.; France and Germany 4 years 1 month.

Fothergill, Frederick (1918–19); Rifleman, Rifle Brigade and King's R. Rifle Corps; France 3 months.

Foulger, Wilfred (1915–19); Sergeant, Honourable Artillery Company; France 14 months, Italy 12 months, Austria 1 month.

Fountain, Harry Charles J. (1916–19); Sergeant-Clerk, R.A.F.

Fowler, John George (1914–19); Sergeant, London Rgt.; France 2 years.

Fowler, Harold Elliott (1917–19); Corporal, R.E.; France 15 months.

Fowler, Joseph (1914–19); Sergeant, London Rgt.; France 9 months, Salonica 6 months, Palestine 1 year.

Fowler, William Fortune (1918–19); Seaman, R.N. Experimental Station.

***Fox, Charles James** (1914–16); Sec.-Lieutenant, R.W. Kent Rgt.; France 16 months; Killed in action, 22nd July, 1916.

Fox, Henry John (1914–19); Lance-Corporal, London Rgt. and Rifle Brigade; India 3 years 5 months.

Fox, James George (1914–19); Sergeant, Middlesex Rgt., Royal Fusiliers and Intelligence Corps; Gibraltar 7 months, Egypt 9 months, France 3 years 2 months.

Fox, John (1916–19); Air Mechanic (1st Class), R.N.A.S. and R.A.F.

Fox, Julius (1916–19); Sergeant, R.G.A. and Royal Fusiliers; France 1 year, Palestine, Egypt and Salonica 1 year 8 months.

Fox, Sidney Solomon (1915–19); Private, R.A.M.C.; Salonica 3 years 4 months.

Fox, Thomas Francis (1914–20); Lieutenant, Middlesex Rgt. and Indian Army Reserve; India 3 years 11 months, Mesopotamia 1 year.

Fox, Walter (1914–18); Private, Middlesex Rgt.; Gibraltar 6 months, Egypt 8 months, France 9 months.

Fox, William Henry (1916–19); Aircraftsman (1st Class), R.A.F.

Foxcroft, John George (1916–19); Air Mechanic (1st Class), R.A.F.; France 12 months.

France, Robert (1915–19); Sergeant, London Rgt.; France 1 year 9 months, Salonica 6 months, Palestine 1 year.

Francis, Tom (1914–19); Sec.-Lieutenant, R.W. Surrey and R.W. Kent Rgts.; India 1 year 9 months.

Francis, William Alfred George (1916–19); 2nd Corporal, R.E.

Frankis, Percy (1915–19); Private, R.A.M.C.; France 2 years 11 months.

Franks, Lawrence Lazarus (1915–19); Captain, R.A.M.C.; France 2 years 11 months.

Fraser, Robert (1916–19); Gunner, R.G.A.

***Free, Ernest Robert** (1916–18); Sec.-Lieutenant, Honourable Artillery Company and R.G.A.; France 9 months; Died, 16th July, 1918.

Freeborn, Sydney (1915–19); Private, R.A.M.C.; France 6 months, Salonica 6 months, Egypt and Palestine 1 year 8 months.

Freeborough, Charles (1914–19); Mentioned in despatches; Lieutenant, 15th Hussars and R.E.; France 3 years 3 months, Germany 4 months.

Freeman, Albert Maskell (1914–19); Corporal, R.A.S.C.; France 4 years.

Freeman, Arthur James (1916–19); Lance-Corporal, R.E.; France 1 year 8 months.

***Freeman, Francis Basil** (1914–16); Sec.-Lieutenant, R. Warwickshire Rgt.; France 14 months; Killed in action, 1st July, 1916.

Freeman, George Joseph (1916–18); Sergeant, R.G.A.

Freeman, William Bede (1915–19); Company Quartermaster-Sergeant, R.E.; France 2 years 11 months.

Freemantle, William Henry (1914–19); Sergeant-Major, Army School of Musketry and Light Gunnery.

French, Alfred Ernest (1915–19); Sapper, R.E.

French, Clement Charles (1915–19); Sergeant, R.A.M.C.; Lemnos 2 months, Egypt 3 years 1 month.

French, Edward John (1914–16 and 1917–19); Sergeant, London Rgt. and R.A.F.; France 9 months.

French, Edward William (1914–19); M.C., Mentioned in despatches; Lieutenant, acting Major, Army Cyclist Corps.

French, Sydney James (1915–19); Lieutenant, London Rgt.; France 7 months.

Freudemacher, Sydney Gordon (1914–19); Company Quartermaster-Sergeant, Oxfordshire and Buckinghamshire Light Infantry; France 2 years 8 months.

Friend, James Gardiner John (1917–19); Acting P.O. Mechanic, R.N.A.S.; France 2 months.

Friend, Sydney Richard (1917–19); Air Mechanic, R.N.A.S.

***Froome, Charles William** (1914–16); D.C.M.; Company Sergeant-Major, London Rgt.; France 1 year 8 months; Killed in action, 1st July, 1916.

Frost, Tom (1914–19); Lance-Sergeant, Middlesex Rgt.; India 4 years 6 months.

Fry, Percy James (1916); Rifleman, London Rgt.

Fuller, Leonard Samuel (1914–19); Staff-Sergeant, R.A.M.C.; France 3 years 10 months.

Fullerton, William (1915–19); Armourer Staff-Sergeant, R. Buckinghamshire Hussars and R.A.O.C.; France 1 year 11 months.

Fullford, Edwin Frank (1915–18); Sapper, R.E.

Fulton, John Owen (1914–19); Lieutenant, London Rgt.; France 16 months, Salonica 6 months, Egypt and Palestine 9 months, Italy 3 months.

Furlong, Walter John (1915–19); Sapper, R.E.

Furner, Thomas Ross (1914–19); Lieutenant, Royal Fusiliers, R.A.S.C., R. Welch Fusiliers and Tank Corps; France 15 months.

Furze, Reginald James (1914–19); Lance-Corporal, R.F.A. and R.E.; France 3 years 11 months.

Gallery, George (1914–17); Private, London Rgt.; France 3 months.

Galsworthy, John Ford (1914–17); Sergeant, London Rgt.; Malta 8 months.

Gardner, Herbert (1915–19); Sergeant, R.A.M.C.; France 2 years 8 months.

Gardner, Joseph Thomas (1915–19); Lance-Corporal, London Rgt.; France 2 years.

Garton, Frederick George (1914–19); Lieutenant, R.W. Surrey Rgt. and Oxfordshire Hussars; France 6 months.

Gascoigne, Edward (1915–19); Private, London Rgt.

Gaskin, Leonard Hugh (1915–19); Sergeant, R.A.M.C.

Gasser, James George (1914–19); M.S.M.; Company Sergeant-Major, Seaforth Highlanders.

***Gatehouse, Herbert Charles** (1914–18); Sergeant, R.A.M.C.; France 3 years 7 months; Died, 6th November, 1918.

Gatehouse, Robert (1914–19); Corporal, E. Surrey Rgt.; India 3 years 2 months, Mesopotamia 15 months.

Gatter, Frank (1915–19); Sec.-Lieutenant, Honourable Artillery Company, Machine Gun Corps and Tank Corps; France 16 months.

Geard, Cecil William (1915–19); Regimental Sergeant-Major, R.A.M.C.; Gallipoli and Palestine 3 years 6 months.

Geen, Lesley Stevens (1914–19); Air Mechanic (2nd Class), London Rgt. and R.A.F.; France 4 months, Egypt 1 year.

George, Benjamin James (1914–19); Company Sergeant-Major, Seaforth Highlanders; France 3 years 8 months.

George, Taliesin (1917–19); Seaman, H.M.S. Champion; North Sea 17 months.

George, William Ewart (1916–19); Corporal, R.N.A.S. and R.A.F.; France 2 years 2 months.

Germaney, William Thomas (1915–19); M.M.; Corporal, R.A.M.C.

***Gethin, Percy Francis** (1914–16); Sec.-Lieutenant, London and Devonshire Rgts.; France 7 months; Killed in action, 28th June, 1916.

Gibbs, Albert Edward (1915–17); Regimental Sergeant-Major, R.A.M.C.

Gibbs, Frank Archibald (1918–19); Corporal, R.A.F.

Gibson, James (1915–19); M.M. and Bar; Sergeant, R.A.M.C.

Gibson, John (1914–19); M.S.M.; Regimental Quartermaster-Sergeant, London Rgt.; France 3 years 8 months.

Gibson, John Rowland (1915–19); Lieutenant, London Rgt., R.F.C., and R.A.F.; France 6 months.

Gibson, Stanley Rutherford (1916–19); Lieutenant, R.G.A.; France 9 months, Malta 4 months.

Gidwell, John (1914–19); Sergeant, King Edward's Horse and Lancashire Fusiliers; France 2 years 3 months, Germany 2 months.

Gilbert, Harry Charles (1916–19); Corporal, R.N.A.S. and R.A.F.

Giles, Ernest Edward (1916–19); Sapper, R.E.

Giles, Frederick Chaston (1914–19); Sergeant, London Rgt. and R.E.; France 2 years.

Gill, William James (1914–19); Sergeant, London Rgt.; France 8 months, Salonica 7 months, Palestine 1 year.

Gilliard, Ernest William (1915–19); Telegraphist, R.N.V.R.

Gillham, Frederick James (1916–17); Lance-Corporal, R.W. Surrey Rgt.

Gillham, George William (1915–19); Private, R.A.M.C.; France 18 months, Italy 14 months.

Gillon, Charles (1916–19): Chief Petty Officer, R.N.A.S. and R.A.F.

Gimson, Percy John (1914–18); Corporal, R.F.A.; France 11 months.

Gingell, Leonard Victor Hand (1915–19); Lieutenant, Wiltshire Rgt. and Machine Gun Corps; France 18 months.

Glass, Henry Douglas (1916–19); Corporal, R.A.F.; Salonica 1 year 8 months, Egypt 4 months.

***Gleadall, James** (1914–16); Private, Middlesex Rgt.; Egypt and France 3 months; Killed in action, 15th September, 1916.

Glennie, Charles (1914–19); Corporal, Middlesex Rgt. and R.A.F.; Gibraltar 3 months, France 1 year.

Glover, Albert Joseph (1915–19); Bombardier Signaller, R.F.A.

Godden, Walter Lewis (1918–19); Private, R.W. Kent Rgt. and Somersetshire Light Infantry; France 3 months.

Godfrey, Ernest Allan (1914–18); M.C.; Lieutenant, London Rgt. and R. Marine Light Infantry; France 5 months.

Godfrey, Henry Arthur (1915–19); Corporal, R.A.S.C.; France 2 years 8 months.

Godman, Arthur Andrew (1915–19); Sergeant, R.A.M.C.; Serbia 3 months, Salonica 2 years 7 months.

Godwin, Gilbert Arthur (1915–19); Flight-Sergeant, R.A.F.

Goffin, Frederick Stanley (1915–19); Corporal, London Rgt.; France 2 years 6 months.

Göhns, Charles Alfred (1915–19); Corporal, R.A.M.C., Royal Fusiliers and Intelligence Corps; France 2 years 4 months.

Goldfarb, Maurice (1916–19); Corporal, R.A.S.C.; Macedonia 1 year 10 months.

Golding, Frederick Joseph Othello (1916–19); Corporal, London Rgt.; France 9 months, Germany (Prisoner of war) 8 months.

Goldstein, Simon (1915–19); Lance-Corporal, Rifle Brigade.

Goldthorpe, Frederick James (1916–19); Third Writer, R.N.

Goode, William Henry (1916–19); Private, R.F.A. and Border Rgt.; France 2 years 1 month.

Goodger, Percy Albert (1916–19); Lance-Corporal, R.A.O.C.; France 1 year 8 months.

Goodhead, Fred Hubert (1914–19); Sergeant, London Rgt. and R.E.; France 10 months.

Goodison, Arthur Leathley (1915–19); Corporal, R.A.M.C.; Egypt 3 years 1 month.

Goodland, Percy Harold Edward (1914–19); M.S.M.; Sergeant, Coldstream Guards; France 3 years 11 months.

Goodwin, Alfred John (1914–19); Sergeant, R.A.M.C. and London Rgt.; France 2 years.

Goodwin, Robert Percy (1914–19); Lieutenant, R.A.M.C. and Suffolk Rgt.; France 15 months, Salonica 15 months.

Goose, Thomas Halley (1914–19); Mentioned in despatches; Sec.-Lieutenant, Inns of Court O.T.C.

Gordon, Alexander (1916–19); Sapper, R.E.; France 8 months.

***Gordon, Graham Henry** (1914–16); Private, R.G.A.; France 1 year 7 months; Died of wounds, 4th October, 1916.

Gosling, Charles Frederick (1914–19); Company Quartermaster-Sergeant, Middlesex Rgt.; Gallipoli 3 months.

Gostling, John Albert Norman (1918–19); Corporal, R.A.F.

Gould, Albert (1915–19); Sec.-Lieutenant, London Rgt., R.E. and Tank Corps; France 3 years 1 month.

Gould, Thomas Andrew (1916–19); Signaller, R.G.A.; France 2 years.

Graham, Twentyman (1916–19); Corporal, R.E.

Grant, George Compton (1915–19); Rifleman, London Rgt.; France 2 years 6 months.

Grant, Herbert Percy (1914–17); Corporal, E. Surrey Rgt. and R.D.C.

Graves, Harold (1915–19); Sec.-Lieutenant, R.G.A. and R.F.A.; France 15 months.

Gravestock, Walter John (1915–19); Corporal, R.A.M.C.; Egypt 3 years 1 month.

Gray, Ben Thomas (1916–19); Sapper, R.E.; France 8 months.

Grayston, Henry Francis (1915–19); Sec.-Lieutenant, R.A.S.C.; France 2 years.

Green, Albert Arthur (1914–19); Private, Middlesex Rgt.; India 4 years 3 months.

Green, Charles Henry (1916–19); Sec.-Lieutenant, R.G.A., R.N.A.S. and R.E.; France 1 year.

Green, Charles Samuel (1918–19); Driver, R.E.; France 4 months.

***Green, Louis** (1916); Pioneer, R.E.; France 3 months; Killed in action, 24th August, 1916.

Green, Peter (1917–19); Sergeant, London Rgt.

Green, Samuel (1916–19); Signaller, R.F.A.; France 18 months.

Greenan, Frank (1914–19); Private, R.A.M.C.; Gallipoli 4 months, Egypt 8 months, Palestine 1 year 9 months.

Greengrass, Frederic (1915–19); Staff-Sergeant, R.A.M.C.; Balkans 2 years 10 months.

Greenshields, John Benjamin (1916–19); Sapper, R.E.

Greensmith, Eric Bosworth (1914–19); Captain, Royal Fusiliers and Nottinghamshire and Derbyshire Rgt.; France 1 year 11 months, Germany (Prisoner of war) 7 months.

***Greenwood, Alfred George** (1914–17); Lance-Corporal, Middlesex Rgt.; France 3 months; Killed in action, 10th April, 1917.

Greenwood, Harold (1915–19); Private, R.A.M.C.; Salonica 16 months, Bulgaria 5 months.

Greenwood, John Henry (1918–19); Mechanic (2nd Class), R.N.

Greenyer, Leslie Vincett (1915–19); Sapper, R.E.; France 1 year 10 months.

Gregory, Arthur John Castell (1915–19); Lieutenant, R.E. and R.A.O.C.; France 3 years 10 months.

Gregory, Charles Thomas Walter (1916–19); Corporal, R.E.

Grey, Alfred Lewis (1915–19); M.M.; Sec.-Lieutenant, London Rgt., R.E. and Tank Corps.

Griffin, George Edwin (1917–19); 2nd Corporal, R.E.; France 1 year 8 months.

Griffiths, Benjamin John (1915–19); Lieutenant, Gloucestershire and Welch Rgts.; France 1 year.

Griffiths, Daniel Fred (1916–19); Stoker Engineer's Writer, H.M.S. Gibraltar.

Griffiths, Edwin George (1916–19); Private, R. Sussex Rgt.; France 2 years 4 months.

Groom, Alfred George (1914–20); M.S.M.; Corporal, London Rgt.; France 4 years.

Gross, Stanley Abraham (1918–19); Private, Royal Fusiliers; Egypt 6 months.

***Groves, Leonard** (1916–17); Private, London Rgt.; France 1 year; Killed in action, 24th July, 1917.

Grubb, Walter Thomas (1914–19); Lieutenant, R.N. and R.A.F.

Gully, Francis Robert Curtis (1914–19); Gunner, R.G.A.; Private, Labour Corps.

Gunter, Thomas James (1914–19); M.M.; Lance-Corporal, R.E. and Oxfordshire and Buckinghamshire Light Infantry; France 2 years 3 months.

Gurr, Herbert William (1916–19); Leading Aircraftsman, R.A.F.

Gurton, William Henry (1914–19); Lance-Corporal, R.A.M.C. and R.E.; Malta 15 months, Egypt 3 months, Macedonia 2 years 6 months, Russia 2 months.

Gutteridge, Trevor Frank (1915–19); M.S.M.; Corporal, R.A.M.C.

***Guy, Harold Courtney** (1915–17); Private, Grenadier Guards; France 10 months; Killed in action, 23rd July, 1917.

Gwyther, Lewis Mansel (1916–19); Sapper, R.E.

Gymer, Alfred (1916–19); Corporal, R.A.S.C.

Haddy, Alfred John (1916–19); Lance-Corporal, R.E.

Hadida, Jacob (1916–19); Sapper, R.E.; France 2 years 9 months.

Hague, Charles Hoardon (1914–19); Lance-Corporal, R.E.; France and Italy 4 months.

Hague, Frank Thomas (1916–19); Lance-Corporal, R.A.O.C.

***Hale, Reginald Alfred** (1916–18); Lance-Corporal, Surrey Yeomanry and R. Berkshire Rgt.; France 7 months; Killed in action, 3rd October, 1918.

Hales, Bernard Claud (1914–19); D.C.M.; Company Sergeant-Major, London Rgt.; France 12 months, Salonica 7 months, Palestine 12 months.

Haley, Frederick John (1916–19); Sapper, R.E.

Haley, Harold Percy (1915–19); Company Sergeant-Major, Army Gymnastic Staff.

Halifax, Henry Christopher (1918–19); Sergeant, London Yeomanry and Yorkshire Hussars.

Hall, Edward Cecil (1914–18); Lieutenant, London and Dorsetshire Rgts.; France 11 months, India 6 months, Palestine 2 years.

Hall, Frank Gardner (1915–19); Mentioned in despatches; Captain, R.F.A.; France 17 months, Italy 5 months.

Hallam, James (1914–19); Company Quartermaster-Sergeant, London Rgt.; France 6 months.

Halliwell, George Albert (1916–19); Gunner, R.G.A.

***Hamer, Walter Henry** (1916–17); Lance-Corporal, Royal Fusiliers; France 2 months; Killed in action, 21st May, 1917.

Hamilton, Frederick William (1916–19); Sapper, R.E.

***Hammond, Arthur Joseph** (1914–15); Private, London Rgt.; France 3 months; Killed in action, 25th May, 1915.

Hammond, Sydney Alexander (1914–19); M.M.; Sergeant, London Rgt.; France 3 years 3 months, Germany (Prisoner of war) 9 months.

Hampton, Frank (1914–19); Private, R.A.M.C.; France 1 year, Salonica 3 years 6 months.

Hancock, Ernest Thomas Gordon (1915–19); M.C.· Lieutenant, R.G.A.; France 17 months.

***Hancock, John Leonard** (1916–17); Corporal, Royal Fusiliers; France 5 months; Killed in action, 16th June, 1917.

***Handley, Herbert Eustace** (1914–15); Sec.-Lieutenant, London Rgt.; France 2 months; Killed in action, 25th May, 1915.

Handley, William Luke (1915–19); Lance-Corporal, R.A.M.C.; Egypt 1 year 11 months, Palestine 16 months.

Hansen, Harry (1915–19); Private, R.A.M.C.; France 2 years.

***Hard, William Thomas Stanley** (1914–18); Lieutenant, Middlesex Rgt. and Royal Fusiliers; Gibraltar, Egypt and France 1 year 8 months; Killed in action, 23rd March, 1918.

***Harden, William Frederick** (1916–18); R.N.V.R.; Service at sea; Missing, blowing up of H.M.S. Glatton, 16th September, 1918.

Harding, Wesley Eldred (1914–18); Lieutenant, Durham Light Infantry and Gloucestershire Rgt.; France 5 months.

Harding, William Victor (1917–19); Sergeant, R.G.A.

Hardy, Edgar Charles George (1916–19); Sapper, R.E.; France 3 months.

***Harland, George** (1914–17); Sergeant, Middlesex and London Rgts.; Gibraltar, Egypt and France, 2 years 3 months; Killed in action, 3rd May, 1917.

Harlow, Richard (1917–19); Regimental Sergeant-Major, London Rgt.

Harman, Thomas Alexander (1916–19); Lance-Corporal, R.E.

Harper, David (1916–18); Private, Staffordshire Rgt.

Harper, George Alfred (1916–17); Private, London Rgt.

Harris, Frank (1916–19); Corporal, King's R. Rifle Corps and Machine Gun Corps; France 8 months, Mesopotamia 16 months.

Harris, Henry Bolton (1918–19); Air Mechanic, R.A.F.

Harris, Henry James (1916–19); Able Seaman, R.N.V.R.

Harris, Henry Thomas (1917–19); Sergeant, R.A.F.

Harris, Herbert (1915–19); Sergeant, Liverpool Rgt.

***Harris, Herbert Cecil** (1914–16); Mentioned in despatches; Captain, R.W. Kent Rgt.; France 13 months; Killed in action, 3rd July, 1916.

Harris, Pinkus (1917); Rifleman, King's R. Rifle Corps.

Harris, Percy Gerrard (1915–19); Corporal, R.A.M.C.; France 3 years.

Harris, Walter William (1915–19); Air Mechanic (1st Class), R.A.F.; France 3 years 1 month.

Harrison, Arthur William (1916–19); Bombardier, R.G.A. and R.F.A.; France 1 year 9 months.

Harrow, Percy Avery (1916–19); Private, Middlesex Rgt. and Lancashire Fusiliers; France 6 months, Prisoner of war 8 months.

***Hart, Albert Richard** (1914–17); Lance-Corporal, Middlesex Rgt.; Gibraltar 4 months, France 1 year 9 months; Killed in action, 23rd February, 1917.

***Hart, Ernest** (1914–15); Sergeant, Norfolk Rgt.; France 5 months; Killed in action, 13th October, 1915.

Hart, William Percy (1915–19): Mentioned in despatches; Staff-Sergeant, R.A.S.C.; France 2 years 9 months.

Hart, William Samuel (1914–19); Acting Quartermaster-Sergeant, London Rgt.; France 4 years 2 months.

Hartshorn, James (1916–19): Bombardier, R.G.A. and R.F.A.; France 1 year 9 months.

***Haselden, Edgar Adolphus** (1914–16); Captain, W. Yorkshire Rgt.; France 2 months; Died of wounds, 9th July, 1916.

Haslam, Walter Truman (1916–19); Sapper, R.E.

Hasler, Douglas William (1915–19); Private, R.A.M.C.; France 2 years 11 months.

***Hatcher, Edward William** (1914–16); Lance-Corporal, London Rgt.; France 16 months; Missing, 1st July, 1916.

Hathaway, J. L. (1914–19); Sec.-Lieutenant, Hampshire Rgt.; France 11 months.

***Hattam, Harold Colin** (1915–17); Lieutenant, Suffolk Rgt.; France 3 months; Killed in action, 26th September, 1917.

Hatten, Ernest Walter (1915–19); Corporal, London Rgt.; France 9 months, Salonica 6 months, Palestine 12 months.

***Hatton, Frederick James** (1915–18); Corporal, R.F.A.; France 2 years 1 month; Killed in action, 4th April, 1918.

Hatton, Sydney Frank (1914–19); Sergeant, County of London Yeomanry; Egypt 8 months, Sinai 8 months, Salonica 8 months, Palestine 15 months.

***Haward, Alfred Edward** (1916); Private, London Rgt.; France 4 months; Killed in action, 8th October, 1916.

Haward, Reginald Walter (1916–19); Sergeant, R.A.F.

Hawes, Arthur George (1914–17); Regimental Quartermaster - Sergeant, London Rgt.

Hawkes, Ernest Warren (1914–17); Staff-Sergeant, R.A.M.C.; France 16 months.

Hawkes, William George Warren (1915–19); M.S.M.; Acting Quartermaster-Sergeant, R.A.M.C.; France 3 years 7 months.

Hawkins, Eric Arnold (1916–19); Rifleman, London Rgt.; Salonica and Macedonia 9 months, Egypt 1 month, Palestine 14 months, France 8 months.

Hawkins, Harold William (1915–16); Sergeant, R.W. Surrey Rgt. and Army Gymnastic Staff.

Hawkins, Leonard (1915–19); Flying Officer, R.A.F.; Egypt 3 years.

Hawkins, Philip Albert (1915–19); Corporal, R.F.A.; France 2 years 11 months.

Hawkins, Reginald Henry (1915–19); Private, R.A.M.C.; France 6 months.

Hawksworth, John Herbert (1914–19); M.S.M.; Sergeant-Major, R.A.M.C.; France 2 years 1 month.

Hayes, Philip Charles (1916–19); Private, R.W. Surrey Rgt.; France 2 years 4 months.

***Haynes, Henry Hellas** (1914–17); Corporal, R.N. Lancashire Rgt.; France 17 months; Killed in action, 16th June, 1917.

Haynes, Charles Richard (1915–19); Lieutenant, E. Surrey Rgt.; France 3 months.

Hayward, Albert Henry Dennis (1917–19); Driver, R.F.A.; Mesopotamia 3 months, Palestine 1 year.

***Head, Wilfred Arthur** (1916); Private, London Rgt.; France 3 months; Died of wounds, 16th September, 1916.

***Heard, Ernest Henry** (1916–18); Corporal, London Rgt.; France 13 months; Killed in action, 2nd October, 1918.

Heard, John Frederick Leonard (1916–19); Lieutenant, Honourable Artillery Company and R.G.A.; France 2 years.

Heard, Percy Albert (1915–19); Corporal, R.E.

Heather, Edwin (1914–19).

***Heatly, Henry Francis** (1914–15); Lieutenant, Yorkshire Rgt.; France 5 months; Killed in action, 22nd February, 1915.

Hellicar, George Huntley (1914–19); Twice mentioned in despatches; Captain, Lancashire Fusiliers; France 3 years 10 months.

***Helyar, Samuel Ebenezer** (1916–17); Lance-Corporal, S. Staffordshire Rgt.; France 6 months; Killed in action, 27th September, 1917.

Hemingway, John Ford (1914–18); Private, R.A.M.C.; France 8 months.

Henderson, John Robert (1914–19); Sergeant-Major, R.F.A.; France 3 years 11 months.

Henderson, Ralph Bushill (1915–19); Mentioned in despatches; Acting Lieutenant-Colonel, R.G.A.; France.

Henderson, Robert Francis Gurney (1916–19); Sapper, R.E.

Hennessey, Edward Thomas (1916–19); Corporal, R.E.

Hennessey, Hendry Ernest (1918–19); Private, London Rgt.

Hennig, Conrad Wilfred (1914–19); Corporal, E. Surrey Rgt. and R.E.; India 1 year, Mesopotamia 1 year.

Hennion, Frederick Joseph (1914–19); Sergeant, R.A.O.C.

Henstridge, Charles Leonard (1914–19); M.C.; Captain, Middlesex and London Rgts.; Gibraltar 6 months, Egypt 8 months, France 2 years 9 months.

Herbert, George Charles (1914–19); Sergeant, Middlesex Rgt.; Mesopotamia 8 months, India 3 years 3 months.

Herbert, Thomas Edwin (1918–19); Rifleman, London Rgt.

Herbert, William Frank (1914–18); Lieutenant, London Rgt.; France 5 months.

Herrick, Percy Edwin (1916–19); Private, London Rgt.; Salonica 5 months, Egypt and Palestine 14 months, France 5 months.

Herring, Albert Thomas (1916–17); Gunner, R.F.A.; France 6 weeks.

Herring, Victor Roland (1914–17); Private, Oxfordshire and Buckinghamshire Light Infantry; France 3 months.

Hewett, Wallace Horatio (1914–19); Sergeant, London Rgt. and Machine Gun Corps; France 1 year.

Hewish, Edward Alfred (1916–19); Corporal, R.A.F.; France 2 years 2 months.

Hewitson, Stanley Robert (1915–19); Sergeant, R.A.M.C.

Hewitt, Stanley Edward (1914–17); Sec.-Lieutenant, Royal Fusiliers; France 1 year 8 months.

Hewlett, Alfred Henry (1914–15); Rifleman, London Rgt.; France 4 months.

Hewson, George (1917–19); Sergeant, R.A.O.C.; Baghdad.

Hewson, Sidney Thomas (1916–19).

Heyes, Joseph (1914–19); Sec.-Lieutenant, Essex Rgt.; Gallipoli 4 months, Egypt 1 year, Palestine 3 months, France 18 months.

Hibbert, Clifford (1914–19); Lieutenant, R.F.A.

Hickford, Herbert Arthur (1914–19); Sergeant, Middlesex Rgt.; India 4 years 6 months.

Hicks, Alfred (1916–19); Sec.-Lieutenant, R.G.A.; France 16 months.

Higdon, Reginald Cecil (1914–19); Flight-Sergeant, Middlesex Rgt. and R.A.F.

Higgins, Peter Joseph (1915–19); Lance-Corporal, R.A.S.C.; France 2 years 8 months.

***Higginson, George Neal** (1914–16); Mentioned in despatches; Lieutenant, Royal Fusiliers and Lancashire Fusiliers; France 1 year; Killed in action, 23rd November, 1916.

Higgs, James William (1914–19); Captain, Middlesex Rgt., Trench Mortars and Intelligence Corps; Gibraltar 6 months, Egypt 9 months, France 8 months, North Russia 12 months.

High, Edward Hayhow (1915–19); Driver, R.A.S.C.; Macedonia 1 year 10 months, Russia (Batum) 3 months.

Hilditch, Norman Salmon (1916–19); Warrant Schoolmaster, R.N.

Hiley, Ernest John (1917–19); M.M.; Rifleman, London Rgt. and King's R. Rifle Corps; France 1 year 2 months.

Hiley, Francis Ernest (1916–19); Sergeant, R.A.F.

Hill, Arthur Edwin (1914–19); Sergeant, E. Surrey Rgt. and R.E.; France 2 years 5 months.

Hill, Albert John (1915–19); Sergeant, King's R. Rifle Corps and Oxfordshire and Buckinghamshire Light Infantry; India 3 years 1 month.

Hill, Frank Cyril (1915–17); Private, London Rgt.; France 3 months.

Hill, Henry (1917–19); Private and Aircraftsman (1st Class), Rifle Brigade and R.A.F.

Hill, Henry William (1916–19); Corporal-Instructor, R.E. and Tank Corps.

***Hill, Jack** (1915–18); Corporal, London Rgt.; France 1 year 9 months; Killed in action, 28th March, 1918.

***Hill, Sidney Ernest** (1914–16); Sergeant, London Rgt.; France 10 months; Killed in action, 23rd May, 1916.

Hillier, Charles Sheppard (1918–19); Private, London Rgt.

Hills, J. T. (1914–18); D.C.M., Mentioned in despatches; Company Sergeant-Major, London Rgt.; France 1 year, Macedonia 6 months, Palestine 1 year, Germany 1 month.

Hindell, William Arthur (1915–19); Sapper, R.E.

Hindson, Joseph Carruthers (1916–18); Private, Middlesex Rgt.; France 14 months.

Hitchings, Charles (1914–19); Sec.-Lieutenant, R.A.M.C. and R.A.F.; France 6 months, Salonica 6 months, Palestine 2 years.

Hocken, Wilfred Arthur (1918–19); Private, Rifle Brigade, London Rgt. and R.D.C.

Hodge, Joseph Horton (1916–19); Lieutenant, R.G.A.; France 2 years 10 months.

***Hodges, Horace Sydney** (1914–17); Company Sergeant-Major, Middlesex Rgt.; France 4 months; Died of wounds, 5th October, 1917.

Hodges, William John (1916–19); Corporal, King's R. Rifle Corps, Hampshire Rgt., Labour Corps and R. Inniskilling Fusiliers; France 1 year 8 months.

Holdich, Karl Pascal (1914–19); Private, R.A.M.C.; Balkans 2 years 1 month.

Holland, Frederick Hamilton (1914–19); Lieutenant, R.A.M.C. and R.A.O.C.; Salonica 1 year.

Holland, Frederick Walter (1914–19); Staff-Sergeant, London Rgt. and R.A.O.C.; Salonica 2 years.

Holland, Horace Edward (1914–19); Sergeant, Berkshire Yeomanry and R.E.; Egypt 6 months, Gallipoli 2 weeks.

Holliman, Charles Stanley (1917–19); Bombardier, R.G.A.; France 16 months.

Hollman, John (1914–19): Company Sergeant-Major, London Rgt., King's R. Rifle Corps and British W. Indies Rgt.; France 3 years 5 months, Italy 4 months.

***Holloway, Fred** (1915–17); Lance-Corporal, London Rgt.; France 5 months; Killed in action, 17th June, 1917.

Holloway, Frank Horace (1914–19); Mentioned in despatches; Private, Middlesex Rgt.; Gibraltar 5 months, France 3 years 6 months.

Holloway, Robert John (1915–19); Sec.-Lieutenant, Artists' Rifles and Liverpool Rgt.; France 4 months, Salonica 4 months.

Holmberg, John (1915–19); Corporal-Mechanic, R.F.C. and R.A.F.; France 2 years 3 months.

Holmes, John William (1914–19); Acting Regimental Quartermaster-Sergeant, London Rgt. and Rifle Brigade; Burma 3 years 6 months.

Holroyd, Cyril (1914–17); Sec.-Lieutenant, London Rgt. and Labour Corps.

Holway, Ernest (1916–19); Sapper, R.E.

Holyoake, Leonard William Charles (1916–19); Corporal, Army Cyclist Corps, Yorkshire and Lancashire Rgts. and R.E.; France 1 year, Italy 6 months, Salonica 8 months.

Homer, Ernest (1915–19); Private, R.A.M.C.

Honeysett, James Stanley (1914–19); M.S.M., Mentioned in despatches; Regimental Sergeant-Major, London Rgt. and Intelligence Corps; France 4 years 4 months.

Honeywood, Bertram George (1916–19); Sapper, R.E.

Honnor, Albert John (1914–19); Mentioned in despatches; Lieutenant, Hampshire Rgt. and Garhwal Rifles; India 4 years 2 months.

***Hook, Edgar** (1915–18); Sergeant, Oxfordshire and Buckinghamshire Light Infantry and R. Inniskilling Fusiliers; France 5 months; Killed in action, 4th August, 1918.

Hooker, James (1914–16); Sergeant, London Rgt.

Hooper, John William (1914–19); M.S.M.; Sergeant, R. Warwickshire Rgt.; France 3 years 11 months.

Hopkins, Frederick (1914–19); M.S.M.; Regimental Sergeant-Major, R.A.M.C.; France 3 years 3 months.

Hopkinson, Ernest (1915–19); Sergeant, R.A.V.C.; France 3 years 9 months.

Hordley, William Howard (1915–17); Corporal, R.A.S.C.

***Horn, Charles Bennett** (1915–18); Private, R.A.M.C.; Died, 17th July, 1918.

Horne, Frederick Andrew (1914–18); Acting Captain, R.F.A.; France 2 years 9 months.

Horne, Sidney Meers (1916–19); Leading Mechanic, R.N.A.S. and R.A.F.

Horniblow, Edward Charles Thomas (1916–19); Sergeant, R.E.

***Hornsby, William** (1914–17); Sec.-Lieutenant, Duke of Cornwall's Light Infantry and Somersetshire Light Infantry; France 11 months, Egypt and Salonica 11 months; Killed in action, 21st August, 1917.

Horonzick, Solomon (1915–16); Private, Bedfordshire and Suffolk Rgts.

Horsford, Algernon (1914–19); Lieutenant, Middlesex Rgt.; France 2 years.

Horsley, Francis (1915–19); Telegraphist, R.N.V.R.

Horton, Harold (1914–19); M.C.; Captain, Middlesex and Gloucestershire Rgts.; Gibraltar 7 months, Egypt 9 months, France 2 years.

Hosken, Frank (1915–19); Flight-Sergeant, R.A.F.

Hoskin, William Alexander (1914–19); Company Sergeant-Major, London Rgt.; France 3 months, Prisoner of war 10 months.

Howard, Cecil Thomas (1915–19); Private, R.A.M.C.; France 2 years.

Howe, Albert Henry (1918–19); Air Mechanic (3rd Class), R.A.F.

Howe, Arthur William (1915–19); Private, R.A.M.C.; France 7 months.

Howell, Leonard Colston (1914–19); Sergeant, Middlesex Rgt.; India 4 years 5 months.

Howells, Albert Henry (1918–19); Private, R.A.F.

Howells, Stafford J. (1916–19); Lieutenant, R.N.V.R.

Howitt, John Edward (1914–19); Sec.-Lieutenant, Oxfordshire and Buckinghamshire Light Infantry, Wiltshire and R. Berkshire Rgts.; France 9 months.

Hoxey, George Morris Frederick (1914–19); Sergeant, R.F.A.; France 1 year 10 months, Salonica 6 months, Palestine 1 year 8 months.

Hubert, Charles Richard (1915–19); M.S.M., Mentioned in despatches; Sergeant-Major, R.A.M.C.; East Africa 3 years.

***Huddart, Alfred** (1916–18); Private, Nottinghamshire and Derbyshire Rgt.; France 13 months; Killed in action, 23rd March, 1918.

Huggins, Claud Arthur (1915–19); Sec.-Lieutenant, R.G.A.; Macedonia 1 year 11 months.

Hughes, Charles Henry (1916–19); Bombardier, R.F.A. and R.G.A.; France 1 year 11 months.

Hughes, Owen (1916–19); Acting Sergeant, R.E.

Hughes, William James (1915–16); Private, London Rgt.

Huitt, Henry Robert (1915–19); Sergeant, R.A.M.C.

Hulland, William Everard (1915–18); Company Quartermaster-Sergeant, 2nd City of London Yeomanry; France 2 years.

Humby, Leonard Percival (1916–18); Private, R.A.M.C.

Humphreys, George Fowler (1914–18); Mentioned in despatches; Lieutenant, Middlesex Rgt.; France 16 months, Italy 4 months.

Humphreys, Thomas Arthur (1916–19); Sergeant, London Rgt.

Humphreys, William Arthur (1915–19); M.M. and Bar; Acting Company Sergeant-Major, R.E.; France 3 years 8 months.

Humphries, Louis (1915–19); Captain, R.A.O.C.; France 3 years.

Humphrys, William Arthur (1916–19); 2nd Corporal, R.E.

Hunt, Alfred John (1916–19); Sapper, R.E.

Hunt, George Lacy (1916–19); Private, R.F.A., Border Rgt. and Labour Corps; France 1 year 9 months.

Hunt, Reginald Clarence George (1917–19); Corporal, R.N.A.S. and R.A.F.

Hunt, Samuel Syrus (1918–19): Sergeant, London and Middlesex Rgts.

Hurd, Rupert Fred Stanley (1914–19); Sergeant, Oxfordshire and Buckinghamshire Light Infantry; France 15 months.

Hurley, Frederick William (1916–19); Corporal, R.E.

Hurren, Sydney Alfred (1916–19); M.C.; Lieutenant, R.G.A.; France 1 year 8 months.

Huskins, Thomas 1914–19); Sergeant, Royal Fusiliers.

Huskisson, Stephen Samuel (1915–19); Sergeant, R.E.

Hussey, Thomas Alfred (1915–19); Sergeant, R.A.M.C.; Italy 1 year 9 months.

Hutchinson, Fred (1917–19); Private, R.A.S.C.; France 18 months.

Hutchinson, George Knight MacGowan (1914–19); Captain, E. Surrey Rgt., Duke of Cornwall's Light Infantry and Corporal, R.E.; France 2 years 8 months.

Hutchinson, Henry William (1916–19); Meteorological Assistant, R.N.A.S. and R.A.F.

Hutchinson, Norman Oscar (1914–19); Private, Middlesex Rgt.; Gibraltar 6 months, France 3 years 5 months.

Hutchinson, Walter (1914–19); Sergeant, Middlesex Rgt. and Royal Fusiliers; Gibraltar 7 months, Egypt 8 months, France 1 year 8 months.

***Hutson, Frank William** (1915–17): Private, London Howitzer Brigade; France 2 years 9 months; Accidentally killed, 3rd November, 1917.

Hutton, John (1918–19); Corporal-Instructor, R.A.F.

Hymans, Alfred (1916–19); Private, King's R. Rifle Corps, Durham Light Infantry; France 2 years.

***Hymans, Louis Henry** (1916–17); Lance-Corporal, Royal Fusiliers; France 10 months; Died of wounds, 21st September, 1917.

Hyslop, Albert (1915–19); Sergeant, R.A.M.C.

Iden, William Arthur (1916–19); Sapper, R.E.; France 18 months.

Inder, Jack Prescott (1915–19); Armourer Staff-Sergeant, R.A.O.C.; Egypt 3 years 6 months.

Innes, Angus Hardie (1914–19); Company Quartermaster-Sergeant, London Rgt.; France 14 months, Salonica 13 months, Palestine 5 months.

Instrell, Alan Wilfred (1914–19); Sergeant, R.F.A. and London Rgt.; France 10 months.

Ireland, William George (1916–19); Private, London Rgt. and Machine Gun Corps; France 6 months, Salonica 6 months, Egypt and Palestine 9 months.

Irvin, John George (1916–19); Private, London Rgt.; France 1 year 9 months.

Jack, Robert Hunter (1915–19); Lieutenant, Essex Rgt.

Jackson, George Thomas (1916–17); Private, Suffolk Rgt.

Jackson, Henry Frederick (1917–19); Lance-Corporal, R.A.O.C.

Jackson, Stanley David (1915–19); Lieutenant, Middlesex, R.W. Surrey, R.W. Kent and Suffolk Rgts.; Salonica 1 month, Italy 16 months.

***Jackson, Walter** (1916–18); Private, London Rgt.; France 3 months, Egypt and Palestine 10 months; Died, 13th October, 1918.

***Jago, George Frederick** (1915–18); Driver, R.A.S.C.; Mesopotamia 1 year 7 months; Died, 30th November, 1918.

James, Arthur Henry (1915–19); Lance-Corporal, R.A.M.C.; Egypt 4 years 5 months.

James, Arthur Lloyd (1916–19); Corporal, R.E.

James, Frederick John (1917–19); Sapper, R.E.

James, John (1914–19); Captain and Quartermaster, R.A.M.C.; France 2 years 9 months.

James, John Ernest (1914–18); Private, Royal Fusiliers, London Rgt. and R.A.P.C.; France 1 year.

James, Philip Gilbert (1914–19): Corporal, London Rgt.; France 6 months.

***James, Sidney Whitehouse** (1915–18); Air Mechanic, R.N.A.S.; Italy 9 months; Accidentally killed, 9th June, 1918.

Janau, Henry Victor (1918–19); Acting Sergeant, Royal Fusiliers; France 9 months.

Jarvis, Albert John (1916–19); Sapper, R.E.; France 14 months.

Jarvis, Francis Reid Adalbert (1915–19): 2nd Corporal, R.E.

Jarvis, Walter Thorning (1918–19); Private, R.A.F.

Jay, Henry Eric (1914–19); Sergeant, London Rgt. and R.F.A.; France 2 years 9 months.

Jay, Walter James (1916–19); Sergeant, R.A.S.C. (M.T.) and S. Wales Borderers.

Jeal, William Percy (1914–19); Company Sergeant-Major, London Rgt. and Durham Light Infantry; France 1 year, Salonica 6 months, Egypt 1 year.

Jeans, Harold William (1915–19); Lieutenant, Middlesex and R.W. Surrey Rgts. and Labour Corps.

***Jefcoate, Frank** (1915–19); O.B.E., Mentioned in despatches; Captain, Suffolk Rgt. and R.F.C.; Egypt and Palestine 3 years 1 month; Accidentally killed, 14th February, 1919.

Jefford, William Edward (1916–19): Sergeant-Mechanic, R.A.F.

Jeffs, Charles (1915-19); Private, R.E. and R.A.M.C.; France 16 months.

Jehu, Frederick Charles (1915–19); 2nd Corporal, R.F.A. and R.E.; France 3 years 6 months.

Jelbart, Percy (1916–19); Pioneer, R.E.; France 2 years 5 months.

Jenkin, Herbert Edward (1916–19); Sapper, R.E.; France 3 months.

Jenkin, Stanley (1914–16): Private, London Rgt.; France 7 months.

Jenkins, Edgar Charles (1915–19); Signaller, Royal Fusiliers; France 2 years 6 months.

Jenkins, Emrys Robert (1916–19); Driver, R.A.S.C. (M.T.); East Africa 2 years.

Jenkins, Ernest Ivor (1914–19); Company Quartermaster-Sergeant, R.E.

Jenkins, Joseph Clay (1914–19); Sergeant, R.A.M.C.; Salonica 1 year.

Jenman, Cyril James (1914–19); Lieutenant and Quartermaster, R.A.M.C.; France 3 years 10 months.

Jenn, Frank Yeo (1916–19); Sec.-Lieutenant, R.G.A.

Jennings, Sidney (1914–19): Company Quartermaster-Sergeant, Seaforth Highlanders; France 2 years 7 months.

***Jennings, Sidney James** (1915–18); Lieutenant, E. Surrey Rgt. attached R.E.; France 2 months; Missing, 30th March, 1918.

Jennings, Thomas Albert (1917); Private, R.A.O.C.

Jenrick, Gilbert Blackmore (1914–19); Captain, Middlesex Hussars and Duke of Cornwall's Light Infantry; France 2 years.

Jenvey, Henry Charles (1916–19); Mentioned in despatches; Lieutenant, R.G.A.; France 1 year.

Jeremiah, Trevor Richards (1917–19); Air Mechanic (2nd Class), R.N.A.S.

***Jessop, Robert** (1914–16); Private, Middlesex Rgt.; Gibraltar 7 months, Egypt 8 months, France 4 months; Killed in action, 9th September, 1916.

***Jeynes, Thomas George** (1914–16); Corporal, R. Warwickshire Rgt.; France 16 months; Missing, 1st July, 1916.

Johnson, Frederick Burleigh (1916–19); Sapper, R.E.; France 7 months.

Johnson, George Benjamin (1915–19); Staff-Captain, Leicestershire Rgt. and General Staff; France 3 years 2 months.

Johnson, Henry Shephard (1916–19); Sapper, R.E.

***Johnson, James William** (1914–17); Lieutenant, Middlesex Rgt.; India 1 year, France 8 months; Missing, 30th November, 1917.

Johnson, Leonard Charles (1914–19); Sergeant, Surrey Yeomanry.

Johnson, William (1914–19); Lieutenant, Bedfordshire Rgt. and Royal Fusiliers; France 3 years.

Johnson, William Francis (1916–19); Ordinary Seaman, R.N.V.R.

Johnston, Irving (1914–17); Lance-Corporal, Durham Light Infantry.

Johnstone, Alexander (1916–19); Corporal, R.E.

***Jolly, Ernest Robert** (1916–17); Corporal, E. Surrey Rgt.; France 3 months; Killed in action, 2nd October, 1917.

Jolly, John Arthur (1914–19); Corporal, City of London Yeomanry and Machine Gun Corps; Gallipoli 5 months, Egypt 16 months, Salonica 8 months, Palestine 8 months, France 8 months.

Jones, Arthur Benjamin (1915–19); Italian Medal, 1918; Lieutenant, R. Welch Fusiliers and R.G.A.; France 6 months, Italy 12 months.

Jones, Arthur Cyril (1915–19); 2nd Corporal, R.E.; France 1 year 9 months.

Jones, Arthur Lewis (1916–19); Rifleman, King's R. Rifle Corps; France 2 years 4 months.

Jones, Arthur Tyler (1914–19); M.S.M., Mentioned in despatches; Staff Sergeant-Major, London Rgt.

Jones, Bertram William (1916–19); Sapper, R.E.; France 3 months.

Jones, Charles (1916–19); Corporal, R.E.

Jones, David John (1915–19); Private, R.A.S.C.; France 2 years 1 month.

Jones, Edward (1914–19); Lance-Corporal, Middlesex Rgt.; Egypt 2 weeks, India 3 years 9 months, Mesopotamia 7 months.

Jones, Edgar Isaiah (1914–19); Sapper, London Rgt. and R.E.; France 2 years 10 months.

Jones, Frank (1916–19); Sapper, R.E.

Jones, Isaac George (1915–16); Private, R.A.M.C.

***Jones, Herbert Frederick Chamberlain** (1914–17); Lance-Corporal, London Rgt.; France 4 months; Killed in action, 16th May, 1917.

Jones, John Edward (1915–19); Acting Staff-Sergeant, R.A.M.C.; France 3 years 8 months.

Jones, Jonathan Leonard (1915–19); Private, Honourable Artillery Company; France 2 years 3 months.

Jones, John Stoddard (1914–19); Private, Middlesex Rgt.; Gibraltar 6 months, France 14 months.

***Jones, Joseph Sydney** (1915–19); Corporal, R.A.M.C.; Egypt 3 years; Died, 5th April, 1919.

Jones, Leonard Hay (1915–19); Sapper, R.E.

Jones, Percy Wynn (1914–19); Lieutenant, Middlesex Rgt. and R.A.S.C.; Gallipoli 6 months, Palestine and Egypt 3 years 10 months.

Jones, Robert Ellis (1915–18); Sergeant, R. Welch Fusiliers.

Jones, Robert Pritchard (1915–19); Private, R.A.M.C., R.E. and Royal Fusiliers; France 2 years 4 months.

Jones, Thomas (1916–19); Gunner, R.G.A.; France 1 year 9 months.

Jones, Thomas (1916–19); Sub-Lieutenant, Artists' Rifles and R.N.V.R.

Jones, Thomas John (1915–19); Corporal, R.G.A.; Salonica 2 years 3 months.

Jones, William Henry Lake (1915–19); Captain, London and Middlesex Rgts. and General List; France 15 months, Italy 14 months.

Jurd, Reuben Henry Arthur (1914–18); Private, Royal Fusiliers and Machine Gun Corps; France 2 years 3 months.

Kane, John Charles (1917–19); Corporal, R.N.A.S. and R.A.F.

Keay, Edmund James (1914–20); Captain, acting Major, Machine Gun Corps; Gallipoli 6 months, Egypt 8 months, France 3 years.

Keeffe, Francis Leo (1915–19); Awarded Certificate of Merit for the invention of an automatic filler for Lewis Gun magazines; Armourer Staff-Sergeant, R.A.O.C.

Keeley, Albert Edward (1915–19); Lance-Corporal, London Rgt.; France 1 year 9 months.

***Keeling, Albert Ernest** (1914–15); Lance-Corporal, London Rgt.; France 3 months; Missing, 16th May, 1915.

Keep, William Harry (1914–19); Sapper, R.E.; France 4 years 5 months.

***Kelly, John** (1916–17); Private, London Rgt.; France 1 year; Killed in action, 19th July, 1917.

Kelly, Malcolm James (1916–19); Acting Sergeant, Lincolnshire Rgt. and R.A.F.; France 2 years 9 months.

Kelly, Patrick Thomas (1914–19); Sub-Conductor, R.A.O.C.; France 4 years.

Kelly, Robert John (1914–18); Company Sergeant-Major, London Rgt.; France 3 months.

Kemp, Percival Hepworth (1914–16); Private, Oxfordshire and Buckinghamshire Light Infantry; France 8 months.

Kemp, Walter Sicklemore (1916–19); Staff-Sergeant, R.E.

Kemsley, Wilfred (1918–19); Private, London Rgt.

Kenny, Michael Thomas (1915–19); Sergeant, R.A.V.C.; France 1 year 10 months, Italy 14 months.

Kent, Alfred Larkin (1914–19); Sec.-Lieutenant, London Rgt. and R.A.F.; France 6 months.

Kent, Herbert John (1914–19); M.C., Mentioned in despatches; Lieutenant, London Rgt. and Machine Gun Corps; France 2 years 6 months.

***Kenyon, Harry Thomas James** (1915–17); Private, R.A.M.C.; France 1 year 7 months; Killed in action, 17th August, 1917.

Kern, Bertie Charles (1916–19); Staff-Sergeant, R.E.

Kerrison, Harold Wesley (1914–19); Private, Middlesex Rgt.; India 2 years 9 months.

***Ketcher, Percy Thomas** (1914–16); Private, London Rgt.; France 1 year; Died of wounds, 29th March, 1916.

Key, Charles William (1917–18); Corporal, R.G.A.

Keys, Francis Herbert (1915–19); Lieutenant, London and E. Surrey Rgts.; India 3 years.

***Keys, William** (1914–15); Sergeant, Seaforth Highlanders; France 6 months; Missing, 9th May, 1915.

Kilner, Charles Arnold (1914–19); Flight Cadet, London Rgt. and R.A.F.; France 12 months.

Kimber, Albert Richard (1914–19); Lance-Corporal, London Rgt.; France 18 months.

King, Charles (1915–19); Lieutenant, Honourable Artillery Company and London Rgt.; France 10 months.

***King, Charles William** (1914–16); Sergeant, London Rgt.; France 4 months; Killed in action, 24th December, 1916.

King, Francis (1916–19); Air Mechanic (1st Class), R.N.A.S. and R.A.F.; France 10 months.

King, George (1916–19); Corporal, R.A.S.C.; France 2 years 3 months.

***King, Henry Alfred** (1915–18); Sec.-Lieutenant, R.G.A. and Indian Army; India 2 years 11 months; Died, 4th November, 1918.

King, Henry George (1915–19); Private, London Rgt.; France 18 months.

King, Lawrence Aubrey (1914–17); Private, Middlesex Rgt.; Gibraltar 6 months, France 1 year.

King, Malcolm Percy (1914–18); M.M.; Sergeant, Cameron Highlanders; France 2 years 6 months.

King, Percy William (1914–19); Lieutenant, Manchester Rgt. and R.A.F.

King, Sydney Thomas (1914–19); Sergeant, R.F.A.; France 3 years 11 months.

Kirby, John Charles Anthony (1916–19); Sergeant, R.E.

Kirkby, George (1914–19); D.C.M., M.S.M.; Corporal, County of London Yeomanry.

Kirkham, Harry (1916–19); Private, R. Sussex Rgt.; India 2 years 1 month.

***Kirkwood, John** (1914–15); Lance-Corporal, London Rgt.; France 2 months; Killed in action, 3rd May, 1915.

Kitchen, Albert Edward (1915–19); M.M., M.S.M. and Mentioned in despatches; Sergeant-Major, R.A.M.C.; France 3 years 6 months.

Kitchener, John Parkinson (1915–19); Squadron Quartermaster-Sergeant, R.A.S.C.

Kitcher, Bertram George (1916–19); Corporal, R.E.

Knell, Thomas Harold (1916–19); Lance-Corporal, R.A.O.C.; France 2 years 7 months.

***Knight, Hugh Alfred William** (1915–16); Private, London Rgt.; France 6 months; Killed in action, 15th September, 1916.

Knight, Sidney (1916–19); Sec.-Lieutenant, Rifle Brigade; France 10 months.

Knights, Edward Henry Thorne (1914–19); Lance-Corporal, Middlesex and E. Kent Rgts.; India 3 years 3 months, Mesopotamia 11 months.

Kynaston, Thomas Victor (1914–19); M.M.; Corporal, R.E.; France 4 years 1 month.

Lacey, George Herbert (1914–19); Sec.-Lieutenant, London Rgt.; France 2 years 9 months, Egypt and Palestine 6 months.

Lacey, Robert Vincent (1914–19); Sergeant, London Rgt.; France 2 years.

Lack, Frederick William (1915–18); Air Mechanic, R.N.A.S.

Lake, William Lancelot (1914–17); Colour-Sergeant, London Rgt.

Lakeman, Henry S'Bire (1914–19); Staff-Sergeant, Hampshire Rgt.; India 4 years 9 months.

Lambert, Arthur Eli (1915–19); Lance-Corporal, R.E.

Lancaster, Frank Knowles (1915–18); Sergeant, R.A.V.C. and R. Lancaster Rgt.; France 2 years 1 month.

Lancaster, George Edward (1915–19); Sergeant, R.A.S.C.; Salonica 3 years 4 months.

Lancaster, Louis James Alfred (1918–19); Private, R.A.F.

Landels, Walter (1915–19); Private, Seaforth Highlanders; Mesopotamia 2 years.

Lane, Albert Norman (1914–19); M.C.; Lieutenant, Oxfordshire and Buckinghamshire Light Infantry and Machine Gun Corps; France 4 years.

Lane, George William (1916–19); Sapper, R.E.; France 8 months.

***Lane, Harold Victor** (1914–18); Corporal, London Rgt.; France 15 months; Died of wounds, 29th March, 1918.

Lane, Henry Clifford (1916–19); Private, R.A.S.C.; Salonica 2 years.

Lang, Reginald William (1915–19); Company Sergeant-Major, Middlesex Rgt.

***Lang, Sidney Drummond** (1914–17); Sec.-Lieutenant, Yorkshire Light Infantry; France 1 month; Died of wounds, 23rd February, 1917.

Langford, Alfred Gray (1917–19); Lieutenant, R.F.A. and R.A.S.C.; France 9 months, Palestine 1 year.

Langford, George William (1914–19); Mentioned in despatches; Lieutenant, London Rgt. and Machine Gun Corps; France 3 years 6 months.

Lansdall, Percy George (1914–19); Corporal, Hertfordshire and Essex Rgts.; France 2 years.

Large, Reginald Francis (1915–19); Private, R.A.O.C.; France 1 year 11 months, Italy 15 months.

Large, Richard Passingham (1914–19); Corporal, Essex and Cheshire Rgts., and R.A.P.C.; Egypt and Palestine 1 year 11 months.

***Lassetter, Alfred Ernest** (1916–17); Private, Royal Fusiliers; France 5 months; Missing, 17th February, 1917.

Latham, Frederick Clarence James (1914–19); Lieutenant, Suffolk Rgt.; Egypt 18 months, France 18 months.

Latham, George (1915–19); Corporal, R.F.A.; France 2 years 9 months.

Latter, William Walter (1915–19); Sergeant, R.A.M.C.; France 1 year 8 months.

Launder, George Edgar (1918–19); Air Mechanic (3rd Class), R.A.F.

Laverty, James Haswell (1914–19); Sergeant, Middlesex Rgt.; India 4 years 11 months.

Lawday, Harold (1918–19); Aircraftsman (2nd Class), R.A.F.; France 2 months.

Layer-Parker, Robert (1914–19); Lieutenant, City of London Yeomanry, R.F.A. and R.A.F.; Egypt 6 months, Gallipoli 3 months, France 8 months, Palestine and Syria 11 months, Mediterranean 1 month.

Leach, Charles Herbert (1914–19); Sec.-Lieutenant, Oxfordshire and Buckinghamshire Light Infantry; France and Germany 1 year 8 months.

Leach, Frederick James (1916–19); Private, London Rgt. and R.A.P.C.; France 18 months.

Lean, Robert Graham (1915–19); M.S.M., Mentioned in despatches; Company Sergeant-Major, Army Gymnastic Staff; France 2 years 5 months.

Leaper, William Bambrick (1915–19); Lance-Corporal, R. Inniskilling Fusiliers and R.A.S.C.; France 1 year 8 months, Prisoner of war 8 months.

Leaphard, Edmund Percival (1916–19); Sergeant-Major, R.A.F.

Leaver, Hubert Russell (1915–19); Mentioned in despatches; Lance-Corporal, R.A.M.C.; Dardanelles 2 months, Egypt 6 months, Macedonia 2 years 6 months, Bulgaria 2 months, Caucasus 2 months.

Lee, Horace Stevenson (1915–19); Sec.-Lieutenant, London Rgt., Machine Gun Corps and R.W. Kent Rgt.; France 6 months.

Lee, James Percy (1915–19); Corporal, R.A.O.C. and Essex Rgt.; Egypt 3 years.

Lee, William Ernest (1914–19); Sergeant, Oxfordshire and Buckinghamshire Light Infantry; France 9 months, Prisoner of war 1 year 10 months.

Leedale, Stanley Hinde (1914–17); Private, London Rgt.; Malta 8 months, Egypt 6 months, Gallipoli 3 months, France 8 months.

Leese, William Heath (1915–19); Sergeant, R.A.M.C.; Egypt 3 years.

Legerton, Claude William Saxby (1914–19); Sec.-Lieutenant, Middlesex Rgt. and Machine Gun Corps; India 2 years 10 months, France 8 months.

***Legg, Walter Ambrose** (1915–17); Lance-Corporal, London Rgt.; France 5 months; Killed in action, 30th November, 1917.

Leggett, Sydney James (1915–19); Lieutenant, London Rgt. and R.F.A.; France 4 months.

Leigh, Eusebius (1914–19); Sergeant, London Rgt. and R.D.C.

Leighton, John William James (1914–19); Staff-Sergeant, R.A.M.C.; Egypt and Palestine 1 year.

Lello, William Paul (1916–19); Private, Middlesex Rgt.; India 18 months, Mesopotamia 6 months.

Lerry, Frank Herbert (1915–19); Lance-Corporal, Honourable Artillery Company (Infantry); France 10 months.

Levene, Solomon (1916–19); Corporal, Royal Fusiliers; France 18 months.

Lever, John (1914–20); M.C., Mentioned in despatches; Lieutenant, Royal Fusiliers; France 2 years.

***Lewin, Henry George** (1915–18); Private, London Yeomanry; France 15 months; Killed in action, 27th April, 1918.

Lewis, Charles Langton (1915–19); Corporal, R.A.M.C.; France 3 years 2 months.

***Lewis, Ernest** (1914–17); Private, London Rgt.; France 2 years; Killed in action, 15th March, 1917.

Lewis, Edward George (1916–19); Private, R.A.M.C.; Salonica 6 months Palestine 18 months.

Lewis, Louis Clinton (1914–17); Company Quartermaster-Sergeant, London Rgt.

Lewis, Sidney Herbert (1914–19); M.M.; Sergeant, London Rgt.; France 8 months.

Licence, Russell Ewart (1914–19); Croix de Guerre (Gold Star) (French); Captain, Essex and Warwickshire Rgts., and Durham Light Infantry; France 2 years 7 months, Germany 4 months.

Lidington, Ernest (1914–19); Lieutenant, Oxfordshire and Buckinghamshire Light Infantry; France 2 years 3 months.

Lilley, Ernest George (1916–19); Sergeant, R.G.A.; France 1 year.

Liming, Leonard Hiam (1915–19); Mentioned in despatches; Company Sergeant-Major Instructor, London Rgt. and Army Gymnastic Staff; France 8 months.

Lindsell, Alfred Edward (1916–19); Sergeant, Hampshire Rgt.; France 2 years 3 months, Germany 4 months.

Ling, Albert (1916–19); Sec.-Corporal, R.E.

Ling, Martin (1914–19); Private, London Rgt.; France 6 months, Salonica 7 months, Palestine 1 year 7 months.

Linklater, Philip (1916–19); Corporal, R.A.M.C.; France 1 year 9 months, Germany 9 months.

Linn, Albert Thomas (1916–19); Sapper, King's R. Rifle Corps, Rifle Brigade and R.E.; France 2 years 2 months.

Little, Andrew John (1918–19); Sapper, R.E.

Littler, John (1914–17); Sergeant, Yorkshire Rgt.

Livens, Albert Henry (1915–19); Sec.-Lieutenant, R.G.A.; France 7 months.

Livsey, Arthur Leonard (1914–19); Lieutenant, Northamptonshire Rgt.

Llewhellin, George Edmund (1914–19); Lieutenant, London and Norfolk Rgts.

Lloyd, Evan Addis (1914–19); M.S.M., Mentioned in despatches; Regimental Quartermaster-Sergeant, R. Welch Fusiliers; France 3 years 4 months.

Lloyd, Henry James (1918–19); Private, London Rgt.

Loarridge, Herbert Sydney (1916–19); Signaller, Machine Gun Corps and E. Surrey Rgt.; Mesopotamia 13 months, India 14 months.

Lockeyear, Henry James (1914–17); Sergeant, London Rgt.; Malta 8 months, Egypt 3 months, Gallipoli 4 months, France 8 months.

Lockley, Frederick William (1915–19); Mentioned in despatches; Sergeant, R.A.M.C.; Egypt 3 months, France 6 months, Mesopotamia 2 years 5 months.

Lodge, Charles John (1914–19); Sapper, R.E.

Lofthouse, Raymond (1916–19); Rifleman, King's R. Rifle Corps; Greece 4 months, France 17 months.

Long, Herbert William Fortescue (1916–19); Sec.-Lieutenant, R.N.A.S. and R.A.F.

***Long, William Ernest** (1916–18); Sergeant, London Rgt.; France 3 months; Died of wounds, 25th April, 1918.

Loosemore, Percy (1916–19); Chief Petty Officer, R.N.V.R.; Minesweeping 2 years 6 months.

***Lord, Ernest William** (1914–16); Private, Gloucestershire Rgt.; France 7 months; Killed in action, 21st January, 1916.

Lord, William Clement (1915–19); Sergeant, London Rgt. and Army Gymnastic Staff.

Lorimier, Walter John (1915–19); Gunner, Honourable Artillery Company; Egypt 10 months, Palestine and Syria 2 years 1 month.

Lovesay, George (1916–19); Gunner, R.F.A.

Lowry, Arthur Patrick (1914–19); Private, Middlesex Rgt. and R.A.S.C.; Gibraltar 6 months, Egypt 18 months, Palestine 1 year, France 1 year.

Lucas, Fred (1915–18); Corporal, Rifle Brigade; France 1 year.

***Lucas, Maurice Thomas** (1914–17); Private, Middlesex Rgt.; Gallipoli 5 months, Egypt and Palestine 10 months; Killed in action, 19th April, 1917.

Luke, Francis (1916–18); Pioneer, R.E.; France 1 year 9 months.

Lund, Robert (1916–19); Corporal, R.F.C. and R.A.F.; France 2 years.

***Lunn, Rupert Hugh** (1915–17); Private, Essex Rgt.; Gallipoli, Malta and Egypt 18 months; Missing, 26th March, 1917.

Lyne, Charlie (1915–19); Corporal, R.A.M.C.; France 2 years 8 months.

***Lynes, Norman** (1914–16); Private, Middlesex Rgt.; Gibraltar and Egypt 17 months, France 4 months; Missing, 16th September, 1916.

Lyon, Frederick William (1914–19); Mentioned in despatches; Company Quartermaster-Sergeant, R.A.S.C.; Malta 15 months, France 3 months, Salonica 8 months, Palestine 18 months.

Lyons, William (1917–19); Driver, R.F.A.; France 2 years.

***McAlister, Harry Percival** (1914–17); Company Sergeant-Major, Rifle Brigade; France 3 months; Killed in action, 31st July, 1917.

McArthur, William (1916–19); Corporal, R.G.A.

Macaulay, Dugald (1916–19); Sapper, R.E.; France 9 months.

McCall, Alexander (1916–19); Warrant-Officer, H.M.S. Blenheim; Malta 2 months, Mudros 1 year 8 months, Brindisi 6 months, Black Sea 3 months.

McCall, Thomas Vincent (1915–19); Warrant-Officer, R.N.; North Sea 3 years.

McCarthy, John William (1915–19); Private, R.A.M.C.; Salonica 6 months, Palestine 1 year 11 months.

McCauley, Vincent Joseph (1915–19); Mentioned in despatches; Captain, R.G.A.; France 15 months.

McDiarmid, John Joseph (1917–19); Corporal, R.N.A.S. and R.A.F.

McDonald, John Tolmie (1916–19); Lieutenant, R.G.A.; France 4 months.

McDonald, William James (1916–19); Sergeant, R.G.A.; France 2 years 5 months.

McFarlane, Leonard (1916–19); Air Mechanic, R.N.A.S. and R.A.F.; France 1 year 9 months.

McGibbon, Reginald George (1915–19); Sergeant-Instructor, Norfolk Rgt. and Army Gymnastic Staff.

McGuire, John Charles (1915–19); Corporal, R.A.S.C. and Norfolk Rgt.; France 3 months.

McHaffie, Arnold Ewart (1915–19); Private, R.A.M.C.; France 2 years 3 months.

McHarrie, Walter Cowley (1915–19); Staff-Sergeant, County of London Yeomanry and Army Gymnastic Staff; Palestine 1 year 7 months.

Machin, George (1914–19); Lance-Corporal, Bedfordshire, E. Riding, and Middlesex Yeomanry.

McInley, Ernest Stuart (1915–19); Gunner, R.G.A.; Salonica 6 months, Palestine 18 months.

McInnes, Latimer (1916–19); Sapper, R.E.; France 9 months.

McKee, James (1914–19); Corporal, Middlesex Rgt.; Gibraltar 6 months, France 3 years 6 months.

McKeon, Ralph Frederick John (1916–19); 2nd Corporal, R.E.

***McKimmie, Alexander Ian** (1914–17); Lieutenant, Seaforth Highlanders, W. Yorkshire Rgt. and R.A.F.; France 10 months; Killed in action, 23rd May, 1917.

McKimmie, John (1914–19); Sergeant, Middlesex Rgt.

McLaughlin, Neil James (1915–19); Private, R.A.V.C.; France 2 years 8 months.

McLeish, Peter (1917–19); Signaller, R.F.A.; France 1 year.

McPherson, Graeme (1917–19); Corporal, R.E. and R.A.S.C.; France 5 months, Italy 12 months.

Macpherson, William (1915–16); Private, Royal Fusiliers.

***Macrae, Farquhar Mathieson** (1914–15); Private, London Rgt.; France 4 months; Missing, 9th May, 1915.

McVey, James Stephen (1915–19); Lieutenant, R.A.V.C. and Machine Gun Corps; France 12 months, Egypt 12 months, Salonica 4 months, Prisoner of war 7 months.

Maddock, Frank Arthur (1916–18); Sapper, R.E.

Maiden, Bertram Heath (1916–18); Lance-Corporal, N. Staffordshire Rgt.

***Maidment, Edwin Arthur** (1916–18); Private, R.G.A.; France 15 months; Died, 16th April, 1918.

***Maidment, Hubert George** (1914–16); Sergeant, Royal Fusiliers; Malta, Gallipoli and Egypt 17 months, France 5 months: Killed in action, 15th September, 1916.

Major, Stephen James (1914–19); Sergeant, R.F.A.; France 10 months.

Makepeace, Bernard (1914–19); Corporal, King's R. Rifle Corps, R.N.A.S. and R.A.F.; France 6 months.

***Maley, Robert James Hudson** (1914–15); Private, London Rgt.; France 2 months; Killed in action, 25th May, 1915.

***Mallpress, Victor Kenneth** (1914–15); Private, London Rgt.; France 2 months; Killed in action, 25th May, 1915.

Malone, Joseph Thomas (1916–19); M.C.; Lieutenant, Irish Guards and Inniskilling Fusiliers; France 14 months.

Mangold, Charles Frederick William (1915–19); Private, R.A.M.C.; France 6 months, Salonica 6 months, Palestine 1 year 8 months.

Mann, Herbert Henry (1915–19); Sergeant, Essex Rgt.; Gallipoli 3 months, Egypt 14 months, Palestine 1 year 8 months.

Mansley, Edward John (1915–19); Sapper, R.E.; France 7 months, Salonica 7 months, Palestine 1 year 8 months.

Mapham, Neville (1914–19); D.C.M.; Staff-Sergeant, R.A.V.C.; France 3 years 9 months, Germany 4 months.

Maple, John James (1917); Rifleman, King's R. Rifle Corps.

Marchant, James Albert (1917–19); Corporal, London Rgt.

Marchant, Sidney Henry (1914–17); Private, Middlesex Rgt.

Margetts, Charles Ernest (1916–19); Lance-Corporal, R.A.S.C.; Salonica 2 years 6 months.

Markall, Edward Charles (1916–19); Bombardier, R.G.A.; France 1 year 8 months.

Markham, Percy (1914–19); Company Sergeant-Major, London Rgt.

Markland, George Berry (1916–19); Sec.-Lieutenant, R.A.S.C. (M.T.); Salonica 10 months.

Marks, Alfred Pearce (1916–19); Gunner, R.G.A.

Marks, Louis Charles (1916–19); Sapper, R.E.

Marley, Arthur James (1915–19); M.S.M., Mentioned in despatches; Regimental Sergeant-Major, Yorkshire Light Infantry.

Marlow, Arthur Albert (1914–19); Rifleman, London Rgt. and Rifle Brigade; British Burmah 4 years.

Marrington, Robert Harry Custance (1915–19); Private, R.A.M.C.; East Africa 3 years.

Marsh, William John (1916–19); Private, R.E. and Tank Corps.

Marshall, Faithful James Barratt (1915–18); Lieutenant, London Rgt.

Marsland, David Clement (1916–19); Sec.-Corporal, R.E.

Marston, Roscoe Frederick (1914–19); Corporal, Royal Fusiliers, R.E. and Labour Corps; France 2 years 1 month.

Martel, Ernest (1914–19); Mentioned in despatches; Warrant Officer, R.N. Division and R.N.; Dardanelles 6 months, Cameroons 12 months, North Sea 12 months.

Martin, Ernest William (1915–19); M.M.; Battery Quartermaster-Sergeant, R.F.A.; France 2 years 9 months.

***Martin, William Edwin** (1916–18); Corporal, Nottinghamshire and Derbyshire Rgt. and Royal Scots; France 10 months; Died of wounds, 20th April, 1918.

***May, William John** (1914–17); Corporal, R.E.; France 2 years 7 months; Died of wounds, 6th July, 1917.

Maslen, James Robert (1914–19); Colour-Sergeant, Middlesex Rgt., Indian Labour Company and Staffordshire Rgt.

Mason, Herbert William (1914–19); Acting Sergeant, Middlesex Rgt. and R.A.O.C.; Gibraltar 6 months, Egypt (Western Frontier) 11 months, France 9 months.

Mason, William Charles (1914–19); Lieutenant, R.A.M.C. and Middlesex Rgt.; France 2 years 9 months.

Mather, John Henry (1916–19); Private, London Rgt.; Salonica 6 months, Egypt 1 year 8 months.

Mattey, Sidney Batt (1915–19); Sec.-Corporal, R.E.

Mathews, Frederick William (1916–19); Sapper, R.E.; France 8 months.

Matthews, Frederick John (1915–19); Corporal, R.A.M.C.; Egypt and Palestine 3 years.

Matthews, William Edward (1916–19); Sapper, R.E.

Maunder, Gilbard Coysh (1917–19); Corporal, R.A.O.C.; Mesopotamia 4 months, India (N.W. Frontier) 4 months, France 1 month, Egypt 1 month.

Mawbey, Henry Frederick (1915–16); Lieutenant, Army School of Musketry and Light Gunnery.

Maxfield, Sidney Thomas (1916–19); Sapper, R.E.; France 2 years.

May, Gilbert (1918–19); Aircraftsman (2nd Class), R.A.F.

Maynard, Charles George Gordon (1915–19); Private, R.A.M.C.; Corfu 2 months, Malta 6 months, Salonica 2 years 5 months.

Meades, Charles (1915–19); Able Seaman, R.N.V.R.

Mears, George Harold Rudolph (1914–19); Trooper, County of London Yeomanry and Cavalry Rgts.; Egypt 10 weeks, Gallipoli 3 months.

Meaton, Charles (1915–19); Private, R.A.M.C.; Corfu 3 months, Salonica 2 years 8 months.

Medley, Philip Ernest (1916–19); Gunner, R. Marine Artillery.

Meek, Harold (1916–18); Corporal, S. Wales Borderers; France 4 months.

Meigh, Harry (1914–19); Lieutenant, R.F.A. and R.E.; France 3 years.

Melles, Robert Ernest (1916–19); M.B.E.; Lieutenant, R.G.A.

Melsom, Horace Herbert (1914–19); Corporal, R.E.

Melton, William James Ward (1916–19); M.S.M.; Company Quartermaster-Sergeant, R.W. Surrey Rgt.; France 16 months, Italy 3 months, Germany 2 months.

Mendoza, Daniel (1917–19); Sergeant, Honourable Artillery Company, County of London Yeomanry and Royal Fusiliers; Egypt 6 months.

Mercer, Richard (1915–19); Lieutenant, R.A.O.C.

Merck, Thomas Henry (1915–19); M.S.M.; Sergeant, R.A.M.C.; France 2 years 7 months.

Merriman, Albert Wilson (1915–19); Rifleman, London Rgt.; France 2 years.

Mersh, Leonard James (1914–19); Lieutenant, London and E. Surrey Rgts., and R.E.; France 13 months.

Mewis, Neville Charles (1914–19); Mentioned in despatches; Company Quartermaster-Sergeant, R.E.; France 3 years 2 months.

Meyrick, Benjamin (1916–19); Gunner, R.G.A.; Mesopotamia 1 year 7 months.

Meyrick, Evan Daniel (1916–18); Sapper, R.E.; France 15 months.

Mickleburgh, Fred Percy (1916–17); Rifleman, London Rgt.; France 9 months.

Miles, Albert George (1916–19); Private, King's R. Rifle Corps; France 2 years 3 months.

Miles, Charles Frederick (1914–19); M.C., Twice mentioned in despatches; Major, R.F.A.; France.

***Miles, Francis James** (1914–17); Gunner, R.G.A.; Salonica, Egypt and Palestine, 8 months; Died of wounds, 6th November, 1917.

Miles, Robert William (1914–19); M.C., D.C.M., Mentioned in despatches; Captain, R.F.A.; France 4 years 3 months.

Miles, William Warren (1916–19); Lance-Corporal, E. Surrey Rgt.; India 16 months, Aden 7 months.

Milledge, George Ernest (1915–19); Corporal, London Rgt.; France 4 months.

***Miller, Ernest Septimus** (1914–15); Trooper, City of London Yeomanry; Gallipoli 1 month; Killed in action, 21st August, 1915.

Miller, Reginald Oliver (1914–19); Sergeant, London Rgt. and S. Wales Borderers; France 6 months.

Millett, Arthur Sobye (1918–19); Private, R.A.F.

Millie, William Henry (1915–19); Sec.-Lieutenant, R.F.A. and R.A.S.C.; France 4 months.

Mills, Frederick John (1915–19); Twice mentioned in despatches; Company Sergeant-Major Instructor, London Rgt., Army Gymnastic Staff, E. Surrey Rgt. and Officer Cadet Battalion.

Mills, Sidney Francis (1915–19); Sergeant, R.A.M.C.; North Russia 1 year.

Mills, William Reginald Copeland (1916–19); M.S.M., Mentioned in despatches; Private, Royal Fusiliers and Labour Corps; Salonica 2 years 2 months.

Milner, Alfred Stanley (1914–19); Company Sergeant-Major Instructor, Army Gymnastic Staff.

Milnthorpe, Robert (1915–19); Private, R.A.M.C.; France 2 years 3 months.

Minihane, Edward James (1915–19); Sergeant, R. Irish Rifles.

Minns, Leonard Alexander (1915–19); Private, Honourable Artillery Company and Machine Gun Corps; France 14 months, Italy 13 months.

Mitchell, Frank Henry (1916–19); Sapper, R.E.; France 6 months.

Mitchell, James (1916–19); Private, London Rgt.

Mitchell, John (1914–19); Sergeant, R.F.A.; France 2 years 2 months.

Mitchell, John Augustus (1916–19); Sapper, R.E.; France 2 months.

Mitchell, Sidney George (1916–19); Sergeant, King's R. Rifle Corps.

Monaghan, Joseph Cuthbert (1915–19); Gunner, Honourable Artillery Company.

Money, Joseph William (1916–19); M.M. and M.S.M.; Sergeant, London Rgt. and R. Dublin Fusiliers; France 18 months.

***Monkhouse, John Arthur** (1914–17); Lieutenant and Quartermaster, R.A.M.C.; France 14 months; Died, 23rd January, 1917.

Moody, Arthur (1914–19); Private, London Rgt.

***Moody, Thomas** (1914–16); Lieutenant, London Rgt.; Malta 6 months; France 1 year; Killed in action, 1st July, 1916.

Moore, Percival (1916–19); Lieutenant, N. Staffordshire Rgt, R.E. and London Rgt.; France 1 year.

Moore, Percy (1915–19); Private and Air Mechanic (2nd Class), London Rgt. and R.A.F.

Moore, Robert Henry (1914–20); Mentioned in despatches; Captain, R.G.A. and Tank Corps; France 2 years 4 months.

Moore, Thomas Joseph (1915–19); Bombardier, R.G.A.; France 1 year 8 months.

Moore, William Edward (1915–19); Colour-Sergeant, Oxfordshire and Buckinghamshire Light Infantry and R. Warwickshire Rgt.; France 1 year 8 months.

Morant, Henry (1914–18); Corporal, London Rgt., R.D.C. and R.A.P.C.

Morgan, Albert Owen (1916–19); Sec.-Corporal, R.E.

Morgan, Edward Mottis (1916–19); Sapper, R.E.; France 1 year 8 months.

***Morgan, Emlyn Thomas** (1914–16); Lieutenant, London Rgt.; France 2 months; Died of wounds, 7th February, 1916.

Morgan, Ernest Walter (1914–19); Sergeant, London Rgt. and Rifle Brigade; India and Burma 3 years 6 months.

Morgan, Frank (1915–19); M.C.; Lieutenant, R.G.A.; France 1 year 9 months.

Morgan, Henry George (1914–16); Staff-Sergeant, Dragoon Guards and R.A.V.C.; France 18 months.

Morgan, Henry Thomas John (1916–19); Corporal, R.A.F.

Morgan, James Thomas (1915–19); Lieutenant, R.E. and R.G.A.: France 3 years.

Morgan, Leonard (1916–19); Gunner, R.G.A.; France 7 months.

Morley, Frederick (1914–19); Company Quartermaster-Sergeant, R.W. Kent Rgt.; France 15 months.

***Morris, Arthur Evan** (1916–17); Lance-Corporal, R. Welch Fusiliers; Mesopotamia 4 months; Killed in action, 15th February, 1917.

Morris, Ernest Albert (1916–19); Lance-Corporal, Rifle Brigade and Training Reserve; France 2 years 1 month.

Morris, Harry (1914–18); Sergeant, London Rgt. and King's R. Rifle Corps.

Morris, Patrick Michael (1915–19); Corporal, Irish Guards.

Morris, Wilfred Percival (1916–19); Corporal, R.W. Kent Rgt. and Royal Fusiliers; France 9 months.

Morrison, Robert Craigmyle (1915–19); Corporal, R.A.M.C.

Morrow, Harold Ernest (1914–19); Captain, R.E.; France 16 months.

***Morton, Crowther** (1914–15); Private, London Rgt.; France 7 months; Killed in action, 24th October, 1915.

Morton, Edward (1914–19); Sec.-Lieutenant, Middlesex Rgt.; Gibraltar 6 months, France 3 years.

Morton, Ronald Coster (1914–19); Captain, R. Sussex Rgt.; Mesopotamia, 1 year 4 months.

Moscrop, William (1914–19); Gunner, R.F.A.; India 1 year 10 months; Mesopotamia 2 years 3 months.

Moss, Harry Claude Robbins (1918–19); Private, Middlesex Rgt.

Moss, Stanley Harold (1915–19); Sergeant, Middlesex Yeomanry and Royal Fusiliers; France 12 months.

Mounter, Henry Laurence (1915–19); Flight-Sergeant, R.F.C.

Mountford, Ebenezer James William (1914–19); Captain, City of London Yeomanry and R.A.S.C.; France 6 months.

Moyes, Albert Henry (1917–19); Signalman, R.N.V.R.

Mumford, Francis Albert Edward (1915–19); Driver, R.A.S.C.; France 3 years 2 months.

Munday, William (1914–19); Staff-Sergeant, London Rgt. and R.A.M.C.; Egypt 3 years 4 months.

Munden, Harry George (1914–20); Private, Middlesex Rgt.; Gibraltar 6 months, France 4 years 6 months.

Munnings, Rowland James (1914–19): Sec.-Lieutenant, Rifle Brigade.

Munro, Percy Edmund (1915–19); Sergeant, R.A.M.C.

Murch, Frederick William (1914–19); M.S.M.; Sergeant-Major, R.A.M.C.; Egypt 6 months.

Murch, Thomas Alfred (1914–19); M.S.M., Mentioned in despatches; Regimental Quartermaster-Sergeant, London Rgt.; France 14 months, Macedonia 7 months, Egypt, Palestine and Arabia 12 months.

Murfitt, Basil William Hallett (1916–18); Sapper, R.E.

Murgitroyd, Arthur (1916–19); Corporal, R.G.A.

Murphy, Patrick (1916–19); Sapper, R.E.

Murrell, Ben (1915–19); Sec.-Lieutenant, R.G.A.; France 2 years 1 month.

Murrell, George Austin (1915–19); M.S.M., Mentioned in despatches; Company Sergeant-Major Instructor, School of Musketry.

Myers, Samuel (1915–19); Sergeant, R.F.A.; France 2 years.

Myers, Morris (1917–19); Rifleman, King's Royal Rifle Corps; France 2 years 6 months.

Nagle, Cyril Alexander (1914–19); Sergeant, R.A.M.C.; France 3 years 5 months.

Napper, Eleazer (1918–19); Private, Suffolk Rgt.

Nash, Walter (1916–19); Gunner, R.G.A.; France 2 years 4 months.

Nash, William Henry (1914–17); M.M.; Corporal, Oxfordshire and Buckinghamshire Light Infantry; France 2 months.

Nathan, David (1917–19); Private, R.A.S.C.; Salonica 1 year 7 months.

Naylor, James Joseph (1916–19); Corporal, R.G.A.; Palestine 1 year 9 months.

Neal, John Frederick (1918–19); Corporal Gunnery Instructor, R.A.F.

Neal, Jabez Nathaniel (1915–19); Staff-Sergeant, R.A.M.C.; India 2 years 10 months.

Neat, Martin Luther (1916–19); Sapper, R.E.

Nebel, George Henry Lewis (1914–19); Company Sergeant-Major, R.E.

Nelson, Albert (1914–19); Sergeant, London Rgt. and Surrey Yeomanry; Malta 6 months, Gallipoli 4 months, Egypt 4 months, France 6 months.

Nelson, George (1916–19); Sergeant, R.A.F.

Nelson, George Frederick (1916–19); Flight-Sergeant, R.N.A.S. and R.A.F.

Nelson, William (1915–19); Corporal, R.A.M.C.; France 2 years 8 months.

***Nevey, Frank** (1916–18); Sec.-Lieutenant, London and W. Riding Rgts.; France 16 months; Killed in action, 12th October, 1918.

***Newbold, Richard Hanson** (1914–16); Sergeant, London Rgt.; Gallipoli 13 months, France 6 months; Killed in action, 7th September, 1916.

Newham, James Daniel William (1915–18); Sec.-Lieutenant, London and N. Staffordshire Rgts.; France 5 months.

Newman, Percy Rowden (1914–19); Private, Middlesex and London Rgts.; Gibraltar 7 months, Egypt 9 months, France 1 year 10 months, Prisoner of war 8 months.

Newnham, Arthur William (1917–19); Air Mechanic (2nd Class), R.N.A.S. and R.A.F.

Newport, Percival (1916–19); Corporal, R.A.V.C.; France 2 years 1 month.

Newton, Gilbert Ford (1916–19); Mentioned in despatches; Sec.-Lieutenant, Honourable Artillery Company and E. Surrey Rgt.; France 15 months.

Nicholls, Frederick Charles (1916–19); Private, R.A.M.C.; Salonica 4 months, Egypt 1 year 7 months.

Nicholls, Thomas Walter (1914–16); Lance-Corporal, Oxfordshire and Buckinghamshire Light Infantry.

Nicholson, Arthur Herbert (1915–19); Flight-Sergeant, R.A.F. and R.N.A.S.; France 18 months.

Nicholson, Frank Howard (1916–19); Sergeant, R.N.A.S. and R.A.F.

Nicholson, Thomas (1918); Private, Honourable Artillery Company.

Nicol, Paul Hemsley (1914–19); Company Sergeant-Major, London Rgt.; India 3 years.

Nightingale, Herbert Paul (1914–19); Private, Middlesex Rgt.

Nightingale, Leslie Roy (1914–19); Sergeant, Middlesex Rgt.

Nisbet, Thomas (1916–19); Sergeant, R.W. Surrey Rgt.

Nisbet, William Henry (1917–19); Gunner, R.G.A.

Nisbett, Percival Frederick (1914–19); Regimental Quartermaster-Sergeant, King's R. Rifle Corps.

Nixon, George (1914–19), Mentioned in despatches; Sergeant, London Rgt.; France 4 years 1 month.

Noakes, Edward John (1914–19); Private, London Rgt.

Nobbs, Alfred Leopold (1915–19); Captain, Oxfordshire and Buckinghamshire Light Infantry and Rifle Brigade; France 6 months.

Norman, Everett Alexander (1914–19); Company Sergeant-Major, Army Gymnastic Staff; France 11 months.

Norman, John Edward (1916–19); Sergeant, R.N.A.S. and R.A.F.

Norris, Edward (1916–19); Private, London Rgt.; France 2 years.

Norris, Frederick William (1915–19); Sergeant, R.W. Surrey Rgt.

Norris, Percy Charles (1916–19); Sec.-Corporal, R.E.

Norton, Patrick Oliver (1916–19); M.C.; Sec.-Lieutenant, Gloucestershire Rgt.

Nugent, Samuel (1918–19); Sergeant, R.A.F.

Nunn, Frederick Leslie (1916–19); Company Quartermaster-Sergeant, R.W. Surrey Rgt. and R.E.

Nunn, Herbert William (1914–19); Battery Quartermaster-Sergeant, R.F.A.; France 2 years.

Nurse, Walter (1915–19); M.M.; Lance-Corporal, R.A.M.C.; France 2 years 11 months.

Nyland, Thomas (1915–19); Captain, R.F.A.

Oakey, Alfred James Henry (1914–19); Lance-Corporal, Middlesex Rgt.; Gibraltar 6 months, France 3 years 6 months.

Oakshette, Henry Montague (1916–19); Sec.-Corporal, R.E.

Obendorf, Henry Philip (1916–19); M.M.; Rifleman, London Rgt. and King's R. Rifle Corps; France 16 months.

Odam, Norman John (1914–19); Company Quartermaster-Sergeant, London Rgt.

Odell, Charles Herbert (1918–19); Private, R.A.M.C.

Odle, George Edward (1918–19); Private, R.A.M.C.

O'Dwyer, Stephen Joseph (1917–18); Private, R.A.S.C.

Ogle, Thomas William (1917–19); Private, R.N.A.S. and R.A.F.

Oke, William (1916–19); Sapper, R.E.; France and Germany 2 months.

Ore, Arthur William (1916–19); Lance-Corporal, R.E.; France 2 years.

***Ore, Joseph Frederick** (1914–16); Lance-Corporal, Middlesex Rgt.; Gibraltar 6 months, Egypt 7 months, France 7 months; Killed in action, 7th October, 1916.

Orford, Richard (1918–19); Corporal-Mechanic, R.A.F.

Orton, Alfred James (1917–18); Private, R.A.S.C. (M.T.).

Osborne, Alfred George (1914–19); Sergeant, R. Welch Fusiliers.

Osgood, Percy William (1915–19); Sergeant, R.A.M.C.; Egypt 4 months, France 2 years 10 months.

Osman, Alfred Charles (1915–19); Private, R.A.M.C.; East Africa 2 years 5 months.

O'Sullivan, Frederick (1916–19); Croix de Guerre (Belgian); Sergeant, R.E.; France 2 years 6 months.

O'Sullivan, John William (1915–19); Sapper, R.E.

Owen, Frederick William Poyntz (1915–18); Private, R.A.M.C.; France 2 years 4 months.

Owen, Henry George (1914–16); Company Sergeant-Major, London Rgt.

Owen, John Oswald (1915–20); Corporal, London Rgt. and R.D.C.

Owen, Launcelot Poyntz (1915–19); Flight-Sergeant i/c Cadet Squadron, R.A.F.

Owen, Robert (1915–19); Gunner, R.G.A.; Salonica 2 years, France 4 months.

Owen, Sidney Albert (1916–19); Corporal, R.E.; France 12 months.

Owens, Goronway (1914–19); Sec.-Lieutenant, London Rgt. and R.G.A.; France 6 months, Salonica 1 year 8 months.

Oxford, George William (1917–19); Sergeant-Schoolmaster, R.N.A.S. and R.A.F.

Packer, Harry Sidney (1916–19); Sec.-Corporal, R.E.

Packer, William George (1916–19); Sergeant-Major, R.A.O.C.

Page, Charles Balderson (1914–19); Lance-Corporal, Nottinghamshire and Derbyshire Rgt., Oxfordshire and Buckinghamshire Light Infantry and Yorkshire Light Infantry; Egypt 1 year.

***Page, Harry Thomas** (1916–17); Private, Honourable Artillery Company; France 1 month; Died of wounds, 11th May, 1917.

Page, William Washington (1915–19); Lance-Sergeant, R.A.S.C.; East Africa 2 years.

Pagett, Robert Percy (1916–19); Sapper, R.E.

Pain, Frederick Ernest Watchurst (1916–19); Sergeant, R.A.F.

Paine, Archie Charles (1914–19); Sapper, R.E.; France 6 months, Salonica 6 months, Egypt 1 year 9 months.

Palk, Frederick Arthur (1915–19); Sapper, R.E.; France 3 months.

Palmer, Alfred (1916–19); Corporal, R.A.V.C.; Egypt 5 months, Salonica 2 years 6 months.

Palmer, Ernest Edward Linton (1916–17); Private, London Rgt. and Somersetshire Light Infantry; France 5 months.

Palmer, Henry (1914–19); Sapper, Middlesex Rgt. and R.E.; Gallipoli 4 months, Egypt and Palestine 3 years 3 months.

Palmer, John George (1914–19); M.S.M., Mentioned in despatches; Quartermaster-Sergeant, R.A.M.C.; Egypt 4 years 2 months.

***Palmer, Lancelot** (1916); Private, London Rgt.; France 3 months; Killed in action, 15th September, 1916.

Panton, John Hubert (1915 19); Lieutenant, Inns of Court O.T.C. and Duke of Cornwall's Light Infantry; France 18 months.

Pardoe, Harold Horton (1916–18); Private, R.A.F. and Lincolnshire Rgt.; France 1 year 10 months.

Parker, Albert John (1915–19); Lance-Corporal, R.A.M.C.; France 5 months, Salonica 2 years, Malta 2 months.

Parker, Albert Victor (1914–19); Sergeant-Instructor, London Rgt. and R.E.; France 1 year 9 months.

Parker, Emanuel Alexander (1916–19); Leading Mechanic, R.F.C. and R.A.F.; France 3 years.

Parker, Edwin John (1915–19); Sergeant, Somersetshire Light Infantry; France 1 year.

Parker, Francis James Harris (1914–19); Sec.-Lieutenant, Middlesex and Hampshire Rgts.; India 4 years 11 months.

Parker, Froud Stanfield (1915–19); Gunner, R. Marine Artillery; Egypt 10 months, France 2 years.

Parker, Joseph Francis (1915–19); Sergeant, R.E.

Parker, Norman Leslie (1915–19); Lance-Corporal, London Rgt.; France 7 months, Salonica 9 months, Palestine 16 months.

Parker, William Henry (1917–19); Private, R.W. Surrey Rgt.

Parkes, William Robert (1915–19); Sergeant, R. Sussex and Suffolk Rgts.

Parkhouse, Herbert (1914–19); Captain, London Rgt.

Parkin, George Edwin (1914–19); Signaller, London Rgt.

Parr, Ernest Alfred (1915–19); Lieutenant, R.A.M.C. and Labour Corps.

Parr, Frederick John (1916–19); Sapper, R.E.; Mesopotamia 1 year 7 months.

Parry, Roy Edgardo (1914–19); Captain, 15th Ludhiana Sikhs (I.A.R.O.); India 1 year 6 months, France 11 months.

***Parry, Thomas Ellis** (1914–16); Sec.-Lieutenant, London Rgt. and Lancashire Fusiliers; France 11 months; Missing, 23rd October, 1916.

Parsons, Alfred Hingley (1916–19); Driver, R.F.A.; Mesopotamia 17 months.

Parsons, Henry Bowen (1914–19); Mentioned in despatches; Sergeant, Middlesex Rgt.; Gallipoli 4 months, Egypt 18 months, Palestine 2 years.

Parsons, William James (1916–19); Sapper, R.E.

Partington, George (1914–19); Guardsman, Coldstream Guards; France 3 years 9 months.

Partridge, Frank Edwin (1916–19); Corporal, R.G.A.; France 12 months.

Pascoe, Joseph Ellary (1914–17); Company Quartermaster - Sergeant, London Rgt.

Patrick, Ernest Isaac (1917–19); Gunner, R.H.A.; South Africa 6 weeks, India 1 year 7 months, Egypt 1 month.

Patten, Charles James (1914–19); Sergeant, R.F.A.; France 2 years 8 months.

Paulson, Charles Lawrence (1918–19); Sergeant, Machine Gun Corps.

Pavey, Cecil James (1915–19); Corporal, R.A.M.C.; France 1 year 11 months.

Payne, Arthur Frank (1917–19); Petty Officer (1st Class), R.N.

Payne, George James (1914–19); Sec.-Lieutenant, Oxfordshire and Buckinghamshire Light Infantry, R. Warwickshire Rgt. and Machine Gun Corps; France 1 year 7 months.

Payne, William (1914–19); Lieutenant, Middlesex and Norfolk Rgts., and Indian Army; Mesopotamia 3 years 1 month, India 16 months.

Peacock, Edward (1916–19); Sapper, R.E.

Peacock, Robert Horace (1914–19); Mentioned in despatches; Captain, Leicestershire Rgt. and Machine Gun Corps; Egypt 1 month, France 3 years.

Peal, Edgar George (1915–19); Lieutenant, Honourable Artillery Company and Wiltshire Rgt.; France 8 months.

Peal, Francis Charles (1916–19); Sec.-Corporal, R.E.

Pearce, Horace (1917–18); Sergeant, King's R. Rifle Corps.

Pearce, William Frederick (1916–19); Flight-Sergeant, R.N.A.S. and R.A.F.

Pearce, William George (1916–19); M.M. and Mentioned in despatches; Sec.-Corporal, R.E.; France 2 years 3 months.

***Pearse, Cecil George** (1914–18); Sec.-Lieutenant, R.F.A.; Died, 20th October, 1918.

Pearse, Reginald Claude (1914–19); Sergeant, R.F.A.

Pearson, Frederick Ernest (1916–17); Private, R.A.M.C.

Pearson, Frederick James (1916–19); Mentioned in despatches; Lieutenant, R.F.A.; France 12 months.

***Pearson, George Frank** (1915–16); Private, London Rgt.; France 12 months; Killed in action, 16th September, 1916.

Pearson, Harry Arthur (1916–19); Lance-Corporal, London Rgt.; France 5 months, Salonica 6 months, Egypt and Palestine 1 year 7 months.

***Pearson, Walter** (1914 and 1915); Private, Duke of Cornwall's Light Infantry and Honourable Artillery Company; France 10 days; Killed in action, 25th August, 1915.

Peck, Frederick (1916–19); Corporal, R.A.M.C.; Egypt, Palestine and Syria, 15 months.

Peck, Stanley (1918–19); Rifleman, London Rgt.

Pegg, Herbert William (1914–19); M.M.; Company Quartermaster-Sergeant, Warwickshire Rgt.; France 3 years, Italy 10 months.

Pegram, Francis (1918–19); Aircraftsman (2nd Class), R.A.F.

Pelmear, Andrew (1915–19); Lieutenant, Adjutant, Indian Army, Arab Labour Corps; India 10 months, Mesopotamia 8 months.

Pennington, Frederick Cameron (1918–19); Lance-Corporal, R.E.

Perkins, John Henry (1915–19); Sergeant, R.E.

Permain, Frederick (1914–19); Band-Sergeant, Hampshire Rgt.

Perring, Allen John (1914–19); Company Sergeant-Major, London Rgt.

Perry, Arthur William (1916–19); Gunner, R.F.A.; France 1 year 10 months.

***Perry, Edward James** (1914–16); Sergeant, Middlesex Rgt.; Gibraltar 6 months, France 12 months; Killed in action, 26th June, 1916.

***Perry, Herbert Henry** (1914–18); Sergeant, London Rgt.; France 10 months, Salonica, Egypt and Palestine, 18 months; Killed in action, 14th October, 1918.

Perry, Samuel Roberts (1915–19); Corporal, R.A.M.C.; Corfu 3 months, Salonica 2 years 8 months.

Perryman, Frank Marley (1914–19); Sergeant, London Rgt.; France 9 months.

***Pert, Leonard Harry** (1916–17); Private, Rifle Brigade; France 8 months; Killed in action, 3rd May, 1917.

Philbrick, Harry Alfred (1914–19); Lieutenant, Hampshire Rgt. and Indian Army Reserve; India 3 years, Mesopotamia 2 years.

Phillips, Alfred John (1918–19); Private, R.A.S.C.

Phillips, Edgar (1914–19); M.M.; Bombardier, R.F.A.; France 3 years.

Phillips, Edgar Needham (1916–19); Sergeant, R.A.S.C., R. Welch Fusiliers and S. Wales Borderers; France 11 months.

Phillips, Edwin James (1915–19); D.C.M. and Médaille Militaire (French); Captain, R.A.S.C. and Tank Corps; France 3 years 3 months.

Phillips, Henry John (1916–19); Sapper, R.E.; France 1 year 10 months.

Phillips, Richard (1918–19); Sapper, R.E.

Philpott, Stanley Alfred (1916–19); Lance-Corporal, London Rgt. and Rifle Brigade; France 11 months.

Philpott, Stanley John Francis (1916–19); M.C.; Captain, R.G.A.; France 2 years 6 months.

Phipps, John Henry (1916–19); Chief Mechanic, R.N.A.S. and R.A.F.

Phipps, Sydney John (1916–19); Sec.-Lieutenant, R. Sussex Rgt., Rifle Brigade and King's R. Rifle Corps; France 14 months.

Pick, Noel Ewart (1916–19); Corporal, R.E.

Pickard, Lewis William (1915–19); Mentioned in despatches; Sec.-Lieutenant, Honourable Artillery Company and London Rgt.; France 12 months.

Pickbourne, Leonard (1915–19); Acting Corporal Interpreter, R.A.M.C. and Headquarters Infantry Brigade; France 3 years 9 months, Germany 8 months.

Pickering, Harry (1916–19); M.M. and Bar, Twice mentioned in despatches; Private, E. Kent Rgt.; France 18 months.

Pickett, John Frederick (1916–19); Lance-Corporal, London Rgt.; France 1 year 9 months.

Pierce, Leslie (1914–19); Lieutenant, Grenadier Guards, Devonshire Rgt. and W. African Frontier Force: France 12 months, Nigeria 15 months.

Pipe, James (1914–19); Mentioned in despatches; Lieutenant, R.E. and R.G.A.; France 2 years 8 months.

Pitts, George William (1916–19); Sec.-Lieutenant, R.G.A.

Player, Joseph Leonard (1916–19); Corporal, R.A.F.

Pleydell, Reginald Walter (1915–19); Corporal, R.A.M.C.; France 3 years 8 months.

Plowright, Frank (1914–19); Lance-Sergeant, Middlesex and E. Kent Rgts.; India 4 years, Mesopotamia 5 months.

Pocock, Albert Victor Carley (1916–19); Sergeant, R. Sussex and R.W. Surrey Rgts., Labour Corps and E. Lancashire Rgt.

Pollard, Percy John Wyatt (1914–19); M.M.; Company Quartermaster-Sergeant, Bedfordshire Rgt.; France 3 years 6 months.

***Pollock, William** (1916–18); Private, S. Staffordshire Rgt.; France 16 months; Missing, 27th May, 1918.

Pond, Leslie Harry (1918–19); 3rd Clerk, R.A.F.

Poole, Percival William (1916–19); Sapper, R.E.; France 8 months.

Pope, Archibald (1915–19); Private, R.E. and Tank Corps.

***Pope, Thomas Charles** (1914–16); Sergeant, London Rgt.; Malta 9 months, Gallipoli 3 months, France 7 months; Killed in action, 7th October, 1916.

Porter, Bertram Alexander (1916–19); Signaller, R.G.A.

Porter, George Edward (1914–19); M.C. and Bar; Captain, Honourable Artillery Company, Devonshire Rgt. and Tank Corps; France 3 years 11 months.

Porter, Leslie Vernon (1916–19); Lance-Sergeant, Berkshire Yeomanry.

Porter, Percy George (1915–19); Sergeant, R.A.M.C.; France 3 years 9 months.

Postle, Frank William (1914–19); Regimental Quartermaster-Sergeant, London Rgt.; Malta 8 months, Gallipoli 5 months, Egypt 3 months, France 12 months.

Potbury, Maurice Stephen (1916–19); Corporal, R.G.A.; France 2 years 2 months.

***Potter, Walter Joseph** (1916–17); Rifleman, King's R. Rifle Corps; France 1 year; Killed in action, 19th September, 1917.

Potter, William Simpson (1914–19); Staff-Sergeant Instructor, London Rgt.; France 7 months.

Poulter, Henry David (1914–18); Bombardier, R.F.A.

Poulton, Francis William (1914–19); Regimental Quartermaster-Sergeant, London Rgt.

Povey, Walter Joshua (1918–19); Corporal-Instructor, R.A.F.

Powell, Arthur James (1916–19); Sergeant, R.E.

Powell, Arthur Robert (1916–19); Sergeant, E. Kent Rgt.; France 2 years 1 month.

Powell, Enoch Edward (1914–19); Captain, Surrey Yeomanry.

***Power, William Joseph** (1915–17); Private, City of London Yeomanry; France 2 months; Died, 17th February, 1917.

Powley, Ernest William (1916–19); Sapper, R.E.

***Pragnell, Archie Ernest** (1914–17); Sec.-Lieutenant, London Rgt.; Drowned at sea, 30th December, 1917.

Prangnell, Ernest George (1914–19); Sergeant, R.W. Surrey Rgt.; India 2 years.

Pratt, Alfred Edward (1915–19); Twice mentioned in despatches; Captain, Liverpool Rgt.; France 3 years 3 months.

Preece, Victor William Magnadge (1916–19); Sapper, R.G.A. and R.E.; France 2 years 3 months.

Prentice, Albert (1914–17); M.M.; Sergeant, Oxfordshire and Buckinghamshire Light Infantry; France 3 months.

Prescott, Arthur George (1915–19); Quartermaster-Sergeant Instructor, Honourable Artillery Company and Machine Gun Corps; France 5 months.

Press, Archie (1914–19); Sergeant, R.A.M.C.; France 12 months.

Pressey, George (1915–19); Corporal, R.E.

Preston, John Thomas (1914–19); D.C.M.; Staff-Sergeant, R.E.; Gallipoli 9 months, Egypt 3 months, France 3 years 3 months.

Price, Gilbert John (1915–19); Corporal, R.F.A.; France 1 year 11 months.

Prince, Albert (1914–19); Lieutenant, Hampshire Rgt.

Prince, Arthur (1915–19); Lance-Sergeant, R.A.V.C.; Egypt 3 years 4 months.

Pritchard, Alonzo Dominic (1916–19); Sergeant, R.A.O.C.

Pritchard, Wilfred Arthur (1915–19); Victualling Assistant, R.N.; North Sea (Minesweeping) 9 months.

Probert, William Thomas Oliver (1914–19); Company Quartermaster-Sergeant, R.A.S.C.

***Procter, Alexander Duncan Guthrie** (1915–16); Sec.-Lieutenant, Royal Fusiliers; France 5 months; Killed in action, 7th July, 1916.

Proom, Thomas S. (1915–19); Private, R.A.M.C.; France 2 years 9 months.

Prowse, Percival Harry (1914–19); Quartermaster-Sergeant, Middlesex Rgt.; France 15 months.

Pudney, Lawrence Sydney (1916 19); Sapper, R.E.; France 9 months.

***Pugh, Harold George** (1914–15); Private, London Rgt.; France 2 months; Killed in action, 26th May, 1915.

Pugh, William James Frederick (1918–19); Air Mechanic (3rd Class), R.A.F.

Pull, Ernest (1914–15); Engineer, R. Naval Reserve, Active list of Officers, H.M.S. Cressy and Proserpine.

Pullen, Samuel Fletcher David John (1916–18); Private, Rifle Brigade and R. Lancaster Rgt.; Salonica 17 months.

Pulpher, Sydney Clive Ernest (1916–19); Sapper, R.E.; France 2 years 9 months.

Punter, Charles Edgar (1914–19); M.S.M., Mentioned in despatches; Regimental Quartermaster-Sergeant; R.W. Surrey Rgt.; France 3 years 7 months.

Purnell, Archibald John (1918–19); 2nd Private, R.A.F.

Purtill, John Henry (1916–19); Sapper, R.E.

Purser, William (1914–19); Regimental Quartermaster-Sergeant, R.E.; France 9 months.

Pyle, Alfred John (1916–19); Sergeant-Mechanic, R.A.F.

Quarry, Philip John (1915–19); Sergeant-Instructor, Middlesex Rgt. and Machine Gun Corps; France 17 months.

Quayle, Joseph Graham (1916–19); Private, R.A.S.C. (M.T.); Italy 13 months.

Quennell, Arnold (1914–17); Sergeant, London Rgt. and Rifle Brigade.

Randall, Wilfred William (1915–19); Sapper, R.E.

Rankin, Robert (1915–19); Sec.-Lieutenant, R.G.A.; Salonica 13 months.

Rawlings, Herbert George Gladstone (1915–19); Sec.-Lieutenant, R.N.A.S. and R.A.F.; Gibraltar 1 year 8 months, Malta 14 months.

Ray, Frank Crafer (1914–19); Captain, Leicestershire Rgt.

Rayner, Cyril Leslie Gordon (1914–19); Lieutenant, London Rgt.; France 9 months, Salonica 6 months, Palestine 14 months.

Rayns, Francis William (1916–19); Sapper, R.E.; France 8 months.

Read, Charles Ernest (1915–19); Private and Gunner, R.A.M.C. and R.G.A.; France 1 month, Salonica 7 months, Palestine 1 year 8 months.

Read, Henry Thomas Oscar (1915–19); Corporal, R.A.M.C.; France 2 years 10 months.

Read, John Robert William (1916–19); Leading Aircraftsman, R.A.F.

Redfearn, Cecil John Newby (1914–19); Corporal, Suffolk Rgt. and R.A.S.C.; France 1 year 9 months.

Redfern, James Whitmore (1916–19); Sapper, R.E.

Redford, Albert Charles (1916–19); Corporal-Mechanic, R.N.A.S. and R.A.F.; France 1 year 9 months.

***Reed, William John** (1914–17); Sec.-Lieutenant, R.A.M.C. and Devonshire Rgt.; Lemnos 8 months, France 6 months; Died of wounds, 28th October, 1917.

Reeks, Frederick (1916–19); Private, R.A.S.C. (M.T.); France 2 years.

***Rees, Hugh Glyn** (1915–16); Private, London Rgt.; France 6 months; Missing, 16th September, 1916.

Rees, John (1916–19); Lance-Corporal, R. Welch Fusiliers and Intelligence Corps; France 2 years 4 months.

Rees, Victor Hubert (1914–19); Lieutenant, London and Middlesex Rgts. and Machine Gun Corps; France 3 months, Mesopotamia 2 years.

Rees, William Henry (1914–19); Company Sergeant-Major Instructor, Middlesex Rgt. and Army Gymnastic Staff; France 8 months.

Reeve, Lawrence Robert (1915–19); Private, London Rgt.; France 6 months, Salonica 6 months, Palestine 1 year 8 months.

Reeve, William Robert (1914 19); M.C.; Lieutenant, London Rgt. and E. Surrey Rgt.; France 14 months, Salonica 1 year 10 months.

Reeves, Hubert (1916–19); Sergeant, R.N.A.S. and R.A.F.

Regan, Harry (1915–19); Sergeant, R.A.M.C.; France 2 years 2 months.

Reid, Michael (1916–19); Sapper, R.E.

Reidy, Maurice Joseph (1916–19); Lance-Corporal, R.A.M.C.; Salonica 2 years, Constantinople 2 months.

Relf, Ernest Walter (1914–19); Company Quartermaster-Sergeant, King's R. Rifle Corps; France 17 months.

Rennie, James Halliburton (1916–19); Corporal, R.E.

Rewell, Reginald Howard (1914–19); Sec.-Lieutenant, London Rgt., R.E. and R. Sussex Rgt.; France 13 months.

Reynolds, Arthur John (1916–19); Sapper, R.E.; France 1 year 8 months.

Reynolds, Henry O. (1916–19); Sapper, R.E.; France 2 months.

Reynolds, Walter Edward (1914–19); Sec.-Lieutenant, R.F.A.; France 1 year 11 months, Salonica 8 months, Egypt and Palestine 10 months.

Reynolds, William Fraser (1915–19); Lieutenant, R.G.A.; Palestine and Syria 7 months.

Reynolds, Wilfred Gordon (1916–19); Sapper, E. Surrey Rgt. and R.E.; France 2 years 9 months.

Rhymes, William (1916–19); Corporal, Leicestershire Rgt.

Rich, Julius (1916–19); Corporal, London Rgt.; France 1 year 9 months, Prisoner of war (Germany) 9 months.

Rich, Percy George (1916–19); Private, R.A.M.C.; France 1 year 10 months.

Rich, William John (1916–19); Sergeant, R.N.A.S. and R.A.F.

Richards, Arthur Clements (1915–19); Sapper, R.E.; France 3 months.

Richards, Alfred George (1914–19); Sergeant, London Rgt.; France 8 months.

Richards, Evan Thomas (1915–19); Sergeant, R.A.M.C.; France 2 years 10 months.

Richards, Leslie Claude (1916–19); Gunner, R.G.A.; France 2 years 6 months.

Richards, William Overton (1918–19); Private, London, Bedfordshire and Suffolk Rgts.

Richards, William Percival (1915); Private, R.A.M.C.

***Richardson, Harry Bertram** (1914–15); Sergeant, Highland Light Infantry; France 3 months; Killed in action, 26th September, 1915.

Richardson, James John (1914–19); M.S.M.; Sergeant, Hampshire Rgt.; India 9 months, Mesopotamia 3 years 6 months.

Richardson, Thomas James (1915–19); Mentioned in despatches; Flight-Sergeant, R.A.F., and Sergeant, R.A.O.C.

Rickatson, Louis Alfred (1916–19); 2nd Corporal, R.E.

Ricketts, John (1915–19); Corporal, Middlesex Yeomanry and Middlesex Rgt.; France 6 months.

Ricketts, Joseph (1915–19); M.B.E., Twice mentioned in despatches; Captain, R.E.

Ridd, Herbert William (1915–17); Sapper, R.E.; Mesopotamia 16 months.

Ridge, Timothy (1918–19); Private, Middlesex Rgt.; France 4 months.

Ridge, William Joseph (1915–19); Sergeant, R.E.

Ries, Rudolph (1916–19); Private, Middlesex Rgt.; France 1 year 10 months.

Rigby, Stanley (1914–17); Sergeant, Lincolnshire Rgt.; France 3 months.

Rigg, Leonard Allen (1915–18); Corporal, R.A.M.C.

Rignall, John Richard (1914–19); Mentioned in despatches; Sergeant, London and Yorkshire Rgts.; France 10 months.

Riley, Charles Sidney (1918–19); Aircraftsman (1st Class), R.A.F.

Rilstone, Richard (1916–19); Lance-Corporal, London Rgt.; France 11 months, Greece 3 months, Macedonia 4 months, Egypt 2 months, Palestine 10 months.

Ringland, Elliot Conway (1914–19); Corporal, Middlesex Rgt.; Gibraltar 6 months, Egypt 6 months.

Ringrose, William John (1916–19); Air Mechanic (1st Class), R.N.A.S. and R.A.F.; France 18 months.

Rintoul, Edwin Richard (1914–19); Captain, London and Middlesex Rgts.; France 11 months.

Rippin, Ronald Alexander (1914–19); Officer Cadet, London Rgt. and O.T.C.; France 9 months.

Ritchie, George Arthur (1914–19); Sergeant, London Yeomanry and Imperial Camel Corps; Egypt 7 months, Serbia and Salonica 5 months, Egypt and Palestine 2 years 10 months.

Roake, Alfred (1914–19); Sec.-Lieutenant, Middlesex Rgt. and R.F.A.; France 2 years 6 months, Gibraltar 6 months.

Robbins, Harry George (1915–19); Warrant-Officer, H.M.S. Glory at Murmansk in North Russia 10 months, H.M.S. Phaeton in the North Sea 18 months.

***Roberts, Charles Henry Hill** (1914–16); M.C.; Lieutenant, London Rgt.; France 16 months; Killed in action, 15th September, 1916.

Roberts, Francis Stanley (1914); Private, Devonshire Rgt.

Roberts, Mary Alexandra (1914–19); Staff Nurse, Territorial Force Nursing Service.

Roberts, Henry Keating (1915–19); Leading Aircraftsman, R.A.F.

Roberts, Sidney Herbert (1916–19); Sec.-Lieutenant, R.E.

***Roberts, Thomas** (1914–15); Sec.-Lieutenant, Cheshire Rgt.; France 2 months; Killed in action, 24th May, 1915.

Robin, Norman Ollivier (1915–19); Captain, Middlesex Rgt. and Remount Service; France 2 years.

Robinson, Arthur (1914–19); Corporal, London Rgt.; France 14 months, Prisoner of war (Germany) 2 years 1 month (Holland) 5 months.

Robson, John George (1918–19); Sec.-Lieutenant, London Rgt. and General Staff of Eastern Command.

Robson, John Thomas (1916–19); Lance-Corporal, R.E.

Rockley, Douglas (1914–19); Sergeant, R.A.M.C.; France 3 years 9 months.

Rodgers, Reginald Joseph (1915–19); Lieutenant, R.G.A.; France 2 months.

Rodnight, William Bertie (1915–17); Private, London Rgt.; France 6 months.

Rodwell, Edward (1914–19); M.S.M.; Quartermaster-Sergeant, London Rgt.; France 3 years 5 months.

Roethenbaugh, Ellen (1914–19), R.R.C.: Sister, Territorial Force Nursing Service; Malta 1 year, France 3 years.

Rogers, Frank Edwin (1915–19); Sergeant, R.A.M.C.; France 2 years.

Rogers, Frederick George (1916–19); Sapper, R.E.; France 8 months.

Rogers, Henry William (1916–19); Rifleman, King's R. Rifle Corps, Rifle Brigade and London Rgt.; France 2 years.

Rogers, John Edward (1915–17); Private, Royal Fusiliers; East Africa 2 years.

Rogers, Percy Charles (1914–19); Lieutenant, Nottinghamshire and Derbyshire Rgt., R.A.F. and Oxfordshire and Buckinghamshire Light Infantry; France 1 year 11 months.

Rogers, William Alexander (1916–19); Lieutenant, London Rgt., R.A.M.C. and R.E.; Mesopotamia 16 months.

Rogerson, Frederick Joseph (1916–19); Corporal, R.E.

Rollinson, Bertram (1915–20); Corporal, R.A.M.C.; Mesopotamia 3 years 5 months.

Rood, William John (1916–19); Sec.-Corporal, R.E.

***Rose, Arthur Gurney** (1914–16); Private, London Rgt.; France 11 months; Died of wounds, 12th February, 1916.

Rose, Charles Jackson (1916–19); Sergeant, R.A.F.

Rose, Evan Arnold (1915–19); D.C.M.; Company Quartermaster-Sergeant, R.E.; France 2 years 10 months.

***Rose, Tom** (1915–16); Lance-Corporal, R.F.A.; France 8 months; Died of wounds, 2nd August, 1916.

***Rosen, Joseph** (1914–18); Corporal, London Rgt. and R.E.; France 2 years 10 months; Died, 25th November, 1918.

Rosewarne, Vivian Samuel (1916–19); Lance-Corporal, R.E.

Rosser, Frank Thorne (1918–19); Mechanic, R.N.

Rostron, John (1915–19); Lance-Corporal, London Rgt.; France 5 months, Salonica 7 months, Palestine 13 months, Belgium 3 months.

***Rotenberg, Benjamin** (1915–17); Lance-Corporal, R. Wiltshire Yeomanry; France 4 months; Killed in action, 9th April, 1917.

Rothen, John Neville (1915–19); Sergeant-Instructor, R.G.A. and R.E.; France 18 months.

Rousseau, Albin Charles (1918–19); Sergeant, Somersetshire Light Infantry.

Routley, Walter Stanley (1918–19); Signaller, R.G.A.

Rowe, Sydney Daniel (1915–17); Corporal, R.A.M.C.; France 9 months.

Rowe, Thomas Edwin (1916–19); Lieutenant, R. Naval Division and Lincolnshire Rgt.; France 1 year 7 months.

Rowley, Daniel Thomas (1916–19); Air Mechanic (2nd Class), R.A.F.; France 2 years 4 months.

Rowson, John William (1915–19); Sergeant Gunnery-Instructor, R.F.A.

***Rowson, Tom Hollingsworth** (1915–16); Sec.-Lieutenant, London Rgt.; France 3 months; Killed in action, 15th September, 1916.

Rowthorn, John (1916–19); Lieutenant R.G.A.; France 1 year 10 months.

Rumney, Horace Hales (1916–19); Rifleman, King's R. Rifle Corps; France 6 months, Salonica 17 months.

Rush, Cecil Arthur (1914–18); Sec.-Lieutenant, Royal Fusiliers, N. Lancashire Rgt. and Machine Gun Corps; Overseas 9 months.

***Russell, Charles Edward** (1914–15); Private, Grenadier Guards; France 1 month; Missing, 10th March, 1915.

***Russell, Frank** (1914–16); Private, Middlesex Rgt.; Gibraltar, Egypt and France; Killed in action, 16th September, 1916.

Russell, Samuel Charles (1918–19); Corporal, R.A.F.

Russell, William Andrew (1916–19); Private, London Rgt.; Salonica 6 months, Palestine 1 year, France 6 months.

Rutledge, William Thomas Robinson (1915–19); Lance-Sergeant, R.A.M.C.; Salonica 2 years 9 months.

Ryan, Thomas (1915–19); Private, R.A.V.C.; France 2 years 9 months.

Ryder, Frank (1914–19); Sec.-Lieutenant, Middlesex and E. Kent Rgts.; Mesopotamia 2 years.

Rylatt, Harold (1918–19); Leading Aircraftsman, R.A.F.; Archangel 11 months.

Sager, Jacob Frederick (1917); Private, R.A.M.C.

Saintey, John Sidney (1916–19); Sapper, King's R. Rifle Corps and R.E.; France 1 year 7 months.

St. Leger, Amy Kilner (1914–19); Royal Red Cross, Twice mentioned in despatches; Matron, Q.A.I.M.N.S.; France 4 years 6 months.

Sale, Edward William (1914–19); Lieutenant, R.F.A.; France 3 years 6 months.

Salkeld, James Boustead (1914–19); M.M.; Sergeant-Major, London Rgt.; France 15 months, Macedonia 7 months, Palestine 12 months.

Salmon, Frank (1914–19); Lieutenant, Middlesex Rgt. and R. Welch Fusiliers.

Salmon, Horace (1916–19); Armourer Staff-Sergeant, R.A.O.C.; France 2 years 11 months.

***Salmon, Vernon Edgar Thomas** (1917–18); Private, Honourable Artillery Company; France 6 months, Italy 10 months; Died, 3rd November, 1918.

Samuel, Benjamin (1914–19); Company Sergeant-Major, Essex Rgt. and Rifle Brigade; India 3 years 3 months.

Sands, Frederick James Roberts (1915–19); Private, R.A.M.C.; Egypt 2 years 10 months.

Sands, Percy Robert (1915–19); Sergeant-Major, R.A.M.C.; Italy 18 months.

Sarginson, Joseph (1916–19); Sapper, R.E. and Tank Corps.

***Sarll, Albert Brian Colin** (1914); Private, London Rgt.; France 2 months; Missing, 1st November, 1914.

Saunders, Arthur (1916–18); Lance-Corporal, London Rgt.; France 1 year 7 months, Prisoner of war (Germany) 9 months.

***Saunders, Frank John Bryan** (1915–16); Private, London Rgt.; France 3 months; Killed in action, 31st August, 1916.

Savage, Harry George (1918–19); Private, R.A.F.

Savill, Ernest Clayton (1915–19); Medal for Defence of Amiens (French); Corporal, R.A.S.C. (M.T.); France 3 years.

Sawdy, Harry Edward (1914–19); Sergeant-Instructor, London Rgt. and Machine Gun Corps.

Sawyers, Arthur Ascanius (1914–19); Private, R.A.M.C.; France 8 months. Salonica 3 years.

Saxby, William Edward (1915–19); Air Mechanic (acting 1st Class); R.N.A.S. and R.A.F.

Saxon, Ernest William (1914–20); Captain, County of London Yeomanry, Reserve Cavalry Rgt. and R.A.O.C.; Sierra Leone 7 months.

Sayle, John Daniel (1916–19); Corporal, R.E.

Scadden, Thomas (1916–19); Sergeant, R.E.

Scales, Walter Thomas (1917–19); Private, R.N.A.S. and R.A.F.

Scanlan, Thomas Martin (1916–19); Petty Officer, R.N.V.R.

Schierloh, Philip Eugene (1915–19); Battery Quartermaster-Sergeant, R.F.A. and Labour Corps; France 3 years.

Schodduyn, Lucien Paul (1915–19); Interpreter; France 3 years 4 months.

Schorfield, John (1915–19); Corporal, R.E.

Schwartz, George Leopold (1914 and 1916–19); Private, Middlesex Rgt.; France 17 months.

Scott, Arthur Chard (1914–19); Sergeant, R.A.M.C.; France 4 years.

Scott, Henry James (1915–19); Captain, R.G.A.; France 16 months, Germany 3 months.

Scott, Thomas (1915–19); Corporal, Durham University O.T.C. and R.E.

Scott, Walter Dodson (1915–19); Staff-Sergeant, R.A.M.C.; Egypt 1 year, Mesopotamia 2 years 5 months.

Scott, William John (1915–19); Private, R.A.M.C.; Egypt and Palestine 2 years 10 months.

Scrivens, Arthur George (1915–19); Lieutenant, R.G.A.

Seabrook, Samuel Ernest (1916–19); Regimental Sergeant-Major, R.A.S.C.

Seaman, Arthur Henry (1918–19); Sapper, R.E.

***Searle, George Amos Everitt** (1914–15); Private, Oxfordshire and Buckinghamshire Light Infantry; France 6 months; Killed in action, 24th September, 1915.

Sedwell, Samuel (1915–19); Lance-Corporal, R.A.M.C.; France 2 years 7 months.

Selby, Arthur Ernest (1916–19); Sergeant, R.A.F.

Selley, Hubert (1916–19); Lieutenant, London Rgt.; France 5 months.

Sevier, Thomas James (1914–19); M.M., M.S.M.; Sergeant, R.A.M.C.; France 2 years, North Russia 1 year.

Shafran, Mark Emanuel (1918–19); Lance-Corporal, Royal Fusiliers; Egypt and Palestine 6 months.

Shambrook, Reginald John (1915–18); M.M., Mentioned in despatches; Corporal, R.A.M.C. and 3rd Intelligence Corps Company; France 2 years 10 months.

Sharpe, Henry Edward (1915–19); Sergeant, London Rgt. and R.D.C.

Shaw, Joseph Henry (1914–19); Lieutenant, Royal Fusiliers and N. Staffordshire Rgt.; France 1 month.

Shaw, Lewis Frederick (1914–19); Lieutenant, London Rgt. and R.A.S.C.; France 12 months.

***Shea, William Devereux** (1916–17); Private, London Rgt.; France 7 months; Killed in action, 30th October, 1917.

Sheather, Henry Stephen (1916–19); Sec.-Corporal, R.E.

Shelley, Harry (1914–19); M.C.; Regimental Sergeant-Major, London Rgt.; France 1 year 9 months.

Shennan, Thomas Patrick (1916–18); Sapper, R.E.

***Shepherd, Harold Ernest** (1914–18); Sec.-Lieutenant, Honourable Artillery Company and R.F.A.; Died, 30th December, 1918.

Shepherd, Owen David (1915–19); Gunner, R.G.A.; France 2 years 10 months.

Sheppard, Alfred (1916–19); Private, E. Surrey and Middlesex Rgts.; France and Germany 2 years, Italy 4 months.

Sheppard, William George (1916–19); Sapper, R.E.

***Sherard, Paul** (1916–18); Sapper, London Rgt. and R.E.; France 10 months; Missing, 21st March, 1918.

Shiels, Samuel David (1916–19); Sergeant, R.E.; France 1 year 8 months.

Shilvock, Albert Charles (1914–19); Mentioned in despatches; Sec.-Lieutenant R.F.A.; Gallipoli 3 months, Egypt 9 months, France 2 years 4 months.

Shimmin, William Alfred Moore (1914–17); Lance-Corporal, London Rgt.; France 4 months.

Shingleton, Jolley Samuel (1916–19); Bombardier, R.G.A.; East Africa 2 years.

Shinnick, Jeremiah (1915–19); Private, R.A.M.C.; France 2 years.

Short, Edward Parker (1914–19); Lieutenant, Devonshire Rgt., Yorkshire Light Infantry and Machine Gun Corps; India 15 months, France 4 months.

Shorthouse, Francis James (1914–18); Staff-Sergeant, R.A.M.C.; France 16 months.

***Shrewsbury, James** (1914–15); Sergeant, King's R. Rifle Corps; France 3 months; Killed in action, 16th October, 1915.

Shrimpton, Albert George (1916–19); Sapper, R.E.; France 18 months.

Shuard, Robert William (1916–19); Sec.-Lieutenant, Middlesex and S. Staffordshire Rgts.; France 1 year.

Shuttleworth, Allan (1917–18); Corporal, E. Surrey Rgt.

***Siebert, Stanley Prentice** (1916–17); Sec.-Lieutenant, Rifle Brigade; France 9 months; Died of wounds, 21st September, 1917.

Silley, Frederick Samuel (1915–19); Captain, O.T.C. and Devonshire Rgt.; France 9 months.

Silvano, Thomas Charles Lloyd (1914–19).

Silverston, Jack (1916–19); Sapper, R.E.

Silverstone, Israel (1918–19); Sergeant, R.A.F.

Simmonds, Albert Ernest (1915–19); Pioneer, London Rgt. and R.E.; France 2 years 11 months.

Simmonds, Walter Harold (1915–19); Private, R.A.M.C.; France 2 years 6 months.

***Simmons, Richard Ernest** (1914–17); Sec.-Lieutenant, Middlesex Rgt. and R.G.A.; Gibraltar 6 months, France 16 months; Killed in action, 5th December, 1917.

Simmons, William Richard (1914–19); Corporal, Oxfordshire and Buckinghamshire Light Infantry and Machine Gun Corps; France 2 years 9 months.

***Simons, Leon** (1915–17); M.C.; Captain, Royal Fusiliers; France 10 months; Missing, 17th February, 1917.

Simons, Michael (1914–19); Private, Yeomanry and Machine Gun Corps; Egypt 15 months, Gallipoli 4 months, Salonica 5 months, Palestine 13 months, France 8 months.

Simons, Michael (1916–19); Victualling Assistant, R.N.

***Sizeland, Charles** (1914–16); Sec.-Lieutenant, Yorkshire and Norfolk Rgts.; France 9 months; Killed in action, 12th October, 1916.

Skinner, Leslie Thomas (1915–19); Corporal, R.A.M.C.; Salonica 2 years.

Slarks, Frederick Roberts (1915–19); Company Sergeant-Major, R.W. Kent Rgt.; France 2 years 6 months, Italy 3 months.

Sleight, Walter Guy (1918–19); Company Sergeant-Major, Middlesex Rgt.

Sloman, Charles Shapcott (1914–17); Company Sergeant-Major, London Rgt.; France 3 months.

Small, Frederick George (1916–19); 2nd Corporal, R.E.

Smith, Andrew Hare (1915–19); Lance-Corporal, R.A.M.C.; France 3 years 5 months, Italy 4 months.

Smith, Albert John (1914–16); Private, R.W. Surrey Rgt.

Smith, Arthur Mitson (1916–19); Gunner, R.G.A.; Salonica 2 years 3 months.

Smith, Charles Frederick (1914–19); Schoolmaster-Sergeant, London Rgt.; France 7 months.

Smith, Ernest Sidney (1918–19); Private, London Rgt.

Smith, Frederick (1915–19); Sergeant, R.W. Surrey Rgt. and Royal Fusiliers, France 1 year 7 months, Italy 14 months.

Smith, Frederick Charles (1915–19); Croix de Guerre (Belgian); Sergeant, R.A.M.C.; France 3 years 1 month.

***Smith, Frederick William Ascough** (1916–17); Private, Middlesex and R. Sussex Rgts.; France 9 months; Killed in action, 20th September, 1917.

Smith, George Alexander (1915–19); Lieutenant, R.A.M.C. and R.F.A.; France 1 year 7 months.

***Smith, George Gibson** (1915–19); Lance-Corporal, R.A.M.C.; Salonica 1 year 10 months; Died, 17th January, 1919.

Smith, George King (1918–19); Private, London Rgt.

Smith, Murray James (1914–19); Lance-Corporal, London Rgt.

Smith, Percy Jack (1914–19); M.C.; Lieutenant, R.N.V.R.

Smith, Reginald (1915–19); Lance-Corporal, R.A.M.C. and Devonshire Rgt.

Smith, Richard Harold (1914–18); Sec.-Lieutenant, R.G.A. and R.F.A.; France 18 months.

Smith, Stanley Frank (1914–19); Sergeant-Instructor, London and Norfolk Rgts., Army Gymnastic Staff, and British Military Mission, U.S.A.; France 2 months.

Smith, Thomas (1915–17); Sergeant, R.A.M.C.; Egypt 1 month, Salonica 8 months.

Smith, Thomas Charles Newell (1914–19); Lance-Corporal, Grenadier Guards.

Smith, Walter John (1914–19); Lieutenant, R.G.A.; France, Salonica and Italy 3 years.

Smith, William Alfred (1914–19); M.M., Mentioned in despatches; Corporal, London Rgt.; France 4 years.

Smith, William Henry (1916–19); Sapper, R.E.; France 2 years.

Smith, William Thomas (1916–19); Sapper, R.G.A. and R.E.; France 2 years 4 months.

Smither, Wilfred Cecil Stephen (1914–19); Mentioned in despatches; Sergeant, R.A.M.C.; France 2 years 11 months.

Smyth, Paul Cranfield (1914–19); Lieutenant, Middlesex and Manchester Rgts.; Gibraltar 6 months, Egypt 6 months, France 12 months.

Snee, Edward Andrew (1914–19); Corporal, R.A.M.C. and R.E.; France 2 years 6 months.

Snell, Douglas Hobling (1915–19); Sergeant, R.E.; France 3 years 4 months.

Soames, Basil Charles (1916–19); Sapper, R.E.; France 7 months.

Soko, Arthur Stanislas (1915–19); Staff-Sergeant, R.A.M.C.

Solomons, Samuel (1916–19); Flight-Sergeant, R.A.F.

Sommerton, Harold Charles (1917–19); Corporal Clerk, R.A.F.

Soper, William Thomas (1914–19); Lieutenant, Hampshire Rgt. and Indian Army; India 4 years.

South, Herbert James (1916–19); Sec.-Corporal, R.E.

South, Richard Walter (1915–19); Corporal-Instructor (Wireless), R.A.F.

Southerst, Christopher Guest (1914–19); Sec.-Lieutenant, London Rgt., Royal Fusiliers and R.E.

Southron, Thomas William (1916–19); Mentioned in despatches; Lieutenant and Inspecting Ordnance Officer, R.E. and R.A.O.C.

Spanner, George Charles (1917–19); Lance-Corporal, Labour Corps.

Spary, Cyril Horace (1914–19); Private (Laboratory Foreman), R.A.O.C., Middlesex Rgt. and R.A.O.C.; Gibraltar 5 months, Egypt 9 months, France 5 months.

Spary, Harold Bertram (1914–18); Sergeant, Oxfordshire and Buckinghamshire Light Infantry; France 10 months.

Spaven, Frank Wilson (1915–19); Private, London Rgt. and Machine Gun Corps; France 2 years.

Speight, Bert (1914–19); Lieutenant, Middlesex and Lincolnshire Rgts.; Gibraltar 5 months, France 3 years 3 months.

Spencer, Herbert (1915–19); Sergeant, Yorkshire Light Infantry; France 18 months.

Spicer, Bertram Frank (1915–19); Gunner, R.G.A.; Salonica 2 years 7 months.

Spilsbury, Vincent Charles (1916–19); Sapper, R.E.

Spooner, Alfred John (1916–19); Sapper, R.E.; Mesopotamia 2 years 2 months.

Spreadbury, William Henry (1915–19); Private, R.A.M.C. and Dorsetshire Regt.; India 6 months, Palestine 9 months.

***Springbett, George Thomas** (1915–16); Sergeant, R.W. Kent Rgt.; France 5 months; Died of wounds, 17th September, 1916.

Squire, William Daniel (1915–19); Captain, R.A.M.C., R.F.A. and R.A.F.; France 4 months.

Stacey, Harold William (1915–19); Sapper, R.E.

Stacey, Ralph Llewellyn (1914–19); Corporal, Oxfordshire and Buckinghamshire Light Infantry; France 2 years 7 months.

Stagg, Alfred (1916–19); Company Sergeant-Major, Motor Machine Gun Corps and Tank Corps; France 2 years 6 months.

***Stainton, Robert Meres** (1915–16); Lieutenant, R. Lancaster and York and Lancaster Rgts.; France 11 months; Killed in action, 1st July, 1916.

Staley, William (1914–19); Mentioned in despatches; Sergeant, 15th Hussars; France and Germany 3 years 5 months.

Stanbury, Henry (1915–19); Staff-Sergeant, R.A.M.C.; France 2 years 8 months.

Standfield, Phillip Edward (1915–19); Sergeant, London Rgt.; France 3 years.

***Stanfield, William Arthur** (1915–17); Sergeant, R.A.M.C.; Egypt 2 years 3 months; Accidentally killed, 1st October, 1917.

***Stannard, George Westcott** (1914–16); Corporal, Grenadier Guards; France 17 months; Killed in action, 15th September, 1916.

Stannard, Herbert Harry (1915–19); Private, R.A.M.C., and Sapper, R.E.

***Steel, John** (1915–16); Lieutenant, R.N.V.R.; Killed in fire on H.M.S. Peel Castle, 7th February, 1916.

Stent, Sydney (1914–15); Private, Kent Cyclist Bn.

Stephens, Francis Radnor (1915–17); Corporal, Honourable Artillery Company; France 12 months.

Stephens, James (1916–19); Aircraftsman, R.N.A.S. and R.A.F.

Stephenson, John (1915–19); M.C.; Lieutenant, Durham Light Infantry.

***Steven, Archibald** (1914–16); Sec.-Lieutenant, Gloucestershire Rgt.; France 8 months; Killed in action, 25th October, 1916.

Stevens, Claud Richard (1916–19); Sapper, R.E.; France 8 months, Germany 2 months.

Stevens, Harold Walter (1916–19); Corporal, Northumberland Fusiliers, Rifle Brigade and R. Inniskilling Fusiliers; France 1 year 8 months.

***Stevens, Henry John** (1914–15); Sergeant, Durham Light Infantry; France 7 months; Killed in action, 10th March, 1915.

Stevens, Thomas Leslie (1918–19); Rifleman, Rifle Brigade.

Stevens, William Thomas (1914–19); M.C.; Lieutenant, London and E. Kent Rgts.; France 2 years, Germany 12 months.

***Stevenson, John Connell** (1914–18); Mentioned in despatches; Sec.-Lieutenant, Middlesex and R.W. Surrey Rgts.; Gibraltar and France 1 year 10 months; Killed in action, 24th August, 1918.

Stocker, William James (1915–19); Lieutenant, R.G.A.

Stokes, Robert Biggin (1915–19); Gunner, R.G.A.; France 9 months.

Stone, Fred Norman (1914–19); M.C.; Lieutenant, London Rgt.; France 10 months.

Stone, George (1914–17); Private, E. Surrey Rgt. and R.D.C.

Stone, Hector John (1917–19); Sergeant, R.A.O.C.; France 1 year 10 months.

Stone, Lionel (1916–17); Rifleman, London Rgt.; France 6 months.

Stotesbury, Charles Herbert (1917–19); Corporal, R.E.

Stow, Frederick William (1915–19); Private, London Rgt., and Sapper, R.E.

Strang, Edgar Percival (1916–18); Private, Honourable Artillery Company, Royal Scots and Labour Corps.

Strange, Thomas (1914–19); Staff-Sergeant Instructor, London Rgt. and Army Gymnastic Staff; Malta 7 months, Gallipoli 3 months, Egypt 2 months, France 9 months.

Straw, Albert Gerald (1916–19); Sapper, R.E.; Salonica 4 months.

Strawbridge, Harry (1916–19); Corporal, R.E.

Strawson, Cyril Walter (1915–19); Corporal, R.A.M.C.; France 1 year 10 months.

Streather, John Herbert (1914–16); Private, Middlesex Rgt.; Egypt and France 18 months.

Stretton, Donald (1915–19); Acting Corporal, R.A.M.C.; France 10 months; Egypt and Palestine 1 year 9 months.

Strong, Albert Edward (1915–17); Private, R.A.M.C.; France 4 years 3 months.

Strong, Charles Frederick (1916–19); Captain, Honourable Artillery Company, Nottinghamshire and Derbyshire Rgt. and General List.

Stuart, Albert Henry (1917–19); Captain, R.N.A.S. and R.A.F.

Stuart, Cecil William (1916–19); Sapper, R.E.

Stubbs, John Alfred (1914–19); Sergeant, Royal Fusiliers; France 1 year.

Sturgess, Alfred Walter (1916–19); Lance-Corporal, R.E.

***Sturtridge, Frank** (1914–16); Sergeant, London Rgt.; France 9 months; Killed in action, 30th April, 1916.

Styles, Sydney Alphonso (1918–19); Private, R.A.F.

Sudds, Frederick Henry (1916–19); Lance-Corporal, R.E.; France 3 months.

Sudds, James Edward (1916–19); Corporal, R.A.M.C.; France 2 years 11 months.

Summersby, William (1915–19); Sapper, R.A.M.C. and R.E.; France 18 months, Egypt and Palestine 1 year 8 months.

Swaffer, James (1916–19); Sapper, R.E.; France 9 months.

Swain, Alexander Walter (1916–19); Médaille de Sauvetage Français; Lance-Corporal, London Rgt. and R. Dublin Fusiliers; France 17 months.

***Swallow, William Hugh** (1915–19); O.B.E., Mentioned in despatches; Major, R.A.O.C.; France 1 year 7 months; Died, 21st February, 1919.

Swanborough, Frank Edward (1918); Private, R. Marine Engineers.

Sweeting, Frederick William (1915–17); Leading Mechanic, R.N.A.S.; Mesopotamia 10 months.

Swift, Harry James (1916–19); Sapper, R.E.; France 3 months.

Swindale, John Stephen (1916–19); Sec.-Corporal, R.E.

Swindell, Harold Radford (1916–19); Air Mechanic, R.N.A.S. and R.A.F.

Symes, Cecil Harry Herbert (1914–19); Sergeant, London Rgt. and R.D.C.

***Symons, Alfred** (1914–18); Corporal, London Rgt.; Salonica 4 months, Egypt and Palestine 14 months; Killed in action, 30th April, 1918.

Tailby, Mark Alfred (1915–18); Sergeant, R.F.A.; France 5 months.

Tait, John Alexander (1914–19); Lieutenant, R.F.A.; France 12 months.

Tams, Eyoub Theophilis (1916–19); Private, Middlesex Rgt.; France 1 year 11 months.

Tanfield, Clement Robert (1914–19); Regimental Quartermaster-Sergeant, Machine Gun Corps and County of London Yeomanry; Palestine 12 months, France 9 months.

Tangye, Charles Henry Warren (1914–18); Sergeant, Oxfordshire and Buckinghamshire Light Infantry; France 15 months.

Tanner, William Curnow (1915–19); Sec.-Corporal, R.E.

Tant, Sydney Francis (1918–19); Corporal, R.A.F.

Tarran, William (1914–19); O.B.E., Mentioned in despatches; Major, E. Surrey Rgt.

Tavener, Percy Samuel (1915–19); Corporal, London Rgt. and R.E.; France 3 years 2 months.

Taylor, Alfred James (1915–18); Lance-Corporal, London Rgt.

Taylor, Bert (1914–19); M.S.M.; Quartermaster-Sergeant, R. Sussex Rgt.

Taylor, Charles Harry (1917–19); Lance-Corporal, R.A.O.C.; Italy 1 year 8 months.

Taylor, Charles Robert William (1918–19); Rifleman, London Rgt. and King's R. Rifle Corps; France 3 months.

***Taylor, Frank Henry** (1916–17); Private, E. Kent Rgt.; France 3 months; Killed in action, 27th February, 1917.

Taylor, Frederick George (1915–17); Sergeant, Honourable Artillery Company.

Taylor, Frederick John (1918–19); Corporal, R.A.F.

Taylor, Harry (1914–19); Lance-Sergeant, Honourable Artillery Company; France 2 months.

Taylor, Harry (1915–18); Mentioned in despatches; Lieutenant, W. Riding Rgt.; France 8 months.

***Taylor, Luke Thompson** (1914–16); Sec.-Lieutenant, Inns of Court O.T.C. and Loyal N. Lancashire Rgt.; France 9 months; Died of wounds, 3rd June, 1916.

Taylor, Oliver Charles (1915–19); Corporal, R.A.F.; Eastern Mediterranean 17 months.

Taylor, Oscar Anthony (1916–19); Corporal, R.E.

Teagle, Horace Claude (1915–19); Corporal, Honourable Artillery Company, Royal Scots and Labour Corps.

Teague, William James (1915–19); Private, R.A.M.C.; Egypt and Palestine 2 years 2 months.

Teasel, Hugh Wolsey (1914–19); Corporal, Middlesex Rgt. and A.P. Department; Gibraltar 6 months, Egypt 9 months, France 2 years 10 months.

Tedeschi, Guido (1914–19); Lance-Corporal, Middlesex Rgt. and R.A.M.C.; Macedonia 2 years 3 months.

***Terrell, Victor James** (1915–16); Private, London Rgt.; France 9 months; Missing, 1st July, 1916.

Thew, Alan Wellwood (1915–19); Lieutenant, County of London Yeomanry and R. Sussex Rgt.; Russia 12 months.

Thicthener, James Henry (1914–16); Lance-Sergeant, London Rgt.

Third, Henry McPhail (1915–19); Sergeant, R.A.M.C.; Egypt 3 years.

Third, James Bonella (1914–19); Sergeant, London Rgt.; France 12 months, Salonica 6 months, and Palestine 12 months.

Thirlwall, Harry Archibald (1914–19); Sec.-Lieutenant, Middlesex Rgt.; Gibraltar 6 months, France 2 years 4 months.

Thirtle, Harry George (1914–19); Lance-Corporal, London Rgt.; France 4 years.

Thoday, William Henry (1916–19); Sergeant, R.E.

Thomas, Christmas (1915–19); Rifleman, London Rgt. and R.A.M.C.; Egypt 2 years 6 months, Palestine 12 months.

Thomas, David Talbot (1916–19); Sergeant, R.E.

Thomas, Francis Leo (1914–19); Trooper, Middlesex Yeomanry and Imperial Camel Corps; Egypt 1 year 10 months, Gallipoli 5 months, Palestine 2 years 6 months.

Thomas, Frederick Monro (1914–19); Mentioned in despatches; Rifleman, London Rgt.; France 17 months; Salonica 5 months, Palestine 13 months.

Thomas, Frederick William John (1914–19); Lieutenant, R.A.; France 1 year 9 months, Salonica 5 months, Egypt 14 months, Palestine 5 months.

Thomas, George Arthur (1916–18); M.M.; Sec.-Corporal, R.E.; France 2 years 6 months.

Thomas, Harry (1918–19); Sec.-Lieutenant, R.A.O.C.

Thomas, James Gauntlett (1914–18); Sergeant, London Rgt.; France 2 years 6 months.

Thomas, James Percy (1915–19); Company Sergeant-Major Instructor, Honourable Artillery Company and Corps of the School of Musketry.

***Thomas, John Glasson** (1915–17); Battery Sergeant-Major, R.G.A.; France 10 months; Killed in action, 11th August, 1917.

Thomas, John Henry (1916–19); Corporal, R.A.F.; France 9 months.

Thomas, John James (1915–19); Lieutenant, R.N., R.N.A.S. and R.A.F.; France 2 years 9 months.

Thomas, Lewis John (1916–19); Sapper, R.E.; France 3 months.

Thomas, Norman John Francis Charles (1917–19); Private, R. Warwickshire Rgt. and Air Mechanic, R.A.F.

Thomas, William (1914–19); M.S.M.; Sergeant, London Rgt. and Royal Fusiliers; Malta 4 months, France 4 years 2 months.

Thomas, William Henry (1915–19); Private, R.A.M.C.; France 3 years 9 months.

Thompson, Alfred Alexander (1915–18); Gunner, R.G.A.; Salonica 1 year 9 months.

Thompson, Frederick Capon (1914–19); Lieutenant, Royal Fusiliers; France 2 years.

Thompson, Frederick Harold (1914–19); Company Quartermaster-Sergeant, London Rgt.; France 1 year 7 months.

Thompson, Frederick Wilberforce (1918–19); Corporal, R. Marine Light Infantry.

Thompson, Joseph (1915–17); Sergeant, London Rgt.

Thompson, Joseph Charles (1916–19); Sapper, R.E.; France 12 months.

Thompson, Percy Albert (1918–19); Private, R.A.F.

Thompson, William (1914–19); Sec.-Lieutenant, London Rgt.; France 6 months, Salonica 6 months, Palestine 12 months.

Thompson, William (1915–19); Private, R.A.M.C.; Italy 1 year 10 months.

Thompson, William John (1914–19); Regimental Quartermaster-Sergeant, London Rgt.; Gallipoli 3 months, Malta 2 months, Egypt and Palestine 3 years.

Thompson, William Wood (1914–19); Sec.-Lieutenant, R.A.M.C. and Machine Gun Corps.

Thorne, Sidney James (1915–19); Private, County of London Yeomanry, Middlesex and R. Sussex Rgts.; France 18 months, Italy 3 months, North Russia 11 months.

***Thornton, Harold Victor** (1915–18); Lieutenant, Essex Rgt. and R.A.F.; France 9 months, Italy 2 months; Killed in action, 10th May, 1918.

Thornton, Hubert (1916–19); Sergeant-Mechanic, R.A.F.; France 2 years 11 months.

Tibbitts, Harold George (1915–19); Lance-Corporal, R.E.; France 3 years 4 months.

Tibbs, Charles Henry (1915–19); Staff-Sergeant Instructor, R.A.O.C.; France 3 years.

Ticehurst, Arthur George (1914–19); Lieutenant, London and S. Lancashire Rgts.

Timms, Francis John (1915–19); Captain, R. Warwickshire Rgt., R.E. and R.G.A.

***Timpson, Wilfrid Mansfield** (1916–17); Private, R.A.M.C.; France 5 months; Killed in action, 12th May, 1917.

Tinniswood, Lewis Beattie (1916–19); Private, R.A.F., Nottinghamshire and Derbyshire Rgt. and Cameron Highlanders; France 2 years 4 months.

***Todman, Charles Vincent** (1914–18); Sec.-Lieutenant, London Rgt. and R.A.F.; France 10 months; Killed in action, 3rd August, 1918.

Todds, Walter (1914–19); Captain, County of London Yeomanry, Labour Corps and General Staff; Egypt 1 year 7 months, Salonica 8 months.

Tomkin, William Edward (1916–19); Sapper, R.E.

***Tongue, Andrew Leslie** (1916–18); Sec.-Lieutenant, Honourable Artillery Company and R.F.A.; France 10 months; Killed in action, 28th May, 1918.

Tonkin, Richard Woodward (1916–19); M.S.M.; Squadron Quartermaster-Sergeant, R.A.S.C.

***Tovey, Robert Charles** (1915–18); Private, City of London Yeomanry and R.F.A.; France 8 months; Died of wounds, 17th October, 1918.

Tovey, William Henry (1914–19); M.M.; Sec.-Lieutenant, R.F.A.; France 2 years 6 months.

Towers, James (1915–19); Warrant Schoolmaster, R.N.

Towler, Frank (1916–19); Sapper, R.E.; France 4 months.

Townsend, James Ernest (1915–19); Sergeant, R.A.M.C.

Townson, Frederick (1918–19); Corporal, R.A.F.

Trace, Roland (1914–18); Lieutenant, London Rgt.; France 6 months.

Trasler, George Price (1914–19); Mentioned in despatches; Sergeant, R.F.A. and Central Research Laboratory, Mesopotamia; Dardanelles 6 months, Mesopotamia 3 years 4 months.

Treacher, Joseph Jacques (1915–19); Lieutenant, R.A.O.C. and R.G.A.; France 3 years.

***Treadwell, George Reuben** (1914–17); Major, E. Lancashire Rgt.; Dardanelles 4 months, Mesopotamia 7 months; Killed in action, 5th February, 1917.

***Tremeer, Sidney Charles** (1914–17); Lieutenant, Royal Fusiliers and Bedfordshire Rgt.; France 1 year 7 months; Died of wounds, 18th May, 1917.

Tremmeer, Frederick Henry (1915–19); Private, E. Surrey Rgt.; India 1 year 9 months, Mesopotamia 15 months.

Trenchard, Clement (1914–19); Captain, London Rgt., Somersetshire Light Infantry and R.A.F.; France 2 years.

Trevenen, Arthur Henry (1915–19); Warrant-Officer (1st Class), R.A.F.; Egypt 2 years 7 months.

Trezise, James Edwin (1914–19); Sergeant, London Rgt.

Trivett, Albert (1916–19); Private, London Rgt.; Salonica 6 months, Palestine 13 months, France 3 months.

True, James Jesse (1915–19); Sergeant, London Rgt.

***Truman, Thomas Charles** (1916–18); Private, R.G.A.; France 1 year 9 months; Died of wounds, 10th April, 1918.

Tuck, Henry James (1914–19); Mentioned in despatches; Sec.-Lieutenant, Royal Fusiliers and R.G.A.; France 2 years 7 months.

Tucker, Ernest William (1915–19); Staff-Sergeant, R.A.M.C.

Tucker, Harry Edgar (1914–19); Corporal, London Rgt.

Tucker, William (1914–18); Corporal, London Rgt. and R. Inniskilling Fusiliers.

Tucker, William Alexander (1916–19); Air Mechanic, R.A.F.

Turnage, Robert George (1914–19); Captain, London Rgt.; France 11 months.

Turner, Archibald Worsdale (1914–17); Sergeant, London Rgt.

Turner, Edward (1914–19); Mentioned in despatches; Quartermaster-Sergeant, R.A.M.C.; France 10 months, Mesopotamia 18 months, India 5 months, Egypt 6 months, Palestine 9 months.

Turner, Ernest Lewis (1917–19); Corporal, R.A.F.

Turner, Henry (1914–17); Sergeant, King's R. Rifle Corps and Oxfordshire and Buckinghamshire Light Infantry; India 18 months.

Turner, John (1915–19); Corporal, Honourable Artillery Company; France 3 years 6 months.

Tyers, Archibald Neville (1916–18); Sec.-Lieutenant, R.G.A.; France 6 months.

***Udall, William Gaius** (1916–17); Private, R.E.; France 7 months; Died of wounds, 22nd April, 1917.

Uden, Walter (1914–19); M.S.M., Twice mentioned in despatches; Regimental Quartermaster-Sergeant, R.A.M.C.; France 4 years 4 months.

Uglow, Harold George (1917–19); Sec.-Lieutenant, R.G.A.

Underwood, Reginald Sidney (1915–19); Company Sergeant-Major, Norfolk Rgt. and Army Gymnastic Staff; France 11 months.

Upham, William Lewis (1917–20); Lance-Sergeant, R.A.O.C.; Egypt 2 years 7 months.

Urquhart, George Stanley (1914–19); Lieutenant, London Rgt. and King's R. Rifle Corps; France 2 years, Italy 5 months, Germany 1 month.

Usher, Reginald Ernest (1915–19); Sergeant, R.A.M.C.; France 2 years 7 months.

Vanderhook, Solomon (1914–19); Lieutenant, Oxfordshire and Buckinghamshire Light Infantry, Gloucestershire Rgt. and R.A.F.; France 13 months.

Varney, Walter Vernon (1915–19); Corporal, R.E.; France 3 years 4 months.

Vaughan, Sidney Percy (1914–19); Corporal, Middlesex Rgt.

Vearncombe, Reginald (1915–19); Corporal, R.A.M.C.; France 3 years.

Veness, Edmond (1916–19); Schoolmaster, R.N.

Venning, Harold (1914–19); Mentioned in despatches; Lieutenant, R.G.A.; France 3 years.

Vernon, Gordon Cayley (1916–19); Sapper, R.E.

Verrall, Albert George (1914–19); Sec.-Lieutenant, London Rgt. and Machine Gun Corps; France 7 months.

Verrells, Henry Victor (1915–19); Sergeant-Instructor, Army Gymnastic Staff.

Verrells, William Streatfield (1915–19); Company Sergeant-Major-Instructor, R.A.M.C. and Army Gymnastic Staff; France 12 months.

Verrier, Frederick John (1916–19); Corporal, R.E.

Vince, Robin Coles (1915–19); Corporal, R.A.F.

Vincent, Percy Claude (1917–19); Private, R.A.S.C.; France 1 year 8 months.

Vine, Henry (1916–19); Corporal, R.E.

Wade, Ernest George (1914–19); Lieutenant, Middlesex and E. Kent Rgts., and Rajput Light Infantry; India 3 years, Mesopotamia 10 months, Aden 8 months.

Wade, William (1916–19); Private, R.A.M.C.; Mesopotamia 2 years 8 months.

Wagstaff, William James (1914–18); Regimental Quartermaster-Sergeant, London Rgt.

Wagstaffe, George William (1916–19); Sergeant, R.E.

Wait, Albert Owen (1915–19); Private, R.A.M.C.

Waldridge, Charles Frederick (1916–19); Sec.-Corporal, R.E.

Waldron, Percy (1914–19); Lieutenant, Leicestershire Rgt.

Wale, Richard Robert (1914–17); Corporal, London Rgt.; France 15 months.

***Wale, Sydney John** (1914–17); Sergeant, London Rgt.; France 4 months; Killed in action, 21st May, 1917.

Walkem, Charles Batt (1916–19); Sergeant, R.A.O.C.; France 2 years.

Walker, Charles Albert (1914–19); Sec.-Lieutenant, R.E.

Walker, Frederick Joseph (1916–19); Bombardier, R.G.A.; France 1 year 10 months.

Walker, George Harold (1914–17); Company Quartermaster-Sergeant, E. Surrey and R. Sussex Rgts.

Walker, Harold Stanley (1915–19); Sergeant, Yorkshire Light Infantry; France and Germany 10 months.

***Walker, John Alexander** (1915–16); Private, R.A.M.C.; France 2 months; Killed in action, 24th December, 1916.

Walker, John Reece (1915–17); Private, R.A.M.C.

Walker, Samuel Keith (1915–19); Sec.-Lieutenant, R.A.S.C. and Egyptian Labour Corps; France 3 months, Egypt 3 years.

Wall, Cyril Ernest (1915–17); Sapper, R.E.

Wall, Frank Athelstan (1916–19); Gunner, R.G.A.

Wall, John Albany (1915–19); Corporal, R.A.M.C.; India 2 years 8 months.

Walling, Leon Edward (1916–18); Corporal, R.E.; France 2 years.

Wallis, Josiah (1916–18); Sapper, R.E.

Walls, Alfred George (1914–18); Sergeant, R.F.A.; France 3 months.

Walls, Edward William (1914–19); Mechanist Sergeant-Major, R.A.S.C.

Walsham, Charles (1915–19); Private, R.A.M.C.; France 12 months, Salonica 15 months.

Walshe, Cecil (1915–19); Lieutenant, Honourable Artillery Company and R. Warwickshire Rgt.; France 1 year 7 months.

Walter, William George (1914–19); Sergeant, Leicestershire Rgt.; France 3 years 5 months.

Walters, Fred (1916–19); Sapper, R.E.; France 2 years.

Walton, William (1915–19); Private, R.A.M.C.; France 2 years 9 months.

Ward, Alfred John (1914–19); Mentioned in despatches; Company Quartermaster-Sergeant, London Rgt.; France 6 months, Salonica 6 months, Palestine 1 year 9 months.

Ward, Charles Samuel (1915–19); Mentioned in despatches; Company Sergeant-Major-Instructor, R.W. Surrey Rgt. and Army Gymnastic Staff; France 1 year 10 months.

Ward, Ernest (1914–19); Sec.-Lieutenant, Hampshire Rgt.; India 2 years, Palestine 2 years.

***Wardley, Miles Edward** (1914–17); Sec.-Lieutenant, London Rgt. and Royal Fusiliers; France 16 months; Killed in action, 29th April, 1917.

Wardman, Oswald (1915–19); Private, R.A.M.C.; France 16 months.

Ware, James Herbert (1915–19); Lieutenant, Honourable Artillery Company, London Rgt. and Machine Gun Corps; France 15 months.

***Wareham, Frederick William** (1914–16); Lieutenant, R. Warwickshire Rgt.; France 8 months; Killed in action, 1st July 1916.

Waring, Frederick George (1914–19); Regimental Sergeant-Major, R.A.M.C.; East Africa 15 months.

Warner, Hugh (1918–19); Private, R.A.F.

Warr, Edward Ernest (1915–19); Company Sergeant-Major, Essex Rgt.; France 1 year 10 months.

***Warren, Alec Francis** (1914–16); Private, Middlesex Rgt.; Egypt and France 12 months; Killed in action, 15th September, 1916.

Warren, Frederick Charles (1914–19); Staff-Sergeant, R.A.M.C.

***Warren, Harry** (1914–17); Sec.-Lieutenant, Hampshire and Dorsetshire Rgts.; France 1 month; Killed in action, 7th July, 1917.

Warren, Stanley William (1918–19); Corporal, R.A.F.

Warren, Thomas Henry (1915–19); Sergeant-Instructor, London Rgt. and Army Gymnastic Staff; Mesopotamia 13 months.

Washington, William (1916–19); Sec.-Lieutenant, R.A.S.C.; Salonica 3 months, France 18 months.

Waskett, William (1915–19); Quartermaster-Sergeant, London Rgt.; France 7 months, Salonica 9 months, Egypt 3 months, Palestine 1 year 9 months.

***Waterland, Douglas** (1914–15); Sergeant, London Rgt.; France 2 months; Killed in action, 26th May, 1915.

Waterman, William Charles (1915–19); Sergeant, R.A.M.C.; France 2 years 7 months.

Waterworth, Tom Powis (1915–19); Private and Flight Cadet, London Rgt., R.E. and R.A.F.

Watkins, Henry Miles (1916–19); Corporal, R.E.

Watson, Robert William (1918–19); Sergeant, Bedfordshire Rgt. and Royal Fusiliers.

Watson, Stanley Joseph (1915–19) Corporal, London Rgt.

***Watson, Sydney Thomas** (1914–18); Company Sergeant-Major, London Rgt.; France 5 months, Palestine 16 months; Killed in action, 28th March, 1918.

Watson, William Arthur (1916–19); Corporal, R.N.A.S. and R.A.F.

Watson, William Percy (1915–18); Lieutenant, London Rgt.; France 6 months.

Watt, George Robert (1914–19); M.C.; Lieutenant, R.F.A.; France 3 years 4 months.

Watts, Bertram James (1916–19); Gunner, R.G.A.

Watts, Percy Frederick (1914–19); M.C.; Captain, Bedfordshire and Hertfordshire Rgts.; France 1 year 8 months, Germany 8 months.

Way, Herbert Edward (1916–20); Lieutenant, R.A.S.C.; Mesopotamia 16 months.

Way, William George (1915–18); Company Sergeant-Major, R.F.A. and E. Kent Rgt.

Weatherley, Charles Alfred (1916–19); Sergeant, R.N.A.S. and R.A.F.

Webb, Charles Albert (1915–19); Corporal, London Rgt.; France 13 months, Salonica 6 months, Palestine 15 months.

Webber, Edward Charles (1915–19); Lance-Corporal, R.E.

Webber, Perceval Ernest (1914–19); Private and Sapper, Middlesex Rgt., Imperial Camel Corps and R.E.; Dardanelles 4 months, Egypt and Palestine 4 years.

Webber, William Charles (1915–17); Private, Honourable Artillery Company.

Webster, Henry George (1914–19); Quartermaster-Sergeant Surveyor, Middlesex Rgt. and R.E.; Gibraltar 6 months, France 3 years 9 months.

Wedge, John Longmore (1916–19); Bombardier, R.G.A.

Weinstein, Hyam (1916–19); Private, Middlesex Rgt.; France 1 year 11 months.

Welch, Arthur Frederick Chilman (1914–19); Regimental Quartermaster-Sergeant, London Rgt.; France 2 years.

Weldon, John Thomas (1915–19); Rifleman, Rifle Brigade; France 3 years 3 months.

Wells, George Henry (1914–19); Sergeant, Oxfordshire and Buckinghamshire Light Infantry; France 1 year 10 months.

Wesley, Arthur Frederick (1914–19); Mentioned in despatches; Lieutenant, Labour Corps.

***West, Charles Edward** (1915–18); Private, London Rgt.; France 5 months, Salonica 7 months, Palestine 9 months; Died of wounds, 28th March, 1918.

West, Herbert (1916–19); Sergeant, R.N.A.S. and R.A.F.

West, John William (1914–18); Private, London Rgt.

***West, William Frank** (1914–15); Private, London Rgt.; France 3 months; Died of wounds, 12th May, 1915.

Westcott, William Henry (1914–19); Company Quartermaster-Sergeant, London and Middlesex Rgts.; Gibraltar 7 months, Egypt 9 months, France 2 years 8 months.

Weston, Allan (1915–19); Lieutenant, R.H.A. and Napier's Rifles; India 3 years 10 months.

Weston, Charles Edward (1915–19); Captain, S. Wales Borderers; France.

***Weston, Frederick George** (1914–18); Mentioned in despatches; Company Sergeant-Major, London Rgt.; France 2 years 1 month; Killed in action, 28th August, 1918.

Weston, Leonard Charles (1914–19); Lieutenant, London and R. Warwickshire Rgts.; France 1 year 10 months, Germany 3 months, Italy 1 month, Asia Minor 1 month.

Weston, Sidney James (1914–19); Private, Middlesex Rgt.; Gibraltar 8 months, Egypt 9 months, France 2 years 8 months.

Wethey, Charles Henry (1915–19); Private, R.A.M.C.; France 5 months, Salonica 8 months, Egypt 1 year 7 months.

Wexler, Louis (1918–19); Private, Labour Corps.

Whatley, William Ernest (1917–19); Private, R.A.M.C.; France 17 months.

***Wheatcroft, Frederick George** (1915–17); Sec.-Lieutenant, E. Surrey Rgt.; France 4 months; Killed in action, 26th November, 1917.

Wheeler, Arnold (1915–19); Lieutenant, Inns of Court O.T.C., R.W. Surrey and Suffolk Rgts.; Egypt 18 months.

Wheeler, Frederick George (1914–19); Staff-Sergeant, R.A.M.C.; France and Germany 3 years 6 months.

Wheeler, Walter Harold (1916–19); Sapper, R.E.; France 1 year 8 months.

Whelan, John (1916–19); Private and Air Mechanic (2nd Class), R.A.O.C. and R.A.F.

Whelan, William (1915–19); Sapper, R.E.

Whitaker, Richard Harold (1914–19); Trooper, City of London Yeomanry; Dardanelles 3 months, Salonica 7 months, Egypt 18 months, Palestine 16 months, Syria 6 months.

Whitbread, Harold William (1915–19); Corporal, R.A.M.C.; France 16 months.

White, Arthur (1914–19); Rifleman, London Rgt.; Salonica 7 months, Egypt and Palestine 1 year, France 17 months.

White, Edwin Charles (1915–17); Rifleman, London Rgt.; France 3 months.

White, Harold Harry (1914–18); Sergeant, London Rgt.; France.

White, Jack Foster (1914–18); Sec.-Lieutenant, Middlesex Hussars and R.A.F.; Egypt and Sinai 1 year 10 months, Dardanelles 4 months, Salonica 10 months, Palestine 6 months.

Whitebrook, John Cudworth (1915–19); Lieutenant, Monmouthshire and Manchester Rgts.; France 8 months.

Whitehead, Norman (1914–19); Lieutenant, R.G.A.

Whitehorn, Edward (1916–19); Sapper, R.E.; France 7 months.

***Whiteley, Frederick Joseph** (1914–16); Sergeant, Rifle Brigade; France 1 year 7 months; Killed in action, 18th August, 1916.

Whiteman, Harry (1914–19); Mentioned in despatches; Lance-Sergeant, Grenadier Guards; France 3 years 5 months.

Whiting, Leopold Augustus (1915–19); Sec.-Lieutenant, R.H.A., R.G.A. and Labour Corps; Egypt 2 years.

Whitlock, Arthur Edward (1914–19); Sec.-Lieutenant, Hampshire and London Rgts.; India 2 years 3 months, Palestine 1 year 9 months.

Whittaker, William (1914–19); Sec.-Lieutenant, London Rgt. and R.G.A.; France 5 months, Salonica 1 year 9 months.

Whittle, John Edward (1918–19); Corporal, R.A.F.

***Wholey, Frederick** (1914–16); Lance-Corporal, Middlesex Rgt.; Gibraltar 6 months, France 15 months; Killed in action, 16th September, 1916.

Wicks, Wilfred James (1916–18); Rifleman, London Rgt. and R. Irish Rifles France 7 months.

Widdicombe, Horace Manfred (1915–18); Sergeant, R.F.A.; France 10 months.

Wightman, Frank Herbert (1915–19); Chief Petty Officer, R.N.

Wilcox, Benjamin Richard Kingston (1916–19); Aircraftsman, R.N.A.S.

Wilcox, James John (1914–19); Sergeant, R. Marine Light Infantry.

Wilcox, Robert Henry (1915–19); Warrant Officer, R.N.; H.M.S. Lucia 7 months, H.M.S. Furious 1 year 7 months.

Wild, Laurence (1914–18); Rifleman, London Rgt.; France 1 year 10 months.

Wilkins, Bernard Horace (1914–19); Lieutenant, R.E. and Royal Fusiliers; France 8 months, Salonica, Bulgaria, and Turkey, 2 years 2 months.

Wilkins, George Leslie Ernest (1916–18); Lieutenant, Lancashire Fusiliers and Royal Fusiliers; France 2 years 5 months.

Wilkinson, Rupert Ruthven (1916–19); Private, Welch Rgt. and R.A.S.C.

***Wilkinson, William Alfred** (1915–17); Sec.-Lieutenant, R.F.A.; France 8 months; Killed in action, 2nd December, 1917.

Wilks, William Thomas (1914–17); Sergeant, R.A.M.C.

Wille, Henry John Standen (1915–19); Sergeant, R.A.V.C.

Williams, Clifford Sydney (1915–19); Silver medal of the Order of King (Grecian) George I., 1st Class; Corporal, R.A.S.C.; Egypt 2 months, Salonica 3 years.

***Williams, Daniel John** (1915–17); Sec.-Lieutenant, R. Welch Fusiliers and Machine Gun Corps; France 3 months; Killed in action, 2nd October, 1917.

Williams, Harold Howell (1916–19); Sergeant, R.G.A.; France 18 months.

Williams, Harry (1915–18); Sergeant, R.A.M.C.

Williams, Harry Morse (1914–16); Sergeant, Scottish Borderers; France 6 months.

Williams, Herbert Owen (1916–19); Corporal, R.A.S.C.

Williams, John (1916–19); Sapper, R.E.

Williams, Robert Alfred (1914–19); Captain, Grenadier Guards, R. Warwickshire Rgt. and King's R. Rifle Corps; France 14 months, Germany 5 months.

Williams, Sidney Arthur (1915–19); Sergeant, R.A.O.C.

***Williams, Sydney Mansel** (1914–17); Lieutenant, London Rgt.; France 4 months; Missing, 15th June, 1917.

Williams, Walter Archibald (1914–19); Lieutenant, R.F.A.

Williamson, Arthur Gilbert (1915–19); Lance-Corporal, R.E.

Willis, Arthur Walter (1915–19); Lieutenant, R.F.A.; France 3 years, Germany 3 months.

Willis, Douglas John (1915–19); Private and Aircraftsman (1st Class), London Rgt. and R.A.F.; France 6 months.

***Willis, William Frederick Bucknole** (1914–16); Sec.-Lieutenant, Oxfordshire and Buckinghamshire Light Infantry; France 16 months; Killed in action, 23rd July, 1916.

Willmer, Reginald Arthur Pyemont (1914–19); M.M.; Private, Manchester Rgt.; Gallipoli 2 months, Egypt 13 months, France 16 months.

Wills, Walter Wellington (1914–19); Sergeant, Middlesex and E. Lancashire Rgts.; France 17 months.

Willson, Alfred Graffham (1918–19); Rifleman, King's R. Rifle Corps.

Wilmot, Ernest Fitzwilliam (1915–19); Sergeant, R.A.S.C.

***Wilson, Cecil Fred** (1915–18); Lieutenant, Honourable Artillery Company and Hampshire Rgt.; Palestine and France 2 months; Died of wounds, 27th July, 1918.

Wilson, George Douglas (1914–19); Lance-Corporal, London Rgt. and R.D.C.

Wilton, Ernest (1915–19); Private, Honourable Artillery Company; France 2 years 6 months, Germany 1 month.

***Winbush, Edward Thomas** (1915–17); Lieutenant, R.F.A.; France 1 year 9 months; Killed in action, 24th September, 1917.

Winder, Harry Howell (1918–19); Corporal, Rifle Brigade, London Rgt. and R.A.P.C.

Winder, Herbert Burns (1916–18); Gunner, R.G.A.

Winfield, Cyril Charles (1915–18); Private, Royal Fusiliers, Black Watch and Scottish Horse.

Winn, George Edmund Wells (1916–17); Private, Essex Labour Corps.

Winn, Henry William (1916–19); Sec.-Corporal, R.E.

Winn, Leonard (1917–19); Sergeant, R.A.O.C.; Italy 2 years.

***Winter, James Frederick** (1916–18); Lance-Corporal, R.G.A. and R.E.; France 2 years; Killed in action, 28th October, 1918.

Winter, William Percy (1916–19); Sapper, R.E.

Wisdom, Alfred (1916–19); Warrant Schoolmaster, R.N.

Witcombe, Sidney Frank (1915–19); Mentioned in despatches; Lieutenant, London Rgt. and R.E.; France 3 years 8 months.

Witney, Arthur Harry (1914–19); Battery Quartermaster-Sergeant, R.F.A.

Witty, Harry Walter (1914–19); Corporal, Middlesex Rgt.; Gibraltar 6 months, France 3 years 6 months.

Wood, Arthur Ernest (1914–19); D.C.M.; Corporal, London Rgt.; France 2 years 9 months.

Wood, Arthur John (1918–19); Private, R.W. Surrey Rgt.

Wood, Benjamin (1916–19); Sergeant, R.A.S.C. and A.P.C.

Wood, Frederick (1918–19); Private, Essex Rgt.

Wood, George Hamilton (1917–19); Air Mechanic (2nd Class), R.A.F.; France 2 years.

Wood, George William (1914–19); Corporal, London Rgt.; France 18 months.

Wood, Percival Edward (1915–18); Trooper, King Edward's Horse; France 17 months.

***Wood, Randolph Amos** (1914–17); Sergeant, London Rgt.; France 2 years 4 months; Killed in action, 22nd November, 1917.

Wood, Sidney Albert (1914–19); Company Quartermaster-Sergeant, Oxfordshire and Buckinghamshire Light Infantry and R. Warwickshire Rgt.

Wood, William Thomas (1916–19); Lieutenant, R.E. and R.A.O.C.

Woodgate, Walter George (1916–19); Sec.-Corporal, R.E.

***Woodhouse, Fred** (1914–16); Company Quartermaster-Sergeant, R. Berkshire Rgt.; France 16 months; Killed in action, 2nd October, 1916.

Woods, Elias Charles (1918–19); Private, R.A.M.C.

Woods, Ernest John (1916–19); Bombardier, R.G.A.

Woods, Frederick Harrison (1914–19); Sergeant, E. Surrey Rgt.; India 12 months, Aden Field Force 2 years.

***Woods, John William** (1914–17); M.C.; Captain, Coldstream Guards; France 2 years 2 months; Killed in action, 14th April, 1917.

Woodward, Frank Cecil Charles (1915–19); Sec.-Lieutenant, R.A.S.C. and R.G.A.; France 2 years 3 months.

Woolf, Harry (1917); Private, R.A.M.C.

Woollett, John Castle (1914–17); Regimental Quartermaster-Sergeant, R. Irish Fusiliers.

Woolley, Sidney (1915–19); Lance-Corporal, R.A.M.C.; Adriatic 3 months, Salonica 2 years 8 months.

Workman, George James (1916–19); Private, Middlesex Rgt. and R.A.M.C.; France 4 months.

***Worner, Percival Seymour** (1915–16); Sec.-Lieutenant, Devonshire Rgt.; France 6 months; Killed in action, 4th September 1916.

Wotton, Arthur Edward (1917–19); Mechanic (1st Class), R.N.A.S. and R.A.F.

Wren, Harry (1915–19); Staff-Sergeant, Middlesex Rgt.; France 12 months.

Wright, Frank (1915–19); Lance-Corporal, R.E.

Wright, Samuel Charles (1914–19); Staff-Sergeant, R.A.P.C.

***Wrigley, James** (1915–17); Sec.-Lieutenant, R.A.M.C. and R.G.A.; France 1 year 8 months; Killed in action, 29th September, 1917.

Wroot, Ezra (1916–19); Corporal, R.G.A.

Wyatt, William John (1915–19); Private, R.A.M.C.; Albania and Corfu 3 months, Salonica 2 years 6 months.

Wyles, Stephen (1916–19); Sapper, R.E.; France 9 months.

***Wynne, John Andrew** (1915–16); Private, London Rgt.; France 4 months; Killed in action, 22nd May, 1916.

Wyse, William John (1914–20); Company Quartermaster-Sergeant, Devonshire Rgt.

Yalden, Edward Charles (1915–19); M.C.; Sec.-Lieutenant, Middlesex Rgt.; France 7 months.

Yarham, Edwin Moss (1916–18); Lance-Corporal, London Rgt.

Yates, John William (1916–19); Lance-Corporal, R.A.M.C., R.A.S.C. and R.A.O.C.

Yorke, John Paley (1916–19); Twice mentioned in despatches; Captain, R.E.

Young, Arthur Roland (1914–19); Private and Air Mechanic (3rd Class), Middlesex Rgt. and R.A.F.; Gibraltar 8 months, Egypt 8 months, France 2 years 8 months.

Young, Charles (1914–19); Gunner, R.F.A.; Italy 14 months.

Young, Fred (1917–18); Gunner, R.G.A.; France 12 months.

Young, Joseph Bernard (1914–19); Company Sergeant-Major, London Rgt.; France 8 months, Salonica 8 months, Palestine 12 months.

Young, Norman Malcolm (1916–19); Private, R.W. Kent Rgt.; India 2 years 3 months

Young, Stephen John (1914–18); Staff-Sergeant, R.A.M.C.

Young, William John (1915–18); Sergeant, London Rgt.

Zaktrager, Myer (1915–19); Mentioned in despatches; Sergeant, R.E.; France 3 years 9 months.

Zeffert, Abraham (1918–19); Lance-Corporal, Royal Fusiliers.

***Zoller, Herbert Sidney** (1916–17); Private, London Rgt.; France 5 months; Killed in action, 7th June, 1917.

***Zoller, Victor** (1916–18); Private, R.G.A.; France 1 year 8 months; Killed in action, 25th April, 1918.

Stores Department

Arnold, Charles William (1915–19); Private, 24th Bn. London Rgt., R. Irish Rifles and Irish Rgt.; France 18 months.

***Bain, Archibald James** (1915–17); Rifleman, 6th Bn. London Rgt.; France 4 months; Missing, presumed killed, 21st May, 1917.

Barratt, Arthur George (1915–19); Company Quartermaster-Sergeant, 16th Bn. Rifle Brigade; France 18 months.

***Beale, Reginald Charles** (1914–15); Private, 24th Bn. London Rgt.; France 2 months; Killed in action, 26th May, 1915.

Beere, James Henry (1918); Rifleman, 15th Bn. London Rgt.

***Bennett, Charles** (1916–19); Private, 3/4th Bn. R. W. Kent and Cheshire Rgts.; France 7 months; Died, 21st January, 1919.

***Benson, Edward Thomas** (1914); Gunner, R.F.A.; France 2 months; Died of wounds, 15th November, 1914.

***Berridge, Percy** (1915–18); Gunner, R.F.A.; Salonica; Died, 14th April, 1918.

Blake, Horace James (1915–19); Private, R.A.M.C.; France 12 months, Italy 5 months.

Bounds, Henry (1915–19); Regimental Staff-Sergeant, R.A.M.C.; France 3 years.

Brennan, Arthur Henry (1916–17); Sergeant, 24th Bn. London Rgt.

Briant, George Faulkner (1915–19); Corporal, 3/13th and 2/25th Bns. London Rgt., 23rd Bn. Cheshire Rgt. and Trench Mortar Battery; France 1 year.

Briggs, Thomas William (1915–19); Gunner, R.G.A.; France 1 year.

Brookes, Edward George (1915–19); Sergeant, R.G.A.; France 15 months.

Brooks, William George (1918–19); 1st Private, No. 8 School of Arms, R.A.F.

Brown, Charles Godfrey (1915–19); Mentioned in despatches; Sergeant, R.A.S.C.; France 3 years 1 month, Italy 6 months.

Bulcraig, Francis John (1914–19); M.M., Mentioned in despatches; Drum-Major, 23rd Bn. London Rgt.; France 4 years.

Butler, Henry Bartle (1915–19); Private, R.A.O.C.; Egypt 2 years 7 months.

Cairns, Robert (1915–19); M.S.M.; Company Sergeant-Major, R.A.S.C. and Labour Corps; France 3 years 1 month.

Chambers, Arthur Percy (1917–18); Private, Northamptonshire Rgt. and R.D.C. France 2 months.

Charlton, Arthur W. (1916–19); Lieutenant, A.P.C., A.P.D.

***Clark, Arthur** (1915–16); Rifleman, 16th Bn. London Rgt.; France 11 months; Died of wounds, 10th October, 1916.

***Clarke, Frederick William** (1914–15); Private, Coldstream Guards; France 1 month; Killed in action, 25th January, 1915.

Cole, Robert Nash (1916–19); Lieutenant, R.N.A.S.

Collier, Charles Henry (1915–19); Guardsman, Coldstream Guards; France 2 years 4 months.

Court, Sidney Herbert (1916–19); Corporal, R.N.A.S. and R.A.F.; France 2 years 10 months.

Curtis, Albert (1914–19); Corporal, R.A.S.C.; France 4 years 1 month.

Cuthbertson, Lawrence (1914–19); Twice mentioned in despatches; Captain, 9th and 10th Bns. London Rgt., R. Welch Fusiliers and S. Lancashire Rgt.; Overseas 3 years 2 months.

Daniels, Walter (1914–15); Private, 2nd Bn. Rifle Brigade; France 9 months.

***Davey, William Alfred George** (1914–15); Rifleman, 18th Bn. London Rgt.; France 6 months; Killed in action, 29th September, 1915.

Dawkins, William Royd (1914–19); Sergeant, R.A.M.C.; Salonica 3 years 1 month, France 9 months, Turkey 4 months.

Dennis, William Frederick (1915–19); Corporal, R.F.A.

Duncan, Hamilton Ford (1914–19); Signaller, 302nd Brigade R.F.A.; Egypt 6 months, France 6 months, Salonica 6 months, Palestine 18 months.

Dundon, Arthur (1915–19); Corporal, R.F.A.; France 2 years.

Dunscombe, Herbert Upton (1915–17); Private, 15th Bn. London Rgt.; France 15 months.

Elbourne, Ernest Hugh (1915–19); Staff-Sergeant, R.A.O.C.

Ellis, Jeffrey Rudlen (1916–19); Aircraftsman (2nd Class), R.F.C. and R.A.F.; Palestine 18 months.

Firman, Harley (1914–19); Sapper, 5th London Brigade, R.F.A. and R.E.; France 3 years 11 months.

Fordham, William (1914–19); Lance-Corporal, 1st Bn. Duke of Cornwall's Light Infantry; France 1 year 7 months, Germany (Prisoner of war) 2 years 6 months.

Fox, Thomas Augustus (1914–19); Sergeant, 4th Bn. R. W. Surrey Rgt., Corps of M.P.; France 6 months.

Gates, Charles J. (1916–19); Lance-Sergeant, Royal Fusiliers and A.P.C.

Gates, Leonard Thomas (1914–19); Bombardier, R.F.A.; France 2 years.

***Goss, Samuel** (1916–18); Driver, R.H.A. and R.F.A.; France 15 months; Died of wounds, 13th June, 1918.

Hales, George Leo (1915–17); Private, R.A.M.C.; Gallipoli 6 months, Egypt 5 months.

Haley, Andrew Daniel (1914–19); Regimental Sergeant-Major, London Mounted Brigade Field Ambulance, R.A.M.C.; France 14 months.

Halfpenny, Edwin Joseph (1915–19); Private, 2/3rd Field Ambulance, R.A.M.C.; France 1 year.

Hammant, George John (1915–19); Mentioned in despatches; Private, R.A.M.C.; France 3 years 3 months.

Hampson, Charles (1915–19); Private, R.A.M.C. and 95th R.F.A.; France 2 years 5 months.

Harraway, Charles (1915–19); Private, 7th Bn. Wiltshire Rgt.

Harris, Philip Frederick (1914–19); Rifleman, 16th Bn. London Rgt.; France 1 year 7 months.

Harvey, Charles Samuel (1914–18); Gunner, R.G.A.; France 4 years 2 months.

Hatton, Robert (1915–19); Rifleman, 6th Bn. London Rgt. and Labour Corps; France 3 years 1 month.

Hawkes, William David (1915–19); Private, R.A.O.C. and 2nd Bn. R. Irish Fusiliers; France 1 year 10 months, Prisoner of war 10 months.

Herbert, William John (1916–19); Sergeant, R.F.C.; Salonica 2 years 7 months.

Hollingsworth, Albert Edward (Junior) (1915–19); Corporal, R.A.S.C., Horse Transport; Palestine 2 years, Egypt 8 months.

***Hollingsworth, Frank Edison** (1914–16); Private, London Rgt. and Sec.-Lieutenant, Argyll and Sutherland Highlanders, R.E. and R.F.C.; France 1 month; Missing, 15th September, 1916.

Horne, Lawrence Victor (1915–19); Private, 1/8th (Cyclist) Bn. Essex Rgt.

***Howard, Stanley Finbow** (1915–17); Lance-Corporal, 15th Bn. London Rgt. and 11th Bn. Rifle Brigade; France 3 months; Killed in action, 20th November, 1917.

Howell, Sidney Ernest (1914–19); Rifleman, 11th Bn. London Rgt.; Gallipoli 8 months, Palestine and Egypt 2 years 4 months.

Hutt, Edward John (1916–19); Clerk (2nd Class), R.N.A.S. and R.A.F.; France 2 years 6 months.

Juleff, Stephen James (1915–19); Corporal, R.A.F.; France 3 years.

Kates, Edward James (1916–19); Corporal, R.A.F.; France 10 months.

Keeble, Walter Edward (1916–19); Company Sergeant-Major, 14th Bn. R. W. Surrey and Middlesex Rgts.

Kelly, Harry (1915-19); Steward (2nd Class), Leading Seaman, H.M.S. Lord Nelson; Ægean Sea and Mediterranean 1 year.

Kemp, Frank Nathan (1915-19); Sergeant, R.A.M.C.; France 2 years 11 months.

King, Byron Charles (1915-19); Lieutenant, R.A.S.C.; France 3 years 10 months.

King, John Jackson Porteous (1917-19); Corporal, R.A.M.C.

Knight, William Ernest (1916-19); Sergeant, A.P.C.

Lane, Arthur Edward (1915-20); Flight Sergeant, R.A.F.; France 3 years 5 months.

Lane, Leslie Charles (1917-19); Lance-Corporal, Honourable Artillery Company; France 2 years.

Linnington, Henry James (1915-19); Corporal, R.A.M.C.; France 8 months, Italy 16 months.

***Lloyd, Richard** (1915-18); Private, Labour Corps and R.A.S.C.; Salonica 2 years; Died, 16th January, 1918.

Lucy, Charles Robert (1917–19); Rifleman, 5th and 16th Bns. King's Royal Rifle Corps.

McDonald, Frank (1915-19); Sergeant, 290th Bde. R.F.A.; France 18 months, Palestine 2 years, Egypt 8 months.

Magenis, Bert (1914-17); Corporal, R.F.A.; France 2 years 1 month.

Marsh, Walter James (1915-19); Staff Quartermaster-Sergeant, R.A.O.C.; Salonica 2 years 10 months.

Mitchell, Walter Herbert (1915-19); Corporal, R.G.A.

Moore, William George (1917-19); 2nd Private, R.N.A.S. and R.A.F.

Morris, Eric (1914-19); Rifleman, 18th Bn. London Rgt.; France 3 years 10 months.

Neave, Bertie John (1915-19); Private, R.A.M.C.; Mesopotamia 5 months, India 2 years 8 months.

Newman, Frederick John (1914–19); Sapper, 3rd Bn. Coldstream Guards and R.E.; France 3 years 9 months.

Norman, John (1914-19); Corporal, 6th Dragoon Guards, attached 1st Life Guards, and 3rd Bn. Argyle and Sutherland Highlanders; France 2 years 6 months.

Orchard, Frederick George (1914-19); Acting Quartermaster-Sergeant, 1/1st and 2/3rd London Field Ambulance, R.A.M.C.; France 3 years 5 months.

***Overton, Herbert Alfred** (1914-16); Private, 15th Bn. London Rgt.; France 16 months; Died of wounds, 18th September, 1916.

Paul, William George (1915–19); Driver, 100th and 231st Bdes. R.F.A.; France 2 months, Salonica 3 years 6 months.

Perry, Hubert Charles (1916-19); Sergeant, R.G.A.

Pickett, Samuel (1915-19); Gunlayer and Signaller, 110th and 291st Bdes. R.F.A.; France 2 years 9 months.

Player, Arthur Henry (1915-19); Staff Sergeant-Major, R.A.S.C.; British East Africa 2 years 2 months.

Plummer, Percy A. (1915-19); Private, R.A.M.C.; Salonica 2 years 11 months.

Potter, John Daniel (1915-19); Sapper, R.E.; France 13 months.

Prince, William Harold (1915-19); Drummer, 15th Bn. London Rgt.; France 2 years 1 month.

Richards, N. A. (1915–18); Staff-Sergeant-Major, R.A.S.C.

Roe, George Edward Frank (1915-19); Mentioned in despatches; Lieutenant, R.E. and R.A.S.C.; France 5 months, Italy 1 year 9 months.

Rowles, George (1915-17); Private, 1st Bn. Northamptonshire Rgt.; France 3 months.

***Salmon, Henry John** (1916–18); Private, R.A.S.C. and Machine Gun Corps; France 7 months; Died, 27th November, 1918.

Samuel, Lionel (1915-19); Lance-Corporal, 16th Bn. London Rgt.; France 2 years 6 months.

Scott, Arthur (1915-19); Gunner, R.F.A.; France 17 months, Italy 6 months.

Scott, George John (1915-19); Gunner, 2/6th London R.F.A., Guards Div. Artillery; France 2 years 3 months, Germany 5 months.

Shorting, William (1914-19); Driver, R.A.S.C.; France 4 years.

Smith, Horace (1915-19); Acting Sergeant, R.A.M.C. (Sanitary Section); France 3 years 10 months.

Smith, Stanley Edward (1916–19); Clerk (2nd Class), R.N.A.S. and R.A.F.; France 1 year 9 months.

Smith, William Robert (1916–19); Corporal, Royal Fusiliers; France 4 months.

Snell, George (1914–19); Private, 10th Bn. London Rgt.; Palestine 18 months, Egypt 18 months.

***Stagnell, Herbert** (1916–17); Rifleman, King's Royal Rifle Corps; France 1 month; Killed in action, 9th April, 1917.

***Standerwick, Edwin William** (1914–18); Lieutenant, 4th Bn. Essex Rgt.; Killed in action, 19th April, 1918.

Steele, Frank Bertram (1914–19); Sergeant, 2/A Batty. Honourable Artillery Company; France 1 year 8 months.

Stevenson, Harold (1916–19); Able Seaman, H.M.S. Glorious; North Sea 2 years 3 months.

Teevan, George Harris (1914–19); Driver, 7th London Bde. R.F.A.; France 3 years 3 months.

Thorogood, Henry Frederick (1915–19); Private, 9th Bn. E. Surrey Rgt. and Machine Gun Corps; France 3 years 4 months.

Townsend, Walter Edward (1915–19); Lance-Sergeant, Royal Fusiliers.

***Tuffey, William** (1914–15); Private, 7th Bn. Gloucestershire Rgt.; Dardanelles 2 months; Killed in action, 8th August, 1915.

Vickers, Sidney (1915–19); Private, 10th Bn. Tank Corps, 2/2nd County of London Yeomanry and 7th Bn. King's Own R. Lancaster Rgt.; France 2 years 8 months.

Viney, Arthur (1918–19); Private, 32nd Bn. Middlesex Rgt. and R.A.O.C.

Wallbank, Walter Francis (1916–19); Sergeant, R. Irish Rgt., R.F.A. and 13th Bn. King's Liverpool Rgt.; France 1 year 3 months.

Wallis, Thomas (1915–16); Private, 16th Bn. Middlesex Rgt.

Warton, Joseph Jerome (1915–19); Private, R. Welch Fusiliers; France 3 years 1 month.

Weston, Arthur (1916–19); Sergeant, Royal Fusiliers and A.P.C.

White, Alfred (1916–19); Private, 2/1st Bn. Cambridgeshire Rgt. and 17th Bn. Essex Rgt.

***White, Charles** (1914–15); Private, 2nd Dragoon Guards; France 4 days; Accidentally killed, 18th September, 1915.

White, Harry Thomas Thornton (1917–19); Corporal, Royal Fusiliers and A.P.C.

Whitehead, Charles (1915–19); Gunner, 8th London Bde. and 20th Corps Trench Mortar Bde.; Palestine 1 year, France 1 year 10 months, Syria 3 months, Egypt 6 months.

Wilkins, Herbert John (1915–19); Sergeant, R.A.M.C.; France 2 years 5 months.

Wilkins, John Thomas (1915–19); Corporal, R.A.M.C.; India and Mesopotamia 1 year 9 months, Egypt and Palestine 5 months.

Willden, Arthur (1915–17); Lieutenant and Quartermaster, R.A.M.C.; France 11 months.

Willden, John Henry (1915–19); Captain, R.A.M.C.; Gallipoli 7 months, Egypt and Salonica 2 years 6 months.

Williams, Sidney Thomas (1916–19); Sergeant, R.F.C. and R.A.F.; France 17 months.

***Williams, William Alfred** (1914–17); Sergeant, Middlesex Rgt.; France 1 year 8 months; Killed in action, 17th March, 1917.

Wilson, Charles Ernest (1915–18); Private, 10th and 1st Bns. London Rgt.; France 9 months.

Wilson, Walter Ernest (1915–19); Lance-Sergeant, R.A.M.C.; France 2 years 3 months.

***Wilton, Albert Edward** (1914–15); Private, 1st Bn. Coldstream Guards; Missing, 25th January, 1915.

***Wood, Henry Oxley** (1915–16); Private, 2/7th Bn. Middlesex Rgt.; France 1 year 7 months; Died of wounds, 12th September, 1916.

Wood, William C. (1916–18); Sapper, R.E.

***Woodcock, James** (1914–16); Lance-Corporal, 12th Bn. Middlesex Rgt.; France 14 months; Killed in action, 26th September, 1916.

Worthy, Alfred John (1914–19); Corporal, 301st Bde. R.F.A.

Yeomans, Henry (1914–19); Gunner, Honourable Artillery Company; Palestine 17 months, Egypt 2 years, Syria 5 months.

Youatt, John (1915–19); Sergeant, Acting Quartermaster-Sergeant, R.A.M.C.

Young, Frederick (1915–19); Private, R.G.A. and R.A.M.C.

***Young, George** (1916–17); Rifleman, 5th Bn. Rifle Brigade; France 9 months; Died of wounds, 21st November, 1917.

Parliamentary Department

***Beardmore, Henry Oswald** (1914–16); Private, 24th Bn. and 25th (Cyclist) Bn., London Rgt.; France 18 months; Killed in action, 15th September, 1916.

Dimmick, Frederick Charles Eugene (1917–19); Twice mentioned in despatches; Captain, R.A.F. and Air Ministry; Numerous flights to France.

Hanscombe, Hugh James (1914–19); Captain, Royal Fusiliers, S. Lancashire Rgt. and General List; Gallipoli 14 days.

Fawcett, Sam (1914–19); Corporal, R.A.M.C., 2/1st London Field Ambulance; France 2 years 11 months.

Asylums and Mental Deficiency Department.

Central Administrative Staff

Budd, Thomas William (1915–19); Sergeant, R.A.M.C.; France 3 years 9 months.

Farrer, George Arthur (1917–19); Sergeant, R.A.F.

Gerrard, Philip (1914–19); M.S.M., and Twice mentioned in despatches; Warrant Officer Class 1 (Staff Sergeant-Major), Middlesex Rgt. and R.A.S.C.; Gallipoli 4 months, Egypt 15 months, Palestine 1 year 11 months.

Goldie, Donald (1915–19); Sergeant, Inns of Court O.T.C.

Laxton, William James (1916–19); Private, Royal Fusiliers; France 1 year 6 months.

Leeming, Walter Spencer (1915–19); Sec.-Lieutenant, R.A.M.C. and R.A.F.; France 2 years 10 months.

Pickering, William Frederick (1916–19); Sergeant, R.A.S.C. and Border Rgt.; France 3 months.

Pathological Laboratory

Mann, Sydney Andrew, B.Sc., A.I.C. (1915–20); Mentioned in despatches; Captain, R.A.M.C., 93rd Sanitary Section; 1st London (City of London) Sanitary Co., R.A.M.C.; Egypt and Syria 3 years 3 months.

Mott, Sir Frederick Walker, K.B.E., M.D., F.R.S., F.R.C.P., LL.D. (1914–19); Mentioned in despatches, K.B.E.; Brevet Lieut.-Colonel, R.A.M.C.

Partner, Frank (1914–19); Acting Sergeant, R.A.M.C.; France 3 years 10 months.

Banstead Mental Hospital

Ansell, Albert Edward (1915–19); Private, 2/5th Bn. E. Surrey Rgt. and R.D.C.

Attrill, Alfred (1917–19); Private, 5th Bn. Royal Fusiliers and Labour Corps; France 1 year.

Austin, John Algernon (1918–19); Corporal, R.A.S.C.

***Bailey, John Edmund** (1915–18); Private, 3rd Bn. R. Welch Fusiliers; France 2 years; Died, 9th January, 1918.

Barber, James Oswald (1917–19); Private, R.F.A. and R.A.O.C.; France 2 years 2 months.

***Bateman, Charles John** (1915–18); Corporal, R.A.M.C.; Salonica 2 years 10 months; Died, 16th March, 1918.

Bell, Gilbert Fenwick (1914–19); M.M.; Sergeant, 6th Bn. Border Rgt., 14th Bn. Northumberland Fusiliers; Gallipoli 11 months, France 3 years 7 months.

Bonwick, William (1914–19); Private, 4th Bn. R. West Surrey Rgt.; Gallipoli 4 months, India 3 years 4 months.

Boreham, William Stanley (1914–19); Sergeant, 8th Bn. West Riding Rgt. and Essex Rgt.; Palestine 2 years.

***Bown, Victor** (1915–17); Gunner, R.F.A.: France 1 year 8 months; Killed in action, 10th August, 1917.

Burgess, James Thomas (1917–19); 2nd Air Mechanic, R.A.F.

***Butler, Stanley Harold** (1914–15); Private, 8th Bn. West Riding Rgt.; Gallipoli 6 weeks; Died of wounds, 13th August, 1915.

Byram, William Mason (1914–19); Mentioned in despatches; Sub-Conductor, R.A.O.C.; France 4 years 8 months.

Candler, Thomas William (1914–19); Gunner, R.A.M.C. and R.F.A.; France 3 months, Egypt 3 years 10 months.

Carpenter, Albert Cornelius (1916–19); Gunner, R.G.A. Siege Battery; France 5 months.

Carter, Francis James (1914–19); Gunner, R.F.A.; France 3 years 3 months.

Caselton, Walston (1914–17); Private, 2/5th Bn. E. Surrey Rgt.

Clarke, Geoffrey (1915–20); Mentioned in despatches; Lieut.-Colonel, R.A.M.C.; France 4 years.

Cloughton, Sidney (1916–19); Private, R.G.A. and R.A.M.C.

Collyer, William Edwin (1915–16); Private, 3rd Bn. R. Welch Fusiliers; Gallipoli 4 months.

Cook, Charles St. George (1914–19); Mentioned in despatches; Regimental Sergeant-Major, 21st Bn. Machine Gun Corps; France 2 years 9 months.

Cope, John (1914–19); D.S.M.; Chief Petty Officer, Minesweeping, North Sea.

Cox, James (1915); Private, 1st Dragoon Guards; France 3 months.

Cox, William Thomas (1914–19); M.S.M.; Sergeant, R.G.A.; France 4 years 3 months.

Crissell, Alfred James (1915–19); Private, R.D.C. and R.A.M.C.

Critchley, William Henry (1917–19); Private, 2nd Bn. Bedfordshire Rgt.; India 1 year 5 months.

Davis, Frederick (1914–19); Private, National Reserve and R.D.C.

Edwards, Arthur (1914–19); Private, R.A.M.C.; France 10 months.

Elms, Harry (1914–19); Mentioned in despatches; Acting Sergeant, 1st Bn. E. Surrey Rgt.; India 3 years 6 months, Mesopotamia 18 months.

Elsey, Ernest Richard (1916–19); Private, R. Sussex Rgt.; France 5 months.

Emmett, Robert (1914–15); Private, 2nd Bn. Worcestershire Rgt.; France 3 months.

***Farrow, Mark** (1914–18); Private, 2nd Bn. Devonshire Rgt.; France 2 years 5 months; Missing, 26th to 31st May, 1918.

Farrow, Roland Frank (1915–16); Driver, R.A.S.C.

Fluck, Alfred John (1916–19); Lance-Corporal, Sherwood Foresters; Egypt 1 year.

Fraser, Charles (1918–19); Private, R.A.M.C.

Garland, William Edward (1915–19); Lance-Corporal, R.A.M.C.; Malta 3 years 4 months.

Gibbs, Solomon Richard (1917–19); Private, R.A.M.C.

Gibson, Edward Oscar Spencer (1914–16); Gunner, R.F.A.; France 10 months.

Gibson, Robert Henry Knox (1914–19); Bombardier, R.F.A.; Mesopotamia 1 year, France 2 years 3 months, Egypt 1 year 3 months.

***Gould, Percy John** (1914–15); Private, 9th Bn. E. Surrey Rgt.; France 6 months; Died of wounds, 26th September, 1915.

Gowin, David Coleman (1915–19); Sapper, Electrical and Mechanical Co.; France 3 years 6 months.

Green, Henry Constantine (1914–19); Corporal, R.A.S.C.; France 4 years.

Hesselden, Thomas (1915–19); Private, R.A.M.C.; France 2 years, Italy 1 year.

Hodson, Charles William (1914–19); Driver, R.F.A.; France 4 years 6 months.

Horne, Joseph Scott (1914–19); 1st Air Mechanic, E. Surrey Rgt. and R.A.F.

House, William Edward (1914–18); Lance-Corporal, R. West Surrey Rgt.

***Ingram, Albert** (1914–15); Private, 9th Bn. E. Surrey Rgt.; France 6 months; Missing, 26th September, 1915.

Jeffries, Alfred George (1915–19); Private, R.A.M.C.

Jones, William (1914–19); Sergeant, E. Surrey Rgt.; India 2 years 6 months, Mesopotamia 2 years.

Kendall, Godfrey William (1914–19); Corporal, R.F.A.; France 4 years, Italy 5 months.

King, Frank (1915–19); Private, R.A.S.C. (M.T.); France 2 years 5 months.

Kirkland-Whittaker, Rev. Harry (1915–19); Captain, R.A.M.C.

Kitcherside, George Henry (1914–19); Private, Royal Marine Light Infantry; North Sea 7 months, West Coast Africa 3 years.

Lane, Harry (1916–18); Gunner, R.G.A.; France 1 year.

Langridge, Harry James (1914–19); Private, 3rd Bn. E. Surrey Rgt.

Lawrence, George (1914–19); Staff Sergeant, R.A.M.C.; France 4 years 8 months.

Layzell, Willie George (1914–17); Company Sergeant-Major, 6th Bn. Bedfordshire Rgt.: France 18 months; Discharged unfit, 12th September, 1917; Died of illness incurred on active service, 14th January, 1918.

Low, Cyril Edwin (1914–19); Private, 2/5th Bn. E. Surrey Rgt.; India 18 months, France 15 months.

Lufflum, George Henry (1914–19); Acting Staff Sergeant, R.G.A. and Military Provost Staff Corps; France 4 years.

McAndrew, John (1915–19); Corporal, R.A.M.C.; Malta 2 years, France 18 months.

Maltby, James (1914–17); Private, 5th Bn. E. Surrey Rgt.

Marshall, Joseph Robert (1914–19); Corporal, Cavalry Machine Gun Corps; France 4 years 2 months.

Martyr, Arthur Waterer (1914–19); Corporal, R.A.M.C.; France 3 years 4 months.

Massara, Joseph John (1915–19); Private, R.A.M.C.; France 1 year.

Mays, Thomas John (1915–19); M.M.; Corporal, R.E.; France 2 years 4 months.

Middleton, Charles Bailey (1915–19); Private, 1st Bn. Border Rgt.: France 2 years 6 months, Egypt 4 months.

Miles, Edward (1914–19); M.S.M.; Regimental Quartermaster-Sergeant, 8th Bn. W. Riding Rgt.; Gallipoli 6 months, France 3 years, Egypt 4 months.

Moore, William Charles (1914–19); Pioneer Sergeant, 5th Bn. E. Surrey Rgt.; India 3 years, Mesopotamia 18 months.

Mortimer, James (1915–19); Gunner, R.G.A.; France 2 years 6 months.

Nash, Jeremiah (1916–19); Lance-Corporal, 12th Bn. R. West Kent Rgt., M.F.P.

Newitt, William (1914–19); Lance-Corporal Bandsman, 13th Bn. R. Scots Fusiliers; France 2 years 2 months.

Newman, Alfred Horace (1914–19); Corporal, 8th Bn. W. Riding Rgt.; France 1 year, Gallipoli 2 months, Egypt 4 months.

Owen, Sam (1914–19); Sergeant, 1st Bn. Loyal North Lancashire Rgt.; France 3 months.

Perkins, William Michael (1915–19); Private, R.A.S.C.; France 3 years 2 months.

Peters, Robert Sharp (1915–19); Driver, R.F.A.; France 1 year 10 months.

Phillips, Edward (1915–17); Private, R.A.M.C.

Pink, John (1915–19); Driver, R.A.S.C., M.T.; France 3 years.

Priest, George (1915–19); Private, R.A.M.C.; Dardanelles 3 months, Egypt 16 months

Rawlinson, John (1915–19); Private, 3rd Bn. E. Surrey Rgt.; Salonica 3 years 2 months, France 6 months.

Reed, William (1915–19); Private, R.A.M.C.; Mesopotamia 6 months, India 3 years 4 months.

Ricketts, Edward (1915–19); Private, 11th Bn. E. Surrey Rgt.; France 1 year 11 months.

Robinson, Walter (1914–19); Private, Leicestershire Rgt.

Rose, Ernest Percy (1915–19); Gunner, R.G.A.; France 2 years 10 months.

Ruthven, Morton Wood (1915–19); Captain, R.A.M.C. Special Reserve; France 2 months.

Sales, Albert Henry (1915–19); Sapper, R.E.; Palestine 1 year, France 2 months.

Salter, William George (1914–19); Corporal, 12th Lancers; France 13 months.

***Seal, Albert** (1914–15); Private, 2nd Scots Guards; France 6 months; Died, 15th May, 1915.

Shepherd, Robert (1916–19); Private, R.A.M.C.

Size, Albert Edward (1916–19); Sergeant, E. Surrey Rgt. and A.P.C.

Slater, George William (1915–19); Private, R.A.M.C.; France 3 years.

***Smith, Charles** (1914); Private, 5th Bn. E. Surrey Rgt.; Died, 29th November, 1914.

Smith, William Henry (1914–19); Sergeant, 3rd Bn. Liverpool Rgt.

Spreadbury, Albert (1914–19); Sergeant, 5th Bn. E. Surrey Rgt.; India 2 years 8 months, France 16 months.

Stallwood, Thomas Frederick (1915–19); Sergeant, R.A.M.C.; Mesopotamia 2 years, Salonica 3 months, India 1 year.

Stones, John (1915–19); 2nd Class Officers' Steward, 12th Escort Flotilla.

Stribbling, Andrew (1915–18); Sergeant, 5th Bn. E. Surrey Rgt.

Sugars, Albert James (1915–19); Private, R.A.M.C.; France 4 years.

Swain, Frank (1915–19); Private, R. Irish Fusiliers; France 2 years 4 months, Prisoner of war 8 months.

Turner, Albert (1916–19); Private, 29th Bn. Middlesex Rgt.

***Vaughan, Dr. Robert William Walter** (1914–17); Lieutenant, R.A.M.C.; France and Serbia 2 years 6 months; Killed in action, 23rd May, 1917.

Wallace, Mary Fanny (1915–19); Sister, T.F.N.S.

Waterman, Frank Edward (1914–19); Staff Sergeant-Major, 15th Field Butchery; France 4 years 5 months.

Weatherley, James John (1915–19); Sergeant, R.H.A.; France 4 years.

***Webb, Arthur James** (1914); Private, 2nd Bn. Grenadier Guards; France 4 months; Killed in action, 29th December, 1914.

West, Percy (1916–19); Private, 2/5th Bn. Durham Light Infantry; Salonica 2 years 3 months, Russia 4 months.

Wilson, Frederick James (1914–19); Corporal, 9th Bn. E. Surrey Rgt.

Winkworth, Harry Hall (1914–19); Sergeant, 15th Bn. Durham Light Infantry; France 1 month.

***Wiscombe, Frank** (1915–18); Private, 2nd Bn. Wiltshire Rgt.; France 2 years; Wounded and missing, 8th May, 1918.

Wootton, Dr. Leonard Henry (1915–19); M.C.; Major, London Field Ambulance; France 9 months, Salonica 3 years 6 months.

Bexley Mental Hospital

Adams, William Frank (1914–17); Sergeant, Manchester Rgt.; France.

Allan, James (1915–19); Private, R. West Kent Rgt., R.D.C., Royal Fusiliers, R.A.S.C.

Andrews, Alfred Leslie (1915–19); Corporal, R.E.

Ball, Stanley Richard Thomas (1914–19); Sergeant, R.F.A., Indian Labour Corps; Gallipoli 6 months.

Banham, George William (1914–16); Private, 14th Bn. London Rgt.; France 4 months.

Bates, Frederick George (1915–17); Private, R.A.S.C.

Bowden, Samuel Thomas (1914–19); Sergeant, R.A.M.C.; France 3 years 8 months.

Carr, Arthur (1915–19); Lance-Corporal, R.A.M.C.; France.

Carran, John Paisley (1914–19); Private, R.A.M.C.; France 3 years 9 months.

Cartwright, Bertram James (1914–19); Private, R.A.M.C.; France 3 years 9 months.

Cliffe, Peter (1916–19); Bombardier, R.G.A.; France 3 years.

Coppard, William James Edward (1915–17); Private, R.A.M.C.; France 17 months.

Curd, Albert Alvah (1914–19); Private, Royal Defence Corps.

Curtis, Arthur Reginald (1915–18); Lance-Corporal, Oxfordshire and Buckinghamshire Light Infantry, Worcestershire Rgt., M.F.P.; France 15 months, Dardanelles 4 months.

Darvell, David (1914–19); Private, 2nd Life Guards.

Deely, Patrick John (1914–19); Sergeant, R.E.; France 3 years 3 months.

Draycott, Arthur George (1915–19); Corporal, R.A.M.C.

Eastwood, Ernest (1915–19); Corporal, R.A.M.C.; France 1 year, Salonica 1 year 9 months.

Everest, George (1914–19); Sergeant, Middlesex Rgt.

Fackrell, Albert Arthur (1914–19); Private, R.A.M.C.; France 4 years 3 months.

Farrant, Henry William (1914–19); Corporal, 4th Bn. Middlesex Rgt.; France 4 years 6 months.

***Faulks, Edgar** (1915); Lieutenant, R.A.M.C.; France 1 month; Killed in action, 26th September, 1915.

Fitzgerald, Patrick (1914–19); Sergeant Drummer, 5th Bn. E. Kent Rgt.; Mesopotamia 3 years 4 months.

Ford, Edward Matthew (1915–19); M.S.M.; Sergeant, R.E.; France 3 months, Salonica 3 years 2 months.

Frost, Arthur William (1917–19); Private, R. Irish Rifles; France 17 months.

***George, John Alfred** (1916–18); Gunner, R.G.A.; France 2 months; Died of wounds, 25th January, 1918.

Gosling, Thomas William (1916–19); Gunner, R.G.A.; France 2 years.

Gough, Ernest Douglas (1914–19); Private, R.A.M.C.; France 2 years, Egypt 1 year.

Green, Samuel Henry (1915–19); Sergeant, R.A.M.C.; Egypt 4 years.

Groom, Percy Andrew (1916–19); Lieutenant, London Rgt., Leicestershire Rgt., Tank Corps; France 16 months.

Guppy, F. H. (1914–19); M.C., Médaille des Epidémies (en vermeil); Captain, R.A.M.C.; France 5 years.

Ham, Albert Frank (1915–19); Sergeant, 11th Bn. R. West Kent Rgt.; France.

***Hampton, Albert** (1914–18); Private, R.A.M.C.; Salonica 2 years 6 months; Killed in action, 13th April, 1918.

Harber, Charles Percy (1917–19); Private, R.A.M.C.

Harding, James Bowerman (1915–19); Corporal, R.A.M.C.; France 6 months, East Africa 2 years 6 months.

***Hicks, John George** (1914); Private, 2nd Dragoon Guards; France 2 months; Died of wounds as prisoner of war, 9th December, 1914.

Higdon, Albert (1914–19); Private, 5th Bn. E. Kent Rgt.; Mesopotamia 3 years 3 months.

Hodgson, Sam Milnes (1915–19); Private, R.A.S.C.

Hosmer, James William (1914–19); Private, R.A.M.C.; France 2 years, Dardanelles 6 months.

James, Alfred John (1914–19); Sergeant, 5th Bn. E. Kent Rgt.; Mesopotamia and India 4 years 3 months.

Jealous, Sidney (1914–16); Lance-Corporal, Norfolk Rgt.; France.

Jeeves, Ernest Charles (1914–19); M.S.M.; Sergeant, R.A.M.C.; France 3 years 7 months.

Jones, Frederick James (1915–19); Private, R.A.M.C.; Mesopotamia and India 3 years 9 months.

King, John James (1915–19); Sergeant, R.A.M.C.; France 3 years 6 months.

***Kirk, Randall** (1914); Private, Coldstream Guards; Died of wounds whilst a prisoner of war, 14th September, 1914.

Knight, Leo George (1914–19); Private, 14th Bn. London Rgt.; France 10 months, Salonica 6 months, Palestine 14 months.

Langley, Edgar (1916–19); Gunner, R.G.A.; France 5 months.

***Lawrence, William** (1914); Stoker, H.M.S. Hogue; Drowned at sea, 22nd September, 1914.

Loveland, William (1914–19); Private, R. West Kent Rgt.; Mesopotamia.

***Luker, Alfred** (1914); Private, Northumberland Fusiliers; France; Killed in action, 9th September, 1914.

Lynn, William (1914–19); Lance-Corporal, R.D.C.

MacDonald, Ranald (1915–19); O.B.E.; Major, R.A.M.C.; Port Said.

McKinnon, Alexander (1915–19); Sergeant, R.A.M.C.; Gallipoli 7 months, Egypt 1 month, Salonica 8 months.

Marshall, Ernest (1917–19); Rifleman, Rifle Brigade; Salonica 1 year, Russia 2½ months.

Mason, Henry (1915–17); 2nd Corporal, R.E.; France 1 year, Egypt 1 year 8 months.

Meacham, William (1914–19); Private, Coldstream Guards; France 3 years 8 months.

Murray, Henry (1915–17); Private, R.A.O.C.

O'Brien, Patrick John (1914–15); Private, 12th Lancers; France.

Odell, Albert Alexander (1914–19); Corporal, R.F.A.; France.

Owen, William (1915–19); Private, R.A.M.C.; Hospital ship 16 months.

Palmer, Walter Bennett (1914–19); Sergeant, 7th Dragoon Guards; France 8 months.

Parker, George Edward (1915–19); Private, Army Cyclists' Corps, Labour Corps; Salonica 8 months, Malta 4 months.

Pepler, Henry William (1914–19); Private, R.A.M.C.; France 3 years 6 months.

Piper, Alfred Frank (1914–19); Corporal, R.A.M.C.; Hospital ship 2 years 2 months.

***Poffley, Alfred George** (1915–18); Private, R.A.M.C.; Died 23rd January, 1918.

Proudfoot, Alexander (1914–17); Corporal, Royal Defence Corps.

***Rafter, John** (1914); Private, Irish Guards; France 3 months; Killed in action, 9th November, 1914.

Rattee, George (1917–19); 1st Cook's Mate, H.M.S. St. George.

Roberts, George Duncan (1915–19); Sergeant, 26th Bn. Royal Fusiliers, Lieutenant, 9th Bn. Royal Sussex Rgt.; France 18 months.

Roberts, William (1914–19); Private, South Lancashire Rgt.; France 2 months, Prisoner of war (Germany) 4 years 2 months.

Roome, John Herbert Edward (1914–19); Petty Officer (1st Class), H.M.S. Edward VII. (Actæon); Minesweeping all time.

Russell, Archibald (1914–19); Corporal, R.E.; France 3 years 10 months.

Samson, Edgar (1915–20); Private, R.A.M.C.; India.

Seaman, Sidney (1914–19); M.M.; Corporal, R.F.A.; France 3 years 6 months.

Sharman, John Frederick (1914–19); Trooper, 2nd Life Guards, Machine Gun Guards; France 4 years.

Shaw, George Frederick (1915–19); Flight Sergeant, R.A.F.; France 15 months.

Sims, Charles (1915–19); Private, R.A.M.C.; France 3 years, Egypt 5 months.

Skevington, Dexter Thomas (1915–19); Private, R.A.M.C.; France 3 years 8 months.

Smith, Ernest William (1914–19); Private, 2nd Bn. Suffolk Rgt.; France 2 months, Prisoner of war (Germany) 4 years 2 months.

Smith, Frederick Charles (1917–19); Private, 1/8th Bn. Middlesex Rgt., 7th Bn. City of London Rgt.; France 7 months.

Spittles, James (1914–19); Private, R.A.M.C.; France 2 years 7 months.

Stansfield, Thomas Edward Knowles; C.B.E.; Hon. Lieut.-Colonel, Hon. Consultant for Nervous and Mental Diseases to the Eastern Command, R.A.M.C.; Gave service locally from October, 1914, extended to area south of Thames, 1915; Commissioned August, 1917, appointed to whole of command.

Stokes, William Orton (1914–19); Sergeant, R.A.M.C.; France 4 years.

Tait, Robert Ferdinand (1914–19); Private, R.A.M.C.; Hospital ship 2 years.

Terry, Edward Percy W. (1914–19); Sergeant, R.F.A. and R.G.A.; France 15 months, Salonica 1 year.

Thomson, Frederick C. (1915–19); Private, R.A.O.C.; France 2 years 10 months.

Thorp, Frederick Hudson (1914–19); Trooper, 2nd Life Guards, Machine Gun Guards; France 1 year 7 months.

Turner, Arthur (1914–19); Stoker, R.F.R. Dardanelles 2 years 6 months.

***Walker, James** (1914); Lance-Corporal, R. Sussex Rgt.; France 1 month; Died of wounds, 15th September, 1914.

Waller, Edwin John (1916–19); Gunner, R.G.A.; France 2 years 3 months.

Whitehurst, William (1915–19); Private, R.A.M.C.; France 3 years.

Williams, James Thomas (1915–19); Staff Sergeant, R.A.M.C.; Malta 3 years 4 months.

Winchcombe, Thomas Sawyer (1914–19); Sergeant-Major, R.F.A.; France 3 years 11 months.

Windmill, Charles (1917–19); Private, R.A.M.C.

Witts, Francis William (1914–19); Company Sergeant-Major, Wiltshire Rgt.; Dardanelles 2 months, Egypt 8 months, Palestine 3 years.

Wood, Thomas (1914–19); Bombardier, R.F.A.; France 3 months, Salonica 3 years.

Woods, Alfred Edward (1914–18); Private, Loyal N. Lancashire Rgt.; France 2 years 5 months.

Wright, William Edward (1914–19); Twice mentioned in despatches; Regimental-Quartermaster Sergeant, London Rgt.; France 6 months, Salonica 6 months, Palestine 1 year 9 months.

Yates, Walter Edmund (1914–19); Private, 1st Bn. Leicestershire Rgt.; France 11 months, Mesopotamia 2 years, Palestine 1 year.

Young, Harry (1915–19); Private, R.A.O.C.; France 3 years 6 months.

Cane Hill Mental Hospital

Adams, William (1915–19); Driver, R.F.A. and R.A.S.C.; France 3 years 6 months.

Allen, Albert Edward (1916–19); Lance-Corporal, R. W. Kent Rgt. and M.F.P.; India 1 year, Mesopotamia 1 year 11 months.

Aprile, Napoleon Percy (1914–19); Corporal, R.A.M.C.

Ayles, Victor Harry (1915–19); Sergeant, R.F.A.; France 1 year 7 months.

Ayling, Stephen (1914–19); Corporal, R.D.C. and R.A.M.C.

Battams, Joseph Thomas (1916–19); Corporal, R.F.A.; Egypt, Palestine and Syria 1 year 7 months.

Beadell, William Henry (1918–19); Private, Labour Corps; France 9 weeks.

Bellis, Frederick Thomas (1914–18); Gunner, R.G.A.; France 2 years.

Boniface, Ernest Edward (1916–19); Private, Middlesex Rgt. and Labour Corps; France 16 months.

Bossom, William Alfred (1918–19); Private, R.A.M.C.

Briggs, William Thomas (1914–19); Private, R. Sussex Rgt.; France 16 months.

Buckland, Frank Ethelbert (1914–19); Sergeant, R.A.M.C.; France 2 years 1 month, Egypt and Palestine 2 years 2 months.

Burgess, George Edward (1914–19); Bombardier, R.G.A.; France 7 months.

Burnell, John Thomas (1914–19); Sergeant, R.F.A. and R.G.A.: France 3 months.

Burton, Charles William (1915–19); Private, R.A.V.C. and Gunner, R.F.A.; France 2 years 7 months.

Coffey, Harold Frederic (1916–19); Corporal, R.A.F. and 3rd Bn. London Rgt.

Cook, Albert (1914); Private, 7th Reserve Cavalry Rgt.

Coomber, William (1916–19); Private, E. Surrey Rgt.; France 1 year 8 months.

Cooper, Charles Albert (1914–19); Trooper, R. Horse Guards; France 7 months.

Cooper, John (1916–19); Gunner, R.G.A.; France 1 year 10 months.

***Cordery, Herbert Thomas** (1914–15); Corporal, 1st Life Guards and 6th Dragoon Guards; France 6 months; Killed in action, 11th February, 1915.

Corfield, William (1915–19); Private, R.A.S.C; Gallipoli 2 months, Egypt 3 months, France 2 years 10 months.

Curtis, William (1917–19); Stoker (1st Class), R.N.; Convoying to Canada and Portugal 9 months, Black Sea 10 months.

Cusack, George Joseph (1914–19); Corporal, King's Royal Rifle Corps, E. Surrey Rgt. and 18th Bn. London Rgt.; France 3 years 2 months.

De Rose, Albert Edward (1916–19); Private, R.A.M.C.; France 2 years 1 month.

Dollimore, Stanley Hubert (1915–19); Lance-Corporal, Royal Fusiliers; France 18 months.

Duke, James (1914–15); Private, R.W. Surrey Rgt.; France 4 months.

Evison, Edward (1914–19); Driver, R.H.A.; France 4 years 4 months, Germany 3 months.

Ford, William (1914–19); Corporal, R.A.S.C.

Greenaway, Andrew (1914–19); Lance-Corporal, Grenadier Guards, E. Surrey Rgt. and M.F.P.; France 4 years 4 months.

Grinham, Sydney James (1917–19); Private, Suffolk and Northamptonshire Rgts., and Labour Corps; France 1 year 11 months.

Hancock, Allen Coulter (1914–20); M.C. and two Bars; Major, R.A.M.C.; France 4 years.

Hayler, George (1914–19); Private, R. Marine Light Infantry; South America and Falkland Isles 2 years 3 months, North Sea 1 year 10 months.

Henty, Frederick (1914–16); Private, R.D.C.

Hinton, Francis George (1916–19); Lance-Corporal, E. Surrey Rgt., R.E., Essex Rgt., and Oxfordshire and Buckinghamshire Light Infantry; France 2 years.

Hiscox, George Price (1915–19); Sergeant, R.A.S.C.

Horne, Walter John (1916); Private, R.F.A. and R. Irish Fusiliers.

Huggett, John (1914–19); Sergeant, E. Surrey Rgt. and Essex Rgt.; France 6 months, India 3 years.

Hussey, Henry (1915); Private, Gloucestershire Rgt.

Hutchings, William Alfred (1914–19); Gunner, R.F.A.; France 6 months, Dardanelles 5 months, Palestine 3 years 7 months.

Inkersole, William (1914–19); Sergeant, Royal Fusiliers; France 15 months.

Jordan, William (1914–19); Sergeant, E. Surrey and Essex Rgts.; Mudros 5 months, Egypt 2 years, Palestine 7 months, Salonica 6 months.

***Joyce, Herbert George** (1916–17); Private, R. W. Surrey Rgt.; France 9 months; Missing, presumed killed, 25th September, 1917.

***Key, George William** (1915–17); Bombardier, R.F.A.; France 16 months; Killed in action, 14th October, 1917.

Lakeman, Mabel Grace (1914); Sister, Territorial Nursing Service.

Lane, George Thomas (1914–19); Corporal, R.D.C. and R.A.M.C.

Lee, William (1914–17); Private, 20th Hussars.

Lloyd, Robert (1914–17); Private, 10th Hussars, R. W. Surrey and R.D.C.

Lowe, Thomas Edward (1914–17); Gunner, R. Marine Artillery.

McEntire, Ronald Gordon John (1914–16); Captain, R.A.M.C.; France 18 months.

Millwood, Frederick James (1916–19); Gunner, R.G.A.; Mesopotamia 2 years 4 months.

***Moore, Edward Charles** (1917–18); Air Mechanic, R.A.F.; France 1 year; Died, 29th November, 1918.

Morres, Frederick (1915–19); Captain, R.A.M.C.; Hospital Ship 5 months, France 3 years 1 month.

Noake, Thomas Albert (1914–19); Private, R. W. Surrey Rgt. and Rifle Brigade; India 3 years 2 months.

Norman, George (1914–19); Sergeant, Bedfordshire Rgt. and R.A.M.C.; France 3 years 6 months.

Page, Walter Thomas (1918); Private, R.A.F.

Parsons, Thomas (1914–17); Private, National Reserve, R.D.C. and R.A.M.C.

Perry, Francis (1914–19); Company Quartermaster-Sergeant, Northamptonshire and R. W. Surrey Rgts., and Labour Corps; India 2 years, France 2 years 7 months.

Poulter, Wolsey (1915–16); Private, R.A.M.C.; Mesopotamia, 1 year.

Purdy, Robert (1915–19); Private, R.A.V.C. and Gunner, R.F.A.; France 3 years.

Randall, Herbert Eustace (1914–19); Lieutenant, Rifle Brigade, Yorkshire Rgt. and R.A.F.; France 6 months.

Ransom, John (1914–19); Sergeant, 16th Lancers and Military Mounted Police; France 3 years 7 months.

***Rice, Harry Charles** (1914–15); Private, 4th Bn. R. W. Surrey Rgt.; Died, 11th July, 1915.

Richards, Benjamin (1916–19); Private, E. Surrey Rgt. and Yorkshire Rgt.; France 2 years 3 months.

Rose, Albert Edward (1914–19); Private, R. Marine Light Infantry; South Africa 4 years, Royal Yacht 5 months.

Rouse, Harry (1916–19); Private, Rifle Brigade and Machine Gun Corps; France 1 year 7 months, Italy 15 months.

Russell, Arthur (1914–16); Private, Surrey National Reserve (The Queen's) and R.D.C.

Russell, Peter (1914–19); Private, R. Marine Light Infantry.

Samuel, Harry (1916–19); Sergeant, Middlesex Rgt. and Royal Fusiliers; France 1 year 7 months.

Saunders, Alfred Edward (1916–19); Private, E. Surrey Rgt. and Labour Corps; France 7 months.

Sleight, William (1914–15); Private, R. W. Surrey Rgt.

Treanor, Eugene (1915–19); Corporal, R.A.M.C.; France 4 years.

Walker, William (1914–19); Corporal, R. W. Surrey Rgt.

***Warren, Alfred** (1915–16); Rifleman, King's Royal Rifle Corps; France 3 months; Died of wounds, 25th August, 1916.

Webster, Walter (1914–19); Private, National Reserve, Rifle Brigade and R. W. Kent Rgt.; India 2 years 6 months, Mesopotamia 16 months.

Wesson, Walter (1918–19); Acting Corporal, R.A.F.

Wheeler, Charles Ernest (1915–19); Lance-Corporal, M.F.P.; Egypt 18 months, Syria 3 months, Palestine 13 months.

Wheeler, Thomas (1914-19); Private, Royal Marines; S.W. Africa 16 months, Portsmouth Coastal Patrol Boats 17 months, East Africa 8 months, Northern patrols 13 months.

Williams, George (1914–18); Corporal, R.D.C.

Wood, Henry (1916–19); Private, R. W. Surrey Rgt. and Labour Corps; Balkans 2 years 6 months.

***Wright, Leslie** (1914–18); Sergeant, Leicestershire Rgt.; France 2 years 3 months; Missing, presumed killed, 22nd March, 1918.

Claybury Mental Hospital

Abbott, Harold William (1914–19); Corporal, R.F.A.; France 2 years 3 months, Italy 15 months.

Aimes, John (1914–19); Private, Middlesex Rgt. and R.A.M.C.; France 3 years 3 months.

Anderson, Thomas (1914–19); Private, R.A.M.C.; France 3 years 4 months.

Arnold, James (1915–19); Corporal, Essex Rgt. and R.D.C.

Baker, Albert (1917–19); Rifleman, 16th Training Reserves and Rifle Brigade; France 11 months.

***Baker, Thomas Heasman** (1915); Gunner, R.F.A.; Salonica 3 months; Died of tuberculosis, 6th December, 1915.

Baker, Wilfrid (1916–19); Gunner, R.G.A.; India 3 years.

Barnes, Albert (1917–19); Private, R.A.S.C.; France 1 year.

Bennett, Arthur Robert (1914–19); Sec.-Lieutenant, R. Marine Light Infantry, Essex Rgt. and R.A.F.; Dardanelles and Egypt 7 months, France 18 months.

Blackmore, Noah (1914–19); Sergeant, Grenadier Guards; France 3 years 4 months.

Bloomfield, Curtis James John (1914–19); Sergeant, E. Kent Rgt., Machine Gun Corps and Labour Corps.

Blundell, Herbert Henry (1916–19); Private, Bedfordshire Rgt.; France 1 year 9 months.

Brady, Walter John (1914–18); 3rd Class Medal Russian Order of St. George; Bombardier, R.F.A. and R.G.A.; France 2 years.

Butler, Henry Mantle (1917–19); Private, R.A.V.C.

Caward, Thomas Edward (1915–19); Staff Sergeant, R.G.A., R.H.A. and R.F.A.; France.

Chappell, William (1914–19); Private, Bedfordshire and Suffolk Rgts.; France 4 years.

Childs, James (1915–19); Sergeant, Essex and Middlesex Rgts., Royal Fusiliers and R.D.C.

Clements, Walter (1918–19); Private, R.A.F.; France 5 months.

Cox, Edward Jonathan (1917); Private, R.A.M.C.

Cox, Frank (1916–19); Corporal, Norfolk and Bedfordshire Rgts.; France 18 months.

Curtis, James (1916–19); Private, Yorkshire Rgt. and Labour Corps.

Dawson, Frederick (1916–17); Private, Bedfordshire Rgt.; France 5½ months.

***Dawson, Owen Samuel** (1914–15); Private, Cameronians; France 5 months; Killed in action, 6th January, 1915.

***Diamond, Frank** (1916–17); Private, Norfolk Rgt.; France 4 months; Died of wounds, 19th May, 1917.

***Edlin, Bertram Alexander** (1914): Private, Bedfordshire Rgt.; France 2 months; Killed in action, 13th October, 1914.

Edwards, Arthur Henry (1916–19); Corporal, Essex Rgt.; France 3 years.

Ellis, Thomas William (1917–19); Private, Home Service Employment Bn., attached Northumberland Fusiliers.

Elvin, George Daniel (1914–19); Corporal, Rifle Brigade; France 4 years 4 months.

Faggetter, Ephraim James (1916–19); Private, Essex Rgt. and Labour Corps; France 9 months.

Feldwick, William Edward (1914–19); D.S.M.; Lieutenant, R.N., R.N.A.S. and R.A.F.

***Fitzgerald, Patrick** (1916–17); Private, R.A.O.C. and Worcestershire Rgt.; France 2 months; Killed in action, 26th August, 1917.

Green, George Frederick (1916–18); Private, Essex Rgt. and R. Inniskilling Fusiliers; France 5 months.

Greenaway, Sidney (1915–18); Private, R.A.M.C.; Mesopotamia 17 months, India 5 months.

Gregory, Alfred (1917–19); Corporal, R.A.V.C.; Egypt 1 year, Palestine 14 months, Salonica 2 months.

Gregory, Cyril Charles (1914–19); Sergeant, R.A.S.C.; France 5 months, Salonica 2 years 2 months, Russia 4 months.

Hall, John (1918–19); Private, 16th Bn. R. West Surrey, Middlesex and Suffolk Rgts.

Hall, William James (1914–19); Private, R.E.; France 4 years 5 months.

Hawtin, Ralph (1915–19); Gunner, R.F.A.; France 3 years 3 months.

Hayden, Frederick Wm. (1916–19); Private, E. Surrey Rgt. and Highland Light Infantry.

Hayward, Harold Edgar (1914–19); M.M.: Sergeant, R.F.A.; France and Italy 4 years 7 months.

Henry, James (1914–19); Driver, R.F.A.; France.

Hewitt, Walter (1915–19); Sergeant, Essex Rgt. and R.D.C.

Holland, William (1917–19); Private, 124th Labour Corps; France 2 years.

Hollingsbee, Robert (1915–19); Corporal, Devonshire Rgt. and R.A.M.C.; France 5 months.

Ingram, Charles (1916–19); Rifleman, Norfolk Rgt., Rifle Brigade, R. West Kent and 8th Bn. London Rgts.; France 2 years.

***Jackson, Albert** (1914–15); Lance-Corporal, Durham Light Infantry and Yorkshire Light Infantry; France 5 months; Killed in action, 4th September, 1915.

Jeanes, John Victor (1914–19); M.M. and Bar; Sergeant, Grenadier Guards; France 4 years.

Johnson, William Robert (1914–19); Petty Officer (1st Class), R.N.; At sea 2 years.

Kenny, Stephen Patrick (1916–19); Private, Northamptonshire Rgt.; France 11 months, Salonica 1 year.

Kerr, James Montague (1917–19); Private, 14th Bn. London Rgt.; France 18 months.

***King, Denham George** (1915); Private, Essex Rgt.; Gallipoli 2 months; Died of dysentery, 22nd November, 1915.

King, Frederick Ernest (1914–19); Quartermaster-Sergeant, R.A.M.C.; France 3 years 5 months.

King, Walter (1915–19); Private, R.A.M.C.; France 3 years 3 months.

***Lee, Charles John** (1916–17); Private, R. West Kent and Manchester Rgts.; France 9 months; Died of wounds, 19th October, 1917.

Lovell, Albert Ernest (1916–19); Lance-Sergeant, King's Royal Rifle Corps; France 11 months, Salonica 1 year 9 months.

McAteer, George John (1914–19); Private, E. Kent Rgt. and R.A.M.C.; France 1 year 7 months.

McKowin, Richard Henry (1914–19); Company Sergeant-Major, Oxfordshire and Buckinghamshire Light Infantry and Labour Corps.

Magson, Walter Herbert Harry (1914–19); Private, Rifle Brigade and Devonshire Rgt.; France 4 months, Germany 7 months.

Mead, Albert Edward (1914–19); Private, Essex Rgt. and R.A.M.C.; France 13 months.

Meara, Michael (1914–19); Guardsman, Irish Guards; France 4 years 5 months.

Mitchell, Alfred (1916–19); Corporal, R.E.

Moore, Mark Thomas (1915–19); Staff Sergeant, R.A.M.C., A.G.S. and R.A.F.

Mould, Arthur Alexander (1914–19); Sergeant, R.F.A.; France 3 years.

Nicholls, Herbert Edward (1915–19); Petty Officer (1st Class), R.N.

Page, Alfred John (1915–19); Private, R.A.M.C.; France 11 months, Salonica 2 years 3 months.

Paine, Frederick (1914–19); Mentioned in despatches; Captain, R.A.M.C.; France 5 months, Salonica 2 years, Palestine 10 months.

Parry, Herbert Charles (1914–19); Sergeant, Essex Rgt.

Paveley, Alfred Peter (1914–19); M.M.; Sergeant, R.F.A.; France 2 years 3 months, Italy 15 months.

Pearce, Henry Ernest (1917–19); Private, R.A.M.C.

Petrie, Alfred Alexander Webster (1915–19); Captain, R.A.M.C.; France 3 years 4 months, Mediterranean 6 months.

Purkiss, Arthur (1914–17); Lance-Corporal, M.F.P.

Purkiss, Charles (1918–19); 2nd Private, R.A.F.; France 5 months.

Radley, Frederick Charles (1914–19); Lance-Corporal, Border Rgt.; France 4 years 2 months.

Randall, Walter (1917–19); Private, R.A.S.C.

Rashbrook, Henry Martin (1915–20); Major, R.A.M.C.

Reeves, George Ambrose (1914–19); Guardsman, Grenadier Guards; France 3 months.

Ridgewell, Walter William (1916–19); Gunner, R.G.A.; Mesopotamia 13 months, France 4 months.

Rourke, Daniel (1914–18); Guardsman, Irish Guards; France and Prisoner of war 4 years.

Sangster, Alexander (1914–19); Guardsman, Grenadier Guards and Machine Gun Guards; France 14 months.

Sawer, Frederick (1914–16); Corporal, Royal Fusiliers; France.

Saye, Charles Arthur (1914–19); Sergeant, R.A.S.C.; France 4 years 2 months, Mesopotamia 5 months.

Sharp, William Henry (1914–19); Lance-Corporal, Rifle Brigade; France 3 years 7 months.

Sheridan, Eugene (1915–19); Private, R.A.M.C.

Shipton, Arthur (1915–17); Gunner, R.F.A.; France 1 year 10 months.

Shuman, John Henry (1914–19); Private, R. Scots Fusiliers; France 4 years 6 months.

Shuttlewood, Joseph (1916–19); Private, Middlesex Rgt. and Labour Corps; Salonica 1 year 10 months.

Skingley, Charles Albert (1917–19); Private, 131st Labour Corps; France 2 years.

Smallbone, Walter John (1914–17); Regimental Sergeant-Major, R.A.M.C.; France 18 months.

Smith, Albert George (1914–19); Sergeant, 2nd Dragoon Guards and R.A.S.C.; France 4 years 8 months.

Smith, Charles (1914–19); Sergeant, Royal Fusiliers, E. Kent Rgt., R.A.F. and 31st Training Reserve Bn.; France 2 months.

Smith, Ernest William (1916–19); Private, Norfolk Rgt. and 8th Bn. London Rgt.; France 1 year 10 months.

Smith, Stanley Byron (1914–19); M.S.M.; Corporal, R. Sussex Rgt. and R.A.S.C.; France 2 years 9 months, Italy 4 months.

***Squires, William George** (1914–15); Corporal, R.F.A.; France 9 months; Killed in action, 16th June, 1915.

***Stower, Walter Ernest** (1915–16); Private, Middlesex Rgt.; France 11 months; Killed in action, 20th October, 1916.

Sully, George (1918–19); Bombardier, R.G.A.; France 15 months.

Taylor, Sebert Mark (1918–20); Private, E. Surrey Rgt.; France 2 months.

Toseland, Arthur Joseph (1916–19); Lance-Corporal, Durham Light Infantry and M.F.P.

Wakeling, Alfred Stanley (1915–19); Private, Essex Rgt.; Dardanelles, Egypt and Palestine, 3 years 7 months.

Waller, Mark (1914–17); Driver, R.E.; France 2 years 6 months.

Warbey, Robert John (1914–19); Leading Seaman, R.N.; Mediterranean 18 months.

Ward, Frederick (1917–19); Corporal, 124th Labour Corps; France 2 years.

Wellman, William James (1914–19); Mentioned in despatches; Quartermaster-Sergeant, R.E.

Wells, Thomas Henry (1914–16); Bombardier, R.F.A.; France 18 months.

Whayman, William Ray (1918–19); Private, 16th Bn. R. West Surrey Rgt.

Wheatley, Edwin (1915–19); Corporal, Essex Rgt.; France 2 years.

White, James William (1914–19); Sergeant, R.A.M.C.

White, John (1918–19); Private, W. Kent Yeomanry.

Wild, Joe (1914–19); D.C.M., Mentioned in despatches; Regimental Sergeant-Major, R.E.; France 4 years 1 month.

Willcox, Horace Reginald (1916–18); Rifleman, Rifle Brigade and Machine Gun Corps.

Wilson, Herbert Augustus (1915–19); Corporal, R.A.M.C.; France 3 years 4 months, Germany 2 months.

Wright, George (1918–19); Private, R.A.S.C., M.T.

Wright, Harry (1914–19); Private, Bedfordshire Rgt.; France 4 years 5 months.

Colney Hatch Mental Hospital

Ailward, Charles Henry (1914–19); Staff Sergeant, R.A.M.C.; Egypt, Syria and Palestine 4 years 1 month.

Almond, George Harold (1915–19); Lance-Corporal, R.A.M.C.; France 2 years 11 months.

***Baker, George** (1914); Private, Royal Fusiliers; France; Missing, 23rd August, 1914.

Baker, John William (1914–19); Private, R. Marine Light Infantry.

Barnes, Harold Frederick (1915–19); Private, R.A.M.C.; France 2 years 10 months.

Battrick, Robert George (1915–19); Private, R.A.M.C.; France 4 years 1 month.

Beamon, Charles Henry (1916–17); Private, E. Surrey Rgt.; France 2 months.

Beesley, Fred (1914–15); Private, Essex Rgt.; France 6 months.

Blackwell, Lawrence Arthur (1915–17); Lance-Corporal, R.A.M.C.; German E. Africa 6 months.

Bolton, Charles (1914–19); Driver, R.F.A.; France 4 years 7 months.

Breed, William (1915–16); Sapper, R.E.

Britten, Alfred Charles (1915–19); Lance-Corporal, 3rd Bn. R. Scots Fusiliers.

Budd, William James Reginald (1916–17); 2nd Air Mechanic, R.F.C.; France 5 months.

Burt, Frederick (1915–19); Private, Hampshire Rgt.; Dardanelles, Egypt and Salonica 3 years 7 months.

Calcutt, Ernest George (1914–18); Private, 2nd Bn. Essex Rgt.; France 8 months.

Christer, Albert Edward (1914–19); Regimental Sergeant-Major, Royal Fusiliers.

Church, Henry (1914–16); Private, ·yal Fusiliers; Malta 4 months, France months.

Clark, Albert (1914–19); Corporal, ·meronians; France 2 years 4 months.

***Clark, Arthur** (1914–18); Private, Grenadier Guards; France 4 years; Died, 2nd November, 1918.

Clarke, William John (1914–19); Regimental Quartermaster-Sergeant, Royal Marines; Belgium 2 months, Germany 4 years, prisoner of war.

Coleman, Alfred Henry (1914–19); Gunner, R.F.A.; France 3 years 7 months.

Connolly, Victor Lindley (1914–19); M.C.; Major, R.A.M.C.; France 3 years 10 months.

Cooper, William (1915–19); Sergeant, Royal Fusiliers; France 3 years 2 months.

Cording, George (1914); Private, Middlesex Rgt.; France 2 months.

Corner, Oscar Mead (1914–19); Gunner, R.G.A.; France 3 years 10 months.

Cox, Lewis John (1914–19); Gunner, R.G.A.; France 2 years 4 months.

Daniels, Frank (1914–17); Private, Grenadier Guards.

Davis, Hubert Frank (1914–19); Private, E. Kent Rgt.; France 4 years 6 months.

Davis, William Job (1915–19); Private, R.A.M.C.; France 3 years, German E. Africa 8 months.

Day, James (1915–19); Horsekeeper, R.A.V.C.; Salonica 3 years 6 months.

***Dickens, Charles Albert** (1914); Private, Royal Fusiliers; France 1 month; Missing, 14th September, 1914.

Digweed, Barry James (1916–19); Corporal, Durham Light Infantry; Salonica 2 years.

Dilworth, John (1915–19); Private, R.A.M.C.; France 4 years 1 month.

Downing, Reginald Charles (1914–19); Corporal, R.F.A.

Dyson, William George (1915–17); Sergeant, R.A.M.C.

Edinborough, Leonard George (1916–19); Private, Middlesex Rgt.; Salonica 2 years 4 months.

Emery, Herbert Thomas (1915–19); Staff Quartermaster-Sergeant, R.A.O.C.; Egypt, Salonica and Palestine 3 years 7 months.

Foster, Thomas (1914–19); Private, Middlesex Rgt.; France 3 years 7 months.

Freeth, Albert (1916–19); Corporal, W. Kent Yeomanry; France 2 years 3 months.

Garratt, Thomas (1914–19); Private, Sherwood Foresters; France 4 years 5 months.

Gatward, Allison Bertie (1916–19); Sergeant, 32nd Training Reserve Bn., and 4th and 11th Bns. Middlesex Rgt.; France 9 months.

Ginn, Benjamin (1914–19); Corporal, Northumberland Fusiliers; France 10 months.

Green, Ralph Lionel (1917–19); Private, R.A.M.C.

Harris, William Leonard Hepworth (1917–19); Private, Honourable Artillery Company; France 1 year.

Hart, Edgar John (1915–19); Private, 23rd Bn. London Rgt.; Egypt 3 years 6 months.

Head, William (1915–19); Sapper, R.E.; France 3 years 4 months.

***Henderson, William Richard** (1914); Trooper, 1st Royal Dragoons; France 2 months; Missing, 30th October, 1914.

Higgs, Thomas (1915–19); Private, R.A.M.C.; France 4 years.

Holding, Horace Frederick (1915–19); Corporal, R.E.; France 2 years 4 months.

Horne, Henry Frederick (1915–19); Corporal, R.E.; France 2 years 5 months, Salonica 8 months.

Humber, George (1915–19); Sapper, R.E.; France 3 years 6 months.

***Humphreys, Maxwell Mark** (1914); Lance-Corporal, S. Wales Borderers; France 2 months; Missing, 31st October, 1914.

Hunt, Charles Robert (1915–19); Private, R.A.M.C.; France 3 years 9 months.

Hunt, Harry David (1914–19); Lance-Sergeant, Duke of Cornwall's Light Infantry; Egypt 3 years 6 months.

Hutchings, Walter John (1915–19); Private, R.A.M.C.; France 4 years.

Jarman, Alexander George (1916–19); Private, Durham Light Infantry; France 7 months.

Jenkins, Jonathan (1916–19); Gunner, R.G.A.; Mesopotamia 2 years 5 months.

Jepps, Frederick (1916–19); Private, Middlesex Rgt. and 97th Labour Corps; Salonica 2 years 2 months.

Keenan, Daniel (1915–19); M.M.; Staff Sergeant, R.A.M.C.; France 3 years 7 months.

Kimmens, Harry (1916–19); Private, Middlesex Rgt.; France 2 years 1 month.

Kirby, Walter J. (1916); Private, E. Kent Rgt.

***Lamont, John** (1917–18); Private, 14th Bn. London Rgt.; France 9 months; Killed in action, 12th March, 1918.

Lincoln, Frederick (1915–19); Corporal, R.A.M.C.; France 3 years 7 months.

Ludlow, Ernest Herbert (1916–19); Private, R.A.S.C., King's Royal Rifle Corps and Royal Fusiliers; France 2 years 6 months.

Mabbot, Charles (1915–19); Private, R.A.V.C.; France 1 year 9 months.

Macarthur, John (1914–18); Captain, R.A.M.C.; Gallipoli 6 months, France 18 months.

McCombie, James Cameron (1914–15); Lance-Corporal, R.A.M.C.

Manno, Edward Blake (1916–19); Private, R.A.M.C.

Moore, Archibald John (1917–19); Horsekeeper, R.A.V.C.; France 2 years.

Moroney, John Edward James (1914–19); Battery Sergeant-Major, R.F.A.; France 1 year 9 months.

Munro, George (1915–19); Corporal, R.A.M.C.; France 4 years.

Murphy, Daniel William (1915–19); Private, Northumberland Fusiliers; Salonica 14 months, France 6 months.

Norris, George William (1916–19); Lance-Corporal, R.E.; France 1 year 5 months.

Parnis, Henry William (1914–19); Captain, R.A.M.C.; France 4 years.

Pedrick, Frank Barter Frost (1916–19); Private, Bedfordshire Rgt.; France 2 months.

Perry, George (1918–19); Pioneer, R.E.; France 3 months.

Philip, James (1914–18); Corporal, 2nd Dragoons; France 2 years 6 months.

Phipps, Alfred George (1916–19); Private, R.A.M.C.

Phipps, Harry (1915–19); Sapper, R.E.; France 3 years 3 months.

Razzell, John (1917–19); Private, E. Kent Rgt.; France 1 year 7 months.

Reynolds, Freddy (1916–19); Gunner, R.G.A.; France 6 months.

***Reynolds, John** (1915–18); Private, R.E.; France 2 years; Accidentally killed, 15th July, 1918.

Robinson, Walter (1914–19); Sergeant, Suffolk Rgt.; Dardanelles and Palestine 3 years 7 months.

Russell, George Henry (1914–19); M.S.M.; Company Quartermaster-Sergeant, R. Irish Fusiliers; France 2 years 6 months.

Saunders, Alfred Harold (1914–19); Private, 18th Hussars; France 4 years 7 months.

Saunders, Frederick Charles (1915–19); Saddler, R.A.V.C.; France 3 years 4 months.

Sharpe, James (1915–19); Sapper, R.E.; France 2 months, Salonica 3 years, Rumania 1 month, Dobruja 3 months.

Sides, Henry (1914–16); Private, R. Berkshire Rgt.; France 5 months.

Skipper, Frederick (1916–19); Private, E. Kent Rgt.; France 2 years 5 months.

Smith, Walter (1917–19); Private, Norfolk Rgt. and Labour Corps.

Springford, Edwin John (1915–19); Lance-Corporal, Norfolk Rgt.; India 3 years 5 months.

Staker, James (1915–19); Horsekeeper, R.A.V.C.; France 3 years 6 months.

Stone, Henry James (1915–19); Private, R.A.M.C.; France 13 months, Hospital ships, Mediterranean, 2 years 4 months.

Stower, A. (1918–19); Gunner, R.G.A.; France 5 months.

Surgey, Charles (1915–19); Sapper, R.E.; France 3 years 4 months.

Thomas, John William (1916–19); Private, Royal Fusiliers; France 4 months.

Thompson, Charles (1916, 1918–19); Private, 366th Reserve Employment Company, Durham Light Infantry.

Thurlow, Alfred (1915–19); M.M., Mentioned three times in despatches; Company Quartermaster-Sergeant, R.E.; France 3 years 6 months.

Travel, Albert (1914–19); Able Seaman, H.M.S. Empress; North Sea and Mediterranean 4 years.

Treasure, Edward Henry (1915–19); Private, Middlesex Rgt. and R.A.S.C. (M.T.); France 3 years 4 months.

Turner, Albert Llewelyn (1916–19); Gunner, R.G.A.

Turner, Sidney (1914–17); Sergeant, Royal Fusiliers.

Wakenell, Walter Frederick (1914–19); Trooper, 2nd Dragoon Guards.

Walton, William John (1917–19); Private, Royal Fusiliers; France 2 months.

Whelan, Peter (1915–19); Private, R.A.M.C.; Salonica 4 years 3 months.

Wilson, Albert Edward (1916–19); Sergeant, Northumberland Fusiliers.

Wilson, Charles (1914–19); Trooper, 17th Lancers; France 3 years 4 months.

Wilson, Herbert (1918–19); Private, R.A.F.

Woodwards, Harry (1914–15); Private, Grenadier Guards; France 5 months.

Wrenn, Edward Jerome (1915); Corporal, Gordon Highlanders.

Wright, Jesse (1915–19); Sapper, R.E., and 1st Air Mechanic, R.F.C.; France 8 months.

Hanwell Mental Hospital

Allen, Arthur Ernest (1916–19); Private, Royal Fusiliers and Labour Corps; France 13 months.

Arnold, Edgar Frank (1914–19); Sub-Conductor, R.A.O.C.; Palestine and Egypt 15 months.

Atterwill, George Henry (1915); Sapper, R.E.

Ayres, John Edward (1914–19); Private, 17th Lancers; France 4 years 4 months.

Baker, John Herbert (1914–19); Private, Middlesex and Norfolk Rgts.

Bennett, Benjamin (1914–18); Private, Royal Fusiliers; France 15 months.

***Birch, Harry** (1914–17); Private, Hampshire Rgt.; France 3 years; Missing, 26th August, 1917.

Bishop, Thomas (1914–19); Private, R.A.M.C.; France 3 years 3 months, Mediterranean 5 months.

Bonner, William (1915–19); Gunner, R.G.A.; France 17 months.

Bray, Henry James (1916–17); Private, Middlesex Rgt.

***Brill, Walter Percy** (1914–17); Lance-Corporal, Middlesex Rgt.; France 2 years 9 months; Killed in action, 30th November, 1917.

Brown, Donald (1914–19); Staff Quartermaster-Sergeant, R.A.S.C.; France 3 years.

Butler, George (1914–19); Sec.-Lieutenant, Middlesex Rgt.; France 2 years 6 months.

***Butler, Tom** (1915–16); Corporal, Machine Gun Corps; France 5 months; Died of wounds, 9th September, 1916.

Byles, Albert James (1914–19); Sergeant, Royal Fusiliers; France 4 years.

Cawsey, John (1916–19); Corporal, Military Port Police.

Chapman, Henry (1914–19); Lieutenant, 9th Bn. London Rgt. and Dorsetshire Rgt.; France 2 years 7 months.

Choat, Ernest (1914–19); Lance-Corporal, Royal Fusiliers, R.E., and Essex Rgt.; Gallipoli and Egypt 6 months.

Clarke, Henry Stanhope (1914–19); Leading Seaman, R.N., Portsmouth; At sea about 2 years.

Couppleditch, William Charles (1914–19); Private, Royal Fusiliers; France 2 years 6 months.

Crewe, George (1914–19); Staff-Sergeant, R.A.O.C.; Greece 3 years 6 months.

Cronyn, Edward Michael (1914–16); D.C.M.; Sergeant, Royal Fusiliers; France about 1 year.

Danby, Thomas (1915–19); Private, R.A.M.C.; France 2 years 7 months.

Davis, Alfred Edward (1914–19); Sergeant, R.E.; France 14 months, Salonica 2 years, Italy 6 months.

Deamer, Edward (1914–19); M.S.M.; Staff Quartermaster-Sergeant, R.A.O C.; Salonica 6 months.

Deering, Herbert Henry (1914–19); Sergeant, R.A.S.C.; France over 4 years.

Dunstone, Henry Cecil (1915–19); Sergeant, R. Lancaster Rgt.; France 3 years 6 months.

Eames, George William (1914–19); Corporal, Lancashire Fusiliers; France 1 year 11 months, Gallipoli 8 months, Egypt 2 months.

Elliott, Arthur John (1916–19); Private, Royal Fusiliers and Labour Corps.

Ellis, Joseph (1914–19); Bombardier, R.F.A.; France 4 years 7 months.

Elstone, William Thomas (1915–19); Private, R. W. Kent Rgt.; France 2 years, Italy 6 months.

Farress, Arthur Edward (1916–18); Rifleman, King's Royal Rifle Corps; France 10 months.

Fearnley, Charles (1916–19); Private, Middlesex and Suffolk Rgts.; France 17 months.

Ferris, Henry George (1916–19); Gunner, R.F.A.; France 15 months.

***Fish, William Frederick** (1915–17); Private, R.A.M.C.; Salonica 9 months; Died 24th May, 1917.

Fletcher, John (1916–19); Gunner, R.G.A. and R.F.A.; France 10 months.

Fletcher, Sidney James (1914–19); Pioneer, Middlesex Rgt. and R.E.; Gibraltar 5 months, France 13 months

Fuller, Edward Arthur (1914–19); Private, Royal Fusiliers; France 3 years.

Glenister, Charles James (1914); Private, Nottinghamshire and Derbyshire Rgt.

Godden, Charles Henry (1914–19); Lance-Corporal, Royal Fusiliers; France 3 years 4 months.

Graimes, Frank Edward (1914–17); Private, Royal Fusiliers and R.E.; Gallipoli about 2 months.

Greeney, John (1914–17); Private, R.A.O.C.; France 2 years.

Hankins, Frank Reginald (1915–19); Private, Middlesex Rgt. and R.D.C.; France 3 years 2 months.

Harrison, James William (1917–19); Gunner, R.G.A.

Hearn, Harry (1914–19); Sergeant, R.A.O.C. and Somerset Light Infantry; France 4 years.

Hedge, Charles Athelstone (1914, 1916–19); Private, Bedfordshire Rgt., Royal Fusiliers, Middlesex Rgt., R. W. Surrey Rgt., and Labour Corps; Macedonia and Greece 2 years 2 months.

Hedge, William Alexander (1914–19); Able Seaman, H.M.S. New Zealand; At sea 4 years 2 months.

Henbury, Alfred (1915–18); Sergeant, Yorkshire Light Infantry.

Holdaway, Albert James (1914–18); Sergeant, Middlesex Rgt.; Gibraltar 3 months, France 2 years 9 months.

Hopkins, Arthur William (1915–19); Private, Royal Fusiliers and R.A.F.; France 18 months.

Horsman, Herbert (1914–16); Private, Royal Fusiliers.

Jennings, James (1914); Private, Middlesex Rgt.

Kidd, Leonard (1916–19); Private, R.A.F.

King, John (1914–19); Corporal, Middlesex Rgt.

Kingham, Edward Havelock (1914–20); Regimental Sergeant-Major, Middlesex, Suffolk and Essex Rgts., and Labour Corps.

Kynaston, Harry (1916–19); Private, Middlesex Rgt., Argyle and Sutherland Highlanders, Seaforth Highlanders, Highland Light Infantry, Scottish Rifles; France 1 year.

Laker, George (1914–19); Private, Middlesex Rgt.; France 6 months.

***Lediard, Frederick Samuel** (1914–18); Private, Royal Fusiliers; France 2 years 8 months; Killed in action, 28th August, 1918.

McCarthy, John (1915–19); Staff-Sergeant, R.A.O.C. and R.G.A.; Gallipoli 3 months, Egypt 2 years 1 month, Palestine 13 months.

Marshall, Thomas (1915–19); Staff-Sergeant, R.A.O.C.; France 3 years.

Martin, Harry (1914–19); Sergeant, R.E.; France 18 months.

Matthews, Albert George (1915–19); Private, Middlesex Rgt. and Labour Corps; Egypt 11 months, France 3 years 2 months.

Maynard, Leonard Harry (1915–18); Sergeant, Middlesex Rgt.; France 1 year 8 months.

Meadows, Sydney Frank (1914–17); Private, Military Mounted Police and Labour Corps; Egypt 15 months.

Meese, Clifford Christopher (1914–19); Regtl. Quartermaster-Sergt., R.A.M.C.; France 2 years 6 months.

Miller, Alfred (1914–19); Lance-Sergeant, Northumberland Fusiliers.

Miller William James (1914–19); Staff-Sergeant, R.A.M.C.; Salonica 2 years 8 months.

***Mitchell, Charles John** (1915–16); Corporal, Royal Fusiliers; France 1 year; Missing, 7th October, 1916.

Mitchell, Octavius (1914–19); Gunner, R.F.A.; France 15 months.

Monger, William George (1915–19); Private, R.A.V.C.; France 4 years.

Morrison, William Charles (1914–19); M.S.M.; Sergeant, Lincolnshire Rgt. and R.E.; France 3 years 6 months.

Moul, Arthur William (1915–19); Private, R.A.S.C. and R. Welch Fusiliers; Egypt, Dardanelles and Salonica about 3 years, France 11 months.

Mulroy, George (1914–19); Private, Royal Fusiliers; France 3 years 8 months.

Newton, Ernest James (1917–19); Air-Craftsman (1st Class), R.N.A.S. and R.A.F.

Nicholls, Bert (1916–19); Signaller, R.G.A.; France 2 years.

Nunn, John (1914–19); Farrier Quartermaster-Sergeant, R.F.A.

***O'Flynn, Dominick Thomas** (1915–18); Twice mentioned in despatches; Captain, R.A.M.C.; France 3 years 7 months; Died, 21st June, 1918.

Oram, John Henry West (1914–19); Stoker (1st Class), H.M.S. Europa and H.M.S. Redwing; Mediterranean 3 years 4 months.

Packham, William Richard (1915–19); Rifleman, 16th Bn. London Rgt.; France 1 year, Salonica 6 months, Egypt and Palestine 1 year.

Partridge, Alfred Ernest (1914–19); Belgian Croix de Guerre; Sergeant, Duke of Cornwall's Light Infantry; France 4 years 2 months, Italy 4 months.

Payne, James William (1914–19); Corporal, Royal Fusiliers; Gallipoli 7 months, France 2 years.

***Peel, Thomas William** (1914–16); Sergeant, Middlesex Rgt.; Gibraltar 8 months, Egypt 6 months, France 4 months; Died of wounds, 12th September, 1916.

Pike, Alfred (1914–19); Sergeant, Royal Fusiliers and Middlesex Rgt.; France 1 year.

Plumridge, Reuben (1916–19); Corporal, Kent Cyclists and R.A.M.C.

Poole, Francis (1914–19); M.C., Twice mentioned in despatches; Captain, R.A.M.C. and Scots Guards: France 3 years 2 months.

Pratley, Walter (1915–19); Private, Royal Fusiliers; Dardanelles 5 months, France 1 year.

Price, Samuel Joseph (1914–19); Corporal, R.A.M.C.; France 4 years 1 month.

Pusey, George Alfred (1915–18); Private, R.A.M.C.

***Ridgewell, Alfred** (1915–16); Private, Middlesex Rgt.; France 9 months; Missing, 15th July, 1916.

Rogers, Albert William (1916–19); Corporal, R.A.F.; France 2 years 4 months.

Rose, George Thomas (1914–19); Private, Bedfordshire Rgt. and Labour Corps; France 1 year.

Ryall, Percy (1915–19); Private, Somerset Light Infantry; Dardanelles, Egypt and Palestine, 4 years 2 months.

Saggars, Ernest Henry (1916–19); Private, R.W. Surrey Rgt.; France 1 year 10 months.

Scott, Frank (1914–19); Private, R.A.O.C.; France 10 months, Salonica 3 years 2 months.

Sheath, Frederick William John (1914–19); Sapper, London Yeomanry and R.E.; Palestine and Syria 10 months.

Smith, William John (1914–19); Sub-Conductor, R.A.O.C.; France 4 years.

Snowdon, John (1915–19); Corporal Shoeing-Smith, R.A.V.C.; France 1 year.

Spence, Thomas Henry (1914–19); Captain, R.F.A. and R.G.A.

Strong, Harry (1917–19); Gunner, R.G.A.; France 7 months.

Taylor, James (1916–19); Corporal, Tank Corps; France 2 years 4 months.

Taylor, James Alfred (1914–19); Corporal, R. Irish Rgt.; France 4 years 3 months.

Thewless, George Frederick (1915–20); Gunner, R.G.A.; France 1 year 4 months.

Tilbury, Joseph (1915–19); Sapper, R.E.

***Townsend, Frederick Thomas** (1916–17); Private, Middlesex Rgt.; France about 6 months; Died of wounds, 18th August, 1917.

Trask, Henry (1915–19); Driver, R.A.S.C.; France 3 years 9 months.

Tucker, Frederick John (1914–19); Petty Officer (1st Class), R.N.V.R.

Warren, Arthur James (1916–19); Gunner, R.G.A.; France 9 months, Italy 16 months.

Warren, Samuel George (1915–19); Sergeant, Northumberland Fusiliers; Malta, Mesopotamia, Italy, Salonica and France, 3 years 6 months.

Webb, Albert James (1914–19); Private, R.A.M.C.; Dardanelles 11 months.

Wellings, Norman (1914–19); Sergeant, R. W. Kent Rgt.; France 3 months.

Wells, Charles William (1914–19); Corporal, Middlesex Rgt.; Gibraltar 7 months, France 4 years

***West, William** (1914–15); Private, Royal Marine Light Infantry; France and Dardanelles 9 months; Killed in action, 6th May, 1915.

Wheeler, William (1914–19); Sergeant, Royal Fusiliers; France 1 year.

***Williams, Victor** (1915–17); Private, Royal Fusiliers; Egypt 5 months, France 13 months; Missing, 24th April, 1917.

Woodbridge, Bernard (1914–19); Private, Royal Fusiliers; France 1 year.

Woodcock, Herbert George (1916–19); Private, Royal Fusiliers and Machine Gun Corps; Salonica 2 years.

Horton Mental Hospital

Adams, Ernest Edward (1915–19); Private, Labour Corps and E. Surrey Rgt.; France 2 years 1 month.

***Alderton, Arthur** (1915–16); Private, 14th Bn. London Rgt.; France 8 months; Killed in action, 1st July, 1916.

Appleby, Henry Thomas William (1914–19); Gunner, R.F.A.; France 3 years.

Armstrong, George (1917–19); Private, R.W. Surrey Rgt. and Shropshire Light Infantry; France 3 months.

Barnes, Percy Stanford Clark (1914–17); Sergeant, Northamptonshire Rgt.; France 2 years.

Barnett, Joseph Edward (1916–17); Private, Middlesex and Devonshire Rgts.

Basford, William Singleton (1918–19); Air Mechanic (3rd Class), R.A.F.

Bayliss, Albert (1915–19); Regimental Quartermaster-Sergeant, R.A.M.C.; France 3 years 3 months, Italy 1 year.

***Bell, Walter** (1914); Lance-Corporal, S. Wales Borderers; France 2 months; Killed in action, 30th October, 1914.

***Bennett, Arthur Ernest** (1916–17); Lance-Corporal, E. Surrey Rgt.; France 1 year; Died of wounds, 5th August, 1917.

Blake, William (1915–19); Musician, H.M.S. Barham; Grand Fleet 3 years 8 months.

Blench, Thomas Henry Middleton (1916–19); Lance-Corporal, Royal Fusiliers; Balkans 2 years 2 months.

Blunden, Walter Jacob (1914–19); Gunner, R.F.A.; France 4 years, India 7 months.

Briggs, George Edward (1917–19); Private, R.A.M.C.; France 1 year 7 months.

Bromley, Alfred (1915–19); Private, R.A.M.C.; France 2 years 9 months.

Brown, Charles (1917–19); Regimental Sergeant-Major, R.A.M.C.

Brown, William Abram (1914–19); Sec.-Lieutenant, R. W. Kent Rgt.; France and Germany 2 years 8 months.

Buckland, George (1914–19); Sergeant, E. Surrey Rgt. and Rifle Brigade; India 3 years 4 months.

Bulley, Charles (1914–19); Private, King's Royal Rifle Corps; France 1 year 3 months.

Burdon, William Harry (1917–19); Private, R.A.S.C.; France 16 months.

Butler, Lewis (1914–17); Lance-Corporal, King's Royal Rifle Corps; France 2 years.

Callaghan, Denis (1915–19); Belgian Croix de Guerre; Sergeant, R.G.A.; France 1 year 8 months.

Chandler, William (1915–19); Gunner, R.G.A.; France 3 years.

***Channel, Walter** (1916–17); Sergeant, R.W. Surrey Rgt. and Machine Gun Corps; France 6 months; Died of wounds, 6th August, 1917.

Chaplin, Harry Herbert (1915–19); M.M., Mentioned in despatches; Rifleman, King's Royal Rifle Corps; France 3 years 9 months.

Cheek, Thomas Elisha (1916–19); Gunner, R.G.A.; France 8 months, Italy 16 months.

Churchman, George Victor (1915–19); Private, R.A.M.C.; Salonica 2 years, Bulgaria 8 months.

Clarke, Harvey (1914–19); Corporal, R.A.M.C.; France 4 years 2 months.

***Clifford, William** (1914–17); Gunner, R.G.A.; France 13 months; Killed in action, 20th July, 1917.

Conningsby, Charles William (1914–19); Able Seaman, H.M.S. Magnificent and H.M.S. Cyclops; Grand Fleet 4 years 3 months.

Cook, Edward (1915–19); Private, Royal Fusiliers; France 3 years.

***Coombes, Harry Frederick** (1914–18); Private, Dragoon Guards; France 17 months; Killed in action, 25th March, 1918.

Cornish, Albert William (1916–19); Corporal, R.A.F.

Cotterell, William George (1917–19); Private, R. W. Surrey Rgt. and W. Yorkshire Rgt.; France 9 months, Italy 15 months.

Cox, Abraham (1917–19); Corporal, London and W. Riding Rgts.; France 1 year 10 months.

Cox, George (1917–19); Corporal, R.A.M.C.

Dawkins, Cyril Henry (1916–20); Private, R.A.M.C.; Mesopotamia 3 years 4 months.

Day, David John (1916–19); Lance-Corporal, Cameron Highlanders; France 18 months.

Doggrell, Charles (1915–19); Private, R.A.M.C.; Malta 5 months.

***Downie, George Hunter** (1914–16); Private, Dragoon Guards; France 13 months; Died of wounds, 16th March, 1916.

Dudley, Frederick (1916–19); Gunner, R.F.A.; France 17 months.

Field, Charles Joseph (1915–19); Private, R.A.M.C.; France 1 year, Italy 2 months.

Fletcher, George (1916–19); Private, Royal Fusiliers and Labour Corps; France 2 years 1 month.

Fowler, George Victor (1915–19); Staff-Sergeant, R.F.A. and R.E.; France 10 months.

Frankcombe, William Arthur (1914–19); Sergeant, London Rgt.; France 9 months.

***Friday, Lewis James** (1915–17); Private, R.A.M.C.; France 1 year; Died of wounds, 25th May, 1917.

Fry, Frank (1914–19); Private, E. Surrey Rgt. and R.D.C.

Fry, Tom (1916–19); Private, Durham Light Infantry; Salonica 2 years 6 months.

***Gaunt, George** (1916–17); Private, Leicestershire Rgt. and R.E.; France 1½ months; Killed in action, 23rd October, 1917.

Gilden, Frederick Charles (1914–19); Lance-Bombardier, R.F.A.; France 2 years 6 months.

Goodchild, Albert (1916–19); Corporal, R.A.O.C., R.F.C. and R.A.F.

Hamilton, Henry (1914–18); Private, E. Surrey Rgt. and R.D.C.

Harding, William Gilbert (1916–20); Private, Machine Gun Corps; India 2 years 8 months.

Harris, Ernest St. Leger (1917–19); 2nd Corporal, R.E.

Harrison, George (1914–19); Sergeant, R.H.A.; France 3 years.

Haynes, John (1914–19); Private, E. Surrey Rgt. and R.D.C.

***Hepworth, Percy Walker** (1914); Stoker, H.M.S. Hawke; Grand Fleet; Missing, believed drowned, 15th October, 1914.

Hill, Frank (1914–19); Lance-Corporal, E. Surrey Rgt., R.D.C. and Suffolk Rgt.; France 3 months.

Hodge, Arthur William (1916–19); Private, Suffolk and Norfolk Rgts.; France 9 months.

***Jenkins, George Albert** (1914–15); Private, Royal Lancers; France 9 months; Died of wounds, 17th May, 1915.

Jenner, Arthur Leonard (1914–19); Corporal, R.A.M.C.; Egypt and Gallipoli 13 months, Macedonia 15 months.

***Johnson, Ernest Ralph** (1914–17); Company Sergeant-Major, King's Royal Rifle Corps; France 2 years 5 months; Killed in action, 15th October, 1917.

Johnston, Hugh (1916–19); M.M.; Sec.-Lieutenant, Hunts. Cyclists and Bedfordshire Rgt.; France 9 months, Italy 4 months.

Justice, Harry (1915–19); Corporal, R. Berkshire Rgt.

Kent, Horton Victor (1914–19); M.S.M.; Conductor, R.A.O.C. and R.F.A.; Balkans 3 years 6 months.

Langford, Harry (1914–19); Private, Hampshire Rgt.; France and Prisoner of war, 4 years 3 months.

Lomax, Joseph (1917–19); Corporal, R.A.M.C.

Lord, John Robert (1915–20); C.B.E.; Lieut.-Colonel, R.A.M.C.

Miles, Henry Frederick William (1915–16); Corporal, King Edward's Horse; France 9 months.

Mills, Alfred Walter (1914–19); Mentioned in despatches; Regimental Sergeant-Major, E. Surrey Rgt.; France 2 years 4 months, Italy 2 years.

***Moth, Ernest Solomon** (1914); Rifleman, Rifle Brigade; France 6 weeks; Died of wounds, 25th October, 1914.

Oliver, Michael John (1917–19); Sergeant, R.A.M.C.

Oliver, William John (1915–19); Private, King Edward's Horse; France 6 months.

Paice, William Robert (1914–19); Sergeant, E. Kent and E. Surrey Rgts.

Pearn, Oscar Phillips Napier (1914–19); Captain, R.A.M.C.

Pottle, William Thomas (1916–19); Private, R. Welch Fusiliers and E. Surrey Rgt.; Macedonia 3 years.

Randall, William Arthur (1915–19); Private, E. Surrey Rgt. and R.E.; France 3 years.

Read, John (1916–19); Private and 2nd Air Mechanic, London Regt., Lancashire Fusiliers and R.A.F.; France 2 years 1 month.

Riches, Reginald George (1915–19); Major, R.A.M.C.; Egypt 2 years.

Roberts, Frederick John (1916–19); Lance-Corporal, M.F.P.; East Africa 2 years 7 months.

Roberts, Norcliffe (1915–19); O.B.E.; Major, R.A.M.C.

Robertson, Archibald John (1914–19); Private, R.A.M.C.; Balkans 1 year 8 months, France 5 months.

Russell, Percival Frederick (1914–19); Private R.A.M.C.; France and Germany 4 years 9 months.

Scott, Lancelot James (1915–19); Driver, R.F.A.; France 1 year 10 months, Italy 6 months, Germany 7 months.

Sibley, James John (1915–19); Private, R.A.M.C.; France 2 years 8 months.

Skelly, Albert James (1914–19); Sergeant E. Surrey Rgt. and R.D.C.

Smale, Orlando John (1917–19); Private, Middlesex Rgt. and Labour Corps.

Smith, Oscar Harold (1915–19); Sergeant, Coldstream Guards; France and Germany 3 years 7 months.

Soole, William Arthur (1914–19); Private, R.A.M.C.

Spong, Albert William (1917–19); Gunner, R.G.A.; Egypt 1 year 8 months.

Spong, Robert Sidney (1914–19); Gunner, R.M.A.; France, and at sea 4 years.

Spong, Victor Lawrence Charles (1916–19); Corporal, E. Surrey Rgt.; France 2 years 5 months.

Stevens, George Richard (1917–19); Corporal, Welch Rgt.; France 2 years.

Stevenson, George (1917–19); Lance-Corporal, R.G.A. and Labour Corps; France 18 months.

Stewart, Robert (1915–19); Private, Coldstream Guards; France 11 months.

Stockman, Herbert (1915–19); Private, R.A.M.C.; France 2 years 3 months.

Thomas, William (1915–19); Corporal, Royal Fusiliers; France 18 months.

***Tichener, Harry Oliver** (1914–18); Driver, R.F.A.; France 11 months; Killed in action, 3rd October, 1918.

***Toseland, Frederick Arthur** (1915–17); Private, R.A.S.C. and Highland Light Infantry; Egypt 15 days; Missing, believed drowned, 4th May, 1917.

***Turner, Henry William** (1914–15); Gunner, R.G.A.; Died, 24th September, 1915.

Turrell, Percy John (1914–19); Lance-Corporal, E. Surrey Rgt.; France 11 months, Macedonia 3 years.

Tutte, Henry George (1915–19); Gunner, R.G.A.; India and Mesopotamia 2 years, France 10 months.

Vincent, Reginald (1917–19); Sergeant, R.W. Surrey Rgt. and Labour Corps; France 2 years 1 month.

Vincent, Thomas Francis (1917–19); Private, R.A.M.C.

Ware, Frederick Henry (1917–19); Private, R.A.M.C.

***Weall, Edwin James** (1914–19); Armourer Staff-Sergeant, R.A.O.C.; Gallipoli 7 months; Died, 18th February, 1919.

Wheeler, Harry (1915–19); M.M.; Sergeant, R.F.A.; Egypt 8 months, Gallipoli 9 months, France 2 years 8 months.

Wiles, Charles William (1917–19); Private, Labour Corps; France 18 months.

Winter, Herbert (1914–19); Private, R.A.M.C.; France 3 years 9 months.

Wood, Percy John (1916–19); Private, R.A.S.C. (M.T.); France 1 year 8 months.

Young, Robert Henry (1916–19); Lance-Corporal, Suffolk and Essex Rgts.; France 10 months.

Long Grove Mental Hospital

Acres, Bob (1915–19); Private, Hertfordshire Yeomanry; Egypt 7 months, Mesopotamia 2 years 9 months.

Amis, Herbert (1914–19); Private, Shropshire Light Infantry, Liverpool Rgt. and R. Irish Fusiliers; France 1 year. Egypt 2 months, Salonica 2 years 8 months.

Arkwright, George (1915–19); Lance-Corporal, Dragoon Guards, S. Lancashire Rgt. and Labour Corps; France 10 months.

Askew, Fred. (1916–19); Gunner, R.G.A.; France 2 years 8 months.

Atkinson, Henry Harrison (1915–17); Private, Royal Fusiliers; France 1 month.

Baker, Robert Charles (1916–19); Bombardier, R.G.A.; France 2 years 5 months.

Banyard, Frederick Ernest (1914–19); Private, R. Marine Reserves; H.M. ships 4 years 6 months.

Boniface, Jesse (1914–19); Private, E. Surrey Rgt.; India 1 year 9 months, Mesopotamia 16 months.

Bown, Wallace (1915–19); Gunner, R.F.A.; Mesopotamia 3 years 2 months.

Boxall, William (1915–19); Guardsman, Coldstream Guards; France 2 years 5 months.

Bridgman, William George (1914–19); Sergeant, R.F.A.; France 3 years 6 months.

Briggs, Frederick Herbert William (1915–19); M.M.; Private, R.A.M.C.; France 2 years 5 months.

Broderick, Adrian Joseph (1915–19); Staff-Sergeant, R.A.O.C.; France 3 years 4 months.

Broderick, Thomas (1916–19); Gunner, R.F.A. and R.G.A.

Brown, George Lewis (1914–19); Mentioned in despatches; Regimental Sergeant-Major, R.A.M.C.; France 3 months, Salonica 3 years 2 months.

Brunsden, Herbert James (1917–19); Private, R. W. Surrey Rgt. and Labour Corps; France 17 months.

Burrage, William Percy (1916–19); Private, Middlesex, Devonshire and Welch Rgts.; France 1 year 9 months.

***Butland, Robert** (1916–18); Bombardier, R.G.A.; France 1 year 7 months; Died of wounds, 26th September, 1918.

Callier, Albert Edward (1916–19); Private, 101st Training Reserve Bn., Devonshire and Hampshire Rgts.; India 1 year 10 months, Aden 11 months.

Chambers, James William (1917); Sapper, R.E.

Chapman, Benjamin (1916–19); Bombardier, R.G.A.; Salonica 2 years 6 months.

Childs, Richard (1915–19); Private, Royal Fusiliers and Machine Gun Corps; France 2 years 7 months.

Christian, William Henry (1915–19); Private, R.A.M.C.; France 1 year 8 months.

Claydon, Herbert (1914–19); Bombardier, R.F.A.; France 2 years 8 months, Italy 6 months.

Collins, Edward (1916–19); Private, E. Surrey Rgt.; France 6 months, Prisoner of war 16 months.

Coppard, Herbert Ambrose (1916–19); Private, E. Surrey Rgt.; France 9 months, Prisoner of war 18 months.

Cornford, John Arthur (1916–19); Private, E. Surrey Rgt. and Machine Gun Corps; France 1 year 7 months.

Crompton, Richard (1915–17); Private, R.A.M.C. and London Rgt.; France 5 months.

Cruse, Arthur James (1917–19); Corporal, R.A.F.

Darnell, Arthur Joseph (1915–19); Sergeant, R.A.M.C.; France 15 months.

Dodge, Alfred Frank (1916–19); Private, E. Surrey Rgt. and R. W. Kent Rgt.; India 2 years 11 months, East Persia 10 months.

Doran, Joseph (1915–16); Sergeant R.A.M.C.; France.

Dunstan, Bertram Reginald (1914–19); Trooper, 13th and 11th Hussars; France 4 years 6 months.

Durbridge, Alfred Henry (1914–19); Gunner, R.H.A.; France 4 years 6 months.

Edwards, David Munday (1917–19); Driver. R.A.S.C.

Etherington, James (1914–19); M.M.; Private, E. Kent Rgt., R. W. Kent Rgt. and R.A.S.C.; France 1 year 10 months.

Ferriman, James George (1914–18); Bombardier, R.F.A.; France 1 year 10 months.

Garton, William (1915–19); Private, R.A.S.C.; France 1 year, Salonica 18 months.

Ghent, Frank (1915–18); Private, Devonshire Rgt.; Egypt.

Hadley, Charles Ancel (1914–19); Private, R.A.V.C.; France 3 years 2 months, North Russia 11 months.

Hagger, William Henry (1915–19); Private, R.A.M.C.; France 2 years 10 months.

Hall, Henry James (1915–19); Lance-Corporal, R.A.S.C.; France 3 years 7 months.

***Hambly, Benjamin** (1914–15); Lance-Corporal, 17th Lancers and 2nd Life Guards; France 9 months; Killed in action, 13th May, 1915.

Hardiment, George William (1914–19); Sergeant, Grenadier Guards.

Harvey, Edgar (1915–17); Private, E. Surrey Rgt. and R.D.C.

Hauberg, Horace Otto (1914–19); Private, Bedfordshire Yeomanry, Aircraftsman (1st Class), R.A.F.; Egypt and Palestine.

Heath, James (1916–); Private, 64th Provisional Bn. Suffolk and R. Warwickshire Rgts.; France 5 months, Italy 12 months; Still in hospital.

Hennessey, David (1914–19); Corporal, Duke of Cornwall's Light Infantry; France 6 months.

Hibbert, Reginald (1917-19); Rifleman, Rifle Brigade; France 2 months, Prisoner of war 10 months.

Hignett, Henry Sutton (1914–19); Squadron Sergeant-Major, Shropshire Yeomanry.

Hills, Harold William (1915–19); Major, R.A.M.C.; France 1 year 8 months, Prisoner of war 10 months.

Hood, Thomas Henry (1916–19); Gunner, R.G.A.

Hooper, Walter William (1915–18); Private, R.A.M.C.

Hockey, Alfred (1914–19); Corporal, R.F.A.; France 2 years 2 months, Egypt 3 months.

Huntingford, James (1914–19); Mentioned in despatches; Acting Captain, Devonshire Rgt.; France 4 years 5 months, Turkey and South Russia 3 months.

Irish, Charles George (1915–19); Private, Lovat's Scouts, Cameron Highlanders and Gordon Highlanders; France 9 months.

Jackson, George Arthur (1914–17); Gunner, R.G.A.; France 9 months.

James, Arthur Bollard (1914–19); Sergt.-Major, R.F.A. and Labour Corps; France.

Jerman, Richard James (1914–19); Regimental Sergeant-Major, E. Surrey Rgt. and R.D.C.

***Jibb, Arthur Harwood** (1914–18); Mentioned in despatches; Lieutenant and Quartermaster, R.A.M.C.; France 2 years 3 months, Egypt 13 months; Died of wounds, 12th April, 1918.

Keeling, Frank Wilkinson (1915–19); Mentioned in despatches; Captain, E. Surrey, Border and Manchester Rgts.; Egypt 4 months, France 17 months, Prisoner of war 9 months.

Kerr, Bertrand (1915–19); Corporal, Cameron Highlanders, Officers Cadet Bn.; France.

***Kirkcaldy, Douglas** (1914–16); Sergeant, R.G.A. and Border Rgt.; Gallipoli, Egypt and France 10 months; Killed in action, 1st July, 1916.

***Knights, John Percy** (1914); Private, Sherwood Foresters; France 2 months; Killed in action, 20th October, 1914.

Lake, Arthur Henry Frederick George (1914–19); Gunner, R.H.A., Private, Labour Corps; France 11 months, Mesopotamia 9 months, Egypt 2 years 5 months.

***Lambert, Frederick Charles** (1914–16); Sergeant, Duke of Cornwall's Light Infantry; France 6 months; Missing and presumed dead, 23rd July, 1916.

***Laurence, Nelson** (1914–16); Private, Royal Fusiliers; Malta 5 months, France 1 year 7 months; Died of wounds, 10th October, 1916.

Lewis, Frank George (1915–18); Private, R. W. Surrey Rgt. and R.D.C.

Lipyeat, Thomas Alexander (1914–19); M.M. and Bar; Sergeant, R.F.A.; France 3 years, Palestine 1 year.

***Lowes, William Andrew** (1914–16); Sergeant, R.F.A.; France 13 months; Killed in action, 25th August, 1916.

MacManus, Herbert Patrick (1915–19); Private, R.A.O.C. and Lincolnshire Rgt.; France 2 years 3 months, Prisoner of war 9 months.

Mann, Frederick (1916–19); Private, Durham Light Infantry and Labour Corps; Salonica.

Mapother, Edward (1915–19); Captain, R.A.M.C.; France 9 months, Mesopotamia and India 16 months.

Mathis, Arthur George (1916–19); Corporal, 2/6th (Cyclist) Bn. Norfolk Rgt. and Military Foot Police.

Matthews, Edwin (1914–19); Private, 12th Cavalry Reserve, 9th Cavalry Reserve and Machine Gun Corps (Cavalry); Egypt.

Matthews, George (1914–19); Sergeant, Northamptonshire Rgt.; France 3 years 6 months.

Mesley, William Charles (1914–16); Private, Royal Marine Light Infantry; H.M. ships.

Mitchell, Benjamin (1916–19); Sapper, R.E.; France 2 years 7 months.

***Morley, Charles James** (1914); Private, Worcestershire Rgt.; France 1 month; Killed in action, 16th September, 1914.

Paddon, Alfred George (1914–19); Lance-Corporal, R.E.; Gallipoli 4 months.

Pearce, Frederick Thomas (1917–19); Private, R.A.M.C.

Pearson, Cedric Whalley (1914–15); Private, 12th Cavalry Reserve.

Peat, James (1915–19); Croix de Guerre; Lance-Sergeant, R.A.M.C.; France 3 years 2 months.

***Peters, Walter** (1915–17); Private, R.A.M.C.; France 5 months; Died on active service, 11th January, 1917.

***Plumridge, Walter Joseph** (1914–18); Bombardier, R.H.A.; France; Killed in action, 21st March, 1918.

Porter, Albert (1915–19); Lance-Corporal, R.A.O.C., Nottinghamshire and Derbyshire Rgt.; France 3 years 4 months.

Randall, Frank (1916–19); Lance-Corporal, Middlesex Rgt.

Riley, George Henry (1915–19); Private, R.A.M.C.; France 2 years 5 months.

Robinson, Frederick John (1915–19); Captain, R.A.O.C.; France 18 months, India 17 months.

Roome, Frederick Joseph (1914–19); Corporal, R.G.A.; France 3 years 2 months, Italy 14 months.

Sayers, William Aaron (1915–19); Corporal, R.A.S.C.; France 3 years 2 months.

Sharp, Edward (1914–19); Private, E. Kent Rgt.; France 3 years 6 months.

Shortall, Thomas (1914–15); Lance-Sergeant, Irish Guards; France.

Simpson, Alfred (1915–19); Private, R.A.M.C. and Shropshire Light Infantry; Salonica 2 years, Russia 6 months.

Skilton, Thomas Knatchbull (1914–19); Gunner, R.F.A.; France 2 years 10 months.

Smith, Richard (1914–19); Private, R. Lancaster Rgt.; France 9 months, Salonica 2 years 5 months.

Stainsby, Percy Holland (1916–19); Seaman, R.N.V.R.; Served on H.M. ships 2 years.

Stanyon, William Barton (1916–19); Gunner, R.G.A.; France 11 months.

Stewart, Allan Lauchlin (1914–16); Corporal, R.F.A.; France 13 months.

Sutherland, Margaret (1914–20); Royal Red Cross (2nd Class); Nurse, Territorial Force (Nurses); France 3 years 6 months.

Taylor, George William (1914–19); Sergeant, Dorsetshire and Worcestershire Rgts.; France and Mediterranean.

Tipping, Frank Ernest (1915–19); Gunner, R.F.A.; France 2 years 3 months, Italy 6 months.

Turner, Albert Edward (1915–19); Private, R.A.M.C.; France 2 years 8 months.

***Turner, Henry Dennis** (1914–17); Corporal, R.F.A.; France 2 years; Killed in action, 7th July, 1917.

Walker, Herbert (1915–19); Private, R.A.M.C.; France 3 years 9 months.

Walker, Leslie Thomas (1915–18); Private, Royal Fusiliers; France.

Walker, Thomas (1914–19); Sergeant, E. Surrey Rgt. and Machine Gun Corps; India 3 years 5 months, Egypt 2 months, France 9 months.

***Walton, Percy** (1914–16); Sergeant, R.F.A.; France 1 year 11 months; Killed in action, 18th July, 1916.

Warren, William Thomas (1915–19); Private, R.A.M.C.; France 2 years 7 months.

Webb, John (1917–19); Sapper, R.E.

Webber, Bertram (1915–19); Lance-Corporal, R.A.M.C.; France 4 months, Cross Channel Hospital Ship 13 months.

Webster, Joseph Robb (1915–19); Private, R.A.M.C.; France 1 year 9 months, Italy 15 months.

White, Harry Stanley (1916–19); Driver, R.A.S.C.; France 2 years 3 months.

Wilshire, James Raymond (1914–16); Private, R. Warwickshire Rgt.; France 9 months, Gallipoli 6 months.

Wilson, Joseph (1915–17); Lance-Corporal, E. Kent Rgt. and Machine Gun Corps; France 7 months.

York, Bertram George (1914–16); Rifleman, King's Royal Rifle Corps; France.

The Manor Mental Hospital

***Brook, Frederick Charles** (1916–17); Private, R. Dublin Fusiliers; France 3 months; Killed in action, 16th August, 1917.

Catlin, Albert Arthur (1916–19); Private, R.A.M.C.

Connett, Wilfred John (1915–19); Corporal, R.A.M.C.; France 3 years 2 months.

Hames, William Thomas (1916–19); Mentioned in despatches; Regimental Sergeant-Major, R.A.M.C.; Macedonia 2 years 1 month, Caucasia and Transcaspia 3 months, Turkey 7 months.

Heels, James (1915–19); Driver, R.A.S.C. France 3 years 3 months.

Hunter, William Johnson (1916–19); Air Mechanic (1st Class), R.A.F.; Egypt 18 months.

Keary, John (1914–19); Lance-Corporal, R.A.M.C.

Litteljohn, Edward Salterne (1918–19); Lieutenant, R.A.M.C.; North Russia 10 months.

Louden, David (1914–19); Private, R.D.C.

Partrick, Ronald Alfred (1914–19); Sergeant, R.H.A.; France 3 years 5 months.

***Penfold, George** (1915–17); Gunner, R.G.A.; France 9 months; Killed in action, 4th August, 1917.

Poulton, Charles Welch (1916–19); Second Writer, R.N.; Grand Fleet 1 year, 4th Destroyer Flotilla 18 months.

Rolleston, Charles Ffranck (1918–19); Major, R.A.M.C.

Russell, Charles Arthur (1915–19); Driver, R.A.S.C.; France 5 months, Salonica 2 years 4 months, Russia 4 months.

Seymour, Reginald (1916–19); Staff-Sergeant, R.A.M.C.; Macedonia 1 year 10 months, Serbia, Bulgaria, Russia and Asia Minor, 6 months, Turkey 7 months.

Shuter, Alfred Henry (1914–19); Private, R.A.M.C.; France 4 years.

***Smithers, William James** (1916–17); Private, 5th Bn. Middlesex Rgt.; France 1 year; Killed in action, 28th November, 1917.

Steer, William Henry (1915–19); Driver, R.A.S.C.; France 7 months, Salonica 7 months, Palestine and Syria 1 year 9 months.

Stredwick, Hubert Henry (1914–18); Sapper, R.E.

Strode, Thomas William Ramsden (1914–19); Captain, R.A.M.C.; France 3 years 4 months, Mesopotamia 1 year.

Tolley, Edward Charles (1916–19); Private, Royal Fusiliers; France 4½ months.

Vaughan, Albert Edward (1914–19); Regimental Quartermaster-Sergeant, 11th Bn. Devonshire Rgt.

Watson, Joseph Ambler (1918–19); Staff-Sergeant, R.A.M.C.

Wright, Frederick Herbert (1918–19); Private, R.A.M.C.

Webb, Stephen John (1915–19); Lance-Corporal, R.A.M.C.; Egypt 16 months.

Woodbridge, Alfred William (1916–19); Private, R. W. Kent Rgt.; France 1 year.

Ewell Colony

Adams, William (1916–19); Private, R. Berkshire Rgt., Huntingdonshire Cyclist Bn. and Dragoon Guards; France 1 year.

***Bailey, Thomas** (1914–18); Sergeant, Gloucestershire Rgt.; France 3 months; Killed in action, 25th April, 1918.

Benger, Joseph William (1914–19); Sergeant, R.A.M.C.

Bridgman, Edward John (1915–19); Private, R.A.M.C.; France 2 months, Salonica 3 years 3 months.

Burdett, Charles (1914–15); Petty Officer (1st Class), R.N.; Minesweeping 1 year.

Cates, Harry (1914–19); Private, R. Marine Light Infantry; West Africa 15 months, East Africa 10 months, Arctic Patrol 10 months, Defence Armed Merchant Service 1 year 8 months.

Churchman, Albert John (1917–19); Sapper, R.E.; Mesopotamia 2 years 2 months.

***Childs, James** (1914–15); Private, Hampshire Rgt.; Dardanelles 1 month; Killed in action, 21st June, 1915.

Clark, Alfred (1914–19); Mentioned in despatches, May, 1915; Sergeant, R.A.M.C. France 4 years 8 months.

Clark, James (1915–19); Staff-Sergeant, R.A.M.C.; Salonica 3 years 6 months.

Clifford, Harry (1915–19); Private, R.A.S.C.; France 3 years 4 months.

Coleman, James (1915–18); Private, E. Surrey Rgt.

Coles, Thomas (1914–19); Private, E. Kent Rgt.; France 3 years 8 months.

Collins, Michael Abdy (1915–19); Lieut.-Colonel, R.A.M.C.; Mediterranean 2 years 10 months.

Cook, William Charles (1915–19); Private, R.A.M.C.; France 5 months, Salonica 2 years 4 months.

Cooke, Henry John (1915–19); Corporal, R.A.M.C.; Dardanelles 7 months, Mesopotamia 3 years.

Daniels, John James (1914–19); Corporal, E. Surrey Rgt.; France 13 months.

Davies, James William (1915–19); Sergeant, R.E.; France 3 years 2 months.

Dorrell, Roland Edgar (1917–19); Lance-Corporal, R.E.

Elgee, Samuel Charles (1916–19); Lieut.-Colonel, R.A.M.C.

Elliott, William Thomas (1916–19); Sapper, R.E.; France 2 years 1 month.

Greenslade, Frederick George (1914–19); Sergeant-Major, R.A.M.C.

Herbert, Arthur James (1915–19); Staff-Sergeant, E. Surrey Rgt. and Suffolk Rgt.

***Kennedy, Walter** (1915–18); Sergeant, R. W. Kent Rgt.; France 15 months; Missing, presumed dead, 23rd March, 1918.

Langley, Ernest (1915–19); Private, R.A.M.C.; Mesopotamia 4 months, India 3 years 4 months.

Lightwood, Ralph (1916–19); Corporal, R.A.M.C.

Loader, George Kellow (1916–19); Private, 5th Bn. Durham Light Infantry, Sapper, R.E.; Salonica 13 months.

***Mace, John Martin** (1916–19); Driver, R.A.S.C.; France 14 months; Died, 26th January, 1919.

Morey, Walter John (1915–19); Private, Devonshire Rgt. and Labour Corps; France 1 year.

Murray, James (1914–16); Sergeant, E. Kent Rgt.; France 13 months.

Oliver, David (1914–16): Private, E. Surrey Rgt.

Petrie, Alfred Alexander Webster (1915–19); Captain, R.A.M.C.; Mediterranean 9 months, France 3 years 1 month.

Reardon, Michael (1915–18); Corporal, R.F.A.; France 2 years 1 month.

Scott, William Ingham (1914–15); Lance-Corporal, R.A.S.C.; France 5 months.

Simmons, Sidney (1914–19); Sergeant, E. Kent Rgt. and Army Cyclist Corps; France 3 years 9 months.

Starling, John Matthew (1914–19); Private, R.A.M.C.; France 2 years 10 months.

Thomas, Hopkin (1915–19); Sergeant R.A.M.C.; France 3 years 6 months.

Westbrook, Frederick (1915–19); Sergeant, R.A.M.C.; Egypt 3 years 3 months, Dardanelles 4 months.

Central Station, West Farm, and Estate Railway

Agar, Joseph (1914–19); Private, E. Surrey Rgt., and Aircraftsman (1st Class), R.A.F.

Chandler, Charles (1917–19); Private, Northamptonshire Rgt. and Labour Corps; France 1 year 11 months.

***Daniel, Walter George** (1914–17); Private, E. Surrey Rgt.; France 2 years 3 months; Killed in action, 18th July, 1917.

Elliott, Albert William (1915–19); Private, E. Surrey Rgt. and R.A.M.C.; France 1 year.

James, Henry Herbert (1914–19); Stoker, R.N., R.F.R.; H.M. ships 4 years 4 months.

Hollidge, Samuel Valentine (1916–19); Corporal, Middlesex Rgt. and Labour Corps.

Rowland, William (1914–19); Lance-Corporal, R.A.S.C.; France 3 years 8 months.

Simons, John (1917–18); Private, Labour Corps; France.

Tipping, Henry John (1915–19); Driver, R.F.A.; France 3 years 9 months.

***Watkins, Frederick** (1914–18); Private, 20th Hussars; France 4 years 2 months; Killed in action, 7th November, 1918.

Asylums Engineer's Department

Hoggett, Alfred Christopher (1914–19); Acting Regimental Quartermaster-Sergeant, 2/10th Bn. Middlesex Rgt.; Gallipoli, Sinai Peninsula, Palestine, 4 years.

Johns, Thomas Benjamin (1916–19); Captain, 22nd Bn. King's Royal Rifle Corps, 4th Bn. N. Hants Labour Corps; France, Belgium, Germany, 2 years 9 months.

Mayhew, Alfred Ernest (1915–19); Staff Sergeant, R.E., Military Foreman of Works, R.A.M.C. Sanitary Section, 44th and 10th R.E.; France 3 years 10 months.

Smith, Arthur Frederick (1916–19); Bombardier, R.A. and R.G.A.; France 3 months.

The Temple Press Letchworth England

www.ingramcontent.com/pod-product-compliance
Ingram Content Group UK Ltd.
Pitfield, Milton Keynes, MK11 3LW, UK
UKHW041849190726
13854UKWH00002B/783

9 781843 424727